B
BISHOP
F

Fountain, Gary,
    1949-

Remembering Elizabeth
    Bishop.

$35.00

DATE			

REMEMBERING ELIZABETH BISHOP

Remembering
Elizabeth Bishop

AN ORAL BIOGRAPHY

Gary Fountain and Peter Brazeau

UNIVERSITY OF MASSACHUSETTS PRESS ◆ *Amherst*

Copyright © 1994 by
The University of Massachusetts Press
All rights reserved
Printed in the United States of America
LC 94–14811
ISBN 0–87023–936–8
Designed by Mary Mendell
Set in Joanna by Keystone Typesetting, Inc.
Printed and bound by Thomson-Shore, Inc.
Library of Congress Cataloging-in-Publication Data
Fountain, Gary, 1949–
Remembering Elizabeth Bishop : an oral biography / Gary Fountain and
Peter Brazeau.
p.   cm.
Includes bibliographical references (p.   ) and index.
ISBN 0–87023–936–8 (alk. paper)
1. Bishop, Elizabeth, 1911–1979—Friends and associates—Interviews.
2. Bishop, Elizabeth, 1911–1979—Biography.
3. Poets, American—20th century—Biography.
I. Brazeau, Peter. II. Title.
PS3503.I785Z683   1994
811'.54—dc20
[B]   94-14811
                      CIP
British Library Cataloguing in Publication data are available.

FOR MELISSA

CONTENTS ❦

Acknowledgments ix

Preface xi

A Brief Chronology xvii

1. Childhood, 1911–1927 1

2. Walnut Hill, 1927–1930 20

3. Vassar, 1930–1934 36

4. New York, Europe, and Key West, 1934–1940 60

5. Key West and New York, 1941–1948 88

6. Washington, D.C., and Yaddo, 1948–1951 109

7. Brazil, 1951–1957 127

8. Brazil, 1958–1965 163

9. Seattle, 1966 201

10. Brazil, 1966–1967 222

11. San Francisco, 1967–1969 238

12. Ouro Prêto, 1969–1970 254

13. Cambridge, 1970–1973 269

14. Cambridge and Boston, 1973–1977 308

15. Boston, 1977–1979 341

Afterword by Bonnie Costello 353

Notes 357

Notes on Contributors 383

Index 395

Illustrations follow page 186

ACKNOWLEDGMENTS

Grateful acknowledgment is made to the following for permission to quote from previously published and unpublished material:

Elizabeth Bishop Papers, Washington University Libraries, St. Louis, Missouri: Letters from Barbara Swain to Anne Stevenson and from Julia G. Bacon to Anne Elvin

Farrar, Straus & Giroux: Published poems of Elizabeth Bishop, from *The Complete Poems, 1927–1979* (New York: Farrar, Straus & Giroux, 1980)

Pauline Hanson, From "The Forever Young and Never Free," *Across Countries of Anywhere* (New York: Alfred A. Knopf, 1971).

Houghton Library, Harvard University: Letter from Elizabeth Bishop to Robert Lowell

Mrs. Winthrop Merriam, Sr.: Letter from Julia G. Bacon to Anne Elvin

Alice Methfessel: Published (from *The Complete Poems, 1927–1979* [New York: Farrar, Straus & Giroux, 1980]) and unpublished writings and letters by Elizabeth Bishop

Papers of Marianne Moore, Rosenbach Museum and Library, Philadelphia: Letters from Elizabeth Bishop to Marianne Moore

Frani Blough Muser: Letter from Frani Blough to Elizabeth Bishop

Nova Scotia Hospital, Dartmouth, N.S., Canada: Records, "Statement of Nova Scotia Hospital" for Gertrude Boomer Bishop completed by Grace Boomer Bowers

Manuscripts Division, Department of Rare Books and Special Collections, Princeton University Libraries: Letters from Elizabeth Bishop to Ilse Barker

Alastair Reid: From "Quarrels," *Weathering: Poems and Translations* (Athens: University of Georgia Press, 1988)

Kay Orr Sargent: Letters from Ruby D. Bishop to Miss Bigelow and from John W. Bishop to Helen Farwell

Estate of Barbara Swain: Letter from Barbara Swain to Anne Stevenson

Special Collections, Vassar College Libraries: Letters from Eleanor Prentiss to Elizabeth Bishop; from Elizabeth Bishop to Frani Muser; from Frani Muser to Elizabeth Bishop; from Elizabeth Bishop to Loren MacIver; and from Elizabeth Bishop to U. T. and Joseph Summers; notes by Elizabeth Bishop on "The Baroque Style in Prose"

Walnut Hill School Archives: Letters from Florence Bigelow to Mrs. John W. Bishop; from Ruby D. Bishop to Miss Bigelow; from John W. Bishop to Helen Farwell; from Helen Farwell to John W. Bishop; from Ruth Mulligan to Florence Bishop; and from Miriam Steeves to Miss Girard; college recommendation for Elizabeth Bishop; and confidential information given by John W. Bishop to Ruby Willis

P eter Brazeau began this oral biography of Elizabeth Bishop in 1984. A handsome man of medium build, with curly hair, a thick mustache, and an open, engaging face, Peter was passionate about literature, particularly modern poetry, and people. He was my wife's favorite colleague at St. Joseph College. Peter died in 1986, leaving numerous interviews and notes for this book, and his companion and executor, Jim Harrison, turned to me some time later to pull the pieces together and complete the project.

Although Peter never met Elizabeth Bishop, he did hear her read her poetry once. Peter completed a well-received oral biography of Wallace Stevens (*Parts of a World: Wallace Stevens Remembered*, 1975) before turning to a project on Elizabeth Bishop, but I like to think that the genesis of this book occurred at that reading, when the poetry and the person met before him. Bishop would not have been comfortable with a biographical study of this sort. She was not at ease in public, disdained academic and literary conversation, and, as one of her friends expressed it to me, had a ferocious sense of privacy. She deflected even the most obvious biographical interpretations of her poetry and evoked in many of her friends a desire to protect her. Bishop would be appalled that her unguarded letters to her doctor, Anny Baumann, are now available for others to read. The interviews that Peter conducted for this project demonstrate how adept he was at earning the respect and trust of those who knew Bishop.

The rending and mending of personal ties, in a systolic and diastolic rhythm, is the plot of Elizabeth Bishop's personal life. Bishop gathered friends and lovers to her at various times in various locations, ranging from her childhood in Great Village, Nova Scotia, and Worcester, Massachusetts, to New York City, Key West, Rio de Janeiro, San Francisco, and Boston. Her travels north and south were in part a journey of the heart, a search for community and family. In this book, those who knew Bishop on this journey narrate her story. Their recollections leave two abiding and contrasting impressions, a dominant theme and its counterpoint. On one hand, from early in her life Bishop knew artistically and personally who she was, what she stood for, what she wanted to achieve, and what she believed. She possessed a self-assurance that made her "a thing apart," as one of her Walnut Hill classmates characterized her. She was set in the ways of her genius. But much of Bishop's life is characterized by lack of control, both in the piteous and fortuitous events that were visited upon her and in her own periodic collapses into confusion, depression, and drunkenness. Bishop's life was the product of her will, yet she was also dependent upon the good will, kindness, and direction of others.

Bishop required efforts of affection, to borrow a phrase from her piece on Marianne Moore, but the effort, as one friend recently put it to me, was easily, gratefully, even pleasurably given. As another friend commented, Bishop needed to have things done for her, but performing these tasks was a pleasure because Bishop was a splendid friend. But in some of her relationships, the effort of the affection exacted a toll. Bishop could be a heavy burden, and a scenario of spiraling mutual weakening characterizes Bishop's tragic relationships. Bishop's friends remember her as determined, good humored, witty, broadly intelligent, graceful, and precise in her views, as in her art, but also lonely, dissatisfied, unhappy, and rootless. She was a divided woman. She evoked pathos. My task has been to paint a portrait that strikes the balance—or, rather, describes the drama—between the strength and weakness, freedom and dependence, self-assurance and indecision in Elizabeth Bishop's life.

✦ ✦ ✦

Peter Brazeau completed more than seventy interviews for this book. I have added more than forty others. Peter was a fastidious, probing researcher. Although he and I never discussed this project, it became clear to me from listening to his taped interviews that he had completed vast background research, particularly in the rich collection at the Vassar College Libraries, Special Collections, and in caches of letters he discovered in the course of his interviews. These interviews are detailed and explicit. Each begins with the same question, "Do you remember when you first met Elizabeth Bishop?" From this point the interviews follow the recollections of the interviewees, with an observation leading to a question, leading to another observation, and so on, eventually exploring the period of time when each interviewee knew Bishop. Questions were often based on Bishop's own description of events, either in letters or in other forms of writing, and the interviewee's perception of the same events. Peter had a lengthy list of detailed questions for each interviewee, all of which he managed to cover in the course of conversation. There is an art to his formal informality. I followed his lines of questioning in my interviews.

When Peter died, much of his background research died with him—his notes were spotty and eclectic. He had not transcribed any of the tapes, and he had written less than a page of the text, a draft of an opening paragraph for the book. My initial task was to read the archival material, including hundreds of letters, and Bishop's published and unpublished work. I conducted the interviews Peter had not done, edited the interviews, and wrote the narrative for this book.

To edit the interviews, I first transcribed each word for word, then arranged each into a monologue by moving pieces around so that comments about similar subjects or topics were together, adding transitional words or phrases for continuity. Here and there, for the sake of clarity, pronouns have been replaced with proper nouns, and vice versa. I have taken the liberty of correcting some grammatical errors and have added words to clarify meaning and to make sense of phrases that were truncated, imprecise, or confused in the normal course of conversation or as a result of the question-and-answer format. In several cases, interviewees requested that their interviews be submitted to them before publication, and I have printed their final, edited versions.

✦　✦　✦

Elizabeth Bishop possessed uncanny empathy. Her letters to her Aunt Grace, living on a farm in Nova Scotia, have the same detailed vivacity of her letters to Robert Lowell, but the subjects and the point of view are vastly different. She addressed all of her friends and relatives on their own terms; she did not impose herself. Bishop's empathetic imagination and the breadth of her knowledge and interests prove true the clichéd observation that each relationship is different. No one person saw the whole in his or her relationship with Bishop, as the chorus of voices in a study like this one demonstrates. This study, then, is not an attempt to write the definitive biography of Bishop, if such a biography exists for anyone, but to offer perspectives on the whole. My intention has been to produce a book for the range of readers of Bishop—the person with a casual acquaintance with her writing, the knowledgeable reader, the student, and the scholar—hoping to lead each to a deeper acquaintance with Bishop's life, to provoke thought about the connections between Bishop's life and her literature, and to encourage revaluation of previous interpretations.

One of the surprises uncovered in researching this book was how little Bishop discussed her writing with anyone. Peter and I had hoped to locate people with whom she had discussed her poems either during or after writing them. Such was not often the case with Bishop. Many of her poems had their genesis in events of her life, but they were composed in solitude. Writing was a private enterprise for Bishop, and she was known discreetly to absent herself from discussions of her own work. I hope that this book will form the basis of future studies that will explore through literary analysis those points at which Bishop's life and her writing intersected.

The detailed legwork required by a study of this sort was consistently rewarded by the exhilaration of discovery. The appearance of an address or a person and the uncovering in an interview of unsuspected facts took me down fascinating byways. The serendipity of this project—the person who knew someone else who knew . . . , the letter that was forwarded to the correct address, the random piece of paper that appeared from a folder or drawer—delighted, at the same time that, with its hint of near misses, it alarmed. And, of course, there was the deeply moving portrait that emerged of how Elizabeth Bishop affected those who knew her. One high school classmate, in dire straits, spoke eloquently and passionately about what her friendship with Bishop had meant to her—the richness of her memory offset the poverty of her circumstances. This project was supported by the generosity of those I met. My visit with Ilse Barker, conversing with her over two days, sleeping in the guest cottage where Bishop herself had paid for the plumbing, then spending a morning looking through the paintings in the studio of Bishop's close friend, Kit Barker, is only one example of several comparable incidents—kindnesses offered much in the spirit of Bishop herself, I suspect.

There are many whose direct contributions deserve specific thanks. Peter Brazeau was supported by grants from the National Endowment for the Humanities and the American Philosophical Society, to whom I give my thanks. Three of the many fine students whom I have taught helped early on with transcriptions—Sara Hannafin, Kate Zipser, and Carolyn Meltzer. The librarians at the Vassar College Libraries, Special Collections (the energetic and thorough Nancy McKechnie, in particular); Trinity College Library, Hartford, Connecticut; Washington University Library, St. Louis; the University of Washington Library in Seattle (Gary Lundell in particular); Princeton University Library; the New York Public Library (Lisa Browar in particular); the Rosenbach Museum and Library; and Miss Porter's School Library provided many details and sources. Lola Baldwin and her staff at the Walnut Hill School discovered invaluable material. Rachel P. Belash, Ashley Brown, Paula Deitz, Jonathan Galassi, Robert Giroux, Frederick Morgan, Andrew Motion, Lloyd Schwartz, Mark Strand, Richard Todd, Thomas Travisano, Helen Vendler, and Wesley Wehr provided shrewd and encouraging advice. Sandra Barry and Phyllis Sutherland offered invaluable insight into and information about Elizabeth Bishop's family and life in Nova Scotia. I regret that Alice Methfessel, Elizabeth Bishop's literary executor, declined an invitation to be interviewed for this book, but I thank her for reviewing the text for errors. There were also several people interviewed for this project whose words did not make their way into the final text; my thanks to them for their time and patience.

Jim Harrison, dear friend, provided wise guidance and enheartening confidence throughout this project.

Finally, I thank Melissa Fountain, the most important source of loving encouragement and keen advice for this project, as for so many aspects of my life, to whom this book is dedicated. I hope it is a fitting homage to one of her dear friends, Peter Brazeau.

A BRIEF CHRONOLOGY

11 FEBRUARY 1911— Birth of Elizabeth Bishop

OCTOBER 1911— Death of William Bishop (Elizabeth Bishop's father)

JUNE 1916— Gertrude Boomer Bishop (Elizabeth Bishop's mother) committed to Nova Scotia Hospital in Dartmouth

1916–18— Living with grandparents in Great Village, Nova Scotia, and Worcester, Massachusetts

1918–27— Living with Maud and George Shepherdson in Boston area

1927–30— Attending Walnut Hill School, Natick, Massachusetts

1930–34— Attending Vassar College, Poughkeepsie, New York

SPRING 1933— Con Spirito founded at Vassar College

29 MAY 1934— Death of Gertrude Boomer Bishop

JUNE 1934— Moves to 16 Charles Street, New York City

JULY 1935–JUNE 1936— Trip to Antwerp, Brussels, Paris, Douarnenez with Harriet Tompkins Thomas; joined by Louise Crane in October 1935, and on to Paris, Morocco, London, Seville, and Madrid

DECEMBER 1936–MARCH 1937— First trip to Florida with Louise Crane

JUNE–DECEMBER 1937— Trip with Margaret Miller and Louise Crane to England, Ireland, Burgundy (car accident in July), Paris, Rome, Florence, and Marseilles

JANUARY 1938–JUNE 1938— Visiting Key West; purchases 624 White Street with Louise Crane

DECEMBER 1939— Canoe trip through the Ten Thousand Islands, Florida, with Charles and Charlotte Russell, and Louise Crane

DECEMBER 1941— Takes up residence with Marjorie Stevens on Margaret Street, Key West

APRIL–DECEMBER 1942— Trip to Mexico with Marjorie Stevens

MAY 1945— Houghton Mifflin Poetry Prize Fellowship

AUGUST 1946— North & South published

OCTOBER 1947— Visits Washington, D.C.; Robert Lowell records her reading poetry; first visit to Ezra Pound at St. Elizabeths

NOVEMBER 1948— Bard Poetry Conference, Bard College, Annandale-on-Hudson, New York

FEBRUARY 1949— Trip to Haiti with Virginia Pfeiffer

MAY–JULY 1949— Under care at Blythdale in Greenwich, Connecticut

AUGUST 1949— In residence at Yaddo, Saratoga Springs, New York

SEPTEMBER 1949–OCTOBER 1950— Poetry Consultant, Library of Congress, Washington, D.C.

OCTOBER 1950–JANUARY 1951— In residence at Yaddo, Saratoga Springs, New York

AUGUST 1951— Trip to Sable Island, Canada

FALL 1951— Amy Lowell Travel Fellowship

NOVEMBER 1951— Departs from New York City for South America

MAY–JUNE 1952— Returns to New York City to settle affairs and move to Brazil

JULY 1955— Poems: North & South—A Cold Spring published

DECEMBER 1955–JANUARY 1956— Working on Modern Brazilian Architecture with Henrique Mindlin

MARCH 1956— Partisan Review Fellowship

MAY 1956— Pulitzer Prize for Poems: North & South—A Cold Spring

APRIL–OCTOBER 1957— Visiting New York City with Lota de Macedo Soares

DECEMBER 1957— The Diary of "Helena Morley" published

FEBRUARY 1960— Boat trip down Amazon River with Lilli Araújo

JANUARY 1961— Lota begins work on Flamengo Park

JUNE 1961–JANUARY 1962— Writing *Brazil* for Life World Library; visits New York City December 1961 to January 1962 to finalize text with publisher

FEBRUARY 1962— *Brazil* published

JUNE–JULY 1962— Robert Lowell and family visit Brazil

MAY–JULY 1964— Trip with Lota to Milan, Florence, Venice, and England

FALL 1965— Purchases house in Ouro Prêto

NOVEMBER 1965— *Questions of Travel* published

JANUARY–JULY 1966— Teaching at University of Washington, Seattle

OCTOBER–DECEMBER 1966— Trip to Holland and England with Lota

MAY 1967— Trip on Rio São Francisco River

JULY–OCTOBER 1967— In residence at 61 Perry Street, New York City

25 SEPTEMBER 1967— Lota's death in New York City

DECEMBER 1967–MAY 1969— Living in San Francisco with Suzanne Bowen

APRIL 1969— *Complete Poems* published

MAY 1969— Returns to Ouro Prêto, Brazil with Bowen

AUGUST 1969— Moves into Casa Mariana, Ouro Prêto, with Bowen

MARCH 1970— National Book Award for *The Complete Poems*

MAY 1970— Bowen returns to Seattle

SEPTEMBER 1970— Begins teaching at Harvard; lives in Kirkland House

APRIL 1971— Order of Rio Branco, in recognition of services rendered to Brazil

JULY–AUGUST 1971— Trip to Galapagos Islands, Machu Picchu, and Ouro Prêto with Alice Methfessel

SEPTEMBER 1971— Takes up residence at 60 Brattle Street, Cambridge, Massachusetts

APRIL 1972— *An Anthology of Twentieth-Century Brazilian Poetry* published (with Emanuel Brasil)

JUNE 1972— Reads "The Moose" for Phi Beta Kappa Award Ceremony at Harvard

AUGUST–SEPTEMBER 1972— Trip to London, Stockholm, Helsinki, Leningrad, Oslo, and Bergen with Alice Methfessel

MARCH–JUNE 1973— Teaching at the University of Washington, Seattle

JULY 1973— Four-year appointment as lecturer at Harvard begins

AUGUST 1974— Takes up residence at Lewis Wharf, Boston

FEBRUARY 1976— Books Abroad/Neustadt International Prize for Literature (awards ceremony in April)

MAY 1976— Trip to England and Greece with Alice Methfessel

DECEMBER 1976— *Geography* III published

JULY 1977— Retires from Harvard University

SEPTEMBER 1977–JANUARY 1978— Teaching at New York University

6 OCTOBER 1979— Death of Elizabeth Bishop at Lewis Wharf, Boston

REMEMBERING ELIZABETH BISHOP

CHAPTER 1

CHILDHOOD, 1911-1927

In 1974, at the age of sixty-three, Elizabeth Bishop moved into a handsome, top-floor condominium at Lewis Wharf in Boston. From the narrow balcony she had a view of the harbor. Bishop kept a list of the ships that passed and told one friend, poet and translator Robert Fitzgerald, that if she had been born a boy, she would have been a sailor. Her great-grandfather from Nova Scotia, a captain on a merchant vessel, had sailed the east coast of North and South America and may have docked at the wharves within Bishop's view. Beyond these wharves was South Boston, and across the bay was Revere, the two places where Bishop had spent much of her childhood living with an aunt and uncle. Forty miles west of Boston was Worcester, Bishop's birthplace, where her grandfather and father had been prominent businessmen. Even the building itself on Lewis Wharf reminded Bishop of her origins—the granite had been quarried in Quincy, near the home of her paternal grandmother. Having inherited something of her great-grandfather's itinerant spirit, Bishop had lived in several cities throughout North and South America during her life. With the move to Lewis Wharf, she sensed that she had traveled full circle.

Bishop had lived in Cambridge, Massachusetts, for more than three years before moving to Lewis Wharf. In 1970 the poet Robert Lowell, a close friend, had arranged for her to replace him for a year as a teacher of writing and literature at Harvard, a position that had been renewed yearly. Lowell's offer had been a lifesaver for Bishop, who was unhappy and confused after just having dramatically ended an ill-fated relationship in Brazil, where she had lived for sixteen of the previous twenty years. As had been the case throughout Bishop's life, a friend came to her aid at a critical moment. In fact, a number of broken relationships throughout her life had periodically cast Bishop adrift. Lewis Wharf, then, another in a series of beginnings for her, was perceived by Bishop as probably her final effort in a lifetime spent searching for the regularity, intimacy, and privacy of domestic life. This legacy had been settled upon her as a child.

◆   ◆   ◆

William Thomas Bishop (1872–1911) and Gertrude May Boomer (1879–1934), Elizabeth Bishop's parents, may have met while William was a patient at Boston's Massachusetts General Hospital, where Gertrude was a nurse. In photographs Gertrude appears both direct and cheerful. She was a slender woman with angular yet full facial features. A native of Great Village, Nova Scotia, Gertrude taught school in both Nova Scotia and Cape Breton before training to become a nurse. Her loneliness in Cape Breton (she took her uncle's dog with her after one vacation) and the Gaelic dialect of the region, which she found difficult to understand, made her leave that job. Many men and women moved between Nova Scotia and New England during this period, and Gertrude became a part of this historical migratory pattern. Grace, Gertrude's younger sister, followed in her sister's footsteps. One can also imagine that Boston must have represented for the Boomer daughters the promise of a larger life, and in Gertrude's case, William Bishop must have symbolized this new life.

William Bishop was a large man with slumping shoulders, thin hair, and a somber expression. Elizabeth may have inherited his streak of melancholy, which vied throughout her life with her Boomer liveliness. He was the oldest of eight children (an older sister had died when she was ten days old) and heir apparent to his father's large and prosperous construction firm, J. W. Bishop & Co. John W. Bishop, Sr., had built his business from the ground up, after emigrating from Prince Edward Island and learning carpentry in Rhode Island.[1] He imposed something of the same rigor on his sons, who had to climb the corporate ladder from the simplest jobs. William left high school to join the firm and eventually earned a reputation as one of the best estimators in the business.[2] Like his father, William was independent, and at one point he attempted to strike out on his own in the construction business, although without success.

William and Gertrude married on 22 June 1908 (he was thirty-six and she twenty-eight) in New York City's Grace Church, followed by a honeymoon in Jamaica and Panama. They took up residence in Worcester, and Elizabeth, their only child, was born on 8 February 1911, the day after a heavy New England snowstorm, in a third-floor apartment at 875 Main Street. Elizabeth's birth marked the beginning of an anguishing time for the Bishop and Boomer families. Bright's disease, which may have taken him to the hospital in Boston when he first met Gertrude, struck William shortly after Elizabeth's birth and caused his death on 13 October, at the age of thirty-nine. Elizabeth was eight months old.[3] Although John W. Bishop was eager to take care of any of Gertrude's and Elizabeth's needs, William's death cast mother and daughter adrift, at least in part because of Gertrude's prolonged grieving. She and Elizabeth lived alternately in Worcester, Boston, and Great Village for the first years of Elizabeth's life. Gertrude wore mourning clothes for five years. As Elizabeth watched, helpless and uncomprehending, her mother's grief spiraled into depression and, eventually, into hallucinatory and violent mental illness.

As Elizabeth's cousin Kay Orr Sargent remembers the story from the Bishop side of the family, "Father said there was a tendency toward mental illness in Gertrude's character and that William's death just pushed her over. He said that Elizabeth's father had done very well and had left quite a little money." According to Elsee Layton, whose father ran the general store next to the Boomers' house, Gertrude's instability following the death of her husband was not the first such incident and that at least one similar incident had occurred during her nursing training: "In those days, training was emotionally hard. Something happened while she was studying to be a nurse, and Gertrude left. Afterward, she went back and finished. She left one hospital and went to another."

Gertrude suffered her first recorded mental attack in 1914, when Elizabeth was three. The following year Gertrude and Elizabeth went to live with the Boomers in Great Village, where Gertrude became uncontrollable. Hazel Bowers, a Great Village resident, remembers a friend of Gertrude's, Ruth Hill, telling her about visiting the Boomers at this time: "The Boomers did talk about not being able to control Gertrude and all the noise from her screaming. Once Ruth found Mrs. Boomer crying. Mrs. Boomer said it had been a bad night. It was dreadfully upsetting for the family." Bishop's strongest memory of this period, recorded in her autobiographical story "In the Village," was of her mother's screams when the seamstress arrived at the Boomers' to fit Gertrude for the dresses that would replace her mourning clothes. When Gertrude had a bad spell at night, the Boomers hurried about, protecting Elizabeth from seeing her unstable mother. Also, Bishop told the poet Frank Bidart that her mother had once been discovered holding a knife while sleeping with her, although it was not clear to anyone that she intended her daughter any harm.

When Gertrude became violent in the spring of 1916, the Boomers committed her to the Nova Scotia Hospital in Dartmouth. Elizabeth was five. Gertrude's younger sister, Grace, who had left her nursing job in Boston to attend to her sister in Great Village, completed the hospital forms. In a written statement dated 20 June 1916 and quoted below, Grace briefly described Gertrude's character, stating that as a child she had been "happy and full of fun" and had grown into an adult who was "steady and successful" in applying herself to everyday tasks. Gertrude was at times "very headstrong," at others, mild in disposition. Grace also traced the progressively severe excitability, irritability, and restlessness in Gertrude's temperament, which she had witnessed during the six to eight months before Gertrude entered the hospital at Dartmouth.

Two years ago [1914], Gertrude had a mental attack and was first treated in Deaconess Hospital, Brookline, [where she] jumped out a 2d story window. [Gertrude was] then sent to Dr. Morton's private Sanatorium, Norwood, Mass. [There she] was not suicidal or homicidal, but morbid and depressed, remained about three months and came out practically well. At [the] beginning of [her] sickness [she] seemed to worry over business matters. [She] also imagined she had kidney, heart, and specific diseases, thought she was going to die and became very religious. When she travelled to Boston, [she] imagined she saw people she knew & that she was watched as a criminal. There at times she would be greatly excited and talk about the war, equality of labor, catholicism, being hanged, burnt as a witch or electrocuted. [She] has always been afraid someone was going to take her child away from her.

All winter [1915–16], during her menstrual periods she was very much upset. [Her] memory is excellent [and she demonstrated no] defects in judgment, confusion or self-accusation until [recently]. Lately she complains of not hearing very well, nervous chills, and very weak spells. Now she imagines she is being given electricity or is being mesmerized and hypnotized and that all medicines given her contain poisons. At times [she] wonders why she has to suffer so, and there again thinks she is doing it for someone else. [She] has never really recovered from the shock of her husband's death [and] still grieves for him. About the first of March [1916] [Gertrude] received a business paper which upset her. After receiving [this] business letter, [she] tried to hang herself with the sheet and caught her mother about the throat.

Probably no one will ever know what was in that letter. After Gertrude was admitted to the hospital in Dartmouth, she did not improve, although the doctors had expected that she would with time. Elsee Layton's sister visited Gertrude shortly after she was admitted and found her slipping in and out of reality: "She felt that Gertrude was well cared for. I remember that Gertrude said, 'What does your father mean by sending all us girls down here?' Gertrude was really mixed up, but part of the time she knew." Gertrude spent the next eighteen years in Dartmouth. She died on 24 May 1934, a few weeks before Elizabeth graduated from Vassar College. What did the young Elizabeth make of this tragic story? Elizabeth told Charlotte Russell, whom she met years later in Florida, that "as a little girl she couldn't understand what was the matter with her mother."

Later in her life, Bishop did mention, although always hesitantly, her mother's institutionalization, and two of her friends, Dorothee Bowie and Frank Bidart, recollect their conversations with her.

FRANK BIDART— Elizabeth never saw her mother in the hospital because her family didn't want her to, and by the time she was old enough, Elizabeth was afraid to. Elizabeth told me that each time she went to Vassar, the train passed the hospital her mother was in—she shuddered when she said this. It was a source of pain, but she didn't simply say (as if the question were simple), "Oh, I should have gone to see her." How does one visit a parent not seen since the age of five, in a mental hospital, when you have been taught to think of her as dead? Then, suddenly, when Elizabeth reached the age when she might have been able to come to an independent judgment about the matter, her mother *was* dead.

DOROTHEE BOWIE— Elizabeth talked about her mother's illness but in a bitter way, partly because at the onset, she was so young. She wasn't aware of what was going on. It was a very traumatic time for her. My sense is that once the mother was institutionalized, Elizabeth, out of a kind of self-defense, just pushed it away. She simply wiped it out.

✦　✦　✦

After her mother's institutionalization, Elizabeth continued to live with her grandparents in Great Village. The Boomers' white farmhouse still sits on a small lot at the center of town, on the main road, next to the general store and across the street from the imposing Presbyterian church. Bishop's grandmother had a small garden at the house, and her grandfather drove his cow to pasture and farmed a plot of land outside of town. Some mornings Elizabeth drove the cow up Scrabble Hill on the Old Post Road, which ran north from the Presbyterian church, to a pasture at the Chisholm's farm. From the top of the hill she could see beyond Great Village to the Bay of Fundy, a blue streak in the distance. High tide filled the salt marshes behind the Boomers' house.

By all accounts, the Boomers were kind, loving grandparents. William Brown Boomer (1846–1930) was a simple man who was known throughout Great Village for his generosity of spirit and good humor. "He was kind of jokey," remembers G. Arthur Patriquin, a friend of the Boomers, and particularly of Elizabeth's Aunt Mary. The Laytons, who ran the general store next to the Boomers, "liked Mr. Boomer. He was a gentleman."[4] Descended from farmers—once or twice a year one of his rustic cousins visited Great Village with gifts of bear meat and venison in sacks in the back of his buggy— William Boomer had moved to Great Village to apprentice himself to a tanner. Eventually he purchased the business, essentially a small piece of land with three tanning pits across the street from the Boomers' house. When Elizabeth and her mother came to live with the Boomers, however, local tanning businesses had lost their customers to large chemical tanning factories. Mr. Boomer then made a modest income farming, performing odd jobs around town (including butchering), and working as the janitor at the school and the Baptist church, where he was a deacon. He would slip Elizabeth a peppermint with "Canada" written on it while passing the collection plate in church. According to her poem "Manners," when Elizabeth and her grandfather rode in his wagon, he instructed her to greet everyone they passed on the road, to offer anybody a ride, and to walk up hills to give the horse a rest.

Elizabeth's grandmother, Elizabeth Hutchinson Boomer (1850–1931), was, like her husband, "a home person" who was involved in "church things."[5] She made yeast from the hopvine that grew against the barn, preserved fruits and vegetables, baked bread, churned the butter and tended her garden. Mrs. Boomer was the source of her namesake granddaughter's strong domestic impulse. A short, heavy, and stoop-shouldered woman, she had a glass right eye, which was a novelty among Elizabeth's childhood friends: "Mrs. Boomer had a great sense of humor. When I stopped in after school to play, we'd watch her to see if we could tell which was the glass eye."[6]

Mrs. Boomer's friends remember her talking about arriving in Nova Scotia from England when she was young. Elizabeth believed that her grandmother's forebears were Tories who originally settled in upstate New York, then fled to Nova Scotia at the time of the American Revolution. Anglicisms peppered Mrs. Boomer's speech, and books by British writers were present in the house. Elizabeth traced her first interest in literature to these books. In fact, there was a fortnightly literary society in Great Village to which Elizabeth's mother and aunts had belonged. Each winter was devoted to the study of a single writer, Keats, Ruskin, the Brownings, Milton, Shakespeare, Dante, and Tennyson among them. According to a high school friend, Elizabeth's sense of poetry emerged when she was very young, perhaps during her time with the Boomers.

FRANI BLOUGH MUSER— Elizabeth said she always thought that the first time she got the idea of poetry was from a doctor. She was about four or five or something like that. She had the incipient asthma that was going to bother her later. She had suffered from a lot of colds. Elizabeth was in bed with something or other, and the doctor in telling her what was wrong with her or in asking her to put out her tongue made a couplet, made a rhyme. It surprised her. She was tiny and she had never heard anything like that. She laughed. Elizabeth said she had never heard something so wonderful in her life. So then she began thinking about words that rhymed.

✦   ✦   ✦

Elizabeth Bishop's Hutchinson uncles, the brothers of her grandmother, added educational, literary, and artistic interests to the family. William Hutchinson served as president of Acadia University in Wolfville, Nova Scotia, which he and his brother John had attended. When this career ended because of his blindness, William took an administrative position with the Baptist church. John Hutchinson was a missionary, writer, and translator. George Hutchinson, the oldest of the three brothers, shipped out from Nova Scotia as a cabin boy when he was fourteen. He returned apparently fed up with the sailor's life and determined to become a painter. Photographs show him as a thin, handsome man with a self-confident air. George spent some time painting pictures of ships for their owners in Great Village, then studied in Paris and London. He gained some distinction as a portrait painter in London. In the 1890s (perhaps for two or more years) George Hutchinson set up a studio in Great Village with a friend, Bertram Knight Eaton, and two of Elizabeth's aunts, Grace and Maud, studied painting with them. The Hutchinson eye for art passed from George's portraits and landscapes, through Maud's accomplished sketches, oils and watercolors, to Elizabeth herself, who painted delicate watercolors throughout much of her life. She wrote two poems about George's paintings ("Large Bad Picture" and "Poem"), and she alone seems to have inherited his wanderlust.

After Gertrude entered the hospital at Dartmouth, Elizabeth's favorite aunt, Grace, returned to Boston. Mary, the youngest, was the only Boomer daughter left at home. She was twelve years older than Elizabeth. As a childhood friend G. Arthur Patriquin remembers her, "Mary Boomer was a very pretty, very intelligent girl. Mary used to take care of Elizabeth quite a lot." Elizabeth attended her first year of school, primer class, in Great Village from 1916 to 1917, and she and Mary, who was in her last year of school, walked together to the large white schoolhouse located south of the Boomers' house and across the bridge. Elizabeth could hear the school bell while she ate her porridge, and Mary annoyed Elizabeth by always leaving for school at the last minute.

There were five grades in Elizabeth's classroom. The primer students wrote on slates, and Elizabeth brought a medicine bottle of water and a rag to school each day to clean hers. She had a desk and learned school etiquette— raise your hand, don't scrape your feet, don't gaze out the window, the latter enforced upon Elizabeth one day by the teacher's pointer—and some basic reading, writing, and arithmetic. She seemed a happy, normal child: "Elizabeth was a nice little girl. She was very clever and intelligent. She wasn't shy, just an ordinary girl."[7] Photographs from the time show her healthy, round face, natural smile, and large, dark, attractive eyes. "Elizabeth was pleasingly plump and looked like her Aunt Grace."[8]

Even at the age of six, Elizabeth prided herself on being conscientious, and one day when Mary's tardiness made her late for school, she writhed with embarrassment. As this scene is described in her autobiographical story "Primer Class," it was the kind hand of her teacher, Georgie Morash, who calmed her and reprimanded Mary. Morash was the favorite of many students in Great Village.

CASSILDA CHISHOLM FORBES— We all thought the world of Georgie Morash, a great teacher. We thought she was very pretty—nice skin, nice teeth. She was tall, or she looked so to us. Georgie didn't seem to have any favorites. She was very kind. She was fair. She was sharp in school. You behaved yourself.

In the primary room there was primer class through grade 4. In the morning Georgie would put most of her time on primer and grade 1, and then at recess, 10:30, they'd be through for the morning and go out to play. She could then concentrate on grades 2, 3, and 4. Georgie generally had arithmetic on the board for this class. You were all through with math in the morning and generally your reading lesson in the morning, and then Georgie would teach English and grammar. We always had singing in the morning, and a hymn after dinner. She taught us a lot of music. We would sing each other songs, because the school had no piano or organ.

✦ ✦ ✦

Bishop often said that life in Great Village was like living in the nineteenth century. She fit comfortably into its regularity. She and her cousin Billy, the son of her Uncle Arthur and Aunt Mabel, who lived across the street, would play hide-and-seek around the Presbyterian church. Elizabeth and her friends visited Nate Fisher, the blacksmith, whose shop was next-door to the Boomers' house. "Elizabeth spoke about Nate being good to her when she was a little girl. He made her little rings and things."[9] Nate's shop was vibrant with sights, sounds, and smells for Bishop and her friends.

DONALDA MACLACHLAN NELSON— We used to stop by to visit Nate, the blacksmith. The door would be open most of the time. You'd stand and hear the cling clang and watch him take the metal and put it on the wagon wheel. He would heat up the metal and throw it into the water—steam and that sort of thing. I remember him having the horse's hoof up and this whitish stuff that he was cutting off and the smell.

Every Monday Elizabeth walked to the post office with a package of food, small gifts, and books for her mother at Dartmouth, and, as she described herself in "In the Village," she stayed to the side of the road opposite Nate's shop and avoided other villagers on her walk. According to Hazel Bowers, when Nate Fisher read Bishop's descriptions of her trips to the post office "he mentioned about one place where she said something about him calling her over to look at the parcel, and he said he didn't call her over to be inquisitive. He just called her over to be friendly. She never did stop on her way over. She always stopped on her way back. The grandparents didn't want anybody to see the address where the parcel was going."

The tinsmith's shop of Elizabeth's Uncle Arthur (Uncle Neddy in "Memories of Uncle Neddy") was across the street from the Boomers'. From the ceiling of Arthur's workshop, in the back of the building, hung the tin pails, mugs, and other objects that Elizabeth watched him shape. Arthur, whom photographs show to have been a thin, timid-looking man, let her help with the soldering. In the store at the front of the building there were two chairs, near his fishing rods, where Arthur sat with his friends and talked. Arthur was a skilled fisherman who was known for tying his own beautiful flies. A fascination with crafts and native, primitive objects, first developed in the dark shops of Nate and Arthur, stayed with Elizabeth throughout her life. She also inherited Arthur's interest in fishing.

Arthur scandalized the Boomers, however, and Elizabeth observed many quarrels between him and her grandmother. His bad management of his own finances frustrated Mrs. Boomer. In 1901, the year before he married, Arthur had sold all his own property to pay off his debts. There was an ongoing family debate about a horse Arthur had received as a gift from his mother, sold back to her, then continued to use. His marriage to Mabel Pigott (Aunt Hat in "Memories of Uncle Neddy") did not please Mrs. Boomer, either. There was some question about Mabel's background: "Someone asked Art one time who his wife was. 'Well,' he said, 'she was from Londonderry and so-and-so was her mother, but God knows who her father was.' Mabel was kind of a character too. She could tell more naughty little rhymes and stories, and she would laugh!"[10] Mrs. Boomer complained about Mabel not feeding her own children homemade foods, and Arthur did take advantage of his relatives across the street: "Art was always coming in and getting some eggs or a piece of butter or something. I don't think Mrs. Boomer liked it too well."[11] Elizabeth found Aunt Mabel a fierce, frightening woman, with a sharp jaw, or at least so she is presented in "Memories of Uncle Neddy." According to one of Mabel's friends, "There wasn't a kinder soul in the world than Mabel Boomer."[12]

While Art cut, shaped, and soldered tin in his workshop, he chewed tobacco and took swigs from the bottle of rum he kept near his bench. "Art would more or less go on benders. I can remember my husband and me driving up the road because Art had been drinking and was driving a car. My husband would get Art off the road, make him sit over, and drive Art's car back home. When Mabel would be away, he'd get in real trouble, and Billy, the son, would come over. I'd go over, make some strong coffee, and try to help him get straightened out. After one of his benders, Art would do a good job at his work for a long time."[13] Art once took the temperance pledge, unsuccessfully. He infuriated Mabel. "Mabel couldn't stand drinking."[14] So Art and Mabel would quarrel over his drinking, and occasionally they came to Mrs. Boomer for advice. Elizabeth listened to the rumble of their voices from behind the closed door to the parlor. Once Art showed up drunk at a funeral in Great Village, and Elizabeth watched her grandmother cry with embarrassment. Nevertheless, "when Art was sober, he was the nicest person,"[15] and Elizabeth had an affection for him, although she would later in life cite him as evidence of the hereditary pattern within her family that led to her own alcoholism.[16]

The center of the Boomers' social life was the church, and Art violated their Baptist propriety and pledge of temperance. The small church where the Boomers attended services and Elizabeth attended Sunday school was located on the edge of the village proper. There were also church meetings and hymn sings during the week at the houses of other Baptists. Elizabeth watched the baptisms in the stream that ran through town, and she made two girls of fervent faith, who were baptized in cold water and died from the chill, the subject of her short story "The Baptism." "There was a deep hole where the river ran under the bridge, where the baptisms were held. Generally people would line up on this bridge and watch the baptism, and the Baptists would stand on both sides."[17]

The Baptists in Great Village considered themselves stricter than the Presbyterians. Sunday mornings Mrs. Boomer sat in her rocking chair at the kitchen window and watched the villagers arrive for Presbyterian services; then at the Baptist afternoon service, she and others who had done the same thing commented on what and whom they had seen. Elizabeth remembered one time when her kind and tolerant grandparents were critical of the upbringing of one of Elizabeth's childhood playmates, the pretty, delicate Gwendolyn Patriquin (Gwendolyn Appletree in Bishop's story "Gwendolyn"). They felt her parents were indulgent. In her story, Bishop describes the Patriquins feeding Gwendolyn sweets without any care for her diabetes. Gwendolyn's brother recollects the circumstances of his sister's illness.

G. ARTHUR PATRIQUIN— Gwendolyn, one of my seven brothers and two sisters, was a pretty girl with light hair. She would go out in the fields and pick flowers every day. She was the youngest of the family. I wouldn't say that she was pampered. I don't think that my parents ever went against the doctor's orders. Gwendolyn died when she was nine years old [in 1922] from diabetes. At that time they didn't know what diabetes was. She practically lived on ice cream or fruit, which she shouldn't have had at all. She was bedfast a very short time when she died. The family had expected her to pull through.

Gwendolyn's death occurred when Elizabeth was eleven and was visiting the Boomers during a summer vacation. According to Bishop's story, Mrs. Boomer watched Gwendolyn's funeral from her rocking chair in the kitchen, sending Elizabeth outside to play on the side of the house opposite the Presbyterian church. Elizabeth sneaked into the house to watch the funeral from the parlor window, and she could hear her grandmother sobbing in the background. Suddenly, two men emerged from the church with Gwendolyn's coffin, then left the coffin unattended, leaning against the church by the church door. The stark sight of the coffin sent Elizabeth screaming into the background, followed by her weeping grandmother. A month later Elizabeth and her cousin Billy staged a funeral of their own for Gwendolyn, using Mary's favorite doll, even though Elizabeth knew that if she were discovered with this doll, as she was, she would be severely punished.

Bishop's lifelong struggle between affirmation and denial, ultimately between life and death, took root in Great Village. She did not inherit the Boomers' religious faith; she remained an unbeliever. In its place, she developed a trust in beauty and art. She remembered the sound of Nate's hammer ringing through the Boomers' house and counteracting her mother's screams, the glitter of the solder offsetting the darkness in her Uncle Arthur's workshop, and Mary's doll adorned with flowers prolonging Gwendolyn's beauty and innocence, if only briefly. In each case something crafted and attractive relieved the gloom.

◆　◆　◆

In September 1917, at the age of six and after three years in Great Village, Elizabeth was abruptly moved to Worcester. Her Bishop grandparents wanted to provide her with a better education, and by implication a better upbringing, than that which the Boomers could provide in rural Nova Scotia. The Boomers agreed. Nevertheless, Elizabeth felt as if she were being kidnapped by people whom she hardly knew. She gives the details of moving to Worcester in her autobiographical story "The Country Mouse." In the cramped cabin of an overnight train from Halifax to Boston, her grandfather, with his silver hair and goatee, was an imposing, even intimidating figure. He grumbled all night because he was cramped in a single berth with his wife. The formal language of her grandmother seemed cold and distant to Elizabeth. After a restless night Elizabeth was sick in the morning. She remained in her seat with her grandmother, watching the autumn trees and munching on soda crackers, while her grandfather went to breakfast in the dining car.

When they arrived in Boston, the Bishops' chauffeur, Ronald, drove Elizabeth and her grandmother to Stern's to purchase a new wardrobe (brown), which Elizabeth hated. After lunch, Ronald drove them to Worcester. The Bishops lived in a rambling farmhouse on fifteen acres at the edge of the city. The trolley line went past the front, but there was a feel of the country to the place: an apple orchard, a large barn, where the Bishops kept cows and hens, and a garden. Huge maples lined the driveway, and swings hung from two large horse chestnuts.

John William Bishop (1846–1923), a self-made businessman who never forgot his country origins, could have afforded a far grander house in a fashionable section of Worcester, but a farmhouse suited his taste. He had been born on a farm on Prince Edward Island, immigrated with his family to Rhode Island, where he mastered carpentry, learned all the details of the building business, and founded one of the largest construction companies in the East. J. W. Bishop and Company built scores of college, government, and industrial buildings. And John W. Bishop was very much in charge of every-day details at the company at the age of sixty-one, when Elizabeth came to stay in Worcester. He liked to point out to his grandchildren a mill house in Whitinsville, a town not far from Worcester, in which he had lived as a young man. He told them that he had had bathrooms installed in all the mill houses in that town when he had made his fortune.[18]

John W. Bishop and Sarah A. Foster (1849–1923) had been married for forty-seven years when Elizabeth came to live with them. They had had nine children, but only three (Jack, Marion, and Florence) were still alive. John Bishop was a patriarch devoted to his family.[19] He rented houses on Cape Code when one grandchild became sick from rheumatic fever and needed salt air. He built a house next door to his own for one daughter, so that his family would remain together. He founded a roofing business for a son-in-law so that he would not take a distant job. Elizabeth's cousin Kay Orr, who was four years old when her mother, Sarah, died, was also taken in by the senior Bishops and attended kindergarten in Worcester, as did her cousin Elizabeth. She and Elizabeth were often in Worcester together as children.

KAY ORR SARGENT— Grandpa and Grandma's sprawling, beautiful farm-house, at 1212 Main Street, was in the country, a couple of miles from the center of Worcester. The trolley line stopped one block beyond it. An elderly farmer who had been with Grandpa for years did all the farm work, yet Grandpa knew what needed to be done. He had some earlier experience with farming. At that time the elite of Worcester lived nearer downtown, on the hill in back of Main Street. Grandma and Grandpa weren't sociable people with many friends in town. They had money enough, but not the taste to pursue the social life. Grandpa wasn't mixed up in many civic activities. He was well known in the business circle.

Grandpa was an impressive looking, kindly gentleman. He was smart, honest, and picked some good men to work for him. Grandpa had very loyal employees. Every morning he went off in his chauffeur-driven car. In all the years when I was with them, he was never sick or home from work for a day. He had drive, and plans working in the back of his mind all the time.

Grandpa would come home at a set time, shed his coat and hat, go to his pet chair near the big front window of the billiard room—the family or living room—and have a cigar. If I were around, he'd ask what I had done during the day. Sometimes he would take a walk around the rose and iris gardens, which he loved, if it was still daylight. Every night after supper he sat at the big center table in the billiard room and played Canfield. He read the papers, but I don't remember seeing any books around. There were books in one of those parlors. No one disturbed them. I don't think that the tastes got developed that far.

Grandma was pretty. She was shorter than Grandpa, and heavy, with a placid, sweet expression and disposition, lovely, snow-white curly hair and a pink-and-white complexion. Grandma taught me how to darn and to sew. Her sewing room, where she had her plants and her canary birds, had an all-glass front. By the time I knew her, she knew what she was doing as far as her household was concerned, and, of course, she had brought up several children by then, and I imagine she had done a good deal of the bringing up, too, because Grandpa was traveling so much. There were a cook and a second maid, and the farmer, and occasionally somebody else came in if they had heavy spring cleaning to do. Grandma went to the kitchen every morning and interviewed the cook. I never saw her do anything but take care of her plants and her birds. She was well taken care of. She was a lady.

◆　◆　◆

In spite of all that the wealthy Bishops could provide for Elizabeth, her life in Worcester was fated to fail. As well-intentioned and generous as her grandparents were, Elizabeth sensed duty and obligation rather than love in their affection for her. Kay Sargent remembers that "Grandpa and Grandma were certainly good with my young brother and sister when they were around. I never heard a harsh word to any child, but they were not demonstrative. If Grandpa gave an order, it would have been obeyed." As a result, Elizabeth felt alone in Worcester. The Bishops' rambling farmhouse seemed empty to her. Her Uncle John was distant and forbidding and her Aunt Florence eccentric and odd. According to Elizabeth's recollection in "A Country Mouse," there was one girl next door with whom she became good friends, and she liked her school teacher, but Elizabeth felt out of place in an American school. She had sung "God Save the King" and "The Maple Leaf Forever" each morning in Great Village. Saluting the American flag made her feel that she was betraying Canada. When she told her grandmother that she hoped the Americans would win World War I but did not want to be an American herself,

Mrs. Bishop almost cried, then took to helping her memorize "The Star-Spangled Banner." Elizabeth's happiest moment occurred when her grandfather returned from visiting his office in Providence one day and brought her her own chickens for pets. He thought that a bit more farm life might make her feel more at home. It did, temporarily, but Bishop's unhappiness brought on eczema and asthma. Her cousin remembers how ill Elizabeth was at times.

KAY ORR SARGENT— Aunt Florence was delegated to ensure that Elizabeth and I both got properly put together for breakfast. When Elizabeth was three, I can remember her bouncing up and down delightfully in the middle of Aunt Florence's bed while she was trying to get us dressed. We always played well together; neither of us was fussy or a crybaby. Grandpa had a big barn with cows where we played. He'd had a special pen built, and he bought some bantam hens for Elizabeth. There was a playhouse. In winter we could slide downhill behind the house.

Elizabeth was plump and healthy looking, except that her color was always pale. She was sick a lot. Every once in a while she had a bad attack. She couldn't breathe. Grandpa and Grandma took Elizabeth to one of the few specialists on asthma in Boston. One time they had a trained nurse for her, and Elizabeth was isolated in one smoky room. My grandparents and the doctor were trying some new treatment, which was the only way she could breathe at that point.

♦   ♦   ♦

One day the eczema sores on Elizabeth's skin were so severe that she was sent home from school. Incidents like this one made her self-conscious and shy, even fearful that she was dying. She thought of her father. As she lay in bed with asthma, and her Aunt Florence's dog, Beppo, scratched at the closed door, Elizabeth realized that she was alone in the world. And it is from this period that Bishop traced her own sense of a unique identity. As she narrates the famous story in both "A Country Mouse" and the poem "In the Waiting Room," one February afternoon she was sitting in the waiting room of the dentist's office while her Aunt Florence was inside for her appointment. Florence's cry from pain, the date (February 1918) on the *National Geographic* that Elizabeth was reading, and the unfamiliar people in the room made her suddenly aware that she was different from them all. She was an Elizabeth. And then came the attendant questions: Who is this Elizabeth? Why is she in the world?

Bishop's dismal stay in Worcester lasted less than a year, ending in the spring of 1918. Then she was sent to live with her Aunt Maud and Uncle George Shepherdson in Revere because "the doctors decided they wanted to try sea-level climate for her. Worcester is very high and dry, and she was so sick with this asthma that they thought they would try that."[20] When Ronald carried the sick Elizabeth up the steps of the Shepherdsons' house, Aunt Maud broke into tears.

"Elizabeth went from one extreme to the other in moving from the Bishops' to the Shepherdsons'. The Shepherdsons' house wasn't shabby, but it was lower class."[21] The Bishops provided financial support for Elizabeth during these years because "the Shepherdsons didn't have much money. They needed help."[22] If Bishop's recollections in an unfinished story entitled "Mrs. Sullivan Downstairs" are to be believed, she had a small back bedroom in the five-room, top-floor flat that the Shepherdsons rented in Revere, to which they had moved from South Boston.[23] They lived in a working-class neighborhood occupied by immigrant families, some of whom did not speak English. Their street was unpaved. There were vacant lots between the houses, a few with gardens, one tended by Elizabeth's Uncle George. Maud and Elizabeth grew boxes of pansies on the back steps and other plants throughout the flat. For some holidays Elizabeth was driven to Worcester by Ronald; she spent summers in Great Village with her Boomer grandparents.

"Elizabeth didn't talk much about living with Aunt Maud. I never got any sense that she was that close to Maud. She was more attached to her Aunt Grace. I know that," remembers her cousin Phyllis Sutherland. Grace Boomer worked at Massachusetts General Hospital, lived with the Shepherdsons, and shared responsibilities for taking care of Elizabeth with Maud. Maud was a nervous and shy woman who lived a workaday, poor life. Elizabeth watched Maud sift the ashes to find the unburnt bits of coal and soak old bits of newspaper in water, squeeze them into balls, and dry them to use to start fires. A girl from across the street, Barbara Hunt, was called upon to visit when Elizabeth was too lonely. Maud, who had been a seamstress in Great Village, took in sewing. Maud painted with some accomplishment, and she and Grace took Elizabeth to all the museums in Boston. Maud also played the piano and sang beautifully. She and Elizabeth would sing hymns in harmony.

George Shepherdson is curiously absent from any of Bishop's comments about this time. Ernest Sutherland remembers George Shepherdson as "a nice fellow. A good-looking, very stern man. He'd let you know if he was displeased." A classmate from Walnut Hill School, Barbara Chesney Kennedy, remembers driving Bishop to the Shepherdsons' for a vacation: "Theirs was a two-story house in a modest to lower neighborhood. The living conditions and surroundings made Elizabeth sad. Aunt Maud's husband worked for General Electric in Lynn, Massachusetts. He had been laid off because of the Depression. My father was vice-president of G.E., which made the contrast more acute." Elsee Layton traveled from Great Village with Mary Boomer to visit the Shepherdsons when they were girls and remembers "we had a wonderful visit. We saw a number of good plays. George, a teacher, took us out two Saturdays to where George Washington met his men, Harvard, and the Boston market. George was an awful tease. At one point he wanted Mary to go ahead while we were walking on the street. She was scared that he might just disappear." For whatever reasons, "Elizabeth didn't care for George."[24]

During her years with the Shepherdsons, Elizabeth seems to have missed a good deal of elementary school because of her asthma. Maud stayed up with Elizabeth during her sleepless nights. When she was sick, Elizabeth read and was read to by her two aunts. Maud kept her supplied with new books. Elizabeth also spent her own allowance on books. She particularly liked fairy tales. And thus her interest in writing took root. Elizabeth wrote her first poetry at eight, coached by her Aunt Grace. Like Elizabeth's mother, Grace had taught school in Nova Scotia before going to Boston to study nursing, and she brought good humor and common sense to her relationship with Elizabeth. When she was twelve, Elizabeth won an American Legion prize for an essay on "Americanism." She discovered Walt Whitman on her own at thirteen.[25]

Life at the Shepherdsons' changed for Elizabeth in her early teens. In 1923 Grace Boomer returned to Great Village and later that year eloped with William Bowers. They were married in New Brunswick and returned to Great Village to live on Bowers' large farm. Elizabeth visited Grace during the summer and wrote to her. Grace's responses occasionally included a poem.[26] The same year of Grace's marriage, Elizabeth's Bishop grandparents died, within five days of each other. According to one of Bishop's cousins, "When Grandma died, we arranged a very quiet funeral downstairs because Grandpa was very sick upstairs. He was a startling sight, with his white beard against yellow-brown skin from jaundice. He died five days later [on 2 October 1923]."[27]

The deaths of Elizabeth's grandparents left her Uncle Jack (John Warren, 1880–1934) head of the construction firm and responsible for administering Elizabeth's funds. Elizabeth never liked him. When she lived in Worcester with her grandparents, she found Jack's joking about spankings and other punishments crude. His arguments with her grandmother had frightened her. Nor did she like Jack's wife, Ruby. "Uncle Jack wasn't a fun person, and I doubt if he would have paid much attention to Elizabeth unless she asked him a financial question. Aunt Ruby might have paid a little more attention. Ruby was a selfish person. She was polite and kind, but she wouldn't put herself out too much."[28] Jack Bishop, with his hair slickly parted in the middle, seems to have been a hardened man who was frustrated by his failure to fill his father's shoes. According to one of Elizabeth's cousins, "Uncle Jack had been an alcoholic for quite a while, and he beat it himself. He took to chocolates, and always had a big box beside his armchair. Dad admired Uncle Jack because he had managed to quit. Dad didn't admire him for many things. When Grandpa died, my father said he'd give Jack three years to ruin that business. Jack did it in two."[29] Jack did gain respect in the construction business as an estimator, but as an overall manager, he was a failure.

However stern he was, Jack Bishop took his responsibilities as Elizabeth's guardian seriously. Sensitive to the fact that Elizabeth had few, if any, acquaintances of her own age, he and the Shepherdsons sent her to camp for part of the summer in 1924. At Camp Chequesset, a nautical camp for girls, in Wellfleet, Massachusetts, "there was a certain catering to the expressive person."[30] There, for the first time, Elizabeth met a group of girls who shared interests similar to hers. Friends of hers from Chequesset, some of whom called her "Bishy," remember her as being precociously literary, even having a favorite perch in an apple tree where she would write. Elizabeth wrote poems, songs, and skits which were performed at Sunday evening gatherings. She kept the week's log for her group in verse. The camp turned her into a sailor and a naturalist. In the course of the six summers that Elizabeth spent at Camp Chequesset, she introduced her fellow campers to a number of writers, and they introduced her to the writing of Emily Dickinson, Joseph Conrad, and Henry James. One girl gave her Harriet Monroe's anthology of modern poets, from which Elizabeth memorized lines from Hopkins's "God's Grandeur." At fourteen, in a secondhand bookshop in Provincetown, Elizabeth discovered George Herbert's poetry. At sixteen she bought her own edition of Hopkins.[31]

John Bishop also decided that boarding school would help Elizabeth make friends. Through a friend at Wellesley College, he located the Walnut Hill School in Natick, a town located halfway between Boston and Worcester. He visited Walnut Hill in the early summer of 1926, and Elizabeth was admitted to the ninth grade for September, although her doctor's unwillingness to give her a smallpox vaccination because it might provoke her eczema prevented her from attending that year. Instead, Elizabeth spent ninth grade (1926–27)—or, actually, repeated ninth grade, which she had already taken at Saugus High School—at North Shore Country Day School, in Beverly Farms, Massachusetts, commuting daily by car an hour each way from the Shepherdsons' house in Revere. Her academic record was uneven—she was weak in math and Latin, but she was clearly gifted in English. Five pieces by Elizabeth were printed in the school's literary yearbook, The Owl, among them two brief, precocious essays on Tennyson's Idylls of the King, a Thurberesque story about a hapless traffic policeman, and a magical poem about sky dragons that were turned into subway cars as punishment for eating new stars.

When Elizabeth entered Walnut Hill in September 1927, at the age of sixteen, she took the first steps in shaping a life on her own. During her three years there, the Shepherdsons drifted into the background of her life, and visits with her Uncle John and Aunt Ruby Bishop became an unpleasant family formality. Most important, Elizabeth developed the friendships that Jack Bishop had hoped she would. According to one school friend, "Elizabeth would kind of groan a bit about Walnut Hill, but she liked it enough. It was home to her. She was more at home there with her friends than with her relatives."[32]

CHAPTER 2

When John Bishop visited the Walnut Hill School in the spring of 1926 to enroll Elizabeth, he described his niece and ward as "a lonely little girl."[1] He and other relatives of Elizabeth were eager for her to locate a group of friends, and Walnut Hill seemed a hospitable place for doing so. Its five residential buildings, designed to look like cottages, sat on a hill surrounded by fifty acres of playing fields and woods, just north of Natick, Massachusetts. The central dormitory, Eliot House, had comfortable living and dining rooms and a broad porch where students gathered. The school had a stated concern for the students' health, and there was a program of outdoor physical activity—at least one hour every day. And Walnut Hill was known for sending its graduates to the best women's colleges, such as Wellesley, located two miles east. In fact, John Bishop preregistered Elizabeth for Wellesley when she entered Walnut Hill.

Elizabeth had difficulty adjusting to boarding school life during her first year at Walnut Hill. She was a quiet, dreamy, seemingly preoccupied sixteen year old. To those around her, she seemed very mature in certain areas—she had read more than any of the other students and could recite hymns, songs, poems, and stories with ease—but she did not mix well. Although Elizabeth was a year or two older than her classmates, presumably because of school she had missed as a sickly child, she was quite immature socially, as one of her friends remembers.

MARGARET MANN BEMIS— Elizabeth and I liked the outdoors. There were two tall trees right on the edge of campus we used to climb, sit up there, survey the world, and talk. Someone discovered us up there, and we were hauled in to Miss Bigelow [the principal], who said, "I really don't know how to punish you girls for this, because we've never had this problem before. But young ladies do not climb trees." I think we were put on-bounds for a week or something like that. It never occurred to us that we were doing anything forbidden. I have an idea that we probably went right on climbing trees, figured we could get away with it. We were doing totally harmless things. Very unsophisticated, all of us. Very young for our age.

✦   ✦   ✦

Elizabeth was frequently ill and in the infirmary during her first fall at Walnut Hill; thus her work in Algebra and French was incomplete by the December marking period, according to the school's report. Miss Bigelow noted in a letter to Elizabeth's guardian that she felt Elizabeth had a keen enough mind to do excellent work and earn admission into an excellent college, but "she takes so little care of herself that we wonder whether she will ever reach college."[2] Elizabeth's Aunt Ruby wrote back to Miss Bigelow that she and her husband were pleased to see that Elizabeth's report showed "a little improvement in some things but sorry she had to lose so much time from her classes and studying." She blamed Elizabeth's difficulty in adjusting to school life on her upbringing: "Elizabeth is rather spoiled and has not been made to do many things, but it was so easy to do for her and let things slide; she was always a sort of pathetic child, having to fight asthma and eczema ever since she was a baby. I can only hope that she will do better as time goes on."[3]

In February 1928, during Elizabeth's second semester at Walnut Hill, Ruby Bishop wrote to the school, stating that she was disappointed with Elizabeth's grades and angry that Elizabeth had not written in response to cards and candy that she and John had sent while traveling on vacation to South Carolina: "Elizabeth is heedless and thoughtless of others. . . . She is old enough to take a little responsibility."[4] However, by April, John and Ruby Bishop were "very much pleased to know that Elizabeth is improving in her studies, as well as general school life. . . . As we see her only occasionally, we can see a big change in her from time to time, and believe she is on the right track."[5] Elizabeth was finding friends and becoming a part of the community. Barbara Chesney became a close friend at Walnut Hill, and she remembers the distinctive bearing that set Elizabeth apart from other students at Walnut Hill.

BARBARA CHESNEY KENNEDY— I remember well when Elizabeth and I became close friends. It was at the theater, sitting next to her. We were allowed to go to Boston for an occasional Saturday afternoon, or we were taken as a group to symphonies and plays. Something changed that day and she began confiding in me. She told me about her mother and the dress-maker and that whole story in "In the Village." It made me want to protect her. Elizabeth needed somebody then, and apparently I was it. I probably was the closest friend she had at that time. I don't know that she'd ever had a friend that close before.

Elizabeth and I were the same age. I understood her background. I was born when my mother and father were almost fifty. My parents were the age of Elizabeth's grandparents. Mine was a New England family and hers was Nova Scotia, but it was the same conservative English background. I lived a sheltered life in Pittsfield, and she had too. She felt comfortable with my family and visited us a lot. I also knew her Aunt Florence, who summered near Pittsfield, and I met her aunts Maud and Ruby when I drove her to their homes.

I don't think Elizabeth felt part of our family. She was very independent and at the same time dependent, but always independent in "thought." She didn't like to be center stage. Elizabeth didn't have what you call a stage presence for a large party. She didn't fit in with general conversation and small talk. At the dining room table at my house, for instance, people didn't really know quite how to handle her. When I'd go back home, my friends didn't understand why I preferred seeing her.

Elizabeth was far more interesting and had a lot more to offer and to learn from than other students at Walnut Hill. She wasn't an athlete and didn't do the things that most boarding school girls do. She had nice turns of speech then, often with a catching sense of humor, that always delighted me. Through Elizabeth I became aware of the unexpected word used in a special situation. She seemed to know these things instinctively. Elizabeth also taught me a lot about seeing the little offbeat thing. She had read far more widely than anybody else had. I asked her much later how this came about, and all she could say in explanation was that when she was ill and in bed as a child that she only thought and read. That doesn't answer the whole question. I learned a lot about art from Elizabeth. In my senior year at Walnut Hill or freshman year in college we went to galleries in New York. I remember on one occasion her refusing to go into one because there was a charge and she didn't approve of that for art. I went with her to see an organ play color on a screen. It also gave out smells. She was conscious of new things from an early age, more so than most of us. One could call it being avant-garde.

Elizabeth wasn't run-of-the-mill. She was a thing apart. The gifts and presents she gave me were always most unusual and exquisite. I still have the antique garnet earrings, the tiny cast Beatrix Potter animal figurines, a Limoges Easter egg, Brazilian clay crafts, their Brazilian cook's primitive painting, a monogrammed blanket for my horse—well, you get the point. She had the same feeling about people. They needed to be special and different. Elizabeth never was really comfortable with her Uncle Jack and Aunt Ruby. They were conventional, boring and to her nonunderstanding. Elizabeth had set her heart on a red leather edition of Shakespeare in which each play was separate. Aunt Florence promised to give her the set but then discovered it was too expensive, so she gave Elizabeth another set that had single plays in single books, but they were gray and looked "textbooky." Elizabeth took them back and got half of the red leather set instead. She had taste, and her love and appreciation for good literature was instinctive.

My relationship with Elizabeth was a very strong one, stronger than most relationships and long lasting. It was more intense but not a lesbian one, though I do know that some people were concerned that it might be. Ruby Willis, the math teacher, once called me into her room and asked me if this was a "normal relationship." I don't remember what I said, but fortunately I ignored it. Elizabeth was different and I perceived and appreciated this.

Everybody respected Elizabeth and thought of her as superior, but unapproachable. A lot of people did not understand her. Miss Prentiss, an English teacher, loved her. She always did a "thing" about *Hamlet*, in the gravediggers' scene. She wore false teeth, which highly entertained the girls, but Elizabeth found it embarrassing rather than funny.

✦　✦　✦

Walnut Hill brought discipline and order into Elizabeth's life. Dress was proscribed and the day was an order of events from room inspection and morning prayer through classes and sports to evening study hall. There were formal sit-down meals—once one of her friends was reprimanded for taking a drink of water after having placed her napkin on the table. In time, Elizabeth learned to be tidy and to take better care of herself, as Miss Bigelow had wanted. At the same time, there was a certain leisurely pace about life at Walnut Hill, and Elizabeth and her friends biked to Natick and Wellesley, picnicked on the grounds, and went sledding and skated on the pond at the center of the campus.

Seriousness of purpose pervaded academic life at Walnut Hill. As one of Elizabeth's classmates remembers, "Walnut Hill was all business as far as learning what you needed to know to pass your exams and get into what college you hoped to go to. We worked very hard. The teaching was very good."[6] Elizabeth's curriculum at Walnut Hill each year consisted of English, Latin, French, and mathematics (algebra and plane geometry). She took one year of ancient history, and senior year she studied chemistry. Elizabeth took piano lessons each year, and a yearlong course in harmony during her senior year. Every student attended Bible study each week. At North Shore Country Day she had excelled at French and English, receiving A's in both subjects, yet had difficulty with Algebra I and Latin I (both of which she had taken at least in part the year before at Saugus High School), receiving C's in both. Math remained a difficulty at Walnut Hill, but Elizabeth's performance in Latin seems to have improved. In fact, later in life Elizabeth said that translating Latin had been the best training she had to become a poet.[7]

Frani Blough entered Walnut Hill with Bishop in 1927, and, although she was a year ahead of Elizabeth, became one of her closest friends. Blough was interested in writing and served as editor of the school's literary magazine during her senior year. Also, she loved music; Blough and Bishop played and sang hymns together in the practice rooms on rainy days. She remembers the teachers who were most important to Bishop during these years.

FRANI BLOUGH MUSER— I had a fine time at Walnut Hill mainly because I knew Elizabeth and some people like her. Our rooms were adjacent the first year. We became good friends right away. It was fun to do things together. She had a somewhat reserved manner, but very humorous. Elizabeth was the kind of person who would say, "It is going to be a beautiful sunrise tomorrow. Let's get up at five and go look at the sunrise." Well, that appealed to me, the kind of thing that stretched the rules a bit, because you were not supposed to be off campus at five in the morning.

Miss Daniels—she was a marvelous teacher. Her way of teaching Latin was very strict, but very kind and very sensible. You had to memorize a certain number of words of vocabulary each day, twenty or something. The first thing you did when you marched into the room was write down your twenty words. Then Miss Daniels took up the paper, corrected it, and the next day any that were wrong were added to the new words. After about a week of this, you knew those words forever. She had a basic method of analyzing a sentence in order to translate it properly. It involved analyzing each single word. That kind of attention to detail Elizabeth liked.

The math teacher was Miss Ruby Willis—a real tough nut, very severe and large, a lot of white hair. She kind of glared at you and glowered. She didn't bother me much because math came easily to me. Elizabeth came to blows with her all the time. Miss Willis couldn't stand Elizabeth, of course, because Elizabeth was inclined to be a little bit fresh. Elizabeth couldn't stand Miss Willis because she was such a dragon. Elizabeth hated numbers. She couldn't make the connections.

Walnut Hill was a place that stressed high standards in reading and writing. There was a lot of peer judgment on the quality of literary effort. You'd write something and then you'd leave it on somebody else's bureau to look at. We were all eager at exchanging. Our English teacher, Miss Prentiss, was kind of a trial because she was so spiritual.[8] She would sigh over things, write sentimental notes, that kind of thing. But Miss Prentiss had good taste in literature, and she brought on anybody that showed a sign of any talent. She was devoted. She was good at teaching writing. Miss Prentiss insisted that her girls write about something they knew—a person, your life—and not imaginary material. Elizabeth would groan and say, "Oh, well, that's right. I guess I do owe her something." Miss Prentiss was of course thrilled with having taught Elizabeth.

✦　✦　✦

Elizabeth made a name for herself at Walnut Hill through her writing. As early as November of her sophomore year, her Aunt Ruby mentioned in a letter to the school that Elizabeth was "thrilled with the honor thrust upon her," which, one can assume, was having four pieces accepted for publication in the December issue of the school's literary magazine, the *Blue Pencil*.[9] She was the only one from her class to be appointed to the magazine's editorial board during her sophomore year. Bishop wrote poems, plays, short stories, and book reviews for the *Blue Pencil* during her three years at Walnut Hill. She was book review editor during her junior year and general editor of the magazine senior year. Bishop also wrote plays and songs for various occasions at the school. She was an alto and secretary in the Glee Club. As one close friend put it, "Walnut Hill was for Elizabeth and a lot of people a kind of freedom, freedom of expression. It was good for her and for all of us, if only for the friends we made and people of like viewpoints."[10] Several of Bishop's friends remember some of her activities during her first two years at Walnut Hill.

BARBARA CHESNEY KENNEDY— Elizabeth often came up with a song or a play when it was needed overnight. One of the best things I remember about Walnut Hill was a play we gave, and I believe Elizabeth wrote it. Miss Prentiss coached us. We went looking for a horse and buggy near the school, or at least the buggy, and we carried it on and off the stage. I remember being the leading man with the girl and me sitting on the seat of the buggy kissing. Elizabeth was the villain in large, men's clothes.

At the end of that first act, we had to carry the buggy off the stage, down the middle aisle; of course, everyone was in hysterics. It was the success of the year for the school for all of us—I remember asking Miss Prentiss if we couldn't act in plays all the time.

And, having discovered the buggy, we then knew there was a horse to go with it. The rule in those days was that you couldn't drive in a car with anybody without written permission. Elizabeth decided that there was no rule against going for a ride in a horse and buggy, so we did just this, driving down the back roads for several weekends, until we got caught. Since there weren't any rules to cover this adventure, we got away with it. I realize from Elizabeth's poem "Manners" that she knew a lot more about horses and buggies than I did. She certainly left me with great girlhood experiences. Everything was a bit different, more fun and very enriching.

MARGARET MANN BEMIS— During junior year Elizabeth wrote a little song about a tree that had been planted by the outgoing class, just for fun. This was the kind of thing she would do.

> Poor little tree,
> All the seniors have departed.
> Poor little tree,
> But the juniors are kindhearted.
> Poor little tree,
> We will prize you, water you and fertilize you,
> Make you grow and mesmerize you,
> Poor little tree.

FRANI BLOUGH MUSER— Another little experience of ours was going to hear Edna St. Vincent Millay in Boston. She spoke in Jordan Hall. We thought it was a scream. She was dressed, of course, in some filmy, long dress. Today it would be a caftan, but then, it looked more like somebody about to do a Grecian dance, except it was long. And she sort of grasped a curtain. The whole thing was so calculated and so soulful that we were convulsed. We thought it was the funniest thing we had ever seen. So perhaps we were ready for something more modern than Edna St. Vincent Millay. I remember Prokofiev came to play, at Wellesley and also in Boston. Elizabeth and I both took piano lessons. The piano teacher saw to it that we got to Prokofiev. It was pretty avant-garde for a conservative girls' boarding school in those days. And, of course, we were eager for that kind of thing.

Elizabeth and I put on a takeoff of an 1890s type of melodrama—which we spelled, of course, *mellow drama*, thinking that was very witty—with a girl tossed out by her cruel father, carrying a baby through snow, which was paper. Full of forties stuff, but it was all our own idea. The school, desperate to fill up those Saturday nights, went along with us. There was a Christmas pageant that was put on just before closing down the school for the vacation every year, and Elizabeth and I decided that it was corny and needed to be updated or refurbished. So we wrote a play to take its place. We used to write it in the bathroom after lights-out because that was the only light that could be on. We sat on the floor under the washbasins. It involved a lame boy who comes and presents something to the infant and receives a blessing, like *Amahl and the Night Visitors*. We wrote some songs so that it was a musical. It was still put on in the fifties or sixties.

The great thing about working for the *Blue Pencil* was that you could leave campus and take things to the printer and read proof. Elizabeth and I used to go there together and work on the *Blue Pencil*. It gave you a sense of tremendous importance, freedom, and independence.

✦　✦　✦

In time, Bishop gathered a coterie of friends at Walnut Hill. Rhoda Wheeler Sheehan, who was president of the student government in her senior year, remembers that "Elizabeth had an influence, a very quiet one, not a domineering one, on others. I admired and looked up to her, but there was never any question of not being equals." Joanne Collingwood Disney, who was in Bishop's class and was also a member of the editorial board of the *Blue Pencil*, recollects the effect Bishop had on her.

JOAN COLLINGWOOD DISNEY— Elizabeth was really different from everyone else, in her appearance as well as her ability. She had an almost round face, beautiful blue eyes, and frizzy hair. You couldn't look then look away. The experience of Walnut Hill to me was the experience of knowing Elizabeth. She introduced me to authors I hadn't known before, and if I had known a little about them, I felt closer to them because of her knowledge of them. She was completely at home with the world of literature. Elizabeth was familiar with everything to do with Katherine Mansfield, a favorite of hers— British writers that Mansfield was intimate with, the people around her, and the whole story of her life. She was very much interested in Russian novelists.

I wouldn't have read *The Brothers Karamazov* as soon as I did had it not been for Elizabeth. She also introduced me to John Donne and Ernest Dowson. She was sure that I would like Emily Dickinson very much, and I did. Elizabeth gave me a lovely, blue leather copy of *Alice in Wonderland* and an excellent biography of Beatrix Potter. Elizabeth knew what I wanted to know. She did it all so unostentatiously. That was the beauty of it.

Elizabeth was very modest, although keenly aware of her own . . . I wouldn't use the word "power." There was no question in her mind of her own rightness, or of her being at the center of her own world and being able to find her way through it. She was absolutely sure of that in a way which at that age not many people are.

Elizabeth had such funny and original ways of looking at things and people. On the one hand, Elizabeth was a bit amused by a lot of things. She had a sort of general attitude of amusement toward the foibles of the human race. She was more than anything else amused, but not in an unkindly way. I listened and more or less accepted her way of looking at things. It was a really nice place to be. It was not a place that invited mockery of any kind. Occasionally she was close to cynicism in what I refer to as amusement. She was trembling on the brink of being rather harsh when it was unnecessary.

There was this big gap in Elizabeth's life. Elizabeth didn't talk much about her childhood. It was too difficult. She felt affection for her aunts and they toward her. She really had to grow up all by herself. A terrible sadness would cause her to be despondent. I remember exactly how she looked one time when she was leaving our house in Plymouth, Massachusetts, after a visit. It was a very sad look and stayed with me. Maybe the right word would have kept her there.

✦ ✦ ✦

Elizabeth's sadness was prompted, at least in part, by her feeling that she was different from others and, consequently, that no one cared for her. The adults at Walnut Hill witnessed Elizabeth's sense of her difference surfacing occasionally in her behavior. In May 1929, during her junior year, Elizabeth and another student dressed up in "grotesque costumes," wrapped themselves in bedspreads, placed baskets on their heads, and walked from the campus toward Natick. Before they arrived in town, Elizabeth and her friend realized their foolishness, but on the way back ran into a faculty member, who sent them to the principal's office. Miss Farwell felt that she could understand this kind of behavior from a fourteen year old, but not from the eighteen-year-old Elizabeth. She worried about Elizabeth's inheriting her mother's mental instability and took the liberty to consult a psychotherapist in Boston. A report of this incident and this meeting are contained in a letter from Harriet Farwell, the assistant principal, to John Bishop:

> Dr. Taylor was very much interested in everything I had to say about Elizabeth, but she would like to see her before she can make any final analysis of her case. She did not seem to be worried at all about Elizabeth's heredity. The fact, however, that Elizabeth probably has repressed within her a certain amount of information about her mother, she did consider to be very serious. I feel very sure myself, in fact, I may say positively that Elizabeth knows some if not all of the truth about her mother. It does not make much difference whether it is some or all— either would be enough to make her very unhappy and keep her in an abnormal state of mind. Dr. Taylor feels very decidedly that submerged facts of this kind are dangerous and should be brought out into the open. She would not be willing to try to handle Elizabeth's case unless she were given permission to tell her as much as seemed advisable—all if necessary. . . .
>
> Elizabeth shows many evidences of the fact that she thinks, for some reason or other, she is different from other girls. This kind of a performance is natural in children who try to assert their own personalities when they feel things are not quite as they should be. What Dr. Taylor would try to do would be to make Elizabeth feel that she is like other girls, removing if possible any mystery that may be in her mind, and removing also a possible fear.[11]

✦ ✦ ✦

Apparently Elizabeth had never spoken of her mother with the Shepherdsons or the Bishops. Three years before the costume incident, when John Bishop had visited Walnut Hill with the intention of enrolling Elizabeth for the ninth grade, he spoke frankly with Ruby Willis, a summer assistant to the principal, about the history of Elizabeth's mother's illness and his concerns for Elizabeth's psychological health. Miss Willis took the following notes for Miss Bigelow and Miss Farwell:

> These facts are either unknown to Elizabeth or, at most, only surmized by her, since no one has ever spoken to her about her mother and she has never mentioned her. Elizabeth's mother has been mentally unbalanced for a long period of years, probably since Elizabeth's birth, and has been in an institution in Nova Scotia for the last seven years.

Elizabeth's father died soon after the child's birth. The mother tried to administer the estate, and had many difficulties. Her family knows of no hereditary tendency to insanity. . . . Doctors believe that the mother may recover when she reaches a certain age.

Elizabeth's guardian is most anxious that no mention of these facts shall be made to Elizabeth. She had been a "lonely little girl" and he anticipates much happiness for her at Walnut Hill.[12]

How much did Elizabeth know at this time about her mother? According to Frani Blough Muser, "Elizabeth told me that her mother was in an institution. Then she never mentioned it again. Elizabeth felt that fear of inheriting her mother's illness was a horrible thing, but she consciously did not allow it to be part of her life." John Bishop did meet with Dr. Taylor and gave her permission to go ahead with her treatment of Elizabeth. When Elizabeth went for her sessions, however, she refused to talk openly, and the meetings were discontinued.

✦ ✦ ✦

By the time Elizabeth was a junior and a senior at Walnut Hill, she led an independent life. She was essentially on her own. Two friends recollect the freedom with which she spent vacations during this time.

MARGARET MANN BEMIS— Elizabeth wanted to spend part of the summer of 1929 with Joan Collingwood and me to get away from having to be with her family. We rented a cottage for a month on this spit of land that went out into Plymouth Harbor. A fifteen-foot sailboat went with it. My father and mother were spending that summer in York, Maine; so we decided, without telling them, to sail up the coast from Plymouth to York Harbor. The first night we camped at Narragansett Beach. The next day we were going across Boston Harbor, and there was a schooner race going on. There was no wind, and all these big ships were floating around, and we were floating around in the middle of them. We spent one other night in the boat, then got to York Harbor. My parents were totally surprised and horrified at these three bedraggled females suddenly emerging from the sea. We stayed a day or so there with them, and then we sailed back again.

FRANI BLOUGH MUSER— Elizabeth and I made a walking trip down the Cape out of season—spring vacation, probably. Of course, at our age, you didn't go off by yourself like that, so the school said they would provide a chaperone, the assistant headmistress of the school, Miss Farwell, a stiff little woman. Miss Farwell really bore the brunt of running the school. In fact, she was a very intelligent woman. Maybe she thought it would be fun. And it was fun. We had a delightful time. We took the train down, then we started walking up the Cape, through the very pretty wilderness part north of Brewster. It was all dunes and hills of pine, very deserted. In those days the Cape wasn't what it is today. It was so funny to be walking along with this woman for whom we felt nothing but an amiable scorn. There was a little rooming house you could stay in. We had a three-day walking trip on the Cape with Miss Farwell. That was the kind of adventurous thing Elizabeth and I liked, adventurous because nobody else would have thought of walking anywhere.

The summer after I had graduated from Walnut Hill [1929], I had finished my college boards, which one did at the end of June in those days. Then they let you know about the middle of August whether you were in. So the summer was a time you just wanted to get through, if you were really anxious about your future. I didn't know where I'd go, and Elizabeth said, "Why not come to camp with me?" I thought that was not a bad idea. I'd not been to camp since I was twelve, but I had never learned how to sail. Elizabeth had been there so long that she knew how to sail very well. So I signed up and spent the two months [at camp]. I partook of the camp life, which was very delightful, very low-key. We were both much too old to be at camp. Elizabeth, of course, was very much a kingpin in that setup there, because the people that ran it had known her for a very long time. They were very superior people, a doctor and his wife from New York City. There was a published girl poet in my cabin. There was a certain catering to that kind of expressive person. So we used to write new songs. It was the kind of place where you would read all the time. There was lots of time for reading, and people did. It was respected.

◆   ◆   ◆

Elizabeth's seeming-independence masked her rootlessness, however, as another incident from this same summer illustrates. Elizabeth spent part of August 1929 with her Uncle Jack and Aunt Ruby at their summer home in Harwich Port. A bad attack of asthma forced her to leave in early September. As she was preparing to leave, a shutter fell on Ruby's head causing a bloody cut. In a grisly letter to a friend, Elizabeth described herself snickering to herself as she watched Ruby on the ground.[13] Elizabeth then went to visit her Aunt Florence in Stockbridge for the final weeks of summer vacation.

Florence Bishop, a tall and skinny maiden aunt, had helped take care of Bishop as a child in Worcester. Florence lived with her parents until their deaths, then moved to a small house in Stockbridge, Massachusetts, where she was treated at a local clinic for her list of habitual physical complaints—she was a lifelong hypochondriac—and operated her own bookstore as part of her therapy. Elizabeth indulged her aunt, who liked literature and felt, as a result, that she was the only Bishop who understood Elizabeth. One of Elizabeth's cousins who was staying with Florence at the time recollects Elizabeth's visit that summer.

NANCY ORR MORRILL— I spent a summer [1929] in Stockbridge when Aunt Florence lived there. Elizabeth had been there two or three days before I was there. Priscilla Coe [a cousin] and I arrived together. There was a little theater in Stockbridge that I was interested in. A friend asked me to come to the theater for a day with her to see what was going on. So I asked Elizabeth if she wanted to come. She didn't want to come. Priscilla had a date.

When I came back, Aunt Florence said, "And where is Elizabeth?" I didn't know. I'd been at the theater all afternoon. I said, "Well, she may have gone up to town shopping, Auntie. She'll be back." She didn't come back. It began to get dark. A cousin came over and we patrolled Pittsfield and Lee. And finally I said, "You know, she said to me she was going to go back to school." I wondered if she wouldn't hitchhike. And that's just what she did. She went back to Walnut Hill. The police found her sleeping on the steps.

I don't have any idea what made her do it. Elizabeth was kind of odd. She wasn't a girl that mixed very well. Maybe Priscilla and I were overwhelming to her and she got frightened. Priscilla was a very attractive girl at that age; she had lots of boyfriends. I have to wonder if maybe all these boyfriends didn't scare Elizabeth. Priscilla was much more sophisticated than Elizabeth and I at that age.

✦   ✦   ✦

Miss Mulligan, an English teacher, found Elizabeth wandering around the Walnut Hill campus the next day. Elizabeth told Miss Mulligan that she had traveled by train and by foot, arriving at Walnut Hill late the previous night and sleeping on the porch of Eliot House in a hammock couch. She asked to see Miss Farwell, who was away. Miss Mulligan took Elizabeth home with her, gave her some food, and put her to bed. Elizabeth slept until dinner time. Miss Mulligan phoned Florence, then wrote her a lengthier description of what Elizabeth had told her, which included the following comments:

I think that Elizabeth is beginning to realize what a cruelly thought-less thing she did in running away, and yet she is so intensely individualistic that she keeps saying that she couldn't help it. Unfortunately she seems to have got the idea in her head that people think her odd and that nobody loves and admires her. Apparently her longing for affection seeks compensation in the bizarre. Because I believe it very bad for her to think that she is in any way "odd" or "different"—as such a talented girl is likely to think—I have told her that most people have impulses to run away at times and I have laid the emphasis not on the impulse but in the lack of self-control in yielding to it.[14]

However this particular incident resolved itself, Elizabeth returned to a successful senior year at Walnut Hill. To some extent her antics continued. One night in January 1930 she and a friend sneaked into the gymnasium, which was under construction. They lit the fire in the workmen's stove, tossed in some potatoes, then climbed the scaffolding. From the highest point, Bishop could see the glow of the stove and watch crystals slowly forming on the tall windows of the new building. She and her friend sat there, waiting for other friends to arrive to eat the potatoes, singing hymns. They felt "like drunken cathedral builders."[15]

Elizabeth was a successful and inventive editor of the Blue Pencil during her senior year. To increase the number of submissions, she and others on the staff transformed the school's dining room into a Greek tavern for one evening in April. Elizabeth herself played the proprietor, Ignatius Acidophilus. The whole school was invited, in two sittings, to celebrate the christening of Blupi, a new son in the Acidophilus family. The students arrived in Greek costume and deposited their entrance fee, a literary manuscript, at the door, in a large ballot box borrowed from the Natick town clerk. There were mounds of cream cheese in fancy designs, kettles of spaghetti, and bunches of bananas suspended from the ceiling. The literary staff staged a fight among some sailors in one corner and planted a fake rat beneath the faculty table. When Blupi, a large Humpty-Dumpty doll, was brought before the crowd, the evening concluded with an extemporaneous speech by his proud father.[16] The finances of the Blue Pencil were so strong that year that the magazine sponsored a group of professional puppeteers to perform on campus for the whole school.

In late April, Elizabeth and Barbara Chesney visited Frani Blough at Vassar. This trip convinced Bishop that she wanted to attend Vassar.[17] (Vassar must have looked like a larger version of Walnut Hill to her, although it was to prove to be a far larger, less homey, and more contentious place once Elizabeth took up residence there that fall.) Toward that end, Elizabeth received a good, balanced recommendation from the school concerning the progress she had made in her three years at Walnut Hill:

> Elizabeth Bishop is markedly above average in intellectual interest and attainments. She has read extensively, with a mature taste, and displays so much talent in writing both prose and poetry, that she is regarded by teachers and schoolmates as something of a genius. She is at present the successful editor-in-chief of the school magazine. She has shown originality and initiative in this connection and in various school activities, notably a Christmas miracle play which she helped to revise and in which she acted one of the parts.
>
> She has a keen interest in fine music and plays the piano.
>
> She enters into out-of-door activities with great enthusiasm. Although she was suffering from asthma when she first came to us, this trouble has been largely overcome under Dr. Rackemann's care, and her health is now good.
>
> Since her father's death, when Elizabeth was a child, and her mother's subsequent invalidism (in an institution for mental trouble) Elizabeth has been brought up by her grandmother and partly by an uncle. She has found in school life, however, what a psycho-therapist advised us she should have: friendships and group activities to make her less of an introvert, and healthful outlets for her vivid imagination. We are very much pleased with her development and improvement.
>
> She is attractive in appearance with a personality that makes itself felt. Formerly she was often silent and abstracted in manner; but is now generally alert and responsive. She is high minded and sincere. Altogether we can recommend her highly as a candidate for college, and we feel that she is a girl who needs what college can give her in companionships and in opportunities for self-expression. We have confidence that she will do distinguished work in English.[18]

To prepare for her college entrance examination in English at the end of the school year, Elizabeth wrote an additional weekly practice essay for Eleanor Prentiss that spring, with success: she received 98 percent on her English college board. Barbara Chesney Kennedy remembers Bishop helping her prepare for the exam.

BARBARA CHESNEY KENNEDY— I can see Elizabeth and me sitting in a room while she coached me for the English college boards. They were all essay questions. She coached me in college, too. In English, [my] freshman year at

Smith, I had to write a theme every week. I would always consult Elizabeth by mail and remember her telling me to write about my past or something I knew, to write about myself. In one particular paper she told me to remember what magazines were on the coffee table, as she later did herself with the *National Geographic* in her poem "In the Waiting Room." I regret that I did not save those letters, as she wrote every day.

Elizabeth graduated in June 1930, with thirty-one other seniors (six of whom went to Vassar with her) and thirty special students who had come to Walnut Hill for an extra year's preparation for college. All wore white dresses and jackets for graduation. Elizabeth left a melange of final images behind her. In the graduation portrait of the senior class, she sits hunched, suspicious, a slim smile on her face, her wavy hair pulled tight from front to back. The class poem, "Lays of 1930," written by the editors of the yearbook, referred to "Bishop of the barbarous hair."[19] Her individual senior portrait in the yearbook shows a far younger, boyish Bishop; one thinks of the tree climber. And then there was her senior prophecy: "Miss Bishop, the poet laureate of Nova Scotia. Walnut Hill has proudly placed her bust in the alcove, while she remains in Nova Scotian seclusion."[20]

E lizabeth Bishop arrived at Vassar College in September 1930 with a pot
of Roquefort cheese. "Bishop," as she came to be known to her friends
at Vassar, believed that the best way to develop poems was to record
her dreams, which she did in a notebook, and that eating cheese before
going to bed would make her dreams more vivid and interesting. Throughout her freshman year, the pot of Roquefort sat on the bottom shelf of her
bookcase.[1]

Vivid dreams or not, Bishop did not have a happy freshman year at Vassar.
An undergraduate population of 1,150 was daunting for her, even though
some friends from Walnut Hill were there with her. "Elizabeth was overwhelmed by the size of Vassar."[2] There was something of the rural feel of
Walnut Hill at Vassar, but none of Walnut Hill's intimacy. And one can
imagine how other college students reacted to Bishop's idiosyncratic enter-
prises during that first year—eating Roquefort cheese before bed, sleeping in
a tree one night, or sitting alone in a darkened dormitory room observing
the shadows an old-fashioned lantern cast on the walls.

Two of Bishop's classmates remember her during their freshman year at
Vassar. Shirley Clarke had known Bishop at Walnut Hill, where Clarke had
been president of the senior class. They became even closer friends at Vassar. Eleanor Clark had graduated from high school early and lived in Italy for
the year and a half before entering Vassar. Clark recollects that she "just
wasn't geared to American college life at all" and that Bishop shared her
restlessness.

SHIRLEY CLARKE VAN CLEEF— Elizabeth, Rhoda Wheeler Sheehan, and I
lived in Cushing Hall at Vassar. Freshman year Elizabeth and I lived on the

third floor. (Later we lived on the first floor across the hall from each other.) I had to walk past Elizabeth's usually open door to go down the stairs. Every night I went off campus to get something to eat. Elizabeth was highly critical of this because I was getting awfully fat. Obviously I had to give up my nightly chocolate and doughnuts. So I'd get to the head of the stairs and Elizabeth would say, "Where are you going?" I would turn around and come to her (sometimes darkened) room. She would give me an apple, we'd talk, and I'd forget about eating.

We talked mostly about books and writers, sometimes about what she was writing. I still have the copy of John Donne's collected works that she recommended. Although I, too, was an English major and loved books, I was also enamored of men and parties, and she was curious about my adventures. Once she said to me, "I wish I knew some men the way you do." I remember this because it startled me. I thought she was superior to that sort of thing.

One of the nicest things I remember about Elizabeth was an evening in New York. My father invited us to dine at the Union League Club. He was in his sixties at that time, much older than anybody else's parents. He was a very dignified, old-fashioned gentleman who wore a derby hat and Chesterfield coat and carried a silver-headed cane. He treated Elizabeth with gracious courtesy, and she responded in the same way. My father particularly liked intellectual women. He and Elizabeth talked steadily all through dinner. I don't remember what they talked about. It was enough simply to sit and watch them enjoy each other.

Elizabeth and I didn't always agree. She disliked Miss Lockwood, who was my freshman English composition teacher, and who remained my good friend for many years. But our disagreements didn't really matter. I respected and admired Elizabeth. By the time we got to Vassar I was sure she was going to become a famous poet.

ELEANOR CLARK WARREN— Bishop and I were both very untypical American college freshmen. I was rather solitary and fairly miserable, and Bishop was floundering. It took a lot longer for her to gather her little society, which had very much her stamp on it. At the beginning of the year, we were equally out of it, more or less miserable, bored and unhappy and not wanting to do the things that seemed to be what other people were taking pleasure in.

One winter night Bishop turned up at my room—it must have been nine o'clock in the evening—and we just decided to run away, not with any permanence, but get out of there. We collected what little money we had between us. Bishop wore her uniform, the pea jacket. We got a trolley down to the railroad station and the next train out heading south. The idea gradually arose to aim for my mother's closed-up house in Litchfield County, Connecticut. We spent all the money we had except a few cents to take a taxi from Hudson to the shoreline. The last train out was leaving and stopped at Stamford. So we walked to the center and decided to hitchhike.

So we got on the Post Road and started thumbing. It was snowing hard, almost a blizzard. It was getting toward two or three in the morning. There were just a few trucks still on the road. They didn't stop for us. Finally, a car came and said something like, "Hello, girls." It was the cops. They trundled us off to the police station, and, of course, they didn't believe for a minute that we were college girls. Elizabeth later said the cops told her that they were out looking for a prostitute in a pea jacket. Maybe. We had a time convincing them that we were college girls.

I told them they could call my mother in New York. I got them to let me speak to her first. I must say she really was heroic on that occasion. Of course, it was well past daylight by the time she made it, but they let her take us. We went on to the empty house in Roxbury, bundled up, slept through the rest of the day, and then my long-suffering mother drove us all the way back to Vassar. The thing that made the cops relent was what Bishop had in the pockets of the pea jacket which she always wore: Greek notes, for her Greek class; a magazine published in those days called Breezy Stories, the kind of thing that you get at a stand; and The Imitation of Christ. Those cops were really stumped, but they decided it had to be something beyond the usual.[3]

✦　✦　✦

Bishop struggled academically during her first year at Vassar. As Frani Blough Muser observed, "At Walnut Hill we all knew that Elizabeth was a genius, but that's a small place. Ten geniuses can walk in at Vassar and not be spotted for two years. Elizabeth always wanted to be good. If she was taking part in something, Elizabeth wanted to be doing it well and be an important part of it. So she would stand back and fall back on her own resources until she'd assessed the situation. Sophomore year Elizabeth was still looking things over." During her freshman year, Bishop declared music as her major field of study, hoping to specialize in composition. Having studied harmony and taken piano lessons at Walnut Hill, she felt comfortable enrolling in a second-year course in theory (Analysis of Design) and taking advanced pianoforte lessons. To her surprise, Bishop found herself unable to master complex music theory that first semester. She enrolled in a lower level, introductory course during her second semester and dropped harmonic design. She also had difficulty performing.

FRANI BLOUGH MUSER— Elizabeth was a good musician, but very particular, as she was with writing poetry. You can stretch writing poetry over any amount of time to perfect a word, but you have to have a carefree abandon when playing. At Vassar they put recitals together of all the students every month or so. Elizabeth came out to play her best piece, and she got stuck. She started again, and she got stuck. Then she got up and left. Elizabeth never played in public again. She had too much stage fright.

♦ ♦ ♦

Bishop's poor performance in music alarmed her former music teacher at Walnut Hill, who could not understand why Bishop had not done as well at Vassar as her preparation and her talent had promised. In response to this concern, Bishop's pianoforte teacher at Vassar, Miriam Steeves, sent to Walnut Hill a written evaluation of Bishop's performance for that year:

> I was disappointed in the progress that Elizabeth Bishop made, as I recognized from the first that she apparently had done, and was capable of doing, both musical and intelligent work. She was technically handicapped by an unusual degree of muscular tension, which I believe to have been one phase of an overtense oriented and nervous organization. As it seemed to me that she could not advance much without an improvement in this condition, I worked hard to help her to overcome it, but without, I am sorry to say, a great deal of success. I am sure it was too deep-seated to be altered easily, and I think she was impatient of the slow progress.
>
> The technical difficulty was, however, nothing like such a problem to me, as was the very small amount of ground which she covered in the learning of pieces. In her first semester . . . a Bach Three-part Invention . . . was the only one of the group of only four pieces which she memorized and was able to play.
>
> While I do not think that quantitative or technical standards are the first ones to be considered, I do think that Miss Bishop's work was inadequate in these respects, and it was only by stretching a point in her favor, on account of her difficulty in adjustment, that I was able to give her a C. She complained feelingly of too-short practice periods, and noisy practice rooms. While I sympathized with her on these accounts,

I really could not think them the sole cause of her slight progress; I feel convinced that this was only part of the difficulty which she seemed to have in adapting her quick and imaginative, but too self-conscious self to college conditions. It seems to me that if she is to remain in college, and derive any profit and enjoyment from it she may need special advice and assistance in the problems of adjustment. I wish she might compass the difficulty, as she has qualities which might be assets to herself or to the college.[4]

During her freshman year, Bishop had deviated from the standard curriculum at Vassar to design a program with an emphasis in the arts, including the study of both music and English literature (Shakespeare).[5] With the demise of music, however, came the ascendency of literature. The Vassar curriculum had been recently changed to allow a student to concentrate in an area of particular strength or interest, and Bishop took full advantage of this option. She took three full-year English courses during her sophomore and junior years, and four during her senior year. That English was the correct path of study for Bishop had been clear to her freshman-year English teacher, Barbara Swain:

> My acquaintance with Elizabeth Bishop was purely a classroom one, and very distant at that, since she was an enormously cagey girl who looked at authorities with a suspicious eye and was quite capable of attending to her own education anyway. And I was young; and I liked prickly intractable people, and I certainly let her strictly alone, except for our class sessions about Shakespeare. . . . Every year at mid-term the English Department at Vassar "writes up" its first year students, trying as best it can to say what it sees about them; I remember that I wrote on Bishop's card that she was evidently doomed to be a poet.[6]

Bishop was perceived by at least one classmate at Vassar as "extraordinarily endowed. When she was talking about something she had been reading, it was to the point, it was clear, it was piercing and bright."[7] She also struck some as detached and self-involved: "Elizabeth could have a very pleasant expression, which I really think was not fake. She could look as if she cared about somebody, a sort of a half smile, not a real big smile, a little pleasantness of expression that seemed to express an interest in other people's lives, when in fact you knew that she was frightfully off in her own [world]. She had some basic isolations."[8] Bishop set high standards for her friendships: "Elizabeth was very strong-minded and strong-willed. She wasn't going to do anything that she didn't believe was right, write anything that she didn't believe was right. This is a very good characteristic, and a person you liked to associate with."[9]

Bishop found two important new friends at Vassar: Margaret Miller, who was in Bishop's class, and Louise Crane, who was a year younger. Miller and Crane are a study in contrasts, or, rather, in a contrast within Bishop's own personality. "Elizabeth was very choice in her friends. Compromise was rather against her nature; so friends she made were apt to be sympatico."[10]

Margaret Miller was Bishop's "intellectual equal."[11] One classmate remembers her as "thin, birdlike, with bright eyes and a nice, sharp sense of humor. She was innovative, academic and had a lively mind."[12] Miller studied literature and art history—she also painted and drew—wrote art reviews for the school newspaper, the *Vassar Miscellany News*, and graduated Phi Beta Kappa. Miller was taciturn, shy, and private, like Bishop, and also shared Bishop's arch wit. One day in English class she talked convincingly for two hours about a play after having read only the preface. She and Bishop lived in adjacent rooms during their senior year and edited the yearbook. They discussed books and painting and were each other's most valued critics. Two friends of Bishop and Miller remember how their temperaments suited one another.

HAROLD LEEDS— Margaret was very special in many ways. She and Elizabeth had a very similar curiosity about things and words. Margaret is extremely expressive. We went with Margaret to spend the day at Vassar. Margaret would talk about such things as the marble in the toilet stall and how she and Elizabeth would disagree about what the figuration in the marble [resembled].

WHEATON GALENTINE— Elizabeth [did] a little drawing and made stationery embossed with a rabbit that had an owl riding on its back. The rabbit was galloping, and the owl was just sitting there enjoying it. This was a fossil they had fantasized on the toilet wall.

◆　◆　◆

Bishop herself called Louise Crane her "odd friend."[13] Crane, who "had a big face and huge blue eyes,"[14] had difficulty applying herself to academic study. "Louise was a freshman three years in a row."[15] Crane hired tutors, but she never finished Vassar. As Crane's closest friend from private school remembers, "Louise lived in a Fifth Avenue apartment. When we arrived after school, the Crane family butler would open the door with a gold pocket watch in his hand. 'You're late again,' he'd say to Louise with a frown.

Louise's mother never seemed to be at home—only servants. Louise was unpredictable, foolish, a 'poor little rich girl.' Louise must certainly have felt any attention she got from Bishop."[16] Crane could be taunting and irreverent—she had a strong streak of rebelliousness—as one family friend remembers.

MONROE WHEELER—I was a close friend of Louise Crane's mother because she was an important trustee at the Museum of Modern Art. I can remember one evening in the early days, soon after Mr. Crane had died and Mrs. Crane had moved from Washington and taken this splendid apartment on Fifth Avenue. She was having one of her Thursday evenings—fascinating events when she would have a distinguished person talk and a discussion afterwards, which was the part that she liked. Louise walked in and said, "What's going on here? In Washington we always had charades."

◆　◆　◆

Louise Crane's father had been president of Crane Paper Company, governor of Massachusetts, and a U.S. senator. Mrs. W. Murray Crane was a member of the original committee to organize the Museum of Modern Art, and she provided the funds to found the Dalton School, the progressive private school in New York City. Louise herself was fascinated by modern art and popular music, particularly jazz, and, as heiress to the Crane Paper Company fortune, had the means to pursue these interests. She introduced Bishop to New York City artists and jazz singers. Louise Crane's "sense of humor and sense of adventure" attracted Bishop.[17] Once she and Bishop kept a pet duck in the dormitory. Both Frani Blough and Mary McCarthy spent time with Bishop, Crane, and Miller at Vassar.

FRANI BLOUGH MUSER—Elizabeth was very shy, as is Louise Crane. Louise is one of those people who have intuitive taste. She would look at a picture recently painted by an unknown and say, "I'll take that." For twenty-five dollars. Then she'd say, "Where can I meet this person?" And it would turn out to be Loren MacIver or someone like that. Her taste in painting was impeccable. She had ideas of the same nature. These were in line with Elizabeth's kind of perception, although Louise did not do something creative with it, as did Elizabeth. She had a quick perception, like that you never can analyze in a mathematical genius.

Louise liked to travel, liked houses, and had a lot of money. She was able to carry out ideas in a way that most people can't. Her mother at that time was very active in the Museum of Modern Art and started a series of coffee concerts. They were in the evening and would mix contemporary music with jazz. Louise was especially good on jazz. She was a good friend of Billie Holiday, people like that. Elizabeth met Billie Holiday through Louise.

MARY MCCARTHY— There were several sort of droll characters in the smoking room in Cushing. There wasn't much input from Elizabeth, but she was certainly there. Louise was part of the smoking room life in Cushing. She was known as "Auntie" because she had little old-maidish airs. At Vassar she was a comic butt. Elizabeth was devoted to her, and vice versa.

Bishop had a very good friend, who was a friend of mine, Ev [Evelyn] Huntington [Halpin] '32, a very amusing character. Ev and Bishop went on a walking trip together [to Newfoundland in the summer of 1932]. She told jokes. There were also those slightly off-color songs, mostly borrowed from men's colleges, that were sung up there at the time, and Ev had several.

Elizabeth lived next to the toilets, which was a nuisance. They made a lot of noise when they flushed. She wrote a humorous poem about the toilets, which she recited in the smoking room in Cushing.

> Ladies and gents, ladies and gents,
> Flushing away your excrements,
> I sit and hear behind the wall
> The sad continuing waterfall
> That sanitary pipes can give
> To still our actions primitive.

And then, of course, there was Margaret Miller. She was no part at all of this smoking room life. The ribald side was not her style at all.

✦　✦　✦

Bishop chiefly spent her Vassar summers and vacations with friends. She felt a certain duty to visit her Boston and Worcester relatives periodically, especially for Christmas, her least favorite holiday, but she was essentially on her own during her years at Vassar. During the summer of 1932, following her sophomore year, she rented a cabin at Wellfleet with Barbara Chesney, then was joined by Joan Collingwood and her sister. In August she traveled with Ev Huntington to Newfoundland, where the landscape—the sharp, tall cliffs, the towns built on hills plunging to the sea, the picturesque schooners and fishing boats—dazzled her. Barbara Chesney recollects aspects of the summers she spent with Bishop on Cape Cod.

BARBARA CHESNEY KENNEDY— In the summer of 1930, after we graduated, several of us from Walnut Hill went to visit Rhoda Wheeler at her seashore home in Westport. I received a call from my mother saying that I had been accepted at Smith. A few days later, Elizabeth, Rhoda, and Shirley Clarke were accepted at Vassar. That was June. In the summer of 1930 or 1931, I bought a 1920-something Dodge touring car for sixty-five dollars. Elizabeth and I drove it to Wellfleet to the "cottage" that she and I had rented for two months. Elizabeth had known about the "cottage" or shack by having explored there when she was at the sailing camp in Wellfleet. Elizabeth also bought a Dachshund, which she named "Comus." She immediately got asthma because she was so allergic. In the end, my aunt took care of him for years. We were visited by several friends from Walnut Hill as well as other friends of mine, including a man from Pittsfield who was pursuing me. He is the same man who took over Elizabeth's finances, putting them in a trust in a bank in Pittsfield.

During another summer, we frequently drove over to Truro on sandy roads to the top of sand dunes. We would climb up and down and I would drive the Dodge in as far as I could on a very sandy road. Once the touring car got stuck. We had a pillow from the cottage, which we put under the rear wheel. The car moved, but chicken feathers went all over everybody.

Nobody lived on those dunes. We never saw anyone on the beach when we swam there. Sometimes we would swim in the nude. One time, however, a lighthouse keeper came walking toward us swinging his telescope. He informed us he was just seeing if we were "safe." A memorable event! One summer Margaret Miller painted, at Elizabeth's request, the inside slanting roof of the privy. As one looked up from this "two holer," one saw two angels sitting on two "potties." I wonder how the landlady received that addition. Not much of this would have happened, if Elizabeth had not been behind it all.

I remember very clearly once when we were sitting on the beach at Cape Cod, and Elizabeth said, "If anything ever happens to me, take me to the ocean." I think she was talking about her mental state. The sea would be for recovery. This statement quite worried me at the time.

✦   ✦   ✦

There are a few references to men in Bishop's comments about her Vassar years—a weekend date with a very dull fellow from West Point, a couple of Coast Guard cadets who pursued her and Barbara Chesney one summer (1932) at Wellfleet, and a particularly muscular ice man whom she eyed there the following summer. There was one young man with whom Bishop was involved during her Vassar years, Robert Seaver, from Pittsfield, Massachusetts. Bishop kept Seaver a secret from many of her friends. Barbara Chesney introduced Bishop and Seaver, and Seaver's sister was frequently at home when Bishop visited her brother.

BARBARA CHESNEY KENNEDY— I used to go out with Bob Seaver, and we used to go to Stockbridge to tea, probably during my boarding school time. Bob was a polio victim and walked on crutches. He was rather literary, and I enjoyed talking to him. I remember him telling me that my tastes were improving in the art I was buying when I bought a Dufy reproduction of two ladies in an opera box. I introduced him to Elizabeth before she went to Vassar. She was wonderful from his point of view. He fell in love with her. This was a new thing for Elizabeth; he was the first man she dated. I don't remember Elizabeth ever dating, except for Bob Seaver. As far as I know Bob was the main one at that time.

One night Bob and Elizabeth went out from my house alone. Our house had this big staircase that turned around, so that from the top you looked down into the stairwell with a railing around it. When they returned that night, there was excitement in the air emanating from both of them as I looked down. He had just given her his fraternity pin. I know there was correspondence, and I know Bob went to see Elizabeth in Vassar.

ELIZABETH SEAVER HELFMAN— Robert and I grew up in Pittsfield. He was four years older than Bishop and I and went to Hamilton College, then Harvard Business School, for only a year. After that he got a job as a teacher of history at what was then called the Lebanon School (it is now called the Darrow School) from 1931 to 1932, possibly two years. Then he came home to live and worked in a local bank for the rest of his life—this was unfortunate for him, I think. He was interested in literature. He liked poetry and read a lot. He was quite well read in modern poetry. He was not interested in writing himself, but English literature was one of his big interests in college, although I think he majored in chemistry. My brother had an offer of being a lab assistant at Cornell, but he turned it down. This caused great distress in my family because he said that it didn't offer much of a future and didn't pay anything. That was before he knew Bishop.

Robert was very friendly with a lot of girls, had a lot of girlfriends. He made a great thing of this, partly because when he was thirteen or fourteen he had polio, and he walked with crutches for the rest of his life. He compensated for this by becoming so charming that, for instance, girls would sit out with him rather than dance. Barbara Chesney, who went to Walnut Hill, was a friend of Elizabeth Bishop's there and she brought Bishop to Pittsfield.

Barbara decided that my brother was just the man that Elizabeth should meet. My brother probably met Bishop in the spring of 1931. My journal for 1 October 1931 reads, "What a continually amazing and interesting person is Bish. It's fun to have her here: a person with unique ideas and no insipid gush." Neither of them were people who got acquainted very fast. I was really fascinated by her—in the first place, I saw in her something of myself because we were both very shy and both wanted to be poets. I didn't know too much about her background, except that she had a very difficult childhood and I knew that she was living with her aunt. One of her aunts [Florence] was at the Austin Riggs Center at that time, and later left and ran a bookshop in Stockbridge at the suggestion of the doctors at Riggs, to keep herself busy.

I'd say that at one point Bishop visited every month or so. Usually when she came to visit us, my parents were not there. They would often go off to Pigeon Cove on a little vacation, and that was a good time to ask Bish to come. I was a sort of chaperone. She would stay over for a day or two. Sometimes Bishop would stay at Barbara's house. I didn't have many times with Elizabeth, except with my brother, of course. She was always very pleasant. I loved the way she talked. She didn't talk like other people I knew: her talk had a slightly literary flavor. The notes she wrote afterward simply fascinated me. They were really a little artificial, but she would never come out directly and say, "I had a nice time, thank you." It was always an elaborate literary production.

Bishop was quite antisocial in some ways. She didn't like eating with everybody. She would often skip meals at Vassar and go up among the pine trees and have lunch all by herself. I got the impression that although she was glad that she was at Vassar, she didn't want to take part in the social life in a big way or to be with people very much. She was a very introverted person. My most vivid memory of Bishop is of her sitting up in my mother's bed reading a book. She read half the night. She said it was very restful to read, and that she didn't need to sleep so she'd rather read. She would read in bed until one or two in the morning. She did have some of those terrible asthma attacks when she was there—they were very bad.

I know that she had a great fondness for sailing. I remember her going off one summer with a Vassar friend on a little island somewhere in Boston harbor or off the coast. It was an island that they could only reach by boat.

I can't remember talking with Elizabeth a tremendous amount; I was rather in awe of her. I thought of her as being brighter than I, perhaps because she interested my brother so much. I thought it was very fine for him to have such a nice girl. Although Robert talked to me about Bishop, he never told me any intimate details. I know that they were very involved, and I know that they went to Nantucket together in the winter, during one of Bishop's vacations from Vassar. They went in the winter because there were very few people there then and apparently had a wonderful time. Another winter or spring vacation they went to Cuttyhunk. There was a little inn there—definitely off-season. My brother told me a lot about Cuttyhunk, and I got the impression that they had a simply wonderful time. My journal for 2 January 1932 reads, "Barbara and Bish for supper. A most charmingly intriguing situation, dramatic really, for reasons known wholly to my brother and me, only partly to Bish." This probably has to do with something my brother was doing, possibly his plan to go with Bish to Nantucket. From letters to my brother I wrote from college in 1932, when I was a junior, there is the following reference to Elizabeth: "I'd like nothing better than to have lunch with you on Saturday, but it happens that I am going to Boston. Remember me to Bish, won't you."

✦　✦　✦

Bishop joined the editorial staff of the *Vassar Miscellany News* in her junior year. During this year (1932–33) the *Miscellany News* was one of the hotbeds of political discussion on campus.[18] The country was in the depths of the depression, and in this election year, college campuses were rife with political debate. Bishop's specialty, however, was the newspaper's humor column, "Campus Chat." Two Vassar contemporaries remember working with Bishop on the newspaper.

HARRIET TOMPKINS THOMAS— The "Campus Chat," the most widely read part of the *Miscellany News*, was a humorous commentary on the current campus scene—bits of verse, take-offs, parodies, jokes. The editorial board used to meet on Sunday and Wednesday evenings at about eight o'clock until one or two in the morning, ending up with the fun of the "Chat." We all used to sit around the table in a sort of caffeine drunkenness at the end of the evening and chip in writing it. Bishop's "Chat" contributions were awfully good always, but they were usually written by herself alone over in a corner of the room.

MARY ST. JOHN VILLARD— Elizabeth was a vastly entertaining woman with a warm, pixyish quality that was enchanting. You couldn't really forget her because her humor was so puckish and such fun. She was an absolute knockout as a humor editor of "Chat." Elizabeth did more of that than she did anything else. She was the leaven in the lump of disorder of editorial meetings. We were awfully socialist, carrying torches for the poor, and she was never like that. I worked in the theater with Hallie Flanagan [director of the Vassar Experimental Theatre]. The play that I wrote that was produced in my senior year was a propaganda play, really. Bishop couldn't care less. She was definitely one of the dreamers. There was never any conventionality to her. It was a strength, really, that all the people she played with were politically oriented, and she never seemed to be.

◆   ◆   ◆

A November editorial in the Miscellany News complained about the campus having been "bombarded this fall by political theories . . . a Communist, a Fascist, a Farmer Laborite, and a prophet of the N.R.A."[19] Bishop, of course, kept a distance from all this discussion, although she did attend a speech on campus given by Norman Thomas, whose daughter was in her class. His dullness, she said, turned her away from socialism.[20] "Elizabeth was very much her own person. She would not be taken over by any ism."[21] Yet, Mary McCarthy remembered being convinced of the merits of socialism by Bishop: "I was very, very much to the right. Strangely enough, Bishop wasn't exactly a socialist, but she was closer to their point of view than I. Discussions with her sort of opened my eyes to the socialist argument." Bishop herself said that anyone who visited New York City during the Depression would have had to be blind not to be aware of its effects and that she knew something of poverty firsthand from having lived in Nova Scotia.[22] "Bishop was wildly unpolitical in a completely political time, the depth of the depression. She never had anything to do with politics on campus. Neither did her friends. Louise certainly never did. Margaret Miller never did. She had the brightness also to choose to go down only the alleys that were appropriate for her, and not squander herself as many of us were doing."[23]

Eunice Clark, editor-in-chief of the Miscellany News during Bishop's junior year, was one of these politically oriented people with whom Bishop associated. Under Clark's leadership the newspaper had a decidedly activist and contentious tone throughout the year. Clark proposed that the junior prom be canceled because such a conspicuous display of consumption was inappropriate, if not immoral, given the times. After much discussion in and out of the newspaper about whether a canceled prom would actually be counterproductive because it would curtail business needed by local merchants, a more modest prom was held and fifty cents of the price of each ticket went as a donation to the poor.

EUNICE CLARK JESSUP— I was more identified with political activity than anybody else in my class. I had seen unemployment, runs on the banks, people going bankrupt, my friends' fathers jumping out of windows. We talked our heads off and then wrote editorials. In 1932 we corralled voters for Norman Thomas. By the time I graduated in 1933, the majority of the class thought they were socialists. We got defeated in a campaign to abolish the junior prom on grounds that with all the poverty it was a disgusting show of affluence and indifference. When we failed, we said we'd put on our own party, and that's what we did. We got out a paper, the *Mortem Post*. Bishop wrote for. It was just a lark.

Bishop wasn't garrulous, like me, or pushy. She was a very private, self-sufficient person. She wasn't agitating and wasting her time like the rest of us. From a literary point of view, Bishop was way ahead of any of us. She had a fantastic sense of English style, probably much broader and deeper than many of her English teachers. Bishop represented the classical thing. We were agitating about world affairs, reading newspapers, debating socialism, and Bishop and Mary McCarthy were studying Greek and Latin. They learned a lot more than we did. They were much better students than my gang.

✦ ✦ ✦

It is difficult to imagine Bishop being engaged by this debate over the prom, but the idea of organizing a cabaret to calm the ruffled feathers around campus that had been caused by the debate caught her attention. One evening in early March the main dining room at Vassar was converted into a cabaret hall for all the students. Tables were covered with red-and-blue checked tablecloths, walls were covered with newspapers, and a line of clothing stretched over the orchestra. At one point the lights went out, there was a scream, and a black figure ran toward the door. When the lights went back on, a body was slumped over a table, and newspaper boys, one of them probably Bishop, ran through the hall hawking the latest edition of the *Mortem Post* with the headline "Morgan Mauls Marx." The headline story described J. P. Morgan's murder of Karl Marx over a love triangle. Bishop wrote a poem for the paper. The evening ended with Vassar's President McCracken singing a humorous ballad about the *Miscellany News* and the murder. Bishop and her friends made a profit of $450 for the poor.

Bishop presents her attitude toward the politics of her day in "Then Came the Poor," which was published in a campus literary magazine, Con Spirito, in February of her junior year. The story tells of a socialist revolution from the point of view of a character whose wealthy family flees their mansion as the revolutionary masses approach. The narrator refuses to run away with his family (he finds them unpalatable sentimentalists), blends into the crowd of revolutionaries, and when the house has been divided for the appropriate number of families, ironically ends up living there again because one social-ist needs an extra family member. Frani Blough Muser remembers Bishop making fun of the overly serious political theorizing of the day.

FRANI BLOUGH MUSER— Elizabeth wouldn't be out raising money for good causes or leading a march down the main street. They seemed a little frivo-lous. She was too sophisticated, in a way, to get involved in that kind of organization, which gave her the reputation of being lofty. But, actually, it's just a viewpoint that says this stuff is childish. We did an awful lot of talking. We had an awful lot of theories, but they weren't grounded firmly enough in any action for them to last very long. Of course, the bottom line would be revolution, although we would have been horrified at the word. Violence was not a word that we were familiar with, but we were ready to theorize. That was of course what caused Elizabeth to write ["Then Came the Poor"]. Her attitude was somewhat frivolous in that. Elizabeth stated her standpoint to me at the end of her life better than at the beginning, her feeling that the world was really a terrible mess and people were just something subprimi-tive. The best way to put up with it was to be a bit gay, have a good time, enjoy the good side.

◆　◆　◆

Bishop was instrumental in founding a new literary magazine at Vassar during her junior year. When Eunice Clark became dissatisfied with Vassar's literary magazine, the Vassar Review, she proposed to Bishop and Mary McCar-thy that they start their own.[24] They met off campus, advertised for manu-scripts, and put up their own money to finance the first issue. Mary McCarthy remembers Bishop's pleasure at sneaking off-campus to a favorite illegal spot even before the clandestine meetings of the magazine took place there: "I remember going downtown with Bishop to an Italian speakeasy, Signor Bruno's, where you got a sort of dago red in thick white cups. He would say things that appealed to us like, 'I born poor, I die poor. I born happy, I die happy.' Elizabeth quite liked him." Con Spirito—the name was Bishop's, a pun on putting new life into the old magazine, yet doing it conspiratorially—first appeared in February while the debate over the junior prom was raging.

EUNICE CLARK JESSUP— Bishop was a force in *Con Spirito*. The idea came from me. I was writing stuff that seemed good to me that the editor wasn't putting in the *Vassar Review*. The *Vassar Review* was sort of conservative. The editors of the *Review* published a piece I wrote about the Scottsboro trials. The way I wrote poetry was more radical, more colloquial. It wasn't the *Vassar Review* idea of poetry, and that made me mad because it was [Helen] Lockwood's [an influential English teacher] idea.

Prohibition had just been called off, and Bishop, McCarthy, and I celebrated by going downtown in Poughkeepsie and having some wine. We had our wine and just decided we were fed up with the *Vassar Review* and we'd get something out. *Con Spirito* was a happy thing because it was a conspiracy. It was wonderful. There were no squares to hold us back. It had more spirit than the *Vassar Review*. We put the money up. The faculty didn't approve of it. Anonymity, they didn't think that was right.

✦ ✦ ✦

Con Spirito created a sensation. The *Miscellany News* gave it a good review, as one might have expected, since the conspirators were on the newspaper staff. Some readers wrote letters to the newspaper complaining that the magazine's writing was obscure and incoherent. One reader singled out Bishop's "Then Came the Poor" for this criticism and her poem "The Flood" for being undistinguished.[25] When T. S. Eliot visited Vassar in May to view the Vassar Experimental Theatre's American premiere of *Sweeney Agonistes*, and Bishop interviewed him for the *Miscellany News*, she was pleased when he complimented *Con Spirito*. At least *Con Spirito* stirred up debate about literature and brought into focus political and artistic divisions on campus.

HARRIET TOMPKINS THOMAS— I wasn't part of the *Con Spirito* group, although I published a poem in it. I remember being excited about it and trying to find out who had published what in it. I knew that Eunice was somehow connected with it. We tended to look on the majority of the Vassar students as very unenlightened Republicans that weren't interested really in literature and politics, which seemed to go together in our minds in those days.

✦ ✦ ✦

Bishop received one particularly interesting review as a result of *Con Spirito*. E. Rosemary Paris (class of 1935) mailed two poems and the editorial from the first edition of *Con Spirito* to a friend at Princeton, who wrote back an anonymous review, which was printed in the *Miscellany News*.[26] The reviewer described the writing in the magazine as obscure, pretentious, and slavish in its imitation of Eliot, singling out Bishop's poems, "Three Sonnets for Eyes"—not knowing, of course, who had written them—for some praise, but attacking their imitation of Hopkins as overbearing. The reviewer also commented that the poet did not understand Hopkins's metrics, harsh criticism for Bishop, who would have a paper on the topic published in the next *Vassar Review* (February 1934).

In her anonymous response in the *Miscellany News*,[27] Bishop complimented the reviewer on being informed, honest, and thoughtful, was pleased that he had ferreted out her sources, and commented that his review was the only honest criticism she had seen printed in the *Miscellany News* since she had started reading it. Twelve years later, the anonymous critic sent Bishop his review of her first book, *North & South*, and identified himself as Arthur Mizener.[28]

Although there was an avid group of readers at Vassar, there were not enough to sustain two literary magazines, and in November 1933, after four issues, *Con Spirito* joined forces with its rival, *Vassar Review*. Margaret Miller and Eleanor Clark were added to the editorial board of the *Review* as a result of this merger, and someone on the staff, perhaps Bishop herself, wrote a poem commemorating the literary union:

Epithalamium

Hymen, Hymen, Hymenaius
Twice the brains and half the spaeus . . .
Con Spirito and the *Review*
Think one can live as cheap as two . . .
Literature had reached a deadlock,
Settled now by holy wedlock,
And sterility is fled,
Bless the happy marriage bed.[29]

◆   ◆   ◆

Bishop's most influential teacher at Vassar was Rose Peebles. In the storm of political debate during Bishop's junior year, Peebles represented for Bishop an aesthetic calm. Peebles had been teaching at Vassar since 1909, and she had written an authoritative study of Arthurian romance. She was interested in the aesthetic shape of contemporary novels, the ways in which modern novelists used pictures, prose, and poetry to create syncopated patterns of meaning. She described modern novelists like H. G. Wells, Arnold Bennett, and Virginia Woolf as suggestive rather than didactic writers. This distinction pleased Bishop, who took Peebles's Contemporary Prose Fiction during her junior year. Peebles's use of musical and literary terms appears in Bishop's own essays during her junior and senior years. Peebles also had an intellectually energetic yet tolerant temperament that suited Bishop, as two of her students recollect.

GRETCHEN KEENE SMITH— Rose Peebles had a fair, tolerant, kindly approach to humanity. She was a lovely, quiet southern gentlewoman. Unfortunately, Miss Peebles ran a terribly boring class. She was so well meaning, but she didn't know how to get a conversation going. There happened to be a nucleus of us that were very interested in twentieth-century novels senior year. So we simply took over. If over the dinner table or in the dormitory we started to talk about the books we were reading for Miss Peebles, we would stop and save our ideas for class. Miss Peebles couldn't imagine why we were so lively. At the end of the year, she said we were the most interesting class she had had since 1916.

HELEN MUCHNIC— Rose Peebles was one of my favorites. She was a charming, quiet person, and as a teacher, more interested in letting her students develop their own ideas than imposing her own on them. She encouraged independent work, and I, for one, was especially grateful to her for this when, in a seminar during my senior year, she gave me a free hand in writing a paper on medieval romance. My work on it was not the kind normally approved in academia. Unstructured, wasteful, disorganized, my "research" was absolutely wild. But it gave me a thrilling sense of literary symbolism, and in my first year of graduate study at Bryn Mawr this piece, called "The Coward Knight and the Damsel of the Car," was published in a learned journal, the PMLA (*Publications of the Modern Language Association*).

✦　✦　✦

Arguably the most popular and influential teacher in the Vassar English Department was Helen Lockwood, whose bearing and teaching style were the opposite of Peebles's. The dynamic and aggressive Lockwood taught a course in the Romantic poets and her very popular Contemporary Press, a study of the perspectives and biases of contemporary newspapers and periodicals. Eunice Clark "was closer than anybody in college to Helen Lockwood, who wasn't just interested in social protest, but whose thinking was radical from the literary point of view." Lockwood was close friends with Hallie Flanagan, whose social and political productions at the Experimental Theatre she admired.[30] Lockwood's style was not for all, however, as one student recollects: "I never had Miss Lockwood, one of the reasons being that I had heard she could make students cry. She was ferocious, and I could see that she rather enjoyed that. Miss Lockwood was not for me."[31]

Lockwood's influence was broad, and even Bishop, the last student one would expect to have been interested, felt compelled, as did many English majors, to take Lockwood's Contemporary Press during her senior year. She was miserable in the course. In the fall, Bishop complained about Lockwood's assignments. One required students to list the typical qualities of "the business man," "the 100-percent American," and similar stereotypes. Bishop found assignments like this one puerile. She scoffed at the tone of class discussions: "Press Class is a group of God's annointed."[32] Eleanor Clark talked with Lockwood that year about Bishop's presence in the class.

ELEANOR CLARK WARREN— I can't conceive of why Bishop made the incredible mistake of signing up for Lockwood's course, Contemporary Press. It was quite a disaster all around. Her presence ruined the class for everyone. Bishop was quite authoritative, without saying a word. Lockwood was used to stirring up a great deal of enthusiasm. She could get people passionately interested. Bishop represented the death knell to any such passionate interest in the press, in current events, in any of that. She was quite authoritative in class without saying a word. Her presence was completely stymying and paralyzing to Lockwood.

I was devoted to Helen Lockwood and dedicated my first book to her. Although I wasn't studying with Lockwood senior year, I went to see her a lot. In the middle of the year, I had dinner with her at Alumnae House. Somehow this touchy subject, what was happening that year to her Press class, came up and I told her it was very clear from things people were saying that Bishop sitting in one of those rows was just the death knell to that class. Bishop hated the class, and it was too late for her to get out. She made other people mistrustful of it. That was quite bad, that business.

As a result of the articles and poems Bishop published in the Vassar magazines and newspaper, she earned a reputation for herself as an intellectual by her senior year. Her work received excellent reviews on campus, in the *Vassar Miscellany News*.[33] She won honorable mention in a 1933 national undergraduate writing competition sponsored by *Hound and Horn*. Caricatures of her and three others appeared during their senior year in the *Vassar Review,* the magazine that published the best undergraduate essays, under the heading "The Higher Types." In 1963 the Recorder at Vassar, Julia G. Bacon, went over Bishop's academic folder at Vassar, now lost, and her summary of the comments of Bishop's teachers confirms this portrait of her:

> Miss Bishop was an unusual girl in her undergraduate days. Comments from faculty residents in the houses where she lived are interesting. One said, "egocentric—aloof—responds to beauty in any form." The "egocentric—aloof" comment did not in any way mean that she was defiant or disagreeable. She simply was not interested in community affairs. She had a few close friends who meant a great deal to her and she to them. Her interests were intellectual. Another comment, "real intellectual curiosity and a great deal of ability in her field—a hard worker. Writes well—erratic, but produces."[34]

Bishop's most ambitious project during her senior year was a translation of Aristophanes' *Birds.*[35] At one point she was hopeful that it would be performed on campus. She took four years of Greek at Vassar, including yearlong courses in Homer, the Greek dramatists, and independent study. This sense of the importance of the classics, during these years of political consciousness at Vassar, distinguished her from the Lockwood crowd, although the classical road was not an easy one for her.

FRANI BLOUGH MUSER— Elizabeth and I struggled through first-year Greek together. Still, we had a marvelous time. Miss McCurdy was a dear old lady who was devoted to Gilbert Murray. When it came time for an exam, we took a passage that seemed to be a favorite of hers, opened up Gilbert Murray and memorized it. When we came to the passage on the exam to be translated, that was it. It took a lot of self-control not to be Gilbert Murray verbatim. We had to be careful not to use whilom. Elizabeth and I both got an A-plus that semester.

Later on we hit Phil Davis, who was the handsome god who taught Greek when you got into the dramatists. Twelve hundred girls' hearts fluttered when Phil Davis walked down the hall. He was rough, didn't put up with any of the kind of the thing Miss McCurdy thought was charming. So I sank down to C-minus. Poor Elizabeth got a D. We stuck with Greek in spite of those C's ruining our academic record. It was determination. If you've been brought up in the English tradition of being literary, you've got to know Greek. You don't feel quite respectable unless you do.

✦ ✦ ✦

Bishop's literary focus, albeit timidly and tentatively, began to shift outside of Vassar during her senior year. During the summer of 1933, when she was at Wellfleet with friends and then in Stockbridge with her Aunt Florence, she corresponded with Dudley Fitts and, through him, Lincoln Kirstein about publishing some of her poems in Hound and Horn. Fitts said that her writing was mannered and too derivative from Hopkins and Hardy, comments that angered Bishop. The New Yorker also returned Bishop's work that year. The Magazine published a poem that Hound and Horn had refused ("Hymn to the Virgin," April 1934) and a short story ("Then Came the Poor," March 1934), for which she received $26.18—her first payment and published works.[36] Her article "Dimensions for a Novel" received lengthy notice in the 2 June 1934, New York Sun review of the Vassar Journal of Undergraduate Studies.

Through her contact with the editors of Hound and Horn, Bishop entered into correspondence with Donald Stanford, a poet and graduate student who later became the editor of the Southern Review. Stanford recollects his correspondence and meeting with Bishop during the spring of her senior year.

DONALD STANFORD— I was a first-year graduate student at Harvard in the fall of 1933, and Yvor Winters, the regional editor of Hound and Horn, wrote to me on October 17 telling me to get in touch with Elizabeth Bishop at Vassar. He said that she was a senior who had talent and he suggested that we swap poems. Hound and Horn was considered by many of us to be the best around. So I wrote to Elizabeth, and we exchanged letters for about one year, about twenty letters apiece. She sent me a little drawing of a scene she saw from the tower room that she shared with Margaret Miller. Elizabeth always liked good views.

Elizabeth and I swapped poems. I was writing in conventional iambic verse, the pentameter line. She was writing in free verse or free rhythm. We differed on rhythmic patterns, and we never changed our minds.[37] We never influenced each other very much, except she did drop some phrases that I didn't like in her early poems, and I threw some of my poems in the wastepaper basket, particularly when she said of one of them, "Jesus Christ, my dear boy." Elizabeth wasn't too happy with the poems she sent me, all of which are included in The Complete Poems, 1927–1979, in the section titled "Poems Written in Youth." We discussed "Hymn to the Virgin" before it appeared in The Magazine and I attacked it as being too imitative of Hopkins, too mannered. She defended herself rather fiercely. Elizabeth talked quite a bit in her very first letter and in her later letters about a translation she was doing of Aristophanes' *Birds*. She sent me two or three pages of it in the early letters. She was getting rather enthusiastic about it by the spring of 1934. Elizabeth also sent me a couple of poems by Alan Porter [a teacher at Vassar], whom she admired.

In the spring of 1934 Elizabeth and I arranged a meeting in Boston. She was there to visit relatives. She was much more reticent in person than in her correspondence. Elizabeth was soft-spoken, but a very classy, well-dressed girl—typically Vassar. On the second day we went shopping for books. We were looking for medical books. That surprised me because medicine hadn't come up at all in the letters. Elizabeth hadn't made up her mind at that time whether to go into medicine or literature.[38]

During her senior year at Vassar "Elizabeth was terrified of looking for work or deciding what to do with her life."[39] Her notion of going into medicine, which stayed with her for another year, suggests how very confused she was. Bishop had taken only one course in science at Vassar. Meeting Marianne Moore that spring helped give Bishop some direction. The story of their meeting is virtually legendary. Bishop was preparing an essay on Moore and asked Fannie Borden, a librarian at Vassar with whom she and Miller had taken a course in bibliography, why there was no copy of Moore's *Observations* at Vassar. Borden herself owned copies of Moore's books and mentioned that she and Moore had been friends from childhood. When Borden had first known her, Moore had bright red hair and addressed her friends by the names of animals. Borden offered to arrange for Bishop to meet the poet. Moore agreed and proposed as a meeting place a bench just outside the reading room at the New York Public Library. If the encounter did not go smoothly, it would be easy for Bishop and her to go their separate ways.

Moore, at forty-five, was a figure in the world of poetry, having finished her editorship of the *Dial* five years before. She was noted for her rapid whisper when her interest was piqued, as it must have been when she discovered that she and Bishop shared interests in the idiosyncratic and the exotic. Both were learned, but neither was pretentiously literary, and they must have been relieved to find this quality in each other. Shortly after their meeting, Bishop recommended to Moore a new book on tattooing, at the same time she sent her a copy of a biography of Hopkins by G. F. Lahey, S.J. The two met again to attend the circus later that spring, and Moore brought bags of bread to feed the elephants.

As Donald Stanford recollects, "Elizabeth and I talked about her meeting

Marianne Moore, which was a decisive event in her career. Oddly enough, at the beginning of her letters she didn't think too highly of Marianne Moore. She said that Moore's poems were not successful, but after she met her, she changed her mind and, of course, became a close friend and admirer." Bishop was attracted by Moore's spirit—her devotion to her mother and her perseverance in the face of a small readership and a modest income. She appreciated the fact that Moore's poetry and reviews, although produced slowly and infrequently, were faultless in their own way. By the end of May, Bishop had decided to live and write in New York, where she herself would most easily find reviewing and freelance literary work. Some friends—Miller, Crane, and McCarthy—would also be living there. And there was this glimmer of a new relationship with Moore.

In late May the *Vassarion*, the yearbook that Bishop and Margaret Miller had toiled over throughout the year, came out, to both praise and criticism. As one of the yearbook staff remembers this project, "Elizabeth and Margaret Miller put it out double-handedly that year. They knew what they wanted to do, and we were all glad to have them do it."[40] They created a book that was unabashedly old-fashioned, as if from another era. There was no sense of the debates over politics, literary taste, and junior proms that had characterized their class's years at Vassar. The book was set in typefaces from the 1870s— one cast specifically for this project—and filled with photographs of Vassar from the late nineteenth century. The binding was maroon velvet. In their introduction to the *Vassarion* Bishop and Miller defended their design, claiming that their classmates should feel as much a part of the Vassar of 1870 as of the Vassar of their own years. They appealed to the universal standards of " 'taste, elegance, and wit,' " which they had employed in selecting the old pictures in the yearbook.[41] Their opinion was not shared by all: "There was a lot of criticism of the old-fashioned format, and I tended to take Elizabeth and Margaret's part at the time. I thought it was an amusing way to do it. I have come to think that maybe the critics were right because when I've looked back at the *Vassarion*, I've been disappointed that I didn't see pictures of the college the way it was when I was there."[42]

The death of Bishop's mother in May 1934 came as a pathetic footnote to her final year at Vassar. Bishop mentioned her mother's death as an aside only to her closest friends. Gertrude Bishop died quietly, apparently peacefully, yet as disoriented as she had been when she was admitted into the Nova Scotia Hospital in Dartmouth in 1916, when Elizabeth was five. She was buried next to her husband in Hope Cemetery in Worcester. Bishop had not seen her mother in the eighteen years since their separation. In fact, when she had arrived at Vassar in 1930, Bishop had listed her mother as "deceased" on her information card. Gertrude Bishop's death that spring must have sharpened the sense that Bishop had throughout her senior year at Vassar, that she was on her own.

lizabeth Bishop arrived in New York City in June 1934 knowing neither where she was going to live nor what she was going to do. Mary McCarthy, who had been living there with her husband for a year, located an apartment for Bishop at 16 Charles Street in Greenwich Village. It had a large living room (approximately 14 feet × 22 feet) with rough plaster walls, a bedroom, a bath, and a kitchen. While her apartment was being painted and readied that summer, Bishop briefly visited her Uncle Jack and Aunt Ruby at Harwich Port, Massachusetts, and then spent three weeks alone at a boarding house on Cuttyhunk Island, where she read, wrote, swam, walked the dunes, and went deep-sea fishing for the first time. In late July, Bishop returned to New York. Within the first few days she had typed some of her poems to send to magazines, and she decided that Charles Street was going to be a good place to work. Bishop determined that she could afford to buy one piece of furniture each month if she did not allow herself another vacation that year.

Although she could live modestly, if not comfortably, off the trust her father had left her, Bishop intended to find employment. She read advertisements for jobs in newspapers and resolved to request poems to review from publishers and editors, but, sick to her stomach from fear, she never summoned enough courage to approach them. New York City always intimidated Bishop—it required professional and personal assertiveness she never possessed. On 1 November she was visited by a classmate from Vassar, Gretchen Keene, who had located a job as a reader for a literary agent. Keene must have convinced Bishop that work of this kind could be at least tolerable, for she soon found similar employment.

GRETCHEN KEENE SMITH— I don't quite remember why I would have been staying overnight at Elizabeth's apartment in Greenwich Village, because I didn't know Elizabeth well enough to be really an overnight guest. It was her politeness in mentioning that she had an extra bed that I could use. The apartment was neat, rather attractive, very small, a poet-in-a-garret kind of place. Our relations with each other were simply polite and formal, but we had a good time. Things seemed very tentative in Elizabeth's life at this time. She certainly didn't seem to be a happy person. But we were all just out of college and looking around, so it was not unusual.

I had a job with a very questionable literary agent. She was quite an old lady at the time, at the end of her career, which had started as being an editorial reader and assistant for various publishers. I think in her younger days she had done a number of perfectly good, legitimate things of that nature. But in her older years, when she probably began to lose some of that, she opened an office and advertised for young women to do reading of manuscripts. She was making her money from selling the poor, alone, undiscovered writer a series of courses. I was there for about six months, and I am not unhappy to say that I was fired because I wasn't doing the job that she wanted done. Elizabeth got into very much the same kind of thing a bit later. If I had Elizabeth's talent, I would do a piece on my first job; there were great similarities between my own experiences and the work, the kind of people, and Elizabeth's associations with her boss and the other employed people.

In "The USA School of Writing," set in the late fall of 1934, Bishop describes herself taking a job with a sham correspondence school for fifteen dollars per week. If Bishop's description is true, her boss had recently paid a large fine for mail fraud and was rebuilding the business when Bishop arrived. The offices were located on the top floor of a decrepit building near Columbus Circle. The company advertised for clients in cheap magazines. Her office mate, Rachel, read James Farrell with a passion and harbored an amiable scorn for Bishop, the Vassar graduate.

Bishop claims that she could stomach the tawdriness of the place for only a short period. If Bishop did in fact have this job, she was finished with it by Christmas, which she spent with Margaret Miller and her mother. On Christmas Day she was suddenly struck with a virulent combination of asthma and the flu, and she rushed home to bed. Margaret Miller took care of Bishop for more than a week—making her meals, fetching things for her, and giving her back rubs. Bishop missed a New Year's Eve party with a number of other Vassar graduates at Eleanor Clark's. The gossip from Mary McCarthy was that a professor had been observed in close quarters with an acquaintance with whom Bishop and McCarthy had attended Vassar. Bishop spent the evening in bed and at midnight telephoned the time operator to see if the announcer's voice changed to indicate the new year. It did not.

✦　✦　✦

Marianne Moore attempted to nudge Bishop's writing career along during her first year out of Vassar. Moore recommended Bishop to editors who, within three months of her graduation, requested poems. Bishop demurred, saying that she had little that was serious and worthy of their interest. In early 1935 Bishop read Moore's introduction to three of her poems for the fall issue of *Trial Balances*. Also, Moore mentioned Bishop to the editor of *Life and Letters Today*, and she was included in a list of poets, along with Moore and Leonie Adams, in an article by Horace Gregory. Bishop thanked Moore in the spring of 1935 by taking her to the circus to see bears on roller skates and a Chinese family who played cards and ate while hanging by their hair from hooks. Other friends had Bishop's best interests in mind, as well: Mary McCarthy introduced Bishop to the reviewer Margaret Marshall at a dinner party in January 1935, and Louise Crane introduced her to Virgil Thomson at a party in June.

Bishop also studied in New York during her first year out of college. She and Margaret Miller attended lectures at the New School on, of all topics, "Specimens of Advanced Mathematics," and Bishop took clavichord lessons with Ralph Kirkpatrick. In April 1935 Bishop began a tutorial at Columbia University in reading and translating French, with a special emphasis on modern French poetry. She had a trip to Europe in mind. When Bishop returned to Vassar that spring and mentioned her trip to Europe to senior Harriet Tompkins, editor of the *Miscellany News*, they decided they would travel together. Louise Crane was going to be in Russia and Germany with her mother; Bishop would meet her in Paris.

Bishop did all the planning—she solicited advice from her friends about sites and hotels and made all the arrangements for the voyage. She relinquished the lease on her apartment, placed her things in storage, and on 29 July, Bishop and Tompkins departed from Weehawken, New Jersey, on the SS *Königstein*, with all due fanfare plus one novelty: police were on deck to prevent violence to the Nazi freighter on which Bishop had booked very economical ($155 round-trip) passage.[1]

HARRIET TOMPKINS THOMAS— Elizabeth came back to the *Vassar Miscellany News* in the spring of 1935, when I was editor, and she was going to France. I said I wanted to go to France, too, so we decided to go together. I really wasn't a close friend of Bishop's at Vassar—I think she struck everybody as slightly different—but I admired her poetry very much, and I admired her. I knew there was something special. I thought it would be fun to go with her. Paris just seemed to be the place that everybody headed for in those days. I wanted to be a war correspondent, to be a second Dorothy Thompson and have a great career. I left most of the planning to Bishop. I was struggling in those two or three months at Vassar. Bishop got our boat and arranged the timing. She was quite practical. I was quite surprised. Bishop knew exactly what to do in a very quiet and unofficious way.

When we got on, we found that the boat was a Nazi boat. I remember the scene as we pulled out of New York harbor, one mass of people on the dock raising up their arms in the light, and Bishop said, "Oh, how horrible. It's like the dead." She'd say things like that that were funny and very spontaneous. That was the fun of being with her. We objected to the German men, who all seemed to be bald and earthy, and so were the women. We did find Albert Nock, the author of Our Enemy, the State, on board. Bishop was very taken by him, and so was I. The crossing took about five days and almost a day to go up the River Schelde that goes into Antwerp, where we spent just a morning. Then we went on to Brussels and the World's Fair. That was fun, but I can't remember seeing anything except the paintings [by Breughel, Hugo van der Goes, and others]. Bishop knew about this tiny little pension on an unknown street in Brussels where we stayed. She had done a little reconnaissance before we went.

We stayed in Paris for three or four days. My father gave me a letter of introduction to people, his clients, who had a chateau at Versailles, and Bishop and I went there for lunch. There were twenty-five people, and the whole house was filled with absolutely beautiful furniture, all gold, everything served up to a degree of richness, but there wasn't one single book in the entire house. So Bishop and I of course were very snooty, and I made a remark at the table about this. The hostess heard me, broke in, and reprimanded me about it. I nearly died.

Bishop had heard of Douarnanez from somebody, so we went. It was a charming place, definitely off the beaten path. It was not a place the Parisians would go to, because it was a very simple fishing village in those days. I hadn't been to Brittany before, and I loved the people and the atmosphere of it. I feel now that it appealed to Bishop because it was like Nova Scotia. It was pure Bishop terrain, a place she would naturally love. Bishop was just delightful. She would have insights about people and the things that we saw that were just very gratifying. I do remember Bishop saying that smoking Gauloises, one of the French cigarettes, was like kissing your great-uncle. We spent most of the morning writing or reading or doing something of this sort. We walked all over Brittany, as far as we could go. I got bronchitis and had to stay in bed for three or four days, so she helped to nurse me. I recovered from bronchitis and I felt I must get back and try to get my career started, so I left for Paris.

✦   ✦   ✦

Louise Crane joined Bishop in Douarnanez for a few days after Tompkins left; then they made their way to Paris via Saint-Malo and Mount Saint Michele. The landscape at Saint-Malo—the expanse of sand, the huge rocks, the drapery of green-and-purple seaweed—caught Bishop's eye, and she pictured it as the background for a small operatic masque she hoped to write with Frani Muser, but never finished.[2] Mrs. Crane had arranged for Bishop and Louise to stay at the apartment of the Countess de Chambrun in Paris—the setting of "Paris, 7 A.M."—at a corner of the Luxembourg Gardens. They had seven rooms filled with antiques, and five fireplaces. There was also a cook. Bishop walked in the Luxembourg Gardens, bought a pair of white doves, and painted a large cage pale blue for them, and she and Crane considered taking courses at the Sorbonne. She began clavichord lessons in December, when a portable clavichord she had ordered from Dolmetsch arrived. She had paid for the instrument with the inheritance from the estate of her Uncle John, who had died a year before.

Bishop and Crane had privacy in Paris, that is, a life out of the view of the suspicious and disapproving eyes of Mrs. Crane. As a friend of Mrs. Crane recollects, "I don't know that Louise's mother cared much about Elizabeth. I think Mrs. Crane felt Louise had been carried off by her first affair with Elizabeth. Mrs. Crane always spoke about it lifting her eyes to the ceiling and professing ignorance. Mrs. Crane could only avert her eyes to its romantic overtones."[3]

Bishop had ended her affair with Robert Seaver before leaving for Europe, when he had asked her to marry him. According to Seaver's sister, "a little before Bishop went to Paris in July 1935, my brother did tell me that she had said she didn't ever want to marry anybody, by which I assumed that he had probably proposed to her and been turned down."[4] Bishop and Crane kept up the facade of interest in men to their friends, commenting about the dapper soldiers who lived in their building and grumbling about Harriet Tompkins having gathered all the desirable men in Paris before they had arrived. Crane and Bishop joked about their Parisian maid pitying them because they had no male admirers and thought of sending themselves flowers to regain her respect.[5] Harriet Tompkins Thomas recollects other incidents from this time.

HARRIET TOMPKINS THOMAS— I wrote to Bishop from Paris to Douar-nanez, and she said that my letter was very welcome particularly as contributions from other sources had been very sparse. She counted on getting letters daily. I stayed in a pension in Paris, then moved in with Louise and Elizabeth when they arrived. The apartment of the Count and Countess de Chambrun—they were away—was elegant and quite charming, full of clocks and old furniture.

I discovered Shakespeare & Company while I was walking around, and I was delighted by the place because here were all these books that we had always wanted to read and all the very current ones. I took Bishop there the next day, and she borrowed some books [Yeats, Lawrence, and Owen]. We were reading all the time. Sylvia Beach knew who Bishop was. She must have had an advanced copy of Life and Letters Today and knew that there was a poem of Bishop's in it ["The Man-Moth"]. So then she tried to make friends with Bishop and invited her to this party for André Gide. Bishop told me about it. Bishop and Louise tried to decide what Bishop would wear. I think that they went out and bought a new blue dress for her, and Louise then ordered a car to drive Bishop to the party. Unfortunately, just as Bishop was about to step out of the car, she got cold feet and decided that she couldn't do it. So she went home. I don't think that I was surprised because I was very shy about my French, too, and felt it would be a hard thing to go into this place and speak French. Bishop was really looking forward to the party; that's the rather sad part of it.

Once we invited two gentlemen for tea. We'd met John Thomas in this Russian restaurant called Djigouti, when he had offered us a seat because there wasn't room for us all and then came over and talked to us afterward. He was a very good talker. He could talk all about his experiences in New York and Paris, and about the night life and the low life of Paris. Bishop sort of drew back at this sort of thing. I had the feeling that the conversation wasn't to her taste. Louise invited John for dinner, and he came. John talked about philosophy, because he enjoyed it, and we got into this argument about beauty. Bishop began defending the idea of beauty. For her beauty really was one of the eternal verities, the most important thing in life. Beauty meant a great deal to her.

John was taking the part of the *advocatus diaboli*, arguing that beauty was in the eye of the beholder and that one's ideas of value conditioned what one thought and how one defined beauty. Bishop was trying to argue with him and he was getting the better of the argument because he was a practiced debater. Bishop got very upset, threw off her coat and hat—I don't know why she had her coat and hat on—and went into the kitchen. I found her there ten minutes later drinking a large glass of gin and weeping profusely. She said, "Well, you know, people shouldn't discuss things like that." This was very personal; it meant too much to argue about. She was very, very upset. She felt that he was a Philistine. She really did misunderstand him completely.

I always felt that Bishop didn't want to live life too intensely, that if she did she might somehow break up. She was on guard about a great many things to protect herself against feeling too deeply about something. That was the reason that she was so upset by John, because she really felt deeply about this argument. I was relieved when she went to Spain and Morocco and sent me a postcard that said, "Love to John." She hadn't really taken offense by the whole thing.

◆　◆　◆

Bishop spent January 1936 in the American Hospital, recovering from a mastoid operation. Doctors circled around her, testing her hearing with tuning forks. With her head wrapped in a turban, she thought she resembled Alexander Pope.[6] Once Bishop was well enough to travel, she and Crane spent a week in London, where they saw productions of T. S. Eliot's *Murder in the Cathedral* and W. H. Auden's *Dog Beneath the Skin*—both disappointments to Bishop—then took a boat to Morocco.

There the climate was warm, for Bishop's asthma, and the ambiance was exotic, if not sultry. In Casablanca, Bishop and Crane stayed at a former pasha's palace, in a long, marble room with large beds at each end, looking over a courtyard of lemon and orange trees. Bishop and Crane hired a guide in Marakech who took them to night clubs and lent them his phonograph and records of Moroccan music. In Moulay-Idriss, Bishop liked the risqué dancing of a woman who balanced a tea tray on her head, lay down and rolled over with the tray still in place, then held a cup of tea by her toes and offered it to her. Bishop and Crane drove over the rugged and spectacular Atlas Mountains, then, before departing from Tangier to Gibraltor in early April, spent one evening visiting a Moroccan brothel.

In Seville they encountered a political anomaly—a Holy Week celebration ordered by the communists. The government did not want to disappoint the tourists. After Morocco, however, Spain proved disappointing, except for the Goyas and a few pieces of baroque architecture and design. Even the two bullfights Bishop attended did not impress her. She and Crane traveled through southern Spain, Madrid, Granada, Valencia, and Toledo then, exhausted from being tourists, went to the island of Palma for two weeks, where they lay in the sun and read, while Bishop recovered from an asthma attack. They departed for America two weeks earlier than they had intended, arriving home on 2 June, after a third-class trip with a number of immigrants.

After they returned from Europe, Bishop stayed with Louise Crane, in her family's Fifth Avenue apartment and their home in Dalton, Massachusetts. Then she rented a cottage for the summer in West Falmouth, near the Cranes' house in Woods Hole. Margaret Miller joined her there. Bishop and Miller lived on one dollar a day for groceries. They sailed with Crane in her twenty-foot sailboat to Cuttyhunk Island, where Bishop had stayed the previous summer. The landlady of the boarding house gave Bishop a cat, which she named Minnow.

The cottage sat in an orchard and was surrounded by flower beds and fields. Miller painted and read on the front lawn, while Bishop read and wrote in the back. Miller was working on several canvases; in fact, while Bishop had been in Africa and Europe, Miller had been painting or drawing a portrait of her, apparently winged, entitled *Poetic Furor*. During Bishop's trip, Margaret Miller had sent off poems and at least one article, on Gertrude Stein, for Bishop. Evenings on Cape Cod, Miller and Bishop argued about Marxist criticism of Shakespeare, Cervantes, and other writers, which they were reading together.

In September Bishop returned to New York, staying with Crane before moving into an inexpensive, shabby room at the Chelsea Hotel. She and Crane took Marianne Moore to Coney Island in September. Moore had encouraged Bishop through a period of artistic doubt in August, persuading her to continue writing poetry, instead of going to medical school.[7] She convinced Bishop that her tempo of composition might seem slower than that of other poets, but it was correct for her. Bishop sent Moore pieces to evaluate throughout the fall. Then an unanticipated blow—in November Bishop received word that Robert Seaver had committed suicide. Shortly after his death, a terse, angry note from him arrived. Seaver's sister and Barbara Chesney Kennedy remember some of the events surrounding his death. Frank Bidart remembers Bishop confirming the story to him.

ELIZABETH SEAVER HELFMAN— It was clear to me that Robert and Bishop were very fond of each other. I assumed that they would get married. Robert was very, very sad that summer of 1935 when Bishop was in Europe. He would keep going down to see her aunt at the bookstore in Stockbridge to get news of her. On 10 January 1936 I wrote to my brother: "How does Bishop like Paris? Maybe she will be a bit nostalgic and write well because of it, like Thomas Wolfe." I think that her relationship with my brother worried her because she did care so much about him. That's my theory. In a way she never really wanted to get involved. She said she was never going to marry anyone, and she never did. He was very much in love with her. I don't doubt that. He had so many girls, but she was the only one he really cared for.

Robert died in November of the year she came back [1936], and his death was reported as suicide. My parents would never accept that. Although it was never actually proved, it was reported by the medical examiner as suicide, and I think this was what it was. I wish I knew the circumstances leading up to it. He didn't seem unusually depressed at the time, according to my parents. He was planning a trip abroad in February with his closest friend, who was extremely close to him, especially after Bishop turned him down.

BARBARA CHESNEY KENNEDY— I was home in Pittsfield when Bob killed himself, and I remember going over to see his parents the next morning. Bob and a good friend often went out for shooting practice in the country. His parents couldn't believe that it was suicide. They felt sure he wouldn't do anything like that, but I think he might have. I hadn't seen Bob in over a year, so I didn't know how depressed he was, or whether Elizabeth was the cause of his suicide. I remember being in New York and calling Elizabeth. I asked her if she knew about his death. Very emotionally, she said she did, and that she had gotten a letter from him a day or two afterward saying, "Go to Hell." She sounded very upset.

FRANK BIDART— Robert Seaver wanted to marry her and finally she didn't want to marry him. She broke it off. It was at this point that Seaver killed himself, and before he did, he mailed her a postcard on which he had written, "Elizabeth, Go to hell." It arrived after his death.

✦ ✦ ✦

In early June 1937 Bishop, along with Crane and Miller, again sailed for Europe. The trip over was foggy and unexciting, although the tragic events that followed, which were to change Bishop and Crane's relationship with Miller, were not. The trio visited Ireland first, where neither Bishop nor

Crane trusted the other to hold her legs to kiss the Blarney Stone, then France. On a weekend in mid-July, Crane drove Bishop and Miller through Burgundy to visit churches. They were returning to Paris, when a large car passed them, driving them off the road. Their car skidded out of Crane's control in the sand, turned over, throwing all of them out, then righted itself. Bishop and Crane got up immediately and saw that Miller's right arm, which had been hanging out the window, had been severed between the wrist and the elbow. Bishop thought Miller was bleeding to death.

Two men working in a field nearby came to their aid, and one put on the tourniquet that Bishop credited with saving Miller's life. The driver who had forced them off the road returned and drove Miller, accompanied by Crane, to a doctor in the nearest town, five miles away. Bishop waited at the car, where she was pestered by questions from passersby, among them a priest who said that the accident had occurred because there had not been a man driving. When she arrived in town, Bishop found the medical techniques antiquated and the police's insistence on interviews ghoulish. Crane eventually arranged for the assistance of a nurse from the American Hospital in Paris. Miller was moved to this hospital after four days.[8]

Bishop and Crane took up residence in a hotel across the street from the hospital, where, while Miller recovered, they whiled away the time playing billiards. Initially, Miller's progress was remarkable: she started writing with her left hand within two days of the accident. The wounds healed nicely. Fearing that Mrs. Miller's overly solicitous attitude toward Margaret would impede her progress, Bishop, Crane, and perhaps Margaret herself, attempted to keep the details of the accident from Mrs. Miller. Nevertheless, Mrs. Miller arrived on 4 August. She had suspected only a broken arm and fainted when Bishop met her in Le Havre and told her the details of the accident.[9] At this time, also, complications set in. In mid-August there was a skin grafting operation, which initially seemed successful; however, adhesions developed, necessitating another operation. As Miller's recovery slowed and the pain grew stronger—there was at least one operation to sever nerves—she became melancholic.

When Miller was released from the hospital in mid-September, she, her mother, Bishop, and Crane took an apartment on the Ile de Saint Louis. Mrs. Miller's anxious ministrations toward Margaret seemed to Bishop counterproductive. Margaret became more depressed and withdrawn. Asthma had been nagging Bishop for weeks and became worse in the apartment, so she and Crane traveled to Arles for a week. Bishop was worse there, and she rushed back to the American Hospital for ten days. And then there was a trial.

Miller's insurance covered the medical expenses, but Crane's car insurance would provide greater compensation. For Miller to receive these benefits, however, Crane had to be convicted of negligence, even though the fault was clearly not hers. The legal trick was for Crane to be found guilty without being sent to jail. Mrs. Crane, two lawyers, an insurance man, and all the principals returned in mid-October to the seat of the county in which the accident had occurred. Louise pled guilty to causing the accident before a French judge and received a small fine as a penalty.[10]

Bishop's asthma continued to worsen. When the lease for the Paris apartment was up, the Millers decided to remain in Paris, near Margaret's doctor and a masseur, and Bishop and Crane traveled to Rome, where Bishop's asthma immediately improved. For the first time in three months she did not have to have a daily shot or take some other form of medicine. After Rome, Bishop and Crane traveled to Florence, where Bishop waited for word about whether Mrs. Miller was going to return to New York City. If so, Bishop would stay with Margaret in Paris. No word came. Bishop and Crane left from Genoa for the States on 9 December, leaving Miller and her mother behind.

FRANK BIDART— The person Elizabeth was really in love with in those early years was Margaret Miller. They never had a physical relationship. Elizabeth felt that Margaret was not homosexual. She had been in love with Margaret since they were roommates at Vassar. Once she told me that, after years of being obsessed with Margaret, when she woke up one morning, the knot in her chest always present when she thought of Margaret simply was gone. After years suddenly she was over it. (She told me this trying to assure me that an obsession I had about someone would end.)

Elizabeth never talked about being in love with Louise Crane. She gave the impression that they had some sort of an affair. When Elizabeth had been drinking a lot, or was sobering up, the relationship with Margaret Miller haunted her, and certainly the relationship with Lota [de Macedo Soares] haunted her. The relationship with Louise Crane didn't.

♦   ♦   ♦

When Bishop and Crane arrived in New York City on 24 December 1938, they carried with them several small owls from Italy. One was to have been a Christmas present for Marianne Moore. The owls, however, never made it through customs. Within a month after her arrival, Bishop left New York City for Key West, Florida. Bishop and Crane had stayed at the Keewayden

Club in Naples the winter before. Florida's wildlife had astonished Bishop. She and Crane had fished from boats and the docks, with pelicans and chameleons sitting next to them. There was a richness of birds and animals (tanagers, pelicans, buzzards, turtles, and alligators) and plants (particularly the mangroves and the palms) unlike any Bishop had ever seen. Evenings she walked the shore, gathered shells, and memorized their local names: Ladies' Ears, Job's Tear, and Junonia.

Bishop met Charles (Red) and Charlotte (Sha) Russell at this time. Red embodied Florida's naturalism and wildness to Bishop. She likened him to Tarzan—he wrestled alligators and hunted with a bow and arrow. The Russells introduced Bishop to the naturalist Ross Allen, whom she also saw wrestle alligators, in Fort Myers in February 1937. From these three friends came some of the details in her poem "Florida."

CHARLES RUSSELL— The Keewayden Club in Florida was a winter resort where parents could come for two or three months with their kids and put them in a school right there in the club. So Sha was hired to run the school, and I was hired as recreational director. That's where Sha and I met, in the fall of 1935, when school opened and the club opened, and we were married in the fall of 1936. Lizzie and Louise came down the first couple of weeks in January 1937.

CHARLOTTE RUSSELL— Louise went back to New York and Lizzie stayed down for most of the winter. I always think of them together, Louise and Elizabeth. We used to call her Lizzie, "L" and "L." I would visit her in her little room. We got along just beautifully. She would talk about books, and I was fascinated. She was a very quiet person. People at the inn wanted her to recite poetry, and she didn't want to. I said, "Go on." So she finally did, and she did a very good job. Her poems were fascinating. But, she wasn't outgoing. She could be funny too.

CHARLES— Lizzie wasn't an easy person to know because she was reserved. She was a little aloof and could be very critical of other people, but not going around and criticizing. She was very selective in her acquaintances, critical in that sense.

CHARLOTTE— One time she came when we went up to Fort Myers and watched Red when he wrestled alligators with Ross Allen. He wrestled alligators and snakes and everything. All the way down Ross Allen was saying, in the back of the car with Lizzie, "Lean on me!" Lizzie was rather reluctant to, and finally Ross said, "Well, if you won't lean on me, I'll lean on you." More squeals from the backseat followed. Afterward she wrote a poem on Florida and used quite a bit that Red had told her.

CHARLES— Ross Allen was the card. When she was talking about the alligators in "Florida," she was quoting Ross Allen, what Ross Allen told her that night, that the alligators had five calls, mating call, fighting call. . . .

CHARLOTTE— They all made calls in the backseat.

CHARLES— Ross taught her. He could mimic the alligators so he told her a little bit about their love life. Lizzie kept journals in those days; she always had a notebook. She was always writing.

✦   ✦   ✦

During her first visit to Florida, in late December 1936, Bishop visited Key West. She had heard that the fishing there was better than in Keewayden, and she hired the captain who had taken Hemingway out for years. They caught twenty fish of more than twenty pounds, and she got the largest one of the day, a sixty-pound amberjack. Even more than the fishing and the literary ambience, however, the lovely old houses and the inexpensive lifestyle there appealed to Bishop.[11] Bishop traveled directly to Key West for her second winter, following her return from Europe in January 1938. She rented a large room in a boarding house at 529 Whitehead Street, across the street from the county court, for four dollars per week.

Bishop liked the homey eccentricity, the casual pace, and the general air of friendliness in Key West. The landlady and her husband sat on the porch, just outside her window, talking and singing hymns. There was a boarder, Mr. Gay, who collected odd items in cigar boxes, and Bishop began a story about him. The boarding house was on the edge of Jungle Town, the residential district for blacks. Down the street was a small house in which Bishop saw a bed, a chair, and a French horn painted silver, leaning against the wall, with a painted silver pith helmet hanging above it—all details that made their way into "Jerónimo's House." The gentle voices of the blacks reminded Bishop of the rhythms of her favorite hymns and poems. She was free from asthma. She rode a bicycle around the island every day.

Louise Crane arrived in mid-March, the month Bishop was awarded a *Partisan Review* prize for her story "In Prison." They immediately rented a house. Miss Lula was their landlord. She used a large ear horn, had a fortune teller come each week to read cards for her, and was taken care of by Cootchie—Bishop wrote a poem about her—a tall black woman who looked forty yet claimed she was a great-grandmother. Crane was as much taken by the look and feel of Key West as Bishop. By May they had decided to buy their own house. A simple, tall boxlike white house, a Key West "conch house" at 624 White Street, caught their attention. A second-story roof extended over the front porch, supported by four tall, thin pillars. A modest yard surrounded the house. Across the street was an empty field. The house was located on the edge of the Cuban section of town, where there were a number of food stores and restaurants. Bishop and Crane hired their own housekeeper, Mrs. Almyda, a kind, serious woman who prepared Key West specialities, such as turtle steak and conch. She scurried around the house uttering old-fashioned expressions—"Oh my precious love!" "Oh my blessed hope!" and, when she was surprised, "Oh, hush!"—and must have reminded Bishop of her grandmother Boomer. The Russells visited several times.

CHARLES RUSSELL— For two or three years before the war we would go down to Key West two or three times a winter, before I left the area to go with the Red Cross in 1941.

CHARLOTTE RUSSELL— Red would take a trip and land down there and pick me up. Elizabeth, Louise, and I really had a wonderful time together.

CHARLES— Louise and Lizzie did purchase the house in Key West together. Louise finally sold out her part to Elizabeth. It was a two-story house, pillars on the front, overhanging roof, porch underneath, a typical Key West house, very plain. Of course, they preserved the integrity of it by keeping it just as it was, plain inside. There was nothing fancy, though they had the means, with Louise's help, to furnish it any way they wanted to. They kept it very plain, very severe. Never cluttered. Practically every flat surface was clear. There was a very pristine atmosphere about it, but it was a very comfortable and inviting little house. There were a lot of bookcases in that house.

CHARLOTTE— When I would go down and visit her sometimes, the books would go up the stairs. It was a lovely house with a nice little porch at the side. It was just a quiet little Key West then.

Lizzie got marvelous letters from Marianne Moore every week. She wrote wonderful letters, and she'd read me those that she'd write back. Marianne Moore was just everything to her. She kept Elizabeth working to come up to a certain standard. She'd always say, "I wonder if Marianne Moore would like this?"

◆　◆　◆

Crane and Bishop had a picture of their house painted by the primitivist painter Gregorio Valdes that spring. In fact, they credited themselves with discovering Valdes, a poor, sickly man, who painted signs for a living and had some paintings for sale around town. Bishop first came to know his work when she saw a landscape of his displayed in the window of a barbershop on Duvall Street. She bought it for three dollars. Valdes's painting of 624 White Street captures the crisp, simple symmetry of the broad front of the house. His perspective lifts the house out of the enclosed neighborhood and adds a number of exotic details—a parrot on a perch extending from one of the porch pillars, an oversize monkey (the neighbor's) climbing a palm, and palm trees from another area of Key West. The monkey and palms were Bishop's suggestion. Valdes painted the sky a luminous pink. He was so pleased with this work that he changed the sign on his own house from "Sign Painter" to "Artistic Painter." Two Valdez paintings that Bishop and Crane owned, one that of their house, were exhibited at the Museum of Modern Art in the fall of 1938 in a show of "Unknown Painters" organized by the trustees.

Bishop had a party for her friends to view the painting of her house shortly after Valdes delivered it. He attended, drinking the sherry as if it were wine throughout the afternoon. Charlotte Russell was visiting at the time, and after a few drinks, she and Valdez ran around the house, buzzing, imitating mosquitoes. This was one of many parties that Crane and Bishop threw in their house as they found a range of friends there. Martha Watson and Betty Bruce, whose husband was Ernest Hemingway's right-hand man, became close friends with Bishop and Crane in Key West and recollect aspects of life in the town that made it appealing to Bishop.

MARTHA WATSON SAUER— It was 1938 or 1939 that I first met Elizabeth and Louise. Elizabeth was pretty, with beautiful eyes and lovely skin. She had a wide-eyed look. Our friendship was very pleasant and more than casual because we were interested in each other's health. Asthma had brought me to Key West. Elizabeth and I happened to have allergies to cats and to cold weather. Any time Elizabeth, who had access to much more advanced doctors than I had down here, would find a new medicine, she would write to me and tell me about it. When cortisone came out for use, I got an exultant letter: "At last I can have a cat!"

Elizabeth was a very private person. To use a very old-fashioned phrase, she was a lady, and a lady does not trespass on somebody else's privacy and expects you to maintain your own and hers too. She was delightful, quiet, fun, witty, not physically exuberant, but interesting. One time we were sitting around talking. She said, "You know a funny thing. Did this ever happen to you? You get halfway up the steps and you wonder which foot comes next?" Little quirks like that were fun. One year for Christmas there was a black-and-white postcard for sale at Sloppy Joe's [a local hangout]. It was a woodcut, and Elizabeth painted stars on it and sent it around for a Christmas card. We would talk about art and Key West gossip. There was never any feeling that one shouldn't call because she might be in the middle of a poem. There was no special time set aside in the day for her writing as a dedicated professional prose writer would do. She wrote a poem when she felt one coming on.

Louise was pretty, with a nice personality. She was pleasant, outgoing. I think of her being brisk. Louise was probably a better organizer. She was that kind—managerial and very frank. She was good company, fun.

BETTY BRUCE— Louise was much more energetic than Elizabeth. Also, Elizabeth was a little on the heavy side. Elizabeth had the childlike, innocent quality in her face.

SAUER— When you entered Elizabeth and Louise's house on White Street, you walked right into the living room. There is a stairway to the left and a door leading to a room on the left. The living room was well lighted, with lots of windows, and wooden walls painted white. There were some nice paintings on the walls. It was a bright, sunny, very attractive room, very modestly furnished, just essentials. I remember Elizabeth being exultant because she found some white ceramic doorknobs at Curry Hardware. That's what the houses had before they changed to metal.

Elizabeth had some good paintings. She had a little one by John Ferrin, a friend who came down to visit her. She said he was well known. It was a geometrical design, like Mondrian. Elizabeth introduced me to the French composers, Delius, Poulenc, and Franck. She had records of those, and we would sit and listen to the old gramophone. She had a lot of jazz records.

BRUCE— She also had a lot of German records. Once Elizabeth left her phonograph records and her kaleidoscope with me. The kaleidoscope was a gorgeous old one, and I babysat her phonograph records because she didn't want to leave them in the heat of the house. That was a marvelous collection—Billie Holiday, things that had just been done on a private basis. I took care of a stack about three feet high.

Back then, at night there was the smell of the jasmine and the spicy Gentleman of the Night throughout Key West. The air was like the softness of down at night, maybe like an old-fashioned counterpane. The coffee houses roasted coffee three times a day, and you'd have their smell. The roasting places were in varying locations. The Sanchez coffee house was down on Green Street. Another one was near White Street, where there was another Cuban cigar costillo. There were others all scattered around town. They did it for their own neighborhoods. They roasted it so that it was pungent and fresh, and the fragrance was lovely. The same way with the bread. Cuban bread is fantastic. They did that three times a day, for breakfast, lunch, and dinner. The bakeries were also scattered.

SAUER— You could smell the coffee roasting a block away. The Cuban national lottery—that's all you could hear on the radio in a Spanish voice, number after number after number.

BRUCE— There was a very foreign flavor, as well as the cosmopolitan. You have very basic people who had lived here forever. They were the Bahamians, Cubans, Germans, and Irish.

Even though I was a conch [a native], we in Key West have always welcomed people coming from outside because they brought in new influences. Key West had its own sense of being. It was a place of people who belonged in that place. We felt that this was our island and we were glad you liked it. There was a sense of dignity about it. There was also the business of not minding the other person's business. If you wanted to see people, you saw them; if you didn't want to see them, you didn't have to see them.

A writer would be considered just a regular person. Hemingway spent all of his time on the docks because he liked the people. Elizabeth was a sensitive person. She wasn't terribly happy with herself. She was looking for a place where she could be herself. She wasn't seeking any special appreciation. Key West had no social stamp. People were agreeable to each other. Also, Key West was extremely inexpensive to live in in the late 1930s and early 1940s.

SAUER— Elizabeth loved this openness. One of her best and dearest friends here was Sully, James Sullivan. He worked in metals and made boilers, wrought-iron stairways for the ships. We all loved him. He was old enough to be Elizabeth's father.

When Elizabeth was first on White Street there was a movie house called the Monroe in the 600-block on Duvall Street. Theaters used to have boxes on the sides. Elizabeth went to matinee movies then, and she would take a bucket of ice and a couple of cans of beer and sit on the side there, watch the movie, and drink her beer.

BRUCE— Sully was a great friend of Pauline Hemingway's [Ernest Hemingway's second wife]. He was her right-hand man. He had barely a high school education. There was very little social snobbery of any kind in Key West. That's why a lot of people liked it, because it wasn't people chasing fame.

SAUER— Mrs. Almyda was devoted to Elizabeth. She was a little, wiry woman, a simple woman, a New England spinster type. She used to ring her hands worrying about Elizabeth's health, like a mother hen. They were very fond of each other. I went one time for dinner, when Mrs. Almyda had prepared chicken, and it was so tough that neither of us could chew it. Elizabeth said that it would hurt Mrs. Almyda's feelings if the chicken were not eaten. There was great embarrassment on the part of all three of us. I was the guest, and I couldn't eat it, and Elizabeth was the hostess, and she couldn't eat it, and Mrs. Almyda was ringing her hands.

BRUCE— She wanted everything to be perfect for Elizabeth.

✦   ✦   ✦

During Bishop's second winter in Key West (1938–39), the painter Loren MacIver and her husband, the poet Lloyd Frankenberg, visited Bishop. Bishop had met them through Louise Crane and had spent September and October 1938 sharing their cabin on the dunes near Provincetown. Bishop rented an abandoned grocery store in Key West as a studio for MacIver, where she painted the *Red Kite*, among a number of other works. The Frankenbergs also brought the painter Robert Reitz with them, and Bishop located a studio for him in an abandoned bar—he painted in the bar and slept in the game room.

John Dewey, the philosopher, lived in Key West and liked MacIver's paintings. When he heard that MacIver was visiting, he asked to meet her and was introduced to Bishop. Bishop then met his youngest daughter, Jane, who became a lifelong friend. Bishop also met Pauline Hemingway and a number of other residents.[12]

MARTHA WATSON SAUER— I did see Lloyd Frankenberg and Loren MacIver when they were with Elizabeth. I liked them very much. Lloyd was very good looking—tall, dark, and handsome. He was a very forceful person. We all liked Loren's paintings. They had lovely colors and were rather romantic. Elizabeth said she thought Loren painted the way she did because her eyesight was so poor she couldn't really see what anything looked like. She had already had one hung in the Museum of Modern Art.

BETTY BRUCE— Loren was very quiet. She was tall and thin and had rather straight hair. There is a little shack in somebody's backyard that she painted in. She did *Hopscotch* here and all those shell paintings here, and then she did the one of the Square Roof. They all used to go down to the Square Roof, an old whorehouse.

SAUER— Elizabeth, Louise, and some others thought it was fun to go there. They used to have a few drinks and sit around. I went once with some friends and Elizabeth, and I was never more uncomfortable in my life. It was slumming—there were these black prostitutes sitting around, and there was somebody playing the piano.

BRUCE— It was the thing to do. Pauline Hemingway and all that crowd used to go there.

SAUER— Pauline was a very sociable, congenial kind of person. She was trim, neat, kind of birdlike with bright eyes and an inquiring look, as though she were inquisitive and wanting to know what was coming next. We spent every Sunday at the pool at the Hemingway house during the war. The officers on the PT boats all came in on weekends, and Pauline would invite them and any single girls around.

Jane Dewey was the youngest of John Dewey's three daughters and had a marvelous sense of humor. Elizabeth and Jane were witty, but Jane was really the wit, at times mean. She could be very sarcastic. She wasn't all sweetness and light. Jane and Elizabeth worried about each other. Jane taught physics at Bryn Mawr, and when the war broke out, she went to work for the navy.

BRUCE— She worked on the bomb.

SAUER— Then she worked on the space project at a lab in Maryland. When you spent an evening with the Deweys, Jane did all the talking. She was the greatest gossip for any little tidbit. When Jane and her sister Lucy sat down for dinner, there would be delightful stories, about the man at the paint store, the man at the grocery, and all that.

John Dewey was a most agreeable man. He was a good friend. He always had a card table set up with a jigsaw puzzle on it. He liked to read and doodle. I would try to read his books because I revered him. One day I said, "Mr. Dewey,"—I never had the gumption to call him Dr. Dewey—"I'm trying to read your work, and it's very hard for me." And he said, "Cheer up, it's hard for everybody." Mr. Dewey was comfortable, a pussycat. He also had a nice sense of humor. One time, when he was in his eighties and I was in my thirties, I said to him, "Mr. Dewey, don't you get sick and tired of all the things going on, the war, everything? Aren't you sick of it all?" He said, "No, I want to live forever, because I'm always curious to see what's going to happen next." He and his wife adopted two war refugees from Belgium when he was eighty-one. He liked helping people. He bought my first painting.

STEVE BOYDEN— I probably met Elizabeth and Louise at Pena's Rose Garden, somewhere between 1937 and 1939, because everybody went to Pena's at five o'clock, all the fun people in Key West. Pena's was a gathering place for all the arty types that were moving down here. Elizabeth would come in with Louise and other artists. I didn't know anything about her writing. She was very shy in a strange way, and she didn't talk a great deal, but you liked her immediately. I thought she was a wonderful person. She seemed very genuine. Elizabeth just happened to be with a group of people I knew. Jane Dewey was part of our crowd. She was older than we were. Jane and Elizabeth were both very much alike. They didn't exude personality. I don't mean it unkindly. Quiet sorts.

I went with Martha [Sauer] to a morning party at Elizabeth and Louise's house on White Street in 1937 or 1938. Louise and Elizabeth had mint julep parties. They would crush mint leaves, soak them in the bourbon overnight, and pour this mixture over chopped ice. At one of these parties, I noticed a man sitting with his back to everybody, looking at a fence. I asked Louise who he was, and she said he was a budding writer, Tennessee Williams.

✦   ✦   ✦

James Laughlin, the publisher of New Directions, came to Key West in January 1940 to visit Tennessee Williams and to meet Bishop. He had published three poems by Bishop in 1936, when he was literary editor of *New Democracy* and had regularly requested her work since. In March 1938 he suggested to Bishop that New Directions publish her first book of poems; a year later, when Bishop agreed, he tried to get her to sign a five-book contract with him. Bishop rejected the idea. Given her rate of production, five books sounded like a lifetime's work. In November 1939 Laughlin had wanted to include Bishop in an anthology of five younger poets, but Bishop had balked both at the notion of being in an anthology and at Laughlin's suggestion that she would provide "sex appeal" as the only woman poet in the anthology.[13]

After his visit to Key West in early 1940, Laughlin suggested that Bishop publish in his pamphlet series. Bishop thought she would make more money publishing in individual magazines, suggested that he publish a book of her poems, then retracted the idea when Laughlin continued to argue for the pamphlet series. With this final move, their literary chess game ended. That fall Bishop was invited by Laughlin to a birthday party in New York for William Carlos Williams. Feeling uncomfortable, as she often did in such gatherings, Bishop left before speaking with either Williams or her host.

Laughlin recollects his trip to Key West, aspects of his convoluted dialogue with Bishop over four years, and Bishop's cagey attitude toward the publishing world.

JAMES LAUGHLIN— I first heard about Elizabeth in 1936, when Marianne Moore wrote me that she thought Elizabeth was a very promising poet. Ezra Pound had written to Miss Moore, as I always called her, after I returned from studying with him at the "Ezuversity" in Rapallo. Pound had arranged with Gorham Munson, the editor of the New York Social Credit magazine, *New Democracy*, that I should be allowed to guest-edit two or three literary pages of each issue. Miss Moore sent me her lovely little poem "See in the Midst of Fair Leaves" and persuaded Elizabeth to send me "Casabianca," "The Gentleman of Shalot," and "The Colder the Air," which appeared in the April 1936 issue of *New Democracy*.

What I liked about Elizabeth's work was her crystal clarity. No decorative obfuscation. She pursued the mot juste. She had a sense of craft. One felt that her poems had been deeply thought out and carefully put together. I liked the way she controlled her feelings. She didn't gush. In those early days of New Directions, I was chiefly concerned with publishing experimental work, but I was open to poems in a traditional vein if they were good enough.

I always wanted to do a book of Elizabeth's poems in New Directions, but I managed to muddy the waters for her. I had thought up a stratagem for publishing new poets in group books, which I hoped would sell better than the single-poet first volumes that were not doing at all well in those days—if they ever have. The series was called "Five Young American Poets." They were anthologies of five poets, about forty pages for each, enough for a good showing of a new talent, and, believe it or not, we were then able to sell these hardbound collections for $2.50! What would that be today? Probably twenty dollars. The first collection, in 1940, contained Mary Barnard, John Berryman, Randall Jarrell, W. R. Moses, and George Marion O'Donnell. The second (1941) was Paul Goodman, Jeanne McGahey, Clark Mills, David

Schubert, and Karl Shapiro. For the third (1944): Alejandro Carrion (Ecuador), Jean Garrigue, Eve Merriam, John Frederick Nims, and Tennessee Williams. All good poets, and some of them became famous.

But Elizabeth wanted a book unto herself. She wouldn't play groupie. Throughout her career she was so much the individualist, cultivating her own plot of ground, not becoming a member of a school. I understand that now. But at the time I was stubborn, insistent for my publishing project in which she would have been a star. So I lost the chance, I suppose, to be her first and perhaps her regular publisher. The correspondence about our discussion of the problem—always amicable—is in the library at Vassar.

My next effort to "manipulate" Elizabeth—I use the word advisedly, I was always one to try to get my way—was with the Poets of the Month Series. (The Book of the Month people enjoined me to change the name to Poets of the Year; they claimed the phrase "of the month" belonged to them.) I had always loved typography and fine printing. But I didn't have the money to emulate the French livres d'artiste or the great English press books. I hit on the idea of a series of thirty-two-page pamphlets of poetry, each one printed by a different fine printer, an artist of design. It seems incredible now, but I was able to sell these for 50 cents, or $5.50 for a boxed set to subscribers. The series ran for forty-two numbers and attracted a distinguished list: Delmore Schwartz's verse play *Shenandoah*; Rilke's *Book of Hours*; William Carlos Williams's *Broken Span*; Berryman's first book, *Poems*; Brecht's verse play *The Trial of Lucullus*; Dylan Thomas's *New Poems*; Rimbaud's *Illuminations*; a selection of Hoelderlin; Nabokov's translations of *Three Russian Poets*; Thomas Merton's first book, *Thirty Poems*; and selected poems of Melville were a few of the highspots.

I desperately wanted to enlist Elizabeth for the Poets of the Year Series, but I failed to persuade her. By that time she had finished enough poems for a much longer book, and she wanted the impact of a collection larger than a thirty-two-page pamphlet. We were both politely stubborn. She published *North & South* with Houghton Mifflin and then went to work with my good friend Bob Giroux. Bob is by all odds the great literary editor of our time.

In those earlier years I don't think I had actually seen Elizabeth more than once or twice. My chance to get to know her better came in 1940, when Tennessee Williams, whose plays I had been publishing for some years, invited Gertrude and me down to visit him in Key West. Elizabeth was in Key West that winter with her friend Louise Crane. Tennessee and Elizabeth were congenial. He liked bright girls as long as he didn't have to get involved with them. One of his funniest letters came a few years later from New Orleans where a beautiful but aggressive girl was giving him a difficult time—would

I come down and rescue him? (I fudged on that publisher's duty.) We had some very pleasant dinners with Elizabeth and Louise. I found in Elizabeth a delicacy akin to that of her poems, but also a nice sense of humor. I remember a quiet twinkle.

Tennessee had walked me around the town a bit. I was struck by an old wooden building that had a square roof. The place was indeed known as the Square Roof. It was a brothel where the young ladies were of dusky complexion. It turned out that Elizabeth and Louise had researched the Square Roof in the line of literary duty. "I have a friend there," she told us. "Would you like to meet her? We could pay a call." Not meaning a professional call, but a social one.

Elizabeth arranged the invitation to tea. Tennessee suggested we doll up a bit to show we were chums not customers. It was one of the few times I saw him in a necktie. Tenn was small, but he could look quite handsome when he took off his "shades"; they were his shield from the world. He was shy, but what a smile when he liked someone!

The madam of the Square Roof was elderly. She must have been very pretty once. She had somewhat elegant manners. She enjoyed making polite conversation. I wanted to ask her if Hemingway had ever been a patron of the house when he lived in Key West, but decided I'd better not. A confidential matter. The young ladies were of various dimensions, including one who was quite rotund. A special taste? They were wearing their "church" dresses—their guardian informed us that some were Methodists and some Baptists and that they attended Sunday services regularly. They were not talkative, though Elizabeth and Louise tried to draw them out, but it was evident from their demeanor that they were glad to see us. The madam poured from an antique tea service into flowered cups that were daintily grasped by the young ladies. Oreo cookies were served, my favorites.

Suddenly one of the girls—a light-skinned charmer—inquired if we would like to see her room. A moment's silence, but Elizabeth said that we indeed would. We all traipsed upstairs. I found the girl's room touching and sweet. The bedstead with a high, carved back could have come out of any bourgeois house in the Bordeaux. A fancy, purple silk spread. Lace covers on the pillows. An embroidered flower-print rug. The mirror on the dresser was nearly as tall as a pier glass. Below it a small glass vase with several stalks of jasmine in it. Standing frames with photographs of a handsome family from old people to children. On a small table by the head of the bed a Gideon's Bible. But, most moving of all, sitting propped against the bed pillows, a row of dolls in dresses that surely the owner had stitched. What we saw there in that room touched us all to silence. We trooped downstairs and thanked them all for our visit. They all seemed so cheerful and happy. I've often hoped that an account of our visit to the Square Roof would turn up in one of Elizabeth's poems, but if she ever wrote it, I've never seen it.

✦ ✦ ✦

In late November and early December 1939, two months before Laughlin's visit to Key West, Bishop and Crane went on a canoeing trip with the Russells through the Ten Thousand Islands, off the southwest coast of Florida. Bishop did not much care for canoeing, but she was willing to go when she realized they would be able to sail for a good part of the trip. She also hoped to write an article on what she saw and did.

CHARLOTTE RUSSELL— In December 1939 we all decided that we were going to take a canoe trip. At that time Red had a canoe factory. We were going to get people interested in his canoes by taking them on trips, and Lizzie and Louise wanted to go on the first trip.

CHARLES RUSSELL— We took our canoes down by a little place called Caxambos, the southern end of Marco Island, a very swanky resort area now. In those days it was the last little settlement off the mainland before you got to the Ten Thousand Islands proper. Our first jaunt was from Caxambos to Cape Romano. We went on the inside of the islands, about four or five miles. It was quite apparent at the beginning that Louise was not much of a canoeist. So it took us the better part of the day to go the four or five miles. Louise had a Philco battery radio a little larger than a shoe box. She was in the bow and had the radio on her lap. She'd take a couple of strokes here and a couple of strokes there, and then she'd fiddle with the radio and try to get some music.

CHARLOTTE— Louise was terribly interested in jazz at that time, had done a lot for Ellabelle Davis and things like that. There were lots of jazz musicians she gave money to and helped along the way. We had another couple with us (the Fullers), Red and me, Louise and Lizzie—just three canoes. We slept in tents, Red cooked fish over the fire, and everybody got awfully bitten, especially Louise. Lizzie was fascinated by everything. Nothing escaped her. She was a very astute observer.

CHARLES— When Lizzie wasn't doing anything else, she would sit and write. She was always writing something down. Lizzie liked the whole idea of the frontier kind of experience, getting away from cars and people.

On another day we made our way to the mouth of the passage that goes into Everglades City. We camped there and the next day had to make our way up the pass to Everglades City. So we got into Everglades City after dark, and took the first landing we could find and made camp. It turned out in the morning we were right in front of the city dump. We had friends there bring the cars down and take us home.

◆　◆　◆

Throughout the following year Bishop watched Louise Crane's interest in the jazz, popular, and classical musicians grow. She came into contact with a range of them in New York City. Following the canoe trip, Crane returned to New York, then traveled to Key West for Christmas with three Spanish musicians whose career she was promoting. They were too noisy, energetic, and overbearing for Bishop, who felt they took over the house. Crane loved their animation. At this time Bishop and Crane talked about Crane renting an office on Broadway and starting a recording business. She was beginning to take the idea of becoming of an impresario seriously. Betty Bruce saw Crane in New York during this time and attended one of the series of evening concerts Crane organized for the Museum of Modern Art.

BETTY BRUCE— Louise was very interested in music. Besides the Spanish, she was very, very interested in black musicians. She spent a lot of time in Harlem. One time I ran into Louise Crane when I was in New York City in 1939 or 1940. She invited a friend and me to Harlem with her. We went to a nightclub before a performance, and we just sat around at the table and talked to Billie Holiday.

MARTHA WATSON SAUER— Elizabeth also told a funny story about once when she was backstage in New York, and Billie Holiday—it might have been Maxine Sullivan—was getting ready to go on. Elizabeth said Billie put this stuff on her hair to straighten it. She carefully straightened every hair. When she got it all straight, she twisted it up in little tight curls, and when that was done to her satisfaction, she took it all down, and there she was right back where she had started.

BRUCE— Louise was director of a series of coffee concerts at the Museum of Modern Art. I went to one just because I had met Marina Romero in Key West. It was Marina's friend, a classical guitarist, who gave the concert that night. It was an evening performance, around eight o'clock, at the museum, in the small auditorium they have. It was an introduction to the different phases of music. Louise was backstage.

◆ ◆ ◆

Crane returned to Key West in March 1940 and was " 'the life of the party,' " according to Mrs. Almyda.[14] Bishop rented a small room in a hotel for quiet, so that she could write mornings. During her trip to New York that year (October and November), Bishop was drawn into Crane's new circle of activity. Bishop traveled to the Crane house in Dalton, Massachusetts, with Louise and her Spanish musicians for a concert in Pittsfield. A Williams College professor who attended told Crane that she was a Medici.[15] In November there was also a concert by Ellabelle Davis, followed by a party at the Cranes' apartment on Fifth Avenue.

Bishop must have fully realized that Crane was involved with other women during this period in New York. When Bishop returned to Key West in December 1940, she was touched to discover that during her absence Mrs. Almyda had repainted the floors and some of the walls in the house. Bishop sat on the front porch, ate figs from the trees, and let Mrs. Almyda take care of her. The sunshine and air in Key West had a soothing, salubrious effect.

Bishop sensed that her relationship with Crane was over, and it was at moments like these, when Bishop felt herself abandoned and alone, that she fell into the depressions that her friends from Key West periodically witnessed: "If you saw Lizzie over a long period of time, you knew that it would be very difficult at times, because she would get so depressed. And one could never quite understand what you had done. Elizabeth would get blue quite often. Maybe being alone in Key West had something to do with it."[16] Charles Russell remembers hearing "tales of Elizabeth going overboard during fits of depression. What would bring those on I don't know. Sometimes she would feel neglected, insecure." The artist and writer Mary Meigs remembers Crane's description of her breakup with Bishop.

MARY MEIGS— I first met Elizabeth in the late forties, near the beginning of my relationship with Louise Crane. We met at a party in New York City and, after the party, took a taxi together downtown. Though this was the first time we'd met, I felt immediately at home with her, and I think she felt the same way about me. She had had a long and, finally, unhappy relationship with Louise, not just before me, but before the woman before me—Anny Laurie Chestnut—and this prevented either of us from feeling jealous. In fact, we were more like friendly conspirators who could freely discuss and laugh about both the past and the present. I remember that Elizabeth held my hand and that when I got out of the cab, we kissed each other and I felt happy. I'd been struck immediately by the fragility and delicacy of her mind and the sense of her as a receiver of signals beyond human ears. I didn't see her again until years later, when she was giving her poetry seminar at Harvard and I was living in Wellfleet with Barbara Deming and Marie-Claire Blais. Elizabeth, Marie-Claire, and I had dinner together from time to time in Cambridge and had animated conversations in which Elizabeth was conspicuously more discreet than Marie-Claire and I were. Elizabeth and I belonged to a generation of women who were terrified by the idea of being known as lesbians, and for Elizabeth as poet, the lesbian label would have been particularly dangerous. One of the side effects of lesbians' fear of being known to the world was our fear of being known to each other, so that a kind of caution was exercised (certainly it was by Elizabeth) that no longer seems necessary today.

From Louise Crane I heard about the difficulties of her breakup with Elizabeth, about Elizabeth's despair and her suicide threats. Louise was irresistible to women; she had very blue eyes, full, it seemed, of innocent candor and love of life. She adored people and parties; she wasn't an artist herself, but she was able to spot the unusual talent and to help artists with their careers. She launched Ellabelle Davis as a singer and was passionately interested in Billie Holiday. Her attraction to Harlem life was at the same time a passion for the singers and musicians who interested her. She told me that she had followed Billie Holiday from night spot to night spot, while Billie, who refers to Louise in her autobiography as "a rich white chick," was mistrustful. During this period Louise's mother was suffering all the pangs of the mother of a rebellious daughter who was in some ways exactly like her. Between the two of them they knew almost everyone who was of importance on the New York cultural scene, and Mrs. Crane's salons, in which Louise shared, were proof of this. They lived at opposite ends of the Fifth Avenue apartment—Louise in very simple surroundings and her mother amid the splendor of paintings by great artists, of beautiful old furniture, and china. I remember Louise telling me that her mother sent her to see a psychiatrist. But Louise resisted being straightened out and went on with the life that made her mother so anxious.

I think of Louise's life with Elizabeth as the deepest love relationship she ever had. It was a time of artistic flowering when many of Louise's friends were already perceived as great artists. My feelings now about Louise are gratitude and affection for making me feel at home in her world, even though we were in no way suited to live together. I was austere and strait-laced and ignorant about life, and she was bursting with courage and joie de vivre. We had violent quarrels but eventually became good friends again. As for Elizabeth, I feel acute regret that our paths lay in different directions, that I couldn't accept her invitations to Ouro Prêto or to Maine. She is in the pantheon of the artists whom I admire most—those whose work is mysterious beyond understanding.

✦ ✦ ✦

By July 1941, seven months after having seen Crane in New York City, Bishop had rented out 624 White Street. Crane had lost interest in Key West, and supporting the house alone was too expensive for Bishop. By January 1942, one year after having last seen Crane in New York, Bishop told friends that she had not heard from Crane in months.

I n 1941 Elizabeth Bishop and her friends watched with dismay as the navy moved into Key West. Military housing went up in the field across from Bishop's house at 624 White Street—"two-story, four-family boxes, two up and two down. One pink, one gray, one blue, one green."[1] Bishop complained about the noise from dynamiting and building, the nightly blackouts, and the overcrowding. The navy tore down Pena's Rose Garden, a local hangout, as part of their overall plan to build an air station for sea planes and a submarine base. "The navy brought young married couples who were different from normal Key West types. The whole atmosphere had changed from the privacy we were used to. We no longer had the same quiet way of life."[2]

A new relationship, with Marjorie Stevens, kept Bishop in this changed Key West. By July 1941 Bishop had moved in with Stevens, who lived on Margaret Street. Stevens brought stability into Bishop's life after her breakup with Louise Crane earlier that year; she was a practical companion with good business sense. Stevens efficiently turned her attention to the details of renting 624 White Street to navy personnel, and, eventually, selling the house for Bishop and Crane. Stevens worked as an accountant for the navy, even though she complained endlessly about the inefficient, disorganized bureaucracy. Two friends remember her.

BETTY BRUCE— Marjorie Stevens was a bright, very attractive woman. She had a job with the navy during the war. Marjorie was well educated, but I don't think she was that interested in literature. She was from Boston where her husband was in the publishing business.

MARTHA WATSON SAUER— They weren't divorced. Marjorie said he didn't want a divorce because this way he was free to run around and everybody knew he was legally married. When we met him, he was a proper Bostonian. She was very pleasant, a year or two older than Elizabeth, I would guess. She seemed more grown-up. Marjorie was here for her health also.

BRUCE— Marjorie had very, very bad health—she was tubercular. Lloyd Innis-Taylor, a friend of ours, and she met in the sanatorium in Saranac, New York, and then in 1937 or 1938 they went to Southern Pines, a sanatorium in Pinehurst, North Carolina. Then they came to Key West the first winter. Lloyd came back down from Washington in the later 1940s when Elizabeth was living with Marjorie, and the three of them lived on Margaret Street. They were friends and it was the logical thing. Key West in those days was very, very affectionate anyway. Nobody would have mentioned such a thing. Marjorie entertained and had a very nice house.

SAUER— Marjorie loved parties. She was a wonderful cook. I always think of her riding her bicycle—she was always going somewhere on that bike. I think she may have dabbled in painting, not seriously, just for fun. Marjorie and Pauline Hemingway started a decorating shop in the Caroline House with Maureen Thompson.

BRUCE— Originally Pauline bought it for their shop. The shop was in the front and Marjorie's apartment was in the back. They sold draperies, fabric, and so forth. For a while the store did pretty well. Then Maureen bought out Marjorie and moved it over to another area of town.

✦ ✦ ✦

With life in Key West being transformed by the military, Bishop and Stevens looked to other inexpensive, isolated places as retreats. In September and October 1941 they traveled to Brevard, North Carolina, where Bishop had rented a cabin in the mountains with the Russells the year before. At Brevard, Bishop found native characters as diverting as those she had first known in Key West—a fourteen-year-old cleaning girl who was about to marry and Cordie Heiss, who lived alone in a cabin in the woods and walked eight miles to town every week for her fifty-cents relief money. The Russells recollect time they spent with Bishop during these months in Brevard.

CHARLES RUSSELL— Brevard was a resort, but not in a fancy sense of the word. It was a quiet place up in the Great Smoky mountains, right on the edge of the Pisgah National Forest. It had a sense of remoteness to it. There were a few inns that catered to guests for two, three, or four weeks. They served marvelous meals, homegrown vegetables. That was the place to go from Florida for vacation, to North Carolina and the mountains.

When Lizzie was there we rented a cabin for about five or six dollars a week. It was a couple thousand feet above Brevard itself, with a nice panoramic view of the valley. A few mountaineers would drop by occasionally, but it was really off the beaten path. We had our own spring where we kept our butter and fetched water. I had been operating an aquatic school in that area for several years. Every summer I'd go back for ten days or two weeks.

CHARLOTTE RUSSELL— That little house was just awfully cute. All the people on the hill were regular people. One man who sold liquor would open the top of the door and say, "Anyone want anything?" Of course, Lizzie always loved her liquor, and we got several things from him, and then there was a woman [Cordie Heiss] that sang through the hills.

CHARLES— This woman was retarded, demented. She'd sing classical songs at night as she walked through the mountains. You'd hear her for miles. She lived in a little cabin. She was very fond of Lizzie and invited her to go to tea. Elizabeth described the woman wearing her hat in the little one-room cabin, wallpapered with pages from Life magazine. I'm sure Cordie must be in her notebooks. Lizzie was writing during this visit with us.

CHARLOTTE— She said it was going to be a book, but she'd never get it done on time. She always underestimated herself. She always pooh-poohed whether she could get it done. That was her way. I remember up in the mountains she wrote standing up in a little room.

CHARLES— There was a little lean-to on this one-room cabin we had. It was called "disarobia." Lizzie would work there in the mornings.

Lizzie took the Holly Inn the second year she went up, after staying with us. She was so in love with the place that she decided to go back. That's when Marjorie Stevens went up with her. I stayed down at the camp, and Sha stayed in town at the Darlington Inn.

CHARLOTTE— Mrs. Wright, the woman that ran it, was nice. Lizzie and Marjorie liked her very much. They were very friendly with her. She was very calm.

CHARLES— Mrs. Wright charged Lizzie eight dollars a week. Ridiculously low-priced.

✦ ✦ ✦

Bishop and Stevens traveled to Mexico in April 1942. They had intended to visit for two weeks, but Bishop so liked Mexico's primitivism that they stayed for six months. They first visited the Yucatan, then Mexico City for several weeks. She met the Mexican poet Pablo Neruda while climbing a pyramid at Chichén Itzá. He recommended a place for them to stay in Mexico City and a Spanish tutor for Bishop. The tutor had Bishop translate Hemingway's *Sun Also Rises*. John Dewey had provided a letter of introduction to Otto Ruhle, whom Bishop met in Mexico City. She helped Ruhle's wife polish the English of stories and articles she was writing. One of these articles was about the Mexican government's project of draining salt lakes to retrieve salt. Bishop visited the desolate, eerie salt lakes with the Ruhles in July.

When she and Stevens returned from Mexico in October 1941, Bishop went to New York City and Stevens returned to Key West, where she managed Bishop's house for her, arranging for tenants, cleaning the place, and filing forms with the city rent board. Bishop was miserable in New York. She saw friends (Marianne Moore, Mary McCarthy, Margaret Miller, the Frankenbergs, and even Louise Crane), met E. E. Cummings, and had her portrait painted by Loren MacIver, but she was depressed all the time and suffered from insomnia. Stevens wrote solicitous letters, reminding Bishop how melancholy she became when she was not getting sleep and warning her not to drink when she was too tired. Stevens said that she would look for a job so that she could support Bishop while she wrote, if she decided that Key West would be best for her writing.

Bishop returned to Key West in December 1942 and lived there for a year and a half with Marjorie Stevens. Her depression and drinking continued. Marjorie Stevens encouraged Bishop to find a job, to take her mind off herself, so in August 1943 Bishop became a helper trainee in a navy optical shop. For $5.04 per day she took apart, cleaned, and reassembled binoculars. One end of the shop where she worked was open, and Bishop watched ships and submarines pass throughout the day. The work was tedious, but the workers were friendly; they drank coffee together, played checkers, and bought each other Cokes. Eyestrain from the work made Bishop seasick, and the acids she used to clean the lenses caused eczema. After five days' work, Bishop was honorably discharged.

Bishop was back in New York in the spring of 1944. In May, Stevens wrote that she was controlling her own drinking and that she hoped Bishop was off to a similarly good start. Stevens visited Bishop in New York in the fall, however, and found her in very poor health.[3] She warned Bishop that it was dangerous for her to live alone. Marianne Moore suggested that Bishop take some time at the spa in Saratoga. Stevens encouraged Bishop to return to Key West where Mrs. Almyda could care for her as well as, and far less expensively than, any nursing home. The next two years were filled with such coaxing and cajoling until, one senses, Stevens grew weary and frustrated. By the summer of 1946 her intimate relationship with Bishop had ended and they became casual friends.

◆　　◆　　◆

Bishop was pulled to the North and to the South during the forties. Key West and life with Marjorie Stevens were good for her health. Yet Bishop wanted a literary life, and New York was the center for her literary contemporaries. Stevens herself was notably unliterary, repeatedly asking Bishop to recommend books for her, then putting off reading them. The physical climate of New York—the dirt, the dust, the oppressive air in the summer and the cold of the winter—made Bishop ill, and the people in New York, particularly those who were on the go, aggressively advancing their careers, unnerved her. Still, the place had its compulsory appeal. The writer and art critic Clement Greenberg was an editor of the *Partisan Review* in the early forties, when he met Bishop. He remembers how different Bishop was from other literary people he knew in New York.

CLEMENT GREENBERG— I read Elizabeth's poetry in *Partisan Review* and elsewhere before I met her and liked it. Her poetry was good—open and precise. When I had a chance to meet her, I was delighted. She was over at my place on Bank Street once in the forties. I'd see her here and there, at parties. Elizabeth was interested in painting, and we'd talk about that from time to time. The pictures I had down there on Bank Street—she really looked at them. I won't say she was professional and expert, but she looked at everything with an oriented eye. Unlike Auden, whom I knew better than I did Elizabeth. He was aural.

Elizabeth had a light touch in her address when she talked, was self-possessed, not in a forward way. She was just so agreeable, so amiable, so right—good company. Elizabeth had no business being nice, compared to the other poets I know whose work I admired. Elizabeth struck me as someone without vanity. No professional jealousy, unlike some good poets. She knew all the editors [at *Partisan Review*]. She'd be invited and come to the parties. But Elizabeth wasn't hanging around with the *Partisan Review* crowd.

The literary world was much smaller then in New York. *The New Yorker*, well-run magazine that it was, was high-middle brow. We liked to think that *Partisan Review* was the center of the avant-garde. I became one of the five editors in 1941, until February 1943 when I went into the army. Everybody was a literary editor at that time—Philip Rahv, Dwight MacDonald, Fred DuPee, William Philips, and I, and George L. K. Marsh for a while. Mary McCarthy was around, but not right there in the middle of the editorial life during the days I was one of the editors. We published everything Elizabeth sent us. We were too sophisticated to look for anything other than quality. When it came to politics, of course, we wouldn't publish anything Stalinist or over on the right, either. Politics were not aesthetic. It was taken for granted that they were separate.

I remember Elizabeth because she stood out. Elizabeth wasn't a yacking literary type all the time. She wasn't Delmore Schwartz. You felt with Elizabeth life came first. She wasn't a celebrity figure, one whom journalism could catch hold of. Her poetry did it. She wouldn't have fitted in with the *Partisan Review* crowd. I never felt Elizabeth belonged in any crowd.

The Frankenbergs, and parties at their Perry Street townhouse, were the focal points for a loose coterie of Bishop's friends in New York. Yet as early as 1941 Bishop's insecurities undercut her relationship with even them. Bishop complained that they had changed from the simple, unpretentious people whom she had first known in the thirties. Still, Lloyd Frankenberg remained one of Bishop's strongest advocates, praising her poetry in his book *Pleasure Dome: On Reading Modern Poetry* (1949) and recording her reading several poems for an album that was released to complement the book. Four friends recollect aspects of Bishop's life in New York at this time.

HELEN MUCHNIC— I met Elizabeth through Edmund Wilson, who was a good friend of mine. He introduced us in 1946, having decided, I presume, that we should meet because we were both Vassar alumnae and loved good writing. I then went to see Elizabeth where she lived on King Street, not far from my pied-à-terre on Fourth Street in Greenwich Village. And I remember that what struck my eye when I first stepped into her room, on the fourth or fifth floor of a dilapidated building, was a lovely oval-shaped object hanging from the ceiling. Was it alabaster or exquisitely polished marble? It turned out to be an ostrich egg. There was also an electric burner with a beautifully decorated top, the work of Loren MacIver, its colors the same as those of the dust jacket she had done for Lloyd Frankenberg's *Pleasure Dome*. It did not take me long to realize that this combination of the simple, authentic, and unusual was typical of Elizabeth's taste and judgment in all kinds of ways.

MARY MEIGS— I came to know Loren MacIver and Lloyd Frankenberg through Louise Crane, like so many people I came to know in New York. Louise adored her painting and so did Elizabeth. I certainly did. The subtlety of it interested me. You seemed to be looking through a mist that was an essence of things. Loren had that magic in herself physically, with her red hair falling over her face. She had the most beautiful tweed suit with these extraordinary colors that looked exactly like her paintings.

Loren was under the wing of Pierre Matisse. She showed in his gallery. She was very highly thought of as a painter. But she had this elusive quality, so she wasn't typical at all. She didn't fit with anybody else. She was utterly different. She was extraordinarily like a creature of the woodlands. She was so fugitive, another woman like Elizabeth who expressed herself by innuendo. It was Lloyd who did the talking. He was the mouthpiece. They had big parties, great parties, but utterly simple, just a glass of wine and a bit of cheese.

ROSALYN TURECK— I met Elizabeth through Loren MacIver and Lloyd Frankenberg, whom I knew intimately over many years. I have a very vivid memory of Elizabeth. I associate her with an English appearance and an English type of personality, a combination of delicacy and strength. She was very, very pretty and her great delicacy was implicitly expressed in the way she spoke.

I met Loren and Lloyd through my first husband, Kenneth Klein, the director of the Town Hall, the concert hall in New York City. He and Loren grew up together on the same street in New York. Loren and I have been intimate friends for years. Lloyd looked like every young girl's dream of a poet. He was tall, handsome, and sensitive. He had a beautiful tenor voice, and he was great fun. I remember we used to laugh like mad all the time. Loren gives the impression of a quiet personality, but she has a very intense presence. I wouldn't say she is retiring, but she could be quiet. She is extremely alert and extremely sensitive, like moths' wings. Her art is very subtle, as is her humor.

I saw Elizabeth often. She was one of our regular circle with Loren and Lloyd. I met E. E. Cummings and his wife a couple of times in their apartment. Lloyd and Loren talked often about Cummings. Cummings was very important to them. Lloyd was doing lots of poetry at the time, and Loren had connected with the Pierre Matisse gallery shortly after we met. I regularly went to openings of her exhibitions, and I used to see her paintings in the studio, one by one, as they were finished. All of us used to talk art, painting, and poetry endlessly. We had tremendous fun together, just sitting around talking. Our brains and sensibilities were enough to keep us going deep into the night. We did a lot of laughing at the foibles of artists and people, not raucous but, rather, good-humored laughter.

I had started on my career very young and had played my first all-Bach recitals in 1937, several years before I met Elizabeth. Elizabeth knew I was a Bach player. She had purchased a clavichord built by the great Arnold Dolmetsch some years before we met. I remember her speaking of the instrument with great tenderness. She offered to send her clavichord to me. She said she didn't use it regularly and there was no reason why I shouldn't have it. It was a superb, beautiful instrument of excellent tone and modestly decorated in overall green with gold lettering. Having studied the clavichord since I was fourteen years old, I had great joy in playing it daily. I had it for some time, until I was due to make my first tour in Europe, the winter of 1947, and was to be abroad six months. I therefore sent it back to her. Later, on my return, she said she wished I had kept it permanently. The night before I left on this tour, I packed the entire night, and Elizabeth came to say goodbye. She arrived about midnight, alone, when I was in the midst of packing, and she brought me a present, a compass. Isn't that adorable? I thought that was so witty and so charming. We both laughed about it. Elizabeth had great refinement and true charm. We had a lovely relationship.

HOWARD MOSS— I first met Elizabeth through Loren MacIver. I was taken with her right away. As a person I adored her because she was so completely interesting. There was simply her way of looking at things. Just to take a walk with Elizabeth was to observe in the most casual way a lot of things that you would not ordinarily notice. Also, she was so terribly nice. She didn't seem to be trying to get anything or have an idea of a career. There was something very graceful about Elizabeth, even when things got sort of chaotic. There was a certain wonderful, inherent sense of manners.

Also, I felt and do feel that Elizabeth was a genius. She always tried to avoid that knowledge that she really was a genius. Yet she was too intelligent not to have been aware of that. She was modest, but she was not self-deprecatory. Elizabeth, however, was always troubled by the fact that she was so unprolific. There was always that little comment to herself saying how little she had done, that could be misunderstood as self-deprecatory, but I don't think that was the case.

There were a few times we had dates and she didn't show up. [Once] we had a date for dinner and I came by on King Street, and no one answered the bell. Then another man came to the doorway and he rang Elizabeth's bell. She came down in a bathrobe. She obviously had had dinner dates with both of us and wasn't going to keep either. I was always an admirer, and I didn't know at that time much about her drinking. Of course, I got to know much more later.

I do remember a night at the apartment on King Street, when Mrs. Hemingway was there. That apartment had a tiny terrace, and Elizabeth had planted some seeds from Key West, so there were some Florida plants growing on the terrace. I thought, how wonderful that this Floridian arrangement was here in the city. Elizabeth had a clavichord. She called me once and asked if I would want it. And I said yes.

♦   ♦   ♦

Bishop was subject to periods of debilitating self-doubt and loneliness in the forties. Her friends, including Marianne Moore, were baffled about what to do: "Elizabeth was anxious about Marianne Moore's opinion of her in the way one is about one's mother. Marianne said to us that she was worried about Elizabeth's drunkenness. Apparently at one point Elizabeth had gone to Marianne's absolutely drunk as a skunk, and Marianne was very shocked and took her in like mama. I don't think Marianne relished it in any way, but I think Elizabeth felt free to be a naughty girl with Marianne, because she knew she'd be forgiven, she'd be understood, and she'd be worried about— all very nice things to have happen to you."[4]

Bishop's most helpful confidant and ally was Dr. Anny Baumann. Louise Crane had introduced Bishop to Anny Baumann in the thirties, and Baumann became throughout Bishop's life the mainstay in her struggle with both asthma and alcoholism. According to many of Baumann's patients, she was an acute diagnostician who possessed uncommon compassion and a strong authoritarian bearing. Both qualities attracted Bishop. Three of Bishop's friends who also had Baumann as a doctor remember the loyalty and affection Baumann elicited from her patients.

WHEATON GALENTINE— Dr. Baumann came to this country about 1933. Elizabeth was one of her first patients.

HAROLD LEEDS— She had gone to medical school in Berlin. I think Anny's mother was Jewish. I remember Anny telling me the story of trying to get her mother to leave Germany, and Anny saying, "One day you'll leave and you won't even have a toothbrush." Finally she got a cable from her mother in Spain saying, "Here with my toothbrush but nothing else." That was 1939.

Anny was one of those old European doctors who believed in taking care of the whole person. Anny used to say, "If I can see you once a year, I can keep you in good health."

Anny had been my physician since the middle forties. I had avoided [her] before that, because it always sounded to me like some sort of club. Anny was Louise's [doctor and] Margaret Miller's for a while. I remember it was Loren who convinced me. I was having terrible problems with a torn muscle in my neck. Of course Anny solved it right away. She was a remarkable diagnostician and a great friend.

I think that she loved seeing her patients well. She loved going to Elizabeth's readings. When I had been ill and had major surgery, Anny talked Louise into having a Christmas party for me that Anny called a victory party. Anny sort of orchestrated it and conducted it to a good degree. But I think those were her dividends, because, if you needed her, if you were sick, she was there. Her dividends were the pleasure she perceived in seeing her patients well and functioning.

I knew Anny quite well. She [took] care of poor and hard-working blacks. Anny would take care of anybody. She was a wonderful human being. But I think she found it awfully glamorous if you were as rich as Louise or as famous as Marianne. She was interested in the arts.

GALENTINE— She would always be at a reading or a recital or an opening of a gallery.

LEEDS— In New York City doctors very rarely make house calls. Anny was an exception. If you were very sick, Anny would come see you.

MARY MEIGS— Anny Baumann had this marvelous German presence and a very, very strong German accent of authority. You felt you were in the most perfectly reliable hands you could get into. It was nice to have a woman doctor in those days, too. Anny Baumann was handsome, with blue eyes and aristocratic, decided features. I admired her from afar and was rather scared of her. She was quite authoritarian. She had so much influence over Elizabeth and her treatment of her. Elizabeth appeared to be almost in love with her.

♦   ♦   ♦

In November 1944, in the midst of this confusion in her personal life, Bishop's professional fortunes took a dramatic turn. Jean Pedricki at Houghton Mifflin wrote to her, praising "Songs for a Colored Singer," which she had read in *Partisan Review*, and enclosing an application for the Houghton Mifflin Poetry Prize Fellowship. Marianne Moore, Edmund Wilson, and John Dewey wrote recommendations for Bishop, and on 31 May 1945, after reading 833 manuscripts, the committee (Ferris Greenslet, Katharine White, and Horace Gregory) awarded Bishop the one-thousand-dollar prize and offered to publish a book of the poems she had submitted. The judges felt that Bishop fit in the line of poets, including H.D., Edith Sitwell, and Amy Lowell, whom Houghton Mifflin had published in the past.

Bishop gave fastidious attention to the production of her first book. When she turned in the final manuscript in mid-January 1946, a month late, she also submitted suggestions about the way she would like the book to look, including recommendations for the typeface and the book's shape and binding. Bishop was worried that none of her poems were about the war and suggested that a note be placed at the beginning of the book mentioning that most of the poems were written or begun before 1941. She wanted to approve each step of production, including the location and size of the page numbers and the advertisement blurbs on the dust jacket. One friend of Bishop's who worked for Houghton Mifflin remembers Bishop's reputation there.

U. T. SUMMERS— People at Houghton Mifflin saw Elizabeth as one of the most difficult authors they had ever known. I felt they were especially impatient because they perceived the publication of poetry as something of a personal favor to the author, even though they liked the prestige they hoped it would bring. Elizabeth was exasperating because she cared about every aspect of the production of her books.

After I left Houghton Mifflin, a chief editor called me in 1948–49 to say, "Is there anything you can do with this woman?" Type had been set on some of the first poems she sent in after the publication of *North & South*, and she was making what was considered an awful fuss about some detail of printing. Elizabeth cared fantastically about how every poem looked on the page. Those poems finally appeared with the publication of *A Cold Spring* in 1955. It came out with a reissue of *North & South* and a book jacket she approved of by Loren MacIver.

✦　✦　✦

In the course of the production of *North & South*, Bishop talked herself into believing that there were too few poems in the manuscript and that Houghton Mifflin was not really interested in the book. In the spring of 1946 it appeared that the book would not be published until September, and Bishop was annoyed. Houghton Mifflin argued that supplies were short and late spring was a bad time to issue a book.[5] Marjorie Stevens recommended that Bishop break her contract and publish with some other company. Then Houghton Mifflin rushed the book through for summer release.

That summer Bishop rented her apartment in New York to Steven Boyden, telling him that she intended to travel to Brazil with the money from her prize. Boyden remembers Bishop as both ill and lonely before she left New York: "Every time I went by Elizabeth's apartment, she had terrible asthma. She could hardly breathe. She wasn't going out; she was withdrawn. I took Elizabeth out before I moved into her place because I felt sorry for her. Elizabeth was reticent to go out with me, and she wasn't a great talker, but she appreciated the fact that I tried to be nice."

Bishop traveled to Nova Scotia, not Brazil, that summer of 1946. She received her first copy of North & South on 22 July 1946 and told Houghton Mifflin that she liked everything except the cover. Margaret Miller sent her word that month when the book appeared in bookstores in New York. Bishop visited her Aunt Grace and her grandparents' closest friends, the MacLachlans, in Great Village that summer. However, Bishop cut her trip short, leaving in August by bus—the trip which formed the basis of her poem "The Moose"—because she had to sign the deed for her Key West house. Marjorie Stevens had arranged for the sale of the house. Donalda MacLachlan Nelson remembers her parents' reaction to Bishop's visit that summer. Bishop also visited with her friend Zilpha Linkletter in Halifax.

DONALDA MACLACHLAN NELSON— Elizabeth came back and visited my parents. They appreciated having her come. Mother said Elizabeth was ordinary, like ourselves, and they could talk to her. She and Elizabeth had a lot in common. Mother was interested in music and literature, and she was well read. Elizabeth must have liked Mother and Dad very well, because she wanted to come up here one winter and live with them. She asked the DesBrisays [cousins living in New York City at the time] to try me out on it and see what I would think about it. But Mother and Dad were getting along in age then, and I didn't think it would be a good thing to take all that responsibility.

ZILPHA LINKLETTER— I was in New York for the equivalent of a college term, from September 1945 to April 1946, and it was during early 1946 that I met Elizabeth, through Ella DesBrisay, another person from Nova Scotia who was teaching in New York. I was going to NYU, the campus on Washington Square, and lived on Waverly Place. Elizabeth and I met a couple of times and had dinner and so on. She came to Nova Scotia on a number of occasions, and we renewed acquaintance and always managed to strike a common note. There would be years between our meetings.

On one of those trips to Nova Scotia—probably the 1946 one—Elizabeth was inquiring about her mother. She went to the Department of Health here. The records might be more likely to be there. I think she was trying to find out what she could about her mother's illness. I remember she came into my office. I'm sure it was a trial to her to do it, but she was perhaps driven to do it by some concern about her own upset condition. I had the feeling that she didn't learn a lot, but she didn't say it had been a failure.

✦   ✦   ✦

The first review of North & South to appear was by Ted Weeks in the August issue of The Atlantic.[6] Weeks was critical, arguing that Bishop's poems were intellectually thin. He felt that the collection as a whole lacked an overriding perspective, idea, or scheme. He struck a nerve with Bishop who feared being considered a lightweight thinker. However, favorable reviews by Marianne Moore, Lloyd Frankenberg, Louise Bogan, and Randall Jarrell followed. In the fall of 1946 Bishop herself sent Ferris Greenslet at Houghton Mifflin two of these reviews and encouraged him to take out an advertisement featuring them. Then other distinctions came Bishop's way. Katharine White offered her a first-reading contract with The New Yorker, which would net her 5 percent above the going rate for each poem the magazine published.[7] Bishop took the contract but doubted that the magazine would be interested in her serious poems. Bishop applied for a Guggenheim Fellowship in late 1946, and received $2,500 in April 1947, to work on her next book of poems. She had broken into the ranks of the successful writer.

Bishop's success brought her into contact with a number of prominent writers, among them Robert Lowell. Bishop met Lowell in January 1947 at Randall Jarrell's apartment in New York. Six years younger than Bishop, the tall, thin, disheveled Lowell had already published two books of poetry and had recently been appointed poetry consultant at the Library of Congress for the year beginning in September 1947. He and Bishop hit it off at Jarrell's. Bishop was pleased with the review of North & South that Lowell had published that summer; here was someone who understood her poetry. Lowell could be uncommonly self-effacing and affectionate in his relationship with

Bishop. He considered her among the best poets, a list that included Frost, Williams, and Moore. Yet Lowell also criticized some of Bishop's poems as trivial and self-indulgent. He felt that in North & South there were ten poems that failed to work.[8] Bishop liked hard criticism, when she felt it was true.

Lowell nudged Bishop out of her isolation from her literary contemporaries. When Bishop traveled through Washington, D.C., on her way to Key West in mid-October 1947, she recorded—poorly, unfortunately—some of her poems for Lowell, who had undertaken a series of recordings during his tenure as poetry consultant. In May 1948, returning from Key West, Bishop again visited Lowell in Washington, D.C., staying with Lowell's lover, Carley Dawson (Lowell and Jean Stafford had divorced in April). Bishop and Lowell visited Ezra Pound at St. Elizabeths Hospital at this time.

That summer Dawson visited Bishop in Wiscasset, Maine. When Lowell met them in Stonington, he and Dawson fought, and their relationship ended. Dawson abruptly left Stonington, and Bishop and Lowell were alone there for the final days of his stay—walking in the fog to a nearby cove, meeting with the poet Richard Eberhart, and visiting an island to fly kites. To Lowell's mind, these were intimate days. Bishop claimed to Dawson that she kept Lowell at a distance, not wanting to upset the delicate balance of their literary friendship.[9] She also found Lowell's somewhat chauvinistic, egocentric personality off-putting. Later Bishop told friends that Lowell had in fact proposed to her during this time. After leaving Stonington, Lowell was reported to have told some of his friends that he was going to marry Bishop. Carley Dawson recollects details from that summer.

CARLEY DAWSON— My relationship with Robert Lowell had begun when he was quite new as the poetry consultant. He introduced Elizabeth and me. At that time, I was supposed to be marrying Robert. Elizabeth was so sweet, and she was very pretty, with delicate features, and a small, sort of pouting mouth, not much color in her face, sort of a young girl grown-up and become old without her knowing. I remember that she invited me to stay with her at Wiscasset, and when I got there I was greeted by her saying, "We have to leave right away. These people won't let me stay in the house." I didn't know what the reason was. She was told to get out of the house and I felt that there was some very upsetting reason why this had to be. I never asked. I said, "Where else can we go?" And Elizabeth said, "Well, Cal is going to Stonington. We can meet him there." Stonington was a nice little village. Elizabeth and I went out in a boat fishing. She was trailing a line over the edge, dreaming, and all of the sudden, there was this terrific pull on the line, and the fisherman stopped the boat. It was a small shark. We were there for a number of days before Robert (I never called Robert "Cal") showed up. Elizabeth was vague and she was lost, a waif. She was without cords. She was just floating.

Then Robert showed up and he was acting rather strange. We went out, supposedly on a picnic and to go swimming, and it was then that he acted so odd that I just couldn't think what was wrong with him. He wouldn't talk to me, kept away from me, and all of that. The last I had known we were engaged. All of this was very strange. All three of us had dinner together. That night, Robert came into my room to talk. I knew that the people who owned the boarding house were overhead, and I said, "Please be quiet. Don't disturb the people that own this house." He explained that he was going to a meeting within a few weeks at which all his poet friends were going to be. He said, "You can't come." And I said, "Why not?" "You just can't come."

I understood him to be saying that I wasn't on his level in terms of literature and poetry. That spring Robert and his friends—R. P. Blackmur, John Berryman, and that whole crowd—had given a big luncheon, and they had tested me. I knew that this was going on, and I was so nervous that I gave all the wrong answers. I was seated next to Blackmur, and he kept asking me a lot of questions. I thought this was terribly mean, but of course they were protecting Robert. They didn't know whether I was worthy of him, I presume.

Robert said, "You simply can't go to this meeting." We talked for a number of hours. Then he left, and I didn't sleep. I had never been up against anyone who was schizophrenic before. I went to Elizabeth and said, "Oh, you have to help me." "What is it, darling?" was her response, which surprised me because I had never been on a "darling" basis with her. We had been just good friends, but never anything like that. She couldn't have been nicer, and she was so helpful. I said, "You have to help me get away from here," and told her why. I think she felt I was in terrible trouble and she'd been in so much trouble herself that she reacted to help me. She had a friend, a man who was just as much a drinker as she was, who was recovering from a hangover that morning, but she got him to drive me to the station. He hated driving me but he did it. Elizabeth insisted. And away I went, and that was that.

Robert never talked with me about Elizabeth, except to say that he was very fond of her. I said once or twice, "I wonder why she hasn't married because she's so attractive?" His reply was, "She must be very choosy." I never had the feeling that he had any romantic interest in Elizabeth. There was a woman that he went to see in New York, something that had happened between his first marriage and meeting me, and he said he wanted to tie up the loose ends. I felt extremely jealous about it. His relationship with Elizabeth was a friendship.

◆ ◆ ◆

Bishop and Lowell were together again at the Bard Poetry Conference in the fall of 1948, a gathering of several of the prominent poets of the day organized by Ted Weiss and Joseph Summers. Bishop traveled to Bard from New York City with the Frankenbergs, whom she introduced to Lowell. Several of Bishop's friends remember this event.

U. T. SUMMERS— I began working at Houghton Mifflin late in the winter of 1946. Elizabeth had just won the first Houghton Mifflin Poetry Award, so her name became familiar to me then. When we became friends with Lloyd Frankenberg, through my writing to him about the possibility of his writing a book explaining modern poetry, I became aware through him that Elizabeth was a great poet. In the fall of 1946 we met Elizabeth at Lloyd's apartment. Lloyd and Loren were as much New York glamorous bohemia as there could possibly be. He was a tremendously handsome man and she an extraordinarily talented, gentle, and beautiful woman. We were kind of bowled over by the pair of them, and anybody they would call a great poet I was sure was a great poet. Elizabeth was a little quiet and unglamorous compared to them. She sat very quietly in her chair, in a straight chair—they didn't have any comfortable chairs in the studio at all—and really didn't have much to say at all. She didn't speak much to me.

JOSEPH SUMMERS— She talked like mad to me about Herbert. She was shy, but she knew Herbert cold and was interested in anything anybody was trying to do with him. The basis of our friendship was Herbert, not the Frankenbergs, as far as I'm concerned. Elizabeth said that she loved Herbert so much that for years she had carried a copy of The Temple in her suitcase wherever she went, whether Key West or Paris or wherever, and she finally had to quit because she found out she had started writing seventeenth-century poems rather than twentieth-century poems. That poem "The Weed" is an example: she didn't like that anymore.

U.T.— After we met Elizabeth at Loren and Lloyd's in the fall of 1946 (and almost a year after the publication of North & South), Elizabeth came to Boston to meet her publishers at Houghton Mifflin. She invited us and the painter

Hyman Bloom to drinks in her hotel room and then to dinner at Ye Hong Guey's.

Her second visit was after seeing her aunt in Worcester who told her that her hair was "awful." My memory is that this was somehow tied in with a first reading at Wellesley. She had been or was very apprehensive about it. She slept on our studio couch and ate my frozen fish baked with a cream sauce for supper. With that visit we became real friends. We talked a great deal, all of us, about our childhoods, she about her childhood in Canada, I about mine in Tennessee, Joe about his Baptist family. This was one of the things that we really shared.

JOSEPH— She said that what we had in common was that we all grew up in the nineteenth century in an essentially fundamentalist background. In Nova Scotia as a child alone she was allowed to play with playing cards, but if they saw the minister coming up the front walk, they would grab them from her and hide them under the lace tablecloth.

U.T.— She talked about knowing Wallace Stevens and Hemingway in Key West and about being a friend of Pauline Hemingway's. She didn't like Ernest much. In New York she was always buying clothes for Hemingway's boys in Macy's basement to ship to Pauline. There was some story about Hemingway and Stevens scuffling [in Key West] and a wonderful one about Pauline's mother, who Elizabeth said was a wonderful old woman who was getting slightly [senile]. Elizabeth would say, "How are you?" And she'd say, "Just fine, Elizabeth, my mind's failing something wonderful." Elizabeth was very proud of having brought Ralph Kirkpatrick and Billie Holiday together in New York.

JOSEPH— Elizabeth liked Billie but said Billie was a crazy kind of girl—drink and drugs. Elizabeth loved her songs. Elizabeth said that she thought that Billie was the only person in New York who didn't know who Ralph Kirkpatrick was, and he was the only person in New York who didn't know who Billie was. She got them together; they played beside each other at her place. Billie could not read music, and he would have to play a thing through once, and then she would sing. And Billie said, "That man can really play that thing." Kirkpatrick said Holiday had the most extraordinary gift of phrasing that he'd ever heard in a singer. Once she heard it, she knew exactly how the tune should go. Elizabeth was very proud of that evening. It was a grand evening.

[The Bard weekend] was Ted Weiss's idea. The whole weekend was run on

$125. That's all the cash we had. Those who were paid to give papers were Louise Bogan and William Carlos Williams. We gave $75 to Williams and $50 to Louise Bogan. Everybody paid for their own railway tickets to get there; it wasn't all that much up from the city. We provided beds and fed them, had sort of pot-luck suppers together. Ted said everybody should invite all the poets they knew. The Wilburs were old friends of ours from Cambridge; he and I had shared an office together at Harvard. Dick and Betty Eberhart were old friends. Lowell came because he heard Elizabeth was coming, and Elizabeth came because she heard Lowell was coming.

U.T.— Elizabeth partly came because Lloyd and Loren were coming. They had just been to Europe for their very first trip. It was the first time we'd ever known anyone who was willing to say so completely what they did every single day in Europe, which was part of the fun. They had seen everybody— Picasso, Miro, Jimmy Savo, Elizabeth Bowen. After a party the very first night, Joe asked Elizabeth if she would like something to drink, and she said, "Oh, yes, some milk." He gave it to her and she said, "You didn't put anything in it!"

JOSEPH— There was an enormous crowd and it was most fun. There was one session at night where Williams spoke, and in the morning Bogan spoke. It ended Saturday morning with [a] roundtable [discussion]. One of the things discussed was William Carlos Williams making one of these fatuous remarks that he was full of, about [how] we'd have to write the American beat and the American line and all that sort of thing: nobody could write heroic couplets anymore, nowadays. And Elizabeth said, "Oh, Dr. Williams, you're just so old-fashioned! Cal's been writing marvelous heroic couplets recently." He looked just stricken and said to Lowell, "Cal, is that true?" "Yes, I've been trying," [Cal replied]. It was a wonderful moment. When you get literary people together, they don't talk about imagery and myth and all these high-fallutin things. You get poets together, and they talk about meter, all the time. It's just incredible how technical about lines and rhythms and things the discussion was. [The weekend] was supposed to end [Saturday] at noon, and then nobody wanted to go home. We finally got Lowell off on Monday, I believe.

U.T.— [Everyone] stayed through [Saturday] afternoon. Elizabeth hated reading her poems [so she did not want to read a poem at the final session with the others]. Cal read Elizabeth's poems. I took a nap that afternoon, and I heard reports on the poetry reading, and one of the most amusing moments that was reported was of Kenneth Rexroth's reading a very erotic poem about a woman with red pubic hair.

JOSEPH— It was a sexual poem. And then he stopped in the middle of it and [said], "You know, my wife has red hair." Finally he said, "Well, what do you think of it? Do you think it's corny?" And Lloyd Frankenberg said, "Let him who is without corn cast the first kernel." That sort of dissolved into laughter. Nobody could think of a thing to say.

For breakfast on Sunday we had Lowell, Lloyd and Loren, Elizabeth, and the Wilburs. We all took a very long walk, and I remember falling behind with Lowell and Elizabeth and finding that marvelous. And then they all came back and had lunch. Listening to Lowell talk about the gospel of St. John in very literary-religious terms was wonderful. He and Elizabeth seemed to be very much in love that weekend. He was saying, "Now let me know when you are coming back." And she said, "I don't know." "Let me know where you are," and so on. She was being quite attentive, obviously liking him, and flattered. Later on she told us at one point she loved Cal more than anybody she'd ever known, except for Lota [de Macedo Soares, her companion in Brazil], but that he would destroy her, that he was a violent person and she knew he would destroy her. She said, "He wants to marry me and I couldn't marry him."

U.T.— He liked bright girls very much. That's the only kind he married.

RICHARD WILBUR— We first encountered Elizabeth [at the Richard Eberharts']. We thought her quiet, attractive, approachable, reserved, and once she got talking, of course, it turned out that she had many more definite opinions than she had seemed initially to have. In particular, she had a strong notion as to which was Poe's best poem, and I have since come pretty well to agree with her; her favorite was "Fairy-Land."

CHARLOTTE WILBUR— [Elizabeth was] an extremely attractive woman, but the first thing that struck me was shyness. I also felt that she was not well, that she had something, nothing serious, bothering her. It seemed like asthma. She had that all the time. She looked pale and under the weather. I talked with her a little bit then, but not nearly so much as later.

RICHARD— Rather early after we had first met Elizabeth, she was staying in Boston at the Vendome [and] asked us to lunch. I recall that being a very nice, easy talk. The chief thing she said on that occasion had to do with productivity. She said, "How many poems do you write a year?" And I'm afraid I gave an answer like "Ten or twelve that I can stand." And she said, "Oh, dear, one is good luck for me." She wasn't implying that I was a blurter; there was no implicit judgment at all.

CHARLOTTE— When we saw her at the Vendome, she talked about [North & South, being published]. She just said something ironic and funny, "It's nice to be published." Something like that. And "I'm enjoying my new status."

At a writers' conference at Bard, I felt that I was beginning to know her because of what she brought up. Cal Lowell had not arrived yet, but she knew that he was coming. And there were too many poets around. She and I were at a party, and we got away deliberately from the noise—both of us disliked noise, disliked cocktail parties on the whole, and wanted to sit down and talk to one person. We sat down and started talking about Cal. She did not know until then that I was a Bostonian, had lived part of my childhood on Louisburg Square, and had met Cal somewhere en passant years before, when we were children. He was a little older than I. Elizabeth and I talked about his curious change of accent and how that came about partly because of his dislike of Boston, and I said it came about in me for the same reason. Then for some reason she just said, "Charlee, I am still very much in love with Cal. I always have been in love with him." Then she went on and told about that feeling, how in her mind he was one of the few people she addressed in her poems. She said that he had proposed to her, and she had turned him down. She [did] not go into specifics at that time about mental problems, but [she mentioned] general instability on both sides, on her side as well. Then later we did much more talking as women than we did that time. The ice was broken. Elizabeth was someone who really cared a great deal about men. I'm sure she could have been, had she chosen, bisexual.

RICHARD— I can recall having breakfast with Elizabeth and a couple of others the morning after the first day at Bard. We all tried to account for what we had done the evening before. She said, "Where was Kenneth?" And I said, "Oh, he was out in the graveyard being a natural force." That's the way she liked things put. Later on in that day—I don't know how this came about— the poets present, with no audience whatever, gathered in a room about as big as this. We all sat around, and it was proposed by Ted Weiss, who was our host and running the affair, that each of us read a poem. When it came to Elizabeth, who was sitting with Cal next to her, she said she didn't think she could read a poem. We all said, Oh, Elizabeth, read such and such, read such and such. She said no. And I think it was probably both shyness and the fear of asthma. So Cal took her book and read a poem for her, very well indeed.

I can remember [some time later] Cal's carrying Elizabeth's "Armadillo" poem around in his wallet everywhere, not the way you'd carry the picture of a grandson, but as you'd carry something to brace you and make you sure of how a poem ought to be. [Cal talked] eternally about her merits as a poet. I have a feeling that finally she was the poet he most respected, which was quite apart from his feelings of great affection for her. He wasn't going to carry anyone else around, not even Randall Jarrell, not even Ted Roethke. I think he regarded her as a perfect judge and a splendid model. I heard him say at times, "Oh, God, I'm such a bore. I talk about myself and I'm always ranking people, first, second, third, fourth. I can't get off of poetry." I think Cal must have found Elizabeth in some ways the sort of person he would have liked more often to be in relation to the art, because he had his delicacies and his feelings of what social conversation ought to be, and she talked in his view as a poet ought to talk.

JAMES MERRILL— I met Elizabeth at the famous Bard poetry conference in the fall of 1948. I was teaching there just that year, and upstairs from me lived Joe Summers and his wife, U.T. Joe gave me North & South to read. U.T. was working at Houghton Mifflin then and was one of the people who'd seen the book through. Elizabeth came to the conference, along with Dr. Williams, Louise Bogan, Kenneth Rexroth, Lowell, Mary McCarthy, and others. I remember meeting Elizabeth there, [but] I have no impressions of her whatever, though Elizabeth told me later that at that weekend she had told Cal Lowell she wouldn't marry him. She was always frightened of mental illness, of course, and she didn't want to involve herself with an unstable person, brilliant as he was and as much as she adored him. She told me—I think it was there—that she and Lizzie Hardwick had had to put Cal to bed, he was so drunk, and as they left the room, Lizzie looked back and said Cal looked just like a Greek god. Elizabeth realized the course things would take from then on.

That winter I still was at Bard. I was just bowled over by "Over 2,000 Illustrations and a Complete Concordance," so I asked Elizabeth to lunch in New York. We went to Giovanni's, where I must have been before and she turned out to have been quite often. I naively thought I could spend most of the lunch telling her how wonderful I thought the poem was. It only took a couple of minutes, and whatever we talked about from then on, we were on our own. Elizabeth wasn't affected at all. I think she knew how much she had put into her poems. She must have known they were wonderful. Maybe out of a kind of superstition she didn't want to make too much of them in talking about them.

CHAPTER 6

In November 1948 Elizabeth Bishop attended the famous party for the Sitwells at the Gotham Book Mart in New York. Marianne Moore was there, as well as a number of other prominent writers, including Tennessee Williams, William Carlos Williams, Delmore Schwartz, and Robert Lowell. Bishop had given Moore new white gloves for the occasion, which Moore brought in a box and took out for the group photograph. In this picture, which appeared in *Life* magazine, the gloves lay delicately across Moore's lap. Bishop stands hunched at the edge of the group. Pauline Hemingway thought that she looked as if her head "had been removed and then screwed back on the wrong way."[1]

In the year and a half since the publication of *North & South*, Bishop had met a number of her literary contemporaries. In November 1948, the same month as the Gotham party, Robert Lowell arranged for Bishop to have dinner with the writers Allen and Caroline Tate and himself. In December 1948, on her way to Key West for the winter, Bishop stopped to see Jane Dewey in Baltimore—they visited Poe's grave, in the rain—and then at Lowell's invitation attended a lecture by T. S. Eliot in Washington. On the day following the lecture, she, Lowell, and others were to have dinner with Eliot and Auden. The night before this dinner, however, Bishop's nervousness overcame her.

CARLEY DAWSON— I had a little house that I was renting on O Street and asked Elizabeth if she would like to stay there. I didn't know that she was a lush, and under the stairs was a cupboard where I had an assortment of liquor. It never occurred to me to put them away. I left the house in charge of my maid and a friend to keep an eye on her. When I came back, they said that she had taken a little of everything and the vomit on everything all over the house was something to behold. They cleaned it all up. I said something to Elizabeth about it, like "What had happened about the liquor?" And she said, "I got feeling sorry for myself one night and I started tasting all the different things. I just started, couldn't stop."

✦   ✦   ✦

After a few days in the hospital, Bishop continued to Key West, where she located a large apartment with a screened porch at 611 Francis Street. Shortly after her arrival, Lowell informed Bishop that if Marianne Moore declined the invitation, as he expected she would, Bishop would be appointed poetry consultant for the Library of Congress for the year beginning September 1949. Bishop's formal appointment was made in January 1949. She was to be paid $5,700. Lowell explained the responsibilities as minimal, a daily appearance at the office, but each week's work could be accomplished in two days. Since he planned to have completed most of the recording project, Bishop would have a lot of time for her own writing. Bishop agreed to accept this job, then almost immediately began doubting her decision. Did she deserve the job? Would she be successful in such a public position? What if she were called upon for speeches? Would other writers be critical of her appointment? Wesley Wehr, whom Bishop met in Seattle, Washington, in 1966, remembers Bishop telling him about a prominent writer who criticized her for taking the Library of Congress position.

WESLEY WEHR— Elizabeth said to me in 1966 that when she was given the Library of Congress poetry position, "A" was most resentful. "A" told her in no uncertain terms that "A" felt that he or she should have had the job, because, after all, "A" had a family, and Elizabeth didn't. "A" could be so insecure and competitive that Elizabeth found "A" embarrassing if not offensive. She just tried to avoid "A" whenever possible. This incident demonstrates the level on which Elizabeth could be offended. I'm sure that Elizabeth in her own privacy could be pretty combative.

A short trip to Haiti in February 1949, with Virginia Pfeiffer, Pauline Hemingway's sister, helped Bishop put the Library of Congress into the back of her mind. A bout with asthma that had been bothering her vanished; she took up spearfishing and hiked to local landmarks that were usually reached only by horse. Bishop also attended a lecture on Haitian art by Selden Rodman, the writer and art critic, who had visited Key West in January, when he had arranged for his companion, the writer Maia Wojciechowska, to room with Bishop. When Bishop returned to Key West from Haiti, she entered a very difficult period, with almost tragic results.

MAIA WOJCIECHOWSKA RODMAN— I was the part-time assistant, part-time babysitter for Sarah Palfrey [a tennis professional] at the Casa Marina [in Key West] in 1949. We came in November or December, and then the high season came, and I was occupying a room that the hotel could be renting. I was asked if I could find someplace else to live. I had no idea where to go. This was the time that Selden [Rodman] came from Haiti to visit me in Key West. Selden introduced me to Elizabeth, told her my predicament, and she said, "Oh, she can stay with me." This is how I met Elizabeth, and within a couple of days I moved in with her. I had no idea who Elizabeth was.

When I first met Elizabeth, she seemed bloated. Her face was puffy. She seemed much older, very dowdy, very pale, physically almost sickly. I was indoctrinated by Marjorie Stevens, very shortly after I came, to the fact that Elizabeth was a drunk. Stevens was a very angry young woman. Elizabeth was out someplace during this conversation. This woman said that I must not allow any liquor to come into the house, and that I must prevent any deliveries because Elizabeth was a very cunning drunk and she would call all over the place and try to get liquor. Although Marjorie had canceled all of Elizabeth's charges around town, Elizabeth would still find a way. She would lie. I said, "I won't be here. I won't know." I was going to be out from early morning until quite late at night. What should I do? After all, I was only nineteen and very naive. I'd never known a drunk. I'd never taken care of one. Marjorie said that I must watch Elizabeth. She spoke to me as if I was some hired help. More than being demeaning to me, I felt it was disloyal to Elizabeth to be speaking to me that way. It gave me the impression that Elizabeth was a totally untrustworthy and conniving person, and this from what I thought was her best friend or a good friend. Following as close as I could these instructions, I found a lot of stashed liquor and dumped it into the toilet.

Elizabeth had a very large, airy apartment on the second floor, with a large living room, two bedrooms, and windows [looking] out on the street. Usually the shades were drawn. I remember opening the drapes and windows all the time. She was in the darkness all day. When I returned from work and I asked her what she had been doing, she would say something like, "Well, I was trying to work." Elizabeth was working on something. At one point she explained to me that the way she worked was very painful, that she first wrote a poem in her head, but the act of writing, putting it down, was usually a letdown, so then she either put it away, destroyed it, or rewrote it. It was a painful process.

When it rained, I didn't work. I'd come in, and then it would be like I was part of her day, and she didn't seem to do anything. She seemed to be on a routine that involved so much leisure that it was a foreign life to me. She seemed so unnaturally devoid of life's juices. I had an idea that there was a clique of friends, but they never came when I was there. There was nobody coming in, except for Marjorie. Elizabeth had no social life. Key West seemed to be a good town for drinking. The bars were interesting. It was almost like the Left Bank in Paris in atmosphere. As far as I know, Elizabeth was not going into the bars to do her drinking. She did not live to the possibilities that were there. Why was she not drinking where the people were drinking? She was very much isolated.

I learned nothing about her, but maybe that was part of her style. I thought she might have been rich. I presumed that she was a very lonely person. I do remember sitting with her evening after evening. She had some things that were very nice in her apartment. A couple of very nice drawings. Terrific books. We read a lot. She had a very nice collection of records. She introduced me to blues—Bessie Smith, Billie Holiday. That was a big thing, the records. We played cards. We talked. She asked a lot of questions about me growing up in Poland.

We did talk about Robert Lowell. I was in love with Selden. She indicated that when she was in love with Lowell and he was in love with her, it was madness, not reality. It was either too romantic or too unreal. Maybe she didn't say it in so many words, but she implied that her love for Lowell was never as real as what Selden and I had going. Something of that sort.

Then one day I came home, not all that late, and I found Elizabeth on the floor in the bathroom, her face totally violet. I thought she was dead. I checked for her pulse. She had a pulse. I immediately called Marjorie, and she called the ambulance. Marjorie knew immediately what had happened. Having found nothing in the house to drink, Elizabeth drank the rubbing alcohol. Marjorie was in such a fury. I've never seen anybody so horrible. I kept saying, "What do we do?" And she said, "Everything's taken care of! You do not do anything." The fury of this woman made me almost afraid for my life. Marjorie said that I was responsible. I had killed Elizabeth. Didn't I know that if I had emptied every bottle in the house not to leave the rubbing alcohol? That must have been the love and concern, but it was desperation and so much anger that you couldn't connect it with love easily.

Elizabeth recovered within a few days. She called from the hospital, insisted that I stay, and said that she was going to be there for some time. She was very sweet, wonderful. I think I stayed there for a little while but moved out before she came back from the hospital. Elizabeth made me feel that it wasn't my fault at all. I couldn't figure out Marjorie and Elizabeth's relationship, because Elizabeth never said anything about her being a friend or a dear person in her life who was taking care of her. Maybe that is why she was so sad. People who were close to her never noticed. I think Marjorie was the same way. She was screaming, making all this noise, and nobody asked the important question, What was really wrong?

I never said anything about this incident to anybody. What hurt me is that people talked about it and pointed a finger at me. I thought that lacked grace. This little clique of ladies would come up to me and say, "Oh, you're the one who made Elizabeth drink rubbing alcohol." I said no, and I would explain it all, and they would laugh. When I met Tennessee Williams, he knew the story. Those people were so catty, so mean spirited. There were possibly even two groups not totally friendly to each other and sometimes a little catty. One group of people was not terribly friendly to Elizabeth. One woman in particular had some vile and mean things to say about Elizabeth following Elizabeth's incident with the drinking. Marjorie, Pauline, Virginia, and a couple of other ladies were sympathetic to Elizabeth. Once something made me really cry, because somebody was cruel, and I asked Pauline about it, and she tried to explain to me that there are certain people who are so unhappy with themselves that they are out to crucify other people.

Elizabeth realized that she had to get well after that incident. She said that this was like a breaking point or the low point. I had a feeling that there had been attempts at suicide prior to this incident or a fear that Elizabeth might try to commit suicide. There was a watch going on. After she got out of the hospital, Elizabeth came over to my place. For a week or so I rented this little room that had a toilet inside of it. The toilet was filled with flowers that I had received from a friend. Elizabeth came, and I cooked a dinner. She thought it was absolutely fantastic to have flowers in the toilet. I always thought she was going to write a poem about that. She went on about it in such a way. That was the first time I saw her take pleasure in something.

After being in the hospital in Miami in March 1949, Bishop was admitted in May to a clinic, Blythwood, in Greenwich, Connecticut, where she underwent treatment for alcoholism until going to Yaddo, an artists' colony in Saratoga Springs, New York, in June.

Bishop felt out of place at Yaddo—the young and energetic writers and artists made the place too intense for her. She knew no one. She telephoned Loren MacIver, claiming that she wanted to die. She wandered around Saratoga drunk. One day she was confident that the job at the Library of Congress was right for her and resolved to believe in herself, the next, a compliment from someone at Yaddo about her predecessor at the Library of Congress, Leonie Adams, would set Bishop reeling.

◆ ◆ ◆

Bishop arrived in Washington to begin her job as poetry consultant on 12 September 1949, and, as Carley Dawson recollects a scene from one of her first days there, began her stay there with unsteady footing.

CARLEY DAWSON— I found Elizabeth a room in Georgetown's one boarding house, Miss Looker's—she had wonderful food, apparently. I remember after Elizabeth got there, she called me up and said, "If you love me, bring me something to eat." She wasn't well. I still was so naive I didn't realize that she was an alcoholic. She had drunk a whole bottle of toilet water to get the alcohol. I brought her a bunch of sandwiches or something.

◆ ◆ ◆

Bishop spent her first few days at the library observing Leonie Adams. She admired Adams's efficiency and command of the job. However, even after the first month, Bishop remained confused about exactly what she was to be doing. It seemed foolish, for example, for her to respond to research questions that her assistant, Phyllis Armstrong, could handle much more quickly and knowledgeably. Armstrong was particularly good at rewriting Bishop's letters into bureaucratic language. Bishop and Armstrong also read the racing forms every day; Armstrong always bet on the daily double. Eventually, Bishop settled in, making recommendations for purchases and preparing the second series of recorded albums. She recorded Muriel Rukeyser (in November), Robert Frost (in December, for a second time), Archibald MacLeish, and Dylan Thomas, who she felt was a superb reader. Bishop spent most of her time preparing the leaflets to accompany these and other recordings.

Bishop also continued Robert Lowell's tradition of visiting Ezra Pound in St. Elizabeths Hospital. She brought him books and magazines. At Christmas she gave Pound cologne and found him sitting under a Christmas tree, acting a little crazier than he had been that fall. Pound tried to convince Bishop to order subscriptions to a variety of foreign language magazines, including some in Bengali and Japanese. Bishop suspected he wanted to locate his own name in English script in them. Majorie Brush, whom Bishop met when she was living in San Francisco in the sixties, recollects Bishop telling her about these visits to Pound, which formed the basis of her "Visits to St. Elizabeths."

MAJORIE BRUSH— Elizabeth told me about how awful those visits were, how she suffered visiting Pound because he lived in a room with no doors. He had no privacy whatsoever, so whatever illness he had was exacerbated by this condition. People would go in and out, guards and other patients, and Pound was cross and kind of mean. Elizabeth and I talked about politics. She seemed to understand why Roosevelt had to treat Pound the way he did. Elizabeth felt that it was her duty to go and see him. She wasn't sympathetic to Pound personally.

✦　✦　✦

Bishop learned how bureaucracy worked at the Library of Congress. She also had a bird's eye view of American letters. However, there were public and social aspects to the job for which Bishop was not suited—she did not give a public reading while in Washington, deferred speaking at luncheons, and was so unnerved while planning a meeting of the Board of Fellows in January that she got drunk for two days. Joseph Frank, the biographer and critic, met Bishop during her time in Washington and noticed the detachment she had from her job at the library. Frank attributes this attitude in part to the fact that Bishop did not have the mind of a literary critic.

JOSEPH FRANK— I met Elizabeth during her year at the Library of Congress. I was a newspaperman for the Bureau of National Affairs in Washington. I also was writing literary criticism at the time. I got to know Allen Tate [and] had already published a number of things in the *Sewanee Review*. I have some recollection of Cal Lowell introducing Elizabeth and me. I knew Cal when he held the chair there and the literary people that were coming in the Library of Congress at that time. We did overlap in Yaddo when Elizabeth was there [in 1950]. I left for Europe shortly after I left Yaddo that summer. This was a big experience in my life. I was going to Europe for the first time and I was very excited about it, so she gave me as a departing gift a traveling wallet in which you could put a passport. We were very close friends.

Elizabeth was very reserved, not at all exuberant or outgoing, but very nice, once you got past the first barrier of a certain kind of anxiety of human relations. We got to know each other very well; we had common interests and common friends. We used to have lunch together. There was a literary sort of milieu around the Library of Congress. Sometimes I would work in the library, and I would stop off and see her and say hello. I know she thought [being poetry consultant] was rather odd. [She] was amused at having any kind of official status, and her relation to it was one of ironic amusement. She never knew what she was supposed to be doing or what her functions were.

Elizabeth certainly had lots of anxieties. I'm not so sure they were connected specifically with the job or her official post at the Library of Congress. [She was] very, very much [an anxious woman]. I have a vague recollection of a sense of isolation from her family or her family background. From casual remarks that she made I had the sense that [her background] seems to have left a certain sense of emotional emptiness in her life. Things would slip out in conversation. I remember her speaking about [her father's death]. I had the feeling that her childhood was troubled in all sorts of ways and that she was still under the effect of this. It was there in her sensibility. I always had the feeling that she didn't want to talk about anything personal. She could comment on all sorts of people with great sharpness and wit. She could be very deadly about other people, not to their face, of course, but very little got past her. She was an awful lot of fun to talk to.

I didn't even know if Elizabeth was American or not. I wasn't quite clear because she spoke so much about Nova Scotia. I had the feeling that she didn't feel at home in this country somehow, that she was rather alien from that point of view because [these] early years had shaped her sensibility in such a way. She wasn't a regular fellow—she was more Canadian and more English than she was American. There was not this kind of American casualness about her at all as a person. She was aware of that. She traced it to the different kind of bringing up she had had. She was much more rigorous in some deep moral and social sense than the ordinary American. She was very formal in many ways. Probably the more formalized Latin culture that she lived in in Brazil [beginning in 1951] suited her much more than ordinary life in the States.

In general I don't think Elizabeth had a theoretical interest in literature at all. My sense of her was of these completely spontaneous reactions. I was always impressed and rather surprised at the immediacy of her response and her absolute certainty. If she didn't like anything, you could not get her to reconsider. What she [found] congenial, she accepted, and what she [didn't], she rejected, and that is all there was to it. [She had strong opinions] about literary matters. She always responded to the immediate and the specific. That's the response of an artist.

[This reaction is also] something that you feel in Elizabeth's poetry. There's a response to the concrete, the things themselves, and what they mean to her or how they make her respond somehow. She read a poem about a rooster ["Roosters"], and she told me that it came from the time she was living in [Key West], and that there really had been a rooster like that as the basis of the poem. She began to reminisce about the fact that at the basis of the poem was something she had experienced herself. Writing poetry was just a very personal thing with Elizabeth. She wrote poetry because she felt she had to write poetry. This was a response to experience. It rather surprised her somehow. I don't think Elizabeth had any conception of herself at all as a literary person. This is my reaction because I am in some ways quite the contrary. I think she felt it rather incongruous that someone like herself was a poet. Everybody seemed to admire her poetry. She seemed to be one of the few poets about whom there was very little disagreement.

She was very close to Cal Lowell. She liked him and his work. In some ways—here I'm talking completely off the cuff—she had a liking for things that were harsh. I think she found that quality in his work. There was no easy yielding to certain kinds of facility. This was a very early stage of his writing when [what] he was writing was extremely complex, elaborate. I think she liked the kind of knottiness and also a certain pitiless quality of his sensibility. I know she was greatly concerned about him, because everybody was aware that he would go off. . . .

Elizabeth used to go regularly to St. Elizabeths to see Pound and bring him books of Chinese hieroglyphs and things like that. He would ask her for something, and she would go and get it and bring it. She was laughing that he didn't know how to read these things. He couldn't understand these things and yet he wanted them. I don't think she thought he was really crazy. I do think she admired his poetry.

[Elizabeth's drinking problem] was extremely isolated and sporadic. Every once in a while I had the feeling that she drank too much. I never had the feeling that she was a pathological drinker who had lost control. There were episodes occasionally, then she would stop. There was only one occasion, over all the time I knew her, when she was ill that I was aware of. It may have been the illness that depressed her and then set her off. I didn't see any of it in ordinary contact. Once I had been drinking too much and I [had] a hangover, and she told me that a beer was pretty good for that.

✦ ✦ ✦

Margaret Miller and Virginia Pfeiffer visited Bishop in Washington in the fall of 1949, and the Frankenbergs visited in the spring of 1950. Bishop herself spent some weekends in New York. Bishop also visited Jane Dewey, at her farm in Havre de Grace, Maryland. Dewey was employed at a ballistics testing ground fifteen miles from her house, and when Bishop was there during weekdays, the ground would occasionally shake and a faint boom could be heard in the distance when the laboratory was testing explosives. Bishop attended exhibitions—one of Klee's paintings she saw three times—and regularly visited the National Gallery, where a Delacroix painting of an Algerian girl got her started on a poem. Still, Bishop found that she had virtually no time to work on her own writing during this year. Also, Washington was lonely. The buildings were boring and the weather oppressive—she felt there was no spring, just a brief transition from damp winter to stifling summer. In the course of one of her visits to New York, probably at New Year's, Bishop contacted Maia Wojciechowska, who recollects her overall impression of Bishop's loneliness during this period.

MAIA WOJCIECHOWSKA RODMAN— Elizabeth was in New York, at the Waverly Hotel on Washington Square. We had lunch or dinner, and then she called me up one night, saying that she was dreadfully sick and felt miserable. Could I come and take care of her? I said I would love to. It must have been nine or ten at night. When I arrived she was in her nightgown in bed, totally drunk. I said, "What can I do? You seem to be half asleep." And Elizabeth said, "Well, all I really want is . . . Why don't you lie down in my bed?" I said, "Elizabeth, I think somebody told me about women liking women. Is that what you are saying?" She said she found me so attractive. I told her, "You must be kidding," and I turned this whole thing into a joke. And she said, "All right, this is as far as I'll go with this. I know you're not attracted to me." She let that go. And then she grew very serious and said, "I'm very afraid. I've been drinking, and I'm very afraid I'm in a horrible state of mind. Would you spend the night on the sofa, or in the bed and I'll spend it . . ." I said, "No, no, I'll sleep on the sofa."

I really felt that this was desperation. I suppose she might have felt suicidal. I had no words of comfort. I did not understand. She didn't drink anymore. She got up to go to the bathroom, and she was holding on to furniture. Then she decided she wanted to give me something. She gave me a book of hers signed "My favorite laundress." I kept thinking, Why is she saying this? Did I ever do her laundry? Is she confusing me with anybody else?

I had to go to work the next morning. Elizabeth was still asleep when I left. I left a note with my work number, if she needed me. I said that I knew that we have bad moments and then feel much better. She called me that day, and she said, "I'm fine." She was going to go someplace. She had asked whether I would ever be in Washington and invited me to come to visit. She really appreciated my staying. She said she was sorry she had made a pass at me, which surprised me tremendously, because I thought she was way too drunk to remember. That was the last time I saw her. I thought that that scene in the hotel was one of many nights like that.

◆　　◆　　◆

Bishop went to Yaddo for four months after she had finished at the Library of Congress in October 1950. After the first week, when she was hospitalized for five days for drinking, she was more at home at Yaddo this second time. Walking the grounds of the estate calmed her. She started practicing her clavichord daily. And slowly a group of friends began to take shape there, including the writer Ilse Barker and her husband, the artist Kit Barker, the poet May Swenson, the critic Alfred Kazin, the writer Calvin Kentfield, and the composer Alexi Haieff. Bishop was pleased that Victor Wolfgang von Hagen, an archeologist and explorer, several of whose books on South America she had read, was there as well.

Bishop was particularly kind to Pauline Hanson (the assistant to Elizabeth Ames, the director of Yaddo), whose long war poem, The Forever Young, so impressed her that she wrote to Marianne Moore, Louise Bogan, and Robert Lowell on Hanson's behalf. Hanson remembers Bishop from this visit at Yaddo, particularly her attitude toward her year in Washington. Ilse Barker remembers the warmth of Bishop's relationship with her and Kit, yet the unpredictability of her behavior. Eleanor Clark Warren, Bishop's friend from Vassar, remembers her time at Yaddo in January and February 1951 as a particularly difficult period for Bishop.

PAULINE HANSON— Elizabeth told me she was terribly unhappy at the Library of Congress. She said, "It has kind of taken poetry away from me. I had to read so much I didn't like, it absolutely numbed me." She was greatly honored to have the post, but she said it was all so difficult. She said, "I had wanted to give a fine party. So I invited Carl Sandburg and Robert Frost, two men the same age, fine poets, they would have so much to talk about. When they came, they stared at each other, and they sat each at far ends of the sofa." It was up to the disciples to approach, to choose whom they would go to and kneel before. They just didn't like each other at all. She said it was a terrible party.

Elizabeth did tell me about a wonderful night at some lovely lady's home, a wealthy woman, who loved poetry and had a big poetry party. Dylan Thomas was there. Elizabeth hadn't met Dylan Thomas or hadn't really had time to talk with him. They probably had a drink or two too many. At one point, finding themselves in the butler's pantry, they locked the doors. She said, "We had a wonderful time drinking and talking." She said she loved him. Elizabeth mentioned visiting Pound and what an interesting visit it was, because there was this poor man, this poor poet, and this wife and his mistress, one on one side and one on the other side. She said, "How can a poor man stand that?"

Elizabeth came into a situation at Yaddo that was very relaxing and very comfortable. She was left alone. There was absolutely no visiting studios until after four o'clock. Elizabeth had a room in East House, which has two studies. She had one side and Beauford Delaney, a fine black painter and a wonderful human being, had a bedroom and studio on the other side. Beauford didn't have a cent—he had friends who were very kind to him and had brought him by car—his feet hurt him and he didn't have the right shoes. He emanated warmth and love. There was something maternal about him. Meeting him was important for Elizabeth; he was good for her. They both wanted before-dinner drinks, and for this the two of them got together. There was a connecting door between one side of the house and the other. A guest room usually had a rocking chair in it. While they had Lord knows how many drinks together, they rocked. I don't think they wanted to be invited over to the larger West House where together other people had their drinks. Elizabeth and Beauford liked to be where and as they were.

After dinner Beauford would sing. He had a beautiful voice and was a true artist. (A few years after he left Yaddo, he went to Paris and got a job singing in nightclubs and was an enormous success.) Kit Barker would sing and then Beauford would sing—all in what were very special and relaxed periods. Alfred Kazin was there. I remember him saying desperately to Beauford one night after Beauford got done singing, "Oh, Beauford, if there were only something in the world I could do for you. You don't know what your singing does for me." It was how we all felt. And at the time, I felt Elizabeth was probably buying some of Beauford's work. In a casual, quiet way.

Elizabeth was writing what she knew were some good poems. I know she wrote that one poem ["While Someone Telephones"] about the tree outside East House. She read to me the line "might they not be his green gay eyes." She said, "I was thinking of Robert Lowell, of course." May Swenson came during that time. Elizabeth was very, very generous about other people's work, if she liked it. In the season from late fall to spring, we all sat at one table for meals. Elizabeth and May, standing at the table one evening, were sort of skirmishing about birthdays—you know, who was the older. Suddenly, I heard Elizabeth say to May, "Oh, we're just about the same age. May, I want to say something to you. May Swenson, when I read your work, I'm just green with jealousy." She said it with such love for poetry in her voice. They were both, of course, very, very visual.

My cousin Wallace Fowlie was briefly at Yaddo in that period. He and Elizabeth had met, walked together, in their 1949 visit. She remembered one of their walks with special pleasure—when telling her how much he admired her sestina ["A Miracle for Breakfast"], he had recognized the form and they had together talked about its history. She told me Wallace was, for her, the rare person who could sit at the breakfast table and not talk about aesthetics. He would only talk about the weather. That was the way she was. Poetry was private.

Elizabeth knew that I had written a little poetry book before I came to Yaddo. I never mentioned this to her, and she found out from someone else, probably Elizabeth Ames. Questioned, I said I wasn't a guest at Yaddo, I was just an employee, and didn't want to show anyone my poetry. I think Elizabeth's strong reaction to my little book was just because it was so old-fashioned and different from what she had been seeing. I didn't know anything about poetry. Someone I loved very much was dying, and two lines suddenly came to me: "The fatherhood is mortal and of hate; / the only brotherhood is of the dead" ["The Forever Young and Never Free"]. The two lines became part of the first quatrain. It was because it came like that that the poem was written in quatrains. The poem decided its own form. Without saying anything, Elizabeth wrote to the publisher of The Forever Young, got a number of copies and sent a copy to Marianne Moore, Louise Bogan, and Robert Lowell. When she got Marianne Moore's letter, Elizabeth cornered me and read it to me. She had told me that Moore liked it. I didn't know she had done all this. It impressed me that she was so kind and so generous. Elizabeth was very generous this way.

Word came of Edna St. Vincent Millay's death, and Elizabeth was terribly disturbed about that, talked about it over a period of weeks. She said, "Think of that poor, poor thing all alone in that house and falling down those stairs. Did she do it on purpose or did it just happen?" She spoke of the aloneness.

I began work at Yaddo January 1, 1950. Though Elizabeth had some alcohol problems when she was there in the summer of 1949, it was then Elizabeth Ames invited her to come for the late 1950 visit. This though she knew that if there was trouble in the fall, she'd be the first to bear the burden of it. But she felt strongly about Elizabeth Bishop's poetry. She knew how charming she could be and how much others enjoyed being with her. In the end, I think what decided it was Elizabeth Ames's hope that a long fall-to-spring visit would give Elizabeth the kind of quiet working time she needed. The great generosity of the Trasks brought Yaddo into physical existence. And from the beginning, Elizabeth Ames so well structured how it "works" for artists, its procedures remain much the same. Except for the first and last days of her visit, it did "work" for Elizabeth Bishop. Elizabeth Ames, of course, knew the difficulties that Elizabeth was having with drink that spring. Often Elizabeth didn't come for dinner.

Elizabeth in the beginning was very happy at Yaddo. She had a deep friendship with Beauford, the Barkers were a joy, Calvin Kentfield was devoted to her, and the grounds were fascinating—she loved to walk. Later in her visit things began to change. Beauford's visit ended and William Goyen came for his studio. He was another very sensitive, very talented writer, very intellectual, too. That changed things and probably began to make Elizabeth think of being in New York, and how different things were going to be, there. Katherine Anne Porter then came. So admired, so established. I remember at dinner table how we all stared at her, she was so beautiful and talked so brilliantly.

Elizabeth had about a five-month invitation. She left early. She once said to me that New York City was the wrong place for her, that she needed to be in a place where there were exotic flowers and exotic birds. There were people it was good for her to be with, and there were people and circles that were not good for her to be with, and Elizabeth knew this. If she hadn't been at Yaddo, I don't know what would have happened to her, going directly from the library to New York City. I don't think she would have made it. She came to Yaddo and she met there people it was important for her to meet and be with. It was only with their help and [the] feeling that they had real affection for her that she made it through that spring.

ILSE BARKER— Elizabeth, Kit, and I were at Yaddo together for four months. We knew about Elizabeth before we met her, since, when we were at Yaddo in May to June of that year [1950], Bob Evett, a composer friend of Elizabeth's from Washington, had been a fellow guest. He composed mainly church music, later became an editor at *The New Republic*. He told us that Elizabeth was a wonderful person, and that she was having a terrible time. He said we would enjoy her company and asked us to look after her.

Kit and I arrived in early November [1950], and stayed until early March [1951]. We had a nice house-cum-studio called "Pine Tree" where we worked and had people to tea and gave parties. Elizabeth was often with us there. She was in a way closer to Kit than me, partly because I was so totally involved with my work—finishing a novel I had started at Yaddo earlier that year—partly, I think, because he had a more immediate understanding of people and poetry. I felt at the time that they immediately became friends and felt great warmth for each other.

Elizabeth's visual sensitivity was an important link. She herself painted and would probably have gone on painting if she had not been so modest, deprecating her gift. Kit understood her modesty and was also more able than I was to cope with her alcoholism, something I felt [was] very difficult to deal with. Elizabeth and Kit talked about art and the art of painting and the painters they admired. She liked Kit's work and had a great understanding of his desire for privacy. She also had a special feeling for people with a glass eye. Later, when Kit developed asthma in middle age, they had yet another thing in common. And during all our many meetings, at Yaddo, in London, Sussex, Boston, and Maine, we always had fun together.

I remember Elizabeth's anti-allergy shots. The taxi used to come and take her into Saratoga Springs, and she sometimes took the opportunity of bringing back supplies of bourbon. She was often the worst for drink and did not leave her room for days. I used to worry about her. Was she going to appear for breakfast, lunch, dinner? Was she around? What about inviting her to a party? Would that be good or bad? Most of the time Elizabeth wasn't well enough. If it wasn't her asthma, it was drink. Elizabeth Ames was very good and forbearing, not judgmental. Elizabeth, in that state, must have been a worry, but Elizabeth Ames never let on.

I don't know what had caused Elizabeth's difficulties in Washington except that she had hated her time there, hated anything to do with putting herself in the public eye. Getting away, I think, she felt almost as if she had come out of prison. Katherine Anne Porter was at Yaddo, living in a flat in Saratoga Springs. She used to spend her evenings with us and, despite her considerable age, played Ping-Pong with us. Elizabeth and Katherine were not particularly friendly. I don't think Elizabeth could cope with anybody who was anything other than just a personal friend, and there was a hint of competitiveness in everything Katherine Anne did. Elizabeth still felt easily threatened after Washington and the "public life" she had to lead there.

Elizabeth had not really wanted to come to Yaddo at the time but was persuaded by Bob Evett and other friends. I think Bob told her about us and assured her she would be "comfortable" with us. In the event, I think the stay did help her. She wrote "The Prodigal" during her time at Yaddo, and this was a breakthrough. It was the first poem she had written for a long time. One of the lovely things about Elizabeth was that she was unself-consciously pleased with her poetry when it worked well. She showed us the poem with obvious pleasure.

ELEANOR CLARK WARREN— I hadn't seen Bishop in a long time [before seeing her in Yaddo in 1951]. It was out of season. There were never more than about ten artists in residence at that time of the year. As I remember, Elizabeth didn't eat much, wasn't at many of those meals, she was drinking so much. She'd go down to Saratoga, get herself completely soused, and the bar people would call a taxi and get her sent home. The taxi drivers would just pour her onto her doorstep.

Elizabeth and I got talking a little, times when she was sober. She called one night, rather late in the evening, wanted me to come over, which was really the first gesture she'd ever made toward me for many, many years. I think she just was in desperation—there wasn't much of anybody else there in that season that she could feel any rapport with. She wasn't dead drunk, she wasn't falling-down drunk that evening; I think she was just scared to death of herself. She just wanted some presence to talk to. She just wanted something between herself and the dark. And boy she needed it.

Of course, there wasn't really anything I could do. But what I did do—I was a passionate skier and I had my old car there, and I asked her if she would like to go with me the next day. She said she would and she did, and just the two of us went, she, of course, not skiing. It was a way of doing something else than going to the bar in Saratoga. I enjoyed it very much. We had a nice chatty time going and coming. She was as sober as could be that day and was very companionable. Elizabeth Ames sort of thanked me for taking Elizabeth on that ski day.

♦   ♦   ♦

By March 1951 Bishop was staying in an inexpensive, dingy room at the Hotel Grosvenor in New York. Ilse Barker remembers "visiting her in a most ghastly midtown hotel room between the first of March and the fourteenth. Her room looked out on an air shaft. I think she was past caring. She was in a poor way." Bishop's apartment building on King Street had been torn down two years before. Her psychiatrist, Dr. Foster, whom Bishop felt had been a great help to her, had died the previous fall, and "Elizabeth went into Dr. Baumann's arms when she left Yaddo."[2] Baumann arranged for her own public accountant to work with Bishop to get her finances in order. Bishop had booked passage to Europe on a freighter for the sixteenth of March, but the tax issues with which this accountant was helping her kept her in New York. In May, Baumann took Bishop with her to an exhibition of paintings by a clinic patient of hers at a housing project community center in Queens. Her tactic was to help Bishop focus on the future, not the past, on her potential, not the obstacles. Baumann also prescribed for Bishop Vitamin B shots and female hormones, to control her nervousness and, she hoped, to prevent her drinking.

Baumann seems to have helped. In May, Bishop moved into an apartment more comfortable and cheerful than her hotel room and began planning a trip to Sable Island. *The New Yorker* had expressed an interest in an article on her trip. Bishop's great-grandfather and his crew had drowned off the coast of this desolate, thin island of sand dunes—actually, the tip of a sand bar one hundred miles long—off the coast of Nova Scotia. Bishop was interested in the island's history of such tragedies, its settlements, and the fauna, par-ticularly the herd of wild horses that lived there, one of which her Aunt Grace had bought for her farm in Great Village. Bishop arranged for permis-sion from Ottawa to be taken out on a tender and stay at the lighthouse. She landed on the beach in a dory on 8 August and spent a week walking the dunes, chasing the horses and the seals, reading, and taking notes.

Bishop's article on Sable Island never materialized, and, once she returned to New York, her depression recurred. Dr. Baumann recommended more travel, and another grant made this trip possible. In March 1951 Bishop had been awarded the $2,500 Lucy Martin Donnelly Fellowship from Bryn Mawr College. Marianne Moore, Edmund Wilson, and Katharine White had writ-ten recommendations for Bishop. Bishop booked a trip to Europe for the fall. Joseph Summers saw Bishop in October and heard her talking about her travel plans.

JOSEPH SUMMERS— [A group of us had] agreed to meet at some restaurant or bar and were down in the basement. We were sort of waiting for Eliz-abeth, and she was late. When she came, she was hitting the banisters and ricocheted off the walls. Elizabeth was obviously very tight. I remember she sat down, sort of huffy and puffy, dropped her purse and dropped her hat, this sort of thing. We ate and got through things. It was all right, but Eliz-abeth obviously wasn't really feeling well. Finally, the dinner was about breaking up, and Lloyd [Frankenberg] offered to take her home. The rest of us were thinking about going somewhere, somebody else's house or some bar, and she asked me, "What should I do?" I said, "I think you ought to let

Lloyd take you home." And she said, "Oh, I don't mean that. Should I kill myself?" It was just horrifying.

I made an appointment to have lunch with her the next day at some Viennese restaurant. She gave me very precise instructions on how to get there and what they had to eat. And I went there the next day and she never appeared. I sat there feeling very bad. I was afraid that I might not ever see her alive again. I did feel that she was so desperately unhappy, and then there was the combination of the drinking and possible suicidal tendencies. Elizabeth wrote a couple of cryptic notes. She wrote one note asking me to forgive her, could I forgive her, this kind of thing.

Elizabeth said, "I'll never try to live in New York again," which she did. It was a mistake to begin with. She said it's the loneliest place in the world if you don't have any family or anybody you care about. She had had a ticket to go around the world, just to get out of New York, and before she was supposed to leave, they called up and said that they'd overbooked and they couldn't take her. She said, "Well, where do you have boats going?" And they said, "Well, we have one going to South America." And she said, "All right, I'll come on that one."

In early December 1951 Bishop embarked on the *Bowplate* for a trip around South America. Her plans were indefinite—she would first visit friends in Rio, then continue on the freighter through Tierra del Fuego and around the world, perhaps in four months, arriving in Holland, where Robert Lowell was living. She had no specific destination, but at her first stop, the unexpected occurred. Quite simply and miraculously, Bishop fell in love with a woman in Brazil, stayed, and lived the happiest years of her life.

CHAPTER 7

When Elizabeth Bishop boarded a small freighter, the *Bowplate*, in late November 1951 for a voyage around Cape Horn, she looked forward to an extended reprieve from the past few depressing years on the East Coast. The freighter was a workaday vessel. Ladders and walkways extended over huge crates of machinery on deck for the passengers and the crew to make their way fore and aft. Bishop read, worked on reviews, and polished her article on the trip she had taken to Sable Island in the summer of 1951. Among the other eight passengers, only one caught Bishop's attention, Miss Breen, a tall, unprepossessing seventy-year-old woman from Glens Falls, New York, who had been in charge of a woman's jail in Detroit for twenty-six years. She told Bishop about murders she had solved. Miss Breen had been written about in *True Detective Stories*. She had always wanted to take a trip up the west coast of South America and invited Bishop to inspect the jails with her along the way.

After seventeen days at sea, with Brazil still out of sight, Bishop could smell the coffee beans from Santos, the seaport for São Paulo. Here was the promise of something exotic. But when the coast came into view, Bishop saw only shabby warehouses, weary palms, and freighters clogging the harbor. Brazil looked worn and ordinary. Bishop traveled with Breen to São Paulo for two rainy days of sightseeing, then she took a train to Rio, where two friends, Mary Morse and Pearl Kazin, met her at the train station. Bishop had known Kazin, the sister of the writer Alfred Kazin, in New York City. Morse, who lived in Rio, had visited New York in the forties with her companion, Lota de Macedo Soares, when Bishop had become acquainted with both of them.

Brazil did not impress Bishop at first. Rio seemed more congested than Miami and Mexico City, and she found the relaxed vagueness of the Brazilians enervating. As of early December she was looking forward to continuing her trip on the freighter in January. Then, on Christmas, as a result of an allergic reaction to eating a cashew, Bishop became incapacitated. Her hands and head swelled from edema, closing her eyelids so that she could not see for three weeks, and she developed eczema. She could neither write nor type. The illness lasted five weeks, with the eczema and asthma lasting two weeks after the swelling went down. Lota and her friends took care of Bishop, and Lota herself gave Bishop the use of her Rio penthouse apartment, on the Avenida Atlantica, where works by Alexander Calder and Loren MacIver, two of Lota's friends from her visits to the States, hung. There was also a lovely, broad view of the bay from the front windows.

Lota's attention grew, even though she was spending most of her time at a house she was building in Petrópolis, fifty miles north of Rio. Bishop remained critical of Brazil in her notes to Lota from Rio: "Elizabeth wrote quite a lot, and sometimes Lota would pick up the letter and say, 'No, no, no' because Elizabeth was saying bad things about Rio."[1] There were telephone calls, then more frequent visits by Lota once Bishop was feeling better, and, slowly and genuinely, Bishop and Lota's affection for each other grew. Bishop delayed her trip and finally put it off for good. Several years later, in conversations with the poets Frank Bidart and James Merrill, Bishop described her decision to stay in Brazil.

FRANK BIDART— Elizabeth had been sick in Brazil and Lota had nursed her. One morning, Elizabeth was in bed and Lota came into her room and asked her to stay with her in Brazil. Elizabeth said yes. She was surprised she had said yes. She liked Lota, but she was not in love with her. Over the next few years she really fell in love with Lota.

JAMES MERRILL— Elizabeth went into the whole story of how she settled in Brazil, how there was a mix-up about her travel plans, then she got sick, and her head swelled up. By the time Elizabeth was well enough to travel again, Lota had invited her to stay. Lota said she could very, very easily add a little studio apartment for Elizabeth to the house she was building in Petrópolis. That was really what began the tears [as Elizabeth was telling me this story]. Elizabeth said, "I've never in my life had anyone make that kind of gesture toward me, and it just meant everything."

In late April 1952 Bishop returned to Key West and New York to settle her affairs and to gather her books and clothing. She went to Bryn Mawr for a brief talk—attended by only three students, one of them Ogden Nash's daughter—and a reading, to conclude her fellowship. In New York, Bishop saw Anny Baumann, who found Bishop happier and healthier than she had been in many years. Joseph Frank wrote to Bishop there, telling her not to hide out in Brazil for good. Bishop returned to Rio in early June, to make her home there with Lota for fifteen years.

✦ ✦ ✦

Who was Lota? Mary Morse, Lota's companion before Bishop, recollects many stories that Lota told her about her own upbringing. Also, Rosalina Leão, one of Lota's closest friends, remembers Lota's personality and a story she told them about her upbringing.

MARY STEARNS MORSE— I met Lota in 1941. I was a dancer on the way back [from a tour], and I left the boat at Santos to have time with my cousin living in Rio. On the boat going back to New York from Rio was [the Brazilian painter, Candido] Portinari, who was going for the first time to paint the murals in the [Hispanic Foundation of the] Library of Congress in Washington. Portinari, his wife, his sister, a man in the diplomatic service, and Lota [were all traveling together]. We got to know each other on the boat, and in New York I took them around a little bit—this was the first time Portinari had been there—and then they went to Washington. They came back to New York, and then returned to Brazil. In 1942, a few months later, I decided, as I had finished my dancing career, to visit [Brazil again]. I liked it so much I stayed.

I stayed first with my American cousin and went around in an American crowd—rich parties and luncheons, terribly boring. I got into Lota's crowd. They didn't have anything to do, [or] they had plenty to do but they didn't care about having jobs. Women in that time didn't have jobs very much. Lota was from a very well-known, enormous family. Her mother died the year I got here, and she didn't get along terribly well with her father, Jose Edward, the editor of a newspaper, who also wrote articles. The whole family was in politics. She had an uncle who was an ambassador; the other was a lawyer. Lota's father wasn't particularly interested in her. He helped her out once in a while. She was brought up in a convent in Belgium, and a convent in Rio or Petrópolis. Lota was a devil when she was in Belgium; she and her sister were very rebellious. They were famous as the two Brazilians who had more shoes than anybody else. She used to tell wonderful stories.

Lota didn't work. She had so many talents, but she couldn't seem to direct them in any way. When she was living in the big [family] house before her mother died, it was very boring. She was [eager] to come to Rio. Lota and a friend decided to live in Rio and open a small business of making clothes— blouses, skirts, and things like that. They got seamstresses, and the business was in Copacabana. But it was more a whirl than anything else. They lost money—they didn't know how to keep accounts or anything like that—but they had a marvelous time. They sent out for sodas and sandwiches the whole time and had all their friends [visit].

[When I first knew her] Lota was living in Petrópolis with her mother in a lovely old house, called Fazenda Samambaia. Her father had bought the estate in 1918, and the main house is now protected by the Historical Society. Her mother died the year I came here, and the house had been sold, but the rest of the land went to Lota and her sister. They did not get along and decided to divide the land. With a lawyer they chose which parts they would want, until it came out more or less equal. Lota was finishing a little house on this big tract of land in Petrópolis left to her [by her mother], and so we would go up on weekends. Together Lota and I came up with the idea that because she didn't have any money and was interested in construction, architecture, all that kind of thing, we would develop this land. Le Corbusier came to Brazil and united a group of architects, artists, and writers in the early forties or late thirties, and Lota was part of all that. She was interested in everything—architecture, the visual arts, literature.

We called friends who were interested in developing [the area] and got an agronomist to make a plan for the land. The lots began selling. Lota said, "Now, we're going to choose my friends who are going to buy it. We'll make a wonderful group here." At that point Lota was interested in getting her friends and all the good architects (Enrique Mindlin, Sergio Bernardes, Carlos Leon) to have at least one house there. Carlos Lacerda [a journalist and politician] was one of the first to buy. Sergio Bernardes designed Carlos's house. Lota and I oversaw the building every day. We were living in the little house that she had built near the entrance to the development.

Lota had heard that you could refuse a plan of a house if you didn't like it, even after the person had bought the land. She wanted to do that at Samambaia, but she couldn't, so there are some houses of very bad taste and others that are very nice. Lota was quite a snob. When I came to Brazil, I used just Mary Morse as my name. Lota said, "You can't have a name like that."

And I said, "Why not? What's the matter with it?"

"It's too short."

I said, "Well, I have a middle name, Stearns."

"Well, use your whole name," Lota said. "You come from Boston, right? You're from the old Puritans?"

I said, "Well, as a matter of fact, I am a descendant, but that doesn't mean anything. And they were all rebellious anyway, so I don't think they were a very good sort."

And she said, "You're a Bostonian, a wonderful aristocrat. Also, you're related to Samuel F. B. Morse."

I said, "Not at all."

Lota said, "I'm going to present you that way."

Lota and I built [the house in Samambaia] together. We built it with one head stone man, who did the cement and stone work, and his two or three helpers. Lota had a Jeep at that time, and she and I took trips. We'd get the men to put the stones in a pile, and then we'd put grass in the bottom of the Jeep. The better stones we'd protect so that the lichen wouldn't be harmed. Some of the walls still have their lichen today. Sergio Bernardes came up every week or every two weeks or so in the beginning to see if it was going well. Lota fought with him like mad. He designed an enormous dining room Lota wanted, and she then said, "Ah, Serge, please reduce this dining room. We don't need it. After all, one sits only for lunch and for dinner." He suddenly said, "God, help me with this woman! Please, help me with this woman!" And that was just one of the things he said.

Lota adopted a boy she found in a garage where she was having her car fixed. [First] she just saw Kylso's head and shoulders. He was behind [a counter]. Then she discovered that this beautiful boy couldn't walk. He'd had polio. His legs were doubled. He would just shuffle along. So Lota said to Kylso's father, "What are you doing for this boy?" He said, "I haven't any money." She said, "But I think that something should be done. He should have operations and so forth. I'm going to adopt him."

Lota managed to put Kylso in the hospital. He had two or three operations, and now he walks with a limp and with a cane. He had no education at all. Lota sent him to boarding school. He'd go by train, and at that time the train went right through Samambaia. So we'd wave to him from her house. Vacations he would stay with Lota. She bought a motor scooter in New York and had it sent. She did everything for him.

Finally Kylso married. He began having children—one, two, three, four, five, six. Lota would invite the wife and the children up for the summer, try to build them up, because they were very poor, fill them up with food, give them a new outfit of clothes, and all kinds of things. She put Kylso in contact with Enrique Mindlin, the architect, because he had quite a talent in designing. He became quite a good designer [and drafter, after he was apprenticed to Sergio Bernardes]. He made quite a lot of money. Lota thought it was better for Kylso to stay at Samambaia [than in Rio], so she arranged for a little house for him [and his family]. When I started [adopting] my children, Lota was crazy about them.

I went back to New York for two years [1945–46] during the war and worked for the voluntary service. Lota came up to stay with me in the apartment for those two years. Lota's father paid for her trip to the States, so she had money to spend. She bought everything she could put her hands on, pictures, linens, blankets, and so on. She knew all the shops. Lota was particularly interested in furniture, modern furniture, modern Danish and Swedish design, and lamps. Lota went to all the museums, knew practically everybody in the Museum of Modern Art, knew people in the theater, concerts, and ballet. She was curious about everything. There wasn't anything she missed.

[Lota and I met Elizabeth] in New York. She used to come and visit at the apartment. We used to go out. We saw a lot of Louise Crane, and we went to the family's place [in Dalton, Massachusetts]. We all began to be great friends. Elizabeth had already separated from Louise. Elizabeth was very much alone. She was feeling insecure. I don't think a big city was a place for her ever. She would make friends and then they would desert her. When Lota and I came back to Brazil in 1947, Elizabeth kept on corresponding. Elizabeth had written that she was going to make a visit [on her way] around South America [and wondered if] she could stay with us. Lota had sold her small house and was waiting for the big house to get ready, so we were staying at a friend's when Elizabeth came to stay with us at Christmas time [in 1951]. I had begun building my house because I had decided to adopt children. [When] Elizabeth went to live with Lota in the new house, I was living down [the hill from Lota's new house] in the house that I was finishing.

ROSALINA LEÃO— When I [first] knew Lota, she had fought with her mother. Her father was divorced and put her up in the Hotel Gloria. Alfredo Lage [an art critic] took me there to meet her. She was very funny, so clever, and everybody always was calling her. [Once Lota told me a funny story about when] she went to school in Brussels. She was a tomboy and had a little gun, which the Sister immediately confiscated. When Lota was nervous [or homesick], the Sister would give her two [shots of the gun]. Then Lota would calm down.

Lota was a disciple of Portinari, and I was also, so we met a lot. She was a very interesting painter, but she wasn't [confident] of herself. [When] she went to the United States, she took some lessons with a German expressionist. However, after New York she never painted again. She was so brilliant, so full of ideas. My brother [Carlos Leon] was a very good architect. He also gave classes in architecture. He said that Lota was a born architect. Lota had a marvelous library and read very much. Lota was very kindhearted.

◆　　◆　　◆

When Lota was in New York in 1941, she was introduced to Elodie Osborn, who worked at the Museum of Modern Art (MOMA). Osborn had taken Alfred Barr's first course in modern art at Wellesley College. After graduating, she volunteered at MOMA, then became the director of the Department of Circulating Exhibitions. Lota talked with Osborn about arranging for an exhibition of some of MOMA's paintings in Brazil.

ELODIE OSBORN— I was working at the Museum of Modern Art when Lota came to the States with Portinari, the painter, in 1941. She had decided that she was going to learn something about modern art. Monroe Wheeler was in charge of exhibitions at that point, and he had talked to Portinari, who had introduced him to Lota. Lota said that she was just amazed at what people were doing in the United States and she would give anything to take exhibitions back to Brazil. Monroe told her that I was in charge of exhibitions that go out of the museum.

When Lota came into the office, I thought the sensible thing to do was to take her to lunch and explain what was involved in getting exhibitions out of the country. So we went to a little restaurant in the Rockefeller apartments, which is half a block away from the museum. Lota didn't know English at all, but she could speak French fairly fluently. So we mostly conversed back and forth in bad French on both our parts. When we came to dessert, I asked her if she would like coffee, and she said yes she would, and so of course they brought in a great big cup of coffee. Lota looked at me and she said, "How you drink those pool of coffee?" She explained that they got much more coffee in a thimble in Brazil than came in those "pool of coffee."

Lota was just terribly excited about what women could do in America. That's why she was so taken with me. She was just dumbfounded that I had gotten out of the university and stepped into this job. The idea of making it up as you went along was just something that nobody could do in Brazil. [She was my] introduction to someone who just didn't know that anybody could have a job. You could tell that it was something that was just eating her. She couldn't do anything. She was trying to paint with Portinari. She was trying anything she could do, I suppose. To be frustrated in everything you want to do is pretty terrible.

Lota explained a great deal to me about her own life and why she was quite unhappy. She had a very beautiful younger sister, and the younger sister was interested in parties and entertaining, lots of furs and jewels, lovely clothes and everything. Lota had no pretensions of doing anything like that, so she was looked down on as the ugly duckling. Her father, a very powerful person, owned newspapers in Rio, but he had no respect for her, because she was not the kind of woman that he appreciated. Apparently her younger sister was, so she sailed through life, although she wasn't happy either. I don't remember Lota ever speaking about her mother. She mostly spoke about [how] her father was quite mean to her.

Lota just didn't know how to fit in. She couldn't get a job. She said there weren't any jobs in Brazil. That is what made her angry with her father. He could certainly have seen to it that she had an opening somewhere. This never took place. She thought for a while that she might try to live in New York and see if there was something that she could do or, perhaps, start an exhibition place in the middle of Rio that would give her the opportunity to come to New York and pick out things. We talked a lot about this.

That first time Lota was in New York just a short [while]. When Lota came back, she began seeing a psychiatrist here [and] really understood a lot more about herself after that. We talked about it quite a bit. She understood why she felt she hadn't fit in anywhere. Again, it was her father, who made her feel so totally ugly. In fact, when I tried to take a picture of her, she didn't want her picture taken. Lota was tiny, very boyish. She had a very strong face, wonderful dark eyes, kind of a gruff voice. She was a very handsome woman, an extremely intelligent woman. I suppose that she had no sense that that would carry with people at all. Lota stayed here as long as she could to go to the psychiatrist. Then her father cut off all the money. She had to go home.

You had that feeling Lota was always telling you what to do. She ordered you to do [things]. Lota was a little insistent and tried to move into my life. [She would] insist that I have dinner with her, or do this or do that. I was so involved in the work at the museum I didn't see a great deal of her and let her know that that was out of the question. The poem ["Manuelzinho"] reminded me of how upset Lota would get because people wouldn't or couldn't do what she wanted them to. It would just infuriate her. When I had to go get my passport renewed, Lota came with me. I went to the end of the line. I can remember she said, "What are you doing standing at the end of the line? Go right up there and tell them you want it." I said, "Lota, you can't do that." "What do you mean you can't do that? Look who you are." Well, who was I? In many ways the upbringing of a person like that was so different.

[When] Lota and Morsey [Mary Morse] came to lunch, Lota brought all the pictures of her house in Petrópolis. Lota knew exactly what she wanted— exactly what kind of walls she wanted, how she wanted the stone work to be, and so on. It was an absolutely beautiful house. And she found then, when she was doing that, that she had this ability to deal with spatial things. Her conception of the space was really quite extraordinary. I introduced her to Sandy [Alexander] Calder. She was just crazy about Sandy. He liked Lota very much. Lota said, "You just have to make an exhibition in Brazil." The Calders went to Rio twice.

✦　✦　✦

During her visits to the United States in the forties, Lota met the pianists Arthur Gold and Robert Fizdale, who were in the early years of their career. They frequently saw Lota and Bishop, and on occasion went with them to see Marianne Moore. Bishop advised them on the etiquette of visiting Moore: never mention that you are going to take a cab and always take a subway token from the bowl at the door. In the course of their time with Bishop and Lota, Gold and Fizdale came to see how these apparently contrasting women—one reticent and composed, and the other ebullient, argumentative, even domineering—were, actually, aptly suited for each other.

ROBERT FIZDALE— We met Lota de Macedo Soares in 1944. Arthur then had a studio on Sixtieth Street, just above [the harpsichordist] Sylvia Marlowe's, [where one day] we went for a drink. Louise Crane, an old friend of Sylvia's, was there. We hardly knew Louise, but she [asked us] to come to her place in Massachusetts for the weekend. When we got there, Lota and Mary Morse were there, and it was just love at first sight. Lota was one of the most charming, original, remarkable girls I've ever known. That year we saw them practically every night. It was absolutely delightful.

ARTHUR GOLD— Lota had come [to the United States] because she wanted very much to build a museum of modern art in Rio like the one here. Lota said that she had to make this museum because Brazil was a wonderful place but a very, very "backyard" country. She spoke marvelous broken, very fluent English, but it was always delicious. Lota knew all the people at the museum here and introduced us to all of them. Arthur and I gave our first official concert in 1945. Lota, Morsey, and Edgar Kaufman [director of the design department at MOMA] took us in a taxi to the hall. She was really a dear friend.

FIZDALE— Arthur and I then lived in a studio in Carnegie Hall, which was a bizarre thing to do, a great big beautiful, two-story room with a balcony. We gave a party for Lota. She had a book of somebody's poems that had just come out, and at that party she had asked everybody to autograph it. Her first Christmas—before Elizabeth was on the scene—Lota wanted to give a Christmas party. Four or five of her very good Brazilian friends were spending Christmas and they were going to be lonely. [Before the party someone crept up] behind us and measured our waists and our length because [one of Lota's rich friends] was planning to give us a shirt. This same friend sent us a three-story Christmas tree, and when she came to the party, she brought her private band of twelve samba musicians. It was the most fun I've ever had.

GOLD— We had a total Brazilian year like that, every night. It was that atmosphere, the whole exuberance of that Brazilian life, among other things, that enchanted Elizabeth.

We met Elizabeth through Lota. There was something physically graceful and very elegant about Elizabeth. She had what I call genius hair (vibrant, very alive hair); a delightful smile, when she was familiar with you; and a very warm, rather sad, half-shy and half-loving air. She was very, very soigné, always going to the hairdresser, always looking terribly neat, extremely put together, and her clothes were very, very thought out. Elizabeth loved clothes. They weren't distinguished clothes but always suggested a tiny bit of English elegance—not American jazzy elegance.

[Although] she did have a marvelously mobile face, Elizabeth assumed a passive air a good deal of the time. That was sheer shyness and fright. Elizabeth assumed an unassuming air, because the last thing in the world she was ever going to commit was a vulgarity. It wasn't her style. Every once in a while she'd have a poem in The New Yorker, and I'd write an enthusiastic letter or I'd say that I thought it was a marvelous poem, and she would just turn [my] compliment and say [she was] very glad I liked it, and was very polite and sweet. It was almost as though it was too personal to discuss.

One has to understand Lota to understand Elizabeth because Lota was the most volatile, outgoing, almost exhibitionist Latin type. She was very small, not particularly good looking, but immensely vivacious, and in a sense, everything Elizabeth wasn't. She was Elizabeth's south, the Latin side of her character. Elizabeth delighted in all the exuberance that Lota had, all the enthusiasms in anything from a gadget from the five-and-ten to the great modern house that she built. Lota had all the poetic insights into the details of life that Elizabeth had, but in the Macedo sense, not the Marianne Moore sense.

FIZDALE— We did have several meetings with Elizabeth and Marianne Moore. Marianne Moore was a real character and absolutely enchanting, and there was something marvelously touching about Elizabeth's devotion. To see those two ladies together was quite marvelous because each was so exquisitely considerate of the other and so sensitively attuned to every word the other said. They had such admiration for each other, all perfectly justified and perfectly beautiful.

GOLD— [Once we] had dinner together, and we served a meat loaf. Marianne Moore said it was celestial. We had had a long talk about meat loaf, ground meat versus stewed meat, and Elizabeth said she found steak too lurid. Marianne Moore said [she thought] we should all just live on [our] meat loaf. It was the kind of discussion those girls really loved because it was about nothing. It was two butterflies deliciously hovering over marvelous flowers. Two iron butterflies, because they both were so marvelously aware of the sentences the other was saying and the sentences got more and more refined, more and more beautiful, the wit got sharper and sharper, and a little competition, which was very nice, always was just beneath the surface. It was nice competition because Elizabeth worshiped Marianne. There was never any intellectual talk. Elizabeth and Marianne would have long talks about her poetry in private, but it wasn't considered a thing to think about in public.[2]

FIZDALE— Lota was full of Marianne and Elizabeth, as if she was in the presence of great movie stars. We did a concert at the Museum of Modern Art, and Marianne Moore came, invited by Lota and Elizabeth. Lota sat on the sidelines beaming with the display of all of these poetesses.

GOLD— It was very meaningful for Lota to know Marianne Moore, to know Monroe Wheeler, to know Elizabeth, and to be in artistic circles in America. Lota and Elizabeth were really dependent on each other—Elizabeth for creature comforts, among other things, for good Latin common sense, and Lota because she worshiped American culture.

FIZDALE— Elizabeth, who was fascinated by Brazil and by the Portuguese Brazilian culture, had fallen on the person who was the best representative of it in every way. Lota couldn't have been more Brazilian.

GOLD— And then, of course, and this was one of her strengths, Elizabeth was very provincial. Elizabeth never got over Nova Scotia.

FIZDALE— Elizabeth adored the provinciality of Brazil, a very provincial country, and sort of cherished her [own] provinciality. Elizabeth loved Lota's representing that certain kind of provinciality. Elizabeth chose to live in a small town [in Brazil, Ouro Prêto] and she loved all the details of small town life.

GOLD— But Elizabeth was provincial in a sense that Lota wasn't, because Lota had been brought up in Europe. Lota's French was as good as her Portuguese. Elizabeth always struggled with Portuguese and really had a dreadful American accent in every language. She was always the slightly Henry Jamesian character in a cosmopolitan atmosphere, because the atmosphere of very rich Brazilians is very cosmopolitan. Lota was a society girl, and Elizabeth liked that.

✦ ✦ ✦

Bishop was dreamily contented during her first months in Brazil. The Petrópolis house was so high in the mountains that clouds would drift in and out of the windows. The construction was only half completed, so Bishop and Lota carried oil lamps around at night, stepping over building materials, and huddled in some of the smaller, finished rooms when the wind blowing off the mountains was too sharp. Bishop found varieties of orchids, huge snails and butterflies, and humming birds three-quarters of an inch long whose eggs were the size of pieces of rice. There were also flowers that Bishop had known in Key West, and apple and pear trees she recognized from New England and Nova Scotia. For her birthday in February a man down the mountain gave her a toucan, Sammy (Uncle Sam), who ate from six to ten bananas a day and made a high-pitched gargling sound when Bishop petted his head.

Lota was true to her word, and within a year of Bishop's arrival in Brazil, her studio was completed. Lota had built her house on one of the black granite mountains of Petrópolis, near the base of a cliff and its small waterfall. She had the builders place Bishop's studio behind the house, slightly farther up the mountain, near the waterfall. The studio was a large room, with a fireplace made from gray-blue stone flecked with mica, white-washed walls, and a brick floor. It had a bathroom and a kitchenette. A window overlooked a small artificial pond fed by the waterfall. Here Bishop gathered her books and papers for the first time since she had lived in Key West.

"Elizabeth was very proud of her little studio at Samambaia. She brought all her books as a way of saying, 'I'm staying here.' "[3]

A painting by Kit Barker and a photograph of Marianne Moore were the first things Bishop hung on the walls. In April of her first year in Brazil, Bishop read Marianne Moore's poetry to Lota at night. Beginning and ending the day by reading became a regular feature of their life together. Lota also planned to build a large combined living room and library off the gallery for her own hundreds of books on philosophy, psychology, gardening, and architecture.

As Bishop read and wrote in her studio, Lota worked on the house. Occasionally the work on the house was so interesting that Bishop found it difficult to make her way to the studio. In fact, the house became an architectural showplace, and the number of visitors annoyed Lota after a while. At first, however, she was flattered. In 1954 at the Second Bienal in São Paulo, Sergio Bernardes was awarded a prize for the design of Lota's house, and the house was written about in magazines of contemporary design, where it was presented as a work of art made for a woman of high culture who also loved the natural world.

The focal point of this long, flat house was a glassed-in gallery—the glass was not installed until 1959—where Lota and Bishop hung paintings and drawings, among them Bishop's primitives and MacIvers, a Schwitters collage (which Bishop bought Lota for her birthday in 1953), a Joseph Glasco drawing, and two Kokoshka lithographs. Standing in the gallery, one could look out the back of the house to the waterfall behind, or out the front to a broad, deep valley. Only an aloof Aldous Huxley, who visited in 1958, turned away from this view without an exclamation—of course, angering Lota. The wing with Lota's and Bishop's rooms (completed a year after they moved in) was cantilevered on a boulder at one end of the gallery, and rooms for guests and servants were at the other end. There were stone walls and a stone foundation. Thin lattice girders supported a corrugated aluminum roof, giving the house a spare, geometrical look, quite in contrast to the craggy terrain.

The servants were a large part of Bishop and Lota's life at Samambaia, at times occupying them as much as the house itself. In September 1952, during Bishop's first year in Brazil, Lota organized a wedding celebration for their cook, Lulu, and the gardener, Paulo. Lota, Bishop, and Lulu's former employers dined in the dining room, and the workers ate in the kitchen. Then Lota and Bishop left for a few days, after the atmosphere became intensely romantic (Lulu and Paulo kept locking themselves in the pantry) and cooking went awry—once Lulu served the steak with cinnamon instead of pepper. Their first child was born in February 1955, and they named her Mary Elizabeth, after Lota (Maria Carlota) and Bishop. "Lota had never seen a newborn black baby, and she and Elizabeth were sitting in the living room when the gardener came in with a newborn baby practically fresh from the womb, to have her, the patrone, bless it. Lota said it wasn't beautiful. It was ugly like an orchid."[4] Since Bishop was not Roman Catholic, she could not be a godparent with Lota, but she began a parody of Yeats's "A Prayer for My Daughter" (uncompleted), which began, "My negro namesake in my crib."[5]

The Petrópolis servants amused Bishop. The first cook, before Lulu, had discovered she was an artist while living at Samambaia. Bishop herself felt she was a talented primitivist. However, she spent so much time painting designs on rocks near the house that Lota lost patience and let her go. Paulo had limited success with plants: he killed many, produced odd vegetables—huge radishes and beets, two-legged carrots—and interplanted varieties of corn. And then there was Manuelzinho, the subject of Bishop's poem of the same name, who was more interested in aesthetic variety (cabbages edged with carnations) than productivity. He also painted his straw hats. Lota was exasperated and scornful when Manuelzinho misspent money she had given him for his father's funeral or wasted seeds and vegetable plants.

According to Rosalina Leão, "Lota had a very nice relation with her servants. She was very kindhearted. After all, she adopted the boy in the garage." Rosalina's sister, Magu, remembers that once when she was with Lota in a flower shop, Lota charmed the merchant with her concern for his health. Bishop herself was startled once when in spontaneous disregard of Brazilian social convention, Lota stopped in the middle of the street to hug a truck driver with whom she had had her first communion. Yet some of Bishop's friends, Robert Lowell among them, felt that Bishop was influenced by Lota's typically upper-class attitudes, as Frank Bidart recollects. Joanna dos Santos da Costa, Bishop and Lota's maid in Rio, recollects Lota's genuine kindness toward her.

FRANK BIDART— Lowell once said to me that Elizabeth changed tremendously with Lota, at least in political terms, and that after about five years, Elizabeth became, from the point of view of someone from the States, conservative. Lota was Brazilian aristocracy; it was an oligarchy. Elizabeth clearly had accepted that. The poems she wrote in Brazil, and her poems earlier, seem to me often radical in perception and feeling; but, Lowell said, Elizabeth would defend their friend the governor, that sort of thing. She began to sound like Lota. Lowell didn't find this particularly attractive: it wasn't the bohemian Elizabeth Bishop that he had known in the forties in New York. The only poem, I think, that reflects this is "Manuelzinho," with its whiff of noblesse oblige. The speaker of the poem isn't Elizabeth, but Lota; perhaps the title character is perceived too comfortably as helpless and funny. (This is very different from, for example, "The Riverman.") Her last poem about Brazil (and the last poem she finished) is one with enormous, unameliorated social consciousness, "Pink Dog," which is lethal about a society that informally solves the problem of its beggars, its outcasts and crippled, by throwing them into the river.

MARY STEARNS MORSE— Manuelzinho was a wonderful character [who] had a little hut right near my house, on the way up to Lota's house. He had lived there before the [land was developed by Lota]. There were a lot of poor people in little houses around who would take animals and vegetables to the fair to sell. Manuelzinho was one of Lota's favorites. He was very amusing, the way he spoke. He would come and tell Lota and Elizabeth stories and that kind of thing. Lota liked him as a person, so she let him stay on a piece of land right near her house. He didn't work for Lota. He worked for himself, and he was just on a piece of her land, hoping he wouldn't be put off.

JOANNA DOS SANTOS DA COSTA— Manuelzinho Alves worked outside and inside the house [in Petrópolis]. He cleaned the land around near the house. There's a natural waterfall and a pool; he would clean around that. He would clean down the road—it's long—going up to Lota's house. Lota always liked to see the road well trimmed. He would also work inside the house, cleaning the living room, taking the rugs out, doing the heavy cleaning. I remember his unusual gardens. He mixed up the strawberries with the other fruits, and I was quite horrified with that. I would say, "Oh, Manuelzinho, what are you doing mixing up all these things?" Lota would fight with him about that, but her arguing did no good. Manuelzinho was very calm and he wanted to do things his way. He liked staying at home with his children better than work.

◆　◆　◆

Lota, her new home, the landscape, and all of these people gave Bishop what Lota called a "good shakeup."[6] Within a year and a half of having arrived in Brazil, she and Lota moved into the recently finished wing of the house containing their bedrooms, and Bishop said she was truly happy for the first time in her life. Their intimacy was firmly established. "The Shampoo," a love poem in which Bishop describes herself washing Lota's hair in the pool near her study and which was completed about this time, confirms their affection. Ashley Brown, who met Bishop and Lota in Brazil a few years later, remembers witnessing the scene described in this poem.

ASHLEY BROWN— Elizabeth and Lota got along very well together, had this great ease with one another. I remember well the way Elizabeth used to wash Lota's hair. I saw them as I was coming around the terrace in Petrópolis on a sunny day. There was something about the water [being] very hard in one place and soft in the other, so the [process entailed] some sort of a plastic [container] of water [in addition to the basin that Bishop described in the poem]. Elizabeth used to make quite a thing of it. Lota loved it. It was a ritual Elizabeth made [into] a poem.

♦ ♦ ♦

Bishop's improved spirits had little effect on her asthma, which continued to bother her throughout her first months in Brazil. In August 1952, at Lota's insistence, she began taking cortisone, which brought her limited relief. It also produced an energized state between attacks, which allowed Bishop to work for long periods of time. She wrote industriously that fall, claiming to friends that by October she had completed three short stories and was working on another two.[7] Country life in Petrópolis prompted vivid recollections of Great Village, and in two cortisone-induced sleepless nights she finished "In the Village" (originally titled "Clothes. Food. Animals"). The New Yorker purchased the story for twelve hundred dollars, even though the editors felt it was an experimental piece for them because of its suggested rather than explicit story line. They wrote to Bishop about what appeared to them non sequiturs in her story, and she quipped that she did not "believe they could follow their noses."[8] Bishop wrote "Gwendolyn" in one sitting, the first time she had ever written a story on a typewriter. In the midst of this productivity, in January 1953, she was awarded the Poetry Society of America's Shelley Memorial Award of eight hundred dollars. In the spring of 1953 Brazil's most prominent poet, Manuel Bandeira, a friend of Lota's, translated a few of Bishop's poems for a literary supplement in Rio.

In the fall of 1953, with her fee for "In the Village," Bishop bought herself a black 1952 MG with a red-leather interior. One can readily imagine Lota encouraging Bishop to drive herself around and to save Lota the trips to town and the market, which she disliked. Although Bishop learned to drive, she never did get a driver's license. Lota also introduced Bishop to her artistic friends. She took Bishop to visit the studio of the painter Candido Portinari, where they saw his sketches of murals for the United Nations. Lota had studied with the controversial Portinari, whose vivid paintings of coffee workers, villagers, the homeless, and blacks were considered by some to be insulting to Brazil. Lota had also assisted Portinari with the frescoes for the modern Ministry of Education in 1938. It was Lota's intention to provide Bishop with something of an artistic coterie in Brazil. Bishop, however, felt that the literary friends to whom Lota introduced her in her first year in Brazil were essentially uninterested in her, or were critical of the United States, or were jealous of her. Agnes Mongan, curator of drawings at the Fogg Art Museum, at Harvard, met a number of these friends during her visit to Rio in 1954. Stella Pereira, a close friend of Lota's from Rio, and Mary Morse recollect why Lota's intention to provide a group of artistic friends for Bishop never succeeded.

AGNES MONGAN— In the fall of 1954 I went to Brazil at the invitation of the Brazilian government to give a series of lectures throughout the country on the conservation of valuable paper. I was flown to the various cities outside of Rio, but most of my six weeks in Brazil were passed in Rio. I discovered that the lectures had been suggested by a young Brazilian painter who had passed a year at the Fogg, mostly in conservation. I was introduced to many painters, architects, and print-makers. I met Lota and Elizabeth at one of the receptions following the lecture. They immediately invited me to their Rio apartment and then more than once to their charming house in the country.

Elizabeth and Lota were welcoming without pretensions. Genuine people. Elizabeth's relationship with the gifted Brazilians was distinctly affable. She was eager to have me understand certain aspects of Brazilian life. She introduced me to quite a lot of people, mostly Brazilians aware of their Portuguese inheritance, and, as a result, I went to many other houses I would never have seen otherwise. Elizabeth and Lota put me in touch with lots of Brazilian poets and writers. Elizabeth had a number of acquaintances and friends, mostly through Lota. They were interested in literature and the arts. It was a group of the intelligentsia, not just a social group—architects, painters, poets. I don't remember meeting a banker or a businessman.

Lota was charming, eager to help any friends of Elizabeth's. She was interested in me because I had been a friend of Phillip Johnson, Alfred Barr, Russell Hitchcock, and John McAndrew, all associated with the Museum of Modern Art in New York City. I knew Gropius. I had met Le Corbusier, whom Lota had known in Rio, when he came to Harvard. Elizabeth, Lota, and I had quite a bit of discussion about Le Corbusier because a building by him was to go up next door to the Fogg Museum at Harvard. At that point there was no Le Corbusier building in the United States. We talked about why Corbusier didn't have more commissions in this country [the United States] and how it happened that Harvard had invited him to do a building, that kind of talk. Lota knew an awful lot about the history of architecture.

She and Elizabeth were deeply interested in contemporary Brazilian art and literature. We had long discussions about architecture of particular interest to them because a new wing to the museum in Rio was about to be built or had just been built. Lota didn't approve of what they were doing—she felt that it was a poor building in a beautiful place and that the people who were running it didn't know anything about modern art. Elizabeth and Lota were eager to have me see buildings they approved of.

STELLA PEREIRA— I met Elizabeth through Mary Morse and Lota. I used to walk along the beach to Lota's apartment because I lived [nearby]. I was a great admirer of Lota because she was very gifted. She did not have a diploma, and she was an artist. She did everything she had in mind out of her own disposition and force. A very strong personality, very violent in her moods, but very straightforward, very to the point. She knew exactly what was right. Her directions never wavered.

MARY STEARNS MORSE— Lota admired Elizabeth tremendously. She admired anybody who had done work as Elizabeth had. It was as if she said, "Well, I can't do it, but she can."

PEREIRA— Elizabeth was her alter ego, someone [who did what] she couldn't do. Lota was very warm-hearted, but she hid it. That's why she was so vociferous. And I think she tried to give to Elizabeth as much affection as she was able to. I think that Elizabeth needed it badly. Elizabeth and Lota needed one another for inner support.

MORSE— It was Lota who brought Elizabeth out. Lota said, "This is Elizabeth Bishop, the famous poet." It was Lota who pushed her forth.

PEREIRA— Lota did her best. Elizabeth's temperament didn't help. Because she was Elizabeth Bishop, you didn't dare quite approach.

MORSE— That's very Brazilian. When Robert Lowell was here, there was a party. Elizabeth was quite frustrated because we both were somewhat shy. We didn't speak good English. As a result, people who were expected there didn't come.

PEREIRA— Elizabeth was frustrated, but not surprised, because she expected it, due to the circumstances and due to the reaction of people.

MORSE— I didn't have very much in common with Elizabeth. I had nothing to do with literature, or anything like that. We had everyday conversation. Elizabeth was a wonderful cook. That's why Lota called her "Cookie." Lota was worried about [there being artists around for Elizabeth]. There wasn't very much anyone could do because Elizabeth was shy. The others here are shy. It was hard to get them together. The only one I know of who got together with them was Manuel Bandeira, but I don't know how much. They met once or twice and that was about it. It is very hard.

PEREIRA— And besides they lived in Samambaia most of the time.

✦   ✦   ✦

Bishop's burst of prose writing during her first year in Brazil was short-lived. By the spring of 1954 she claimed that she had not finished a decent poem in two years. When she was elected to the National Institute of Arts and Letters in March 1954, she suspected the Institute had selected her because it wanted a woman. She had been in correspondence with Houghton Mifflin since the spring of 1953 about the final poems for her second volume of poetry, a book she had told them would be ready two years after the publication of North & South in 1946. In the view of the editors at Houghton Mifflin, she had too few poems for a new book. With this mounting frustration over her productivity and the attendant guilt because she was not living up to Lota's expectations, Bishop began drinking heavily. In June 1954, at Lota's insistence, she entered the Strangers Hospital in Rio and started Antabuse treatments. Bishop was willing to admit to friends that she had had a day of drunkenness every month or six weeks prior to entering the hospital, but certainly the episodes were more frequent and longer. Subsequently, when Antabuse supplies were low in Rio, Lota used her influence to locate pilots of airliners who could fly the drug in from other countries.

Bishop's periodic depression and drunkenness did not take Lota by surprise. She had known Bishop during her very difficult period in the forties in New York, and, according to Rosalina Leão, Lota had been warned in Rio about entering into a relationship with Bishop, given her instability. Rosalina Leão recalls how difficulties in Bishop and Lota's relationship developed over Lota's friends and Lota's expectations of Bishop as a writer. Mary Morse recollects the difficulty Lota had with Bishop's drinking.

ROSALINA LEÃO— Lota had a wonderful analyst [who] knew Elizabeth [through a] friend. She advised Lota not to [start the relationship with Elizabeth]. The analyst knew it would be a very difficult relationship and told

Lota that Elizabeth was a psychotic who had a [capacity] for persecuting. But Lota went ahead.

Sometimes I went [to Samambaia]. In the morning I used to wake up early. The order was to be in bed, to have your breakfast in bed, stay as long as possible, and come out for lunch. And so I had piles of books around me arranged by Elizabeth. She would tell me what to read and encourage me. I liked her very much. Elizabeth was very temperamental. Elizabeth was so difficult because she could be so charming, so very, very charming, but could change, not from one day to another, but in ten minutes.

Elizabeth didn't get on friendly terms [with many people]. It was Lota's life and Lota's friends. I think that's what [made Elizabeth at times] feel alone, because she lived very much on her own. She only liked to talk to poets like her and people of the same [interests]. Lota had a lot of friends, and Elizabeth didn't have a center. And then Elizabeth had to put up with endless [visits from Lota's friends]. Lota had lots of friends that were very impulsive—screaming and talking and fighting. And Elizabeth would get extremely upset.

Lota and Elizabeth had a little room where a fire burned, where Lota and I would talk at night. [One time] Elizabeth went to sleep, and Lota and I began talking. And then Elizabeth was furious. She said, "You repeat yourself. I come and I listen at the door, and you're telling over, and over, and over the same stupid things."

Elizabeth could be very furious with Lota because Lota would say, "Go up and write. Go up and write. You are very lazy." Elizabeth told me Lota [thought that writing] was like [going to] school. [For someone like Elizabeth] writing came [very slowly], and Elizabeth was very much afraid that suddenly it wouldn't come.

Sometimes Elizabeth would leave the house and go to the hotel because Lota had a fight with her. Once Lota telephoned me because she was in the house in Samambaia and [Elizabeth was in] the apartment in Leme. Lota said, "Please go there because I've been telephoning and there is no answer. See if Elizabeth needs anything." Elizabeth had been drinking. Lota was terrified because Elizabeth would [fall and harm herself]. I went there. I never saw anyone cry like that. Elizabeth was in bed and didn't want to eat, for a whole week. I couldn't do anything about it. She said she was miserable. Elizabeth said she was an alcoholic and wanted to free herself.

[Elizabeth would become] a monster [when she drank]. [Yet] Elizabeth was wonderful; her knowledge was fabulous. Lota was very, very proud of her. Lota's relationship with Elizabeth was very difficult but very rich.

MARY STEARNS MORSE— Sometimes something would be planned and Elizabeth would be completely [indisposed]. You couldn't count on her. I remember in Samambaia, when she was living with Lota in that house, if she started [drinking] then she couldn't stop, and she would drink anything. Lota would hide the bottles, and she would find them. Or if there weren't any more bottles, she would go to straight alcohol. She tried to hide them under the bed, behind the curtains. For a while Antabuse worked. I don't ever remember a period of six weeks [when she didn't drink]. It was something to get Elizabeth to go to a doctor, to have the tests, to know the quantity of pills that she should take. She finally went, but to get her to take [the pills was difficult].

✦   ✦   ✦

During Bishop's first five years in Brazil, poems and stories appeared at intervals of a few months, with one eighteen-month gap between the publication of "In the Village" in December 1953 and "The Shampoo" in July 1955. Much of Bishop's time during these years was spent on a lengthy translation project. In 1952 she began translating the Brazilian classic *The Diary of "Helena Morley,"* which Lota's friends had recommended to her when she first arrived in Brazil. This diary (first published in 1942) of an adolescent girl in the town of Diamantina from 1893 to 1895 reminded Bishop of life in Great Village. It took her four years to complete the translation, and in April 1956 Bishop visited Diamantina, to gather background information for her introduction and to confirm that the tone of the translation matched that of the place. Bishop found that the mining town high in the mountains had changed little from the time of the *Diary*—the mountainous, rocky landscape was still dotted with waterfalls, there was a crucifix on each hill, and prospectors panned all the streams. Schoolchildren pressed their noses against the windows of the hotel to watch the visitor, the writer, eat breakfast. Mining operations had been modernized, and a British strip miner allowed Bishop to operate one of the huge water hoses and wash away the side of a hill.

Manuel Bandeira provided Bishop with an introduction to the real "Helena Morley," Senhora Augusto Maria Caldeira Brant, who was a youthful, amiable seventy-six year old. Bishop visited Mrs. Brant twice. One visit, Mrs. Brant cooked for Bishop some of the dishes described in her diary. Bishop discovered that Mrs. Brant still possessed attitudes of the simple country girl of her book. "Elizabeth was terribly sweet about those two people, the old banker and his wife. I remember Elizabeth telling the story about their having dinner with them: of when Mrs. Brant picked up the wrong fork and Mr. Brant gently put his hand over hers, laid down the wrong fork, and put her hand on the right fork. Mrs. Brant had been a country girl. That little bit of domesticity moved Elizabeth."[9] Mr. Brant was president of the Bank of Brazil and had been a lawyer, journalist, and member of Congress. He had been exiled in France and England during the tyrannical Vargas regime, where he had learned to read English. He proofread Bishop's translation, suggesting alternative phrasings and correcting her word selection, to Bishop's amusement.

As amiable as these meetings with the Brants were, Bishop's relationship with them soured once the translation was published in 1957. She felt that the Brants became interested solely in making money from the project. No one really profited from the book; Bishop herself received just over two hundred dollars in royalties for the first year of publication. She was angered because the wealthy Brants needed the money least of all. Lota went with Bishop to visit the Brants, and for the second visit Bishop also took Rosalina Leão, to help with the conversation in Portuguese.

ROSALINA LEÃO— Elizabeth, Lota, and I went to see Mrs. Brant. She was fascinating—so very tall and she had such a strong voice. When we arrived, she was darning socks. She was very nice and said, "You are going to stay for dinner."

Elizabeth liked the book very much. She would study so hard to get exactly the [correct] word. Elizabeth took the book to Dr. Brant, and he made corrections of her English. It was so funny. Elizabeth laughed. [Then] the Brants were [bothering Elizabeth about making money from the book]. Mrs. Brant had another book [about the years] after the marriage, but the husband didn't let Elizabeth edit that. It never came out.

◆　◆　◆

Bishop interrupted her translation of the *Diary* in November 1955, to translate *Modern Architecture in Brazil* into English with its author, the architect Henrique Mindlin, a close friend of Lota's. Mindlin had given Fazenda Samambaia two pages in the book, with interior and exterior photographs and floor plans. Bishop felt that she owed Mindlin a favor because he had been willing to claim her as an employee so that she could easily renew her visa. Fearful that a similar book was about to be published, Mindlin plunged Bishop into several weekends of feverish translating, made even more wearisome for her by the technical language of the book. By the end of January 1956, with her head spinning, Bishop had finished some two hundred individual descriptions of Brazil's modern houses, public buildings, and gardens.

By May 1954 Bishop had submitted to Houghton Mifflin enough poems for thirty-two pages of manuscript. Bishop felt that there were enough new poems for a book, but Houghton Mifflin claimed that a book of this size was economically unfeasible. Houghton Mifflin suggested reprinting *North & South* and the new poems in one volume. After some negotiating, *Poems: North & South—A Cold Spring*, was published in July 1955. Loren MacIver designed the dust jacket (a cropped green leaf against a diagonally divided background of blue and white). As pleased as she was with the book, Bishop was tired of Houghton Mifflin. Houghton Mifflin, it seems, was also tired of her. The firm was not interested in publishing "*Helena Morley.*" Bishop admitted to them that it must be difficult to publish a poet who produced so little so slowly. She then instructed her agent, Bernice Baumgarten at Brandt and Brandt, to look for a new publisher on the terms that whoever would publish "*Helena Morley*" would get her next book of poems. By the fall of 1956 Robert Giroux at Farrar, Straus, and Cudahy had accepted the offer.

The publication of *Poems* meant as much to Lota as it did to Bishop. In December 1955 she gave a publication party for Bishop. Lota was proud that one Rio bookstore had copies of the book in its window and that there had been newspaper articles on it. Then, in May 1956 *Poems: North & South—A Cold Spring* was awarded the Pulitzer Prize. An excited reporter from the Rio newspaper *O Globo* telephoned Bishop, shouting the news to her. In her typically self-effacing way, Bishop felt that Randall Jarrell's war poems should have won, and she told him so. However, Bishop was particularly pleased with this award because the Pulitzer was known in Brazil. It confirmed all that Lota had been saying to her friends about Bishop's talent. One local shopkeeper was delighted when he saw Bishop's picture in the paper. He claimed that he brought his customers good luck, for another customer had just won a bicycle. Frank Bidart recollects Bishop telling him how important this prize was for her.

FRANK BIDART—Literary Brazil didn't know who she was. A Brazilian writer had asked Edith Sitwell in London—or perhaps Sitwell was on a trip to Brazil—if Elizabeth Bishop was any good, and Sitwell had said no. Elizabeth said that Sitwell's opinion had done her a lot of harm in Brazil. Then she won the Pulitzer Prize in 1955. Suddenly she became a literary eminence.

✦ ✦ ✦

The Pulitzer was the jewel, although the least lucrative ($500) of three prizes that Bishop won within a year. In March 1956, a month before the Pulitzer, she had been awarded a *Partisan Review* Fellowship ($2,700), and in January 1957 she received the Amy Lowell Travelling Fellowship ($2,000), the only stipulation of this last award being, ironically, that she spend a year living outside the United States. These three awards boosted Bishop's own confidence in herself as a significant writer. Bishop even found that a bad review of *Poems* from the *Partisan Review* (the editors had warned her and denied supporting the review) did not bother her, when, five years earlier, it would have sent her off on a drinking spree.

Bishop's awards made it possible for Lota and her to travel in 1957. Fazenda Samambaia was nearly completed—the new living room-cum-library was done, twenty-seven thousand bricks had been laid for a terrace, and Lota had planted 440 pine trees and a number of flowering trees. The Portinari murals would be unveiled at the United Nations in late summer. So, with the self-confidence from both a Pulitzer and a new publisher for her translation, which would be out within the year, Bishop arrived with Lota in New York in April 1957, for her first extended stay since moving to Brazil five years before.

Bishop and Lota located a small apartment on East Sixty-Seventh Street for their stay in New York in 1957, and they spent the next six months visiting with the friends whom they had not seen in years—Loren MacIver and Lloyd Frankenberg, Margaret Miller, Anny Baumann, James Merrill, Randall Jarrell, Calvin Kentfield, Bob Evett, and Clement Greenberg among them. All noticed that Bishop had changed: "Elizabeth seemed to be happy and healthy. For one thing, she was in pretty clothes. She looked very chic. Her hair was very pretty."[10] Pauline Hanson, who had last seen Bishop during her unhappy stay at Yaddo in 1951, Elodie Osborn, and Joseph and U. T. Summers all noticed the effect Bishop's relationship with Lota had had upon her. Mary McCarthy recollects a literary discussion with Bishop at Hannah Arendt's during this period.

PAULINE HANSON— When Elizabeth arranged for me to come down to New York City from Yaddo in 1957, she had May Swenson for dinner. I met Lota briefly; she was going to a concert given by Arthur Gold and Robert Fizdale. We had a very pleasant evening. Elizabeth cooked a dinner. We sort of sat on the floor, the apartment was so small. Elizabeth had wine for us, and I watched, wondering if she was going to have some. She said. "I see you. I'm watching you watch me. It's not that I stopped drinking; I have absolutely no interest in drinking, I owe it to Lota." She told me it was Lota who helped her take care of the alcohol problem. Elizabeth looked very well, and I sensed that she had a feeling of strength and she knew who she was.

Elizabeth mentioned that Lota apparently came from a very wealthy family and was used to the luxurious, but there was such terrible inflation that it left Lota poor. Lota was building a terribly expensive home. Elizabeth had wonderful pictures of it and showed these pictures to May and me. Lota came in before we broke up. Then, as I was getting ready for bed—Elizabeth had given me her room and was to sleep on the sofa—Lota and she wanted to talk about their evenings. Lota was in bed. Elizabeth went into Lota's room and they talked quietly. I had a feeling that Elizabeth was like a little girl talking to her mother before going to bed.

ELODIE OSBORN— I met Elizabeth in 1957 when she came [to Salisbury, Connecticut] with Lota. [Although Elizabeth's] poetry is so crystal clear and so sophisticated in the organization, she didn't give you that impression when you first met her at all. She was rather soft, and very, very quiet. We all just had a very good time, a lot of laughter. Everybody else did the talking. And yet [I could] see that her thinking was so exact. My husband, Bob, enjoyed Elizabeth very much; they had a great deal in common. He reads a great deal of poetry. We talked about all sorts of things, mostly art and writing. Elizabeth talked about Cal then. That was before we met him.

Lota and Elizabeth seemed to be very fond of each other. They shared so many things together. Lota did tell me—she must have come once without Elizabeth—what a terrible experience Elizabeth's alcoholism had been. Lota had to lock Elizabeth in her room because she drank so much. Lota said, "You won't believe how she behaved. I just decided I was going to cure her by just making it impossible for her to drink." And she did. Lota was very tough with her. Lota said, "I had to do it. She was destroying herself. Otherwise she's never going to do any writing." Lota thought that she was saving Elizabeth for her art. I think Elizabeth must have been grateful.

JOSEPH SUMMERS— [When] we saw Elizabeth [in 1957], she said, "It's just heaven. I don't know what I've done to deserve heaven."

U.T. SUMMERS— We could always tell by Elizabeth's gain and loss of weight [whether or not she was drinking]. When she came to Storrs [Connecticut] and we went to New York to visit her and Lota, Elizabeth was very thin and very beautiful.

JOSEPH— Elizabeth was so proud. She said, "I've lost twenty pounds and I've now got the second-best dressmaker in Rio."

U.T.— Elizabeth talked about how strict her dressmaker was with her. She loved beautifully made things. Elizabeth had the same sense of craftsmanship in clothes that she did in wanting her books to be beautiful. It was one of the reasons she loved the rich with taste. She loved the beautiful objects that they had. Elizabeth and Lota were up in New York as much as anything to buy things to take back to Brazil, both for themselves and all their friends down there who loved American objects.

JOSEPH— Elizabeth brought all these pictures of Samambaia and told stories about Lota, the household, and the adopted son. She made a great point about this boy. Elizabeth said that Lota thought she had done two good things in her life. Lota felt as if she had saved two people, this boy and Elizabeth.

U.T.— [When] Elizabeth came to visit us in Storrs, we had a coffee party in the morning to which we invited all the faculty. I think it was rather painful for Elizabeth.

JOSEPH— I had lots of books lying around and some of them were intellectually pretentious, books that you sort of felt you ought to read and have a hard time getting through. Elizabeth just picked up one after another and she'd look at the cover and say, "Oh, I couldn't read that." There was this sense of the absolute dreck which the modern world was full of, particularly of the intellectually pretentious kind. It's sort of like one [comment she made] to Jarrell about her horror at modern critics, the monsters of cleverness.

U.T.— She brought our girls two of Beatrix Potter's books. She loved those. She'd look through the criticism, then she'd pick up the two books she had brought, read them through again and say, "Now this is really good." I sort of see Beatrix Potter and Elizabeth together. Elizabeth was always interested in our children.

JOSEPH— One of her classic remarks was, "Now that Hazel's learned to talk, you must teach her to edit!"

MARY MCCARTHY— I didn't meet Lota all that often [in 1957], two or three times, maybe. We had lunch, I think, at the Beaux Arts on Sixty-seventh Street, with Elizabeth. I took Elizabeth and Lota to Hannah Arendt's one evening. They liked each other very much. I remember a very charming discussion about truth and poetry that evening. We were discussing how to interpret a line of verse. There were several people in the discussion, and they developed more and more far-fetched and very abstract explanations. Elizabeth finally joined the conversation—she was the last to speak up—and in this quiet, little voice said, "Well, I would think that it was literally true."

Then she put forward her conviction that anything in a poem was true, that it was there because it had happened. The other reasons could be added. I was absolutely struck all in a heap by this. I had never seen poetry in that light. I thought, "Well, of course she's right. Of course she's right." Then she brought up Eliot in this connection, and she [talked about the references to] impotence [in his poetry]. She said, "That's what it's about. It's about impotence." Not symbolic impotence—it's about the thing.

✦ ✦ ✦

Bishop spent part of her first few weeks in New York at the typewriter, correcting copy and writing a new introduction for "Helena Morley." In July she and Robert Giroux discussed the cover and the design of the book, and there was additional discussion about the text in August. Bishop, as always, wanted corrections made throughout production and she bristled when Giroux told her at one point that the changes she wanted would cost six hundred dollars. At first, it seemed to Bishop that her relationship with Farrar, Straus, and Cudahy would be like that with Houghton Mifflin. Giroux, however, proved to be a diplomatic, if firm, editor for her; he knew and appreciated the value of her work. Bishop and Giroux established a strong working relationship and, in time, a friendship.

ROBERT GIROUX— In Brazil, Pearl Kazin had suggested to Elizabeth that she acquire a literary agent to handle the "Helena Morley" Diary. For her earlier books of poetry, Elizabeth had not used an agent. It was my good luck that she and Pearl approached Bernice Baumgarten (Mrs. James Gould Cozzens) of Brandt and Brandt, who had been E. E. Cummings's agent and was a friend. (In 1954 I had suggested to Bernice and published the collected edition of Cummings's Poems 1923–1954 at Harcourt, Brace and Company, where I was editor-in-chief.) Bernice told me that Elizabeth's translation of this young girl's diary of the 1890s had been "a labor of love," and I said I was interested in Bishop's poetry rather than the diary. When Bernice explained that, because Houghton Mifflin had turned the diary down, Elizabeth had decided to give her new poems only to the publisher who took the diary, I asked at once to see it. I regarded Elizabeth as one of our best American poets and was overjoyed to have the chance of acquiring her work.

The diary was a fine and charming book, much better than I had expected. I was certain it would have a slow beginning (which it did) but would not lose money (which it didn't), but of course we would not have done it if we were not also acquiring the poetry. FSG had one of the best poetry lists in

America, with Eliot, Lowell, Berryman, Jarrell, Graves, Neruda, and many others. We had to wait eight years for Elizabeth's new poems, *Questions of Travel* (1965), and it was worth it.

Apparently Elizabeth was convinced that the diary would be popular, and so was Lota. It is still in print after thirty-five years, and a "classic," but it was never the best-seller they had envisioned. I tried in a cautious, diplomatic way to persuade Elizabeth not to get her hopes too high. Our first printing was four thousand copies, and the second was two thousand. After several years the diary was well established and the excellent Ecco Press paperback edition reached a wide audience. Elizabeth's letters showed that after the diary appeared, she became annoyed with "Helena Morley" herself, now an old lady married to a banker, instead of the diary's poor girl in the mining town. She kept pestering Elizabeth about the small royalties, and kept asking why the book wasn't making more money.

Elizabeth made many alterations not only in the galley proofs of the diary but also in the page proofs, which she would not have done in her books of poems. Her contract included the standard allowance for author's alter-ations—10 percent of the cost of composition. (If the setting costs were three thousand dollars, for example, the allowance was three hundred dollars, and any charge above that was the author's responsibility.) Elizabeth's corrections were particularly expensive because she rewrote the page proofs. Though she was angry at being billed for an overage of six hundred dollars, Bernice settled the matter by reminding Elizabeth that she had agreed to this arrange-ment at Bernice's advice. We also had words about the dust jacket. I had asked Harry Ford of Knopf, an admirer of Bishop, who is not only an excellent book designer but also one of the great poetry editors, to design the jacket for the diary. He used yellow, blue, and green colors against a black back-ground to make a most elegant design, but Elizabeth protested against the use of black. It was too late to change, and it was a lesson on the impossibility of understanding differences in matters of taste. Harry and I thought that the bright colors were heightened and made more festive by the black, but I learned that black to Elizabeth was *always* funereal. I made sure that on future books Elizabeth approved all production and design matters in advance.

Our first meeting took place when she signed the contract for both the diary and her next book of poems at the Cosmopolitan Club, where she was a member. I found her to be attractive and rather shy, and I noticed her good manners. She scarcely spoke until finally I mentioned Marianne Moore, whom I knew through Eliot. He had asked me to take her to the opening night of *The Cocktail Party* in New York, while he was in London. On leaving the theater after the performance, we heard the Duke of Windsor say to friends, "They tell me Mr. Eliot wrote this play in verse, but I must say you'd *never* know it!" This made Elizabeth laugh. She then told me how, when she was an undergraduate at Vassar, Marianne Moore had carefully arranged their first meeting outside the doorway of the reference room of the New York Public Library, on the right-hand bench. Thus began my publishing relationship with a great poet, which soon deepened into a friendship that lasted twenty-two years.

During this visit to New York, Bishop also discovered that she had acquired a literary prominence. She was flattered that other poets thought so highly of her, yet was uneasy with their attention. She and Lota twice visited Gold and Fizdale at their house on Long Island in the course of their stay, for a Fourth of July party and a concert in October. Aaron Copland attended the concert, and the pianists ended with Milhaud's *Brasiliera*, in Bishop and Lota's honor. It was during the July visit that Fizdale and Gold glimpsed Bishop's new status in the literary world and the apprehension with which she approached it. John Bernard Myers also recollects meeting Bishop at this time.

ROBERT FIZDALE— Elizabeth and Lota visited us in Southampton [in July 1957], and we had a clambake, with steamed clams and sweet corn. Fairfield Porter then had all the young poets around him, Jimmy Schuyler, John Ashbery, and Frank O'Hara. I asked Elizabeth if she had read their poetry. She said [she had], just a little. They were young; none of them had become famous yet. They were very flattered to meet Elizabeth. I was quite amazed to see the enormous respect that she was held in by all the poets whom we had invited.

ARTHUR GOLD— Frank did a marvelously funny thing. In his Irish way, Frank was almost as exuberant as Lota, but he was frightened at the same time, because Elizabeth could [create a] frigid air around her which affected other people unless they knew her. Frank came on like the original exuberant Irishman and proceeded to kiss her hand and then go right up [her arm], like Groucho Marx, which both delighted and terrified Elizabeth. By this time she had had a little bit to drink and was a little more relaxed. John Ashbery was cool, and Jimmy [Schuyler] was the same personality style as Elizabeth. In fact, they resemble each other in many, many ways.

FIZDALE— Elizabeth really held court. They all absolutely came to pay homage to her. She was very pleased with it, but it made her uneasy. Frank called in the morning after the party and wanted to see Elizabeth again, and she said, "I think we've had enough of Frank O'Hara." She didn't want to cope with this [attention].

GOLD— Elizabeth didn't like great fuss with strangers. Actually, she didn't like great fuss from intimates either—[it] rather enthralled her and threw her at the same time.

FIZDALE— We had a nice relationship with Elizabeth because we hadn't approached her as acolytes. We hadn't met her because we were admirers. We met her because we were madly admirers of Lota. Elizabeth was more relaxed with us because we weren't coming to learn at the feet of the great poet; we were musicians pure and simple at that time. Elizabeth loved music. Elizabeth had a beautiful little green clavichord, the kind you could put on the table, with real gold edges. When she went to Brazil, she lent it to us. We had it for quite a few years. [When] Elizabeth and Lota came to the house in 1945–46, we took the clavichord out to the pool and gave them a little concert under the grape arbor.

[In October 1957] we were playing something of Aaron Copland's at the Guild Hall [near our home]. Aaron came out to stay, and Lota and Elizabeth decided they would come too. We had all arranged to have lunch at a place called the Old Mill in Watermill [New York]. Elizabeth and Lota never got over the fact that when the check came he [divided it]. They did as much as it was possible to do for Copland [when he visited Brazil], and they couldn't believe that it hadn't occurred to him to pay for this rather reasonable lunch. And, of course, they were wildly amused by this.

Elizabeth and Lota loved farce, the ridiculous. They had asked for a fire-place [in the Petrópolis house], which was not traditional down there. It was too hot. The workmen thought that this was crazy, but Lota and Elizabeth insisted. When they had their roof-raising party, with branches on the roof, the way you do here, it was slightly rainy, so Lota [told] Manuelzinho to make a fire. When he did, the house was immediately filled with smoke. When the men had built the chimney for the fireplace, they'd bricked it across the top. Of course, they'd never [built a chimney and didn't want] the rain coming into the house.

GOLD— Lota made Elizabeth's life comfortable [during their visit in 1957]. She was very motherly with Elizabeth. She thought Elizabeth was a genius and behaved like a genius's wife, and it was very, very beautiful to see, because of tremendous concern about Elizabeth's comfort and tremendous concern about her lack of being a prolific writer. We found Lota's worry extremely touching because, in a strange way, Lota had as much genius as Elizabeth did.

[Lota talked about Elizabeth's writing] a great deal. It was a concern [to her that Elizabeth did not write a lot]. She put a lot of stock in the drink. It seems to me that Elizabeth wasn't prolific for various reasons. I know that she would work on a poem for a long time because she was exacting; her poetry is not epic. I think the blockage was really a part of the exquisite nature of her poetry. She was an intimate. To be an intimate is not to be epic.

JOHN BERNARD MYERS— I first met Elizabeth in 1957 when Fizdale and Gold were having a Fourth of July picnic, and they came to pick me up. Elizabeth was in the car. We went to their place. We had lobsters and American flags and so on. We were going along the road and suddenly we passed a hot dog stand, and over the hot dog stand [a sign read], "The Enchanted Cottage." Elizabeth said, "Enchanted, enchanted! One more word I can never use again." She seemed like a very cultivated—not put-on cultivated, but highly intelligent—modest, agreeable, and entertaining human being.

I immediately took to Elizabeth because she had a kind of modesty and because of her very pleasant expression, which I liked very much. She's one of the only poets I can bear to listen to. [At a later date] I heard her read at the YMHA. Fearing that I would not hear well, I got way up in the first row, and I could hear every word she said. She didn't have either a Canadian accent or a New York accent; it was just a very pure way of speaking. Also, it's such a pleasure when somebody speaks and they know perfectly well the weight and value of every syllable.

Another time we were talking about life in Brazil, and she proceeded to make me laugh so loud that I thought I would die. Elizabeth could be deadpan at times. How funny she was about what it's like living daily, on the top of the mountain, with a bunch of [servants] running in and out of the house. Elizabeth told the incident about getting the Frigidaire [in 1958]. She and Lota got this gorgeous big Frigidaire, and she brought the cook [in] and explained the whole thing, and within a couple of days, Elizabeth checked the icebox, and there was practically nothing in it. So she said, "How come you're not [using] the fridge?" And the woman said, "You put the butter in, it's so hard, you can't cut it. You put the eggs in, they're so cold you can't make them make an omelet. You put the milk in, it gets a terribly funny taste. You put the onions in, the onions change." I said, "Well, how did the Frigidaire end up?" They kept the charcoal in there.

I met Lota a couple times. She was a wonderful person, a very finished person, a very elegant woman. She wasn't very good-looking, and she wasn't very tall. She spoke well, [with] a Portuguese accent, but very pleasant. And it didn't take you more than two seconds to figure out, There walks a brain. Also, it didn't take you very long to figure out the number one concern in Lota's life was Elizabeth. More so than her landscape architecture or anything. Lota had given Elizabeth this carefully intense care that she needed. I liked this woman's forthrightness.

There was a kind of symbiosis in which a sensitive person would instantly detect the need of one for the other. It's body language. [They were] more than lovers, a really devoted couple.

♦   ♦   ♦

In 1953 Gold and Fizdale had suggested to the composer Ned Rorem that he contact Bishop about setting some of her poems to music. Rorem wrote to Bishop that year and found her interested, but wary of the project, in part because she had not heard Rorem's music. Bishop had always been interested in musical settings for some of her writing. She had written "Songs for a Colored Singer" with Billie Holiday in mind, and she had worked on two or three operatic, masque pieces in the years following her graduation from Vassar. She sent Rorem some suggestions about settings, but nothing came of their first exchange of letters. Rorem and Bishop met during her visit to New York in 1957, and their collaboration, of sorts, was launched.

NED ROREM— Arthur Gold and Bobby Fizdale said Elizabeth Bishop and I were meant for each other. I had just set to music some poems of Frank O'Hara for two pianos and two voices at their instigation. In those days we were warm acquaintances, and they were friends of Elizabeth Bishop. I was terribly interested, as I always am, in poets for the ulterior motive of "What have they got that I can use?" In theory I like to set poems by living people more or less breathing the air that I breathe from the country that I am in. I wrote to Elizabeth Bishop and she answered, and we had a long correspondence between France, where I was living, and South America.

I did not do anything with her poems, right off the bat. However, she did send me many. One was by George Peele, the sixteenth-century poet, which she thought was musical. I did use it, then took the words out and used the music in another kind of piece, actually in many different pieces. Elizabeth's poems at that time struck me as "prosey," which now is a very good thing. I've set an awful lot of Whitman prose and even Mark Twain, and prosiness is an element that I now like, but didn't then. I thought poems should be "musical," whatever that means, and Elizabeth, like all poets, had her ideas of what "musical" is, and, of course, literary people, with very few exceptions, don't know much about music. Elizabeth Bishop was one of those poets who are interested in the fact that you might set their work to music and are sort of flattered, but are inevitably disappointed. But how can they help but be? They heard their own music when they wrote it. So Elizabeth had a few naive notions, and I knew less then than I know now in a formulated way.

On May 7, 1957—during a hiatus in New York, five days before I went back to France—Elizabeth and I got together, in a smallish apartment where she was staying in New York. Lota was there, fussing around in the kitchen, and then went out to do some shopping. I liked Elizabeth and felt immediately that she was a friend. There was enough difference in our ages at that point—because I was born in 1923—for me to think of her as an older person, a person of accomplishment. I was anxious for us to have a rapport, but you can't force those things. There was a warmth to her. I told her that Virgil Thomson had read me "Visits to St. Elizabeths" at the Chelsea Hotel. It had just appeared in *Partisan Review*. Elizabeth said she could just hear him reading *that* poem, with his little piping voice.

Elizabeth was very interested in my setting words of hers to music. I don't think that anybody else had ever brought the question up with her. We had a long talk, and she gave me a copy of *Poems: North & South—A Cold Spring*. On the airplane [trip], which then took thirteen hours, I read straight through the book as though it were a novel, poem after poem, not going back. I was upset about a love affair that I had had that had just collapsed. Because of this love affair, the poems hit me very differently than they would have a year earlier. By the time I got to France, I was immersed.

That first month back in Paris, I set about six of Elizabeth's poems to music, of which at least one overlaps with Elliott Carter, "Insomnia." Several months later I set "Visits to St. Elizabeths." It hadn't occurred to me when Virgil first read it aloud that it should be set to music, but it did later. So I've done seven of Elizabeth's poems, of which two are published, "Conversation" and "Visits." The others, which I did not publish, are "Casabianca," "Letter to New York," "The Mountain," and "Songs for a Colored Singer" (or at least I planned to do it). They were a little bit too sentimental, too *felt*. I wrote them to express my broken heart, and you can't do that, rather than making a song that is appetizing for a singer to get his or her teeth into.

The world premiere, occurred in mid-May 1959. Bill Flanagan and I gave a series of concerts of American songs, and Patricia Neway did a group of my songs, including "Visits to St. Elizabeths: (Bedlam)." In fact, the night before, "Visits" had been done by Regina Sarfaty at the YMHA. Patricia Neway was nothing if not theatrical, very much of a diva. Whenever we rehearsed, I would be busy looking at the music, and Pat would be doing what she was doing. She had very long hair. The night of the performance her hair was all up in a bun. While she was singing "Visits to St. Elizabeths" she took the hairpins out of her hair one by one, so that by the end of the song she looked liked a gibbering idiot. The audience loved it.

I wanted to write a virtuoso piece in "St. Elizabeths." It's difficult to find good poems for fast songs, let alone theatrical or dramatic songs that are going to sound at least as well sung as when read by themselves. That's what I saw in this. I liked the cumulative repetitions.

I try to make poems more of what they are, to heighten them on their own terms, rather than reinterpret them, and to think up pretty tunes to go with them. Experienced though I am in setting words to music, I have mixed feelings about whether the very process is kosher or not, whether by Schubert or Poulenc or myself. There's something insane about taking a complete work of art and assuming that you as a composer can add something to it. I like to go against words, the way Martha Graham goes against music, to make sharp contrasts.

In 1964, to my great thrill, Columbia Records recorded thirty-two of my songs, including "Visits to St. Elizabeths." They used a Cocteau cover, and there was a lot of correspondence at that time, because Elizabeth was in a state of ecstasy about Cocteau. I asked Cocteau to do the drawing for the cover of the sheet music. He made that cover, misspelling Elizabeth's name, in the French style with an "s" between vowels which sounds like "z." It could be the last drawing he ever made, because he died after that.

It was complicated getting records sent to Brazil, but finally the record arrived there. Elizabeth didn't say it, but she was disappointed. Her reasons were naive. She wondered whether the piece should have been in a major key, rather than in a minor one, or slower, or sung by a man rather than a woman. I felt sort of huffy about her reaction. What Elizabeth didn't hear and never would is the music that she had in her mind when she wrote "Visits to St. Elizabeths." How could she? I'm a different person from her. Our correspondence was never quite the same again. I had thought very seriously about doing some other poems of hers, and would have, but the occasion didn't come quite right. I had even made some notes, from another book of hers [Questions of Travel], for the poem about a gas station ["Filling Station"].

Bishop had also spoken to Rorem in May 1957 about his setting some of Robert Lowell's poems to music. Bishop saw Lowell at least three times while she was in the United States in 1957. Her visit in late July with Lota to Castine, Maine, was the only unfortunate incident during her stay. Castine brought to Lowell's mind Stonington of ten years before, when Bishop had described herself to him as the loneliest person who had ever lived, followed by their time together at Bard College.[11] It had seemed to Lowell then that it was only a matter of time before they would be married. As Bishop and Lota spent time with Lowell in 1957, they sensed that he was entering another one of his manic periods. Lowell was overly affectionate with Bishop, apparently in Lota's presence. After they left, he apologized by letter and, one would assume, in person when Bishop saw him in September in Boston.[12] Bishop assured Lowell that he had not been inconsiderate. She did, however, recommend an analyst in Boston and suggested that he not visit Brazil alone.[13]

Bishop traveled to Maryland to see Jane Dewey during this visit to the States, and to Worcester in June to see her eighty-three-year-old Aunt Florence, who had grown more forgetful than ever. Florence confused the Pulitzer with the Nobel Prize. Rosalina Leão arrived in August for the unveiling of the Portinari murals—she had been one of Portinari's assistants for the project—and Bishop left her and Lota in New York to shop as she traveled to Key West to see Marjorie Stevens, who had just purchased a house. Key West was deserted and steamy; Bishop and Stevens bicycled and swam. Lota and Rosalina shopped for clothing, electric frying pans, spices, books, blankets and pillows, and dinner services, to list only a few items on their shopping lists from friends. There were so many packing boxes in their apartment in New York that Bishop and Lota had to spend evenings out during the final weeks of their stay.

Bishop and Lota ended their visit with a party for forty people (twenty for dinner) in early October in the apartment of Arthur Gold and Robert Fizdale in New York. Alexi Haieff, the composer, Tom Wanning, Eleanor Clark and Robert Penn Warren, Marianne Moore, Louise Bogan, Dwight MacDonald, Monroe Wheeler, Glenway Wescott, Mrs. E. E. Cummings, Loren MacIver, Lloyd Frankenberg, Robert Giroux, Morton Dauwen Zabel, and Anny Baumann attended. Katherine Anne Porter could not attend, so Bishop and Gold and Fizdale visited her before she left. Then Bishop and Lota set off on 15 October on the SS *Mormacstar*. Loren MacIver saw them off with a box of chocolates.

Lota did not like ship travel, so eighteen days at sea was far too long for her. Bishop arranged for Lota to have coffee served in bed mornings, but Lota was incredulous that she had to eat dinner at 11:30 and supper at 6:00. When the ship put in to Savannah, Bishop contacted Flannery O'Connor—Bishop had written her a fan letter in December 1956—but they were unable to arrange a meeting, so she and Lota hired a cab driver to show them the local architecture. Bishop and Lota also went sight-seeing in Aruba, taking a taxi across the island to the tidy town of Oranjestad with its statue of Queen Wilhelmena. On the final leg of the trip, Bishop ran out of books, and Lota's boredom spread to her. They checked the ship's log each day and had two algebra teachers from Minneapolis calculate their day of arrival.

When she arrived in Rio on 3 November, Bishop found, oddly, that she missed New York. Rio seemed drab, dingy, and messy. Customs laws had changed while they were away, and it took them three tedious weeks to reclaim their purchases. Then the cook gave birth to a new baby—Bishop thought it looked more like the handyman than her husband—and the rhythm of domestic life took hold. Bishop and Lota spent Christmas with Rosalina, Magu, and two of their brothers at their house in the sea town of Cabo Frio. They walked the long, deserted beaches, with their salt ponds and windmills, and went deep-sea fishing. Evenings they lay in hammocks while Vivaldi records, which they had finally liberated from customs, played on the victrola. New York drifted away.

In early 1958 Bishop immersed herself in domestic life at Petrópolis. Lota brought her fifteen-year-old nephew, Flavio, to Samambaia for a visit in January, when two of the children and the wife of Lota's adopted son, Kylso, also arrived to escape the summer heat of Rio. The maid's two young children were also running around. Apparently renewed by the six months that she and Bishop had spent in New York in 1957, Lota plunged into work on the house, finishing details in the living-room-cum-library, designing a cabinet for the hi-fi that Bishop had purchased with her Pulitzer Prize money, installing their first electric refrigerator (Bishop made sherbet for the children to test the freezer), enclosing the gallery with glass exterior walls, and starting the garage. In March, Bishop quipped that she and Lota always seemed to live "in a state of broken down luxury."[1]

That same month Bishop also complained to friends that she had not finished a poem in more than a year and a half. The intensity of the landscape and the human character in Brazil, which had seemed new and exotic when she had first arrived, had become commonplace. The novelty of Brazil had worn off. The country, too, she felt, was in horrible shape. Lota and Bishop railed against the symbol of Brazilian irrationality, Brasilia. They questioned the sensibility of building a new capital city, to many the emblem of Brazil's future, in an inaccessible jungle, while sections of Rio went without water and electricity. Lota and her friend Carlos Lacerda, a journalist and politician, spent evenings lamenting the plight of Brazil. In late March 1958, her nerves frayed from all the visitors and weak from a particularly severe bout with asthma—her doctor had mixed her serum incorrectly—Bishop told friends that were it not for Lota, she would not stay in Brazil.

John Dos Passos and Aldous Huxley visited Brazil in August to view Brasilia, and Bishop and Lota avoided the topic in conversations when these two writers visited Petrópolis. John Dos Passos's trip was sponsored by the Brazilian State Department; he was to write an article about Brasilia for *Reader's Digest*. Neither Bishop nor Lota warmed to him, nor to Huxley, for that matter, even though Huxley's wife, Laura Archera, was an acquaintance of Bishop's from Key West. Huxley's dignified silences unsettled even the ebullient Lota, who was uncharacteristically tongue-tied one day when he came to lunch. Bishop characterized Huxley to her friends as a humane man who was, ironically, trapped in his own broad intellect. He wanted to be affable, but was unable. As Bishop wrote, "He's awfully nice—but very remote and silent—and when he does talk it's like reading him."[2]

Bishop traveled with the Huxleys to Brasilia and then to western Brazil, near Bolivia, to see the Indians. They delighted Bishop. Here was the fresh, primitive Brazil with which she had lost touch. The Indians were a friendly, happy, peaceful, even sweet-smelling people. One widower proposed to Bishop, after eyeing her earrings and watch and poking her to make sure that this person in slacks was a woman. Bishop spent several weeks writing an article on this trip with the Huxleys, yet when *The New Yorker* rejected it, she was not surprised. Huxley had not said enough throughout the trip to make it appealing for the magazine. However, Bishop's new sense of the life of these Indians, combined with reading she had started about the Amazon River, provided the impulse and details for "Brazil, January 1, 1502," with its dense foliage, giant flowers, and elusive Indian women who retreat into the jungle, "calling to each other" like birds. The interior got her writing again.

During the next year, Bishop was working on a poem ("The Riverman") based on her reading about the Amazon River. In early 1960 Rosalina Leão mentioned that she was planning a trip down the Amazon, from Manaus to the coastal city of Belem, and Bishop asked to go along. Rosalina was initially concerned about traveling with Bishop, whose mood swings had made her wary, but she recollects a happy trip and Bishop's delight with the people and the landscape of the Amazon. David Jackson, whom Bishop met years later, remembers her telling about purchasing one of her prized possessions while on this trip.

ROSALINA LEÃO— I was going [on a trip down the Amazon] with my nephew, a young boy of about twelve. Elizabeth said she wanted to go. So the three of us went. I was so scared about taking care of the little boy and Elizabeth. Elizabeth, I discovered, is good when she travels. Everything is easy for her.

I had written letters to persons to make contacts. We went by plane. My brother picked us up at Manaus. He drove through town showing us the new Manaus, his partner's house, and this and that. Elizabeth and my nephew were [most excited about] the houses in the river [built] on tall legs [and which can only be reached] by boat. I kicked them. My brother was very nervous about them seeing all the poor [sections of Manaus] when he was showing the wealthier parts of town.

[From Manaus] we took a very nice little boat with 250 passengers down the river to Belem. The trip was around two weeks. My brother told the men at the boat that he was going to travel, so they gave us the nicest cabin and bathroom. The food was horrible, but we had been advised to bring lots of food. For dinner the first day there was something very black. We didn't know what it was and we couldn't swallow [it]. My nephew ate everything. Elizabeth was very clever at cooking eggs and [other simple food].

[One day] we saw dolphins, and so [the next day] Elizabeth brought a ball with her and played with them. Canoes would come out to the river, and even the soda machine [arrived] in a little row boat. I was looking [at the canoes] once and suddenly Elizabeth rushed by and screamed, "I want one of the oars!" It was very funny. A boy in one boat had an oar with a [Brazilian] flag carved into it. "I must have it," she said. Elizabeth bought it and was so very, very happy. [The boy returned to shore by paddling the boat with his hands.] Elizabeth bought a big, beautiful tin basin on this trip. It is made from lots of tin cans—oil [cans, food cans] and things like that— [which are hammered together]. Elizabeth was fascinated by this. [One day] a child on the boat was screaming. Elizabeth went over to see why she was screaming. One parent said that she missed the bath [which she was used to every day to cool her]. So we went to our room, took some oil and bathed the child [in the tin basin].

Elizabeth enjoyed everything and she looked at everything. She took some notes. One day Elizabeth and my nephew went down into the second-class [area]. In Brazil you never do this. There were millions of hammocks, here and there, and they saw a foot coming out here and an arm coming out there. . . . It was an enormous place.

Santarem, [the halfway point], was beautiful and very charming. Elizabeth said Venice is like Santarem. At the hotel there we found a little horse very beautifully made from rubber. My nephew wanted it, and I said, "Oh, let's go down to the [section of town near] the river [where it will be] much cheaper." Near the door in one house was the little horse, and so I talked with [the people who lived there]. They were friendly and I asked if they would sell the horse. [It was a toy of one of the children.] We talked and talked about the food on the boat and how bad it was. And then they gave us [some food]!

DAVID JACKSON— [In her Lewis Wharf apartment] Elizabeth had a marvelous great paddle she had bought in the Amazon. She and her companions were going up river and they came to this little settlement. They had moored out in the river, and out came all these people selling things, among them a little boat the size of a pea pod with this father and son, about eight or nine, on it. They had nothing to sell but a big armchair that took up all the boat, and Elizabeth felt so bad about not being able to find anything that she sort of idly admired the paddle, which was quite beautiful, like lacquer, ivory color, and huge, with a painting on it of the Brazilian flag. They sold it to her. And then she got to thinking about how they would get back. She said this tiny boat went shooting back with the father and the son sort of lying on their stomachs paddling with their hands while she stood on this deck with this big paddle in her hand.

✦ ✦ ✦

By the time Bishop's boat made its way to Belem, its 250 passengers had increased to 700, most of them hanging in the hammocks below deck that Bishop had observed. There was livestock on board—turkeys, dogs, and eleven large green turtles in the lifeboats, which the captain had filled with water. He fed them crusts of bread. Egrets and flamingos flew by or waded near the shore, and hundreds of white herons perched on trees beside the river. At one stop along the river, Bishop played with a Peruvian *quati*, with its long nose and striped, erect tale, which rolled, kicked, and bit like a kitten. According to Bishop's poem "Santarem," when she visited that lovely city with its streets of orange sand, a pharmacist gave her a small, intricate wasps' nest that had been sitting on one of his shelves. When she brought the nest on board, a fellow passenger asked, "What's that ugly thing?"

Travel became more and more of a preoccupation for Bishop during the next few months. In May 1960 she and Lota traveled to the beautiful mountain town of Ouro Prêto, where a friend of Lota's owned an inn. That same month, Bishop applied for a grant from the Chapelbrook Foundation to continue her travels, this time outside of Brazil. She proposed that she needed to distance herself from the source of her current poetry, Brazil, to make her writing more reflective. In September 1960 she received seven thousand dollars. Robert Lowell and Agnes Mongan had supported her application.

Just as Bishop and Lota were planning to travel to Europe and New York City, Lota became more deeply involved with life in Rio than ever before. In the fall of 1960 Lota's close friend Carlos Lacerda ran for governor of the State of Guanabara, the district that had been created out of Rio and the surrounding country when Brasilia became the new capital of Brazil. Lota and Lacerda had been friends for many years, and he owned a house in Petrópolis near Lota's. Lacerda rose to national prominence when his articles and editorials for Tribuna da Imprensa and his involvement with the National Democratic Union coalesced opposition to the repressive regimes of President Getulio Vargas (1937–1945, 1950–54). Lacerda occasionally retreated to the quiet of Lota's house in Petrópolis to write his anti-Vargas editorials.

Lacerda had become a virtual folk hero when, on 5 August 1954, he was wounded by an assassin hired by some of Vargas's followers. The attempt on his life took place outside his apartment house on the Avenida Copacabana, just down the street from where Lota and Bishop lived. One of Lacerda's aides was killed in the assault. In late 1955, while supporting, if not actually directing, a coup that would prevent the inauguration of newly elected president Juscelino Kubitschek, Lacerda took refuge in the Cuban embassy, where Lota visited him. Her visits to Lacerda reminded Lota of similar ones she had made as a girl to bring her father, another vehement opponent of Vargas, cigars at embassies where he had sought asylum. When Lacerda fled to the United States in December 1955, Bishop wrote introductions for him to many of her friends, claiming that he was the most brilliant and interesting Brazilian she had met. Anny Baumann agreed and called him "my Carlos." When he ran for governor in 1960 Bishop and Lota saw him as a savior for Brazil. Lota drove people to the polls.

Lacerda won the election, and in December 1960 Lota and Bishop were taken by official car to the Governor's Palace for dinner. At some point during this month, Lota, with Bishop's help, suggested to Lacerda that a stretch of undeveloped landfill along the coast in Rio be converted into a city park. City planners were building a highway through this area, and Lota suggested that part of the area be converted to beaches, landscaped paths, cafes and restaurants, a boat pond, a playground and a railroad for children, and a dance pavilion. Lacerda admired Lota's will power, her energy, and her taste, and he saw this plan as providing an apt symbol for his administration's concern for a better life for all in Rio. Suddenly Lota was plunged into a major construction project. Her life and her relationship with Bishop were to change dramatically.

Initially Bishop believed that in this new job Lota's talents had at last found their deserved focus. She and Lota took up full-time residence in Rio, and Petrópolis became their weekend residence. Bishop put any plans for travel on the back burner. By April 1961 Lota had the formal title of Chief Co-Ordinatress of Flamengo Park, and she found herself negotiating with military officers, cabinet officials, and entrenched politicians. She was the only woman in Rio in this kind of position. Lota called on her close friend, landscape architect Roberto Burle Marx, and others to draw up the complex development plans, and she coordinated the work of other architects and construction crews. Lota's friend Magu Leão worked with new plantings in the park. She and her sister Rosalina had known Lota and Lacerda for many years and had witnessed the affectionately argumentative edge to their relationship. They understood the challenging job that Lota had undertaken.

ROSALINA LEÃO— Lacerda had a house in Samambaia. Lota and Elizabeth would invite him to talk at night. It was very funny [listening to him and Lota argue]. He was always right and Lota and Elizabeth were wrong. They were very good friends, and when Lacerda came to be governor, he asked Lota [to work for him].

[There were to be] four big roads for cars [through] the "âterró." Lota said, "No, four is too much. Maybe two." Lota's idea was to have a beautiful park for the people. She imagined a family coming to spend a day there. The little children would be in a playground, and the others would have football, volleyball, swimming, a pool for [sailing] boats, a theater, music, and a place to dance. Elizabeth was fascinated and helped Lota quite a lot [to develop these ideas]. Lota told me that Elizabeth had helped her very, very much. Lota sold [her ideas] so well that Carlos immediately understood. Carlos had taste; he loved the idea. But the people that [had wanted to build] the road were furious. So at the beginning Lota had a lot of trouble.

✦　✦　✦

Magu Leão also worked on the park with Lota. She recollects that conflicts with the highway engineers, from whom Lota's plans took space, continued throughout the duration of the project. Lota hired a woman engineer to work with her on the design and execution of her plans. Leão and her fellow workers located and transplanted native Brazilian plants for the park. Lota was insistent on the quality and size of plants, and once sent back trees that she found too small—she was a tough taskmaster. Her strong will led to numerous conflicts with Lacerda, and once Lota sent the workers home and left a note on her door informing Lacerda that she and her staff were on strike because they disagreed with a decision he had made. When he found the note (he was giving a tour of the park at the time) Lacerda yelled that Lota's strike was illegal. All of the workers were under additional pressure to complete this park because Lacerda's tenure as governor extended to only one five-year term.

Lota's job changed the rhythm of her domestic life with Bishop. By June 1961 Bishop was telling friends that she saw little of Lota during the day in Rio. Bishop also missed country life in Petrópolis. Joanna dos Santos da Costa was hired as Bishop and Lota's maid when they took up full-time residence in Rio, and her recollections give a detailed sense of the structure of Bishop and Lota's new daily regimen. Monroe Wheeler, director of publications at the Museum of Modern Art in New York, visited Rio in September 1961. He observed the coterie of politicians, socialites, artists, and architects with whom Lota had daily contact through her new job. He noticed that, as Lota was being drawn into even more social and political prominence, Bishop became something of a detached observer, if not an outsider.

JOANNA DOS SANTOS DA COSTA—I started working for Lota in about 1960, when she began to work on the park. I worked in Rio and also in Petrópolis. I went to Petrópolis with her on weekends or other days because I wanted to cook the food that Lota liked. I didn't always go up to Petrópolis. My main place was in Rio, because Lota had other maids in Petrópolis.

Lota would awaken about seven in the morning. I would take her breakfast to her and then she would go to the living room and do some of her work. She would leave about eight. Sometimes she would only go in the afternoon because she would be tired. She would work in the house, have lunch, and then go to the park and work there. Very often I would take lunch to Lota in the park because she wouldn't have time to come home, she'd be so busy. She had an office in the park. If they had a party or something, it would be there. They even had cocktail parties there.

In town during the day there weren't very many visitors, sometimes for tea or for dinner or after dinner, sometimes foreigners, sometimes Brazilians. They would be people for Elizabeth because Lota didn't have time. [In the evenings] Elizabeth and Lota would sit in the living room, and each one would read separately. They were always reading. Then they would converse a little bit and about 9:30 they would go to bed.

Elizabeth would write a lot when she was alone. She received a lot of mail, and she wrote a lot of letters. Sometimes Elizabeth would forget them in the drawer of the desk and I would remind her that they were there, and she would take them out. [It is my] impression [that she wrote] more letters [than poetry]. Elizabeth often used to read poems to me. She would translate them into Portuguese. [Once] at Christmas time Elizabeth wrote a poem about a man who collected garbage and left little reminders that he would like a tip. Elizabeth showed the poem to Lota and me. Elizabeth told me she was going to take it to the States and have it published there. And so I said, "Ah, you're earning money out of this country because of the garbage collector."

Elizabeth had more inspiration in Petrópolis. She wrote a lot near the waterfall, and also there was a coffee plant where she liked to sit. I could see her from the kitchen. She would talk to herself, and then she would go to her study and write. Sometimes they had fights about going out to Petrópolis for the weekend. Friends from the States used to come and visit Elizabeth, and Elizabeth would say, "No, I'm not going up to Petrópolis because I want to receive my friends." Lota would say, "Why don't you bring them up to Petrópolis?" "Because I want to see them here."

I was happy with Elizabeth and Lota because I loved them so much. I felt as if Lota and Elizabeth's apartment was my home and that they were friends with me. At night I used to go out on the veranda with Lota and look with binoculars at the people on the beach. I was a friend of Lota's, a sort of a part of the family.

I knew that Elizabeth and Lota needed a person like me, even though I was a little bit younger, to take care of them. I understood [Lota] and Elizabeth. I was afraid if somebody else came in they wouldn't understand the two. It wasn't a question of salary. I got so many presents from them and they were so generous in what they did for me. I adored them for that. I could do much more for them than anybody else could do. If all of a sudden Lota and Elizabeth received somebody they weren't expecting, I was there with good-will to do it. Through any misunderstanding or anything like that, I [could be] calm.

Lota and Elizabeth [both ran the house]. I followed Lota's instructions more than I did Elizabeth's. Lota would give the money; Elizabeth would give a little money. Elizabeth was more interested in the kitchen, in the food. I learned a lot from Elizabeth—how to make bread, desserts, and things like that. I cooked a mixture of Brazilian and American food. When there was American food that I didn't know, Elizabeth herself would cook it, and I would learn. Elizabeth was agreeable to be with, and when she had her friends [visiting], she would go to the kitchen and help me with something special she wanted.

Elizabeth and I liked each other very much, and she was usually quite simpatico with me. But sometimes Elizabeth was nervous, and I'm a nervous type, and we'd have our [difficulties]. [Sometimes Elizabeth had extreme moods] and it was very difficult to deal with her. I, too, [then], got in a bad mood. Sometimes when Elizabeth was in a bad mood, I would say to her, "Why are you speaking to me in this way?" And she would say, "No, no, it's not because of you I'm in a bad mood." Or something like that. Sometimes we would fight a little bit, but we were good friends.

MONROE WHEELER— I knew Lota very well when I first came back from Paris to New York in the mid-forties. Lota was exactly like the brightest girl you would meet in Paris. Lota was very worldly and interested in painting, literature, and the theater. The exuberance, warmth, and curiosity in everything that she did made her so many friends and made an immensely happy life for her in those days. She was a very rewarding talker because she knew about everything, and what she didn't know about she was busy informing herself about. And you know, people always like to be questioned by the intelligent questioner. We became great friends immediately.

I went to Brazil and visited Lota [in 1961]. She lived up in the mountains. I'll never forget the drive there, zipping around those mountain curves [with the architect Enrique Midlin driving]. Lota introduced me to Carlos Lacerda and I think probably persuaded him to invite me to spend a weekend at his huge house on an island in the harbor of Rio. Lacerda was a fascinating man, and for this weekend he invited various political associates as well as socialites. It was like [a] two-day picnic. They never stopped the sociability from dawn to dark. Lota was part of the festivities, but Elizabeth just melded into everything. She was, as the British say, rather plain, but always very affectionate toward me, smiling and happy. She looked at me as if she were looking to see behind me to determine if there wasn't something there she could enjoy. There were times when she wanted to work. She secured herself in her cottage, but otherwise she seemed to mix with Lota's friends very happily.

We were talking about mutual friends in New York, and about Brazilian artists and Brazilian architects, because Lota and Elizabeth knew everything about Brazilian architects. It was Lota who introduced me to Burle Marx. I had been introduced to them all because we did an exhibition, "Brazil Builds" [at the Museum of Modern Art]. It was done by Philip Johnson, and he took a young photographer with him to take the pictures. [Lota and these architects] were all close friends, a very jolly little group of people. It was just assumed that everybody had known everybody forever. I have the warmest recollections of those Brazilian architects. It was a quiet time. It was all very informal and cozy, just old friends together. Elizabeth was just an observer.

◆ ◆ ◆

There were fearful moments for Bishop as a result of Lota's new political prominence. In the summer of 1961, for example, Lacerda led the opposition against the new president, Jânio Quadros. Quadros resigned on 25 August, but was succeeded, to Lacerda's chagrin, by his vice-president, João Goulart. In early September, as Goulart moved quickly to neutralize his opposition and centralize his power, Bishop feared that Lacerda and Lota, who was frequently at the Governor's Palace, might be exiled. One day when Bishop went to the movies alone, she found herself crying uncontrollably about the course of events. None of her fears were realized, but Lacerda, and Lota with him, remained in a tenuous political position for some time. Two years later Goulart was so frustrated that he plotted, unsuccessfully, for Lacerda to be kidnapped.

Bishop took on a job of her own at this time. In June 1961 Time Inc. offered her $10,000 plus travel expenses to write the Life World Library volume on Brazil. Bishop was attracted by the stipend and the prospect of having her own Brazil project. Also, the trip to New York in November and December to see the book through production would offer her—and, she hoped, Lota—a reprieve from the chaotic scene that was developing in Rio. As the uncanny events of Brazilian politics would have it, Lacerda left the country at this time, to give his controversy with Goulart time to cool off, and Lota was free to join Bishop.

Bishop began the Time-Life project energetically and on schedule, completing three chapters by August, but, as was often the case with her and schedules, she failed to meet the 15 October deadline for a completed draft and was still writing in New York in early December. She and Lota stayed at Loren MacIver's apartment on Perry Street in Greenwich Village. Bishop visited Marianne Moore and E. E. Cummings, who seemed to her very frail, had dinner with T. S. Eliot, the Lowells, and Robert Giroux, and had teas with the art historian Meyer Schapiro and his wife. Bishop complained about the long workdays at the Time offices and changes that the editors made in her original text. She was offended when the researchers questioned her knowledge about Brazil. She complained to the editors that the writers with whom she worked had changed her text beyond recognition. In January 1962, when she and Lota were back in Rio, Bishop received from Time a nine-page rebuttal to her complaints. In the fall, when Bishop was asked if she would be willing to revise sections for a second printing, her response was a curt, forceful No.

In the summer of 1963, well over a year after *Brazil* was published, David Weimer, from Rutgers University, and his family, traveled to Rio, where he was a Fulbright scholar for a year. He had read Bishop's book to prepare himself for the country, and when he mentioned it to her, her reaction was strong.

DAVID WEIMER— The book on Brazil that Elizabeth wrote for Time-Life had come out not too long before my family and I went to Brazil in July 1963, and it was one of the chief things that my wife and I read in order to learn a little something about Brazil. At one of our early meetings, I thanked Elizabeth for having done it, and she said it was terrible. She said that Time had all this money, and they didn't know what to do with it, so they hired college graduates who didn't know the first thing about writing to serve as sub-editors. Elizabeth had turned in the manuscript and got it back all marked up by some of these "twerps"—that's not her word, but it's sort of the idea. Elizabeth told me how one of them had made a marginal notation saying that someone with "Silva" as part of his name couldn't possibly be a man because the word has a feminine ending. This is just one of the things that made Elizabeth explode. She said she phoned or wrote back saying she had known this man for fifteen years.

I went downtown somewhere in Rio and managed to buy a copy of the book in English and brought it to her just to get her autograph. She said she couldn't simply let me have that. Elizabeth took the book—this beautifully illustrates her perfectionism—went off by herself, and went through every line of every page making changes in the text back to the way she originally had written it. Then she signed it and gave it to me.

Bishop and Lota found themselves quickly confronted by the swirl of Rio life when they returned in January 1962. There was a spate of terrorism in Rio that month, although no one seemed to know who was sponsoring it, a fact which made it even more unsettling to Bishop. In May, Lota was appointed to Rio's equivalent of a city council. Bishop found herself more and more missing Petrópolis. By August she was complaining to friends that there were telephone calls all morning in the apartment when Lota worked at home. Lota worked at her office from 2:00 P.M. to 8:00 P.M., then attended meetings most nights. Bishop put some of the money she had earned on the Time-Life project toward renovating the Rio apartment that year, including breaking through the ceiling and building an addition on the roof of the building. Even this project, as two of Lota's friends remember, was an example of Lota's strong will.

MARY STEARNS MORSE— [The apartment in Rio] was very pleasant. It was on the top floor and had a veranda on two sides. It was small. It had a nice living room. Lota had built a wall to make a little office where Elizabeth worked. There were two bedrooms and another small living room. The larger one at the entrance was only used as the dining room.

Ann Hatfield [whom Lota had met at the Museum of Modern Art] gave ideas about color when she came down to work for Enrique Mindlin on one job. Her wonderful ideas about painting walls made the place look larger. Cold blue [made one wall] recede, so the room looked like a larger space than it actually was. Lota followed Ann's ideas. She painted another wall sort of a cold red. Lota had modern furniture. She brought a lot of furniture from New York. Lota designed chairs.

STELLA PEREIRA— Lota loved form. She loved beautiful form.

MORSE— The apartment had been bought years before when Lota's mother died. Her mother bought two apartments, and I think Lota bought two apartments when the building was going up. She had four apartments there.

Above the top floor, [where Lota's apartment was located], there was an open space covered with tiles. Lota said she was going to make a penthouse, to make some more room for everybody. There was a meeting of the condominium owners in the building, and they said it belonged to the whole building. But Lota began talking with lawyers, and she decided that she was going to do it anyway. So she got the workers in, had a square hole made just inside the entrance door, got a big ladder, and up they went. She had somebody design two rooms and a kitchenette or something like that. Lota had said it was going to be for me when I came on the weekend.

We were always afraid of somebody coming to say, "Are you doing any building? You have to have a license for it, you know." So we kept the ladder hidden and the hole very well closed. When we wanted to take anyone up to look at it, we'd put everything aside, go up the ladder and wander around and dream about what we would like there—a window here, a window there—but scared to death if the doorbell rang that some people would come in and say, "You're doing building illegally." It never did get finished because Lota finally gave up the idea. Lota was that way. She was going to win.

◆ ◆ ◆

A visit from Robert Lowell, Elizabeth Hardwick, and their daughter, Harriet, went sadly awry during the summer of 1962. The Lowells arrived 1 July, staying at an apartment in the Copacabana Palace, not far from Bishop and Lota's apartment, and traveling to Petrópolis with them on the weekends. Bishop met Lowell early each morning on the beach in front of her apartment building for a swim. Lowell and Hardwick had a schedule of readings, dinners, and interviews. Lota and Bishop introduced the Lowells to their friends in Rio, taking them to a club in Rio one evening to hear Vinicius de Moraes play his guitar and sing. "Lowell said, 'That man can sing!' "[3] A trip to Cabo Frio was one of the pleasant times of the Lowells' visit. Bishop and Lowell sat on a cliff, talking and watching the boobies dive.

The Lowells so enjoyed Brazil that they stayed two months instead of the originally planned one, and all went smoothly until mid-August, when Lowell began acting oddly. Bishop noticed that he was drinking too much and was excessive in his speech during a visit with the Brazilian writer Clarice Lispector. During an evening dinner with Bishop, Lacerda, and the composer Nicolas Nabokov (a friend of both Bishop and Lowell), Lowell laughed hysterically, interrupted discussions, and espoused strange political ideas. It was clear to Bishop that he was having a breakdown.

Bishop tried to convince Lowell to cancel the remainder of his trip, but he would not listen. He left for Buenos Aires on 3 September; his condition worsened, while Hardwick and Harriet took a boat home, as had been previously arranged. Keith Botsford, who was in charge of the arrangements for Lowell's trip, returned to Rio. Bishop was terrified that Lowell had been left alone in Buenos Aires—the repressive police might pick him up for drunkenness or his political ranting, beat him up, and throw him into jail. She convinced Botsford to return and helped him locate a psychiatrist there. With the help of a woman who had caught Lowell's eye and several muscular men, Botsford got Lowell to a clinic and, after four days, onto a flight back to the States. Lowell made the trip with his legs and arms bound.

Lota's job continued to set the pace for Bishop's life for the months after Lowell's visit. In January 1963 Lota fought successfully for additional appropriations for Flamengo Park. In March she felt that she had achieved a major triumph: she had convinced the government not to build a large—and to her mind ugly—office building in Rio. In May, Lacerda tentatively decided to run for president in 1965, and there was talk of his appointing Lota as minister of education. Bishop increasingly felt that events were out of her control. She complained that Lota hardly noticed that she was around. Evenings she would sit alone in Samambaia, with the butler in formal attire, having him serve her, or occasionally her and Mary Morse, dinner. Morse and Stella Pereira recollect Bishop's frustration.

STELLA PEREIRA— When Lota took a full-time job, there was no free time. Elizabeth was not having her way, not at all. Elizabeth felt that she was sacrificing Lota.

MARY STEARNS MORSE— Lota not only had to go to work but also had to have meetings with people at night, government people that weren't of any interest to Elizabeth at all. Lota was obliged to keep [good relations] with them. That wasn't Elizabeth's cup of tea. How could she be interested in that kind of thing? It [was] not her mind.

◆   ◆   ◆

Bishop took on Lota's twenty-year-old nephew, Flavio, as a cause at this time. Bishop saw something of herself in this precocious, asthmatic young man who loved jazz and wrote poetry. As one of Bishop's friends remembers him, "Flavio was the best of a family that never quite worked out for Lota. He had the Brazilian gift for meeting people and getting along with them and was so wonderfully polite and intelligent in matters both literary [and] political. I thought for his age he was one of the most intelligent people I'd ever met."[4] Fearing that family and political turmoil in Rio might engulf Flavio, in the spring of 1963 Bishop wrote to several friends in the United States (Joseph Summers and Robert Lowell among them) to try, ultimately unsuccessfully, to locate a scholarship for Flavio to an American university.

David Weimer arrived in Rio at this time and during his year there as a Fulbright scholar was often with Lota and Bishop. He observed Bishop's growing loneliness as Lota became more and more preoccupied with her job.

DAVID WEIMER— I met Elizabeth in Rio early on after we arrived in July 1963. A good friend of hers, Joe Frank, sent a letter on ahead, when he knew I was going to Rio. Latin America wasn't completely new to me because I had been in Panama and Cuba in the navy in the Second World War, but I knew almost no Portuguese when I arrived in Brazil, and here was this vast city, which is cacophonous and vivid and brilliant and primitive and, ultimately, brutal, particularly under the military regime [which came into power the following year]. My wife and children and I were adrift in this astonishing place. To have anyone extend a hospitable hand was just wonderful, and Elizabeth and Lota did so. They had my wife and me over early on after we were there. So we were particularly drawn to them and came to like them enormously. I was there until July 1964. I saw a lot of Elizabeth during that year. She and I became friends.

Elizabeth was always very generous with her time and hospitality. She and Lota took my wife and me and our three children to Governor's Island, in Guanabara Bay, on a speedboat. Here are these two women, living by themselves, not having children, and yet they took us and our kids—what exceeding generosity that was! They did this repeatedly. We stayed at Petrópolis for two weeks at one point. One of my favorite memories of Brazil is that house atop a steep mountain. Elizabeth met us there and showed us around. There was a small lodge or hut where Elizabeth worked a hundred yards in the back of the house. She let me work there while she was gone. There were loads of books, many of which were being drilled by termites and carpenter ants. Elizabeth asked if now and then I would apply a treatment to certain of these books. I used her worm-eaten Oxford English Dictionary, a compact two-volume set. The house itself was wonderful, very modern in design, beautifully laid out. There was in the living room a mobile that Calder had presented to Lota. We had taken our own woman servant from Rio. She served us wonderful Brazilian coffee first thing every morning. One could get very spoiled. We just lived it up.

My wife and I liked Lota enormously. She really was modest and very controlled, in an appealing way, a very reserved person. At the same time, she was very explosive, dynamic, energetic, and outgoing most of the time—a wonderful, enigmatic figure. Lota knew everyone. At that time particularly, Brazil was an elitist, small culture. Lota knew everyone in the world of art and letters, and lots of other areas too. Rio was a very cultivated city in some ways. One of the generous things Lota did was to see that my older son was introduced to Carlos Lacerda, governor of the State of Guanabara at that time. My wife, Mark, and I went to the Governor's Palace one evening. He was meeting with the Council of Ministers. They had just had a rice shortage or a bean shortage, but he took fifteen minutes out from that crisis to come over and meet Mark, because my son had expressed an interest in becoming a lawyer and maybe going into politics. Lacerda was just the sweetest guy imaginable. He said to Mark that it's terribly important that good people go into politics. It was just a wonderful moment that Lota had arranged.

Lota was in Petrópolis for a time with us, either right at the beginning or right at the end. She told some wonderful stories, although she didn't think of them as wonderful. She and Elizabeth had been visited long before by John Dos Passos, whom neither she nor Elizabeth could stand. Aldous Huxley had visited them in Petrópolis. The house has an enormous vista through the mountains, and most people seeing that view would say, "My heavens!" Huxley walked out on the veranda, looked around, turned and came back into the house. He didn't say a word, and that annoyed Lota more than anything else. The funniest thing I remember from that time was when Lota got up one morning and expressed supreme irritation to whoever was around because someone was building a house on the next mountain. You got some insight into the landed aristocracy of Brazil. She was a wonderful person, generous and cultivated, but in that one moment you saw her class.

I saw Lota in action at her job more than once, and you could just see the way she dealt with people. It was an astonishing project, an enormous administrative job, to transform a large section of the shoreline area of Rio. She was obviously highly competent. She was smart, confident, strong willed, knew what she wanted, and set people hopping. At the same time, she exuded a kind of warmth that was wonderful. People really admired her. I was working on city-planning things at the time, and so I was very interested.

Lota wanted very much to get a write-up of the park, including the illustrative material, published in some American magazine. Before I left Brazil, I took a lot of material from her, and tried unsuccessfully to get it published in *Architectural Forum*.

Elizabeth and Lota were about as opposite as could be. They clearly respected one another enormously. Elizabeth was wonderfully witty and intelligent, in a restrained way. She wasn't aggressively witty or self-displaying in the way academic wits can be. She was always underdisplaying. Elizabeth was a sensitive soul, a rather suffering soul, strongly asthmatic, modest, extremely retiring, and decidedly likeable. I had a strong sense that she was fighting her body all the time. Asthma bothered her. She would be sniffling and what not. She may well have had other allergies. Just physically getting through a day must often have been extremely difficult for her.

One of the chief memories I have of Elizabeth is of her great loneliness. She had, of course, Lota, and by that time she had been there many years, so she knew quite a few people. She still gave the impression of being, if not isolated, at least solitary and lonely, as I think she probably was everywhere. Not too long after we met, she called me up one afternoon. We were quite some distance apart, maybe a half-hour by bus in the city, and she just more or less asked me to come over to her place. I was involved in work or something at the time and didn't particularly want to go over, but I did.

Elizabeth was just lonely. I stayed with her two or three hours and chatted with her about this and that, and, of course, once I was there I was glad I had come. It was enjoyable and she was interesting, but I had the feeling from time to time down there that she was a deeply unhappy person in many ways and probably always had been.

Elizabeth seemed forever in flight. Once the question arose as to why she had left New York to come to Brazil, and she said something about the intellectual group in New York being so small and so full of gossip that she just couldn't stand it anymore. After my Portuguese got moderately fluent, I began to be able to detect levels of quality in Portuguese speech by foreigners. I realized that Elizabeth could barely make herself understood in Portuguese. I think she was tone deaf, as far as languages go, at least as far as Portuguese goes. Elizabeth read it fluently, but she couldn't speak it well. My wife and I were always amused when we heard her speaking on the phone to somebody, or speaking to a servant.

Part of Elizabeth's brain was very sure of who she was and what she liked. I was a little startled that year to discover that in fact she was . . . I wouldn't say a snob exactly, but she had elitist attitudes. It was only toward the end of the year or maybe afterward that I began to put her in perspective. There were dismissive remarks she would make about either writers or kinds of writing or kinds of audiences for writing, that sort of thing. It may have been one thing that drew her to Lota, because Lota just breathed that sort of aristocraticness. Lota just took for granted that servants had to know their place. Elizabeth was a genuinely humane and decent person, and also she was a poet, so that the funny things that these servants did were exactly the kind of things she liked to write about with that wonderful sharp wit of hers. She sympathized with them and was compassionate and interested, like the wonderful poem about the seamstress ["House Guest"]. She really knew that seamstress, understood her and sympathized with her, at the same time viewing her with enormous detachment. Elizabeth told us one story about the man and the woman who were the servants up in Petrópolis. She said there would be coffee available in Petrópolis, which either the man servant or the maid would make, but she said that we had better get it early in the morning because they would just keep it on the stove all day letting it boil. Elizabeth said it was sludge by the end of the day. She said this in a way to suggest that it was funny of these people to do that, and at the same time she was a trifle scornful that these people really didn't know how to treat good coffee. That's the edge.

Lota's working on the park for no salary was a part of her elitism. It was all from the top down. Lota was wealthy enough, not hugely wealthy—I think she was land poor. It was very genuine with Lota, something she felt she owed the people, something they deserved. Lota was glad to devote herself to it. That fit Elizabeth; she fit that kind of social stratum.

My wife and I had some friends from the lower-middle class, a public school teacher and her husband, who had been in the Brazil military as an enlisted man for a while and then worked for an airline. When they learned that we were friends of Lota's, and perhaps for them incidentally of Elizabeth's, they looked at us in a very distinctive, new way. When we offered to introduce our friends because they were going to drive us to see Lota and Elizabeth, they said Lota wouldn't be interested in them. We got almost an identical reaction from upper-middle-class friends of ours. The husband was in business, a rather wealthy individual; the wife was an articulate, smart, cultivated person. They both were decidedly reluctant to meet Lota because they thought that she might be scornful of them. Lota's and, by association, Elizabeth's was a distinct, different social class to them to which they couldn't aspire and that made them feel ill at ease.

Elizabeth was drawn to the cultivated, civilized side of Brazil, but there was another side that must have attracted her, just as it did in Key West. Elizabeth had a fund of anecdotes, illustrating this double side, and she really treasured them. One of the first stories she told me was about talking to a woman friend of hers who had an apartment in Rio. Her building backed up, as some of the apartments do, against a great hill. One day this friend came home and found a horse standing in the living room. The horse had been wandering on the hill and had just wandered down onto the balcony of the apartment and then on into the living room. Elizabeth wanted to suggest how Rio and, beyond it, Brazilian society in general had this wonderfully modern, advanced, cultivated, sophisticated, polished, and civilized side, but backed right up against an outrageous natural world.

✦　✦　✦

The loneliness in Bishop's life in Rio was, as it often could be, attended by her drinking. In September 1963 Bishop entered a clinic atop a hill outside Rio for a week's rest. Lota had been sick the weeks before with an intestinal occlusion, then typhoid fever following the operation, and had gone off to Petrópolis to recuperate. Bishop herself stayed in a quiet place, run by Seventh-Day Adventists, that was accessible by cog railway and had a broad and lovely view of Rio. Bishop needed the peace away from the city. In February 1964 Alastair Reid, a writer and translator who was on the staff of

The New Yorker, arrived in Rio at the end of a trip through South America. He sensed in Bishop a lonely artist who craved the companionship of shared artistic sensibilities.

ALASTAIR REID— I met Elizabeth in 1961 when Randall Jarrell, whom I knew and was very fond of, was giving a reading at the YMCA. At the end of the reading Randall asked me to have a drink, and Elizabeth was part of the company. We talked about Rio because I had in mind then to make a pilgrimage to Latin America. I had been living in Madrid. I knew Spanish, and I had begun to translate a number of Spanish and Latin American poets, out of *afición*, from enthusiasm. I had decided it was almost immoral to translate poems that had come from a physical, geographical context that I had never seen. So I decided to go to Latin America and Elizabeth told me about Brazil. She said that if ever I came to Rio, I should look her up.

At the very beginning of 1964 I set out from New York and took a round-trip to Buenos Aires that allowed unlimited linear stops. I made about twenty stops on the way and saw many people. It took three months, and in the course of it I saw Neruda in Chile, Borges in Buenos Aires, and I met Elizabeth in Rio. Howard Moss had told Elizabeth I would be arriving. Howard gave me her phone number before I left. I called Elizabeth early from the hotel and went around the first time for drinks and met Lota, talked for a while, and then Elizabeth said we must do something together. I saw her four or five times. On two occasions we went to the botanical gardens. We actually spent four to five hours there. It was a haunt of hers. She was familiar with the exotic birds there, so it was like introducing me to her friends. We would look at things and then sit on a bench and talk about all kinds of things. We talked as strangers can, as strangers who know about each other and share a wavelength.

The exchange we had was a very vivid one. Elizabeth and I sat side by side and talked about what we were looking at. We would look at plants together and notice together. In other words, we were not so much communicating face to face, as we were both looking at the same thing and talking about what we were seeing. Elizabeth would say, "Do you see that thing there?" I would say, "But do you see how that curve goes? The color, what does that remind you of?" It was the whole business of putting physicality into words. We'd look at the birds especially, and Elizabeth would say, "How do you put that creature into words? How do you put that head?" So we tried out words. How would Howard Moss write this? And how would Richard Wilbur treat this? And we conceived of a very graceful Wilbur poem. When we were talking about writers we liked, read or knew, we would try to relate them to what we were seeing. It's a game. When you find somebody you can do that with—I did that a lot with Howard—it is very joyful. These outings were so utterly in the present. We found that we had such fun doing it that after the first day Elizabeth said, "Well, we'll have to do this again." We went two days later. I felt that we were almost like children wandering in the garden seeing what we could see.

It was then that I got from Elizabeth that essential image of rethinking relationship. If you are sitting side by side and looking at the same thing, you relate through what you are seeing. That becomes the objective correlative. That was what really defined our conversation. The image has always stayed with me, and I used it in one poem, "Quarrels":

> Let us withdraw and watch them,
> but side by side, not nose to nose and wary.
>
> That is the only way we'll disentangle
> the quarrel from ourselves and switch it off.
> Not face to face. The sparks of confrontation
> too easily ignite a rage like love.

I also remember talking with Elizabeth about being in a country that is not your own and how it extends you. It makes you look with far greater attention, far greater scrutiny. You have to notice things. Being in places where you don't know the language, you try and almost lipread what people are thinking. It sharpens your eye and ear. You take in everything because you're not used to it. It's all new to you. I had the sense of us on these two days of outings as being aliens, strangers in a garden.

I noticed a big difference between Elizabeth in the presence of Lota and Elizabeth alone. She was somewhat subdued, and a kind of sparring, although affectionate sparring, went on between them when she was with Lota. Lota was so definitively the authority on Brazil, and when Elizabeth spoke about Brazil, Lota took over and corrected her. At the garden Elizabeth was a quite different person—I found her very animated and funny then. After one outing, Elizabeth and I went back to the apartment and had drinks. Lota came in from work. I remember her being very testy. Lota said we shouldn't be drinking at this time of day. It was about five o'clock. Lota was rather domineering to both of us, as though she disapproved, as though we had been caught, because we came in and were already having a drink. I realized Lota ruled. Lota was very decisive. Elizabeth was very tentative. She suggested things. She didn't make statements. When Lota said something, that was it. Lota at that moment was a figure of some importance and we deferred to that, I with my questions about Brazil and Elizabeth naturally.

Lota went to the office and she had that kind of breadwinning image; her presence smacked of public importance of what she did. Elizabeth was at a loose end in the day. The first day Elizabeth and I went out I thought we would just visit the gardens, but she was clearly spending time. We went out about half past ten in the morning on both occasions and we stayed out for the day. I couldn't actually say that she seemed lonely, but she was only too delighted to be spending all that amount of time. It occurred to me that she had lots of free time and she was very glad to be filling it up and was having a great deal of fun in doing that. I had in the back of my mind, "Am I keeping her away from her desk?" I would think that Elizabeth would want to spend some part of the day at her desk. There was no sense of that.

The first evening I went around, I asked Lota a great deal about Brazil. Elizabeth tuned out because she was not at all interested in politics. Lota was explaining to me the relation of Rio to the rest of the country—why Rio was on such a different wavelength, rather like New York. I had a feeling that Elizabeth was not really interested in any of this kind of talk. It was theoretical and it was not about anything that was actual for her. She never ventured very much in these conversations. I was taking notes for a long piece, which I ended up not writing. I was learning a great deal on that trip. I talked to Lota quite a lot about the political situation at the time, which was very tense. It was one of these catastrophic weeks in which the cruzeira fell from about two hundred to the dollar to about twelve hundred to the dollar. That week was only the beginning of what became inevitable, the collapse of the Brazilian economy.

The whole question of whether Brasilia would "come off" was very much in the air then. Elizabeth was interested in that because it was such an unlikely business to set a capital city right in the backlands. We talked about the improbability of Brasilia. There was in fact no road. They just built airports and flew in materials for Brasilia. In the historical development of a city, first there needed to be a footpath, a donkey track, a road, then a railroad, then ultimately an airport. Building Brasilia was like reversing history. Lota was very dubious as to whether Brasilia could ever become more than a filing cabinet, as to whether it could ever become a human city. How were people going to root themselves or to feel anything for the city? It was just an abstraction.

I had a reporter's interest in Brazil, in the situation. Elizabeth appeared to have no interest in that. She talked about her life there, but always in particularities. In fact, she talked very little about Brazil. Naturally Lota was willing to generalize because that's the level on which she was operating and was deeply involved. In no sense did Elizabeth ignore Brazil, because she was taking in its sights and sounds. No wonder she delighted in "*Helena Morley.*" It was made for her.

Elizabeth and Lota didn't seem a couple to me. Theirs was an improbable relationship, Elizabeth looking almost for an opposite. The theoretical, rational mind of Lota and the intuitive and perceptive Elizabeth. Elizabeth perceived small kinks and details that Lota would just not notice, because her sweeping observation would override them. I wonder if the kinds of curious perceptions that Elizabeth was always registering were communicable to Lota?

✦ ✦ ✦

On 1 April 1964 the political turmoil that had been brewing for years in Brazil came to a head. The military and some governors (Lacerda among them) organized a coup against President Goulart. For forty-eight hours troops loyal to Goulart surrounded the Governor's Palace, where Lacerda had barricaded himself. Lota managed to gain passage to and from the palace. Lacerda also avoided Goulart's troops outside of Rio and had hidden for one night in Lota's house in Petrópolis.

MARY STEARNS MORSE— In the revolution in 1964, when Lacerda was disappearing all over the place, Lota was working in Rio. She said to me, "Morsey, I told Carlos that he could stay at my house if he wants to hide." There was nobody in Lota's house, and I was in my house down the road. [What happened was] very funny.

One night, about 9:30, I was reading, and I heard a car drive by. I said, "I've got to do something about that." I jumped into my Volkswagen and stopped on the way up the hill for Manuelzinho. [I told him to] come with me because somebody had gone up to Lota's house. Manuelzinho came out in shorts, a shirt, a straw hat, and a stick. I thought, "What protection's that? Well, anyway, somebody is coming up with me."

When we got to Lota's house, we saw a big flashlight going around and lights in the kitchen. So I said, "Come up with me, Manuelzinho." I wasn't scared at all. I don't know why. We walked in. I couldn't see who was in the kitchen because the light was so bright. Finally, Carlos looked out and said, "Morsey!! You're crazy!" I said, "Yes, I suppose I am. But what are you doing here, Carlos?" He said, "Lota said I could come up and spend the night." I said, "Certainly you can come up, but why don't you telephone to me, not give me a scare like this?"

Carlos had bodyguards. So I said, "Of course you can stay here. Now let me see if the guest rooms are ready." So I went into the two guest rooms, knowing perfectly well they weren't ready. I saw one bed with a machine gun in the center, so I went back and said to Carlos, "Excuse me. I'll give you the pillows. I'll give you the sheets. And what else do you want?" He said, "We'd like some whiskey." I said, "OK. I'll go down to my house, get some whiskey, bring it back to you, but for God's sake, you make up the beds because I don't want to see that machine gun." He said, "Look, we're here hiding. Don't tell anybody we're here." I said, "No, I won't tell anybody. You can trust me." So I brought up the whiskey and I said, "Good night. Good night. I have to go down and be with the children."

The next morning my gardener said, "Do you know who's next door at the florist? Carlos Lacerda's guard." Lacerda was crazy about flowers. And I said, "Oh, my God. He told me not to tell anybody. What kind of hiding is that?" Well, he only stayed one night.

✦   ✦   ✦

Bishop and Lota were pleased that the military coup had succeeded. Although some civil rights were suspended, at least the communists had been sent fleeing. Bishop was angry with politicians in the United States who failed to understand that political actions such as this one were important correctives in a society as desperate as Brazil's. David Weimer lived in Rio during the coup and observed Lacerda's political maneuverings before and after 1 April. According to Weimer, Bishop's approval of the coup was neither a conservative reaction nor atypical of Brazilians as a whole.

DAVID WEIMER—From Goulart's point of view, Lacerda might have been an unknown quantity. The military came to view him this way, too. He whipped up public sentiment against Goulart, accusing Goulart of all kinds of things and corruption of the government, which helped prepare the way for the military coup, although he was by no means partisan to the military. He was thoroughly a brilliant individual, smart as can be, a very canny politician, and very impulsive. I heard from Lota and a lot of people that Lacerda was very much an entrepreneur, promoting his own political career, but also he had a larger vision than merely that. He would go off on quirky things, like launching thugs against his opponents. In retrospect, I discovered that when he was governor, he hired or had [someone] hire bands of young thugs who would go around and beat up political opponents. Lacerda's newspaper would publish the most scandalous and outrageous things. He was kind of a yellow journalist, but much larger and more competent than that.

I talked to a lot of middle-class Brazilians who welcomed the military coup [of 1964] because Brazil really was moving toward a kind of anarchy at the time. There was a broad spectrum of Brazilian opinion that held [that the military revolution in 1964 was good because it freed Brazil from the communists. Elizabeth's believing this was] not an unreasonable position at the time and doesn't necessarily point to her social elitism. The politics had gotten out of hand. Also, the Brazilian military had had a long history of peaceful takeovers. They had done it several times in Brazilian history, and then, after a short period in power, they had relinquished their power and gone back to civilian rule. So no one expected the terrible results that occurred in fact after that. Also, the military didn't get highly repressive until they'd been in office for almost a year. Then they began to crack down.

✦ ✦ ✦

With this shift in power, Lacerda decided to leave Brazil for a while. If he stayed, he would only begin arguing with the new leaders. Bishop and Lota decided to travel as well, using the Chapelbrook Foundation travel fellowship that Bishop had received in October 1960. In May 1964 they traveled to Milan and Florence, then rented a car and drove to Venice, where they stayed in a hotel on the Grand Canal. Lota soon became anxious to see how events were proceeding in Brazil, so she departed from Milan on 1 June. Bishop went on to England. She was met at the airport by Kit Barker, whom she had not seen since Yaddo in 1951.

Bishop spent three days with Ilse and Kit Barker at their four-hundred-year-old cottage in Sussex, talking, walking, and touring a number of old churches in the area, one where Harold had prayed before the Battle of Hastings. The Barkers had always been among Bishop's favorite friends because of their lack of pretense. She found life with them a welcome reprieve after the turmoil in Brazil. Ilse Barker and Bishop had carried on a regular correspondence, often discussing books, and sometimes Ilse would ask for Bishop's opinions of her own work. During this visit, Barker was struck with how Bishop had changed since when they had first met.

ILSE BARKER— Elizabeth's stay in 1964 was a very happy one. She was in very good form. She didn't drink. She had been really at the bottom of the world in Yaddo in 1950 to 1951, but in 1964 was a person with a home she had left

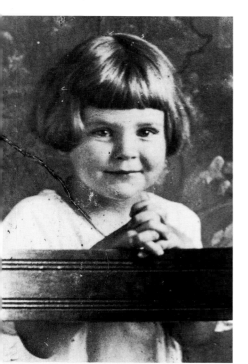

1. Elizabeth Bishop with her grandparents
William and Elizabeth Boomer, 1911
(courtesy of Phyllis Sutherland).
2. Elizabeth Bishop, 1911 (courtesy of
Phyllis Sutherland).
3. Elizabeth Bishop, circa 1915 (courtesy
of Phyllis Sutherland).

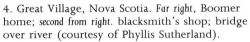

4

4. Great Village, Nova Scotia. *Far right*, Boomer home; *second from right*. blacksmith's shop; bridge over river (courtesy of Phyllis Sutherland).
5. Elizabeth Bishop and her mother, Gertrude Boomer Bishop, circa 1915 (courtesy of Phyllis Sutherland).
6. Elizabeth and William Boomer, Elizabeth Bishop's grandparents (courtesy of Phyllis Sutherland).

5

6

8

7. *Left*, Grace Boomer; a friend (Julia Cochrane) (courtesy of Special Collections, Vassar College Libraries).
8. George Hutchinson, Elizabeth Bishop's great-uncle (courtesy of Phyllis Sutherland).
9. Arthur and Mabel Boomer, with their children (courtesy of Phyllis Sutherland).

10

10. John W. Bishop, Sr.,
Elizabeth Bishop's grandfather
(courtesy of Kay Orr Sargent).
11. The Bishop family, circa
1911. *Second row, left,* Gertrude
Bishop; *second row, center,* Sarah
Bishop; *second row, second from
right,* John W. Bishop, Sr.; *back
row, left,* William Bishop; *back
row, second from left,* Florence
Bishop; *back row, second from
right,* John W. Bishop, Jr.
(courtesy of Kay Orr Sargent).
12. Elizabeth and William
Boomer with Grace Boomer
in front of 55 Cambridge
Street, Revere, Massachusetts,
home of Maud and George
Shepherdson (courtesy of
Special Collections, Vassar
College Libraries).

12

13. *Second row, right,* Elizabeth Bishop at Camp Chequesset, Wellfleet, Massachusetts, 1925 (courtesy of Phyllis Sutherland).
14. *Third row, center,* Elizabeth Bishop, grade 10 (1927), Walnut Hill School (courtesy of Archives, Walnut Hill School).

15. Graduating class of 1930, Walnut Hill School. *Front row, far left*, Margaret Mann; *front row, second from right*, Elizabeth Bishop; *front row, far right*, Joan Collingwood; *second row. fourth from left*, Rhoda Wheeler; *second row, fifth from right*, Shirley Clark; *second row, far right*, Barbara Chesney (courtesy of Archives, Walnut Hill School).

16. Elizabeth Bishop, senior photograph (1930), Walnut Hill School (courtesy of Archives, Walnut Hill School).

17   18

Frani Blough, senior photograph for the 1933 *Vassarion*, Vassar College
(courtesy of Special Collections, Vassar College Libraries).
Mary McCarthy, senior photograph for the 1933 *Vassarion*, Vassar College
(courtesy of Special Collections, Vassar College Libraries).
Center, wearing beard, Elizabeth Bishop during her sophomore year at
Vassar College (1931-32), playing Afanassij in *Uncle's Been Dreaming* by Karl
Vollmoeller, first Hall play. *Far right, standing in profile*, Mary McCarthy (1933
Vassarion, courtesy of Special Collections, Vassar College Libraries).

20

21

22

23

Helen Drusilla Lockwood, associate
professor of English, Vassar College, 1936
(photo by Edmund Wolven, Helen D.
Lockwood Papers, courtesy of Special Collections, Vassar College Libraries).

Rose Jeffries Peebles, professor of English,
Vassar College (1934 Vassarion, courtesy of
Special Collections, Vassar College Libraries).

Staff of the Vassar Miscellany News, 1933
Vassarion. Second row, left, Elizabeth Bishop; front
row, center, Eunice Clark, editor-in-chief (courtesy
of Special Collections, Vassar College Libraries).

The Vassarion editorial and business boards.
Second row, center, Elizabeth Bishop, editor-in-chief;
front row, right, Margaret Miller (1934 Vassarion,
courtesy of Special Collections, Vassar College
Libraries).

"The Higher Types" in the Vassar Review,
April 1934. Clockwise from upper left: Mary E.
St. John, editor, the Vassar Miscellany News; Mary
Crapo, president of the students' association;
Virginia Wylie, chief justice; Elizabeth Bishop,
editor, Vassarion (drawing by Anne Cleveland,
courtesy of Special Collections, Vassar College
Libraries).

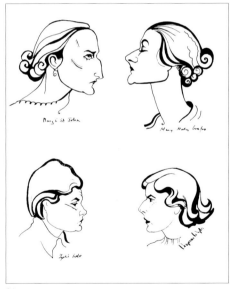

24

25. Marianne Moore, in her
Brooklyn apartment, circa 193
(photo by Charlotte and Arthu
Steiner, the Marianne Moore
Papers, courtesy of the Rosenb
Museum and Library).
26. Margaret Miller, senior
photograph for the 1934 *Vassar*
(courtesy of Special Collection:
Vassar College Libraries).
27. Elizabeth Bishop, senior
photograph for the 1934 *Vassar*
(courtesy of Special Collection:
Vassar College Libraries).

28. Louise Crane and Elizabeth Bishop, New York City, circa 1937 (courtesy of Special Collections, Vassar College Libraries).
29. Elizabeth Bishop, photograph sent to Donald Stanford during her senior year (1933-34) at Vassar College (courtesy of the Donald Stanford Papers, Department of Special Collections, Stanford University Libraries).
30. Robert H. Seaver, 1933 (courtesy of Elizabeth S. Helfman).

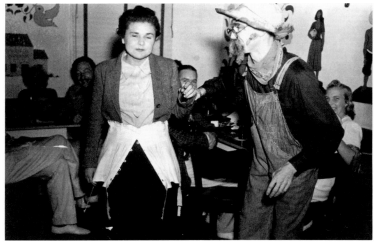

31. Elizabeth Bishop and Louise
Crane, Key West, 1940s. *Left
background*, Maud Shepherdson
(courtesy of Phyllis Sutherland).
32. Louise Crane and Elizabeth
Bishop, Florida, 1940s (courtesy of Charles and Charlotte
Russell).

33. Painting of 624 White Street, Key West, home of Elizabeth Bishop and Louise Crane, by Gregorio Valdes (courtesy of Charles and Charlotte Russell).

34. 624 White Street, Key West, 1993 (courtesy of Beverly Coyle).

35. *Left to right*, Charlotte Russell, Louise Crane, Elizabeth Bishop, Charles Russell, 624 White Street, Key West, 1940s (courtesy of Charles and Charlotte Russell).

36. *Second from left*, George Shepherdson; Louise Crane; Elizabeth Bishop; *second from right*, Maud Shepherdson, in Key West, 1940s (courtesy of Phyllis Sutherland).

35

36

38

39

_oren MacIver and Lloyd Frankenberg (photo by Mark Shaw, courtesy of
ial Collections, Vassar College Libraries).

_eft, Martha Watson (Sauer); Betty Morena (Bruce). Key West, circa 1940
_rtesy of Betty Bruce).

_econd from left, Elizabeth Bishop; third and fourth from left, Lloyd Frankenberg and
_n MacIver; far right, Mrs. Almyda. Key West, 1940s (courtesy of Chester Page).

40

40. Betty Bruce and Steve Boyden, Key West, circa 198 (courtesy of Betty Bruce).
41. Elizabeth Bishop sitting o the steps of the Square Roof, Key West, 1940 (photo by a courtesy of James Laughlin).
42. *Left to right*, Louise Bogan, William Carlos Williams, Jea Garrigue, Lloyd Frankenberg, Elizabeth Bishop, Joseph Summers, Robert Lowell (*in profile*), Richard Wilbur (*in shadow*) at the Bard College Poetry Conference, Novembe 1948 (courtesy of Joseph and U. T. Summers).

42

41

43. *Standing,* Marjorie Stevens; Pauline Hemingway. Key West, 1940s (courtesy of Special Collections, Vassar College Libraries).

43

44. May Swenson, Beauford Delaney, Elizabeth Bishop at Yaddo, fall 1950 (courtesy of Phyllis Sutherland).
45. Lota de Macedo Soares, approximately forty years old (courtesy of Special Collections, Vassar College Libraries).
46. Elizabeth Bishop, Brazil, circa 1952 (courtesy of Joseph and U. T. Summers).

46

48

. View of dining area, home
Lota de Macedo Soares,
zenda Samambaia, Petrópolis,
azil (courtesy of Special
llections, Vassar College
oraries).
. View from front of home of
ta de Macedo Soares, Fazenda
nambaia, Petrópolis, Brazil
ourtesy of Special Collections,
ssar College Libraries).
. Interior view of Elizabeth
shop's study, Fazenda
nambaia, Petrópolis, Brazil
ourtesy of Joseph and U. T.
mmers).

50. Elizabeth Bishop and Robert Lowell
on the balcony of the apartment of Lota
de Macedo Soares in Rio de Janeiro, July
1962 (courtesy of Phyllis Sutherland).
51. Elizabeth Bishop and Robert Lowell
at the Copacabana Beach, Rio de Janeiro,
July 1962 (courtesy of Special Collections, Vassar College Libraries).

52

Front row, *left to right*, Elizabeth Bishop,
fe Humphries, Mrs. Humphries,
nry Reed; *second row*: Robert Heilman,
rothee Bowie. Camano Island,
shington, June 1966 (photo by Ruth
ilman, courtesy of Robert Heilman
ers, University of Washington
raries).

Casa Mariana, Elizabeth Bishop's
ise in Ouro Prêto, as seen from Lilli
újo's house across the street (courtesy
pecial Collections, Vassar College
raries).

Elizabeth Bishop, Wheaton Galen-
, Harold Leeds, Lota de Macedo
res. New York City, November or
ember 1962 (courtesy of Special
lections, Vassar College Library).

53

55

55. Elizabeth Bishop at Louise Crane's house, Woods Hole, Massachusetts, 1974 (photo by Alice Methfessel, courtesy of Chester Page).

56

56. Elizabeth Bishop and Ivar Ivask in Norman, Oklahoma, for the awarding of the Books Abroad/Neustadt International Prize, April 1966 (photo by Astrid Ivask, courtesy of Special Collections, Vassar College Libraries).

57. Left to right: Elizabeth Bishop, Victoria Kent (friend of Louise Crane), Louise Crane. Louise Crane's house, Woods Hole, Massachusetts, 1974 (courtesy of Chester Page).

58

57

58. Richard Wilbur, Elizabeth Bishop, Frank Bidart (seen from rear), John Malcolm Brinnin, Helen Vendler. Duxbury, Massachusetts, 1977 (courtesy of Helen Vendler).
59. Elizabeth Bishop with Miriam Sutherland (daughter of Ernest and Phyllis Sutherland) in Nova Scotia, 1970s (courtesy of Phyllis Sutherland).
60. Left to right, Ilse Barker, Alice Methfessel, Elizabeth Bishop, Kit Barker. North Haven, Maine, 1978 (courtesy of Ilse Barker).

61. Margaret Miller and U. T.
Summers at Elizabeth Bishop Day
celebration, Vassar College, May 1982
(photo by Dixie Sheridan, courtesy of
Special Collections, Vassar College
Libraries).
62. Left, James Merrill; David Kalstone.
Elizabeth Bishop Day celebration,
Vassar College, May 1982. Merrill is
speaking with the author Nancy
Milford (photo by Dixie Sheridan,
courtesy of Special Collections, Vassar
College Libraries).

61

62

to travel, with friends. She was relaxed and enjoying herself. She seemed younger than when we had met at Yaddo and was very talkative. She brought us a set of wonderful Sienese flags from Italy, which were a joy to us for years.

My son Thomas was not yet two, and Elizabeth and I went for lots of walks with Thomas in his pushchair. She had this wonderful feeling for babies and small children. Everything to do with them fascinated her, and she was undemonstratively good with them, which was marvelous, because children like that. They don't like to be picked up by a stranger but want everybody's attention, which she loved to give. One day, as we were sitting on the terrace, she asked me, "How far does your land go?" And like a total idiot, I said, "Oh, as far as you can see." She picked me up on that and wrote a poem for Thomas around my remark.

When she was with us, Elizabeth always felt safe because we didn't know any of the people she knew and who were interested in her. Gossip didn't mean anything to us. Her being a famous poet didn't come into our relationship because we were right outside the American poetry scene. She wrote us, for example, that she'd just won the Pulitzer Prize. We hadn't known, and these honors did, I'm afraid, somewhat wash over us. We never thought of her as the great American poet. She was a friend who wrote beautiful poems. In her many letters she would write about books she'd read, and I would write to her about books I'd read. Elizabeth's reading my work and her criticizing it or encouraging it was a great help to me. I admired her judgment, of course, and it was stimulating when we shared an enthusiasm. I dedicated my third novel to her, and her remarks were always helpful.

◆   ◆   ◆

Bishop had also arranged to meet the poet Anne Stevenson during this trip to England. Stevenson was writing the first book-length study of Bishop's work, for Twayne Publishers. Stevenson and Bishop had corresponded since her first inquiry in 1962, and Bishop had been uncharacteristically forthcoming in providing biographical material about her childhood. She was flattered to be written about.

ANNE STEVENSON— In 1960–61 I was a graduate student at the University of Michigan, studying with Donald Hall. I remember having a huge conversation about Elizabeth Bishop with Don, me arguing that Bishop was a far better poet than Lowell because Bishop noticed everything about her, while Lowell only noticed himself. In those days, such a point of view was heresy. Anyway, one day soon afterward Don walked into my flat, dumped a sack full of books on the table, and virtually ordered me to write the Twayne series book on Elizabeth Bishop.

I had a terrible time finding anything in the library about her. Sometime during the following year, when I was teaching at the Cambridge School of Weston, I went to see Lowell at Harvard. All he would talk about was Elizabeth's insane mother. So I wrote to Marianne Moore, making it clear that I wouldn't be writing a gossipy book or a biography. Marianne Moore wrote back a most wonderful letter—completely typical, ideas all over the place—encouraging me to write tactfully to Elizabeth in Brazil, which I did. During the year 1962–63, Elizabeth and I wrote to each other every other week or so. Those were the letters that were sold, without my knowing it, to Washington University in St. Louis.

I didn't meet Elizabeth until she came to England in 1964, when I was living with my then-husband Mark Elvin in Cambridge, England. I first went to see Elizabeth in a dowdy, dark little hotel called the Pastoria somewhere in London. I'd heard she was a drinker, so I suggested we meet in the bar. How surprised I was when she declared that though she herself didn't drink, she liked to see other people drink. So she bought me a whiskey. I think it might have been easier had she bought one for herself. We were both nervous, meeting after all those letters; for me Elizabeth was a sort of god. The drink relaxed me, but she remained tense. Later she came to visit us in Cambridge, and Mark and I put her straight into a punt. She absolutely loved that. Punting broke the ice.

At that time my daughter Caroline was about ten, and I was a bit fearful of showing Elizabeth about Cambridge with a child in tow. So I gave Caroline money to go swimming in the local pool, telling her to meet us later. Caroline, realizing she was being got out of the way, was furious, and Elizabeth knew it. She immediately suggested that Caroline come with us, adding that she loved children. Of course Caroline immediately began to show off and rather dominated the rest of the day. In the evening Caroline told Elizabeth Bishop all sorts of stories, true and untrue. I was touched by how much Elizabeth Bishop enjoyed her. Elizabeth did love children, and I think she was sorry she never had any. She was a little wistful about this.

We put Elizabeth up in a room at the top of the narrow terrace house we shared with our landlord. I remember the room was covered with green ivy wallpaper. That wallpaper, apparently, was very like the wallpaper in the room Elizabeth had slept in when she visited her grandmother in Nova Scotia. In the morning, when I went up with a cup of tea, I found Elizabeth in a terrible state. The wallpaper had given her nightmares and she had had a bad attack of asthma. Would I mind going around to the chemist [pharmacist] to see if I could find her a hypodermic for her injection? Though she looked desperately ill, she laughed heartily when I told her the landlord's dog had died six months ago. The dead hair must have done it! I was scared to death. I remember sprinting off to Boots and banging on the door at nine in the morning to buy a hypodermic for Elizabeth Bishop. It seemed to do the trick, for she got up for breakfast with us, and I later put her on the train for London.

Always shy and, in a dignified way, modest, Elizabeth was pleased that I took so much interest in her poetry, not her life. I still think that it's indecent to pry into people's private lives, and Elizabeth did, too. Elizabeth never told me anything she didn't want to talk about, and I asked no questions about personal matters. She opened up freely, though, when she spoke of her childhood. Childhood, she believed, was the most important part of every poet's life. Thinking about it later, I wonder if childhood in Nova Scotia didn't hold her together when later she was desperately astray. For me, the poems and stories she set in Nova Scotia are her best. Marvelous. As I began to know her, I realized how much her life had been undermined by misfortune. Her father died when she was a baby. Her mother was insane. During her formative years she was brought up as a single child by an aunt who never (one gathers) understood her. She was tragically isolated. If anyone had a right to a psychodrama, she did, and yet, instead, she focused simply on the way things looked. My image of her is of the sandpiper (from her poem "The Sandpiper") . . . the world was a mist, and then suddenly it was clear again. Elizabeth saved herself by keeping her eyes on grains of quartz and amethyst while the world pounded around her. She preferred the iceberg to the ship every time. No wonder we didn't talk about personal matters . . . not that they weren't there, for they were, all too much. They gave depth to a poetry that never mentioned them because Elizabeth's eyes were fixed, always, on the beautiful shell (the physical world) she perceived to exist independently of herself. Art, for her, was crystalline, a possibility for purity. That's why she didn't sully it with excretions from her own life.

✦　✦　✦

Bishop returned to London from her visit with Anne Stevenson and saw a number of writers at parties—Richard Wilbur, Donald Hall, Robert Bly, Stephen Spender, and several other British poets. Larkin, her favorite, avoided London. Bishop liked Cleanth Brooks, the American cultural attaché, and his southern charm. She enjoyed speaking English again and having witticisms and jokes easily understood. Bishop visited museums and traveled to Darwin's home outside London. She had become an ardent fan of Darwin; she particularly admired his powers of minute observation and comprehensive, systematic thought. For her, Darwin was the lyric and epic poet of science. The weather during the final weeks of Bishop's stay turned to rain and cold (Ascot was canceled), and instead of traveling to Scotland, she left England in mid-July rather than waiting until August. Bishop missed Lota and the Brazilian warmth, and, she had to admit to herself, wondered what had happened in Rio since the revolution.

There was initially good news for Bishop on her return to Rio. In August, Bishop was named the 1964 Fellow of the Academy of American Poets and received an award of five thousand dollars. In November, Randall Jarrell read her poems at the Guggenheim Museum to honor her membership. Robert Lowell introduced Jarrell, saying that Bishop was the best poet of their generation. Flamengo Park had become very popular—a bandstand, dance floor, and boat basin had opened the previous spring—and people recognized Lota on the street and openly thanked her for her work. In January 1965 she was written about in Time magazine.

With this growing public recognition, Lota was showing the signs of strain. In September 1964 she began taking sleeping pills because the park was always on her mind. She had a fight with Lacerda in December and went on strike in January 1965 over his failure to authorize the funds for a children's library and a restaurant in the park. Bishop and Lota became critical of Lacerda. They had grown tired of the political flurry he created over every issue and began to view him as more a political opportunist than a serious political candidate. Ashley Brown, a professor at the University of South Carolina, was a Fulbright scholar in Rio during these months. He attended openings at Flamengo Park, helped Bishop arrange her new book of poems, Questions of Travel, which was published in the fall of 1965, and witnessed Bishop and Lota's change of attitude toward Lacerda.

ASHLEY BROWN— I went [to Brazil on a Fulbright lectureship] early in June of 1964. Flannery O'Connor, who was a close friend, said [that although she and Elizabeth] had never met, they had once spoken over the telephone and exchanged letters, [and that I should] meet her. I had a note of introduction from Flannery and called Elizabeth toward the end of August. She invited me to visit the following night. Elizabeth admired Flannery O'Connor tremendously and wanted to ask a few questions about her. [She wondered if] Flannery really was [the pious] Catholic she seemed to be. I said she was.

Elizabeth was fascinated by someone who could be so totally committed to a religious idea as Flannery was. We discussed Randall Jarrell, Allen Tate, Robert Lowell, and W. H. Auden. I had met Auden a few times, and Elizabeth was slightly acquainted with him.

Elizabeth became very friendly immediately. I suppose she was used to people like myself, a loquacious Southerner. She liked so many different things in Brazil that I did too, such as popular music. Elizabeth sort of liked bossa nova, but she preferred the old-fashioned thing, the samba. We occasionally made wonderful visits to nightclubs in an old-fashioned quarter in downtown Rio. Elizabeth just loved it. These places were completely casual [clubs where] everybody talked to everybody else and listened to the music. Elizabeth had a very real feeling for Brazilian popular culture. [In 1965] Rio was celebrating its four-hundredth anniversary. The carnival was spectacular. Elizabeth, Lota, and I had tickets for the stands they had downtown along the main route.

There's something sort of anarchistic, something rather bizarre and surrealistic, about life in Brazil [that appealed to Elizabeth]. There is a kind of absolute unexpectedness of sights and sounds and smells that is very difficult to describe. Along Copacabana, near the end where Elizabeth used to live, there was a rather sophisticated, Europeanized milieu with diplomatic people. [But you would also run into] people from the northeast of Brazil with their Macumba religion down at the waterfront sending flowers out to sea. Once a week a knife grinder would come around and station himself below Elizabeth and Lota's penthouse. He had this wheel that made whining noises, and he had this great virtuoso feat of being able to play the Brazilian national anthem, an extremely complicated piece of music. Then the maids would take their knives down to be sharpened. Elizabeth found this terribly amusing.

Lota was very much involved with the park during the time I was there and frequently took me to visit it. The park was pretty barren when I first went there. I can remember when they planted the trees. Sometimes when some project would be finished, like a children's pool, there was an opening ceremony. I attended a couple of those. There were a lot of children at the opening of the sailing pond for model boats. Lota got a tremendous kick out of that. She loved children. The park was an incredibly popular thing. People came from all over Rio on a Sunday.

Lota was interested in every last phase of the park, the very angle at which a bridge might go over a road, things like that. She was a perfectionist. Her job usually took up her days. Lota did take on a certain fame. She was in the newspapers from time to time. Elizabeth rather admired all of this, just as though Lota had finally found the proper outlet for all her great talent. At the same time, Lota got terribly bound up with it. Elizabeth said that Lota was overly concerned about this thing. I would be having lunch with Elizabeth at the penthouse, and Lota would be off meeting with officials and so on. Lota was conferring constantly with people like engineers and landscape gardeners. [Sometimes Elizabeth and I] stayed up too late talking, and Lota would berate me, [saying she had] to get up rather early.

[I heard about Elizabeth's drinking] from Lota, although she wasn't the only one [who mentioned it to me]. Every time I went around [to their apartment], there was bourbon for me. Most of the time Elizabeth didn't drink anything at all. Once or twice she had maybe a little bit, and Lota once told me quite sternly that Elizabeth didn't drink very well and not to tempt her. Lota said that Elizabeth simply shouldn't drink at all because of what it led to. Once, relatively late during my year, I arrived for dinner, having been invited, and Elizabeth was pretty well out. She was being looked after, and Lota said she was sorry but that there would be no dinner. Elizabeth had simply been on a little bout that day.

Lota said on a number of occasions that she felt Elizabeth didn't produce enough poetry. What Lota had in mind was certain Brazilian poets who turn out things all over the place. Brazilians have a great deal of respect for literary figures. The Pulitzer Prize was in the newspapers and at one time or another I heard quite a few Brazilians mention Elizabeth; they had not even met her. I said to Lota that she was looking at it in the wrong way. Some people turn out poetry left and right. Elizabeth was the same sort of poet that T. S. Eliot was— when she did something, she did it well, then the problem was solved and she went on to do something else. Everything that she wrote was very beautifully done. Elizabeth was an endlessly meticulous sort of person about her writing. Lota could hardly expect Elizabeth to go into high production. Lota did have this incredible respect for Elizabeth as a writer and somehow felt that Elizabeth should be asserting herself a bit more.

I had a little bit to do with *Questions of Travel*. In the late fall of 1964 Elizabeth was getting the book together. She had been in correspondence with Robert Giroux and [thought that she was not producing] a very large book. I said the size had nothing to do with it really. After all, she had only had two books before, and they came about ten years apart, and now it was about time to have another. Her second book was composed by putting the first one together with it, and I suddenly had an idea which I got from Lowell's *Life Studies*, which was divided into two parts and had a prose memoir in the middle. My suggestion was that Elizabeth take that wonderful story "In the Village," which quite a few people admired and which was not very well known outside *The New Yorker*, and put it in the middle, have the Brazilian things first, and then have other poems, many of which are set in Nova Scotia, follow the story. That would give her another 50 percent in pages. When Lowell moved from the hardcover to the paperback, he added "For the Union Dead." I suggested that Elizabeth move "Arrival at Santos," which comes near the end of *A Cold Spring*, [to be an] introduction to the Brazilian poems. She immediately took up the idea. I should have suggested that she put "The Shampoo" with the Brazilian poems.

There were times when Lota wondered whether the park was ever going to be completed the way she wanted it. I heard Lota getting rather discouraged at times about things. The planning was so involved and vast and intricate. I did [get a sense of the project becoming difficult for Lota in 1965]. The park meant so much to her, and all of a sudden things were going to pieces.

I met Lacerda several times with Lota. Essentially, Lota and Elizabeth favored the revolution [of 1964]; Lacerda did, although some people would say that Lacerda was just following the drift. He was a maverick. On the one hand, Lacerda didn't represent the military people, as such; on the other, he had set himself against the Goulart regime. Of course, he had presidential ambitions. Actually, Castelo Branco [the new president] was a comparatively mild and benign sort of military figure. He was not taken very seriously by a lot of people. Brazilian friends used to say to me, "You have your White House, but we have our Castelo Branco!" It was difficult to tell from one day to the next whether Lacerda was going to run against Castelo Branco. He was absolutely inconsistent at this point. Lacerda's political power really didn't last very long. Lota and Elizabeth began to get very disillusioned about him in a number of ways. They said quite different things about him by June 1965. The atmosphere he created around him was rather hysterical, too. He began to present himself more as an opportunist than anything else. Elizabeth began to hint at it. He was no longer the brilliant, brave young man who was going to do all of this for Brazil.

✦   ✦   ✦

The atmosphere of hysteria mounted. In January 1965 Bishop told friends that Lota came home each night exhausted and pale. She was also arguing with and alienating her colleagues, some of whom called Bishop to complain. There was talk of Lacerda resigning his governorship and running for president in the fall and Lota becoming a member of his cabinet. By February, as Lacerda's decision to run became imminent, Bishop despaired that Lota would ever escape from politics and that they would return to their way of life before Flamengo Park. "In the end, Elizabeth was furious that Lota thought about the park from day to night and that Lota would talk only about the park. That was the beginning of the end of their relationship."[5]

If Lacerda were not the governor, Lota wondered, what would happen to Flamengo Park? Lota and Lacerda came up with a solution that spring: Lacerda decided to create for the park an independently funded foundation that would be beyond political tampering. Developing the plan for this foundation took place over the summer of 1965, and the details were settled in the fall. The poet Mark Strand arrived in Rio as a Fulbright scholar that summer and was witness to some of Lota's fear about the future of her project.

MARK STRAND— [When I went to Rio] in July 1965 as a Fulbright lecturer for the University of Brazil, I knew that Elizabeth Bishop lived there. I had for years been an admirer of her poetry. I was told by Howard Moss, who was my editor and her editor at The New Yorker, that she loved to see Americans when they came through, so I felt no compunction about calling her. We made a date to see each other, for tea at her apartment in Leme, the apartment from whose balcony she wrote "The Burglar of Babylon."

Elizabeth and I had the kind of semiliterary talk that people in the provinces have. What's going on? Do you know so-and-so? Have you read so-and-so's latest book? The Partisan Review was on the table, and the Hudson Review, and Encounter. "Do you subscribe to these magazines?" I asked her. "Yes, I have to. I'm so far away. I subscribe to everything." She asked me, did I know Lowell. I said no. Did I like his work? I liked his work. "Good," she said. I left Elizabeth a copy of my first book, Sleeping with One Eye Open, and she was in every respect gracious and indulgent. There was no reason for a woman of her accomplishment, fame, and I'm sure, busyness, to spend so much time with me.

Elizabeth and I did go out a couple times to meet some poets. She knew a lot of people—Vinicius de Moraes, Cecilia Meireles, Carlos Drummond—and had met a lot of these people through Lota. The people I was meeting through Elizabeth and Lota had more to do with Lota's political life in the park. Elizabeth was isolated and there was not a literary circle for her. Elizabeth was very timid about her Portuguese, although she knew it perfectly. [When I] visited her in Ouro Prêto, we went to a bar where they served coffee and Elizabeth said, "Why don't you do the ordering?" She thought I pronounced Portuguese better. She was always embarrassed by her pronunciation of the language. Anyway, it established, I think, that whenever we were out in public in Brazil, I would do the ordering, the talking, whether it was to the taxi driver, the bartender, the waiter—even though my accent left a lot to be desired.

[Our discussions of literature] were all about preferences. I always thought [that this was so] because I wasn't very literary. Well, then I thought, she's not very literary either. She had the same sort of reticence about literature that I did. We were perfectly free and willing to talk about other sorts of things, like art (Brazilian primitive painters, Loren MacIver's paintings, that sort of thing), which she felt much more at home in discussing, but we rarely talked about literature. It was too touchy. She had to be absolutely sure you adored her work, as Robert Lowell did. She knew I did, but my adoration didn't mean that much to her. I was young. It meant a lot to her that Howard Moss liked her work and bought it. That's the kind of opinion that meant a great deal to her. Once in a while Elizabeth showed me a poem in process, [such as] "Under the Window," about the drinking well in Ouro Prêto. Elizabeth worked so slowly that any discussion of a poem [of hers] would seem frivolous. What you were bound to discuss had already been discussed by her to herself fifty times. It seemed to me she could anticipate anything that I might ask.

At dinners there was a lot of discussion [about the park]. There was terrible fear [from Lota and Elizabeth that Lacerda's successors] were ruining her park. It seemed there wasn't money, there wasn't interest, and it was going to be an eyesore along the water. The park wasn't finished, by any means, either. That was part of the problem. There was a lot going on at Lota's park, but there was general fear and horror because things were not being completed. They had finally gotten the lights up, very late, and I'm not sure that they were the right ones. [All of this] depressed Lota. She was one to take things very hard. She was incredibly passionate. You had a sense of Elizabeth when she was with Lota as a very delicate creature.

✦ ✦ ✦

Events did not work out as Lota and Lacerda had planned. Lacerda's candidate to replace him as governor in the fall of 1965 was defeated. Also, in a maneuver typical of the wiles of Brazilian politics, a bill was passed that disqualified Lacerda, as a former governor, from running for president. Within a year, Lacerda's replacement had reorganized the administrative functions so that the director of Flamengo Park would be his appointee.

According to Magu Leão, by October 1965 it was clear that the foundation that would have protected Lota's position was going to be abolished. As these events occurred, Lota became more animated and, according to some, even more difficult to work with. She alienated the engineer with whom she worked, and in October 1965 she had a falling-out with Roberto Burle Marx. Burle Marx wrote an article for a newspaper in which he denounced her management of the project. He recollects his disagreement with Lota.

ROBERTO BURLE MARX— I [came to know] Lota quite well in 1935 [when] we were at the university. She and Rosalina were studying painting with Portinari. Lota had enormous interest in cultural life. It was very much due to Lota that I did the garden [in Flamengo Park]. Serges Bernardes, a very talented architect, also worked in that park. [When] Carlos Lacerda told her that he wanted to create that big garden, she told him [she would oversee the project] only if I could do it. [Through Lota] I knew Elizabeth Bishop, but I never had any intimacy with Elizabeth Bishop.

[Lacerda asked Lota to take over this big project] because she had very beautiful general culture; Lacerda was a friend and had worked with her father, a newspaperman. Lacerda knew Lota had the general understanding to link art with city planning for the purpose of creating a park in which the cultural qualities would be accentuated. The planning was very complicated, but the whole time Lota and I had a very beautiful friendship. We spoke about all the problems together. Lota thought that the garden and park ought to have cultural qualities. We ought to have places to educate people, little theaters for music, and playgrounds. The idea was to create not a passive park only to be seen, but [one in which] people could play, could do sport and music. [There would be] a beach for people and a theater for children. This intention was unusual because most of the parks [in Brazil] were very much in the spirit of the parks of the nineteenth century; the influence was very strong from Europe or from the United States, in a certain sense. Sport was something that didn't belong sufficiently to those parks. Even the plants that [I chose for the gardens] were plants that belong to the existing landscape [and were native Brazilian flora].

When Lota got power, she began to be a little authoritarian. I had a misunderstanding with Lota due to an associate who told her that he did everything in all the gardens. [This person said that] I was only a figurehead, only a decorative man, and Lota believed him. Lota began to make decisions that I didn't like. Lota imposed her decisions. [I didn't like the design for] illumination, but Lota imposed [her decision]. Lota didn't digest things in a deep way. And I wrote a very strong article against her [in which I did say she was not suited to direct the project]. In a moment that you are furious, sometimes you say much more than you [truly] think, [particularly after] time has passed and you begin to analyze what you think. [Eventually] Lota and I came together, but I lost the intimacy that I had had with her. But I want to underline that Lota was very important for that moment, and she did her best. I had certain difficult moments, but Lota had marvelous culture, and she had a general knowledge of the problems that [one needed to overcome] to create that park.

✦ ✦ ✦

During this political fray, Bishop escaped for vacations to the town of Ouro Prêto. Five years earlier, Lota's close friend Lilli Araújo had purchased an old house in this beautiful eighteenth-century mining town, located two hundred miles north of Rio. Araújo turned the house into a small hotel, Chico Rei, and Bishop and Lota visited her there when she first opened. Araújo witnessed the deterioration of Lota and Bishop's relationship, as drink undermined Bishop and the park project undermined Lota. She remembers Lota visiting her in Ouro Prêto to be free from Bishop, and their fighting by telephone.

Bishop traveled to Ouro Prêto five times in 1965, although each time she felt guilty about leaving Lota alone in Rio with the turmoil of her job. In October, after Bishop remained at Ouro Prêto two weeks longer than she had planned, Lota came to take her back to Rio. Lota had become nervous about Bishop's growing emotional distance. By the end of the year, Bishop had purchased her own house in Ouro Prêto, one of the oldest in the town and in need of much repair. The house needed a new roof, rebuilt walls, a coat of paint, and, at Bishop's insistence, a septic system. There was a legend about the place that an earlier owner had hidden gold in the walls, so the foundation had a number of holes where another owner had been "prospecting." After much pleading from Lota, Lilli Araújo agreed to oversee its restoration. Ashley Brown traveled with Bishop to Ouro Prêto in January and May that year, and to Bahia in July. He recollects the appeal this beautiful town in the mountains had for her.

ASHLEY BROWN— Elizabeth and I took a number of trips into Brazil. We stayed in Ouro Prêto (once for two or three weeks) and had a really wonderful trip to Salvador, Bahia, in July 1965. Elizabeth was always seeing things that I didn't immediately see. She was very farsighted, in fact. I remember once we were in the little penthouse she and Lota had in Rio. I said there was a freighter crossing the bay, and Elizabeth immediately described everything that was on the deck.

Elizabeth had been going [to Ouro Prêto] for quite a long time before I met her. [In January 1965] we spent a couple of weeks there. We stayed at Lilli's little inn called the Chico Rey. Lilli had only four or five bedrooms—it's the most charming inn I ever stayed in—and a fairly good restaurant. We flew up there and had a car with a driver who used to come around in the morning. A couple of times we would take overnight trips from there and stay in primitive hotels. We took along loads of books to read, and of course Elizabeth had a couple of friends in Ouro Prêto.

Elizabeth and I would start off in the morning, maybe after breakfast, in the car and go to some little village where the road was like the bottom of a dry creekbed to look into some old church if we could get into it. We both had eclectic tastes. Elizabeth was extremely knowledgeable about so many things, like folk art, [and she was a good traveling companion because of her] incredible observation of everything, and a sort of humorous construction that she could put on anything. Ouro Prêto has all these churches, and Elizabeth knew every detail about them. She would easily strike up a conversation with very simple people. Elizabeth could move [between] different social levels with a certain amount of ease. She could move among poor people, terribly poor people, without any problem at all.

Elizabeth was a bit extravagant [in her praise of the young artist Jair Afonso Inacio, whom we met working in one church]. She tended to go to extremes about things. Jair was a mulatto and came from Ouro Prêto. He was still very young, [perhaps only twelve years old]. He evidently had a talent for artistic things and had been encouraged and worked with people in charge of what they call the *Patrimonio*, something like our National Trust. Elizabeth and Lota knew several people who were connected with the *Patrimonio*, repainting, for example, those wonderful eighteenth-century interiors of wood. That seemed to be the kind of thing Jair was meant for.

I had the idea that Elizabeth's plan [to purchase a house in Ouro Prêto] was already in her mind [when she and Lota were there in early 1964]. She was looking around. Ouro Prêto was certainly a place where she could get away from the metropolitan environment. I had a sense that she was beginning to lose interest in the Petrópolis house. Once something had been finished, maybe it was time to do something else.

In July 1965 Elizabeth and I flew to Bahia for about a week. One day in Rio I was walking along the Avenida Copacabana and a young man called out to me in English. He turned out to have been a recent student in South Carolina. He went along on this trip with us. We were staying at what at that time was the best hotel in Bahia. Some of the people in the hotel began to be rather curious about us. Elizabeth became very naughty about this. She told some of these people that the student was her son, and other people that he was my son—although he was a bit old for that—and she told other people that she and I were sister and brother.

Lota may have encouraged Bishop to purchase her house in Ouro Prêto in part to keep her in Brazil, for throughout 1965 Bishop considered traveling on her own in the States. Bishop had been approached in the fall of 1964 by the University of Washington in Seattle to fill the Roethke Poetry Chair for the January through June term of 1966. Lota opposed Bishop's accepting the offer, and Bishop herself doubted that she was suited to teaching. However, when she spoke with friends, Bishop offered a number of reasons for accepting the offer: she needed money to restore the house in Ouro Prêto, she had never visited the Northwest, and Lota was so preoccupied that she would hardly be missed. Beneath these reasons there was a single, basic attitude: "Although she was very frightened because she didn't think that she could teach and didn't know what she was going to do there, and she didn't say that she was escaping, Elizabeth *was* escaping."[6] Ashley Brown remembers talking with Bishop about this decision in 1965. Mary Morse and Stella Pereira perceived the way in which the crosscurrent of events during the past few years in Brazil had left both Bishop and Lota vulnerable, with neither able emotionally to support the other.

ASHLEY BROWN— I gently urged Elizabeth [into accepting the Seattle job in the fall of 1965]. She did ask me several times about it, wondering whether it was a good idea, and I proposed that she might enjoy it. In the first place, she had never done any teaching. She'd had no academic connections since she had left Vassar. She knew nothing about the Pacific Northwest. In many ways, Elizabeth really didn't know much about the United States, apart from certain sectors along the eastern coast, all the way down to Key West, of course. She had been living in Brazil most of the time since the early 1950s. The appointment was just going to be for one semester. Another poet was out there at that time, Henry Reed. It was a distinguished Department of English. I'd met the department chair [Robert Heilman], once, and he sounded like a genuinely humane person whom Elizabeth might like being with.

After a great deal of conversation with her over the course of the year, I began to think that maybe she missed the literary milieu in the United States.

I said she might like the change for a few months, and they were going to pay her all this money. Caroline Tate had been out there in the early 1950s, and she'd liked it tremendously. I think I made it sound rather attractive there [to Elizabeth]. Seattle does have an interesting kind of culture of its own, as I kept telling her. She kept bringing up the matter one way or another. I could tell that Lota wasn't altogether happy about it. Lota was tremendously involved in the park. It was taking up more of her time. I had the sense [that their relationship had come to a point where it was easier for Elizabeth to leave].

MARY STEARNS MORSE— [Lota's decline began when] a new government came in after Carlos, and they changed a lot of personnel in the park. Lota couldn't get through the things in the park. She was frustrated. She felt that it was her baby, and she wanted to see it done as she wanted. Lota could be very insistent, and she could be aggressive, too. It may have been a combination of Elizabeth's condition, her problems and saying "I'm going away." Lota was afraid of Elizabeth going away. She saw something that she'd wanted to do all her life slipping away from her, and she saw Elizabeth slipping away too.

STELLA PEREIRA— Elizabeth needed support and she couldn't give [enough]. It's not anybody's fault. Both needed support.

✦   ✦   ✦

Bishop spent ten days in the middle of December 1965 in Ouro Prêto, during which time she gave Lilli Araújo instructions on how she wanted the renovations on her house to proceed in her absence. Then she spent Christmas in Rio with Lota. Lota and Bishop's maid witnessed their days together before Bishop departed for Seattle on 27 December.

JOANNA DOS SANTOS DA COSTA— When Elizabeth was getting her bags ready to leave [for Seattle], she and Lota began speaking in English and fighting with each other. I said, "Look, it's no use, and I want to know what you are fighting about. Speak in Portuguese. Otherwise, I'm going to call Dona Mary [Morse] from Petrópolis, and she's going to tell me what's going on." Lota said, "I don't want to tell you because you have enough problems as it is taking care of us. And I don't want you to be put in the middle."

The next day Rosalina, Magu, and Lota took Elizabeth to the airport, and she left on a night plane. Everything was fine then.

Elizabeth Bishop arrived in Seattle on 27 December 1965, after an exhausting twelve-hour trip. She had left sunny, warm (90 degrees) Rio, to discover Seattle locked in damp winter. It rained and snowed for the first week. By the end of the second week, Bishop had not yet seen Seattle's famed backdrop of snow-capped mountains, and she found herself homesick for Brazil and Lota. A teaching position that had seemed at first a fortuitous escape from the emotional turmoil of life with Lota in Rio looked far less appealing from the unattractive motel room where she took up residence. Bishop called Howard Moss early in her stay: "I'd written something about her, and she said she kept it under her pillow. She cried. She said, 'Well, I really hate it here.' Also, she was having terrible asthma." She also contacted Ashley Brown, who had encouraged her to take the job.

ASHLEY BROWN— I had letters from Elizabeth almost as soon as she arrived in Seattle. Right after Christmas I got a couple of telegrams from her because she realized for the first time that she had to face these classes. She was getting a little panicky. She hadn't particularly thought about teaching until she got there. She was going to be teaching Wallace Stevens and she wasn't really quite sure what she was supposed to be saying. [She asked me to send her] a collection [of essays] on Stevens I edited a long time ago. [Elizabeth also telephoned a few times] about these academic things, how to teach a class and all that.

Bishop warmed to Seattle in time. She found comfort in the Canadians she encountered there and the Canadian money that crossed her palm regularly. Once classes started, students brought her flowers and magazines and called to her from across campus. Colleagues asked her out for meals. Bishop came to see that the English Department was delighted and flattered that she was there. Dorothee Bowie, assistant to the chairman of the English Department, became one of Bishop's closest friends in Seattle. Bowie assisted Bishop with departmental procedures, as well as everyday tasks. Bowie had also been involved in the selection procedure that had brought Bishop to Seattle.

DOROTHEE BOWIE— [Elizabeth was selected] primarily because Roethke had praised her so. Roethke was a very honest man. He had said a couple of times, when he got grants [for visiting artists, that we should] try to get Elizabeth Bishop because she was the best woman poet—of course, very sexist—writing. The department was able somehow to hang on to the money for the Roethke position, which at that time was a very decent salary. The visiting poet got for two quarters Roethke's salary for three quarters. It was rather nice. Henry Reed was the first replacement as poet-in-residence for Roethke. I suggested to the acting chairman in 1964 (Robert Heilman was on leave) that he ask Elizabeth Bishop. He said, "Look, any number of major departments have asked her, and she's always turned them down." I said, "She might just like to be asked." He wrote to her publisher in New York, got her address, wrote a letter, and back came the acceptance, and, of course, the explanation for that was that she so desperately wanted money to fix up the house in Ouro Prêto. To be very honest about it, it was a great coup. In fact, for a while nobody could believe that we had pulled this off.

When Elizabeth first came into my office, I knew instantly that she was terrified. Needless to say, in my twenty years as assistant to the chairman, I had greeted many a frightened newcomer. They don't know what they're walking into. So, I calmed Elizabeth down, did things that I would have done for any number of people. [Within] only five or six days after she was there, she was leaning very, very heavily on me. I'd been around long enough so that none of this bothered me in the slightest. Within a week Elizabeth and I were friends. Elizabeth was a very helpless person in a good number of ways. It was a very simple thing as far as I was concerned. I could do things for her. I thought her worth doing things for. I was not indulgent with her. I was tough with her. I thought she was worth whatever help I could give her.

It wasn't too long after that that I became aware that Elizabeth was a severe alcoholic. She called up one morning and said that she wasn't going to be able to meet her classes. I guess I have a kind of nose for things like that, so I zipped out to the motel and she was skunk-drunk. I felt a kind of responsibility because I was the one who had pushed for that appointment. I brought Elizabeth [to my house] to make sure she ate something. I started to cover [up for Elizabeth].

When Elizabeth would talk with me about her drinking, she said that it had always been a problem. That I believe was true. It just grew. Elizabeth's traumas had very little effect on my feeling for her or my attitude toward her because I have long been convinced that if you pull back the covers on any family, you will find traumas in abundance. If you have a good friend, you take the good with the bad. So Elizabeth had her problems and I knew about them, but in the larger sense, they had nothing to do with this rather marvelous human being that I knew. In her good times she was just really one of the wittiest, funniest, most marvelous people I have ever known. When she'd get with me and my family, it was almost as if she were kind of free. She would talk about cooking. We could have a great time talking gossip about people and laugh. It was during those times that Elizabeth was absolutely herself.

◆　　◆　　◆

As Bishop planned for her classes, she worried that her students would find a modest, old-fashioned teacher like herself a pale substitute for the ebullient, even reckless, Theodore Roethke. What would the students of the liberated sixties think of having to memorize Wallace Stevens's "The Emperor of Ice Cream"? How would they react if she required them to write specific poetic forms, such as sonnets and sestinas? Also, Bishop knew that she was not an academic.[1] In the artist Wesley Wehr, Bishop found one student who was delighted with her approach to poetry. He met Bishop early in her stay in Seattle and observed the slow acclimatization that took place in her relationship with the place.

WESLEY WEHR— I first saw Elizabeth Bishop in Lee's Restaurant on University Way in Seattle, several days before she was beginning to teach at the university. She was having lunch with Henry Reed. Another woman was at their table, and the three of them were talking rather quietly. My first impression was an odd and immediate one. There was a woman who knows exactly who she is. She knew the exact boundaries of her world. I went to the university bookstore the next day to buy a copy of her *Questions of Travel*, out of curiosity, to see what a woman who had made such an immediate and singular impression on me would have written. I was utterly unprepared for what lay before me in those opening pages. Here at last was a kind of poetry so close to what I'd envisioned for myself as a painter, where things are seen as they are, sensitively, absolutely acutely. [Elizabeth's was a poetry of] confidence without the usual vanity.

I'd studied with Roethke, [in both his] poetry workshop and [a class on]

American poetry, for about three years. We had had a little bit of Bishop. The one I remember is "Letter to N.Y.," with the owl taxicab meter. It's the first time I had read that kind of poem by anyone. I wondered who would write a poem about a taxicab in Central Park? I was so inundated with our "Wordsworth whatever it is" out here. Being a student of Roethke's for so many years had meant my tastes lay more toward such poets as Hart Crane, Lorca, Blake, the poets who have changed everything they see into some highly charged personalized expression. I didn't know people wrote poems like Elizabeth's. It seemed very authoritative, very convincing, and somewhat alien to me.

I invited Elizabeth out for coffee after class, and we walked from Parrington Hall to a restaurant down the street. It turned out we had mutual acquaintances. I was surprised how many things Elizabeth said right on our first coffee date. She mentioned longevity. She said, "You know, I've already outlived the normal lifespan of my own family." Then she said she had had some psychiatry, commenting that it didn't help her understand herself any better, but it helped her understand her friends.

Elizabeth had an interesting relationship to being famous. She said, "Oh, it's not that I think that I'm all that good a poet, but I look around at the other poems being written by my contemporaries, and I think, maybe I'm not so bad." I think that she meant that. She just sort of took it in stride. Then we talked about Ned Rorem and his settings of her poetry. We just had a very nice, very chatty time. I was a little surprised and very pleased with how easy it was to talk with her.

It was very soon after that I had a call at my room, and Elizabeth asked if I could come over to her motel room. [She told me to] pick up a six pack and bring it along. Elizabeth answered the door and let me in. She was in her housecoat. I went into the kitchen, clumsily brought each of us a beer, [and when I returned], she was in bed. I sat on a chair next to the bed. She looked at me and said, "I don't know what to do. I'm miserable. I don't know if I can go through with this. I'm thinking of just canceling the teaching arrangement and going home." The weather was terrible. It was January, the worst time of the year, and she was stuck in a God-awful motel room, suddenly confronted with all these students. She missed Lota. It was always, "My dear Lota, I miss her so much." She was devoted to her. She missed Brazil. She knew that the money for the roof [for the house in Ouro Prêto] was very important. She said, "If you were in Brazil and could see how beautiful it is where I live . . ." She was just on the edge of tears, and I sat there next to the bed staring at her. She said, "Oh, I look awful, please don't stare at me. I haven't got my makeup on."

I was a little bewildered because on such short acquaintance she had invited me over and was pouring out this anguish. Then she looked at me and said, "I have a feeling I can trust you." I felt an enormous responsibility came with that word "trust." I wasn't sure what the responsibility meant precisely because other times she would say, "Don't be so protective of me." After that, suddenly, the students started writing, she started liking some of their poems, and the agony started to be replaced by a very very nice time.

✦ ✦ ✦

Early in Bishop's five months in Seattle, the painter Morris Graves organized a dinner party for her to meet some local artists, including Leo Kenney, Jan Thompson and Richard Gilkey, and the poet Caroline Kizer. Beatrice Roethke, Theodore Roethke's widow, also attended. A number of the Seattle painters were interested in Zen Buddhism at that time, and the conversation veered into a debate about whether life had meaning and purpose. Bishop responded in a typical deadpan manner: "Elizabeth looked down at her plate, then up and said, 'Of course, I don't understand what they're talking about, but the shrimp tempura is *simply delicious*.' "[2] At this dinner party Bishop also met Suzanne Bowen [a pseudonym],[3] a young woman who had attended with her husband, an artist. Bishop and Bowen liked each other immediately—Bishop's dry sense of humor drew Bowen to her—and Bishop invited her for tea the next day. They began seeing each other every day, taking walks, going to the zoo, and shopping.

As they spent time together, Bishop and Bowen fell in love. And, as was to be expected in an academic community, Bishop's relationship with Bowen was a topic of comment and criticism. Why was Bishop interested in such a quiet, young—Bowen was half Bishop's age—and, for lack of a better word, unaccomplished companion. Was Bowen simply interested in being seen with a celebrity? Bowen was visibly pregnant at the time, and to some she and Bishop made rather an odd pair. Yet Bishop and Bowen shared a satirical sense of humor that allowed them to deflect any perceived criticisms—they could acerbically mock and mimic Bishop's acquaintances and colleagues. They formed their own society.

Like all Bishop's companions and many of her friends, Bowen became her caretaker, attending to everyday details that could incapacitate Bishop.

WESLEY WEHR— There [were] times when Elizabeth was simply paralyzed by indecision. Her helplessness, whether it was really justified or not, could leave her at an impasse and things had to be done. Elizabeth often needed somebody who could take charge. Elizabeth was lucky that she met someone like Suzanne who can stay calm, efficient. Under the worst circumstances, Suzanne was capable of keeping her wits and proceeding very deliberately. Suzanne suddenly realized that Elizabeth was desperately lonely and home-sick. She just stepped in, very quietly, very efficiently, and saw to it that Elizabeth ate well. She kept her from sinking into herself. If it weren't for Suzanne, God knows how many times Elizabeth would have missed class. Suzanne was absolutely what the doctor ordered and deserves a vast amount of credit.

◆　◆　◆

In February it became clear that living in the motel was not good for Bishop. The wall-to-wall carpeting and heating affected her health, and she was bothered by the constant sound of traffic. Bowen organized a move. Bob Mony, a graduate student in English, located a small apartment on Brook-lyn Avenue, within walking distance of the university, someone donated a couch, and Bishop bought a table at an antique shop. Bowen and a number of Bishop's students did all the moving, sending Bishop downtown for lunch while they were working, and explaining that they did not want her around because they might use foul language. When Bishop arrived at the new apartment, everything was in its place, even her soap and toothpaste. Bishop felt that this was one of the kindest acts ever done for her.

WESLEY WEHR— The motel room wasn't working. Suzanne, Bob Mony, and I got together [to move her into and] to furnish her little apartment on Brooklyn. It was just a little front room, a hallway with a little kitchen and a bathroom right across, and a little bedroom way at the back. It was actually a cell. This gave her some kind of a place of her own. Bob had a nice rug, so that went in. I brought a Bryen watercolor and a brass bed that I'd had for years. Elizabeth had a little phonograph [and some] books. We all went about furnishing that very small apartment.

◆　◆　◆

What kind of teacher was Bishop? Initially, she was both fearful and skeptical. In Brazil, while deciding whether to accept this job, Bishop had told friends that she doubted that writing could be taught. Good writers had natural talent; teachers could perhaps refine what was already there.

Bishop's last contact with college students had been when she was at Vassar in the thirties. She was startled by the students of the sixties in Seattle.

They demonstrated none of the old-fashioned respect that Bishop remembered showing her professors at Vassar, at least to their faces. Her female students discussed birth control with Bishop and commented on her makeup. They seemed unembarrassable. Bishop was also frustrated by what she perceived as her students' poor preparation: "Elizabeth felt she wasn't succeeding at teaching her students what they needed to know as poets. Elizabeth expressed hopelessness that she could teach her students anything. She was appalled and genuinely concerned at the poor training of the students. She talked a lot about how they couldn't punctuate properly. They used words sloppily. They were imprecise and fuzzy in their thinking. She talked a lot about individual students, one who never learned to spell, another whose vocabulary was so limited that he used a word constantly and couldn't think of a better word to substitute. She felt frustrated."[4]

In time, however, Bishop made her peace with the job, which consisted of teaching two sections, one a study of poetry, the other a poetry-writing workshop. She came to see that her students were affectionate, and she was moved that all of them, many of whom worked evenings to support themselves and pay for school, had purchased Questions of Travel. And she discovered some talented students whose work delighted her. "Elizabeth was indeed shocked by the quality of the general students she was meeting. Things had clearly changed since she had been at Vassar, but she found some bright students with whom she enjoyed working."[5] Two of her prize students were Henry Carlile and Sandra McPherson. Wesley Wehr audited the class with these two poets and observed how Bishop brought some of her students to a new sense of style and subject matter in poetry.

HENRY CARLILE— I met Elizabeth in the first class she taught. Though as her student, I never called her "Elizabeth." She was always "Miss Bishop." I was working on an M.A. in English with emphasis in creative writing and had planned on studying with Theodore Roethke. I had studied with him as an undergraduate. Roethke was the first poet to encourage me to write.

Elizabeth was very nervous and uncomfortable with teaching. She arrived with a set of expectations and had to make constant adjustments for the naïveté of her students. She said, "You people have read Shakespeare and Dylan Thomas and Theodore Roethke. What else have you read?" She quoted different poets to us to see if we would recognize them. Most of the time we couldn't. She could make you feel pretty dumb about the things you hadn't read. And she was often genuinely incredulous that we hadn't read something. She said, "Well, we're going to have to work very hard here." We just didn't know as much as she thought we should. Elizabeth said on one occasion outside of class that she felt most students ought to be *discouraged* from trying to write poetry.

Like Theodore Roethke and Henry Reed, who taught the poetry workshop before her, Elizabeth drilled her students in forms. For one assignment she gave us a passage from a short story by Isaac Babel, a description of a church. She said, "I want you to take this prose description and rewrite it as blank verse." She was always interested in details, and I recall this as characteristic of her teaching. Elizabeth disliked hyperbole, any kind of highfalutin, overblown emotion. She criticized the overinflated style of Muriel Rukeyser's poetry. She stressed close observation and accuracy. She often said that there weren't enough "things" in our poems. She said, "Some of your lines are atrocious!" I remember her poem "The Sandpiper" ends with the bird minutely inspecting grains of sand. That's typical of the way Elizabeth noticed things. Her life was often out of control, but her poetry is precise. As if her poetry had to create an order missing from her life.

I remember Elizabeth telling us, "When you use a metaphor or simile, don't use it casually. It should clarify, not just ornament. Make it accurate." I've carried this advice into my own classes and often use her metaphors and similes as examples. The parking meter "like a moral owl" [in "Letter to N.Y."], and "Formosa, the donkey, / who brays like a pump gone dry" [in "Manuelzinho"]. Elizabeth once told us about going to the zoo with Marianne Moore and watching elephants. Elizabeth said, "Look, its skin is like fog." And Moore said, "Oh, I like that. I want that!" Elizabeth told her she could have it. Moore used the simile in her poem "The Monkeys."

Sandra McPherson was Elizabeth's best student in Washington. Like Elizabeth, Sandra paid close attention to language and observed details carefully. She had already written two scholarly papers her professors had urged her to get published. They were dictional studies. One on Shakespeare. I can't remember now what the other was about. Several years later, in Portland, Oregon, she wrote a funny satirical essay on James Wright and Robert Bly, entitled "You Can Say That Again, Or Can You?" It was eventually published in the *Iowa Review*. Elizabeth loved that essay and graciously said that she wished she could write something as witty and entertaining. The essay examined word collocations, dictional mannerisms, exactly the sort of attention to language Elizabeth loved.

I think now that I was lucky to have studied with Elizabeth when I did. Roethke was a great teacher. He could quote hundreds of poems by heart and read beautifully. I still remember a reading he did of Wilfred Owen's

"Strange Meeting." When he got to the line "I am the enemy you killed, my friend . . . ," his voice cracked and he broke down and wept in front of the class. I knew then I wanted to write poetry. I went home after class and memorized that poem. But Roethke was also overwhelming, hyperbolic in ways Elizabeth wasn't. His students worshiped him and imitated some of his worst mannerisms. His spiritual bombast, his confessional manner. Elizabeth, of course, deplored Roethke's influence. Once when I wrote a too-transcendental line, she scratched it out and wrote "No!" in the margin. I didn't appreciate her then as much as I do now.

SANDRA MCPHERSON— When we first met for class, we were all very excited about Elizabeth's being there, and the class was large. She had to have a "write down" to select students. We met Monday, Tuesday, Wednesday, and Thursday first term. She would have conferences on our work. I had one conference in her office and the other right at the end of the term in her apartment. It was a mixed class of graduates and undergraduates. So, it was a little bit of everything—people who were very serious about poetry and wrote heavily iambic sonnets, and people whose work was influenced by Chinese and Japanese poetry. Elizabeth may have wondered about that Asian influence. It's very strong in the Northwest. It's the part of the world we look across the water to. We were more influenced by Chinese and Japanese poetry than we were by European poetry.

One of the first things Elizabeth said was that she had taken some of Roethke's poems to a friend who was a psychiatrist, or maybe to her psychiatrist, who said that Roethke must have been psychotic or some such term, and she didn't see what all the fuss was over Theodore Roethke. This was not a good move to make, for obvious reasons, but it interested me, because I thought it remarkable that she would have the courage to say a thing like that and to go against the grain with that opinion. And I thought, Well, so what if he was a psychotic? Would that be a bad thing? Would that make the poetry not valid? Suzanne told me one day that Elizabeth was afraid of going mad. That was her analysis of why Elizabeth would get upset over Roethke's poems showing that he was psychotic.

Elizabeth thought that she was not a good teacher—she said that in class or she said it to me privately—but she was a wonderful teacher. She was very natural. Elizabeth came into class not as an academic scholar or critic or even someone who demanded that we learn this, this, and this. She came as a practicing great artist, and as a person who seemed to have no affectations. She was a very natural, warm, conversational teacher. She did not seek disciples in any way that I could determine. I felt that Elizabeth was more of a fellow poet than a teacher. I consider writing seeing. She came as a person who wrote and saw for a living. So language and seeing were what her life was centered on. Elizabeth had always been very consistent. I remember her saying more than once, if we would ask her about a poem, "That really happened!"

The first assignment in the class was a ballad. Elizabeth said that in Brazil when the newspapers came out with a sensational story, maybe a murder or something, within a matter of days there was a song written about it, and it became popular. It was a way of perhaps passing news around. I thought it was startling that in that culture anything in the newspaper could be a song. She told us to look in the newspaper in Seattle and come up with a ballad. So I looked in the obituaries and there was one, an obituary for Cpt. Harry Butcher, a tugboatman. I thought this was an odd assignment, and I didn't want to do it, but I did it, and she liked mine. I found it interesting that Elizabeth wouldn't do every poem in class. It wasn't a workshop. She would select certain ones and say, "Now this is the best one; this is a good one . . ." And she would proceed to say why. She did that with my ballad.

Elizabeth wasn't out of sync in Seattle by being a traditionalist and having students write in particular genres. Roethke, as I understood, pretty much gave formal exercises, too. Henry Reed was a formalist. David Wagoner was in between—his assignments were a little different, a little crazier.

For another assignment Elizabeth gave eight unpoetic words or terms that she wanted us to put into a poem. "Space Needle" was one. Here we were in Seattle and that ugly thing was in view at all times, and we didn't especially want to write about it or didn't know how to see it freshly. What I had always liked about Elizabeth's work was that she could write about anything. There was a vocabulary in common things. Anything was material for your sense of wonder and amusement.

About a month into the term we had to read *Biographia Literaria* and comment on it. Mandelstam and Isaac Babel's prose are particular recommendations I got from her. I think that she thought that we were not very well read. Another assignment was to do a poem with a refrain. In response to one blank verse assignment, Elizabeth revised my poem ["To a Night Worker"] for me. She counted all the stresses, and she retyped it. She wondered whether the first foot was trochaic. One line was "Through dark, full-blown you come, hot toothy flower"; Elizabeth's comment was, "OK if flower has one syllable!" I had written for my first line, "Such a red night. Your most colorful hour." She responded, "If you said: 'Such a red night.

And your most colorful hour'—it would work. See it? E.B." For her ear, that "and" was better. For me, the original is still better. I had written in line 7, "You're smoother than crime." She said, " 'You're smooth as crime' would do it," to eliminate the comparison and save a beat. Her goal was to even out the meter. She retyped the poem and she added words. At the bottom she wrote my name as author and then she says "meddled with by E.B." Elizabeth conveyed to me a genuine interest in my work. She treated us with this motherly or grandmotherly concern. She could be irreverent. I have a sense that the voice in her own poetry is amused, and that she was secretly laughing to herself, enjoying things.

The second conference I remember having with Elizabeth was in her apartment. It was in the evening, and she had six or seven or my poems. Certain ones that I thought quite wonderful she ignored and she concentrated on other ones that she did like. She was very gracious and kept asking me nice personal things, like, "What does your father do? What did you do last summer? What do you think of so-and-so in the class? I think he's very gifted but he didn't turn in any poems until just last week, and I don't know what grade to give him." Then she started repeating the questions, and she repeated them all night. I mentioned this to someone, and the other person said she had seen that happen. By the end of the term, there were above five of us who would come every time, because you never knew when she would turn up and when she would not turn up. She was going through something we knew nothing about. Those of us who went, just loved her. Anything she would say, we would want to hear, no matter if we had to go five days a week and she would be there twice. The second term, the spring of 1966, she missed long stretches of class. I think Henry Reed took over for her.

Elizabeth showed me that poetry could be anywhere, though I doubt that she would have used those words. Her poems seem to extend the diction, the homely diction you could use, and objects in that same category. Now when I write and feel that a line is coming out in her voice, it comes out sometimes in an intentionally flattened meter, despite her emphasis on iambic pentameter. When I work on something that has rhymes on the end, and they're not slavish rhymes, I feel that from her I learned to enjoy the flavor of them. And if I miss one, so what? My usual overemphatic meter relaxes a little bit when I put those rhymes on the end. Elizabeth said, "Why always save your best line for last? Put it second to last." She encouraged me to see that the drama of a poem can have a little different shape than I had thought. It doesn't always have to build up to that high point. If you're writing really well, you have high points all the way through the poem. In her work, every place in the poem gives pleasure. It doesn't have to build up to some huge insight.

WESLEY WEHR—From the start Elizabeth worried constantly over her classes. She and Henry Reed were on the phone with each other, [wondering if] these kids had ever heard of iambic pentameter. Elizabeth realized there were going to have to be some very serious technical guidelines. I would be with her the night before the day when she'd be preparing the lesson. She worked very hard to prepare a lesson or a procedure in class. She'd come in prepared, look around at the students, and just know it wasn't the right lesson. She was constantly coming in prepared and then realizing it was too soon or it wasn't the right tactic. Elizabeth had no background. It all had to be her wits, her perceptions, her sensitivity to where the students were and weren't. In this she was extremely conscientious and just at the edge of agony at times because she took this teaching very seriously.

[One day] each of Elizabeth's students was assigned to read a favorite poem to the class. For the most part, they chose either a well-known poem by some modern writer, such as Dylan Thomas or Robert Frost, or a rather sentimental piece they would likely come upon in some magazine. The poems were either overly familiar or simply bad. Finally, the self-appointed rebel in the class had his turn. His favorite poem was filled with obscene words. He half blurted the poem out and stumbled through it as best he could. It didn't come off as shocking, but merely fell flat. When he had finished reading it, he said, "And that, Miss Bishop, is my favorite poem."

Elizabeth answered quietly, "Well, I just don't think that's an especially good poem." He snapped back at her, "You don't like that poem because it's got a lot of obscene words in it." Elizabeth responded, "That's not at all the reason I don't care for that poem. There's nothing intrinsically wrong with those words that you call obscene. After all, they are part of the English language, whether we care for them or not. For that matter, there are a few of them in that so-called poem that I myself have sometimes used, that is, when I felt the situation really called for it." Elizabeth pronounced the words calmly and distinctly. Then she continued, "I just don't think the writer used those words very well. The poem doesn't shock me. I almost wish it did. It just bored me, that's all." There was a smattering of applause from the students. "If a poet sets out to be shocking, [he must] place his words very well, firmly and effectively. You students are in this class to learn how to use words well, not just to toss them about for some haphazard effect. So let me read you something by a writer who knows what he is doing." Then she read us a few excerpts from Chaucer. What the student in class did was also very myopic. He cast her in the role of "Miss Bishop."

[Once Elizabeth told me that Sandra McPherson] was showing signs of becoming a quite interesting young poet. She said, "What I like about her work is that she uses exactly her own materials. Some of the other students seem so reluctant to write about the things around them. The poet's eye, like that of the painter, has to be trained and sharp to notice the fascinating differences between things. Some of my students write poems in which they can easily substitute one word, one object for another. You've seen Vermeer's paintings. The objects in them are very precisely observed and rendered. I'm going to try an experiment on my students tomorrow. I'll bring some ordinary things to class. I'll ask the students to start writing about these objects right there in class. Write down whatever comes into their heads. So often they write much better under time pressures. I'll be curious to see what happens. I've got to do something about shaking them out of their habits. While I'm about it, I can read them some short prose poems by Ponge. He writes about all sorts of things, a match, a telephone, a butterfly, an oyster, a Parisian."

The next day, Elizabeth arrived in class carrying a shopping bag. She spread a newspaper on the classroom table and started taking things out of the bag: an eggbeater, a white canvas tennis shoe, two new potatoes, a fork, a knife, a spoon, and, finally, a package of seeds. She arranged them carefully on the table, somewhat like a still life, and announced, "Now, I want you all to write poems about these objects. For that matter, I think I'll try my hand at it, too." I had done some paintings, some very small ones, and when Elizabeth thought that her students needed to be more concrete, she asked me to bring some things of mine to class one day as an assignment. The students were all to write about these paintings of mine. She came to class another day and said, "We're all going to write a poem, me too, about Seattle today, and I'll give a prize to the student who comes up with the best rhyme for Seattle." Finally, when we read our contributions, we went around the class, and Elizabeth said, "Well, my poem starts, 'I like Seattle, but the weather is getting me down.' "

✦　✦　✦

Bishop did have difficulty with some students. One left the class because of his dissatisfaction. A vocal student frightened Bishop, and she brought another poet-teacher with her to class the next day for support. Bishop was not at all contentious by temperament and eschewed conflict, so she was concerned about how to approach students with whom she had disagreements, particularly those who she felt were talented. When she visited Gretchen Keene Smith, who lived in Seattle and whom she had known in Vassar, Bishop told a story about one such student.

GRETCHEN KEENE SMITH— When I read that Elizabeth was coming to Seattle, I was delighted and so wrote a little note and took it over to the hotel where it said she was staying. It said, "Remember me? Call me up." She did. Elizabeth was much the way I remembered her [from Vassar]. The things I liked about her I still liked about her. We still talked on an impersonal, social level. Elizabeth made amusing references to the fact that she was driven to teaching. She did have to earn a living to some extent. Elizabeth simply said things had been difficult [in Brazil], without going into it. Very impersonal, but without avoiding it exactly. She did say you can't teach poetry. I was surprised that she was making the effort to, because I was sure that as a younger person she would have scorned a teacher trying to teach poetry, but as she explained to me, she had to do something. I admired Elizabeth for handling her job here as well as she did—I saw that she was a conscientious teacher—because it seemed to me that this kind of thing was hard for her to do. It was not a pleasure to her.

Elizabeth told me about a young man who was disrupting the class because he was so insulting to everybody and so superior. He didn't come to class and was rather insulting to her, too. Finally this young man did hand in his assignments late, all at once, toward the end of the [semester], and to her amazement she found that he wrote beautifully. Indeed, he could write poetry. So some of his impatience with the others was because he was a poet and had no patience with this doggerel that was coming up.

Elizabeth had an interview, as she had to, with him, and I was interested in what she said to him and how they got along, because she was still furious at him for having made her life very difficult during the spring term. I'm sure this student caused her pain and probably some drinking bouts. I wish I could remember her words, because they were very good. She just told him that life is not fair, talent isn't fair, and I think she said God isn't fair, but we try to be. When she said talent isn't fair she said, "You have talent." Then she described to him the students who do come to the class, and indeed many of them did not have talent, but they loved their subject. They wanted to know more about it, and they had a right to respect. And I think she made an impression on him.

My husband and I had a sailboat and took Elizabeth out on Lake Washington one afternoon. I didn't know that she had had any experience sailing.

She told us about her summers at camp and that she was something of a gung ho sailor. I was surprised to find Elizabeth being enthusiastic about something. She asked if she could take the tiller, and she was a good sailor. It was a light-wind day, but she really was enjoying it and knew what she was doing. And there was a kind of relaxed childish pleasure she was having that was unlike the Elizabeth that I knew, the careful, quiet, withdrawn person. Her body was in it.

✦　✦　✦

Bishop was ill with asthma and colds throughout her stay in Seattle. On the evening of 9 March she was struck with a virulent strain of the Asiatic flu. This illness began with a sharp headache, which grew to violent pains throughout her body in the course of the night. She called Dorothee Bowie at five A.M. Bowie ordered a cab for her. As she lay in bed in the hospital, her face was as white as her hair. She left the hospital after several days convinced that she had had a heart attack (although the doctors assured her that she had not) and complaining about the twenty-four-dollar cab ride back to her apartment.

While she was in the hospital, Henry Reed, the colleague who became Bishop's closest literary friend in Seattle, took over her last class meetings before spring break. In his sonorous British accent, he read Bishop's poems, which Bishop herself had refused to do, to her students. Reed had been the visiting poet the year before and had stayed on for an additional year. In Bishop, Reed found a like-minded colleague, a brilliant, knowledgeable litterateur who liked to teach the formal elements of poetry. He and Bishop would get together and complain about the plight of teachers of poetry. They drank to excess together. They also went on a diet together: "They dutifully got their armed forces physical conditioning booklet. Henry would call, 'Well, Elizabeth, did you do your sit-ups?' 'Well, did you do yours?' I don't think it lasted very long; knowing Henry, it couldn't have."[6] Bishop and Reed had a similar sense of humor, caustic at times, which came across as a snobbish, elitist air to their colleagues. Henry Carlile, William Matchett, a member of the English Department, and Robert Heilman, the chairman while Bishop was in Seattle, recollect Henry Reed and Bishop together. Dorothee Bowie and her son, Taylor, recollect one unpleasant afternoon when Bishop and Reed were uncomfortably sharp with the poet and translator Rolfe Humphries.

HENRY CARLILE— Henry Reed was handsome, with thinning hair, very English in manner and appearance. He was a wonderful teacher, a great reader of poetry, though he was often "melancholy," as he put it. Away from campus he drank heavily. Most of his students probably didn't know about his drinking, but I witnessed it personally. I don't know the nature of his severe depression. At the time I suspected it had to do with his poetry. He had published only one slim volume of poetry, *A Map of Verona*, and a few translations (of Ugo Betti's work, I think). Once, I saw a manuscript on his coffee table. I don't know if it was poems or translations, but it was battered and must have been at least three inches thick. It had been gone over a lot.

One time my wife, Sandra, and I went to some trouble to fix a nice dinner for him. He had told me that he missed lamb, so Sandra and I got together a lamb roast dinner for him. When I arrived at his apartment, he asked me to drive him to his doctor's office for an antidepressant prescription. Later, at dinner, he picked at his food, hardly ate anything, and asked to be taken home early.

Like Roethke, and later, Bishop, Henry taught forms. He had us do a sonnet, a sestina, a villanelle. Both Elizabeth and Henry deplored the tone that Roethke left at the school. Henry used to say, "If I see the word *salmon* in another poem . . ." This complaint was not directed at Roethke so much as at a couple of other Northwest poets Henry disliked. He told me he had written a parody, though he wouldn't show it to me, in which he had managed to use the words *clam* and *salmon* thirty-two times. He read it once to another student, but not to me. By this time I think he had already decided it was just a throwaway poem.

I loved Henry Reed's teaching. I think he and Elizabeth had similar ideas about poetry. Both were basically modest and precise. They probably commiserated, got together and bitched about the department, the Northwest, the students. In his private comments to me regarding a couple of other students in our class, Henry was very sarcastic. This bothered me at the time, though I said nothing. He was always kind and encouraging about my writing.

WILLIAM MATCHETT— Elizabeth and Henry were both visitors, both poets, and they were thrown together. Henry had been here the year before, and he was broke and very anxious to stay. Bob Heilman was able to pull together a program that would allow him to teach the Victorian novel and stay for another year. This was really an attempt to solve a financial problem for Henry.

He had been very popular in the department and, as the visiting poet, much wined and dined. When the spotlight turned on to Elizabeth the next year, he was a bit jealous and let down. But they soon became friends.

He was a wonderful man and fine with some students, but a very lazy teacher. He was an absolute charmer. My wife and I saw a lot of him in London in the winter of 1970–71. Once he came to his door with his finger holding his place in a copy of *Vanity Fair*. I said, "Oh, Henry, you're reading *Vanity Fair*," and he said, "Oh, yes, old Bob made me teach it that second year and I've always wondered how it came out." There are lots of Henry stories like that.

Elizabeth and Henry may have seemed disdainful of others. Henry was the funniest man I think I've known in my lifetime, but he loved to put people down, in a humorous way. Meeting people was not easy for Elizabeth. Her reticence might have come out as a sense of superiority because people were already looking at her as the great poet. Instead of realizing that she was shy with them, I think they thought she considered herself above them.

ROBERT HEILMAN— Elizabeth and Henry were real cronies. Their friendship appeared in public often as a kind of a shared superiority to the rest of the world, which at times was not altogether pleasant. Since I never knew Elizabeth well enough to claim her as a good friend—Henry I did, because my wife and I saw a lot of him—I was always a little embarrassed by this style of everybody else being stupid.

My wife and I have a cottage up on Camano Island. Every once in a while we'd have a party or a visit from the summer school people. Once Elizabeth and Henry came up and Rolfe Humphries was there. As a young man Rolfe was a very witty, incisive, and even abusive reviewer. By then he was old and tired. He was a guy that you had to like and feel sorry for. Elizabeth and Henry behaved awfully, wandering off in the corners and snickering and that sort of thing. Snide. I don't know whether Elizabeth got drunk; Henry was always a little bit drunk. I remember being terribly embarrassed.

A number of times at parties, my wife and I would be asked to pick Henry and Elizabeth up. They'd get together at the apartment of one of them. Once we waited outside five minutes or so beyond the arranged time of pickup. We could hear them laughing inside and just not bothering to come out. I remember I went in and really lost my temper. I may have been a little harsh about it. Since Henry's career was rather in the wane at that time—he had blossomed much earlier and really wasn't doing much to speak of—a close association with Elizabeth was for him a kind of recovery of some kind of position or status. [This attitude in Elizabeth] would just come out on special occasion[s]. She and Henry brought out in each other that particular tendency to register contempt for the rest of the world.

In denigrating the quality of the students, Elizabeth wasn't doing anything all the rest of us didn't do. You only got one bright student per twenty-five. This was her first teaching [position]. The visiting poets are always shocked to find out what students are like. They haven't been around students. They've been associating with other poets and people like that.

DOROTHEE BOWIE— The party at Robert Heilman's was Elizabeth at the worst I have ever seen her. To this day I don't know what possessed Elizabeth, but she ganged up with Henry and they attacked Rolfe Humphries, a kindly, decent human being. [They were] snide.

M. TAYLOR BOWIE— They spoke in a sort of a circumspect way, casual comments tossed off that were obviously references. It went on the whole day. It was as if Rolfe Humphries wasn't worthy of being in the rest of our company. I remember particularly how uncomfortable Mrs. Humphries was about it. She seemed awfully dignified and decent.

DOROTHEE— I was simply appalled at Elizabeth and Henry Reed, a talented but very frustrated man.

✦   ✦   ✦

Bishop had originally hoped that Lota would join her in Seattle in May 1966. They planned to tour the Northwest, particularly the redwood forests. Bishop wrote letters and cables and made telephone calls to Lota during her months in Seattle, but the details of Flamengo Park kept Lota busy in Brazil. Some of their conversations were contentious, particularly when Lota accused Bishop of failing to take her Antabuse and of drinking too much. Bishop lied to Lota, saying that she was not drinking and had not missed any classes. There was also at least one incident when Bishop was angry with Lota's behavior in Brazil.

DOROTHEE BOWIE— Elizabeth did not [mention that there were difficulties in her relationship with Lota]. I began to [sense this] when she came in one day after she had sent a lot of money to Lota, to tell me that Lota had taken the money and bought a new sports car. Elizabeth just kind of laughed, but it was no laughing matter. It was just heartbreaking to her. When she left Seattle, Elizabeth was torn. The relationship between her and Lota was petering out. And here she'd [had a number of nice things done for her by affectionate friends]. Henry Reed and Elizabeth both got the red carpet. We were indulgent with our visiting poets.

✦   ✦   ✦

Bishop maintained an ambivalent attitude toward Brazil while she was in Seattle. She was relieved to have escaped the turmoil of Rio, but there was not any doubt in her mind about returning to Brazil and Lota. She always viewed her stay in Seattle as a hiatus to give them both some breathing room. In early June, Bishop was awarded a grant for twelve thousand dollars by the Rockefeller Foundation to aid her in producing a book of travel sketches, essays, and critical studies on aspects of life in Brazil. After six months in Seattle with no new prose or poetry, Brazil offered the promise of renewed writing. And, at times, Bishop had reveries about Brazil.

WESLEY WEHR— [There was a] playful side [to Elizabeth]. She told me she knew the man who wrote the music for Black Orpheus. She had a little phonograph in her apartment, and she liked to put on the sambas when it was carnival in Rio, dancing in a housecoat, like she was transfixed. She said, "Oh, if I were there tonight, I'd be dancing," and she started [dancing]. The glazed look of Elizabeth, like she's suddenly back in the crowds at carnival, was incredible. When Elizabeth came out of it, she just looked with a grin and said, "That's what I would have been doing in Rio tonight."

✦   ✦   ✦

Seattle came to represent freedom and independence to Bishop. There she was on her own, away from the watchful, and occasionally tyrannical, Lota. So, in her final weeks of her stay, Bishop was torn, not about returning to Brazil and leaving Seattle, but about where exactly she belonged. One acquaintance detected an aura of homelessness in Bishop during this time.

GARY LUNDELL— Elizabeth felt like she had made friends here, that she would keep in contact with them and she would probably return some day. I remember seeing Elizabeth walk down the street alone, shopping, and sometimes appearing very lonely. I felt that she never did become a resident of Seattle. She always seemed like a visitor, an outsider. [She said that she had taken the teaching job because] the house [in Ouro Prêto] needed a new roof. Even though she was talking about the house that needed work, I almost had the feeling that she wasn't really planning to go back. It was a bit of a puzzle to me.

✦   ✦   ✦

There was also the issue of her relationship with Bowen. Bishop and Bowen had had an implicit understanding throughout their time together that

Bishop was going to return to Lota once her teaching was over. Bowen understood that her relationship with Bishop was different from the long-term, prior commitment that Bishop had to Lota, whatever difficulties Bishop and Lota were encountering. Nevertheless, as the end of her stay approached, Bishop grew distracted and upset, as Henry Carlile observed.

HENRY CARLILE— Elizabeth treated me kindly and encouraged my work, telling me on one occasion to send some of my poems to a magazine. "Not just any magazine," she told me. "A *good* magazine." She disapproved of any kind of vanity publishing. "You should start at the top," she said. Easy for her to say! But we did have a misunderstanding during her second term at the university, when I was taking independent study in writing with her. We were supposed to meet occasionally. She had told me, "When you finish some poems, come in and we'll talk about them." I was pretty much on my own. She would make suggestions from time to time. Very specific suggestions. She had a wonderful ear for poetry, an impeccable sense of diction.

At one point I skipped several conferences with her. I was working part-time as a shipfitter and trying to finish papers for other academic courses. I had also written a number of poems I was still revising. I didn't yet have anything finished enough to show her, so I hadn't seen her for quite a while. Sandra McPherson and I were walking down a street near campus and ran smack into Elizabeth. I must have looked pretty embarrassed. Then she pointed her finger at me and said, "And I want to see *you*. You haven't been in to see me."

Elizabeth had been sick with allergies and, I found out later, had been drinking heavily. During this bad period she got absolutely confused about the amount of work I had completed for our writing conferences. She thought I had handed in some old revisions and hadn't done enough new work. Actually, I had finished more new poems than in the previous quarter's class when I'd received an A from her. Near the end of the second quarter, I submitted a collection of poems for grading. I got my grade and it was a C. I couldn't believe it. I asked her, "What's wrong? What's going on?" And she said, "You're lazy. You didn't do enough work." I said, "Yes I did!" She said, "I'm not referring to the quality of the work. The quality is fine. The quantity is what concerns me. You have to work harder." And I said, "But I *did* work harder. I wrote more poems than last quarter." She said, "You're handing in the same poems all the time." I had given her a few revisions, but most of the poems were new.

I was so upset by the grade I went to see the English Department's director of graduate studies. I showed him the work I had done, and he said she would have to reconsider my grade. Then I talked with Henry Reed about it. He seemed angry with me. He said, "She's having a difficult time. Do you want to put her in the hospital?" Something like that. And I said, "Well, I won't pursue it any further." Elizabeth had been told that she had to reconsider the grade, and she said, "Very well, leave the poems in an envelope on my door." Which I did. She never read them. She just left town. I went back and found the poems where I had left them. At that point I asked Henry Reed what he thought I should do. And he told me emphatically to drop the matter. I decided the grade wasn't that important. I understood there was a lot of personal turmoil in Elizabeth's life and didn't want to add to it. She was in trouble. That was clear.

When Bishop had finished teaching in June, she and Bowen traveled to a cabin at Doe Bay on Orcas Island, one of the San Juan Islands, where they spent several days. They took walks, picked blackberries, gathered oysters, and read aloud to each other. A whale appeared in the bay in front of their cabin every day. When they returned to Seattle, they spent the two days before Bishop left at the apartment of one of Bowen's friends. On 4 July Dorothee Bowie drove Bishop to the airport. Bishop and Bowen had discussed how they could exchange letters without Lota discovering. However, as one would suspect, little escaped Lota's attention.

Elizabeth Bishop returned to Brazil in July 1966, after her five months in Seattle, to find Lota still fighting the battles of Flamengo Park. The governor who had succeeded Carlos Lacerda was attempting to dissolve the foundation that Lacerda had formed to protect the park and Lota's job. Lota was exhausted from her work at the park and from lawsuits that challenged the foundation's legitimacy. Lota's maid recollects what life was like for Lota from before Bishop's departure.

JOANNA DOS SANTOS DA COSTA— When Lota began to be sick, Elizabeth began to be unhappy. Elizabeth spoke very little to me about it, but I knew everything that was going on. The government had changed. The new governor wasn't doing what Lota had hoped he would do for her in the park. There were a lot of things lacking in the park that should be done, and Lota would cry a lot. Lota would go sometimes to the park in the morning and she would come back for lunch, and she wouldn't go back in the afternoon because there was so much pressure and so much disappointment there at this point in her life. Lota saw what was coming and she was very unhappy about it. Then she started treatment with a psychoanalyst, for a long time. I understood what was going on, so I would dance in front of her, sing, tell her stories, and make her invite people to come to cheer her up.

[While Elizabeth was in Seattle] Lota received her old friends. I would try to make her have them for tea, have them for dinner. Sometimes I stayed in Lota's room until eleven o'clock at night talking. Lota wanted Elizabeth to come back. Lota said she was going to go and get Elizabeth. Everything was very happy [when Elizabeth returned]. She came back very happy, brought a lot of presents to Mary Morse's children.

✦ ✦ ✦

Bishop and Lota spent their first days together in Petrópolis but shortly had to return to Rio for Lota to attend to business. The lawsuits challenging the foundation that Lacerda had established came to a head a month after Bishop returned. After a week in Rio, Bishop left alone for Ouro Prêto, where she stayed at Lilli Araújo's inn. Mark Strand remembers that "when Elizabeth came back from Seattle, she went out to work on the house in Ouro Prêto. She didn't come back and stay with Lota. I didn't see her there." When Bishop arrived in Ouro Prêto, she was sick in bed for a week, a collapse precipitated by her confused feelings during this first month. Bishop had instructed Bowen to direct her letters through Lilli Araújo and another friend in Ouro Prêto. In mid-August Bishop received a cable from Bowen about the birth of her son.[1]

That same month, when it became apparent that the courts were not going to uphold the foundation for the park, Lota developed dizzy spells, which caused her to stumble and to fall. And so began the spiraling pattern in Bishop and Lota's relationship: "After Lota began to be sick, Elizabeth's drinking got worse. Elizabeth would begin to be very nervous, and then she'd begin to drink."[2] It may also have been at this time that Lota discovered Bishop's letters from Bowen. Her own illness, fear about Bowen, and Bishop's drinking prompted Lota's close scrutiny of Bishop. Bishop felt that Lota was treating her like a child. Lota accused Bishop of spending the six months in Seattle drinking (and told friends that Bishop had done so), and started forcing her to take Antabuse tablets. Bishop countered that she had taken care of herself in Seattle and could do so in Rio.

Bishop wavered between sympathy and frustration toward Lota. She understood that her own trip to Seattle had exacerbated Lota's condition. Bishop was frustrated, however, because she could not make Lota understand how her violent moods made matters worse for herself. At her most pessimistic, Bishop felt that she had to leave Brazil: "At another time at Lilli's, where Elizabeth was staying, she said that she was going to return to the States, go back to Seattle. She was thinking of divesting herself of everything else she owned with Lota and just keeping her house. This was hers for herself."[3]

Lota's doctor insisted she take some time off, and she was granted a forty-five-day leave of absence from a job where she had become a powerless functionary. Bishop arranged for a trip to Holland and England in late October. Kit Barker was having a show of his paintings in London at this time, and

Lota and Bishop stayed with the Barkers. Joseph and U. T. Summers were living with their family at Oxford.

ILSE BARKER— When Lota and Elizabeth visited us in 1966 Lota was said to have inner ear problems. Kit had suffered from something similar and was sympathetic. Lota and Elizabeth came to Kit's exhibition in London, and Lota found it difficult to remain upright and walk across the gallery because of this giddiness. She had some pills for her condition. On a visit to the house of friends down in Sussex, she had to lie down. Otherwise, she seemed all right, though she did not look well, thin and drawn. But she was charming and had a great inner fire, liveliness. You could feel the power in her, even though she wasn't well. We loved her. She adored Kit, and she was very much his kind of woman, lively, un-English. We could feel that Elizabeth was worried about Lota; she also worried about people not liking her. Even before they visited us, Elizabeth was always afraid we wouldn't like Lota, which was perfectly ridiculous.

JOSEPH SUMMERS— Elizabeth had gone off [from Lota] for the day to Oxford to see us [in 1966]. She had a wonderful day away from Lota.

U. T. SUMMERS— It was one of the best days we ever spent with Elizabeth. We just talked from morning to night.

JOSEPH— She said that traveling to England hadn't done Lota any good, that the doctors probably shouldn't have let Lota go. Lota disliked everything in England—Trafalgar Square was too small, Nelson's monument was too large. Lota didn't really want Elizabeth to be away from her at all. She called in the late afternoon, after Elizabeth had left. I told her that Elizabeth was already on her way home.

U.T.— There was great impatience in Lota's call. Elizabeth had seemed to be so relieved to be away from her for a whole day.

✦ ✦ ✦

In London Bishop had lunch with Henry Reed, who did not seem well, and C. Day Lewis. However, she had to cut her trip short because Lota's condition—her depression, her violent moods, her physical weakness—worsened. Bishop claimed that it was during this trip that she realized for the first time how very sick Lota was.[4] They left London on 11 November, and Lota entered the hospital on her arrival in Rio. She was given insulin shock treatments, then was released from the hospital for Christmas, which she and Bishop spent at Petrópolis. Bishop and Lota had to return to Rio earlier than they had planned after Christmas so that Lota could consult with her doctor. Lota focused on Bishop's Seattle job as an example of how people had betrayed her. Her violent moods increased to a point that frightened Bishop. One evening Lota threatened to throw herself off the apartment balcony. Lota's doctor put her into the hospital, where she was again given insulin shock treatments and kept heavily sedated. She was unconscious most of the time.

Bishop trusted Lota's psychiatrist, Decio de Sousa, but not the doctors in the hospital, fearing that the insulin treatments would kill Lota. De Sousa recommended that Bishop and Lota separate for at least six months, because Bishop had become the focus for Lota's anxiety. In the first week of January 1967, Bishop admitted herself to a clinic, the Casa de Reposuo, for rest and treatment for her drinking. As she recovered, Bishop planned a number of trips that would take her away from Rio. By mid-January, Lota had been released from the hospital and was living in the Rio apartment, under the care of two nurses, the maid, and Mary Morse, who had also attended Lota in the hospital.

MARY STEARNS MORSE— I was taking care of Lota at the sanatorium. I was sleeping on the floor to save money. Joanna was in the apartment and would prepare food, and I would take it to the sanatorium because Lota was very particular about her food. Also, she only liked certain sheets, so we had to wash them.

Lota was on sedatives. I would take her—I don't know whether it was every day or three times a week—to her analyst, but she could hardly walk she was so [weak]. I would take her by taxi and wait for her to have the session there, and then take her back to the hospital because she wasn't ready to come home. [This routine lasted for] at least a month. Elizabeth was getting better from her drunken spell, trying to dry out.

✦ ✦ ✦

At the Casa de Reposuo, located high in the hills overlooking Rio, Bishop was treated by devoted, serious nuns for the worst case of asthma she remembered having since childhood. The steamy summer days made wearing an oxygen mask particularly uncomfortable. At nights she could hear singers from the small slum down the hill preparing for the Carnival. Bishop also received a letter from one of her students from Seattle who had been dissatisfied with her criticism of his writing. He had reread his work and realized that Bishop had been correct after all.[5]

Bishop returned to the Rio apartment in late January, and Lota went to Petrópolis. Their brief separation worked. By early March both Bishop and Lota were stronger. Lota started driving again. They spent time together in Petrópolis, and Lota focused on tasks there. For the time being, her life with Bishop seemed to be as self-satisfying as it had been when they were first together. Still, there were lapses when Lota would awake in the morning crying or have fits of depression or bad temper, and she seemed to be losing her hearing. Doctors suspected arteriosclerosis. Bishop found that Lota's analysis with de Sousa was working—Lota was becoming far less obsessive about Bishop's behavior and her taking Antabuse. She and Lota began turning their attention to the future. Lota began to think about finding another job.

Bishop began to write again. In late May 1967 she took a trip on a steamer down the Rio São Francisco for eight days, to gather information for her book on Brazil. She traveled on a seventy-year-old stern-wheeler that chugged calmly along, stopping regularly to load wood and deliver its cargo of pots and pans. There were a number of animals on board, among them three huge pigs and a sweet-tempered ram with curled horns. There were only fifteen other passengers. Throughout the trip, several of them greeted the diminutive Bishop by patting her on the head. They asked about her family, and when they discovered that Bishop had none, offered their sympathies. The captain was infatuated with a singer of popular romantic songs who had made this trip once, and he played her music loudly for three hours every night.

Although Bishop found this trip far less interesting than the one she had taken down the Amazon, it rejuvenated her. In June she requested that Howard Moss renew her first-reading contract with The New Yorker. At this same time, Lota was planning to take a new job with the city government in Rio. Bishop and Lota seemed to be back on track. Then, suddenly, things fell apart. De Sousa recommended yet another separation, and on the evening of 3 July Bishop left Rio for New York City for several months. What occurred between Bishop and Lota during the final weeks of June to prompt this decision is unclear. Lota's father, with whom she was not close, died in June, and one can only surmise how his death affected Lota. There was also one impulsive, unexplained incident—the night before she boarded the plane for New York, Bishop wrote a holograph will, leaving fifteen thousand dollars to Bowen, with instructions that Lota was not to know of her action.[6] Bishop never told Bowen about this will. Why this sudden fear of death before her flight? Had Bishop and Lota quarreled over Bowen? Lota's maid remembers that "at one point during the year after she returned from Seattle, Elizabeth received a letter from Bowen and Lota saw the letter and said, 'Do you suppose she's coming here?' "[7] Lota's maid got a vague explanation concerning Bishop's departure.

JOANNA DOS SANTOS DA COSTA— Lota's analyst [de Sousa] came and spoke to me at the apartment and said, "Look, the two are back here together now, but one is going away." And I said, "Which one is going away?" He said, "Dona Elizabeth. It's better that they be separated for a while. And Elizabeth has a lot of work to do in the States; so it's better that she go, and Lota will stay with you here." Then Elizabeth said, "Yes, I'm going back because I miss my pupils." Lota didn't like it.

Elizabeth drank a lot [during the period before she left]. I [tried to get her to go to Petrópolis, instead], but she said, "Oh, no. I have to go to the States." Lota was very sad, and I suggested that Lota call Mary Morse to come down [to Rio to be with her].

[After Elizabeth left], Lota tried to work at home, but she was taking a lot of sedatives. I kept an eye on her. Lota would be reading and she would go to sleep in the chair. Lota was invited [to take a new government position], but she didn't accept it. She never liked the man [who offered her the job and was in charge]. She missed Elizabeth very much, and she wanted to go to the States. She wanted to live in the States [if that was where Elizabeth was going to be]. [Lota said that] in one of the letters [she received from Elizabeth], Elizabeth said that she was well and she said, "Lota, why don't you come?"

MARY STEARNS MORSE— I doubt that. That was Lota's imagination, or she was trying to persuade herself.

✦   ✦   ✦

In New York, Bishop stayed in the sparsely furnished apartment of Loren MacIver and Lloyd Frankenberg on Perry Street, not far from where she had lived in the thirties and forties. She was suffering from a concussion she had received from a fall during her last days in Rio. She had a fever from one of her vaccinations and a lingering case of dysentery from her trip on the Rio São Francisco. All her friends had left the city for the summer, and she felt out of place and old-fashioned walking the streets in Greenwich Village. Still, the apartment was quiet, and she intended to complete two or three chapters of her prose book on Brazil. Bishop deepened her friendship with two of Loren MacIver's closest friends, Wheaton Galentine and Harold Leeds. Bishop enjoyed reading and writing in their garden, and she dedicated the poem "Trouvée" to them.

HAROLD LEEDS— I met Elizabeth through Loren, Louise, or Margaret—perhaps at Louise Crane's—when she was living on King Street.

WHEATON GALENTINE— [In 1961] when Elizabeth stayed the first time across the street [at Loren MacIver's, our casual friendship turned into a closer friendship].

LEEDS— It was the summer and fall of 1967, years later, that Wheaton and I saw so much of Elizabeth. Elizabeth stayed across the street at Loren's, but she was really kind of living here. One of the reasons Elizabeth used to like to come here is that she had a faint nostalgia for that period [when she had lived in Greenwich Village]. She liked this house, and she liked Village houses, this four-storied world.

GALENTINE— During the warm weather she'd stay in the garden.

LEEDS— It was that summer that Elizabeth wrote "Trouvée." Wheaton and I were very pleased, not because she dedicated it to us, which she did immediately, but because it was the first thing she had written that summer.

GALENTINE— The episode [upon which the poem is based occurred one] afternoon. Elizabeth arrived late that afternoon, four or five o'clock, and she said she'd just seen the strangest thing. There was a chicken that had been run over by a car on Fourth Street in front of Nicola's [a grocery store]. Individually, we all trotted over to see this bird. There was a lot of jollity about the chicken, conjecturing where it came from. That night she wrote the poem and brought it over the next morning.

LEEDS— Elizabeth would stay at our house a lot during the day because she wasn't very anxious to stay alone. She slept over at Loren's. Elizabeth sometimes drank too much.

Anny Baumann was enormously helpful, loyal, supportive, as she'd always been. We had a service that Anny put us in touch with to have someone to stay with Elizabeth. It wasn't a happy time for anybody.

Elizabeth would see other people here. Elizabeth was seeing Marianne [Moore] regularly while she was staying across the street. She brought Lowell here and he made this sort of crack about Wheaton's plants.

GALENTINE— I like to grow bamboo, a lot of varieties of bamboo, and they never do very well. There was one particularly sad bamboo sitting in the garden in a plot, and he looked at it and said, "I think that plant should be returned to nature."

✦ ✦ ✦

Lota's life remained confused in Rio. She was not interested in accepting a new job offered by a friend in a ministry in charge of supplies and price regulation. The work sounded tedious. Then, because of her illness and the vagaries of Brazilian politics, the job never came to be. The legal debate about the foundation for Flamengo Park dragged on, and Lota continued to submit reports to the courts. She planned to visit Bishop in New York in September. In August, Bishop visited Jane Dewey at her farm in Maryland for three weeks. She returned in far better shape than she had been earlier in the summer, according to Ashley Brown, who saw both Lota and Bishop that summer.

ASHLEY BROWN— I spent most of the summer [of 1967] in Rio. Elizabeth had left before I came. I rented part of a flat just down the street from Lota. I saw Lota very frequently, at dinner two or three times a week. She was indeed very distressed. Lota was not her usual exuberant self, and when I would have dinner with her she would cut the evening short. She seemed rather tired and nervous. Elizabeth had warned me about all this [by letter]. Nothing was going well [with the park] and what Lota hoped would be her lasting monument turned out to be something else. Lota was missing Elizabeth a very great deal. She was worried about Elizabeth.

At the time I was a little bewildered about the situation. Elizabeth had left very suddenly. There was some very general [explanation] about Elizabeth having literary commitments, things she had to look after in New York. Elizabeth didn't take very much with her. Lota was worried about that. Lota wanted to join her as soon as possible. Elizabeth was trying to keep Lota in Rio at least for the time being. Lota was being sedated, obviously. Lota didn't say that [her doctor had advised them to separate], but that was almost the sense that Elizabeth gave me, later on [in letters].

Before I left in early September, Lota gave me winter coats and things like that to carry to Elizabeth. Upon my return to South Carolina, I still had time before the semester started, so I almost immediately went to New York. I saw Elizabeth every day for the week I was there in September.

Elizabeth was looking rather well. She was back in New York, the New York of her youth, and seemed to pick up connections rather quickly. She did [seem happy]. She talked about Lota now and then; she was worried about Lota, and she felt that Lota should not come to New York at that time and should wait at least another month or two. The doctors had told her this.

Elizabeth mentioned [that Lota had been in the hospital in January 1967]. She was under serious medical treatment. Elizabeth mentioned [Lota's insulin shock treatments]. She said that Lota had grown very nervous and depressed, quite seriously at times. [Even though] Elizabeth was concerned about Lota, she [herself] wasn't depressed. There was the sense that they would be reunited in the near future. I had the feeling that Elizabeth thought that she had to gain her distance in order to make up her mind about what she was doing. She seemed to take up with people she'd known in her earlier days in New York rather quickly. One night we went to a discotheque called The Electric Circus. Another evening there was a dinner party with Joseph Summers and his wife at a Spanish restaurant. Emanuel Brasil, a translator at the United Nations, was very close to Elizabeth at this time. Later on Elizabeth went to a great deal of trouble to secure his green card for him and introduced him to any number of people, [including] people at the American Academy of Poets.

✦　✦　✦

Lota became less patient with staying in Rio. She wrote to Bishop and cabled her. Lota pleaded with Bishop to let her come to New York. Bishop knew that Lota should not leave Rio until she was stronger, yet she found Lota's pleas endearing. After Lota told her that de Sousa had approved her coming and Bishop received no response to her cable to him asking if he had in fact said so, Bishop agreed to Lota's request. However, it was clear to Lota's friends in Rio that she was not well enough to travel.

MARY STEARNS MORSE— Lota's doctor said "Don't go." Rosalina said, "Don't go." Everybody said, "Don't go. You're not ready. Wait a little bit, until you're stronger." But Lota insisted and she went.

STELLA PEREIRA— Lota was in my apartment and she asked me, "Shall I go?" I said, "You should not go, and you know that you shouldn't go. But you have to go because you are so powerful." Lota knew that she shouldn't go, but she had to.

MORSE— I took her to the airport. Rosalina wouldn't go, because I think Rosalina had the feeling that something was going to happen. I didn't even want to think about it. I just put her on the plane and that was that. I said, "I hope you have a good trip, that it all goes well." She said nothing.

✦　✦　✦

As soon as Bishop saw Lota descending from the plane in New York that September, she knew that Lota should not have made the trip. Lota looked drawn and haggard, and she acted confused and sad. Lota and Bishop spent a quiet Sunday at the Frankenbergs' apartment, then went out for dinner. Bishop saw that Lota was in a deep depression and suggested that she rest. Early the next morning, Bishop heard Lota walking in the apartment. Bishop got up and found Lota standing on the landing of the kitchen with a bottle of Nembutal in her hand. Lota looked at Bishop, stumbled and then fell forward, down the two steps. Bishop tried to catch Lota and hold her up, but Lota tumbled to the floor, unconscious. Bishop immediately called Anny Baumann, and Galentine and Leeds across the street.

WHEATON GALENTINE— Elizabeth was surprised when Lota did come up.

HAROLD LEEDS— [Early the next morning after Lota's arrival] Elizabeth called and told us to come at once. Lota was in a coma.

GALENTINE— [This was] before five o'clock. Elizabeth had called Anny. At first Anny said that we should call an ambulance and bring her to Lenox Hill. Then Anny made the decision not to go to Lenox Hill. With an emergency, another twenty minutes or so getting up to Lenox Hill could be critical. Two ambulance men carried Lota down the stairway because it's steep.

LEEDS— They put Lota in a chair and carried her down. I remember, [now] with humor, they asked for a chair. There isn't a strong chair in that house.

We all went to [St. Vincent's] hospital. Lota lived [a few] days after that. It was difficult because Anny couldn't have any access [because she was not] on [the staff] in that hospital. Anny knew somebody who was staff in that hospital, so she was very much participating in all of this.

[After] several days Anny called, perhaps to my office, and [asked if] Wheaton [and I would be] home for Elizabeth because Lota had died. She said, "Can you tell her?" I said, "Anny, I don't think I can. Will you?" She said, "Yes, I had planned to come down, but I thought maybe she would be suspicious and you should tell her first." I said, "If I can't deceive her, I will." Anny was of course wonderful that whole summer.

Anny came at six or seven o'clock. I hadn't had the courage to tell Elizabeth, but when Elizabeth saw Anny at the door, [she knew]. Elizabeth stayed [at our house] that night.

✦   ✦   ✦

Bishop did not visit Lota while she was in St. Vincent's. Five days after she took the pills, Lota briefly regained consciousness, and Bishop, Baumann, and others thought that she might pull through, if her heart proved strong enough. Lota died on 25 September, one week after she had been admitted to St. Vincent's. Bishop searched her mind during the week Lota was in the hospital and in the weeks following her death for answers to a range of questions. What could she have done to help Lota during the final afternoon they had spent together? Why had Lota come to New York to do this? What would Lota's friends in Brazil think? Had Lota committed suicide? Had she only erred in taking Valium? An autopsy showed no traces of Nembutal in her blood. Why, if she had wanted to commit suicide, would she have taken the less-powerful drug?

A number of friends in New York came to Bishop's aid following Lota's death, including May Swenson, who lived on Perry Street, and Robert Lowell. There were telephone conversations with Bowen. Bowen arrived from the West Coast one day, but she was intercepted by Baumann, who convinced her to return to Seattle without seeing Bishop. Two friends who visited Bishop during this time remember her groping to come to some understanding of Lota's death.[8]

ELODIE OSBORN— I saw Elizabeth the day after I heard about Lota. I was in New York. I called her and went to see her. Cal was already there. I said I thought I ought to leave, and she said, "Oh, no, please stay. It is much easier if you stay." So I stayed for about an hour or an hour and a half.

I heard all about their own troubles, [Elizabeth's] drinking problem and [Cal's] drinking [and] schizophrenia. It was a mishmash of snippets about how one deals with these things oneself. She and Cal softened the discussion with a little wine, but mostly with a little marijuana, because she said that Cal wasn't supposed to drink. Elizabeth was embarrassed because she had started smoking marijuana. Cal explained how he had gone through a period when his doctor had gotten him off marijuana. Cal told me all about how terrible it was being schizophrenic. The main topic of the conversation was [how] people who are very sensitive and usually rather talented—they didn't admit to being talented—have a much rougher road than other people. Elizabeth talked more about her terribly unhappy childhood than anything. She talked mostly about how awful it was not to have a mother [because she ended up] just not knowing how to make relationships with people. Elizabeth said that not having a mother to turn to [forced her to] go into [herself] much more.

Elizabeth mentioned that [living with Lota during the last years] had not been easy. She said that Lota could not have stood not being in full command, or something of this sort, [and that this factor had precipitated her sickness]. She more or less indicated that [Lota's developing sickness] was partly her own doing, she thought. Elizabeth really didn't know what she was going to be doing, and I worried about her for that reason. I tried to get her to come to the movies with us one night. But she didn't manage to come.

MARK STRAND— I visited Elizabeth at Loren MacIver's shortly after [Lota's suicide], and Elizabeth told me how horrible it was. [Elizabeth told me that] Lota should have stayed in Brazil. She put some of the blame on Decio de Sousa, Elizabeth's and Lota's [psychiatrist]. Elizabeth thought that Decio should not have permitted Lota to come. I defended [Decio, whom I knew]. I don't know whether his purpose was to exercise such control. As far as I knew, Decio was blameless. Elizabeth felt very guilty about Lota's suicide, guilty and angry that it had happened.

✦   ✦   ✦

As one friend who came to know Bishop after Lota's death remembers, Bishop's sense of guilt came from a belief that Lota had accused her of driving her to suicide.

HILARY BRADT— When I stayed with Elizabeth in Brazil [in 1970], we talked a lot, and she kept reliving Lota's death. It was something very traumatic and profound in Elizabeth's life. Elizabeth was wracked with guilt. She said that Lota fixed her with this awful accusing look after she had taken the pills. Elizabeth was standing at the bottom of stairs and Lota then collapsed. Elizabeth felt there was this great accusation just before Lota died.

✦   ✦   ✦

Bishop worried about what others thought. She knew how the rumor mill of New York could feed on a story like this one. She feared that people would think she had driven Lota to suicide through negligence and indifference. Bishop wrote to numerous friends, reciting the events of Lota's death and claiming that nothing unusual had happened the afternoon of Lota's arrival. Their last day together, Bishop said, had been affectionate. However, some of those who knew Bishop's irregular personal history were critical.

ROBERT FIZDALE— [Elizabeth told us that] Lota had been in a sort of sanitarium and she sort of broke out. Lota had been exhausted when she left, and the plane was delayed twelve hours. Elizabeth said Lota just took an overdose of sleeping pills. Lota was in a coma, and Elizabeth kept calling. It was a terrible, terrible thing for all.

ARTHUR GOLD— Elizabeth called it "suicide." One of the reasons Lota killed herself was because the men just simply brushed her aside. Lota's generation was a generation of women absolutely five yards behind carrying the luggage. Elizabeth was going to lead her own life because the love affair was over, which did nothing not to hasten Lota's demise. She wasn't exemplary in the situation. Elizabeth simply didn't handle it as well as Lota might have, had the roles been reversed.

FIZDALE— That's impossible to say. If one person leaves another, and the other one commits suicide, you can never say there's any way to handle that. I think Elizabeth always felt a little guilty that we would judge her treatment of Lota.

GOLD— Which we did.

✦   ✦   ✦

Two days after Lota died, her body was flown to Rio for interment in her family's tomb. By this time, there had been headlines in the Rio newspapers proclaiming "Dona Lota Dies in New York." The plane carrying her body was met by a military guard, three governors, and the head justice of the Supreme Court. More than two hundred people attended her funeral mass the following week. Several articles about her subsequently appeared in newspapers, one of them written by Lacerda.

Anny Baumann had persuaded Bishop not to return to Rio with Lota's body. Bishop returned three weeks later, on 15 November, to attend to the details of Lota's estate. Lota had divided her estate between Bishop and Mary Morse. Morse was executor of the will and inherited the house and land in Petrópolis, excluding, of course, Bishop's possessions there. Bishop inherited the apartment in Rio and seven offices in a building in Rio in which Lota had invested. Lota's sister contested this will, claiming that Lota had not been in sound mental health when she signed it. She argued that as the closest kin, she should be the executor. In part, then, Bishop felt that she was returning to Brazil to protect her interests and her property. She was also concerned about what Lota's friends would think about her responsibility for Lota's death. Following Lota's death, Bishop had fallen in New York and broken her left arm and shoulder. She arrived in Rio looking vulnerable and feeling defensive. She found many of Lota's friends distant.

STELLA PEREIRA— I think that [most of Lota's friends were cold to Elizabeth when she returned].

MARY STEARNS MORSE— I'm sure of it. Rosalina was extremely generous in the way she received Elizabeth. She liked Elizabeth.

Elizabeth treated me badly. [As] the will was made out, Elizabeth was to receive everything in Rio and, naturally, everything in her studio. All her books were hers from Samambaia. Everything in Petrópolis was to come to me, and Lota mentioned the Calders were for me and two engravings by Viedlander. Lota mentioned certain pictures for Elizabeth in Petrópolis. Elizabeth fought with me about these pictures by Viedlander. She said, "But I bought one of these at the Museum of Modern Art here, and Lota bought the other one." I said, "But Lota wrote, and I'll show you here, 'two prints,' because they go together." She was very grabby. I almost fought with her.

STELLA— Lota left a letter [instructing Mary to distribute certain items to] her friends, all her friends.

MORSE— [I was charged to] distribute things. Afterward, somebody insisted they put a plaque with Lota's name in some part of the park. I went to that. They'd written the name wrong, and it was just some little building that didn't have much [significance]. I was so shocked by that.

✦   ✦   ✦

Although Bishop was reticent to talk about Lota's suicide, Lilli Araújo felt that she could understand how, given the stress of the job at the park, which exhausted Lota, that Lota could have mistakenly taken too many pills. As Lota's maid remembers her discussion of Lota's death with Bishop, there was no mention of Lota's having committed suicide.

JOANNA DOS SANTOS DA COSTA— The day Lota went I handed over her medicines because I was happy with the idea of her going. I never thought [that she would commit suicide]. [I thought she would return] with Elizabeth.

[When Elizabeth returned after Lota's death], she said that Lota had arrived very tired. The plane took three hours waiting to get down. She and Lota fought and she didn't know why Lota was so cross with her. She found Lota the next morning, unconscious. Elizabeth said to me, "I didn't mean anything badly. I never realized . . ." She said nothing about [suicide]. I asked several times, "Wasn't it anything else?" She said, "No, no, no. Lota was depressed and her death probably was a result of all the medicine she was taking the last month." It could hardly be.

[Elizabeth stayed in the Rio apartment] four months. She was waiting also for me to find a place to go, and we found one for me to rent. She was also selling the apartment. She sold it very cheaply. Elizabeth didn't leave very much to me to do and didn't talk very much.

✦   ✦   ✦

Although some of Lota's friends were understanding, others were not, and Bishop came to the harsh realization during this brief stay in Brazil that many of the friends she and Lota had had were more Lota's friends than her own. They had liked and been interested in her because of Lota. So with Lota's death something of Bishop's own life had come to an end in Brazil. Rosalina and Magu Leão admit that they were friends with Bishop through, or because of, Lota. The difficult times Lota and Bishop had together upset the Leãos, particularly Bishop's changeability or instability. Lota once told Magu that going home after the day's work to Bishop was frightful, because she did not know if she would be greeted by a cheerful or a contentious Bishop. Rosalina Leão observed Lota's sharp decline during the year before her death—when Magu visited Lota after Bishop's departure for New York, she did not get out of bed—and believes that Bishop's actions had made the bad situation of Lota's job at Flamengo Park worse.

ROSALINA LEÃO— Elizabeth and the park [made Lota depressed and sick]. Lota was very miserable about the park and suffered very much—it was horrible, having all these marvelous ideas and then suddenly the park was out of her [control]. Elizabeth was receiving letters [from Bowen] here, and she and Lota had fights. [When Elizabeth left for New York, she said that] she was fed up with Lota [and did not plan to come back to Rio].

Decio de Sousa asked Lota to be quiet here and wait until all her depression was better. Elizabeth didn't want Lota to go to the United States. We couldn't stop her from going. It was the first time in her life for Lota to be so independent. Lota very much loved company and she had many friends. It was the first time Lota traveled alone.

Elizabeth told me she didn't have dinner for Lota [when she arrived from Rio] and so they went out. [Elizabeth felt that Lota took her not making dinner as a sign], because Elizabeth's tenderness was giving food to people. She loved to make special things and was a marvelous cook. In the night she heard Lota, but she had also drunk and didn't get up. In the morning [she found Lota] on the floor. Dr. Baumann said to Elizabeth that she had to phone [to tell us that] Lota was in the hospital. We were just beginning to see if we could go there, and the notice that Lota was dead came. Lota stayed in the hospital for a whole week, and Elizabeth drank in her bed all the time [and didn't see Lota].

I went to the airport to pick Elizabeth up [after Lota's death]. We were talking and I was sorry for her. It was terrible for her. When she came into the apartment, Elizabeth said suddenly, "Where's that picture that was there?" I told her Lota had given me that picture. [It was] as if she was being robbed. Elizabeth asked me how I could take it by mistake. Elizabeth was very brutal. Suddenly she was looking at everything as if she had been robbed.

Decio made an appointment for me to meet Elizabeth [to talk and reach a reconciliation after Lota's death]. I said to him, "I don't feel like it." I was interested in Elizabeth as Lota's friend.

Bishop had much to do during her month in Rio. She arranged for the sale of Lota's apartment and the offices, and she moved all her possessions from Rio and Petrópolis to Ouro Prêto. She met with Decio de Sousa, and she learned that he and Lota's doctor had insisted that Lota not travel to New York to be with Bishop. De Sousa described Lota as having sneaked away from their care. Bishop had hoped that this meeting would clear the air between them about exactly what had happened. She came away from it, however, angered that events had not been handled better in Rio. And as Bishop encountered more and more people whom she had known in Rio, she became more and more cynical. She likened Lota's friends and family to buzzards circling a corpse.[9]

Bishop knew that she could not stay in Brazil. The specter of Lota was still too strong in Rio, and her own house in Ouro Prêto was only two-thirds completed. Bishop also knew that she should not live alone. She had been in regular contact with Bowen since Lota's death. When Bishop was in New York, she and Bowen discussed by telephone a number of places where they might live together, finally deciding on San Francisco. Perhaps they would return to Ouro Prêto in July 1968, if Bishop's house were finished. So, on 24 December 1967, after several comforting days in Ouro Prêto, walking and conversing with Lilli Araújo and their friend the poet Vinicius de Moraes, de Moraes drove Bishop to the airport in Rio, and she departed for San Francisco, to begin a new life with Bowen.

CHAPTER 11

SAN FRANCISCO, 1967 – 1969

At 12:30 on Christmas morning, 1967, Elizabeth Bishop arrived at the San Francisco airport. Her left arm was still in a sling from a fall several weeks earlier, and she was emotionally shaken from a gruesome month of settling Lota's estate and answering questions about Lota's death. Two hours later, Suzanne Bowen arrived from Seattle, having left her son with her parents. As she would throughout the next two and a half years, Bowen took charge. She arranged for Bishop and herself to stay at the Hotel Canterbury, and the day after Christmas she and Bishop began looking for an apartment.

Although Bishop and Bowen spent several days viewing apartments, they ended up renting the first one they had seen, a large, sunny, top-floor walk-through at 1559 Pacific Street. On one side of their building was a commercial laundry, on the other, a family residence that occasionally erupted with quarrels and shouting. From the bay window at the front of the apartment, where Bishop set up her desk, she caught a glimpse of the bay and the Golden Gate Bridge, to the left of the painting shop and the American Cancer Society across the street.

Bishop moved into the apartment in the first week of January 1968 with three mattresses, a lamp, a coffee pot, and her clothing. She lived a Spartan life there for a week and a half, until Sears delivered a refrigerator and other appliances. Bowen left for Seattle, to gather her son and to collect furniture, which she and two friends drove back to San Francisco in a rented truck. Among these items was the brass bed that had been in Bishop's small apartment in Seattle. Bowen then set about redecorating 1559 Pacific Street, painting the walls and ceilings white, refinishing the floors, and laying black-and-white checked tile in the front living room. She made new curtains and hung kites for decorations.

Bowen became Bishop's caretaker. She was youthful and cheerful. She organized daily tasks, taking charge of everything from preparing Bishop's taxes to raising her hemlines to a fashionable height. Bishop needed and was grateful for exactly this kind of companion. Bishop mulled the events and issues of the last few months—that she had been a scapegoat for Lota's friends in Brazil, that she had been accused by Lota's sister of stealing Lota's jewelry, that only Flavio, Lota's nephew, had been on her side, that Lota's horribly insensitive family and country were responsible for her depression and death, that Lota might not have intended to kill herself, because the stronger drug, Nembutal, was in her hands, and so on. Bishop consoled herself with the thought that Lota at least had wanted to spend her final day with her. When David Weimer visited Bishop early in her stay in San Francisco, he witnessed the effects the previous months had had on her.

DAVID WEIMER— I saw Elizabeth in 1968 in her apartment in San Francisco. It was startling to see her. There was an indescribable sadness about Elizabeth's life. There she was in this sparsely furnished and unattractive apartment after I had seen her in Rio not too many years before, with this beautiful house in the mountains and this rather lovely modern apartment on the beach. Elizabeth still had that arch wit. To open the conversation I said, "What a beautiful city." And she said, "Oh, you mean visually."

We went out to a Japanese restaurant together. She told me of Lota's death, which I had not known of. Elizabeth was still terribly shaken by it—that was very evident. Elizabeth was at pains to suggest that she really wasn't sure how the death had come about, that it could easily have been an accident.

✦　✦　✦

On 1 February, just as her left arm had begun to regain its strength, Bishop, again intoxicated, fell and broke her right arm. When William Alfred telephoned her to inquire about her left arm, "Elizabeth started to giggle. She said, 'Well. I broke the other.' She had such a strange sense of risibility." In time, Bishop and Bowen established the routine for their daily life together, and this regularity helped Bishop's self-control. Bishop wrote at the front of the house, revising drafts of old poems—she wrote no new poems while she and Bowen were together—and then writing letters, while Bowen entertained her eighteen-month-old son at the back. Occasionally Bishop showed Bowen a few lines with which she was pleased and asked for her reactions.

When Wesley Wehr visited Bishop and Bowen in February, he was pleased with how happy they seemed together: "It was nice to see Suzanne and Elizabeth together. Elizabeth had that sense of happiness and well being. She seemed very stable and productive. She was busy working on the anthology of modern Brazilian poetry. It was great to see there was some kind of order and stability."[1]

Bishop and Bowen led a quiet life in San Francisco, going to the movies, listening to music, or simply conversing in the evening. One of the babysitters Bowen hired to watch her son recollects their life at this time.

HILARY BRADT— In early 1968 I was looking for odd jobs, trying to save money to go to Peru. I put up a notice for babysitting in the laundromat, and Suzanne answered. Her son was two then. Suzanne was very formal when I went to meet her and be checked out. When she introduced Elizabeth, she said, "This is Miss Bishop. She's a poet and I'm her secretary." It was almost as if she was distancing me a little bit from Elizabeth. Elizabeth was a sort of motherly, middle-aged lady with gray hair—very warm, charming and friendly, and terribly ordinary. I thought, "Fancy her writing poetry." She wasn't my image at all of a poet. I said, "Oh, you can make a living writing poetry?" Elizabeth said, "Oh, yes. It is sometimes a struggle, but, yes, you can." Eventually I learned who she was.

Their apartment was very bright, very colorful, and full of books, lots and lots of books. This was how Elizabeth and I got started. I was then and am still absolutely crazy about Shakespeare, and we talked about Shakespeare fairly early. Elizabeth also talked a lot about her English relatives. She asked me about myself and was interested that I was English. Elizabeth was certainly an Anglophile.

Elizabeth was very involved with the translation [*An Anthology of Twentieth-Century Brazilian Poetry*]. I discussed that with her. I had no feeling that any new poetry was getting written while I was there, although I remember Suzanne making sure I didn't interrupt Elizabeth while she was working. I never had the feeling that she was under pressure. My parents came over from England for a visit, and I invited Elizabeth to dinner to meet them. And she came. She was so generous with her time, and so kind. I was in my mid-twenties, and I don't think I'd ever had that sort of feeling of admiration and affection for a nonrelative before. I couldn't believe that someone who was famous could be so nice.

Initially, the relationship between Suzanne and Elizabeth seemed completely amicable and happy. I assumed they were just flatmates. Suzanne said the relationship was convenient. She had the child and was looking for some way to live in San Francisco. I had the impression that they were good friends. In time I came to see that Elizabeth needed someone to take care of her. She rather liked to be helpless, I think. Suzanne was the carer who looked after her. Elizabeth was always very deferential to Suzanne. She was under Suzanne's thumb, but she put herself under it. Suzanne was very efficient, very much in command. Elizabeth looked for someone like this.

Suzanne had a quick mind and was frequently teasing. We used to practice in front of the mirror seeing if we could improve our faces with a "face-lift." Elizabeth had this rather pouchy face, and she hated it. She hated the whole aging process. This teasing was very nice. I felt that it was near the edge, but Elizabeth enjoyed it. She enjoyed the attention and also that Suzanne liked the way she looked or was concerned about the way she looked. There was a lot of vanity there, which was surprising. To me, Elizabeth seemed old, and it seemed funny to me that she should worry about that at her age. Elizabeth was concerned about her appearance, and she was usually pretty well-dressed. She was a bit out of character with the rest of San Francisco.

Elizabeth could be delightfully childlike. One sunny weekend, Suzanne, Elizabeth and I took the boy to Golden Gate Park. Some children had marked out some hopscotch squares. I remember Elizabeth had a good aim but was a clumsy hopper! It was rare for me to go out with the two of them—in fact, I can remember no other time—and there was a wonderful feeling of release and happiness.

One reason Elizabeth liked to talk to me was that I was an occupational therapist, and I had experience working in psychiatric hospitals. This both unnerved her and fascinated her. She was always talking to me about the insane people she dealt with, her mother, Robert Lowell, Ezra Pound. Suzanne would tease her, saying that when Elizabeth finally went nuts and ended up in a mental institute, someone like me would come along and say, "Now, Miss Bishop, you're a poet. You should practice writing your poems again in occupational therapy." It was very funny, this sort of scenario, but for Elizabeth, it was much too near the bone, and she laughed, but very anxiously. Suzanne could tease effectively, but close to the bone. I think she knew [just] how close to go in those days when things were happier. Elizabeth was very deferential to Suzanne all the time I saw them together. She was always being careful not to upset Suzanne.

Elizabeth was absolutely, pathologically terrified that she would go insane. Her mother had been mad, and she was afraid that she had inherited it and it was only a question of time. Because she knew I had worked with the insane,

Elizabeth could be less afraid that I would put a label on her. I remember her telling me about her short story, "In the Village," and the scream of her mother. She talked a lot about her mother. Elizabeth said, in subsequent conversations, that she couldn't bear anyone being harsh with or yelling at Suzanne's child because her own mother used to scream because of the madness. That was very poignant. In one of our conversations about death, Elizabeth mentioned people she'd loved who had killed themselves, among them this fellow [Robert Seaver], to whom she had been engaged, and Lota.

✦　✦　✦

Bishop was working on three important projects while she was living in San Francisco. She was coediting a book of twentieth-century Brazilian poetry with Emanuel Brasil, as well as providing some of the translations for this book. Bishop was also attempting to write the prose book on Brazil for which she had received a Rockefeller Fellowship (a book that would never be completed). In October 1968 she submitted a report, substantially written by Bowen, to the foundation defending the slow progress she had made in terms of her personal illnesses and the illness and death of Lota. In early 1968 Robert Giroux suggested that Bishop publish an edition of her collected poems. Bowen, who served as a secretary throughout her relationship with Bishop, typed the manuscript of The Complete Poems. Bishop asked Bowen to review the contract she had signed with Giroux and make certain that she was getting as good a deal as possible. The result, as Robert Giroux recollects, was a rather fiery discussion between Bowen and him.

ROBERT GIROUX— The period immediately following Lota's suicide was, in Elizabeth Bishop's own words, "the worst stretch I remember ever having gone through." These words occur in her letter to Maya Osser, dated January 4, 1968 (this and other searing letters about the aftermath are included in One Art: Selected Letters of Elizabeth Bishop, Farrar, Straus and Giroux, which I spent four years editing). At this sad juncture I suggested to Elizabeth that she put together the first collected edition of her work, and she responded gratefully. She said she wanted to call it The Complete Poems. She felt that all her books had been too short, and she got psychological satisfaction from the prospect of a solid collection. Her two early books, of course, were out of print. The 1969 edition of The Complete Poems of Elizabeth Bishop was a landmark book. It won her the 1970 National Book Award and established her reputation more firmly and widely than ever. In my copy her inscription reads: "For Bob Giroux with love and hopes for a completer poems soon. New York, Lutece [restaurant], May 14th, 1969."

The format was designed by Cynthia Krupat, the daughter of Frani Blough Muser, Elizabeth's classmate and lifelong friend at Walnut Hill and Vassar. Elizabeth loved the rather squarish pages that Cynthia designed, which allowed for long lines of verse without breaks. As for the dust jacket, Elizabeth said her secretary—whose name was not "Suzanne Bowen" and whom I will call X.Y. (as I do in the volume of letters)—would like to try her hand at the jacket. We liked the colorful design submitted and used it. But X.Y. and I had angry words about the contract. To my surprise she phoned and said the contract was not fair (it had been drawn up at Elizabeth's request by a very conservative firm of lawyers in Boston). "In what way is it not fair?" I asked. The problem, she said, was the 7½ percent royalties on "export copies," when it should be 15 percent as on regular copies. Obviously she had no idea that export copies referred only to the few random copies (for which the services of a special export agency were required) ordered by readers living abroad, who wanted the original American edition. Elizabeth was amused by my harsh words to X.Y. and mentioned my "terrible temper" when poet Donald Hall interviewed her.

No doubt X.Y. only wanted to do her best for Elizabeth, but she pounced on a non-injustice. I suggested to Elizabeth that we could drop the export copy clause, covering copies for Brazilians and others in foreign countries, but she said "Not on your life!" so that settled the matter.

✦ ✦ ✦

Bishop and Bowen knew no people when they first moved to San Francisco, and although poetry flourished there in the later sixties, few of the local poets suited Bishop's taste. Nor did she suit theirs. However, Bishop was anxious to meet Thom Gunn, the transplanted British poet, whose use of rhyme and poetic forms was closer to her own aesthetic tastes. When Bishop and Gunn met in March 1968, she was delighted with his amusing sense of humor. They saw each other regularly, participated in readings together and became close friends, although Gunn shared some of the San Francisco poets' skepticism about her writing.

THOM GUNN—I answered the phone one day and there was a very nice man I didn't know, whose name I unfortunately forget, who asked me to come over to have drinks with him and Elizabeth Bishop because she wanted to meet me. Elizabeth had just moved to San Francisco. So I went over and there were Elizabeth and Suzanne, and Elizabeth was drunk out of her mind. We made polite conversation all evening while Elizabeth occasionally grunted out a monosyllable. The next day Suzanne phoned and said that Elizabeth wondered if I would like to try again. This time I was asked over to their place, and we got on wonderfully from then on.

Elizabeth and I talked quite a lot during that year. We lived close to each other, on different sides of Russian Hill. It was about fifteen minutes to go to her place. Though I saw a lot of her, it wasn't so that we spoke much about our private lives. That's what makes a real friendship, a close friendship. One reason why I didn't get to know her better was that Suzanne was always there. I'm not blaming Suzanne, because she was always supposed to be there. She was a very assertive young woman. I got on with her pretty well. However, she was so young, younger than any of us, and she must have felt awkward and out of place.[2]

Elizabeth did tell me various things about herself. Elizabeth told me about Robert Lowell. She said, "He's my best friend." When I met him a few years later, I mentioned that I knew her and he said, "Oh, she's my best friend." It was nice to think that she and Lowell both thought of each other in the same way. Once I was looking at a beautiful old edition of George Herbert that Elizabeth had, in two volumes, and she said that Lowell had given it to her, "but when he gave it to me, he was mad, and I haven't had a chance to return it to him yet." She had an arrangement with him, that if ever he did something absolutely crazy, she was to go to him and try to persuade him not to. When Lowell left Elizabeth Hardwick, she tried to intercede with him to come back to her. She told me this the last time I ever met her, when she came back to San Francisco in 1970 briefly to do some clearing up and she took me to dinner. She also told me that she and Elizabeth Hardwick had a fantasy that one day they were going to run off and open a cocktail lounge called Lizzie's.

Either Elizabeth or Suzanne told me that Elizabeth was working on a poem about a whale in the Seattle Zoo. She and I talked about poets we liked and specific poems that we liked and disliked. We didn't speak about theory. Robert Duncan said he couldn't stand her poetry, but she was such a wonderful person. Elizabeth said to me she couldn't understand his poetry, but he was a terrific person. I was interested that she didn't return John Berryman's admiration at all. She told me she couldn't stand his poetry. When her publisher sent her a copy of his second book of *Dream Songs*, she said to me, "You can have it, I don't want it." So I have her unread copy of this book! I never let Elizabeth know this, but I didn't particularly like her poetry myself at that time. When I first got to know her, I took another look at her poetry. I wasn't greatly struck by it. There seemed to me something, for lack of a better word, that I'll call "deeper" in her that hadn't gotten into the poetry. It wasn't until *Geography III* [1976], with poems like "The Moose" that I saw that side of her. In a sense, with *Geography III* I can find more virtues in the earlier poetry than I could before. It reflects back on the earlier poetry.

Elizabeth and I did do a few poetry readings, because there were tons of great benefits. I remember one in Berkeley where Mark Schorer introduced us and managed spectacularly to knock over a whole pitcher of water. There was a benefit for the students who needed bail from San Francisco State that I especially enjoyed. There were about twelve or fifteen poets who were reading, and I remember a wonderful moment backstage when I passed a joint between Elizabeth and Freewheelin' Frank, the literary Hells Angel, and I thought it was somehow emblematic of where I stood.

✦ ✦ ✦

Bishop gave two readings during the spring of 1968, one in Tucson, Arizona, where her Walnut Hill friend Barbara Chesney Kennedy was her hostess, and another at the Berkeley campus of the University of California. Bishop disliked readings but justified them to friends in terms of needing the money. Bowen managed readings for her throughout their time together—marking the pages of the poems Bishop would read, helping her with comments she made about the poems, encouraging her on the day of the reading, attending to her as the reading approached and her nervousness built, and getting her to the reading on time. On 10 May 1968, Bishop and Bowen left for a trip across the country; Bishop had two readings lined up for the East Coast, and Smith College had invited her to their graduation to receive an honorary degree.

Bishop and Bowen first traveled to Seattle, where Bishop visited with Dorothee Bowie and Bowen left her son with her parents. In Vancouver they boarded a train for Montreal, where Bishop intended to visit her Aunt Mary and Maya Osser, a friend from Brazil who had worked with Lota on Flamengo Park. Bishop and Bowen read to each other and played cards and Scrabble as they traveled. In Manitoba, the conductor stopped them from playing Scrabble because games of chance were forbidden in this province. Further along on the way to Montreal, Bishop developed a bone infection, the lingering result of the extraction of a wisdom tooth in San Francisco six weeks earlier. Bowen wired ahead to have Osser arrange for an oral surgeon to meet Bishop at the hospital. Bishop insisted on Osser driving her to see her Aunt Mary, first, however. During her week in the hospital, Bishop developed an abscess on her upper jaw, which necessitated another tooth extraction. She and Bowen then canceled their trip to Nova Scotia and headed directly for New York City, where they took up residence in Loren MacIver's apartment by the end of May.

Bishop saw a number of friends in New York, including Robert Lowell and Marianne Moore several times, and accompanied Moore to a reading of hers in Lafayette Park, in back of the New York Public Library on Forty-second Street. Moore looked old and weak. Bishop herself did not feel strong in New York—she had one more tooth extracted there—so she canceled her two readings but did travel to Smith College in June to accept the honorary degree. There Bishop saw Helen Muchnic, a professor of Russian, whom she had not seen since they had been friends in New York twenty years before. Bishop mentioned to Muchnic that during her first months in San Francisco the popular singer Donovan had expressed interest in composing music for her poem "The Ballad of the Burglar of Babylon." She signed Muchnic's copy of the illustrated edition of "Ballad" during this trip to Smith, mentioning that she hoped this poem might become a hit song.

HELEN MUCHNIC— After 1947 I lost touch with Elizabeth for many years. Then, suddenly, in 1968, she reappeared when Smith College presented her with an honorary degree, an occasion marked by a reception to which the faculty were invited. There we met again as naturally as if no twenty-year gap had intervened. And that night, Elizabeth [stayed] with us in Cummington, the first of many visits, in the country place that my friend and colleague, Dorothy Walsh, and I had acquired for retirement. This time Elizabeth was accompanied by a young woman who, as she told me, was living through a difficult time. Elizabeth was touchingly solicitous about her, asking what she could do for her, promising to get her things she wanted, etc. As for the honorary degree, she made great fun of the ceremony and would have been much more pleased by the popular success of her ballad ("The Burglar of Babylon") than by the academic honor.

✦   ✦   ✦

Bishop and Bowen returned to San Francisco on 26 July. After the crowds and the dirt of New York, Bishop was happy to be back in prettier, cleaner San Francisco. Her difficulties with her teeth had cleared up, but she had developed an unexplained pain in her side. Also, returning to the place of Lota's death less than a year after the event and seeing so many old friends had depressed her. In August, Bishop and Bowen were visited by Joseph and U. T. Summers, who observed how Bowen was caring for Bishop.

JOSEPH SUMMERS— I was running a seminar at the Clark Library at UCLA for two months [in the summer of 1968], and U.T. and I went up for a weekend to see Elizabeth. It was slightly strained that weekend. We hadn't seen Elizabeth in some time. Elizabeth was not as relaxed as she had been in earlier years. Suzanne was keeping the liquor under lock and key. Part of the difficulty was Suzanne was in the position of a keeper. She was tense, wanting to be sure that Elizabeth didn't get out of hand. U.T. liked Suzanne.

U.T. SUMMERS— She was as nice a keeper as you could possibly have. Suzanne is a woman of a great deal of insight. Suzanne took care of the baby— Elizabeth did the cooking—and Elizabeth loved having the baby. She said, "You know I like babies." That's how she explained that she was living with Suzanne. I had such a good time with Suzanne as well as with Elizabeth. I felt our visit was hard on Elizabeth. She said it was hard to see old friends.

The apartment had real character. They had worked very, very hard at taking up the wall-to-wall carpeting. They had plain floors redone. Everywhere Elizabeth was, once she began to have any money, was very beautiful, because she had an eye for odd and interesting objects and was very aware of her surroundings and on the whole liked things neat. She had beautiful things from Brazil we had never seen, like a little wooden statue of one of the saints, and she had her books with her. Elizabeth did talk about all the things that she had left behind that she did have to go back to get. She talked to us about how Lota's family made it so hard for her to claim her own things.

✦ ✦ ✦

In some ways, the political upheaval of the sixties—Robert Kennedy had been assassinated while Bishop and Bowen were in New York in the summer of 1968—made America as unsettled a place for Bishop as Brazil had been. In California there were the campus protests. In September, Bishop and Bowen rented a television to watch the chaotic Democratic convention, which annoyed Bishop. She felt that the fact that Bowen had registered her to vote in a department store said something about current life in America.[3] Bishop joked to one friend about her lower-class life in San Francisco, driving in a Volkswagen and washing her clothes at the laundromat.[4]

Bishop was not suited for the sixties culture of San Francisco. She thought herself too dated and old-fashioned for Bowen. In August 1968, after she had dinner with Kenneth Rexroth and some of his friends, Bishop was left with the impression that the local poets found her a passé, Eastern-establishment writer. Rexroth had seemed only reluctantly interested in meeting her, and although Thom Gunn had been present, the evening had been a failure.

Robert Duncan, whom Bishop met in October, recollects some San Francisco writers' perceptions of Bishop.

ROBERT DUNCAN— Most people didn't even know Elizabeth was in San Francisco. I had no idea that she was here. It was only in the last year that I met her. San Francisco is an extremely exclusive island of its own. In general the prejudice [against a poet like Elizabeth was the result of her being perceived as passé]. When it comes to that generation, we were fighting for our place, and [poets like Elizabeth] didn't offer anything for us to stem from. If there were a real offense that the West has, its our expressionism and our total lack of distance [from ourselves]. [When I went to Harvard to read when Elizabeth was there, there was] the same insularity that we have. Elizabeth seemed to convey that Lowell was captive of the literary scene he was in.

I had never read [much of Elizabeth's poetry]. While I liked Lowell's work, that early record in which she recites "The Fish" seemed second-class Marianne Moore, and her voice is peculiarly dead on that recording, so I never was [interested in reading further]. Decor and decorum were very important [in Elizabeth's poetry]. The same in her dress, which was always decorous. Very, very good taste everywhere. It was a hard struggle for my generation to find a language that would be appropriate in their work. Josephine Miles would have been immediate to Elizabeth's poetry. Josephine Miles was part of the split [in poetic taste in this area]. There was a split between Rexroth, who was outside the academy entirely and wrote a poetry that really is the prototype of the Western poem, and Josephine Miles, who was writing poems that were closed and anecdotal. That's what I feared I would find in Elizabeth, the anecdotal poem.

Elizabeth herself was so lively. She was the sort of person who had the twinkle of humor always in her eyes and [loved] an amusing situation. Even telling about her visit [to Ezra Pound] in St. Elizabeths, she was amused where lots of other people were outraged.

There never was any letting down of Elizabeth's hair, no self-exposure [at her parties]. Elizabeth was having great fun, but she was sitting down watching it. So there had to be this amused sharing of knowing looks and the kind of indirect jokes. Elizabeth's form of humor is one that I always associated with people that ride through a really hard life. She liked me because I'm very definite and clownish and that was very much what she needed. That was clear at that time. Elizabeth obviously liked to have friendships that were free from literary associations.

The famous story [from my relationship with Elizabeth] is the one of her phoning me to come to a party. I said, "When?" She said, "Tonight." As I turned from the phone, I thought I was just a last-minute fill-in. I went anyway. When I got there, it was just Elizabeth and Suzanne, and Elizabeth said right away that Paul Bowles had sent them a package of hashish from North Africa and they never knew quite what to do with it, so they made brownies from The Alice B. Toklas Cookbook. We sat down to eat brownies. The brownies were very good, as a matter of fact. I remember saying, "Elizabeth, nothing is happening." I was shouting because the sofa where Elizabeth was sitting, across the room facing me, was almost at the horizon, and going home that night was very weird. Elizabeth never forgot that. She told it all over the East.

I didn't feel in any way that Suzanne and Elizabeth were related. It was as if she were taking a partner in order not to have somebody who would intrude upon her own hurt. Everybody knew that she was probably still nursing a hurt. I thought Suzanne was a companion. When people are living together, they have all sorts of family play and little jokes and little gestures of comforting, [which make] you aware of the relationship. There didn't seem to be that kind of sharing going on.

Elizabeth never said anything about her lesbianism. I think the fact that both Thom [Gunn] and [I are] very openly gay was reassuring to her, as if you sort of understood. That recognition is a very odd thing, but you only understand it if you understand what the closet is. In that generation, it was presumed you wouldn't try to break down the reserve at all.

✦   ✦   ✦

In October 1968 Robert Lowell and his friend, the writer William Alfred, invited Bishop to give a reading at Harvard and, when the university was unable to supply funds, paid for her flight and expenses. On 29 December, to celebrate their first anniversary in San Francisco, Elizabeth and Bowen threw a party for forty friends and acquaintances. The party went on until three A.M. One person they invited was the poet Josephine Miles. "When Josephine Miles [who was in a wheelchair] arrived, Elizabeth and Suzanne realized that it would just be too elaborate to carry her up the stairs, so Elizabeth just made some martinis or drinks in a shaker and came down to the car, and they had their social hour in the backseat of the car. If Miss Miles can't come to the party, the party will come to her."[5] Thom Gunn recollects the evening.

THOM GUNN— A tremendous number of very different poets [were] flourishing at that time, and the assortment was very nice. Elizabeth gave a tremendous Christmas party. It was the nicest literary party I've ever been to, possibly the only nice literary party I've ever been to. She asked Josephine Miles, Robert Duncan, Denise Levertov and her husband Mitch Goodman, myself, and other poets, as well. We all had a wonderful drunken time together. We were quite different poets, and Elizabeth had a great sense of making things go. She told amusing stories. She was animated, and contrary to the common image of her, she wasn't ladylike except in a very external manner.

◆　◆　◆

Bishop was far more active in San Francisco in 1969 than she had been during her first year there. Bowen was behind Bishop's more public role. In January, Bishop attended a small party for faculty from San Francisco State University, where the conservative president S. I. Hayakawa had clashed with the faculty and students. In February, Bishop took part in a reading to support the striking teachers. She admitted to friends that her motive for doing so was more friendship for some who were reading, like Thom Gunn, and an interest in meeting other writers from the area—Lawrence Ferlinghetti, Kay Boyle, and Richard Brautigan among them—rather than political idealism. However, Bishop was upset by the gassing, beating, and jailing of student and faculty protestors, particularly when two acquaintances of hers were jailed. The San Francisco State reading reminded her of Vassar in the politically active thirties; some of the writing struck her as more propaganda than poetry. Hilary Bradt recollects attending this reading.

HILARY BRADT— Elizabeth was always ill at ease with life in San Francisco. You couldn't live in San Francisco in those days and not be somewhat involved. One of Suzanne's babysitters was a prominent person in the hippie community, and he would take Elizabeth along to poetry readings. Elizabeth said she really didn't feel these were poems being read. I was with her once when she participated in a reading at San Francisco State University, where there had been a student rebellion. Elizabeth was very generous because she gave this reading, although emotionally she wasn't really particularly involved with the cause. She was just a generous person who would do it because her friends wanted her to rather than because she totally believed in it. There was this sort of embarrassment. She wanted to be part of it, because she was such a nice person, but she was too old for it and was at a different intellectual level. She didn't fit. Elizabeth couldn't disapprove of the student unrest because she was a liberal. But emotionally it didn't gel. She wasn't a born liberal, except for the humanitarian angle. She was so humanitarian. She would cry at the plight of the poor.

Elizabeth was used to being admired and respected because she was Elizabeth Bishop. In San Francisco she was liked because she was a poet, but everyone was a poet in those days. There were people who hadn't heard of her, but they thought it was great she was a poet because they were poets. Elizabeth was as aware as anyone who was living there at that time that this was an important place to be in 1968. Although she didn't feel that she fit in, she was interested to be a bystander.

✦ ✦ ✦

Bowen's most ambitious project for Bishop, which they undertook together in February 1969, was an interview with Kathleen Cleaver, the wife of the black political radical Eldridge Cleaver, who was in hiding. *The New York Review of Books*, where Elizabeth Hardwick was an editor, expressed interest in this project. Bowen arranged the details. Bishop and Bowen met Cleaver at the house of a friend of hers. Bishop found her beautiful, articulate, and defensive. Cleaver's bodyguards mocked Bishop and Bowen. Bishop, of course, was more interested in the person than her politics, wondering how this woman from a black upper-middle-class family had ended up married to a political radical on the run. She gained Cleaver's confidence. When they left this first interview, Bishop and Bowen discovered that their car had been searched.

Bowen transcribed this first interview and submitted the typed manuscript to Cleaver, who had insisted on editorial rights over the text. Bishop herself observed that the manuscript would be reduced by half if the profanities were omitted. She was sick of the general use of profanity, particularly by academics.[6] Two or three additional meetings were needed to complete the interview, but Cleaver herself went into hiding, so the interview came to nothing. And as Robert Fizdale recollects a subsequent event related to this interview, Bishop had something of a bemused attitude toward the whole project.

ROBERT FIZDALE— In San Francisco, Elizabeth interviewed [the wife of] Eldridge Cleaver, who was in hiding, incognito. Elizabeth liked Kathleen, found her very attractive. She was expecting a baby, and Elizabeth had promised to send them a Brazilian christening dress. They're fantastic, embroidered and twenty-feet long. Elizabeth had mailed them this christening dress and had never gotten a thank-you letter from Mrs. Cleaver. When she read that he had escaped [to] Morocco, [Elizabeth asked if] I would call California and see if she had in fact gotten the dress. And, of course, Elizabeth knew how amusing [all of this] was.

✦   ✦   ✦

There were difficult moments in Bishop's relationship with Bowen, particularly during the early months of 1969. The greatest strain occurred when Bowen took a part-time job as secretary to another poet in San Francisco. Bowen discovered that she could not leave Bishop alone. Without Bowen's constant companionship, Bishop turned to drink. Hilary Bradt observed what happened one day while Bowen was away.

HILARY BRADT— The first time that I saw the relationship between Elizabeth and Suzanne in a different way was pretty late in my time in San Francisco. One day Suzanne phoned, very tensely, and just said, "Could you come immediately? There's an emergency." I said, "What's the problem?" And she said, "Come, now! There's an emergency!" She could really be commanding. When I arrived, Suzanne opened the door and she said, "You've got to look after my son. I've got to take Elizabeth to the hospital. She's taken an overdose."

The ambulance men came, and Elizabeth looked awful. She was still on her feet, and they were trying to pull her toward the door, and she was running backwards as fast as she could. She had two ambulance people forcing her. They were being kind. Elizabeth was in her night clothes and looking sort of out of it. She didn't see me or react to me. She looked absolutely terrified.

After leaving the child with my roommate, I drove Suzanne's car to the hospital (she went in the ambulance). I heard her telling the ambulance drivers exactly what pills Elizabeth had taken, I remember her icy control as she detailed how many Valium, how many Librium, how many this, that, and the other. It was an enormous number of pills. It was a near miss. Elizabeth hadn't been left alone for long enough for them to take effect. I sat in the waiting room while Elizabeth's details were being taken. The attendants said, "Middle-aged woman, poet" with absolute scorn in their voices as they wrote it all down. Elizabeth presumably had her stomach pumped. Within earshot, she was vomiting, and Suzanne was screaming at her, "Go on, be sick! Do it, do it!" and other shouted commands. I was disturbed by this since it was the first time I'd ever heard Suzanne raise her voice to Elizabeth, but I assumed it was the right approach to someone who's taken an overdose. But I felt I'd been an interloper, that I'd seen and heard too much.

Elizabeth and Suzanne went away, maybe for a week, after that incident in the hospital. When I saw them again, everything was fine. They were together, and it was just like before, and no one discussed it at that time. They patched it up. It was an inflammable combination.

It was only toward the end of my stay in San Francisco that I was aware of Elizabeth being so careful not to upset Suzanne in what Elizabeth said. They acted very much like a couple about to split up, with one always having to think of what she is saying, in case it upsets the other.

◆   ◆   ◆

In the late spring of 1969 Bishop and Bowen decided to travel to Brazil. Bishop wanted to examine the progress being made in renovating her house. In early May, Bishop attended a meeting in Washington of former poetry consultants to the Library of Congress—she and Lowell were the youngest ones there—and then she and Bowen went to New York City, where they stayed at the Chelsea Hotel. Bishop gave readings at Walnut Hill and at Rutgers and Wesleyan universities. Richard Wilbur was teaching at Wesleyan at this time, and Charlotte Wilbur remembers talking with Bishop.

CHARLOTTE WILBUR— [When] Elizabeth came to give a poetry reading at Wesleyan, she said, "I haven't had a chance to see you at all. Let's go to the ladies room together." So we went down there twenty minutes before she was to appear. Elizabeth stood in front of the mirror and asked me to fix her hair. She said, "I don't like the way it looks. In fact, I look terrible." I said, "Elizabeth, you're nutty as a fruitcake, as usual." She said, "I know I am. That's the problem. I'm nutty and I look it. I look terrible."

Elizabeth also wanted me to help her put on lipstick because her hands were shaking. We had dined with her before the reading, and she hadn't had much to drink. In the ladies room she said, "You know, Charlee, I did all the wrong things in my life. I look at myself and I'm terribly old. I should have married. And what I miss more than anything on earth is not having a child."

Bishop read at the Guggenheim Museum on 6 May, and there was a party for her after this reading at the home of John B. Myers, the gallery owner and writer. Myers had been on the committee that, on the recommendation of James Merrill, had awarded Bishop five thousand dollars from the Ingram Merrill Foundation in December 1968. In April 1969, as Bishop and Bowen were preparing to depart for Brazil, Bishop received a letter from a friend in Brazil, Stella Pereira, who was also a close friend of Lota's. Pereira stated that she would not meet with Bishop because Bishop was returning with another woman. In spite of this ominous sign, Bishop and Bowen left for Brazil on 15 May.

W hen Elizabeth Bishop and Suzanne Bowen arrived in Ouro Prêto in May 1969, they intended to stay for only a few months, then return to locate a house for themselves in San Francisco. They planned to live in San Francisco for nine months each year and return to Ouro Prêto for three months. A year later, when she was still living in Ouro Prêto, Bishop realized that returning to Brazil "was the biggest mistake she had ever made."[1]

Bishop found her house nearly completed. She and Bowen took up residence across the street, in a house owned by Lilli Araújo. From an upper window in Lilli's house, Bishop observed the daily progress on the roof and the cellar of her own house. Set on the side of the steep hill near the edge of the town, Bishop's house has its front door directly on the street and a walled garden to one side. From the back there is a striking view of the surrounding valleys and mountains. Bishop's is one of the oldest houses in this village famous for its baroque churches, and she had it restored to look like the historic landmark that it was, exposing one part of an internal wall to show how the original builders had attached the beams with leather thongs. Bishop named the house Casa Mariana, in homage to Miss Moore and in reference to the town of Mariana down the road.

Bishop was pleased with Araújo's supervision of the reconstruction while she had been away. But when Bishop returned, she abruptly put Bowen in charge of the continuing restoration. Within weeks, Bishop and Bowen had alienated Araújo. To Araújo there seemed little need for her services, nor, for that matter, her friendship. They were concerned with what they perceived as financial irregularities and missing materials, and there was some talk of a lawsuit against Araújo. Araújo herself, in fact, had led a successful lawsuit on

Bishop's behalf while she was absent, when neighbors had erected a fence in the middle of Bishop's side lot. Bowen began meeting every morning with the workmen to give them the day's instructions in her elementary, self-taught Portuguese. They could not understand her and simply went about doing what they thought next needed to be done on the house. At least one of Bishop's friends in Ouro Prêto thought that, intentionally or not, "Suzanne created problems between Elizabeth and all her friends to try to separate them."[2] Araújo watched as Bishop, again drinking too much, began to mistrust many people in Ouro Prêto. Their suspiciousness of others made them the source of some derision in Ouro Prêto. For example, the neighbor against whom they had won the lawsuit attempted to dump water on them over an outer wall.

Bishop found that the alienation she had felt from Lota's friends during her previous trip to Brazil increased when they discovered that she had returned with Bowen: "Elizabeth said that the main reason people in Brazil were angry with her was that she took Suzanne back so soon after Lota's death. She and Suzanne went to the country club, and people cut her. Elizabeth was tremendously upset and bitter about this. People knew Elizabeth had had a relationship with Suzanne before Lota died. Elizabeth felt that in their minds this contributed to Lota's death. Elizabeth said that people there felt that she had murdered Lota."[3] Within a month after their arrival in Ouro Prêto, Bishop and Bowen were visited by Robert Fizdale and Arthur Gold, who were on a concert tour in South America. Bishop and Bowen attended their concert in São Paulo, then rented a car in which Bowen drove Fizdale and Gold to Ouro Prêto.

ROBERT FIZDALE— Arthur and I were going to Argentina to give some concerts [in 1969] and Elizabeth said she could arrange something in Brazil, and did. It was rather a gloomy trip, because in her mind we were very much associated with Lota, and she kept saying that it was a shame we hadn't come there when they had Petrópolis. Many of Lota's friends had turned against Elizabeth, including Stella [Pereira, whom they had met with Lota in New York City], an intimate friend of theirs. It was a question of seeing one or the other; we couldn't see them together. Elizabeth suffered terribly from being made to feel she was an outsider.

We gave a concert in São Paulo that Elizabeth had arranged, and we drove back to Rio and on to Ouro Prêto. We couldn't stay [at Elizabeth's house], but we stayed in a charming hotel. Every day we would do something with Elizabeth and Suzanne. We'd make excursions. One day we waited and waited outside [for them to be ready], and then we went into the house. They were in a fight.

Suzanne insisted on driving. The roads were terrible—at the edge of the mountains there was nothing to protect you—and we were careening along. I thought we were all going to be killed.

ARTHUR GOLD— [These frightening events] seemed to calm Elizabeth down in some strange way. It seemed a sedative to Elizabeth. It wasn't pretty.

FIZDALE— Elizabeth was very cool about it. We were upset. I think craziness was always in the picture somewhere [in Elizabeth's life]. She was attracted to it as well as she was sort of afraid.

[One day] we went to see a church with her, and then she went off in one direction, and we went shopping [and looked at some] paintings and objects. There was a painting that Arthur admired very much. Finally Elizabeth came out of the church where she'd been and she asked the man if we could meet the painter. He said to come back the next day at noon and we would meet him.

When we came the next day to meet the painter, there was this little boy, and Elizabeth said, "Where is your father?" He said, "I am the father." He turned out to be twelve, an undernourished, charming little boy. So we bought the painting, and then Elizabeth took a real interest [in the boy]. He had something like thirteen children in the family, and they were starving. Elizabeth became so enamored of him that she wanted to adopt him, but got the feeling that he would miss his brothers and sisters. Instead she'd have him come every Sunday, during which he ate an awful lot of chocolate cake. She wrote [once] saying she was giving him a scholarship to the art school in the next little town and asked if we would like to contribute. So we wrote back and were frank [about the fact that] we had no money at all. Elizabeth wrote back that the tuition for the year was one hundred dollars, so if we sent fifty dollars then we'd get a painting every year. She would write us letters about our protégé. She loved all of us being art patrons.

GOLD— Elizabeth was as good as one of her poems with this child, so tender and so sweet, and like many people who are shy and diffident, as Elizabeth was, she could become terribly enamored of children, animals, objects, which wouldn't be a challenge to her.

Whenever one talks about Elizabeth, one gets into calamities because her life was dramatic. The real pleasure of Elizabeth was the terribly light wit and ineffably light charm and love of laughter and love of domestic pleasure, and all the cozy things that I like in people.

✦   ✦   ✦

Bishop's moments of good humor became less frequent as the summer went on. By August 1969 the tension between Bishop and Bowen had escalated to a point where they needed to separate for a period. Hilary Bradt visited Bishop and Bowen twice in Ouro Prêto and witnessed their difficulties. Ashley Brown visited Bishop shortly after this temporary separation.

HILARY BRADT— After I took a boat down the Amazon [in July and August 1969], I went to visit Elizabeth. I was in Ouro Prêto twice. Suzanne had gone away the first time, and the second time she was back.

During the first, I just had long talks with Elizabeth. She was living in Lilli's house. Elizabeth talked at great length about her house and we kept visiting and looking at it. She would call encouragement in Portuguese. She sat in Lilli's house watching through binoculars the roof or chimney being put on her house so that she could see every single thing. This is when I got the feeling of the sense of home being so strong for Elizabeth. The apartment in San Francisco was more Suzanne's. It had Elizabeth in it. Ouro Prêto was pure Elizabeth. She adored that house. She was passionate about it.

Elizabeth showed me around the town. That was when I did a lot of the talking with her and I learned about difficulties with Suzanne in San Francisco. She never spoke critically of Suzanne, but she indicated that they weren't always good for each other. That was the first time I discussed the drug overdose in San Francisco with her and told her about being at the hospital and hearing Suzanne shout at her. Elizabeth said she had decided to leave Suzanne at that point. That was when she told me a lot about Lota and about the guilt she felt over Lota's death. With such emotion and pain, Elizabeth told about the accusatory look that Lota had given her at the top of the stairs before she died. She told it to me several times. She would relive it. Lota was the love of her life. Life had never been as good since. That relationship was a real intellectual merging.

ASHLEY BROWN— Before I left South Carolina in June of 1969 to go to Brazil for the summer, I got a cable from Elizabeth from Ouro Prêto. The cable went as follows: "Please bring boubon and baby book." I figured [the first part] out fairly easily—"boubon" is "bourbon." But "baby book," what was that? I thought that maybe Suzanne required it. So I went out and bought a paperback of Dr. Spock.

In August of 1969 I was staying in Rio most of the time with various friends. I thought some very good friends might like to take a trip to Ouro Prêto. They'd never been. So I called up Lilli. Elizabeth wanted to have dinner at this little restaurant she had discovered, a very popular simple place. Everybody had entirely too much to drink. [I was concerned about Elizabeth being drunk in] the presence of a couple of complete strangers, one of whom had a great admiration for her as a poet. The next afternoon we were going over to a little town to see an old church, a couple of local sights, and a factory where they made leather trunks for traveling salesmen. I went to pick up Elizabeth, and I was horrified that Elizabeth was absolutely sodden, just blotto, in the worst sort of way, at Lilli's house. This was early in the afternoon. I was horrified by this degraded position that she had sort of fallen to. She didn't even recognize me at first. For some reason she seemed to think that I was Lowell. She kept calling out for Cal. I tried to sober her up because these friends were coming along. She did sober herself up.

That was the low point in our relationship. Casual conversation [with Elizabeth] was out of the question during those days. [When] we left Ouro Prêto, I gave Elizabeth this paperback Dr. Spock and said I hoped this was the baby book she wanted. The next thing that happened after that was Elizabeth wrote this letter about the baby book [claiming that I had taken it]. I had never seen this thing. The baby book was one of these things that one has or used to have as an infant. It's got family photographs. She said nothing about it while I was in Ouro Prêto. That [letter] really shocked me. At a still later date, in conversation, Elizabeth told me she was very sorry that this had ever happened and she hoped that I would overlook it.

♦　♦　♦

Bowen returned to Ouro Prêto by the end of August, and she and Bishop were reconciled. They took a trip to Bahia for a rest and a change of scenery. The floors of the Ouro Prêto house were being waxed while they were away, and when they returned, they moved in. On 24 September Bowen left for San Francisco to locate tenants for their apartment and to return with her son. Bishop was skeptical about whether she would be happy living with Bowen's child in Casa Mariana. Bishop claimed that Bowen had agreed to find a place of her own if living with the child proved too difficult for her.[4] It was clear to Bishop, however, that although she fought with Bowen, she could not live without her. Bowen dealt with legalities, the workmen, and Bishop's lack of self-control. As soon as Bowen left, Bishop was overcome by her memories of Lota and began drinking. By early October Bishop had admitted herself to a clinic in Belo Horizonte, the city closest to Ouro Prêto, for treatment. She was there for a month.

When Bowen returned, she supervised the additional work remaining on the house. Bishop had decided to have a septic system installed, the first in Ouro Prêto. Bowen gave lengthy instructions to the crew and explained to them the function of the system, but even so, when it was in the ground, the workmen knocked on the door to the house and asked if it was time to fill the tank with cement. One day Bishop and Bowen found a number of women on the street, staring at the place where the tank had been buried. They said they were waiting for it to explode. These are the kinds of stories with which Bishop would have regaled friends during the building of the Petrópolis house. Now they elicited only her scorn.

Bishop visited Mary Morse in November 1969 and was shaken by the hatred in her voice.[5] Bishop felt completely alienated from her previous friends there, and even Brazilian life had lost its attractiveness. When Carnival arrived in February 1970, Bishop was not interested. Yet Bishop did have friends in Ouro Prêto during this time; one of them, the artist Jose Alberto Nemer, saw how kind and supportive Bishop could be to someone who shared her sensibilities. Nemer observed that there were moments when Bishop still found life in Brazil charming and amusing.

JOSE ALBERTO NEMER— [My sister] Linda and I were born in Ouro Prêto. In 1953 we moved to Belo Horizonte. We came to Ouro Prêto for weekends. I used to lecture at the School of Arts at Ouro Prêto. During one weekend in 1969 at a luncheon at the house of a well-known artist, I met Elizabeth. I felt an affinity [with her], something very special, and the same thing happened with her, so immediately she invited me to come to her house, in the afternoon the same day. She was living in a house [across the street from her own house], because her house was being repaired.

Elizabeth was very fragile physically. At first I thought that she was much older than she really was, but afterward I could see that she had vitality and a great inner life. On this afternoon when I came to her house after the luncheon, the cats walked all over me, and Elizabeth said that I shouldn't be bothered by that because her cats were very jealous. All visitors to the house went through that test, the test of the visitor's lap. From that afternoon, a great friendship grew between us.

When Elizabeth moved over to the house, I became so friendly with Elizabeth that I even had a room of my own to use whenever I came to Ouro Prêto. At this time I was spending half of the week in Ouro Prêto, because I had classes on Wednesdays and Fridays, and I would spend the weekend at Casa Mariana. Many times Elizabeth would prepare a very nice dinner and ask me which of my friends I would like to invite. She had consideration for me.

One day I tried to develop [my] literary intentions. I asked Elizabeth for the ideal formula for writing something nice. She smiled with her eyes and replied to the provocation, [saying that writing was] very simple. The only thing I had to do was get a piece of paper and start, "It was ten o'clock when . . ." When Elizabeth died, a journalist friend asked me to write something so that he could create a profile of Elizabeth. So, I wrote,

It was ten o'clock when I awoke as usual at the sound of music. Elizabeth always awoke earlier and turned on the beautiful ballads of Bob Dylan. I woke up with the sound of this music and she waited for me in the dining room for her second cup of coffee. The first coffee was served to her in bed by the maid. It was very strong, bitter, with just a drop of milk, some hot toast, butter, and an orange marmalade which she prepared herself.

Morning in Ouro Prêto started cold, and from the coffee table, we could already see the fog through the hills. Elizabeth rose, opened the door to the balcony facing the view, and looked at the thermometer. Ten degrees centigrade. She came back. She came in and closed the door, leaving her cold breath outside, and laughed at her own curiosity, saying that she resembled one of those old ladies of the British theater who do not think of anything, cannot analyze anything, without knowing what the temperature is.

I wrote many [stories] about Elizabeth and interesting and funny occasions when we lived together. [They show] the clash between a very refined person and very unusual situations. I took a lens and tried to look at everyday life through Elizabeth's perception, [as in the following story]:

Elizabeth always went to Mariana, [which] is more provincial than Ouro Prêto, for a change. Elizabeth loved above all the provincial aspect of the small square. The atmosphere of the city seemed not as heavy as Ouro Prêto's. Sometimes Elizabeth invited a very popular group of guitar players and a singer with the strong baritone voice [from] Mariana to serenade at her house. [One] night they brought a poet with them, who turned this musical evening into a musical literary event. [He was] very naive. Before reciting [a] poem, he would give the name of the poem, and then the name of the author, which was always himself, and then he would describe the situation that had inspired him to write the poem. Elizabeth would joke in a low tone [that she was] becoming jealous. She liked this naïveté, and also she found it humorous.

The poet built to a climax and announced "The Death of the Beloved Mother." Everybody had to be silent and respectful. Only a guitar would accompany [this poem] about the wishes of the dying lady. Elizabeth had an American secretary [Bowen], whom she had discreetly asked to serve dinner. When the poet reached the point at which the coffin is descending [into the grave], the secretary ran into the room holding a scorpion. Everybody ran to see the scorpion. Taking advantage of the break in this evening, Elizabeth and Suzanne served dinner immediately. When all the guests returned to the room, after everybody had had their dinner, they found the poet standing, his mouth open, still shocked with this abrupt interruption. Instead of continuing the recitation, he turned to Elizabeth and said, "Dona Elizabeth, I assure you that this mean scorpion has not bitten anybody, but he poisoned the whole atmosphere of the moment."

Elizabeth loved to work in bed, and many times she would call me and she would ask my opinion. She wanted to change a word and she would consult me, you know, on what I thought she should use to express a certain common experience.

✦   ✦   ✦

In early 1970 Lota's nephew (and Bishop's favorite) Flavio, visited Bishop and Bowen in Ouro Prêto. Flavio was the only relative of Lota's who had supported Bishop during the controversy after Lota's death. In fact, it was Flavio's mother, Lota's sister, who had contested Lota's will. Flavio had testified in court in Bishop's favor. Flavio married in February 1970, and in March he and his wife, Regina, traveled from Rio to Brasilia to take new jobs, stopping at Ouro Prêto, where Regina, a journalist and diplomat, interviewed Bishop.

REGINA CÉLIA COLÔNIA— I entered the Brazilian State Department in February 1968, and I met Flavio that year. Flavio was slender and tall, and he wore very heavy glasses. He was a third secretary and was different from other diplomats because he would drop by where I was working and talk about literature. I was also working for the newspaper *Jornal do Brasil* at the time. I had written poetry and short stories and had won a prize in a short story contest. We also talked extensively about my work as a journalist in the Amazon forest. In 1969, since my marriage was not going very well, I opted for a divorce. At that point we thought that it would be a good idea to marry, and Flavio proposed.

Flavio and I married in February 1970 and moved from Rio to Brasilia a few days after the wedding because the State Department was to be head-quartered at the new capital of Brazil. He was working at the American States Division, and I was posted at the Press Relations Staff of the Secretary of State in the tenure of Ambassador Mario Gibson Barboza. Elizabeth was Flavio's good friend, and she invited us to Ouro Prêto on our way to Brasilia.

Flavio had talked about Elizabeth a long time before we made this visit. Elizabeth was a presence in his life. She used to tell him that he was bright, that he would do something. Elizabeth had also said that she would help him to be accepted at a good university in the United States. Therefore, Flavio sold the small apartment he had in Rio to gather money to come to the U.S., but the invitation was never carried out. On the other hand, Flavio went to court against his mother in favor of Elizabeth over Lota's will. As a result, Elizabeth became the owner of the house in Ouro Prêto, among other assets. Anyway, although Elizabeth was several decades older than Flavio, they appeared to be very good friends.

A petite old lady with white hair, Elizabeth gave me some recipes. One memorable image I have of Elizabeth is when she was baking something for dinner—her hands vigorously stirring flour and cream together—while she was talking about literature with me for an interview I conducted with her for *Jornal do Brasil*. She would go back and forth between the pie and American poetry: "Two cups, and mix this together, and, in addition, Robert Lowell said to me . . ." Anyhow, we had fun working together, and I decided that she was an easy person to interview. The title of the article I wrote about her was "Elizabeth Bishop: Poetry as a Way of Life." As soon as it was published in the Saturday edition of *Jornal do Brasil*—three-quarters of a page, on June 6, sharing the rest of the space, as usual, with Carlos Drummond de Andrade's weekly chronicle—Elizabeth wrote to Flavio to say how much she valued the inter-view. Although she was very critical when judging pieces focusing on her work, she wrote that mine was the best interview she'd had in all her life.

I also portrayed Elizabeth and the charm of Casa Mariana in "A Janela no Ar, a Coruja dos Ovos de Ouro" ("The Window in the Air, the Owl with the Golden Eggs"), a short story included in my *Canção para o Totem* (*Song for the Totem*), a collection that was awarded the Jabuti Prize as the best book pub-lished in Brazil in 1977. This short story is also included in *Sob o Pé de Damasco, sob a Chuva* (Lisbon, 1984), and in *Os Leões de Luziânia* (Rio de Janeiro, 1985).

Flavio had asthma [like Elizabeth]. He always had his little pump aspirator and called it his "portable mother." We had an accident in Ouro Prêto be-cause of this portable mother. Flavio was driving my new car. I was sitting beside him, and Elizabeth was in the back seat. At a curve, Flavio forgot about everything, took out the portable mother and began to use it, and he hit the front of the car coming in the other lane. Nobody was hurt, but because Flavio had just destroyed his own car in an accident in Rio, we were forced to stay a few additional days in Ouro Prêto waiting for my car to be repaired.

We toured Ouro Prêto and the churches with Elizabeth. Elizabeth would talk about the house and what she had done in the Casa Mariana. She related well to the people who were working for her there, and she knew everyone in the city. Whereas Bishop is sometimes described as a lonesome woman with a difficult childhood, Ouro Prêto turned out to be a safe place where people accepted her, not because she was known as a good poet, but because of her as a person. It was an important asset for her.

However, there were a few problems in this colonial haven. Apparently, Suzanne was not that happy to have us there. It seems that she had been nervous and depressed for a long time before we arrived. Furthermore, Elizabeth would talk to me and Flavio against Suzanne: "You know what she said to me? You know what she's done to me?" It was a difficult situation. I was very young at the time, too, so I didn't understand very well what was going on. Elizabeth was saying that Suzanne was very nasty to her, particularly about her not being able to write. So Elizabeth was drinking a lot of beer. Cans and cans of beer from early in the day. I remember Elizabeth in her bed with piles of cans. She was very glad that we were there because she could talk to us and discuss some new things.

We thought that this relationship [with Suzanne] was not a good one for Elizabeth, but it was difficult to talk with her about this subject. We were very young at that time. How could we comment?

✦ ✦ ✦

On 2 March 1970, the month of Flavio and Regina's visit, Bishop won the National Book Award for her *Complete Poems*. William Meredith, Kenneth Rexroth, and Eugene McCarthy were the committee who selected Bishop's book. Robert Giroux called Bishop with the news, serendipitously catching her at a local telephone booth just as she was making a call herself. The Brazilian government and the American consulate each sent a car to drive her to the airport so that she could attend the award ceremony in New York City. Bishop told Bowen to tell the drivers that she had nothing to wear.

Robert Lowell accepted Bishop's award for her on 4 March. As he was preparing to read "Visits to St. Elizabeths," Bishop's poem describing her visits to see Ezra Pound in Washington, Lowell commented that Ezra Pound had never received this award. Kenneth Rexroth, who was seated on stage, stood and objected to hearing anti-Semitic, fascist propaganda. Robert Cromer, the master of ceremonies, commented that Bishop's poem was neither anti-Semitic nor fascist. There was applause. A startled Lowell sat down. A more-collected Giroux remembered to get the check, which Lowell had forgotten, and mailed it to Bishop.

Bishop enjoyed telling stories about people's reactions in Brazil to her winning this prize. Jose Nemer recollects one of them.

JOSE ALBERTO NEMER— When Elizabeth received [the National Book Award], a weekly magazine of the time published a very interesting article on her. Elizabeth and I were drinking at a bar [when] the owner recognized Elizabeth because of this article. He was very proud, and he brought his whole family to introduce them to her, especially his wife. He said, "Oh, you're a celebrity drinking at my bar, imagine." When he introduced his wife, he said, "Oh, this is my wife, and she has also been awarded a prize, for her cooking!"

✦ ✦ ✦

Bishop and Bowen's mutually exacerbating weaknesses got the best of them, and their relationship came apart in the spring of 1970. In March, Bowen was admitted to a hospital in Belo Horizonte. Bishop thought Bowen should return to Seattle for a vacation, where she could be taken care of by her parents. Hilary Bradt and Linda Nemer observed Bishop and Bowen at this time.

HILARY BRADT— My second Ouro Prêto visit is one of the most powerful memories I have of any part of my life. Suzanne was there, and things were very tense between Elizabeth and her. There was some frightful row over one dinner. Suzanne threw the food or the plate at the wall. There was screaming in the course of the night.

The next morning Suzanne wasn't there, and Elizabeth said to me, "Did you hear last night?" And I didn't know what to say. I was not up to the situation. I said, "No, I slept very well last night," or something. Elizabeth said, "Suzanne needs to go to Rio. She needs to get away. Will you go with her? Will you take her today?" I said yes.

We were sitting on the steps in the garden, and Suzanne came out. She had packed her case. She was absolutely rigid. She was so ill, and yet she was practicing such control. I remember Elizabeth looking at her imploringly. There was pleading in Elizabeth's eyes to Suzanne for her to make some sort of gesture that it was going to be all right. Suzanne never made eye contact. She just picked up the bag and said, "All right, Hilary, I'm ready."

I remember the agony in Elizabeth's whole body. I've never seen anyone going through such emotional torment, but so internalized. Elizabeth couldn't reach Suzanne. Elizabeth was desperately worried and wanted to do the best for Suzanne, and what can you do in Ouro Prêto? And even in Rio? There was nothing she could do. Suzanne was going with me because it was the best thing that she could do. But it was the worst thing that Elizabeth could conceive of. Something terrible had happened that last night.

Suzanne was incredibly controlled, because as soon as we left that house, she was acting perfectly normal. We played Scrabble on the train. She joked. She'd been crying—her face was sort of puffed up—but she just wiped those tears away, took a grip on herself, and she seemed normal. I was quite nervous and scared.

LINDA NEMER— During the time that Elizabeth and Jose Alberto became very good friends, I was in Europe. I might have seen Elizabeth twice [when] she was over to our place [with] Suzanne and the boy. I had just returned from Europe when Suzanne was hospitalized in Belo Horizonte. Even though Elizabeth did not know me very well, she telephoned and asked me if as a favor to a very good friend of my brother's I would visit and take flowers to Suzanne at the Santa Clara Hospital. Elizabeth never went to see her, but asked me to try to convince Suzanne to take a holiday in the United States.

I finally convinced Suzanne, and so Jose Alberto and I arranged everything for her to move. I took her to the airport. I presented the passport. They stamped everything and took the packages, and they didn't check the photograph. They thought that I was the one embarking. Meanwhile, Suzanne didn't want to go anymore. I handed her son over to the hostess, and I told Suzanne that her boy was on board already. As soon as she entered the airplane, they closed the door.

✦   ✦   ✦

During the following weeks, Bishop vacillated between guilt and relief. She was sad that Bowen was gone, but she also understood that they had become mutually detrimental. She worried about whether Bowen was receiving the proper care in Seattle. At the same time, she found herself suddenly writing again, for the first time in months, and she finished "Crusoe in England," her lengthy autobiographical poem about the loss of Lota. When she received one thousand dollars from the estate of her Aunt Florence,

Bishop hired an engineering firm from Belo Horizonte to work on her house.

Bishop did not give up on her relationship with Bowen. At the same time she had new locks placed on the apartment in San Francisco, she also hoped they might be able to live together again, or at least live near each other, and be happy. She still loved Bowen.[6] James Merrill visited Bishop in Ouro Prêto during the summer of 1970 and observed Bishop's confusion and loneliness.

JAMES MERRILL— I finally did go to Brazil [in 1970]. That trip turned Elizabeth and me into fairly close friends. I'd gone to Peru with my brother and his wife. They went to the Amazon and I flew to Brazil. Elizabeth met me in Belo Horizonte. We spent the night in that city, because Ouro Prêto was another two or three hours. She was with Linda Nemer at the airport. They had left a child's birthday party and took me back to it. There was a cake shaped like a soccer field, mostly eaten. This sort of thing Elizabeth adored. She said these were the kind of people that Lota would never let her know. All of Lota's friends were polylingual, and there was never a chance to speak Portuguese.

We drove to Ouro Prêto the next day with Linda, who then must have gone back to Belo Horizonte, because Elizabeth and I were alone for a good four or five days. The house was always full of samba music. She adored the music, and she had a lot of records and favorite singers that she played, and either gave me some or had me buy two or three that she especially liked.

Elizabeth's letters had been full of hints about how expensive liquor was in Brazil and how particularly welcome I'd be if I brought some duty-free bourbon with me. I hadn't realized what a problem it was for her, and during our first evening alone we must have killed the better part of a bottle, drinking old-fashioneds by the stove. That's when Jose Alberto Nemer, a painter who was sleeping in the house [while] he was teaching art, came in and looked rather horrified because Elizabeth was talking about Lota and she was crying. "Don't worry, Jose Alberto," I understood her to say, "I'm only crying in English." Elizabeth had gone into the whole story of how she settled in Brazil, how there was a mix-up about her travel plans, then she got sick, and her head swelled up. By the time she was well enough, Lota had invited her to stay, and said she was building a house in Petrópolis and that she could very, very easily add a little studio apartment to it for Elizabeth. That was really what began the tears. Elizabeth said, "Never in my life had anyone made that kind of gesture toward me, and it just meant everything."

Elizabeth did [talk about the death of Lota]. The way I understood the story is that when Lota telephoned from Brazil to say that she was coming, she told Elizabeth that her doctor had said that she was well enough to travel, which was not the case. I didn't get the impression from Elizabeth that there was an overdose. I had the impression that Lota was taking tranquilizers or [some other kind of pills], but she hadn't, to Elizabeth's knowledge, taken more than she usually took. [Elizabeth was] not explicitly [suffering from guilt]. There was every sense of a very, very strong attachment. Part of that evening's conversation was Elizabeth saying how she didn't like being typed as a lesbian. As evidence to the contrary, she talked about the young man with whom she'd had an affair in New York.

I was there about a week altogether. Elizabeth said every two or three days a several-page, single-spaced letter from Suzanne, who was back in America, would come. We took an excursion to a prison town. We looked at churches. We went to a concert one evening in Ouro Prêto. We had an evening, or part of one, with Lilli. There was a party at someone's house.

There was a lot of drinking, aside from our own tête-à-têtes. Elizabeth had invited six or eight people to dinner on perhaps the fifth night, and by then Linda had come back. Elizabeth didn't appear all that day, and I cooked the dinner. I entertained the guests. Elizabeth did not appear. By the time I [left], she was still a bit weak but seemed to be in better shape than she actually was. She had planned to go on to Rio with me and spend a few days there, but that was out of the question.

Before I had left [for Brazil], a strangely shaped package came from a stove works in the state of Washington, and I was about to send it back when a letter came from Elizabeth saying a part of [her] stove needed to be replaced and she had asked them to send it to me. Would I mind bringing it along? It was quite heavy. She goes on a bit in a letter about it and said, "I had better stop or I will end up telling you the first dirty joke I ever heard." When I got there, I said, "What was the dirty joke?" And she said, "Well, simply name three parts of the stove." And the answer is "lifter, leg, and poker." Elizabeth gave me a little tin stove as a going-away present, with little pots with real beans and real rice in the pots, very much her kind of gift, when you think of what the stove means [in "Sestina"].

Bishop stayed in Belo Horizonte under medical care for ten days after Merrill's departure. Part of the time she was with the Nemers. One can only imagine how gruesome her life would have continued to be if she had stayed alone in Ouro Prêto for much longer. This time Robert Lowell came to the rescue. He recommended her to replace him for a year at Harvard. In May,

Bishop had received a letter from Morton Bloomfield, the chairman of the English Department at Harvard, offering her two courses in the writing program (one advanced poetry writing and the other of her choice). Bishop decided in early June to accept the offer, although she was not enthusiastic about returning to teaching. She had given a reading at Harvard in the fall of 1968, when she was living in San Francisco, and had visited Lowell's classes. If she had to teach, Harvard seemed to her the best place to do it.

Some days Bishop thought that Bowen might be able to join her in Cambridge, that they might be able to continue their life together. Other days Bishop feared that Bowen would show up in Cambridge unannounced and there would be threatening replays of their worst times together. Bishop was also fearful about teaching again, but she knew she had to leave, to travel, or she would drink herself to a slow death. Thus in early September 1970 Bishop traveled to Rio to have clothes made for her trip to Boston, to see lawyers, to pay her taxes, and to renew her passport. Just before leaving Brazil, she considered calling Harvard to see if anyone had in fact signed up for her courses and to ask if they still wanted her. Bishop did not make this telephone call and departed by plane for Boston, to begin teaching at Harvard on 28 September.

CHAPTER 13

CAMBRIDGE, 1970 – 1973

Elizabeth Bishop arrived in Cambridge, Massachusetts, late at night on 24 September 1970. She first stayed in a hotel, then moved to an uncomfortable, stuffy room in the graduate center at Harvard, which brought on her asthma. Bishop finally located a suite of rooms on the second floor of Kirkland House, a residential building on the Harvard campus. Although a bit gloomy and depressing, these rooms were inexpensive (six hundred dollars for the semester). Here she became friendly with a graduate student living down the hall who was writing his dissertation on nineteenth-century children's literature and a law student living next to her who asked advice on teaching freshman composition. Bishop's appointment was for only one semester; her life in Cambridge during these few months was tentative. Within three years, however, uncertainty gave way to permanence, as Bishop found a new companion, purchased her own apartment, and had her contract at Harvard extended to her retirement.

Early in her time at Harvard, Bishop reacquainted herself with the writer William Alfred, who had known her, through Lowell, since the late fifties and had last seen Bishop when she read at Harvard in October 1968. The poet Frank Bidart had seen Bishop before her reading in 1968, "wearing her mink stole, looking a little like a matron from Scarsdale. She didn't look like what one thinks of as a poet." He met her, at Lowell's prompting, during her first semester at Harvard.

WILLIAM ALFRED— Cal arranged Elizabeth's reading [in October 1968]. Harvard didn't have the money to pay her fare, so Cal and I sneakily paid her fare so that she could come. Elizabeth gave a lovely reading, just as a kind of favor to us. Then she let us know that she might be willing to come to

Harvard to teach. Cal and I thought it would be wonderful to have her here and we asked around in the English Department. They said they'd give their eyeteeth to have her come. Elizabeth was [originally] to be jointly here with Cal.

Elizabeth decided she would live in Kirkland House [where] I was a tutor. She lived where I used to have my suite. She had fun, and the kids adored her. She came for dinner [shortly after she arrived in Cambridge with] two graduate students living with me—they were rather dashing—and a poet. We went to Mother Anna's in the North End. She had a baptism of fire [into the] real Harvard Square. [One of the] students had just come out of a catatonic breakdown. [The poet] was talking about the fact that there was a conspiracy of silence against him. Elizabeth would say, "Do you like your shrimp scampi?"

Our friendship was merry. Elizabeth was just endlessly energetic in her friendships. She was always trying to see what she could do for you. I felt the privilege of her notice as a very great gift, a freely given gift, and felt honored. She had an old-fashioned code of what was expected of somebody who was a real person. I don't think it had to do with anything other than human kindness. Elizabeth could take something she'd read or bought in the store and tell you about it or talk about some preposterous behavior by somebody. She was just very good company. She had the gift of making you feel that you were her intimate. Once at Kirkland House, Elizabeth just said, "I'm blue." She fell off the wagon (most of the time I knew her, she was on Antabuse), and I fell off the wagon. We both got blue-eyed drunk.

The delicacy with which Elizabeth would speak was the same delicacy with which she would write a poem, write a postcard, decorate a house, or pick out a gift. Because I'm Roman Catholic, [she gave me] a little shrine that the poor sell for people to put into their houses. It says, "All this I did for you. What are you doing for me?" It's a holy picture of the Virgin Mary superimposed [on] a holy picture of the crucified Christ superimposed on a wooden cross in a clear glass wine bottle. The instruments of the Crucifixion, the spear and various things for raising Him on the cross are pieces of wood. It says, "Souvenir from Bahia" [and is] tightly wound with tin foil, which they probably got out of candy bars. Elizabeth said that this piece was touching because [something] really deep in spirit was made out of nothing.

FRANK BIDART— I met Elizabeth in 1970, when she came to Harvard to replace Lowell. He wrote me a letter saying that I should call on her; and wrote her saying that he had asked me to. Obviously I couldn't have had a better introduction. Elizabeth was staying in Kirkland House then, a month or six weeks after she arrived. We met at her room, and then went out for lunch—we just immediately got on. With me she was extremely easy, and very warm, very funny. I was quite worried about going to meet her; just because I was Lowell's friend, and shared his opinion of her work (she was his favorite poet among his contemporaries), didn't mean we'd hit it off. I do think the fact that I was close to him mattered a lot. In a way, she wanted to get back into much better touch with him. Elizabeth trusted me because she knew Lowell trusted me.

That first day she was extremely generous about Lowell, grateful to him. She was diffident about her work and reputation. She felt that because she had been out of the country so long she was unfashionable, half-forgotten. (Years later, visiting my apartment, she plucked *The Modern Poet*, a volume of essays edited by Ian Hamilton, off my shelves. There were essays on Lowell, Plath, Berryman, Jarrell—nothing on her. She scanned the table of contents, then putting the book back said, with woe in her voice: "It's like being buried alive.") She was very affectionate about Lowell, and said that when she first met him he was unkempt, but handsome as a movie star. (With delight she told a story I had never heard before: around 1946 a movie producer actually tried to get Lowell to go to Hollywood for a screen test.) Many times she had gotten something—a grant or a prize, or her present Harvard job—because he worked to get it for her; sometimes she had only learned years later that he had anything to do with it.

Somehow it came up that in an interview he had said that she was one of the four greatest women poets who ever lived. The praise was spoiled because women were placed in a separate category, cordoned off: far better just to be considered a poet, however low the ranking.

In later years, as others have written, considerable tension developed in Bishop's feelings about Lowell. Some of the ground of this anger seemed clear at the time: when he planned to come back to America in 1973, his return (despite his offer not to return if it did) seemed to threaten her job, which she needed. (Brazil—where she became so unhappy she couldn't stay for more than a few months at a time—was by now a kind of black hole for her; and she needed the money.) People who never read poetry knew who Lowell was and what confessional poetry was; though Lowell himself was ironic about "confessionalism" and the flood of bad poems about parents, often full of Lowellisms, filling the magazines, hegemony breeds loathing. Bishop herself had greeted *Life Studies* with a great tribute, printed on the hardcover jacket; now, in the early seventies at Harvard, in the heyday of his fame, she felt suffocated. (Such reasons ignore the residue, the traces of promises, failures, blindnesses, angers left after a friendship of twenty-five years: "heavy as frost, and deep almost as life.") The loyalty, what was obviously love between them was never quite broken; but in the final years it existed in a crucible.

A few weeks after first meeting Elizabeth—after we had seen each other several times—when I called one day she said that she had been sick, but I could come by. At the door, she was in her robe, without makeup, straightforward but full of self-reproaches about the fact that several days earlier she had begun drinking and at last stopped only when she was so sick she couldn't continue. Alice Methfessel, the secretary at Kirkland House, now was bringing her food and trying to get her well. Elizabeth was shaky: more or less sober, but ravaged, with a terrible cough (she was asthmatic). She was ashamed, but didn't want to be alone. So we talked. She talked about the painful things in her past that tormented her, events that she never discussed when she wasn't drinking or struggling in the aftermath of drinking.

Perhaps at this point I should bring up something that I am tormented by: almost nothing I've said about Elizabeth's life would she want said. That's why, after her death, I decided I didn't want to be the source of anything that appeared in print about her drinking, sexual life, etc. But the intensity of interest in her work, and the nature of contemporary biography, made revelations that she would have found intolerable in her lifetime inevitable. I just don't want to be their source. What I could do was treat these subjects in as un-flamboyant, adequate a way as I was capable, once they had already become part of the record. At this point, Elizabeth would gain nothing from my silence. That's the peace I've made with myself on the issue.

I think it would be stupid of anyone to attempt to locate a single "reason" for her drinking (as if it had a single cause), to condescend to her by "explaining" what she couldn't explain or devise a strategy to escape. So what I am about to say is not an explanation of why she drank: it's the experience I had. There was in Elizabeth the "lady" who liked to talk about food, travel, things you've seen, what happened to you, friends—and, to a lesser degree, books. To be in her presence was constantly to feel her originality, freshness of perception, vulnerability. The "lady" wasn't boring or self-important; Lowell said that she was more fun to be with than anyone. But enormous ranges of her feeling she seemingly couldn't bear to express—even, I think, with her closest friends—unless she was drinking: subjects like Lota, especially Lota's death; her own sexual life; those she had been in love with; betrayals; guilt; her mother; drinking itself. When she drank it seemed that she had ripped down the self-possessed facade of her life, the poise that intelligence and luck and accomplishment had given her. She descended into an inferno of still-alive, wholly unreconciled feeling, the wholly present past.

At times Elizabeth could simply drink socially; at times one drink made her drunk; at times she drank for days and only stopped when her body collapsed, often ending in hospitalization. Without fail she was furious with herself for having inflicted this on herself and those who cared for her, especially Alice. She was terrified Alice would leave her because of it. The thing she couldn't stop doing threatened to kill the relationship that she felt she couldn't live without.[1]

◆ ◆ ◆

Bishop's unresolved relationship with Bowen was much on her mind in Cambridge. In early October, Bishop traveled to San Francisco for five days to close the apartment she and Bowen had shared. Dorothee Bowie, Bishop's friend from Seattle, met her there and helped her pack. In early November, Bowen arrived at Harvard and was waiting for Bishop after one of her classes.[2] Bowen had taken up residence in a boardinghouse in Cambridge and planned to apply for college in the area. Bishop was, as she had always been, of two minds; she was both attracted to Bowen and frightened by recollections of some of their time together. Bishop notified the Harvard security police about Bowen and asked that she not be allowed near her apartment.[3] Yet Bishop also claimed she paid for some of Bowen's tuition to a local college for that academic year.[4] Bishop and Bowen met occasionally.

Bishop came under the pressure of renewed professional obligations, specifically reviews and readings, during her first months in Cambridge. In the spring of 1970, while she was still living with Bowen in Ouro Prêto, she had written to Howard Moss to inquire about being appointed the poetry reviewed for *The New Yorker*. Moss was delighted with the idea. He had sent her a stack of books during the summer, and Bishop had spent some time reading them, but "she just sat there as they mounted up, tried to begin things and just couldn't do it."[5] She had failed to complete the review in Ouro Prêto, and had brought the books and her draft with her to Cambridge. When Anne Stevenson, whose study of Bishop's writing had been published four years earlier, visited her one afternoon that fall, she witnessed the effect this obligation had on Bishop.

ANNE STEVENSON— Elizabeth Bishop and I met for lunch a couple of times when I was at the Bunting Institute (must have been 1970) and she was living in Kirkland House. We were better friends this time. In 1964 I had been a worshiper. In 1970 I was older and we talked a lot about bringing up children and teaching. She found teaching difficult. "I am really best when I talk about what I think," she said. "That's the only way to teach. If you prepare too much, you just talk artificially." We spoke a little about Wallace Stevens, whom Elizabeth was teaching at the time. I remember agreeing with her that Stevens wasn't such a philosophical poet as he made out. What he enjoyed was playing around with all those words and ideas.

Elizabeth seemed impressed that in my book about her work I'd compared her to Wittgenstein. "Perhaps I've been a philosopher all my life without knowing it," she laughed. Yet she was suspicious of academics, and at the same time she was afraid that she didn't know enough to be an academic. Elizabeth didn't believe, either, that she had a grasp of abstract ideas. How she hated theorizing! I remember we laughed about "the theory boys," as my mother used to call them. She believed that what matters in art is "seeing things." She was a word painter, the look of things isolated her from the confessional craze.

At the time I had two small children; lots of laundry, I complained, and no washing machine. "Well," said Elizabeth, "Why don't you come put your laundry in the Kirkland House laundrette down in the basement, and then we'll have tea in my rooms?" So I drove to Kirkland House with the laundry, stuck it in a machine and went up to see Elizabeth. When she opened the door, I saw she was greatly distressed. "I'm sorry, Anne," she said, "I've had some very bad news. I don't know how to tell you." What happened? Well, she had been appointed poetry reviewer for The New Yorker, and she wanted to do the job, but she didn't think she could. She told me she didn't have the cast of mind to be a reviewer. "You know, I've got all these poems and articles and everything piling up, and I can't look at one of them." And she burst into tears. There I was, left speechless, a cup of tea in my hand. "I'm sorry," she kept sobbing. "I just can't do it. I can't face it any more. I have to go back to Brazil." Feeling utterly useless, I tried to say something about getting some sleep and making decisions tomorrow. "The New Yorker doesn't matter," I tried to soothe her. "Why should you waste your talent reviewing for The New Yorker?" At this she began crying so hard I knew I was saying the wrong thing. So I put down my teacup and left the room. I remember running downstairs, pulling my laundry out of the washing machine and putting it in the dryer. When I went back upstairs, I found that Elizabeth had locked her door. I was hurt, but I think, really, she was overcome with embarrassment at her show of emotion—to me, of all people, who envied her, and had said so, for being perfectly in control. After that, although I phoned her and we talked (not mentioning the incident), I never saw her again.

Elizabeth, you know, was far too nice. To write reviews you've got to be witty and cynical, and she didn't want to knock anyone, not even those writers she despised. She just wasn't a reviewer. And why should she be? She loved to sit down with friends and laugh at things. That's why she liked the Brazilians; she could laugh with them, and they didn't pull out a lot of academic, critical stuff.

✦   ✦   ✦

It was clear to some of Bishop's friends that she had sharp, often sarcastic opinions of other writers. "Elizabeth had savagely clear standards. If somebody was pompous or vulgar or stupid or self-important, woe be unto them. And there would be times when you would hear Elizabeth's opinion, and it would be quite terrifying, and I would think to myself, I hope I'm never on that operating table."[6] Yet Bishop lacked the temperament to be a critic, to make public pronouncements on other people's work. As one friend remembers her during this time, "Elizabeth would have had a wonderful time writing absolutely scathing reviews, because no one could be funnier or more devastating, but she wouldn't have wanted to publish them. Her reticence would have kept her from publishing."[7]

William Alfred remembers that "Elizabeth was supposed to write a review for The New Yorker on the Western poets, the California poets. She said, 'I finally told them for once and for all that I'm not going to do it. I came across this poem by Brautigan. It said something to the effect, "I was thinking of you so much this morning when I got on the bus that I bought two bus tickets." Now, that's rather charming, but it's not a poem. How am I going to criticize that?' " The New Yorker never saw a review from Bishop. Bishop told one friend that "after three years she finally wrote and said she couldn't do this and was relieved of her position, never having contributed anything to the magazine."[8] Howard Moss remembers the circumstances differently.

HOWARD MOSS— Elizabeth wanted to be the poetry reviewer for The New Yorker, and that was all arranged. She was the one who broached it. I thought it was such a good idea because it would follow in the tradition of Louise Bogan in a certain way, a woman poet. We sent books to Brazil, and she told me she was thinking of phrases. We received nothing. They just never arrived. And that went on for three years. I think she just couldn't do it. Eventually, I thought, well, if this goes on, chances were the whole poetry review would be killed, since there was a terrible lack of reviews in any case. So we decided to act as if it were over, and Elizabeth never mentioned it herself.[9]

✦   ✦   ✦

There was at least one other incident that occurred while Bishop was teaching at Harvard when she found herself unable to complete a commissioned piece.

ANNE HUSSEY— In 1975 Elizabeth had signed a contract to write an introduction to Sylvia Plath's letters to her mother, *Letters Home*. She called me up one day and said, "You've got to come in here." So I drove to Cambridge. She said, "You've got to sit down and read these things." Elizabeth showed me Sylvia Plath's letters to her mother in proof, and she said, "I don't know what to do. I signed a contract, it sounded all right, but now I've read the letters, and the letters are insipid and stupid and superficial." She could not believe that they had been written by anyone who was capable of writing the kind of poetry that Sylvia Plath had written in *Ariel*. Elizabeth said, "I'm in tears. How can I possibly write an introduction to this? This is simply awful." I couldn't disagree with her.

She said, "You were growing up in the fifties. You were in college in the fifties. Is this what it was like?" (In some ways, it was—in some ways it may have reflected the contradictions in Sylvia Plath's nature.) Elizabeth found appalling the girlishness, immaturity, and naïveté that Sylvia Plath's letters to her mother indicated and continued to indicate throughout her life, so that even when she was going through hell in London, about to do herself in, she was still writing cheery letters home to her mother. Elizabeth felt she would be compromising herself and her reputation to attach her name to something like this. The project put her in Stillman Infirmary, she was so upset by it. She got out of the contract medically. She had her doctor call Harper and Row to say that she was physically unable to meet the commitment.

✦   ✦   ✦

Bishop never felt at ease with poetry as a profession. During her first semester at Harvard, Bishop gave a reading in Chicago for *Poetry* magazine with Richard Howard, who noted the sarcastic wit that Bishop could turn toward the public elements of a poet's life.

RICHARD HOWARD— Elizabeth and I performed together at the Poetry Day reading sponsored by *Poetry* (Chicago) in November 1970. Elizabeth didn't like to give readings. I remember how she sat in a corner of the vast Cadillac, being driven by some earnest matron to the occasion—it was held in a high school auditorium—with her back to me, looking out at Chicago; it was raining, and she was apprehensive. She sat holding herself together, and I think she would have liked a drink. We passed a restaurant with a luminous sign that came on and off with great regularity. The sign said: "B & G Foods, A Meal a Minute—B & G Foods, A Meal a Minute . . ." Elizabeth turned to me—it was the first effort at conversation there had been—and said, "A meal a minute! . . . Gobble, gobble, gobble!" She responded to excess, she was amused by the preposterous, and when she saw it in something like that sign, she could be roused out of preoccupations as dreary as the imminence of a reading.

At the party afterward, Elizabeth said, "When I get to a party, I don't like to move around. My system is to find a chair I like and get into it and have people bring me drinks and sit next to me and talk to me." I did that. She was doing fine. I guessed she wasn't supposed to be drinking, but the reading was over. Saul Bellow was coming to talk to her, and I left her. There was something about the way she looked, something about the way she sat in that chosen chair in her tie-silk print dress, something that made me think this was a woman in trouble—but I knew nothing.

My sense of it was that Elizabeth preferred people to be stricken—she liked them vulnerable, or rather she liked some acknowledgment of vulnerability and even failure in one's manner. I think she found my manner rather too slick, too triumphant. As we left the breakfast party next morning—every meal was a party—I had to visit a friend on the other side of town, and I excused myself. As I got into the taxi, I heard Elizabeth ask Daryl Hine, "Well, where's he going—to another reading?"

✦   ✦   ✦

Bishop was not a dynamic teacher. For some of her students at Harvard, this quality was a strength in the classroom; for others, it was a weakness. Bishop was pleased that fifty students enrolled for her poetry-writing course during her first semester at Harvard, and she thought the quality of their manuscripts high. Bishop selected one-quarter of these students for her seminar. She was to teach a number of future poets at Harvard, some of whom recollect their varied experiences in her classroom.

JONATHAN GALASSI— I was in Elizabeth Bishop's class in the fall of 1970. I had taken Lowell's class the year before. Then I wrote a piece in the *Harvard Crimson* about her, to advertise a reading she was giving that season. She was touched by the piece. She said the secretary in Kirkland House, Alice Methfessel, showed her the article and said, "This is what your Mr. Galassi has written about you." Miss Bishop said, "It brought tears to my eyes." That broke the ice between us.

In class Miss Bishop was very formal. She reminded me of my grandmother, and I think, honestly, that was really part of what attracted me to her. She had some of the same sort of bearing, quite reserved but also very warm underneath. She called all the students by their last names. Her manners were almost willfully old-fashioned, but not in any precious way. In Robert Lowell's class I had been too intimidated to say much, because I had been so conscious of his Olympian reputation. Lowell cast a shadow that was immense in those days. His every movement was subject to speculation and gossip among the literary students. Lowell very often praised Elizabeth Bishop. She set a kind of standard for him. What I remember most about Lowell's class was his reading of sonnets by Milton and Wordsworth. I was impressed by the way he gave life to the poems, but there was no real way of knowing him. Miss Bishop was reserved, yet there was no sense of the imposition of a great figure. I could absorb her remarks much more readily.

Miss Bishop was very concerned that the students be aware of tradition. They should know, for instance, what metric forms were all about. She felt that you had to have absorbed the tradition before you could write on your own in any genuine way. She had us imitate forms. We had to do a poem that imitated another poet's style. We had to write a sestina, and take a prose passage and turn it into verse. Miss Bishop never pretended to like something that she didn't like. I once sent her a rather obscure poem about a mountain in New Hampshire, and she wrote back, "I really could do with a little explanation, I'm afraid." In class I wrote that "Life at 4:30 is like life at 9," and she said that simply wasn't true. She wanted accuracy and truth in the smallest details. When she praised something, you did feel that she really did like it.

Miss Bishop was not a professional teacher. She wasn't a manager of people. But I thought she was the best teacher I ever had because there was no discontinuity between her self and her presentation of herself. I really was taken by the persona of this artist because there was absolutely no pretension about her. She didn't advertise herself in any way. I still feel she embodies the ideal of the artist for me because she showed herself as a normal person. She was a great poet, but that wasn't her calling card. She was a person first.

KATHA POLLITT— I audited Miss Bishop's writing seminar in the spring of 1972. I had to take various courses to finish a required major, so I couldn't

take her course for credit. Miss Bishop was a person of absolutely no pretension, social, intellectual, or otherwise, as a teacher. She was completely
accessible. She was never condescending. I think in a teacher you want a little
bit of distance, especially in a teacher of something like music or poetry or
dance. You need to look up to your teacher, the way that the dancers of the
New York City Ballet look up to Balanchine. Miss Bishop had that, and I liked
that in her. I was in her class when she had a terrible episode of asthma and
was in the infirmary. She was very sick, and I drew her a get-well card. There
was something about her that I felt allowed one to be a little playful.

I thought Miss Bishop was wonderful. In our class meetings where you all
sit around the seminar table with your awful student poems, Miss Bishop
would always find something very tactful to say. I was sort of a Young Turk
and believed in telling people what you think, and what Elizabeth Bishop
didn't say to someone who I thought had written a bad poem, I thought was
being tactful. It may be that to another person she was quite waspish. In my
Young Turk way, I would have been delighted if Miss Bishop had lit into my
fellow students, or even into me. That was not her style at all. I thought she
was immensely kind and had a very amused stance toward her job. She grew
up before there was the self-serving industry of writing programs and came
from another century in terms of what the apprenticeship of a writer should
be. Teaching a writing seminar must have seemed to her like a very strange
thing to have ended up doing. She approached it with great good grace and
good humor.

I was also in Robert Fitzgerald's class. He was also a wonderful teacher,
although he wasn't as simple, as socially simple, as Elizabeth Bishop was in
her classes. He was a more formal professorial type. He was also an immensely kind teacher. I remember one student musician bringing in a poem,
some absolutely meaningless rock lyric—this was when rock music was
great poetry—and Robert Fitzgerald sort of gamely trying to make something of it and being slightly dithering, but completely charming. Robert
Fitzgerald was very interested in le mot juste. He would fix on the word. In a
poem of mine I had written that a sail "threads the horizon." In a conference
he said to me that when a sail comes up over the horizon, it's not threading
it; it's more like the needle itself. Maybe "nicks" was a better word. He loved
that kind of tremendously pointed and focused attention. I don't remember
Miss Bishop doing quite so much of that.

Miss Bishop was a very valuable teacher to me, although having said that, I
have to say that I remember very little of what she said, but that's true of my
other teachers as well. All this advice and line analysis that everyone spends

so much time giving you goes in one ear and out the other, because you're on your own track really, or at least I was, for better or for worse. She was the kind of teacher with whom you took out what you brought to it. During the course of the year, I had a conference with her in her office, and she said to me, "I hope you take this very seriously because you are very good." This statement was like a talisman that I have carried about forever. It was the most valuable thing anyone ever said to me. It was exactly what I needed to hear, and I am profoundly and deeply grateful.

Miss Bishop was a terrific reader, and she was a great inspiration to me. She read her poems in a very down-to-earth, person-to-person way. She didn't have any irritating mannerisms. She didn't posture in any way. She barely raised her voice. I thought she was great, because what she was saying is, I am here and I will read you these poems I have written, but these poems are made objects, they are written on a page, and that is where their real life is. It is thanks to her that I never feel stage fright when I read my poems, because I can recognize I am not an actress and that the way I read my poem, whatever it is, is what people are here for.

BRAD LEITHAUSER— Elizabeth Bishop was not an inspired teacher. The whole thing was a chore. She was dutiful. I also studied with Lowell. He enjoyed a retinue. It made Elizabeth uneasy to have two or three people hanging around after class. She was very friendly, but she wanted to set limits on things. She liked to have her dealings with students precisely set out— see me at 2:30 at Kirkland House, that kind of thing. We got along quite well, [but our relationship] was businesslike, in the sense that I wanted to be a writer and we talked about writing. One of the reasons she was interested in me, even though I hadn't traveled much at that time, [was that] I was interested in travel and places in a sincere way, and I liked animals.

Elizabeth didn't really direct the class and would sort of run out of ideas. There would be a sense of fatigue in class. She would let us out early. There was also her persona, which I gather she had been building for years, of really playing a kind of schoolmarm. Elizabeth would sit with a great kind of aplomb and make remarks like "Oh, dear!" and "My heavens!"

I don't think Elizabeth was a terribly popular teacher. I know there was an awful lot of frustration. She gave out C's, which didn't please people. This is not to say there wasn't a group of people completely enchanted with her, as I was. On the whole, I think a lot of people came away disappointed.

PEGGY ELLSBERG— As a teacher, Elizabeth was rather ineffectual. I had been in seminars with Lowell for two years, and I was to go on to be in seminars with him for two more years. He was commanding—maniacal in a way, but very commanding. Elizabeth was just the opposite. She was demure and reticent. She used to dress in expensive Italian silk outfits and beautiful suits, and was immaculately put together.

The advanced writing seminar was a very big deal at Harvard. Eight or ten kids would be chosen to be in this master class to study with a fabulous poet. For years it had been Lowell, and now it was Elizabeth Bishop. To be in this class was the ultimate honor, and those of us who were in it imagined ourselves to be quite the inner sanctum. It was an important experience.

It would not have been Elizabeth's choice of a way to spend Tuesday afternoons. Lowell doted on the attention, but Elizabeth felt it was a heavy responsibility. And she discharged that responsibility in an almost school-marmish way. She would come in kind of late and keep her eyes low, and she would say, "Good afternoon, boys and girls." Of course, when you're twenty-one, and you think of yourself as extremely sophisticated, hearing yourself called boys and girls is a shock. Elizabeth saw this as teaching school. The more eccentric students were not that appealing to her. Whereas Lowell tended to prefer people who seemed capable of pulling a gun one day, she liked students whose gifts were of a less threatening order.

Elizabeth gave funny, foppish assignments. You had to write a translation, a sestina, things that Lowell would never in a million years tell you to do. We had to memorize a little ditty by Coleridge about iambs and dactyls. She loved it. I already knew about dactyls and thought it was rather pedantic. It was a very different experience from being in a class with Lowell, where you were made to feel like one of the Olympians. In Miss Bishop's class you were made to feel like a schoolgirl.

Elizabeth struck me as old-fashioned and conservative. I don't think that she had very tolerant critical taste; in fact, I don't think she was really interested in other people's poetry. Lowell could sit all day and talk about who was better than whom. Elizabeth didn't give a hoot about that kind of judgment. She really was an observer of the most unflinching accuracy. When her own soul entered a piece of poetry, it was as though by a hidden back door. Lowell seemed much more fixated on his own soul and ways of expressing it.

I can remember almost every minute of every class I ever sat through with Lowell. With Elizabeth Bishop they are a big blur. Her presence in the class-room was negligible. You almost couldn't see or hear her. She tried to dismiss class early as often as possible. Elizabeth missed a number of classes because she had asthma, and I remember thinking at the time that she seemed depressed. One memorable thing was that one day she turned to me and Jonathan Galassi and said, "Will you come and have a coffee with me afterward?" The three of us went trotting down to C'est Si Bon. She had a huge cup of black espresso and poured tons of sugar into it. I had a sense of her not really wanting to be alone after class. I could understand that, the way after you've been through a high-stress experience you want to go out for a drink with somebody, or you want to get on the phone with somebody.

✦ ✦ ✦

With Bishop's return to the United States came reunions with friends from the past. In late October 1970 Bishop visited Jane Dewey in Maryland. Dewey was preparing to retire to Key West. She seemed feeble to Bishop, who contacted Martha Sauer in Key West to locate a doctor to keep an eye on Dewey. In late November, Loren MacIver had a show of her paintings in New York, which Bishop attended. MacIver also seemed old and infirm, and Lloyd Frankenberg was ill. The aging of her friends and, by implication, of herself, Lota's death, and her confused relationship with Bowen swirled through Bishop's mind during this fall and winter.

Bishop's first semester of teaching at Harvard ended in January 1971. She traveled to Ouro Prêto that month, where she found herself curiously lonely—at first Ouro Prêto seemed too quiet after the busyness of Harvard. Harvard had offered her a teaching job for the following year, and in February she decided to accept. With the prospect of a longer stay in Boston, Bishop decided to try to sell the house in Ouro Prêto. She was visited by her longtime friend Frani Muser and her husband that March, and in the spring she was awarded the Order of Rio Branco by the Brazilian government for her support of Brazil and Brazilian culture. In May, Bishop was sick with typhoid fever, according to her own account, and admitted herself to the hospital in Belo Horizonte for eight days, thus forestalling a planned trip to an international poetry conference in Rotterdam followed by a trip to Greece to visit James Merrill.

In late May or early June 1971 Bishop returned to Cambridge, in part to locate an apartment for the next academic year. With the help of Alice Methfessel, Bishop rented an apartment at 60 Brattle Street, on the edge of Harvard Square, near the Loeb Theater. Methfessel, the secretary of Kirkland House, had helped Bishop when she moved to Kirkland House by supplying some basic domestic items—a lamp, a blanket, etc.—to help furnish her Spartan rooms. Methfessel was kind to Bishop. In late November 1970 when Bishop returned on a late flight from New York, Methfessel waited for her, after her own delayed flight had arrived a short time earlier. When Bishop arrived in Cambridge in June 1971, weak from typhoid fever and other amoebic infections, she stayed with Methfessel, who fed her, kept track of her temperature, and nursed her back to health. Later that month Bishop and Methfessel traveled to Rockport, Massachusetts, where a relative of Methfessel's had a house. By the end of the month, as a result of Methfessel's attention, Bishop was feeling better than she had felt in some time and was working hard on a couple of pieces of writing. Helen Vendler and Julia Strand both observed the pleasure and security that Bishop's relationship with Methfessel brought into her life, as did Hilary Bradt, who had not seen Bishop since the turbulent weeks with Bowen in Ouro Prêto.

HELEN VENDLER— Elizabeth adored Alice. She thought Alice was so beautiful, and she was so touched when Alice did anything for her. I remember an incident in which Alice reached over and buttoned a button that had come undone on one of those button-down-the-front dresses. Elizabeth looked so delighted that Alice had noticed and done something for her. Alice was, of course, an efficient and practical person; it made Elizabeth feel a lot safer that somebody was indeed looking after her. And Alice seemed extremely fond of Elizabeth. It seemed a very lucky relationship that Elizabeth had found in this unpropitious atmosphere—Harvard, the English Department, a new city to live in, all that.

JULIA STRAND— There was a kind of maternalism on Alice's part, a lot of concern that seemed to be played out. I just remember a general sense of Alice being a keeper. Elizabeth had a bit of a "know-nothing" attitude. She would never claim herself to be an intellectual or even literary. I suppose in some way choosing that kind of mate was a way of underscoring that. The conversations never veered toward ideas. I don't think that if you hadn't known they were lovers, you would have [surmised]. There [were none of] those little gestures.

HILARY BRADT— When she first came to Boston, Elizabeth was feeling out of it. She didn't feel that she fit. I remember her saying that all the students wanted to write free verse, and she wanted them to do iambic pentameter. She refused to give in. Elizabeth just felt she was an old-fashioned fuddy-duddy that no one wanted to listen to. She hated teaching. She didn't have any self-confidence. She felt that she was a bad teacher, that no one wanted to listen to her. She sort of let drop that in fact the class was well attended.

That's why Elizabeth was so happy with Alice. She felt that she had really found her niche. Elizabeth put it to over to my husband and me that she'd finally found it, that Alice was it. Alice was calm. Alice didn't throw dinner plated around, didn't scream. When my husband and I met Alice, she was very cool, very elegant, rather distancing, and took care of Elizabeth without emotional overtones of possessiveness and all the problems she'd had with other lovers. It's like a marriage; someone finds someone else emotionally stable after rocky marriages.

Once Alice came into Elizabeth's life, she perhaps didn't need her other friends as much. Although Alice was politely friendly, she seemed cool toward us, and I felt a bit unwilling to phone up and invite ourselves over. Perhaps my needs were less too, since I had just got married. We had a couple of meetings with Elizabeth after she got back from South America. Since we were hoping to go to the Galapagos Islands, we wanted to hear all about them. As always, Elizabeth was as interested in our plans as in telling us about her own trip, and was as warm and friendly as ever.

✦ ✦ ✦

In August, Bishop and Methfessel traveled together to Peru, to see Machu Picchu, and the Galapagos Islands, which Bishop particularly liked. Following the visit to the Galapagos, Bishop spent a short time in Ouro Prêto. An arts festival that had been in progress since the spring was concluding in August, and Bishop found herself involved in an unfortunate aspect of it. In March the bohemian Living Theater had arrived in Ouro Prêto for the arts festival. Bishop met some of the actors, and they gave her two of their plays to read. The plays reminded her of the kind of propaganda she had read while she was at Vassar in the thirties. The group got itself into some sort of legal trouble and in August asked Bishop to testify on their behalf. As Ashley Brown recollects, Bishop became anxious about her acquaintance with these artists.

ASHLEY BROWN— I saw Elizabeth early in the summer of 1971. She was already trying to sell the house [in Ouro Prêto]. When I got to Rio, she had sent a note to me that also included a kind of ad for the house. The note seemed to indicate that things were very bad in some way or another up in Ouro Prêto. I took the first plane up to Belo Horizonte and a taxi over there.

It seemed that the Living Theater had been inhabitants for some time in the area. Ouro Prêto had become a kind of Katmando [during an arts festival]. They had gotten themselves a very bad reputation in Ouro Prêto, which is a conservative, old-fashioned town by Brazilian standards, even American standards. Imagine some very old-fashioned community in Alabama and all these people flaunting themselves. They were being denounced by the priests from the pulpits. Elizabeth had gone off for a month or so, and she'd lent the house to some member of the company with whom she was acquainted. Apparently, while she was gone, her house got this terrible reputation. Hence, she did.

Elizabeth maintained, in an almost paranoic sort of way, that she was being persecuted, the police were opening her mail, and other things, too. Also, this happened to coincide with a rather bad period in the military regime, the nadir almost. People were being arrested and sometimes thrown into awful jails, maltreated, and some of these things had happened with a couple of those people in the Living Theater Company. Elizabeth was in an absolutely paranoic state. She was completely by herself up there. I stayed a few days, and things seemed to get a little bit better. The mail seemed to arrive after all.

✦ ✦ ✦

Bishop returned to Cambridge in early September 1971 to arrange her apartment on Brattle Street. She bought a Ping-Pong table, which she placed in the front hall. "Elizabeth said that she had to have a Ping-Pong table, and there was no room in the apartment for a Ping-Pong table and a dining table. You could eat off the Ping-Pong table, she said, but you couldn't play Ping-Pong on a dining table."[10] William Alfred recollects details of this apartment.

WILLIAM ALFRED— [The Brattle Street] apartment [building] is a series of dentists' offices, so you couldn't imagine Elizabeth's apartment being pretty. You walked into a very large hall, and there was a merry Ping-Pong table that could be turned into a dining table. She had a small bedroom, which was also her study, facing out toward the Loeb Theater. I never pass there without looking up and wishing she was still there. And then there was a living room with beautiful *santos* like [the one she gave me], little stone things, and everything lovely and fascinating. She had simple, modern furniture. [Once] Elizabeth made me one of those Brazilian meals, with black beans and oranges and sausage and everything else. I was worried about a friend that day, and as I left she said, "You look kind of blue." I said, "Oh, no, I'm full of beans." And Elizabeth said, "I know you're full of beans, but you still look blue."

✦ ✦ ✦

In the fall of 1971 Bishop was a judge for the Amy Lowell Traveling Fellowship, an award she herself had received in 1950. Bishop served on this committee with William Alfred and Richard Wilbur, who recollects working with her and seeing her in Cambridge during her years at Harvard.

RICHARD WILBUR— For a while, Bill Alfred, Elizabeth, and I were judges for the Amy Lowell Traveling Fellowship. It was a great amusement to have a three-way correspondence with those two about the applicants and the merits of the applicants. There was never any exulting in the badness of the candidates, never any cruelty in what Elizabeth had to say. She would sometimes manage quite a lot of indecision—on the one hand, on the other hand—and then suddenly become downright. There's one postcard I have from her from that period in which toward the end of the card she suddenly says, "But she is so *bad!*"

✦   ✦   ✦

The fall of 1971 was a difficult one for Bishop. Lota's nephew, Flavio, killed himself.[11] Also, Bishop was struck with the worst attack of asthma she experienced during her time at Boston. In November she was driven to Vassar for a reading, and animal hair in the car started her wheezing. After she returned to Boston, she was admitted to Peter Bent Brigham Hospital in the middle of the night and was placed in intensive care. Her closest friends feared that she was dying. A broncoscopy was performed, during which three caps on her teeth were knocked out and pieces of enamel were chipped off two other teeth. This emergency procedure worked, but Bishop was blunt with her doctors about their expertise: "When Elizabeth came out of the general anesthetic, the caps on her teeth were gone. The doctor said, 'You're all right. We cleaned out your lungs. We found some gravel in your lungs. I don't know how it got there.' Elizabeth said, 'Well, I know how. You knocked out my teeth with that thing you rammed down my throat.' "[12]

After a week, Bishop was moved to the Harvard Health Services. Frank Bidart brought her ice cream and read to her. Students popped up at her bedside; Methfessel came for lunch every day; and William Alfred took Bishop's classes during her four-week absence. Jane Shore came to know Bishop during this time.[13]

JANE SHORE— I met Elizabeth Bishop in September 1971. I was appointed a Fellow in Poetry at the Radcliffe Institute, now called the Bunting Institute, in Cambridge, Massachusetts. I had a grant to write poetry for two years and was encouraged to audit classes at Harvard, if I felt like it. The previous June I had received my M.F.A. from the Iowa Writers Workshop and couldn't believe my good luck at the chance of being given two years to write, *and* at the place where Robert Lowell was currently teaching. I had hoped to sit in on his famous "open poetry workshops," but Lowell was in England that fall semester, and I was very disappointed that I would miss him altogether. But I remember Kathleen Fraser, one of my teachers at Iowa, telling me that a wonderful poet named Elizabeth Bishop was teaching at Harvard, and that I should try to work with her. I knew nothing about Elizabeth then. I hadn't read even one of her poems. When I arrived at the Radcliffe Institute, however, there was an invitation from Elizabeth to come to her house for coffee. I was thrilled that Elizabeth had extended this courtesy to me, a total stranger.

I asked Elizabeth permission to sit in her undergraduate poetry writing workshop. I can see now that I was looking for a mentor. From the first day in her workshop, one could easily tell that she was uncomfortable as a teacher. She announced to the class that she had asked W. H. Auden how she should teach a writing class. Auden advised her to teach metrics and make her students do formal exercises and memorize poems, all of which Elizabeth thought were good ideas. Now, despite her general discomfort in the class-room, it was a great pleasure—even a reprieve, if you will—to study with her, having just been at Iowa where others had used the classroom mostly to talk about themselves. In this initial regard I was fascinated with Elizabeth, a truly great poet acting with such restraint, integrity, and inimitable humor. I think that Elizabeth taught best anecdotally; that is, she would weave personal knowledge of poets in with a concise, critical take on a particular poem or on their work in general, and this method spiced things up a bit, made her accounts both personal and historical.

At first I thought her reading list peculiar—it included Nadeshda Mandel-shtam's *Hope Against Hope* and Edwin Newman's (the television announcer and journalist) *A Civil Tongue*. I believe she assigned Newman's book, which was a best-selling paperback at the time, because it was about using English correctly, accurately. Bishop assigned Mandelshtam's book because she wanted us to know how easy we poets in America had it, in terms of having the freedom to write about anything without fear of political reprisal. She'd said this in an understated way, and in perhaps two sentences. This was the closest to a lecture that I heard her give.

To say the very least, Elizabeth's poems were not in vogue. Now we know that her peers, and others of a deeper understanding, knew her stature. But I remember the ubiquity of poets such as James Tate, W. S. Merwin, Diane Wakoski, and Anne Sexton. With that modernity of style and voice such a presence, Elizabeth's work seemed of another age, if you will. Many poets, especially young ones, strove for a kind of jazzy surrealism that was hip at the time. I bought Bishop's *Collected Poems*, began reading her poems and was struck by their clarity and stunning images. However, I was so afraid I would get so intimidated and awed by Elizabeth Bishop, the famous (though under-rated) poet, that I would freeze around her and not be able to speak with her, be a friend, as it were. I thought perhaps it was best at the time to stay slightly distant from her work and get to know her as a person instead, but of course eventually she became a central presence in my thinking about poetry and in my memory of those years. I can hardly claim to be alone in this!

I wasn't interested in writing the traditional forms that Elizabeth had assigned our class, but I did give her other poems in free verse that I was writing. She commented on them, made notes on the accuracy or inaccuracy of my language, technical things, very succinct, wonderfully observed, di-rectly useful. If the rhythm or meter was off, she'd pencil a shaky little *x* in the margin after the offending line. Her responses were low-key, minimal, "old fashioned" as a school teacher's—again quite the opposite of what I'd experi-enced at Iowa, where the primary form of criticism was to tear poems to shreds. And where the egos of both poet teachers and budding student poets were necessary to elevate the importance of the poems we were examining. The cult of personality. With Elizabeth there seemed to be almost a complete lack of ego compared to what I'd recently been through.

Naturally, Elizabeth could be very passionate about criticizing our work. She and I once had a disagreement about my use of the word "unravel" in my poem. I think that I'd said that a "ribbon of traffic unraveled into the winter morning" and Elizabeth vehemently (for her) took exception to this word, saying that the verb was imprecise—she just couldn't *see* it. She once faulted the work of a poet whose work I'd admired and whom she was curious about—I'd brought his book to her apartment to show her and I was sur-prised that after reading his poems the one thing she objected to was his unremitting use of caesura in line after line, that is, the overuse of a device that, in her opinion, should be sparingly used. At the time, these seemed like small things to learn, and yet they were large for me. It was the care and attention to the small details that I learned from her, I think, almost by osmosis. But her method of criticism, at least in my experience, was col-laborative rather than an attack. That was criticism on the page. In the classroom, there were silences, but slowly, as the class progressed, students began participating more, the way I had heard that they had in Lowell's classes, a kind of participatory audience. Add that to a protective attitude people seemed to cultivate toward Elizabeth, even a need to defend her— "She is a great poet!"—and you have a sense of the atmosphere.

The early seventies was a very vital time for a poet to be at Harvard: Lowell, Bishop, Robert Fitzgerald, Bill Alfred, Octavio Paz, Peter Taylor were there. When Elizabeth Bishop became ill and was unable to meet her classes, her writer-friends would pinch-hit for her and take turns teaching. It's a time one can continually draw aesthetic sustenance from, aside from the emotional dimensions of being a young poet around such large presences.

One would both interact with Elizabeth and yet keep a bit of a formal, observing distance. I speak only for myself here, but I think others would recognize the accuracy of what I am remembering. I seemed to have personalized things about Elizabeth from early on. A specific instance comes to mind. Early in that fall semester when I first met her, Frank Bidart phoned me and said, "Elizabeth wants to see you. Would you like to visit Elizabeth?" She had recently had a severe asthma attack and was recuperating at Harvard's Stillman Infirmary. I had only recently met Frank through Elizabeth, and I felt quite shy about seeing her in the hospital, but I went with him anyway. Frank brought her a couple of desserts—custard cups that she particularly loved that Sages Market made then. When we got there, Elizabeth seemed weak, but happy to see us. She was embarrassed because the doctors had knocked a couple of her teeth out in inserting a breathing tube down her throat. I remember her saying that the hospital food was great and that the chef had been Rommel's former chef. I think it was that same afternoon that "Jimmy" Merrill came to pay a get-well call on Elizabeth. I almost fainted when he walked into the room. Yet for all Elizabeth's apparent accessibility and the complete opposite of that, her moodiness, in all honesty, I was timid and stayed away— partly because at this point in her life Elizabeth, this *amazing* poet in our midst, had an almost desperate talent at making friends (and acquaintances) attend to her, help her do her shopping, drive her places, in fact, become quite indispensable. I was afraid of becoming a "hanger-on." Of course, there were reciprocities—to be around Elizabeth was to have experiences you couldn't indeed otherwise have. Yet in effect I kept my distance.

✦   ✦   ✦

Bishop recovered from this illness by January 1972. In fact, Methfessel had her cross-country skiing that month. She also gave readings at Bryn Mawr, Princeton, and the University of Oklahoma. Bishop received honorary degrees in 1972 from Brown and Rutgers.[14] Bishop was asked to deliver the Phi Beta Kappa poem at Harvard on 13 June, two days before the Harvard graduation. Throughout the spring she had been working on "The Moose" for that occasion, and, as was often the case with Bishop and deadlines, she still had work to complete as the date for the reading approached. Jane Shore remembers Bishop working on the poem that spring: "When I went into Elizabeth's study once on Brattle Street, I saw a cork bulletin board over the desk. On the board was a poem that was cut in pieces. It was a long poem, and I think it might have been 'The Moose.'" Frank Bidart was with Bishop as she completed the poem, which she did finish on time and deliver successfully.

FRANK BIDART— Elizabeth never showed me drafts of poems at as early a stage, or in as much detail, as Lowell did. A new poem was mostly finished by the time I saw it. The first uncompleted poem I saw was "Poem." Elizabeth was already living on Brattle Street, so it was her second year in Cambridge. Two or three spots still were giving her trouble, and she had variants handwritten in the margins. I still see her standing over her kitchen table, puzzling over what became "A specklike bird is flying to the left. / Or is it a flyspeck looking like a bird?" The other rough passage, written and rewritten over the next few weeks, was the great passage about "art 'copying from life' and life itself," in the last stanza. The problem here, of course, is how to use such abstract, even academic language and not have it swallow up, flatten, banalize the poem; it's characteristic of her that she felt both the necessity of it, of reaching this level of generality, and had to find some way to put a "skin" on such language, ground it in the skepticism and specificities of her own speaking voice. (She struggled in the same way with the "literary interpretations" passage in "Santarem.")

There are two instances in which I think I was useful to Elizabeth. After she had sent "The End of March" to The New Yorker, she was unhappy with the last stanza and rewrote it again and again. She dictated a set of final changes to me over the phone; clearly it was improved. I retyped the stanza so I'd have a clean copy with the changes. (By now it was too late to incorporate them in The New Yorker.) Geography III was set by Farrar, Straus, and Giroux from magazine copies of the poems. When page proofs arrived (I don't think there was a separate set of galleys) the poem had the magazine ending; I was upset. By now the poem was just old enough that Elizabeth had forgotten that she hadn't been able to let it go without revising it; and now she couldn't find the revision. So the single typed copy I made was the source of the version in the book.[15]

In some sense, for Elizabeth, getting a poem right was almost a Platonic act; once she was satisfied, the details over which she had struggled so much ceased to have some of their reality. (There is an important stanza break missing in "Over 2,000 Illustrations and a Complete Concordance" in her first *Complete Poems*, which she didn't notice for years; David Kalstone caught it.) She also had a confident, decisive, original sense of details: she told me once that she had to fight with *The New Yorker* for years before they would let her use a dash at the beginning of a line.

Finishing "The Moose" was a crisis: she had promised a new poem for the annual Phi Beta Kappa ceremony during Harvard's graduation week. About a week before it was to be read to hundreds of people, "The Moose"—long, intricate, begun at least fifteen years earlier—still wasn't completed. She had never promised a poem by a deadline before. It was the only new poem she had. Her insecurity about academia, fed by the fact that she hadn't begun to teach till late in life, became terror. (I've heard that Frost, before delivering his Phi Beta Kappa poem, was in a similar panic.) Elizabeth, Alice, and I had made plans to go to Bermuda for a weekend; both insisted we must go. Elizabeth took the poem with her.

On the plane, as she showed me the lines for the first time, it became clear that the poem already—except for a handful of connectives, a handful of phrases—was there. In *Return of the Jedi* there's a wonderful image of a planet that isn't finished. There's the sphere, but there are all these gaps and holes in the sphere as it hangs in the air. Elizabeth's stanzas were like that. She would have the first line. She would have the last line. She'd have maybe two lines near the end and maybe even several phrases in the middle, but not quite enough to make the rhymes and the lines come together. What she needed was an audience to lead through the narrative line of the poem: in decipher-ing her handwritten corrections for me, having again to move from the beginning of the poem through to the end, having to talk out what the stanzas filled with gaps needed to accomplish within the narrative frame, she filled the gaps. Later many phrases again were changed; but when the plane reached Bermuda, she had a continuous draft of the whole.

✦　✦　✦

After graduation at Harvard, Bishop traveled to Ouro Prêto. She thought about selling some of the manuscripts of her own poems, which she kept there. In January 1972 she had seen the manuscript of her poem "Faustina" on display at the Lamont Poetry Room at Harvard. The poem was on a sheet that also contained one of Marjorie Stevens's grocery lists. The manuscript seemed illegible to Bishop, but it made her conscious of how valuable her personal papers were. Linda Nemer, who had been visiting her in Boston, returned to Ouro Prêto with her that summer and helped her fire up the fireplaces and stoves to dry out the house. As Bishop worked through the musty papers she had gathered there, she had an asthma attack.[16] When Bishop returned to Cambridge that summer, she was still suffering from the asthma attack, and Methfessel nursed her back to health. In August, Bishop traveled with Methfessel to England, Sweden, Norway, and Leningrad. Still recovering from her asthma attack, Bishop ended the trip in a wheelchair.

In the fall semester of 1972 Bishop had her first significant conflict with a student. A young African-American man, whom Bishop characterized to friends as "psychotic," accused her of racism, even calling her a "white bitch."[17] James Merrill recollects a conversation with Bishop about this incident, and both Monroe Engel and Anne Hussey reflect upon the details of this one incident in terms of Bishop's style of teaching.

JAMES MERRILL— Elizabeth and I would talk sometimes a little about her students. There was one funny conversation. I called [and] she said, "Oh, you've just caught me as I was taking my grades to the dean." I said, "Did you flunk anybody?" And she said, "As a matter of fact, I did." This was a course she was giving in letter writers. They read Jane Carlyle, Byron, and [a number of others]. She said there was a black man in the course whom she perhaps ought not to have admitted from the start. The students were asked for a paper at the end of the semester. They could write about any other letter writer that hadn't been discussed in the class. She imagined that he perhaps would take George Jackson's letters from prison. But, no, he chose Lady Mary Wortley Montagu. Elizabeth sighed: "When I came to the part in the paper where he said Lady Mary Montagu ought to be cut up in little pieces and burned in cooking oil, I had to flunk him."

MONROE ENGEL— Elizabeth had been involved in an unfortunate contretemps with a black student. He filed a complaint. She'd made some harsh statement in class about his work, which the student assumed was motivated in part at least by the fact that he was black. I'd be astonished if that was true. It seemed to have been more likely that Elizabeth thought his work was no good and didn't hesitate to tell him so and wasn't diplomatic about it and he attributed [her judgment] to racism. I remember thinking it was impossible that Elizabeth had been motivated by the student's [being black], but I could imagine her saying something to him that was painful. The incident was investigated and not acted on.

Elizabeth could be tactful sometimes, but she tended to be blunt. She asked me once what courses I was teaching, and I was teaching a course on twentieth-century English and American novels. She asked which novels I was teaching, and when I listed among others Norman Mailer's *American Dream*, she said, "You are?" That was it. She didn't want to hear any more. That was the end of the discussion. Mailer's was the one novel on the list I was least certain I wanted to teach myself. Elizabeth moved right into my own vulnerability.

Elizabeth [could show] incredulity that you didn't know something that she thought you should know. The first time I heard her read the poem about fire balloons ["The Armadillo"], I said to her, "What is a fire balloon?" "You don't know what a fire balloon is?" And then she proceeded to tell me in a way that made it impossible for me ever not to know again. It wasn't the usual intellectual put-down. It had to do much more with experiential things that you would assume to be a part of everybody's common experience.

If there was a poem she didn't much like [by a student], she might correct spelling and grammar and then say no more. One of the things that made the less-good students uncomfortable with her was that she was paying attention to their spelling and punctuation, and, without saying it, probably making it apparent to them that she thought the work was intrinsically not worthy of real consideration. That's of course not the best way for a teacher to [deal with any student].

Elizabeth was [not] a great teacher for a wide range of people. Her interests were not catholic. They were very strongly focused on the things that meant something to her. There were far fewer students clamoring to be in Elizabeth's class than in either Robert Lowell's or Robert Fitzgerald's. I don't think Elizabeth was a significant presence in the lives of many students. Relatively few people were aware of the fact that she was here. Elizabeth was a very significant presence, however, in the lives of a few. Some students who weren't directly influenced by Elizabeth, though, as they might be influenced by Cal or Robert [Fitzgerald], nonetheless, felt that they learned something just from getting a sense of how she managed her life. There's something to be learned from a writer who plows a narrow path deep. Harvard is a big place. It would have been different if she'd been the only poet teaching here, but as an additional, extraordinary example, the kids were privileged beyond belief to have her.

ANNE HUSSEY— Elizabeth didn't like direct confrontation, and she occasionally did have some problem students that were hard to get rid of. I think they felt her lack of respect rather immediately, principally by silence or by very brief comment. Elizabeth might say something like, "Well, I don't know about that," and then go right on to something else, but nothing directly confrontational. She was a very kind person. Elizabeth could always sense if somebody was in trouble and didn't want to hurt a young person who somehow had drifted into the class by mistake. Occasionally there would be a problem and she would have to talk to the head of the English Department and let their dismissal happen that way.

We were also in the era of the poetry workshop. Lowell said, "We are not making chairs here. There is some similarity. We are making something and we hope it will stand up, but it's not a chair." The psychological T-Group [therapy group] aspect of a writing workshop is something Anne Sexton loved, but Elizabeth detested. She felt that sort of thing should be inherent in the work or in the writer's self-examination, but a T-Group did not make literature. Elizabeth felt that whatever the experience is, the problem in writing is one of presentation, and that's what she addressed and in a sense that's what Cal addressed as well. They were very much the same in that respect. One of Elizabeth's difficulties was that the students at this time could not accept criticism, and this was devastating to her. They would not rework things. They were very articulate vocally, but not so articulate on the page. They would feel that this is me, therefore it's good, and if you criticize it, you're criticizing me and I have to defend myself against it. Elizabeth was coming up against this sort of thing, particularly later in her years at Harvard, when she was having a little more difficulty controlling the class and a little more difficulty concentrating when she was in fragile health. It was a combination of her changing and students changing.

✦   ✦   ✦

In the fall of 1972 Bishop requested a permanent teaching appointment at Harvard. Robert Lowell complicated this matter for her by announcing in the fall of 1972 that he would be returning to Harvard to teach for the following academic year. Bishop feared that the English Department would not want both Lowell and her there at the same time. Lowell felt guilty because he did not want to jeopardize Bishop's job security.

Bishop was in a precarious position among the academics at Harvard. She was a member of the Writing Program, which was a part of the English Department, but the Writing Program was considered by some of the department's academics an inferior part of the department. Bishop met the director of the Writing Program, the novelist Monroe Engel, during her second fall term at Harvard. She attended a dinner at his house, located around the corner from her apartment, and although Engel's kindly manner put her at ease, the academics present made her nervous. "Elizabeth didn't fit into the academic world. But there was no need for her to, because she wasn't conceived of really as a member of the department. She was an extra. Elizabeth was after all not a natural joiner. I can't imagine one of my regular academic colleagues choosing to have a Ping-Pong table rather than a dining room table."[18] Bishop's was "an off-the-ladder appointment, and her salary did not come out of regular departmental funds. Lowell's appointment was like that, too."[19]

In December 1972 the English Department voted to approve a term appointment for Bishop, guaranteeing her a teaching position there until her mandatory retirement in 1977. Monroe Engel recollects the factors involved in this decision.

MONROE ENGEL— I wouldn't be astonished if [Elizabeth's difficulties with some students] hadn't tempered the enthusiasm for reappointment, particularly since I don't think she had broad support in the department. I don't think there was opposition, but I would assume that if some number of senior members of the department [were asked] whether they thought Elizabeth's appointment [should be extended], they would have said "Sure," but it would not have been a matter of high priority. Her health and some psychological instability [were perceived too as] risks.

I think there were a number of senior members of my department who would have been happy if she hadn't been here. They took those complaints from students very seriously to confirm feelings [of doubt they already had about her]. I don't think there was pressure, though, [to have her removed]. I think [Elizabeth's statements to friends that some were trying to have her removed] came at a time when Elizabeth was feeling strong personal pressure.

◆　◆　◆

Bishop was uneasy around academics.[20] She had little interest in literary theory, as Penelope Laurans Fitzgerald, who was teaching at Yale, recollects from one conversation: "The single question Elizabeth ever asked me having to do with Yale was, 'What is deconstruction?'" When I finished my ten-minute explanation, her only comment was, "Oh dear."[21] When Dana Gioia studied with Bishop, he saw how very skeptical the academic faculty at Harvard was of her. Helen Vendler, who was teaching at Boston University, received a sense of the kind of criticism Bishop liked when they first met.

DANA GIOIA— I arrived at Harvard in the fall of 1973 to pursue a graduate degree in comparative literature. I chose Harvard because it was one of the few places where one could still study literary history. I found Cambridge an exciting and engrossing milieu. During my second year, however, I began to doubt whether becoming a professor of literature was the best career for doing what I really wanted—to write poetry. My interest in literary theory, my fascination with scholarship, and my own unhealthy delight in playing with critical ideas were all creeping into my writing in bad ways. I was beginning to write poems to be interpreted rather than to register on the imagination, emotions, and intuition.

Midway through my second year at Harvard, I decided to leave academics. I then had to decide what I wanted to get out of Harvard during my last term. The obvious choice would have been to take Robert Lowell's seminar on nineteenth-century poetry. It was a celebrated course among Harvard's lite-rati. But I already knew Lowell slightly and his work quite well. Elizabeth Bishop, however, was a more mysterious figure. Whereas Lowell was a cultural hero at Harvard, Bishop was considered an eccentric minor figure. There were only a few people, like Lowell, who were convinced of her importance. The undergraduates mostly considered Bishop a quaint, slightly dowdy poet who was there due mainly to Lowell's charity. The faculty also generally considered Bishop a bit of an embarrassment, a poet who had seen better days. She had recently published very little and took no active part in literary life. Her colleagues also assumed, quite rightly in some respects, that she could not teach. She made it no secret that she was teaching because she needed the money. They also knew that she found her colleagues mostly boring. The typical departmental conversation intimidated or annoyed her.

When I told my adviser that I was taking a class with Elizabeth Bishop, he tried fervently to talk me out of it. He made it clear that he would not willingly sign my card for her class. He said that it was not a serious class, that she was not a legitimate scholar, and that I wouldn't learn anything. (He did not know I was a poet.) I then made a Faustian bargain. I signed up for his notoriously dull course in prosody, and I pretended that if I didn't take Bishop's seminar, the course I would substitute was at the same time as his chronically undersubscribed class. My petty intrigue proved successful, though I am now slightly ashamed to confess it. My other teachers made critical remarks when they learned that I was taking Bishop's course. I was a resident tutor, so I met a great many faculty members in the humanities. Bishop's name would often elicit a polite chuckle. My teachers couldn't understand why anybody who was an aspiring scholar would waste time with Bishop. One notable exception was Robert Fitzgerald. Robert knew that hers was the class I should be taking. Only the writers recognized Bishop's merit—and not even all of them.

Studies in Modern Poetry, a two-hour class in a gloomy basement, was not a cheery affair. There were only a half a dozen students, and they generally did not take the coursework very seriously. Bishop's approach to literature was initially shocking to me, because we did not approach poems in the formal academic way I had learned in the previous six years. We did not look for themes, paradoxes, symbols, or mythologies. Almost all the class discussion focused on explicating the literal, surface sense of the poems. We examined poems line by line, often word by word. At first I thought her method eccentric, but gradually I realized how much I learned from this scrupulous approach, how many exquisite details I had missed in poems I thought I had known. Her approach also emphasized exactly what I liked about poems—their mixture of sense and sensuality. The other students were not prepared for her casual style of teaching—they were used to focused seminar classes, organized lectures, or Lowell's high-octane monologues. After class some students would make slighting comments about her teaching, but I was grateful for her unorthodox literalism.

Miss Bishop's classes were essentially conversations about the poems she assigned each week. There were no lectures or prepared presentations. She was unnervingly modest, especially by Harvard standards. She would be the first person to admit when she didn't understand something in a poem. She also sometimes reminisced about the poets. She once told a long anecdote about driving somewhere with William Carlos Williams and his wife. They were talking about poetry, and Bishop mentioned an obscure seventeenth-century poem to the good doctor. She couldn't believe Williams had never heard of the poem. She told us this incident proved that Williams was not very well read. No one in the class volunteered that we hadn't ever heard of the poem either.

Miss Bishop liked to relate poems to the real world. When she found a flower in a poem by Williams, for instance, she would ask if we had seen the flower in question. If anyone in the class didn't know the flower, she would describe it. When we read Lowell's "For the Union Dead," she asked if we had seen the state house and the other places in the poem. She told us to take a subway downtown to visit them. I did exactly what she suggested and quickly learned that Lowell's early poetry, which had always struck me as abstract and literary, was actually rooted in local Boston history and topography. It was liberating to have somebody say the most obvious and central thing about poetry—that it should somehow correspond to life. She also gave pop quizzes in which she would ask us to tell what a poem literally described. She wanted only an exact paraphrase with no interpretation.

Let me give you an example of the importance she placed on understanding the details of a poem. When we studied Wallace Stevens's "The Emperor of Ice-Cream," Bishop asked if we knew what *deal* was (the wood of the dresser in the poem). She became angry when nobody in the class could explain the word. She said she wanted us to look up every word we didn't know. To her, deal was one of the poem's most ingenious details. She explained what deal furniture was and discussed what sort of person would own it. She was reading Stevens's poetry sociologically. I had been taught not to do that. She also made us memorize poems every week. That old-fashioned exercise was important to me. I felt that Bishop was onto something essential about the sensuality of poetry that I'd almost forgotten. Hers was a profitably confusing class because it made me question many assumptions that I had picked up in graduate school about how one discussed and evaluated poetry. She made me remember the value of simplicity and directness. She also made me recognize the paramount importance of understanding every detail on the surface of a poem.

Miss Bishop thought that criticism was in general a mistaken enterprise. I saw her point, even if I couldn't always agree. She frequently made asides about a dim-witted collective entity she scornfully called "the critics." The one critic she adored, however, was Randall Jarrell. She was delighted one afternoon to discover me carrying a copy of his *Poetry and the Age*. From that point on she mentioned Jarrell frequently and admiringly in class. Bishop loved his way with words. She would often quote a passage from Jarrell in class and savor it for the sheer quality of its language. Bishop also admired Helen Vendler's book on Stevens's longer poems, *On Extended Wings*. She frequently consulted it in class when she didn't understand a passage. She could also be very caustic. She would curtly dismiss poems she didn't like. She could never forgive a poem for being dull. But you never felt that she was being self-serving in her criticisms. She was just talking candidly about what she enjoyed and what she didn't.

By the end of the semester, Miss Bishop and the students were not on terribly good terms. They didn't always come to class. They didn't memorize their weekly poems. I became something of a bright spot in an uningratiating routine. After the class, we would go out for tea and talk. I think my being well-mannered in an old-fashioned, if slightly stiff, way made her feel comfortable. Bishop believed in degrees of intimacy. The more fixed the limits of intimacy were, the more relaxed, generous, and open she became. The casual etiquette of the seventies allowed no defined degrees of intimacy. She felt that she was living in a slightly barbarous age. The fact that I wrote poetry only came out gradually in our relationship. I think she appreciated my good manners in not showing poems to her. We had a friendship that didn't resemble a standard teacher-student relationship. We talked about everything *except* our common academic subject. My conversations with her were the sort I would have with a nonliterary friend. We might talk a little about the novels we were reading, but we were more likely to talk about music, animals, gardening, or travel. She positively hated literary shoptalk. She told me a funny story about that. She went to a dinner party and was horrified to learn that she would sit next to Northrop Frye. She leaned over and said, "I don't like to talk about literature." He replied with great relief, "Neither do I." They ended up talking about Canada.

When I told Bishop I was leaving Harvard to go into business, she was—to my surprise—both delighted and encouraging. When I had told my other teachers, two of them shut the door and spent an hour trying to talk me out of the decision. They felt I was making a mistake and worried that I was doing it because of money. My literary friends warned that I would stop writing. They couldn't understand that I was leaving academia to get a certain amount of mental freedom as a writer. Fitzgerald and Bishop were the only two teachers who openly approved. Bishop told me the university was often not a good place for a writer. It did not always give a writer the kind of nourishment that he or she needed. Genuine writing grows naturally out of your life, which is necessarily different from other people's lives. You need to follow the course of your life, even if it leads to places like Brazil or the business world. She never doubted that I would continue writing, and her confidence was reassuring. She emphasized that a writer does not have to follow intellectual fashions.

Bishop's contrarian identity was especially important to me. She could be personal without being subjective. I admired her refusal to commit herself to a single aesthetic position, either stylistically or thematically. Instead she opened herself to the full range of experiences in her own life. I was from California, where the Beat aesthetic, though already twenty years old, was still dominant. The early seventies was a trendy time in poetry, the heyday of Confessional and Deep Image poetry. The few poets I knew back then who read Bishop dismissed her as a domestic formalist who lacked contemporaneity, political engagement, and experimental energy. Most young poets weren't reading her at all. I had first read her much earlier without any ideological preconceptions—back in high school—because I had enjoyed hearing Ned Rorem's setting of "Visits to St. Elizabeths" so much that I had looked up her work. She was one of the first contemporary poets I had read, and she shaped my notions of what new poetry should sound like. I admired the diversity of styles and material that she could handle with equal authority. Her work demonstrated how an idiosyncratic and original imagination could find unity in seemingly dissimilar things. The quiet exactitude of her work showed that emotions didn't have to be screamed to be genuine.

One always had a sense of the contradiction in Elizabeth Bishop's life. She appeared very genteel and upper-middle class on the outside, yet her life had been very bohemian and unrooted. She combined the freedom of bohemian culture with the civility of certain middle-class traditions. This synthesis allowed her to feel comfortable in the world without bearing all of the weight of its conventions. I admired the way in which the best parts of the bohemian and the bourgeois naturally coexisted in her character without affectation. I learned something important from her in that respect about creating the life one wants to lead rather than merely accepting the conventional choices.[22]

HELEN VENDLER— The first thing that brought me to Elizabeth's attention was a review I did of *An Anthology of Twentieth-Century Brazilian poetry.* I loved the Drummond de Andrade poems that she had translated—they were a real discovery. I felt that she had given an important poet to English. I first met Elizabeth at John Brinnin's house at Duxbury. I was too timid to say anything to her. It's always hard the first time you meet a poet whose work you like very much. I was in the general conversation in which she was taking part. Then Elizabeth said to me that she had found my book on Stevens [*On Extended Wings: Wallace Stevens' Longer Poems*] very useful in teaching her class at Harvard because it talked concretely about what was being done in the poems in terms of language and form. I was taken aback by this compliment, which I didn't expect, and touched by the generosity of her saying that. From then on I felt at ease with her.

On another occasion, Anne Sexton, Robert Lowell, and Elizabeth Bishop were at John Brinnin's house on a Sunday afternoon. Elizabeth asked me if I had ever written poetry. I said that I had from the time I was six until I was twenty-seven, but that then I had stopped. For the first time I said that I felt very guilty about having stopped. Perhaps I should have gone on writing poetry, but I was writing my thesis, had my first full-time job, and was married and having a baby. There were so many reasons not to write. All of them laughed and said I should immediately ease my mind of grief. Elizabeth said, "You couldn't help it. If you were going to be a poet, you were going to write no matter what." She further explained that writing would take authority over being busy or whatever because if you didn't write you immediately would feel it by your condition of body or soul. They variously chimed in and said you either became terribly sick or you had headaches all the time or you couldn't sleep, and then you discovered that if you wrote you felt all right again. Elizabeth felt that there was a real somatic connection between either having to write or else not feeling right somehow, either spiritually or physically.

✦   ✦   ✦

Bishop found a sympathetic and supportive colleague in the English Department in the poet and translator Robert Fitzgerald and in Penelope Laurans. Fitzgerald, who held the Boylston Chair of Rhetoric, understood Bishop's position as a writer in an academic institution.

ROBERT FITZGERALD— Elizabeth may have felt that I was not quite of the freemasonry of poets and writers, that I was quite affected by my position at Harvard. It no doubt identified me to some extent with the academic side of everything. Although we became really quite good and warm friends, I always felt that there was this little fly in the ointment between us. It was of course mixed in with pronounced gratitude toward me because, for one reason or another, every now and then Elizabeth would have drawn attention to herself from the professional academics, and that attention was not always grateful on either side. There were complaints about Elizabeth's teaching, for example. I would be talking with the chairman of the English Department, and he would pull out of his desk a long, elaborate letter, received from some undergraduate at the end of the year, complaining about the way Elizabeth conducted her classes. I can't remember now what the substance of the complaints were, but there were several of them.

PENELOPE LAURANS FITZGERALD— Elizabeth's attitude toward Harvard was ambivalent. She would have liked to be there as a permanent poet-in-residence, but without having to teach. She needed Harvard; it was very important to her, rooted her, and provided her with security. It also, however, was a source of pressure for her because it forced her to do what was stressful and uncongenial for her—that is, to teach.

The reason teaching was so difficult for Elizabeth had to do with her decisiveness. Elizabeth was not an embrasive person. She separated the world sharply into what she liked and what she didn't; her tastes were brilliant, but narrow. Of course, this is often the way of genius—genius is dogmatic, imposing, not embrasive. Elizabeth's crisis with teaching happened because she took it seriously, she wanted to do it well, she wanted to perform in the right way to be "worthy" of Harvard, and yet because she was a genius, she simply couldn't be who or what she wasn't. Much more ordinary people, of course, can manage that, but Elizabeth could not.

The way to appreciate Elizabeth as a teacher was simply to value the opportunity to observe her genius, learn from her tastes, and the most mature and able students could and did do that. There were a number of students who greatly admired and appreciated the chance to study with Elizabeth and gained much from it. But it is also true that Elizabeth was hard on the less-gifted students, and she was even sometimes hard on accomplished students who did quite fine work that did not fit the range of her tastes—and that is discouraging when you are young. As a teacher you have not to be dishonest, but you have to bring people along, and Elizabeth was not somebody who brought people along. Work to her was either original or fine according to her tastes or it was no good, that was it, and she was not able to see things in other than black-and-white, or to dissemble.

ROBERT— Of course, I knew that Elizabeth was not an academic, that she was not a trained teacher. Various things about what she was not had to be admitted and had to be accepted. My point always was that Elizabeth was a very fine and wonderful poet, and we had to have her and keep her no matter what. This was the gist of these occasional, recurrent episodes, when Elizabeth would have to be defended against concerned attacks from various members of the department.

Elizabeth knew that I had done this. Once I remember meeting her in a waiting room at the airport. She was flying with Octavio Paz and Marie Jo to New York, and we all got together while we were waiting. I walked with them to the gate when they were leaving, and just before they departed, Elizabeth turned to me and said, "Of course, I know that you are responsible for my being here." Well, that really was not so in the beginning, but as time went on I put my weight, whenever it was indicated, in favor of her, no matter how odd her teaching might have seemed to this or that person. My point was that above all things we needed her as we needed Lowell. Harvard was the place where the difficulty of these people had to be embraced and their genius had to be allowed to flourish.

Not renewing Elizabeth's contract was certainly in the air. That was again a great anxiety to her because of what she thought she needed from Harvard, the attention to her health. Elizabeth was very interested during all her time at Harvard in the privileges that the Harvard Health Services afforded to people in her position. She was terribly worried sometimes that after her retirement she would not come in for the privilege of using the infirmary and the staff.

PENELOPE— I think that too much can be made of Harvard's coldness to Elizabeth and to some extent to Cal and its other writers. There was a kind of division between the close band of people who were writers at Harvard and the rest of the department, but that is pretty natural; in fact, since the rest of the department was hardly a cohesive whole, and the writers were a tighter band, it's more that the writers had an identity and the rest of the department didn't. The writers took care of their own. When Cal got sick, mostly Bill Alfred but also sometimes Robert and Monroe were there to help; and Robert, Monroe, and Bill were always there when Elizabeth needed help. Of course it is true that the hiring and firing power was not with the writers and that that mattered a lot. And that the powers-that-be worried about what students thought. It was their job to do that. After all, a school is a school.

There was a little bit of the notion among some that Harvard, rich and powerful as it is, owed the writers something. I am not denying that there were certain folk in the department who were narrow and rigid and would have found it easier not to reappoint Elizabeth. After all, she was not as famous then as she now is, and she was not a universally successful teacher. But there were other faculty members I know who honored Elizabeth, valued her presence tremendously, and knew exactly how lucky Harvard was to have her. Pushed a little here and there, as institutions must be, Harvard really gave Elizabeth quite a lot. It is important to see the whole situation with balance.

ROBERT— I persuaded Elizabeth to do something for the writing program in a way of an introduction to Gwendolyn Brooks when she read at Harvard. This was really quite magnificent. Elizabeth's mind was so interesting—she made such interesting connections. She had a point to make, and the point was to liken Gwendolyn Brooks and her minority to Robert Burns and his dialectical minority, and she prepared and delivered this introduction with great care. I was terribly impressed by it. The place was the little auditorium in Hilles Library, which we often used for our readings, and I remember Elizabeth saying, as she began her introduction, that she never thought she would be appearing at Harvard, at this august place. That was a little token of how she felt about Harvard.[23]

✦　　✦　　✦

Bishop complained to friends, and friends complained for her, that she was poorly treated by the English Department. Were her complaints justified? A number of colleagues and friends recollect incidents of Bishop's treatment, and her comments.

JANE SHORE— I didn't realize how badly Elizabeth was being treated by the Harvard English Department until I saw it with my own eyes. At a lunch meeting of the writing faculty at the beginning of the semester in a reserved room at the Faculty Club, a senior member of the department walked in and said in a mocking tone, "Oh, the *poetry groupies* having lunch!" It was so crude. He'd said this in front of Robert Fitzgerald, Bill Alfred, Monroe Engel, and Elizabeth! It was clear then to me how the department felt about writers. For a moment or two everyone was very quiet, shocked. When the professor walked out, Elizabeth turned to me and said under her breath, "And I was very happy to see that he had a large *stain* on the back of his pants."

It was at another one of these lunch meetings that I remember [the following] incident. As was usual, the younger Briggs-Copeland Lecturers were present—Robert B. Shaw, Alexander Theroux, and myself. Alex had just finished reviewing a book about famous last words—the last words famous people said moments before they died. Alex was very funny and entertaining as he recounted the best quotes for us. He said there was a great quote by Lady Mary Wortley Montagu, and that her last words were something like, "Well, it's all been *quite* amusing." Elizabeth announced to us—in her slightly aristocratic and quizzical tone—"That's how I feel. I wish I'd said that!"

LLOYD SCHWARTZ— Certainly whatever good things you could say about the Harvard English Department at that time, with only a few notable exceptions did the faculty go out of their way to make their great poets feel comfortable. Teaching at Harvard didn't do Elizabeth's health any good. She was stuck in the basement of Kirkland House, in this dingy, whitewashed classroom with ceiling pipes and windows at the very top. It was damp, stuffy, and uncomfortable. Awful for her asthma. Robert Lowell held his "office hours" in a windowless seminar room under the Quincy House dining hall. I think they wouldn't have dared, for all his problems, to have got rid of him, but they clearly felt it was easier to drop Elizabeth because she was quiet, shy, and a woman. At that time, women at Harvard were still really second-class citizens.

JOSEPH SUMMERS— Elizabeth said there was somebody at Harvard who she thought was a real monster, just an evil man. He hated her and didn't know what to do with her anyway, and he wouldn't give her a term appointment because she was so near retirement, and they would have to pay [her a] pension. He said something very crude about [her being] old and [Harvard's being unable to] afford her. He sent her a note that arrived Christmas Day that said she was not hired for the next year and she wouldn't get a term appointment. She was as [angry and] fearsome as I remember her [being] about anybody. Finally something was worked out.

ROBERT B. SHAW— At one point I think Elizabeth wanted to teach more courses than members of the department wanted her to teach. They felt they were saddled with another uppity writer because they had had so many problems with Lowell—he was ill so often. I heard a senior member of the department use the word "hoggish" to describe Elizabeth Bishop because she was asking for an extra course to teach. There was a real antipathy, at least with some people, not toward Elizabeth personally, but toward her as another problem. They thought all their problems were concentrated in the writing side of things and she was just a manifestation of that. This was all in the context of Lowell having been there for several years and having given them all kinds of crises. They thought they had one difficult poet to worry about to begin with and that they had been suckered into signing on another difficult poet.

◆ ◆ ◆

John Hollander, who was teaching at Yale at the time, summarizes the attitude of many of Bishop's friends toward Harvard's treatment of her: "If what I know is correct, Harvard treated Elizabeth miserably. I remember writing somebody in the Harvard English Department at the time and just saying that this was an outrage. They had one of the greatest national resources there, and they acted as if they didn't." William Alfred felt that the unsettling discussion of a term appointment made Bishop suspicious even of those who were her strongest advocates at Harvard: "It pulled the guts out of her, the shuffling back and forth. It was awful. I had a feeling that Elizabeth had somehow the notion that Cal and I had failed her with regard to Harvard. There was no meanness with it, but there was a kind of a coolness toward me. I think she thought that Cal and I should have fought harder, but we fought as hard as we could."

Bishop taught only the first semester during the 1972–73 academic year. In December 1972 she was a judge for the translation category of the National Book Award. She and the poets John Hollander and William Meredith awarded the prize to Allen Mandlebaum for his translation of Virgil's

Aeneid. Hollander remembers what it was like working with Bishop on this committee.

JOHN HOLLANDER— Elizabeth Bishop was one of the very last poets of generations before mine that I considered in any way parental whom I ever got to know a little. I admired her poetry from afar for so long. The first time I really spent much time with her was at a party that David Kalstone and I gave for her in New York after a reading she and James Merrill did [in March 1973]. I was impressed by her elegant and powerful composure. We were on a National Book Award translation panel. Elizabeth was marvelous on that. I had the feeling of her perceptions and her discourse being on a welcome high wavelength. She was very good about cutting through humbug. Elizabeth didn't dominate the conversation. She was just very, very forceful.

✦   ✦   ✦

Bishop had several readings in February and March 1973, at Bryn Mawr College, Wellesley College, the University of Virginia, the University of Oklahoma, and at the YMHA in New York with James Merrill. From late March until mid-June, she was a visiting professor at the University of Washington in Seattle, where she spent time with her friends from her previous teaching engagement there in 1966. During her tenure at Seattle, Bishop traveled to Portland State University to give a reading as the Nina May Kellogg lecturer. She was invited by Henry Carlile, who was living and teaching in Portland with his wife, Sandra McPherson.

HENRY CARLILE— I picked Elizabeth up in Seattle and drove her down to Portland. She didn't really like to give poetry readings. She didn't think she was a strong reader and seldom enjoyed the performance part of poetry. But the audience was so appreciative she seemed to enjoy herself. She was incredibly good. She read quietly, undramatically, and the audience loved it.

She was very kind to Sandra, our daughter, Phoebe, and me. She was good with Phoebe. She did have reservations about putting children on stage with poetry. Sandra and I had encouraged Phoebe to write poetry. Phoebe had written some very precocious poems, following her mother's example. Dick Bakken, a poet and one of my colleagues, had already published some of Phoebe's poems in a children's anthology entitled *Miracle Finger.* Sandra had shown Elizabeth these poems, but Elizabeth disapproved of publishing children's poetry.

Elizabeth had brought some gifts for Phoebe. There was a ladybug in a magnetic ring. You detached the ladybug and moved it around inside a glass of the water with the ring. And there was a little paper pill. You placed it in a glass of water and it blossomed into a flower. Elizabeth liked tiny things. She loved Wesley Wehr's minimalist landscapes.

Methfessel met Bishop in Seattle at the end of her teaching term, and together they toured places in the Pacific Northwest. In February 1973 Bishop had contracted for a condominium on the top floor of a warehouse that was being renovated on Lewis Wharf in Boston. She had taken the floor plans of this apartment with her to Seattle to show her friends. So when she and Methfessel returned to Cambridge following their trip through the Northwest, Bishop looked forward to future stability. In her three years at Cambridge, she had found herself a permanent job and home, a new companion and community of friends, and, however uneasy it made her feel, an active life as a public poet.

CHAPTER 14

CAMBRIDGE AND BOSTON,

1973 – 1977

Elizabeth Bishop was uneasy about Robert Lowell's return to Harvard to teach in September 1973, after his absence of three years. The six-foot, disheveled Lowell was an outgoing man, a legendary presence in Cambridge who was easily spotted and recognized as he loped through Harvard Square. Bishop was inconspicuous in appearance and presence. In fact, Brad Leithauser was surprised to find Bishop at Harvard when he studied with her in 1971: "I met Elizabeth Bishop when I was applying to her writing course. I told her I had thought she was dead, which amused her greatly. With Alice, years later, she would remark, 'This is the fellow who thought I was dead.'"

Lowell remained for Bishop one writer whose appreciation of her work she deeply valued.

RICHARD WILBUR— I have a letter from Elizabeth in which she is saying, "Here is my address. Here is my telephone number. I have heard recently of more than one time that you were in Cambridge and you haven't come out to see me, and this evening I have had the ridiculous idea that you were cross with me for some reason or other. Now I know that's not true because I've just received your new book in the mail. But please, when you come next, come out and see us." Elizabeth often struck that note, the note of loneliness, even when she was in a ménage of some kind or another, but especially when she was not.

CHARLOTTE WILBUR— Do you know what the reason for her loneliness was? That's something that she said to me at one time. The women she lived with really had no interest in poetry and her work whatsoever, [except for] Lota. That's one reason why she continued to be in love with Cal.

At John Brinnin's [once] people were talking about a poem of hers that had appeared somewhere. There were perhaps six or seven other people discussing this poem in glowing terms in front of her. She listened for a while and then got up. I went inside to go to the bathroom. Elizabeth followed me and said, "I want to talk to you. There are moments when I cannot stand to talk about poetry, and particularly about mine. I don't like to be in a group of people."

✦　✦　✦

Professional disagreements crept into Bishop and Lowell's relationship in the 1970s. In 1970 Lowell had published in *Notebook* a sonnet that paraphrased a letter that Bishop had sent to him. Bishop considered this sonnet an unforgivable violation of her privacy: "I remember Elizabeth telling about not wanting to write Lowell any more letters because he was using them in his poems and distorting what she said. She was horrified by that."[1] In 1973 Lowell published *The Dolphin,* for which he drew extensively on his correspondence with Elizabeth Hardwick.[2] As William Alfred remembers this incident, he and Bishop were strong opponents to Lowell's publication. Also, Joseph and U. T. Summers witnessed how Bishop's ambivalent feelings toward Lowell in the 1970s could place her in awkward social positions.

WILLIAM ALFRED— Elizabeth, Esther Brooks, and I were the only people who would dare tell Cal that he ought not to print the material from his wife's letters. He knew it. Cal first sent us mimeographed copies, and I wrote in my letter, "You cannot print what is on page 'so-and-so.'" He said, "All right, I won't print that one," but he pretended I'd got the pagination wrong and it was another poem. Elizabeth just said to him, "You mustn't do that." She was absolutely superb during that business. Cal adored Elizabeth, but I think he was a little angry at that time. He was a little angry at me, too. He said, "You just don't understand. I have to tell the truth, and this is my way of telling the truth."

JOSEPH SUMMERS— When we were [at Harvard], Elizabeth was doing alternate terms with Lowell. Elizabeth used to say, "Now, what do you think of Lowell?" Then she would say, "I can't, I won't say anything." Elizabeth was terrified, I think, of being quoted, because she liked him so much, but she didn't like a lot of those later poems.

U.T. SUMMERS— Elizabeth said with respect to that book that he was a megalomaniac.

JOSEPH— I once said to Cal, "I sometimes think that *Imitations* is the most original book you ever wrote." He didn't think it was funny. Elizabeth said, "He's not satisfied with being the best living poet. He wants to be the best poet that ever lived and he wants to be all of them. That's crazy."

U.T.— Lowell was an easy man to worship at the feet of, but I think that Elizabeth made him feel in touch with reality.

♦   ♦   ♦

To the students of Bishop and Lowell, there was a vast difference in their teaching styles. Anne Hussey studied with both Bishop and Lowell at Harvard, after she had studied with Anne Sexton at Boston University. Hussey recollects not only differences in teaching personality and teaching style among the three but also the competitiveness that occasionally rose to the surface between Bishop and Lowell.

ANNE HUSSEY— I had started writing in 1969, and I'd had one poem published in the *Sewanee Review,* my first publication, and one published in *The New Yorker,* my second. I was panicked into a state of requiring more education. I studied for a year with Anne Sexton at Boston University, and after that I heard Elizabeth Bishop was at Harvard, at which point I applied to the Graduate School of Arts and Sciences to be a special student in the fall of 1971. I was told by the chairman of the English Department that the only way I could be at Harvard and study with Elizabeth Bishop was to get her permission.

Not knowing Elizabeth and not knowing anything about her—I had read and very much admired her work—I wrote her and sent some poems, and I got a lovely letter back. She had even noticed that the date of her letter was my birthday and wished me happy birthday in the letter. She couldn't understand really why I would want to be in her class—she took it for granted that I was a professional—but she said of course she would be delighted to have me. I showed the letter to the Graduate School of Arts and Sciences and they said it looked all right.

Two days before classes were supposed to start, I had a letter from the Graduate School of Arts and Sciences saying the chairman of the Department felt very strongly that "persons such as yourself" did not belong at Harvard (meaning married women who had children and lived in the suburbs). In spite of the fact that the professor had agreed to have me in the class, the professor now had to request specifically that I be in the class. I had to track down Elizabeth Bishop, leaving messages for her all over the place. Finally she called and said, "What on earth is going on here?" I read the letter to her, and she said, "Oh, for God's sake!" which endeared her to me immediately. She phoned the Graduate School of Arts and Sciences and that was the end of it. I was in the class.

I found interesting the contrast between studying with someone like Anne Sexton and Elizabeth. With Anne Sexton, class was drama. She was immersed in the psychological and the personal. With Elizabeth everything was rather quiet in class, and yet she was dropping information if you were there to pick it up. Elizabeth's and Anne's personalities were very different. Anne was "let it all hang out" and Elizabeth was "let's keep it all in." Anne was very loud, often common, and liked to dominate the room; Elizabeth's domination was of a very different nature, quiet and dignified. As a hostess, Elizabeth could just come into a room and make everything work smoothly. Anne was a person who always wanted to tip something over, spill something, shake it up.

I had never encountered such a big mind as Elizabeth's. It covered philosophy, literature, art, music, medicine, biology, and natural history, and more. Her memory was prodigious. I think if you put Elizabeth alone in a room for a month, she could quote for the entire time without ever repeating anything. She could quote poem after poem after poem after poem from beginning to end. Elizabeth made us memorize and recite in class. She felt everyone should have an enormous store in their heads of memorized literature, songs, or hymns. She was so grateful if anybody knew anything. She even had somebody recite the words of a hymn in class, just because it was the only thing that he knew.

One went away from Elizabeth's class with sixteen hours of work to do, if one wanted to pick up on what Elizabeth had said. She didn't say, "Go read this," but I was at a point of absorption where every nugget she dropped I was picking up. In Anne Sexton's class everything happened in class and not too much happened outside of class, except you did your own thing. With Elizabeth, what happened in class was rather formal, quiet, and subtle. There was a good deal of tension. Nobody wanted to appear stupid. But there was a great deal to do after she had finished. You couldn't possibly get it all done before the next class. Elizabeth gave me the Harvard Advocate Prize for the person in the most advanced class who showed the most promise. It was one hundred dollars. She called me just before Christmas in 1971 to tell me that she wasn't sure I'd get it, because I was a special graduate student, but that I was the first choice for it.

I also studied with Lowell, both after and simultaneously with studying with Elizabeth. After that first year, I had applied to what was then called the Radcliffe Institute (now the Bunting Institute). I received the Fellowship for 1973–75, and I continued to sit in on her classes until I left the Boston area in the summer of 1976. Elizabeth asked me to be there as support.

In 1973 Lowell too was at Harvard. I sat in on his Romantic Poetry class and what was called his conference hours. Elizabeth never got into somebody's work with both hands and turned it upside down the way Lowell did. Lowell would mix up a work, turn it around, and come out with something that sounded very much like Lowell, but that was a very much better piece of work. Elizabeth never would interfere with the writer's philosophy or the writer's idea or vision. She had enormous respect for anybody who wrote anything sincerely. I felt this with all her students, even the ones who were limited. She never insulted them. She never tore them down, but there was always this unspoken respect that we were all in one place trying to do something, trying to make something and to make it better. With that in mind, she respected each person, and the way you distinguished between what she appreciated and what she didn't appreciate was by the amount of time she spent on a piece of writing, whether she discussed it at all or dismissed it. She never would pick something up and say, "Well, this is nothing." Lowell could do that, and he could be extremely hurtful if you weren't pretty tough. And he could be very hurtful to some people who were very professional, who had published books and were professors.

I felt that I had to watch out not to let Lowell take over because he could take anybody's work and turn it into his own work and make it wonderful Lowell work, but it was no longer your work. I showed him poems that were pretty finished and that I was pretty stubborn about. I would listen very carefully because everything he had to say was important, the way everything Elizabeth had to say was important, but it was important in a different way. He was extremely historical; everything reminded him and reminded him. A small discussion of a small piece could turn into an endless monologue on historical figures. Lowell was very, very close to the top of his own hierarchy of poets, and he may have placed Elizabeth off to the side, in a class by herself, but at a comparable level. He respected her that much. He would say that hers was perfect work and that Elizabeth had an extraordinary ability to make what was complicated seemingly simple.

The nature of Elizabeth's criticism of my poetry was usually very, very tiny. It would have to do with the placement of a comma or perhaps the title, and her main criticism of my work was that I tended to end my poems with a chord. I guess I got this from Dylan Thomas, who felt that everything ought to be driving toward the last line. Elizabeth said it was all right to do that sometimes, but not to do it every time, not to close so hard.

That's not the kind of thing I got from Lowell. The structure of the whole piece was very important to him. It was to Elizabeth, as well, but she saw it, took it for granted, and if it wasn't there, she would move on to something else. But Lowell would insist upon a certain structure. I don't mean just formal form—a poem had to have an imaginative structure or a progression. Lowell felt a tremendous lack if the poem did not get from here to there somehow. He would say that "we had not moved anywhere," that "we haven't gone anywhere." Lowell would categorize things. He would say, "Well, I can see this as a prose piece," or "I can see this as part of a dialogue in a play, but of course it's not really a poem as it is now." He could see the possibilities in the thing and he would tell you what they were from his point of view. He was almost sculptural in his approach.

You had to get from Elizabeth a sense of proportion that was inherent in everything she said, did, and everything she wrote, but not directly stated. She would occasionally say that one line was a little flat compared to the rest of the poem or point to an inappropriate detail. This is the way she related to me and my work. She taught me to be very careful. I showed Elizabeth poetry that was worked on more than a lot of undergraduate work that was just written in five days. It's possible that an undergraduate might have needed something different, more to do with subject or approach or voice.

Normally Elizabeth would have seen my poems first. There was one occasion when I happened to show Cal a poem first, "Baddeck," the title poem of my book. I actually wrote that for his class. I'd sensed that the work that I had shown him was perhaps too short or too quick. He seemed to appreciate writing that had more structure and history behind it. My family and I had been to Nova Scotia largely because Elizabeth had grown up there and talked about it, and I was absolutely taken by Alexander Graham Bell, his museum, and his grand, sophisticated experiments in this wild setting. I wrote it very quickly. Then I found myself taking out engineering books from Widener Library to make sure that my facts were right. Lowell admired the poem. He spent much of the 2½ to 3 hours talking about it. Before I even had a chance to show it to Elizabeth, Frank [Bidart] had called her up right after class. She was "a little disappointed" that I hadn't shown it to her first. So there was a feeling of competition.

Actually, the competition between Elizabeth and Lowell was much bigger than that, much bigger than Harvard. You're dealing with enormous ego here, enormous sensitivity and fragility on all sides. Lowell had become a public figure in the fifties and sixties, was in the news, and had instant facial recognition in the Square. When Elizabeth came to Harvard, she had always been so private that nobody recognized her. I wouldn't have recognized her. Pictures on the back of her books were so old that they hardly resembled her. Elizabeth did enjoy being recognized. After she had been at Harvard for a while, she won some big prizes that were in the news—the Neustadt, the American Academy. Heads would stir. When we walked into the auditorium for Seamus Heaney's reading, heads were turning to see her. She was pleased. She would probably never admit that she was pleased. Later in life she did appreciate being noticed, so long as it was not an intrusion.

✦   ✦   ✦

Jane Shore joined the faculty of the Writing Program in 1973. She observed the proprietary role Lowell could take toward Bishop and the inconspicuous role Bishop assumed at Harvard.

JANE SHORE— In 1973 I got a job teaching poetry-writing at Harvard, as a Briggs-Copeland Lecturer, and Elizabeth and I were in fact colleagues. Then there was even more to talk about. We shared the same poetry students. We were part of the same community, and by that time, of course, I had read Bishop's work in depth and felt more comfortable with her. In fact, Bishop had replaced Lowell as my favorite poet. One would never discuss her own work with her, however—I tried to. Instead, she wanted to talk about a recent trip she'd taken in which she'd seen some blue-footed boobies. There were times when I would want to call Elizabeth on the phone, to talk about school or just (for me) shyly to gossip a little, but I was unsure which Elizabeth would answer the phone—the funny, friendly, confiding person, or the person who was quite cold and who did not want to talk to me. I blamed this on myself, as I was not a close friend of Elizabeth's. At times, I attributed this coldness to her often being ill, but now, in retrospect, it isn't far-fetched to attribute Elizabeth's "moodiness" to her drinking. In any case, I often felt discouraged and stayed away, and debated with myself about calling her.

On occasion we would meet after class at a little cafe in Harvard Square. I was being psychoanalyzed at the time and was pretty open about it with my friends, including Elizabeth, who had some experience in this area, too. I remember her telling me that her doctor had once told her that "given my childhood, I shouldn't have survived, but I did."

I finally got to attend Lowell's open poetry workshop in 1973. I walked into the basement room in the dormitory where the class was held. The seminar table was packed with people, mainly adults, poets from the community, very few undergraduates. The only empty chair in the room was next to Lowell's. I was terrified to sit down. Lowell turned to me with those pale blue-gray eyes, and asked, "Who are you?" When I said my name, Lowell said, "Oh, *Elizabeth* has told me about you." It was unclear what he meant, what she'd said. He asked me if I'd brought a poem to the workshop for him to critique. (The week before I'd given the same poem to Robert Fitzgerald, who had praised it, and I thought it would be great if Lowell liked it, too.) Lowell read my poem to the group, and although he seemed genuinely to like a line or two that he read aloud a few times, and the title, he basically thought my poem was bad. He said something to me like, "And *what* were you trying to *do* here?" And I said, "I was trying to imitate Elizabeth Bishop." And Lowell said, "Well, you *didn't*!" He didn't say this in a mean way; he'd intended this remark to be funny—and the class and I laughed. Yet I found his workshops to be too psychologically charged, in terms of what people had wanted from Lowell. Like myself, many of the poets around the table had come to sit at the feet of the master. Some were Lowell's genuine friends. Some had come out of curiosity, and some, like me, wanted to be praised, discovered. But I felt uncomfortable and nervous, and after a few more workshops, I didn't return.

During the time I taught at Harvard, the English Department invited Gwendolyn Brooks to give a major reading. There was a dinner for the writers at the Harvard Faculty Club. As I recall, the older writers at the table began recounting childhood memories about Halloween, what it was like in "the old days." There was an awkward and embarrassing moment at the table when Elizabeth began talking about her childhood. Elizabeth said that as children, she and friends used to dress up in costumes and smear burnt cork or coal on their faces. Then she realized that she had just described blackface, and Gwendolyn Brooks was right there to hear it. This was a horrible faux pas. I'm sure this remark was unintended, because Elizabeth would never have purposely said something like this. Later that evening, at the reception after the Brooks reading, I gathered up my courage and finally told Elizabeth how much I loved her poetry. I blurted it out. She seemed both pleased and embarrassed. I had to tell her at that moment, you see, because Elizabeth was standing off by herself, while everyone in the room was making a huge fuss over Gwendolyn Brooks, and Elizabeth Bishop was such a great poet and no one was making a fuss over her.

✦ ✦ ✦

Bishop settled into a busy life of friends and travel during her fourth year at Harvard. In September 1973 she delivered an article on Marianne Moore for a meeting of the English Institute in New York. Moore had died the year before. Bishop had completed the article in the latter, hot days of the summer in Methfessel's air-conditioned apartment. She and Methfessel traveled to Rockport two or three times that summer, then to Great Village in October, where Bishop was pleased that Muir MacLachlan at the general store recognized her. Bishop also gave a reading at Dartmouth College that month.[3] Bishop's friends Octavio and Marie Jo Paz were again at Cambridge that year, and in November the Barkers visited. Ilse Barker recollects the Halloween party Bishop gave: "John Malcolm Brinnin, Bill Read, Frank Bidart, Peter Taylor and his wife, Monroe Engel, and the Pazes were there. We spent half a day in Elizabeth's kitchen in Brattle Street carving pumpkins for the Halloween party. Thomas was given this wonderful mask. Elizabeth greeted us at the door with this hand stretched out, a leather glove filled with ice cubes, and there were bats and things all around." Barker also noted a certain unhappiness in Bishop during her family's visit: "Although Elizabeth did love her good students, teaching was still something that bothered her fundamentally. In fact, she said, 'I can't go on.'"

Bishop's sadness during this time found its expression in her poem "Five Flights Up," which began as a dream. It is about Alice Methfessel's apartment, the source of all the items in the poem, including the annoying man outside shouting at his Corgies. However, Bishop was embarrassed by this poem—it seemed slight to her, particularly after so many months had elapsed since she had published "The Moose." In comparison to the popular "confessional" poets of the day, who seemed to Bishop to turn out poems at a prolific rate, Bishop felt that she was irregular and erratic. That fall Bishop met Lloyd Schwartz, and she appreciated his interest in her poetry.

LLOYD SCHWARTZ— Elizabeth was hard to get to know because she was so protective of her privacy. Frank Bidart introduced us after her first Harvard reading [1970], and the only thing I could say to her was how much I had always admired her poems. She was gracious, but her poetry seemed the last thing in the world she wanted to talk about. I met her a number of times over the next couple years. At one party, at Frank's apartment, I screwed [up] my courage and invited her to lunch. We went to Ferdinand's, a little French restaurant in Harvard Square, not far from where she was living. We had a pleasant, chatty, but hardly intimate lunch. Elizabeth insisted on picking up the check. I was a little embarrassed, since I had invited her. She said that I was just a young teacher, just starting out—she knew I didn't have any money. The only other thing I remember talking about was that we both complained about being stuck in Cambridge over the Christmas holidays. She suggested—I thought only out of politeness—that we might get together sometime after Christmas.

One morning—it must have been just after New Year's (1974)—the telephone rang and it was Elizabeth. I'm not sure she ever called me before. She was clearly agitated. She was terribly apologetic and embarrassed about "disturbing" me, but she had fallen down a flight of stairs the evening before at the Casablanca, just down the street from her apartment on Brattle Street. She had broken her collarbone and was in Stillman Infirmary at Harvard. She kept repeating how much she hated to impose, and how embarrassed she was, but would I mind terribly coming to her hospital room and picking up her house keys, then going over to her apartment—all of five minutes away— to get her purse and her glasses, collecting her mail, and getting some papers that she needed and bringing them back to Stillman? She kept saying that she never would have bothered me, except that I was literally the only person she knew who was in town.

Of course, I was glad she had called me and happy to be able to do something for her. I didn't live very far away—it was absolutely no trouble— I'd have been happy to come in from New Hampshire. I got the things she asked for and stayed and talked to her at the hospital for several hours. I asked her if she'd like me to bring her mail the next day and if she minded having a visitor. She said she'd love it.

I came to visit Elizabeth every day. I brought her mail. Letters, especially letters with poems from people she didn't know, she asked me to read for her. I remember one particularly awful poem called "Garbage" that was so funny I had to read it aloud, and we were both roaring with laughter. But suddenly we weren't talking just about poetry, or the poetry world, but about personal things—how she was feeling, health in general, things like that— pop music (which we both loved) and the movies. Elizabeth was suddenly eager to know details of my personal life, which I was perfectly happy to confide to her. And of course we gossiped about people we knew. That's really how we became friends.

When Frank Bidart was editing his issue of *Ploughshares*, in 1974, Robert Pinsky and I were his associate editors. Frank wanted to have something about Elizabeth in that issue, and he knew how interested I was in her. But he also had the chance to publish an essay already written by David Kalstone— part of the chapter on Elizabeth he later published in *Five Temperaments*. I thought Frank should go ahead with the Kalstone piece, that if I were going to write anything on Elizabeth, it wouldn't be just a critical essay, that what really needed to be done was a new book. The only book at that time was Anne Stevenson's, which had been published years before, long before any of Elizabeth's extraordinary new poems began to appear. Then it occurred to me that if I could even think about writing a book, I could also think about writing a dissertation (I'd been stuck on my old thesis topic for seven years). The more I thought about changing my thesis topic and writing about Elizabeth, the more excited I got. But I was also nervous about how Elizabeth would react to the idea of a friend writing about her—that she might feel this was a kind of invasion. And I knew I couldn't go ahead without asking her permission first.

I finally called her up, and when I asked her what she thought about this idea, she said she was flattered. She seemed excited about someone writing a dissertation on her. It wasn't the first, but it may have been the first she knew about, and certainly the first written by someone she knew. I think she secretly wanted the academic seal of approval. She actually volunteered to help me as much as she could. She said if I had any questions, we could meet from time to time to discuss them—which we did. She was very helpful and full of delightful and fascinating anecdotes, although I remember one question I had about the tricky grammar of "Rain Toward Morning" and she answered by saying, "Isn't it obvious?" The dissertation, in fact, was a great opportunity to talk to her about the one subject we couldn't talk about as friends—her poems. I don't think anyone was ever sadder to end a dissertation, because after it was finished, we could never really talk about her poetry in detail again.

I gave Elizabeth a copy of the dissertation, but she didn't look at it right away. She seemed a little nervous about it—partly because she may have been afraid of what I might say, and partly, I think, because one side of her basically mistrusted all academic work. Then she had another asthma attack and had to be hospitalized. She brought the dissertation with her to the infirmary and read it there. She told me that it cheered her up, which really touched me. In the hospital, she gave me as a present her own reading copy of *North & South*, with a poignant little autobiographical verse in it that reads:

From North to South;
    "   South " North;
& back again,
    "   "   "   , to

Lloyd Schwartz, with love—

Cambridge, September 1975

✦   ✦   ✦

For two weeks in July 1974, Bishop and Frank Bidart rented a house on North Haven Island in Maine, where Methfessel joined them for part of the time. Bishop had read an advertisement for the house in the newspaper. This was the first of five summers she rented this house. "Elizabeth adored bringing out the human side of literary people. She felt there were better things to do than to play shop, like playing Ping-Pong and forcing Frank Bidart to go on nature walks at North Haven. It amused her at times to see how inept literary people were in any conventional human sense. Frank knew the names of only two flowers."[4] Bishop was joined at North Haven that summer and subsequent times by the novelist Celia Bertin and her husband, Jerry Reich, who along with two of Bishop's neighbors on the island, Tom and Barbara Thacher, recollect life with Bishop on North Haven.

CELIA BERTIN— I think it was in 1973 that I asked John Brinnin to bring Elizabeth for dinner to our place on Marlboro Street. I had read Elizabeth's poetry and was interested in meeting her. She was the woman I admired most. I had Brazilian friends in the diplomatic service who knew Lota. Elizabeth, Alice, John Malcom Brinnin, and Bill Read came for dinner. I liked Elizabeth very much because she didn't talk much. She was exactly what I thought a poet should be. She was a little old lady with white hair, but she was very special. You could see that. There was so much in this little body. You could feel it.

The evening was very nice and we said we were going to see each other again, and we did. Alice and Elizabeth invited us to Alice's apartment in Cambridge. Then, rather soon after, Elizabeth was going to North Haven and she invited us. That was 1974. The year after, Elizabeth was alone in North Haven because Alice was in business school, and she didn't want to be alone. I was finishing a book, and Elizabeth asked if I would like to stay with her. Of course, I was delighted.

I loved seeing Elizabeth in the kitchen in North Haven. It became a poetical place, the way she cooked, the way she talked about little things, the way she bought things—her relationship with the man who was bringing the lobsters. Elizabeth had a marvelous way of relating to simple people that I loved very much. Maybe it was easier for her because they didn't know who she was. She loved real people. That is one of the reasons she didn't like social life. It was marvelous to be with her alone because she enjoyed everything—flowers, little walks, new places.

JERRY REICH— Elizabeth had such a talent for living in the day and making the day a celebration. She didn't reminisce much with me, but she was always interested in everything. At the dinner table we talked about recipes, books, and movies. We played Scrabble, Backgammon, and "forgotten women poets." Elizabeth did crossword puzzles and would be proud to have finished that week's in a day.

BERTIN— Elizabeth always associated me with Brazil, with foreign things, because I was foreign. Elizabeth mentioned Lota to me almost as if Lota was still living. "Oh yes," she said, "Lota would say that, too." Of course, all kinds of memories from her time in Brazil came back with me. I was a great friend of Janet Flanner [who wrote from Paris for *The New Yorker* as Genêt]. I discovered when Janet came to Boston to visit that Elizabeth didn't like her at all for private reasons that were probably very foolish, something that happened in the past at a party given by Virgil Thomson. Elizabeth had been there with Lota, and Janet got too interested in Lota.

TOM THACHER— One thing [that] Elizabeth did particularly enjoy [at our house in North Haven was] a hymn sing. She and Alice arrived a little early one Sunday night, and Elizabeth started recalling how much she loved the gospel hymns of her youth and proceeded to start belting them out without any accompaniment.

The only excursion we had with Elizabeth was the result of having heard her lament that she had not been able to get off the island on which we were living and go to some of the other islands. We were glad to press into service a pair who sailed in one day from Sutton's Island with their sloop. These people were always accompanied by two dogs, and we did not know that Elizabeth was allergic to dogs. We all got aboard this thirty-eight-foot sloop in a rather strong breeze and set sail for Winter Harbor on Vinalhaven, maybe five miles away. Elizabeth looked troubled on sighting the dogs. The barking rose. She removed herself from the cockpit, where the dogs were kept, and to a further cockpit. Eventually she moved forward and spent the balance of the trip in front of the mast looking stolidly forward and not aft at the dogs.

We had forgotten about the difficulties of approaching another friend's house, which sits at the top of an escarpment on the island. We formed a human chain pulling Elizabeth. We picnicked at the top.

BARBARA THACHER— There was a pony tethered on a long lead nearby. When we took a walk after lunch, we saw this nice-looking pony grazing, so we walked near it thinking we might pat it. As soon as it saw us within range, it came barging at us. If it hadn't been anchored to this iron stake, there's no telling what it might have done. We were very close. The animal stopped about a foot away.

TOM— It almost pulled the chain out. Our friend offered Alice and Elizabeth a ride back to North Haven by another route in a metal rowboat with a small outboard motor. Its freeboard was about four inches above the water, and as the wind came up, water came into the boat from time to time, with Elizabeth and Alice valiantly bailing. Everyone finally got over to North Haven.

BARBARA— When we were saying goodbye, Elizabeth thanked us and said the day had been eventful. Then she said, ruminating, "It's rare that you meet an unpleasant dog and an unpleasant horse in the same day."

✦ ✦ ✦

Bishop moved into her apartment at Lewis Wharf on 8 August 1974, and Methfessel moved into Bishop's vacated apartment on Brattle Street. The contractors had run six months behind schedule; then, when the apartment was finally ready that summer, there had been a carpenters' strike, and Bishop had been unable to have her bookshelves built. When she finally arrived, however, she was very pleased. Bishop told friends that the most exciting aspect of her Lewis Wharf apartment was watching the ships in Boston Harbor from the front windows.

Bishop had packed boxes the previous spring in Ouro Prêto, and it took them months to arrive at Lewis Wharf. Even as late as February 1975 she was complaining that she was still unpacking. Bishop told friends that she hoped this would be the last time she would have to move. At Lewis Wharf, Bishop did create her final home, with a feeling all her own, as several people observed.

HELEN VENDLER— I admired Elizabeth's taste. Her apartment was so beautiful. There was a *santo* in a glass case, a ship's figurehead on the wall, and a wooden birdcage, like the ones she writes about in "Questions of Travel." There was a small shadowbox that she had made to represent a drowned girl, with stickers of winged cherubs in the sky and a shoe on the beach. Elizabeth had the crudely carved, balsa wood figure of a head, a Brazilian thanks offering for recovering from illness, which she later gave to Robert Lowell and which he wrote about in "Thanks Offering for Recovery." There was a huge Venetian mirror, and books, of course, all around. It was an apartment in which each thing had been chosen by someone with an eye. There aren't many places like that—each thing you rested your eye on had its own aesthetic claim. It was a pleasure to sit in the room and let your glance rest on the *santo* or on the figurehead or the birdcage.

DAVID KALSTONE— [Visiting Elizabeth's apartment at Lewis Wharf] was like reading one of her poems. It was up to you to immerse yourself in the details. You were not instructed. The two things that sent shivers through me were the small painting that she describes in the poem called "Poem," the painting the size of a dollar bill, which was in the kitchen, in a very inconspicuous [place], and the twin paintings of her mother and her Uncle Arthur [as] children posed in echoing positions, one leaning on the chair, the other on the table. They are the companion pieces described in the story "Memories of Uncle Neddy." Elizabeth's Aunt Grace had sent these paintings to her in Brazil. Elizabeth had a landscape by Loren MacIver. She talked about how interested she was in MacIver's painting and [what] a shame [it was] that it was more or less out of fashion. There was that sense of someone not necessarily living among her memories or dwarfed by her memories, but somebody who was very much in a setting that meant a great deal personally to her.

PAULA DEITZ— Lewis Wharf was a rather gutsy place to live. It took a lot of flair to live there. The building has a medieval feeling. The high windows down at the end of Elizabeth's apartment were quite narrow, and you almost felt as if you were in a small castle room. You looked out over the water, and there were other warehouses across the slip so that it felt like a fortress. Everything in the living room had a rough feel to it. The interior was raw brick. There was nothing dainty. A place like that has a kind of forthright independence. It's a special taste. There was definitely a motif of strong colors or stripes, woven pieces in stripes. One could say there was an ethnic theme. It was very subtle and personal.

PEGGY ELLSBERG— Lewis Wharf wasn't the chic, desirable kind of place it is now when Elizabeth moved in. Then it was one of the just-refurbished buildings on the Boston waterfront, which was not the charming, quaint neighborhood it is now. By the time Elizabeth died, it had become fashionable.

You walked down a brick path to the arched doorways of the building. You went up a flight. The hall was quite dark, but new and fresh. You had the feeling that not many people lived there yet. In the foyer of Elizabeth's apartment there was a table for you to put your keys or mittens or whatever on. Then you walked into a room that was filled with light. One wall was in part a big window that opened onto the water. Her apartment was beautifully and delicately decorated. Lots and lots and lots of books. On the left was a very well-appointed kitchen. She was a superb cook.

Soon after she moved in—actually, Elizabeth was still moving in—she invited me to Lewis Wharf. I was twenty-four years old, something like that. I'd sold some poems and I had money burning a hole in my pocket. I had bought myself a black cocktail dress as I walked through downtown Boston to get to her place. Elizabeth always made nice food when I visited. Sometimes it would be onion soup or fried bananas or crepes. On that day she'd made crème caramel and a big pot of excellent coffee. Elizabeth was as usual nicely dressed and had prepared for my visit. I felt very aware of being just a kid, and yet that day Elizabeth's own girlishness really struck me.

Elizabeth was unpacking, and the first thing she wanted to know was what was in my package. She made me go into the other room and try it on. And she was so filled with admiration: "Oh, it's so nice. I want one just like it. Where did you get it?" I started to learn on that day that she could talk for hours about shopping and clothes and how much it cost and where could you get it on sale. As my teacher, she had been such a *mysterium tremendum* to me, but out of the classroom she was like a wonderful, cozy girlfriend.

This apartment really had her mark on it, with lots of folk art touches. Elizabeth knew I was a Catholic. She wanted me to see her statues, her *santos*. She started taking them out of their boxes and laying them out. She said she kept these on their little stands, and some of them she kept in a glass case. Elizabeth said she changed their clothes according to the holy seasons. She had little outfits for them and straw hats. Some of them had little purple or black accessories they wore during Holy Week. That was during the winter. The next time I went back it was April, and she had them all dressed for Easter.

That summer I went back, and she took me into her bedroom to show me something there. She told me to close my eyes, lie on the bed, and then look up. She had a beautiful set of marionettes of the Holy Family on the flight into Egypt—the Blessed Mother on the donkey holding baby Jesus, Joseph, and I seem to remember some of the Wise Men. She had hung them from the ceiling. They were primitive, Latin American puppets—plain, in faded outfits. They were hung so that from the pillow of the bed you could see them perfectly. This way, she said, when she woke up in the morning, that's the first thing she saw.

That was the time when she showed me her ship journal—a log of the boats and the ships that went by. Elizabeth loved to see the boats. She had a telescope and a small clock on the window, and she had this nautical diary. It was on a stand, like a Bible stand. She would write down the time of day, the name of the boat, the kind of boat and how many masts, and which way it was going. She liked to keep track of details like that.

✦   ✦   ✦

Teaching at Harvard in the 1970s was for Bishop like attending Vassar in the 1930s. Both were periods of heightened political awareness and activism. Both were times when an artist like Bishop, who eschewed the overtly political and polemical in poetry, felt out of step. Robert B. Shaw became Bishop's colleague in the Writing Program at Harvard in the fall of 1974. He observed Bishop's reaction to the spirit of the time.

ROBERT B. SHAW— I met Elizabeth in October 1968, when she gave a reading at Harvard. She was very intrigued at my middle name [Burns]. She had seen my initial and had asked what it is for. In the fall of 1969 the staff began work on a special issue of The Harvard Advocate on John Berryman. Some other people on the magazine and I were great fans of the Dream Songs, which were coming out in those years. The magazine has a history of occasional special issues. There had been one on Lowell in the early sixties, and a rather famous one further back on Faulkner. I was the one who did the correspondence with all the contributors for the Berryman issue, so I wrote and asked Elizabeth if she would give us either a little prose tribute or a poem. She gave us the little poem "Thank-You Note." I think I may be the only person alive who commissioned a poem from Elizabeth Bishop.

Elizabeth knew who I was when I came back to Harvard to teach in 1974 as a Briggs-Copeland Lecturer. I've always thought that Elizabeth might have been a lot happier at a smaller place, perhaps at a place like Vassar, because I think a lot of her ideas of what college was like, or should be like, were ones that she had really picked up as a student and had never felt the need to get beyond. I know Elizabeth felt the students didn't read enough on their own, as a lot of us felt. She found it hard to accommodate their taste. Elizabeth wanted to have them read Marianne Moore and Auden. She was not very much interested in the poetry of John Lennon or Richard Brautigan, that kind of thing. She was appalled at the level of usage that she found in student writing, and I remember some conversations with her about this or that book on usage. I imagine this issue had its frustrations, because it's awfully hard single-handedly to correct the style of a generation.

Elizabeth thought there was a kind of decline in manners among younger people. I remember her complaining to me very bitterly once about a student who was doing a project on Eliot. She remembered in talking to the student that she had an old issue of the *Partisan Review* that had just the perfect essay, and she described all the hassle she went through finding this twenty-year-old copy in her effects. Finally, Elizabeth delivered the article to the student, and what bothered her was that there was not much of what she thought was an appropriate display of gratitude. To some extent Elizabeth felt victimized by having to teach at all, and so when incidents like that occurred, there was a stronger emotional reaction on her part that maybe other people might feel.

Students had to be admitted to the Writing Program. It was very selective, and there was some kind of numerical limit on the number of people in fiction or poetry that we would take based on who was available to teach them. There were various other specifications about literature courses and a final project, which was equivalent to an honors thesis. Elizabeth and I and others would usually be among the readers of these and would grade them. There was at least one case when I read the thesis of a student for whom Elizabeth had been the adviser, and I liked it a little better than she did. Monroe Engel had to be a sort of mediator and work out a grade. We submitted our different readings and then Monroe had to call us on the phone. I remember deciding some of the prizes with Elizabeth. She took that kind of thing seriously. She had obviously read the manuscripts very carefully and made notes on the ones she had thought were potentially winners.

Elizabeth liked the students who were literary. That is, she paid more attention to work that showed traces of a person having read something. Beyond that she tended to pay attention when she saw her own predilections, which you see in her own writing, in the writing of her students. She certainly appreciated nicety of description and minuteness of observation. In so far as she allowed you to guess at her preferences, she tended to favor writing that was more anchored in the concrete than any that was mystical or speculative. That was what we were disagreeing about on this thesis. A woman had done what I thought were some rather interesting translations of

Persian mystical poetry, and I think it was a little too mystical for Elizabeth, a little too abstract from her point of view.

Elizabeth would talk about just how different it was going to college in the Depression, and how people she knew weren't able to get through because their parents couldn't foot the bill. I don't think she was eaten up by guilt at having got through when these others didn't, but she was very aware of it. She was aware that she had had in some ways a very privileged life, although very unhappy in many ways. At a party I remember, people had been talking about politics. Of course everything was in great turmoil in the late sixties, especially around Harvard, and there was a lot of student agitation. Somebody said, "What does Elizabeth think of all this?" Octavio Paz said Elizabeth's politics were of the 1930s. In so far as she had political or social interests, Elizabeth was concerned with economic justice, that people have enough to eat.

At that first reading I went to, Elizabeth read "Manuelzinho." That's a poem about which some people have said Elizabeth is being very condescending toward the peasant. I didn't get that in her voice at all. It was less complicated. She was seeing it humorously and humanly. For her the fact was that some people had a lot of money and some people had none. What does that do to human character? That was her interest when she approached these subjects in writing, just to render that.

People did run into a snobbishness with Elizabeth sometimes. I saw her at the Gardner Museum once for a concert. Yo-Yo Ma, who was still a Harvard undergraduate but was already very well known, and two other young musicians were playing. It was some kind of memorial to Mrs. Gardner. They were serving champagne afterward. Elizabeth appeared with a couple. She was sitting, looking very delightedly at Yo-Yo Ma, and she said afterward that he always looks so happy when he plays. One virtuoso looking at another. I asked Elizabeth if she was going to have some champagne. She said, "Well, no. It's American champagne. We're going to go off and have some French champagne." I've heard stories like this from other people. It's very hard to quite put your finger on the tone. It was not just a sort of snobbish comment. It was a little more naive than that. It was sort of, "Aren't I lucky," to some extent, as if she forgot that maybe it wouldn't sound politic to say it out loud.

✦   ✦   ✦

Many found Bishop's seeming neutrality on political issues appealing, as was the case with the poet and editor Frederick Morgan: "Elizabeth was the kind of person who was quite secure writing her poems. There they were. She was nonideological. That's why I liked her." The women's movement and gay rights movement were important parts of the social and political land-scape in Cambridge during the early seventies. Bishop viewed both with skepticism.

FRANK BIDART— Elizabeth considered herself a feminist, and had since she was young; she viewed SOME developments in the contemporary feminist movement with skepticism (particularly the development of women-only collections or anthologies), but she was passionately feminist, and could be bitter about how the world had treated her because she was a woman. Late in her life, in a mood of anger, self-doubt, and bitterness, she told me that she felt she would have written much more had she been a man. She brought up how little she had written in contrast to Lowell (his *Selected Poems* had just come out, and in particular once again she was overwhelmed by "Waking Early Sunday Morning"). I can't quote her words exactly, but she felt that certain kinds of directness and ambition—because of gender—had been denied her, had been impossible.

The skepticism she felt about the gay rights movement was based on her sense that straight society would never truly accept homosexuality, that sooner or later it would punish writers for "coming out." She was worried that the candor of what I had written would at some point be used against me professionally, and in warning me said that she "believed in closets, closets, and more closets." One must remember that for the vast majority of her life, in both social and literary terms, not to be in the closet was to be ghettoized; people might know or suspect that one was gay, but to talk about it openly in straight society was generally considered out-of-control or stupid. (Bishop thought famously polemical works like *The Well of Loneliness* weak, simplistic, an embarrassment.) Out of her distrust of the straight world she didn't want people to know she was gay. She certainly didn't want people to talk about it. The irony, of course, is that everyone at least in the literary world did know, and didn't care; but she could never believe that this was the case.

◆　　◆　　◆

At least one of Bishop's students perceived her "schoolmarmish" appearance as a means of hiding her sexuality: "The old maid is sort of an asexual being, and it never raises the question of whether you are straight or gay, because you're the old lady schoolteacher."[5] As Katha Pollitt remembers Bishop's appearance, "There was an aspect of the way Miss Bishop presented herself that permitted a dismissal of her as a sensual, passionate, and deeply feeling person." In reality Bishop's private life was far different from this appearance, as Lloyd Schwartz recollects.

LLOYD SCHWARTZ— Elizabeth's sexual life was inevitably more surprising and complicated than most people assume. In fact, she was also very attracted to men and could be very affectionate with men, even in a physical way. When I was in Brazil in 1990, I heard stories about Elizabeth's friendship with the famous Brazilian poet Vinicius de Moraes, whom she'd translated (he's best known here not as a serious poet but for writing the original Portuguese lyrics to "The Girl from Ipanema"). Vinicius had a reputation for being a womanizer. It was reported to me with authority that Elizabeth and Vinicius would stay up drinking at the Chico Rey, the inn where they'd both be staying (she while her 150-year-old house was being renovated), then spend the night together.

Elizabeth said she'd written "Songs for a Colored Singer" with Billie Holiday in mind and that the last of the four songs was inspired especially by "Strange Fruit"—only Billie Holiday, she thought, could sing the line in her poem about the "conspiring root." She'd always hoped someone would set the poem to music so that Billie Holiday would record it. Elizabeth rarely talked to me about her private past. But one evening at Lewis Wharf in the late 1970s, we got onto the subject of New York, and she started telling me about when she and [a woman friend—name withheld] were living together. It seemed a rather lighthearted time. They'd go to the jazz clubs practically every night. [Her friend] was also a big Billie Holiday fan, and they'd gotten to know her by staying around after her last sets. One night, Elizabeth told me with her familiar nervous laugh, she had returned from some social engagement and found [her friend] home in bed—with Billie Holiday! She was so upset, she chuckled, that she threw Billie Holiday out of the apartment.

When Bishop was living in San Francisco, she resisted suggestions that she march in a gay rights parade. Brad Leithauser recollects Bishop's reactions to the gay liberation movement.

BRAD LEITHAUSER— The whole women's movement and gay liberation movement left Elizabeth Bishop in a peculiar position because she always insisted so much on her privacy. They made her uneasy. She spoke disparagingly of the "women poets." She [gave the] feeling that women were getting attention, which they should have gotten all along, but the wrong women. Elizabeth Bishop spoke approvingly of Auden. She said it was so much braver what he did than someone like Allen Ginsberg. It was obvious that Auden was gay, but the notion was that she didn't want to make an issue of these things.

✦   ✦   ✦

As Jane Shore recollects, Bishop's reactions to feminism made for complex reactions to her fellow poets, such as Adrienne Rich: "Diving Into the Wreck had just come out, and Elizabeth said, 'My God, I've been a feminist since way back. I don't feel that you have to write about sex that way.' She liked Adrienne Rich, felt that she was a very intelligent woman, but said, 'I could never use [sexuality] as a subject or write about things as baldly as Rich does.'" One evening Bishop invited Rich to a party at Lewis Wharf, and during the gathering, Rich presented her ideas forcefully.

MONROE ENGEL— My wife and I went to Lewis Wharf [one evening] with Adrienne Rich. Adrienne's overtness and the way in which she argued her position [about lesbianism] made Elizabeth somewhat uncomfortable. But that evening Elizabeth sat down next to Adrienne and told her how much the prose book [Of Woman Born: Motherhood As Experience and Institution] had meant to her, which was an astonishment to me. It wouldn't have occurred to me that Elizabeth would even have read it. She had read it all, however, and wasn't going to keep that a secret from Adrienne. She wanted Adrienne to know how much it had meant to her. There were a number of other people there, as well, which made this even more remarkable. Adrienne [told] us afterward that she too had been surprised, because she was sure that her politics must have made Elizabeth somewhat uncomfortable.

PENELOPE LAURANS FITZGERALD— I remember the evening Elizabeth had a group of us to Lewis Wharf for dinner with Adrienne Rich. I admired Rich— at least through Diving into the Wreck—later her work became too polemical for me. I remember that night thinking that she was very, very nice. But I also remember that she and Elizabeth were engaged in a discussion—Adrienne was trying to persuade Elizabeth to be in an anthology of American women poets—and Elizabeth was having none of it. She was not, she said, a "woman poet"—she was a poet, plain and simple. She did not see the issues in political terms, and she had no interest in doing so. In certain ways Elizabeth was not very sure of herself, but in others she had the confidence to stick by who she was and how she saw the world. There was this wonderful thing about Elizabeth—she was incapable of putting on a front, of being anyone or anything but herself.

LLOYD SCHWARTZ— Elizabeth was not naive about literary politics. She just didn't want to get involved in controversies, although she had some strong opinions that she never changed. For example, she refused to be published in women's anthologies. In the 1930s, she said, being in a woman's anthology was a form of segregation. Why, then, should she change her position now? She felt she had been a feminist before it was fashionable—she didn't want to seem to be getting on a bandwagon. One evening, near the end of a pleasant party at Elizabeth's apartment, Adrienne Rich asked her about this policy of hers. One of the things she said was something like, "But Elizabeth, don't you want to have a bigger audience?" Elizabeth responded by saying that she thought that her audience was large enough. She obviously felt a little wounded. It was a tense moment. Then Adrienne changed the subject—she clearly knew she was not going to get any further. She had made her point. She was, of course, right in a way, but she must have realized that her question was bound to make Elizabeth feel uncomfortable, especially at a social gathering.

RICHARD HOWARD— Adrienne Rich had been to see Elizabeth in Boston and had attempted to persuade her to be more forthcoming about her sexual orientation. Elizabeth did not regard the enterprise with favor. After Adrienne's visit, I remember her describing her new domesticities at Lewis Wharf. "You know what I want, Richard? I want closets, closets, and more closets!" And she laughed.

✦　✦　✦

In December 1974 Bishop gave a reading at the Pierpont Morgan Library in New York, and following the reading Louise Crane gave a party in her Fifth Avenue apartment for Bishop. Crane suggested that Bishop stay at a guest house that she owned in Fort Myers Beach, Florida, where Bishop's friends Charlotte and Charles Russell lived. Bishop traveled to Florida for a vacation for the first time since the 1940s.[6]

The following winter Crane's house in Florida became the refuge to which Bishop escaped when it appeared to her that her relationship with Methfessel was about to end. Methfessel was considering marrying, and the prospect of losing Methfessel and being alone initiated the worst crisis of Bishop's final years. As early as June 1975, when Bishop visited the Strands and Pazes in Mexico, her friends were noticing her depression. Robert and

Penelope Fitzgerald also recollect being with Bishop and Methfessel during this period.

JULIA STRAND— Mark and I shared a house with Octavio and Marie Jo Paz in Quernivaca when Elizabeth came down [in June 1975]. The Mexican government was paying for some TV extravaganza on poetry. Joseph Brodsky and Elizabeth were two poets involved. Elizabeth was very depressed. She seemed to be drinking a lot. She had had problems with Alice the year before [and she was] talking about how old she was. [She mentioned] how awful it was to be old. She was very low. Marie Jo was holding her hand through that. People around her were concerned about her.

ROBERT FITZGERALD— Elizabeth suffered over Alice's possible marriage for a long time. I remember her on the telephone saying, "I have never been so unhappy in my life."

PENELOPE LAURANS FITZGERALD— Knowing the difficulties of Elizabeth's life, that is hard to believe, although I am sure that is the way it felt to Elizabeth at the time, perhaps for the very reason that she had been through so much and losing Alice at this point in her life was the final straw she could not take. After all, as you get older, it becomes more difficult to form relationships and people's dependencies become more intense. If Elizabeth lost Alice, it was unlikely she would find someone else she felt as strongly about, who would be so devoted and so practical and full of good sense.

One day when we were at Lewis Wharf and Elizabeth was very low, Robert stayed and listened to her confidences and consoled her while Alice and I went out to buy food. Slowly in this or that way the situation became clear to me. Alice was still very young when she met Elizabeth, and she had to worry about making a life. There was always a certain tension having to do with Alice's understandable need to remain independent and consider her future and Elizabeth's sharp dependency on Alice and her need to have her full attention and time.

At one point Alice, in her quest for independence and career, had started business school, and while she was there, she met somebody and considered marrying him. This was devastating to Elizabeth, but completely understandable on Alice's part—Alice had, after all, to contemplate a long life without Elizabeth. And then there was also the point that being with Elizabeth wasn't easy, as she was a consuming person with serious health problems. All of this would strain the relationship of any two people, no matter how devoted, which Alice and Elizabeth certainly were. At the moment I am describing, this imbalance was the central fact of the relationship, putting it in jeopardy and making Elizabeth miserable. But later, after Alice effectively had made her decision and Elizabeth could be more confident in her presence, the balance righted in this respect. Alice was wonderful. Elizabeth owed a great deal to her patience, devotion, and practical sense, and she knew that.

✦ ✦ ✦

When Bishop slipped into depression during this period, she began calling friends late at night.

HELEN VENDLER— Two or three times when she was drinking, Elizabeth called me late at night. A couple of times were in that period when she thought she would lose Alice. All one could say was, "You never know. Probably she'll come back." That sort of thing. She said that Alice's mother wanted her to get married and that she was afraid Alice would. Another time Elizabeth said her life had been a failure. One could only say that in many respects it hadn't been. I could conceive of her feeling that she had not written all the poems she had it in her to write. It's a very small corpus. She must have felt that very keenly, especially with Lowell pouring out poem after poem. She must have felt in some way that she hadn't lived up to her talent or hadn't fully exercised her talent.

✦ ✦ ✦

Bishop's most important writing from this period is her autobiographical poem "One Art," whose subject is the possible loss of Methfessel. The poem took shape in November and early December of 1975, before Bishop traveled to Florida for her second stay at Crane's house. She also worked on "One Art" in Florida. Frank Bidart discussed "One Art" with Bishop during this period, and Helen Vendler relates the tone of that poem to Bishop as she knew her during this period.

FRANK BIDART— The period when she thought she would lose Alice certainly was the most terrible period in Elizabeth's life during the years I knew her. And I think her way of working her way out of it was writing "One Art." It did look "like disaster." And the poem is also the desperate attempt to tell herself that it isn't disaster. "One Art" was 70 to 80 percent finished when I saw it. My memory is that there were two or three stanzas that weren't finished. There was a draft with a list of rhyme words, and I think I suggested a rhyme out of that. It was already a villanelle; the present ending was basically as it is. We talked about the punctuation of "Write it," whether to italicize the "Write," how to do that. Elizabeth was very open about the occasion that drives it.

I think Elizabeth was magnificently inconsistent. On the one hand, she could talk a blue streak about how people shouldn't be writing all these confessional poems, and yet when she had to do it, she did it, and without apology. At a certain level, the aesthetic position was quite irrelevant to Elizabeth. I also think she was able to cut off certain parts of her mind in order to make the poem. For example, someone once said something to her about how "Crusoe in England" is a kind of autobiographical metaphor for Brazil and Lota. She was horrified by the suggestion. And obviously the poem is. I certainly never said to her, "Elizabeth, 'One Art' is a confessional poem," but on the other hand, she was entirely straightforward about how it was directly related to what was happening in her own life. I don't think she wanted to confront the way that contradicted her stance. One evening at her apartment, Elizabeth had just shown Octavio Paz the poem, and he was amazed at both how wonderful and candid it was; that evening he said to me in astonishment: Why, it's a confessional poem.

HELEN VENDLER— There was something very cold about Elizabeth. You sensed her as a chilly person, not that she even perhaps wanted to be, but there was some residue of the person who could turn off. You felt that she could opt into privacy, which is perhaps common to solitaries, intellectual people, creative people, some certain temperaments. I don't mean that it isn't a widespread character trait. There is something about "One Art" that reminds me of that part of her, where she says [in effect], "I've lost it. I'm all by myself. Nobody's going to be able to take care of me. I'm not going to be able to hold onto anything. I am an encapsulated, isolated child." Elizabeth had a place she could go in which she was all alone as a kind of frigid little girl. She could be enticed out of it, but then she would go back into it, back into her own aloneness.

◆　◆　◆

Bishop became suicidal during her stay in Florida in December 1975 and January 1976 as Frank Bidart remembers: "Elizabeth once told me on the phone from Florida that, that day, she had wanted to throw herself under a car. She would see cars go by, and she had a tremendous impulse to do it. Without Alice life seemed intolerable. Of course I can't know how much of this was theater to convince Alice to come back. But I was scared to death."

Her close friend from Walnut Hill and Vassar, Rhoda Wheeler Sheehan, joined her in Florida at this time.

RHODA WHEELER SHEEHAN— I was [in Fort Myers Beach] for ten days. Elizabeth had obviously been drinking too much when I got there. I was trying not to have her drink. I wasn't bringing anything into the house. Elizabeth spent a lot of time in bed. She showed me the poem she was writing. It really sounded terrific.

Elizabeth and I had some nice times. Elizabeth had some very nice, mature ladies there whom she knew. We went out for meals and went for drives through the countryside, which took her mind off [things] a bit. I rented a car and we drove to Naples and Sarasota, trying to keep on the move. When we went to Naples, I had a friend there and Elizabeth and I went to call on her. She turned to Elizabeth [and asked], "And what do you do?" And Elizabeth commented, "I teach writing." She said, "Oh, penmanship?" Of course Elizabeth [loved it].

But when I had to go back, Elizabeth was very anxious. When I had to leave, she begged me not to go—I had a job and a family. It was right after that [that Elizabeth took the overdose]. That made me feel terrible.

◆　　◆　　◆

The overdose of which Sheehan speaks was a combination of alcohol and pills Bishop took in December 1975. A. L. Francis, who was employed by the Crane family, was present when Bishop was discovered.

A. L. FRANCIS— I was working on the house on the beach, and Charlotte [Russell] had gone across the street. Then she came running over to me—I was the only one there at the time—and said that Elizabeth had fallen on the floor. Charlotte wanted to know if I could help get her back in bed. So I went right over, and after a little struggle—Elizabeth was out cold, right beside the bed—did get her back on the bed. She was dressed in her normal clothes for daytime.

Elizabeth was just left to lie there and sleep this thing out. If I'd thought she was in any danger, either Charlotte or I would have called the rescue squad. Nobody ever mentioned any suicide. I got the opinion at the time that she might have been an alcoholic, and this was a regular thing, but then she took [some] pills to knock herself out so she could get some sleep, but she didn't make it to the bed.

◆   ◆   ◆

Bishop returned to Boston in mid-January, and Frank Bidart met her at the airport. The severe effects of her depression lasted into February 1976. During one visit to New York that month, when Bishop was consulting Anny Baumann, she received news of being awarded the prestigious Books Abroad/ Neustadt International Prize for Literature. However, as Chester Page, an assistant to Louise Crane, remembers, even this award failed to help her.

CHESTER PAGE— In February 1976 Elizabeth stayed the night with Emanuel Brasil on Perry Street. The poor dog of Emanuel Brasil's had to be tied outside because of [Elizabeth's] allergies. Elizabeth had just gotten over this streak of depression and had been told by Anny Baumann that she should not be alone. A friend and I took them to dinner. Elizabeth seemed quite relaxed and charming.

She was talking about the crazy things that people asked poets. Some girl had asked Mark Strand, "How do you get your ideas? Do they come to you, or do you make them up?" Elizabeth talked about Marianne Moore's protégé, a man named Lester Littlefield, and how Marianne managed everything from his laundry list to everything else. She told how once she had arrived late at the apartment on Cumberland Street and Mrs. Moore opened the door with the comment, "Lester is always on time. Elizabeth is always late." Elizabeth told us about a concert Sylvia Marlowe gave in Brazil and in a little hall where you could hear the sounds of a soprano vocalizing during the concert. Afterward, Sylvia removed her wig and Elizabeth and some other people dismantled the harpsichord for a midnight flight somewhere. As a special favor, Elizabeth had taken Sylvia to see the Christ of the Andes. She didn't know that Sylvia had a deathly fear of heights. Sylvia had to lie in the back of the car all covered up. Elizabeth didn't tell her until late that the two guides were heavily armed because of robbers at the top. Elizabeth also told about being in Brazil once when there was the funeral of Carmen Miranda, a national event. Throngs of people gathered along the roadways.

The day after our dinner, I read in the Times that she had won the Neustadt of ten thousand dollars, so I called her up to congratulate her. Elizabeth said that she had known about it the night before, but she didn't feel that it was proper to mention it. Dr. Baumann said that if the prize had happened just a week earlier, it would have made no difference, it would hardly have registered. Elizabeth had been that depressed.

Bishop remained in New York until March. Before leaving, she fell and tore a leg ligament. Methfessel met Bishop at the airport, upon her return to

Boston. As Frank Bidart remembers the conclusion to this incident, the rift in their relationship was quickly mended.

FRANK BIDART—I don't remember that there was any sort of big declaration one way or the other. It was clear at some point that Alice decided to give up the man she intended to marry. Suddenly they were together, going on a trip or something together, and there was just no more talk about him. After that Elizabeth was a little unhappy at how extremely candid she had been during this period. For months she had called up a number of people late at night, drinking too much, in despair talking for hours. When things abruptly were resolved, it was as if there had been no crisis.[7]

✦ ✦ ✦

In 1976 a number of awards came Bishop's way. She was elected to the American Academy and Institute of Arts and Letters, under the sponsorship of Agnes Mongan, who was curator of drawings at the Fogg Art Museum.

AGNES MONGAN—I retired from Harvard in 1972, so when Elizabeth came to Harvard, I was often away from Cambridge, but we did see each other occasionally for lunch or dinner. At that time, I was chairman of the House Committee of the American Academy of Arts and Sciences. I wanted very much to have Elizabeth elected as a member of the Academy. I began circulating at Academy meetings, mentioning her among the gentlemen members (at that point there were only a very few women members). I invited her to a meeting about poetry and introduced her to several gentlemen members interested in poetry. Because of my many travels, I did not get my proposal in on time. It was postponed to the next meeting of proposed members. She was then elected to membership. In a very short time, she was an accepted and valued member.

✦ ✦ ✦

In February a setting of some of Bishop's poems, *A Mirror on Which to Dwell*, by Elliot Carter, was performed for the first time at the Hunter College Playhouse in New York City. "Elizabeth liked Elliot Carter personally, and she liked him as a composer, but she didn't much like those settings. She said, 'I really don't think my poems go with songs. They're very different. They're so different.' She got very perplexed about it."[8] In April, Bishop traveled to Oklahoma for the presentation of the Books Abroad/Neustadt International Prize for Literature. Marie-Claire Blais and John Ashbery were on the selection committee.

MARIE-CLAIRE BLAIS— John Ashbery and I worked very hard to get Elizabeth the Neustadt. There were representatives from twelve countries on the committee. My first choice was Ann Hebert from Canada, but I saw I had no chance because she was a French Canadian and her major novels had not yet been translated, which made it difficult to present her. The second choice I had on my list was Elizabeth Bishop. Ashbery was for Robert Lowell first, and then he changed his mind. He was so wonderful because he added his words to mine. I love Robert Lowell, but I thought it was time to have a woman for that prize. It was a long, long fight—[the members of the committee had their own favorites]—and finally Elizabeth got it. We sent her a cable. She was tremendously happy. This was just before things became hard for her. She was sick after that.

JOHN ASHBERY— [In 1948] when I read Elizabeth's poem "Over 2,000 Illustrations and a Complete Concordance," [I wrote my only] fan letter, and I got a very nice postcard from Maine from her during the summer. I didn't meet her until 1950. Emma Swann, a poet whom I knew, asked me if I would like to meet Elizabeth Bishop and James Agee for drinks at the Hotel Earle on Washington Square. I was very excited but also intimidated by meeting these two great writers. I really didn't say much, nor can I remember much of the conversation, except that Elizabeth was very charming. I can only remember that Elizabeth said [something] about all the rooms at the Hotel Earle [opening on] the air shaft.

I wrote my first sestina, "The Painter," inspired by "A Miracle for Breakfast" in North & South. I was affected in other ways than just the form by her poem. [I was attracted by] her slightly surreal combination of urban landscape and seascape. I always admired a kind of patina that Elizabeth's poems seemed to have, a kind of fine powdery texture. And it seemed to me that Elizabeth's work always looked beautiful as an object on the page. I found the shape of the letters and the stanzas and the ways the lines fall exciting.

I only saw Elizabeth a few times [often at parties, after she moved to Boston]. She came to a reading that I gave at Wellesley in the spring of 1976. I was very surprised and a little nervous that Elizabeth had come to the reading. She said something that I always liked about my poetry, that it had a semiabstract quality. I like that because I think that everything is semiabstract, and I think that poetry ought to pay attention to that. Elizabeth called me one afternoon from Boston and seemed very upset about teaching. She wanted to know how I managed to do it. I think she had been drinking. She said, "I just can't do all this; I can't compare Walt Whitman and Emily Dickinson." And I said, "Well, who can? I understand, I'm in the same boat." I'm a poet who's not really a teacher, and I have to teach. I tried to reassure her.

I was asked to be a juror [for the Neustadt], and my first thought, I think, was Elizabeth Bishop. It turned out that Marie-Claire Blais, who was also on the jury, had also nominated Elizabeth, and it was the first time that two jurors had nominated the same person. At first it didn't really seem as though this [would] make any difference, because the other people from Europe, Africa, and South America, were very intent on their own candidates. There was a sort of pitched battle among them, and there were a number of ballotings, where each time there would be fewer people, like musical chairs. Marie-Claire Blais seemed rather timid and nervous, and she came to me, and asked what we should do. I said we should just hang in and see what happens. Finally it almost happened by default, everybody else being canceled through the internecine struggles that were going on. I think I stood up and made the point that this was after all 1976, the American bicentennial, no American had won the award before, and also that Elizabeth Bishop was a woman and no woman had ever won it.

Three months later I had to [return to Oklahoma] and give a talk presenting Elizabeth Bishop, and that bothered me because I don't give lectures. I wrote it out on the plane going out there. I remember that my speech was not of the desired length, only I didn't realize this until just before the ceremony was about to take place. I think I only lasted for about ten minutes.

Elizabeth and I were put up in a hotel on the campus, and Elizabeth invited me over to show me her suite. She said, "Isn't this extraordinary?" There were two bedrooms and two bathrooms, this bar with several stools, a living room, and lamps hanging from chain swags. Elizabeth was looking somewhat bewilderedly around at the garish furnishings of the room, especially at this red shag carpet that covered all the floor and went up the sides of the bar. And she contemplated it and said, "It looks like chopped red cabbage," which seemed so much like the precise descriptions you get in her poetry. Someone had sent her there an invitation to contribute to a magazine for writing by older writers, sixty-five and older, and she said, "My goodness, I was only sixty-five the other day. They're in a big hurry to induct me into this senior citizen group."

◆   ◆   ◆

Frederick Morgan and Paula Deitz visited Bishop at Lewis Wharf shortly after she had received the Neustadt. Bishop had a letter from Lowell conspicuously displayed on her table and brought out the certificate and the silver feather that the committee had awarded her. "Elizabeth was droll about the award. She was very pleased, but also amused as any of us would be by flying out to Oklahoma and the fanciness of the whole thing."[9]

In December the Carter settings were again performed at a special session of the Modern Language Association Convention held on Bishop's work. Bishop read her poems, then escaped with friends to a local delicatessen while papers on her work were being delivered. That same month *Geography III* was published. It had been eleven years since Bishop's last book of poems, *Questions of Travel*, had been published, and *Geography III* contained fewer poems than any other book of hers. Bishop felt guilty about publishing a book of only nine poems, but her publisher and editor, Robert Giroux, was perfectly happy with it. He understood that Bishop was not prolific. Bishop spoke with Frank Bidart about feeling guilty because of her modest output.

FRANK BIDART— Elizabeth wished she had written more. Before publication she worried that *Geography III* was too short. As I said earlier, she once said to me she felt that if she had been a man she would have written much more. Of course I was dismayed: one of the great things about her work is that she *didn't* write too much, that there is such concentration, perfection, about so much of it. But in certain moods—particularly when she was drinking—she could be savage about her work, and no assertion that she was a great writer (and she is, without question, a great writer: and she had many friends who knew that) seemed to reconcile her to what she had done.

Elizabeth wanted to write and talked a lot about having begun a long elegy for Lota. She was very worried about the way it would or wouldn't be candid. In the background of all this, I suppose, was a certain inevitable competitiveness with Lowell, the fact that he was so prolific. She felt very ambivalent about the fact he wrote so much; but she also envied it. The elegy for Lota (so far as I know, never written), mired in so many contradictory aesthetic and personal emotions for Elizabeth, brought these issues to a head.

In the years I knew her—the last nine years of her life—she didn't (so far as I know) write every day, or in any kind of regular pattern. When she went to North Haven she took manuscripts with her and might come back at the end of the summer without much being written, if anything. When an idea for a poem possessed her, she carried it as far as she could, and then might let the fragments lie waiting to be finished for immense lengths of time. She was, at the same time, an infinitely careful craftsman (I don't think she'd object to the traditional word), and believed in at least the possibility of something like inspiration. Once, when I told her how great the end of "At the Fishhouses" is, she said that when she was writing it she hardly knew what she was writing, knew the words were right, and (at this she raised her arms as high straight above her head as she could) felt ten feet tall.

In January 1977 Bishop received the National Book Critics Circle Award for *Geography III*.[10] In spite of this and other recent successes, this new year was overshadowed by disappointments for her—worsening physical health and mandatory retirement from Harvard. In the spring of 1977 Bishop suddenly started feeling physically weak. She traveled to New York to see a specialist recommended by Anny Baumann.[11] In June a doctor finally discovered that she was severely anemic. Bishop was missing 60 percent of her red corpuscles, more than two quarts of blood. She told one friend that she had a "hiatus hernia. She had gone into severe anemia and they had discovered some source of internal bleeding. That was very scary because she had gotten so extremely weak and they hadn't been able to find out what it was. Then she was on a special diet of bland food. She had to eat lots of small meals and chew very well for the hernia. She couldn't take very much on her stomach at once."[12]

Bishop also retired from Harvard that spring. As Joseph Summers remembers, "Elizabeth was furious at Harvard about the retirement business." Although retirement at Harvard was required at sixty-six, it was possible to extend one's contract for up to two years at the recommendation of the department and the dean. As much as Bishop disliked teaching, she wanted the income for the extra two years. Bishop made an appointment with the chairman of the English Department to request the extension, and the department recommended Bishop's request to the dean. It was denied. "Elizabeth was very angry at Harvard when she requested to stay on. I think she felt that the rules could have been bent, or that they had been bent for others. She was very much hurt. Elizabeth knew her own quality and couldn't quite conceive being shown the door. It's hard to take in that somebody else would be hired in preference to you for the following year, if you were herself. She had a powerful sense of her own quality."[13] Unfortunately for Bishop, in this case her illnesses and unpredictability provided the compelling counterargument.

Robert Lowell died from a heart attack on 12 September 1977. His sudden death was a shock to all. As Ilse Barker remembers, "Elizabeth rang me the morning after Lowell died, four o'clock her time, just to talk. I was just a friend. Cal Lowell didn't mean anything to me. It wasn't for my sake. I should imagine she spent the night up emotionally disturbed, calling people." Lowell's death left unresolved certain issues in his relationship with Bishop.

LLOYD SCHWARTZ— Elizabeth was terribly upset when Lowell died, partly because they really hadn't resolved the increasing tension in their friendship. Elizabeth didn't care for his last poems all that much. In Houghton Library, I read her letter to him about *The Dolphin*, which was careful but essentially praising. That was not her attitude in private about the book. She didn't like any kind of privacy being exposed, and of course, Lowell knew she didn't. She had been quite nervous about her response to *Imitations*, the only one of his books he dedicated to her, and probably one of the last books in the world she'd have wished to be dedicated to her. Elizabeth's attitude about translations was quite rigid, and she considered *Imitations* a series of almost willful mistranslations. Not her idea of translating at all—though in practice she was more flexible than you'd think.

On Lowell's birthday Frank Bidart invited some people over for a small party. Elizabeth and Lowell engaged in a hilarious conversation that dominated the whole evening—about who had the worst dental experience. It was one-upsmanship at its most exuberant and teasing. They were sitting next to each other on Frank's couch saying, "Well, if you think that's bad . . ." Everyone was in stitches. They were ironic, slightly cynical, willing—even eager—to be self-deprecating, if that made the joke better. They obviously had a tremendous sense of rapport, because even at a time when their relationship was strained, they could still finish each other's punch lines. It was like Mike Nichols and Elaine May at a party where they obviously knew they were the center of attention and had just taken over the stage. I'm sure part of what attracted Lowell so much to Elizabeth was her dry sense of humor and ironic wit.

♦   ♦   ♦

Bishop felt that she had lived much of her life in Lowell's shadow. This attitude surfaced in a meeting Bishop had with Jonathan Galassi in the spring of 1978. At this time Galassi was working as an editor at Houghton Mifflin and was poetry editor for the *Paris Review*.

JONATHAN GALASSI— In 1978 I took Elizabeth Bishop out to lunch in Boston one day. We spent several hours, and at one point she started talking about her feelings about Robert Lowell. She said that you couldn't talk to him in the last years, that he became a monologue. She felt that Lowell had cut himself off. What also gradually emerged was a sense, hidden under all her modesty, that she had not been appreciated to the extent that she deserved in comparison with her male peers. I think there's truth in that. I remember I wanted to do a *Paris Review* interview with her, and she said, "Well, they should have interviewed me at the same time they interviewed everybody else." There was a clear implication that she had been neglected. Eventually I got her to agree that Helen Vendler could conduct the interview, but Elizabeth unfortunately died before it could be done. Subsequently we did run an interview based on a conversation with Elizabeth Spires that had originally been published in the *Vassar Quarterly*.

♦   ♦   ♦

Bishop's own illnesses weighed heavily on her during 1978, increasing her sense of weakness and vulnerability, as a number of friends who saw her that summer recollect.

HELEN MUCHNIC— Only once did Elizabeth talk about herself with me. This occurred in the evening of her visit to us in Cummington in 1978, the visit that, sadly, was to be her last. She and I were alone in the kitchen. The others had gone to bed. I was doing the dishes. Elizabeth sat nearby sipping whiskey and water. It was probably the drink that induced her to speak as she did that night, accusing herself of selfishness, of demanding too much of others, accusations that contradicted everything that I had seen of her. But she was profoundly unhappy, and nothing I said could console her, diminish her sense of unworthiness and guilt. She started to cry, and then said bravely, "I'm not usually like this. I don't really feel sorry for myself." Finally, I helped her upstairs to bed, hoping that her gloomy mood was indeed an aberration and that her brave remark was not just stoicism.

CELIA BERTIN— The last time I was at North Haven, in 1978, I was very, very concerned because Elizabeth wasn't able to walk anymore. She was walking around the house and porch, but she never went down to the beach as she used to. My favorite memories of being with Elizabeth at North Haven are walking on the beach together. Elizabeth wasn't even able to cross the meadow. I was very surprised because I looked on her like a little bear, she was so strong.

ILSE BARKER— North Haven was the most beautiful and peaceful place. Elizabeth and Alice stayed in an old clapboard house with a very nice, big living room full of old-fashioned things, among them a picture painted by Mrs. Petit's grandfather. There was a dark, big dining room in which Elizabeth worked. The meadow in front of the house sloped to the road; beyond the road were raspberry bushes and a path down to the beach where we— Alice, Thomas, and I—swam. Elizabeth and Kit sat on the sand. She obviously loved the place and enjoyed showing it off. We picked blueberries and raspberries, and Elizabeth made puddings and pies. She loved cooking and domestic tasks, and enjoyed living in a house instead of an apartment as she had been doing. She and Alice grew small beds of flowers by the back door.

Elizabeth had everything planned for our five days. One day we went to the little town of North Haven to collect lobsters she had ordered from a fisherman. Another day we went to a special beach where we dug clams, then went home and all worked away at cleaning them. Another day we crossed the island. In its very center we came to a farm where you could buy fresh vegetables. Elizabeth knew the farm people. Later, Kit painted this farm in the middle of that flat, sea-enclosed land. We walked through lovely woodland to the other side, where we looked across to Vinalhaven and the schooners sailing between the islands. There we helped Alice to pick up sea glass and sand dollars. Kit made drawings and watercolors of the sand dollars we brought home and sent one to Alice. On the last day Elizabeth took us for a lovely boat trip to Vinalhaven and between the islands and fishing grounds.

I remember the dining table strewn with papers where Elizabeth was working on a poem. We went to the library, where she wanted to look up a reference, a verse or something biblical. While we were with her, she managed to finish "North Haven," the poem for Lowell. She read it to us and walked about with it in her hand. I found it very moving that she felt she could hardly bear to put it down, that it was part of her. She put it beside her plate at dinner. In fact it made me write a poem later about her walking about with the poem in her hand, as if she couldn't part with it. You had that feeling it really was part of her and she liked to have it around with her for a while. This made me remember the time she finished "The Prodigal" when we were at Yaddo in 1950–51. But she was also working on other, unfinished poems.

Elizabeth didn't seem well. She had no trouble with asthma (Kit was having rather a bad time), but there were all sorts of things that weren't right. She'd been in hospital in Boston just before coming to Maine. There was something wrong with her blood; she had anemia. Elizabeth and Alice had arguments about what she should or shouldn't drink because of this blood problem. Alice said, "Elizabeth, you've had enough. Remember what the doctor said."

✦   ✦   ✦

Bishop accepted the Berg Professorship at New York University (NYU) from September 1977 to January 1978. She traveled to New York, frequently driven by Methfessel, for two days each week to teach two courses, one on modern British and American poetry and a second on poetry writing. NYU provided a comfortable apartment, and there were a number of people in New York with whom she could socialize and associate, yet Bishop disliked these months. She found her students very weak and the commute exhausted her. Celia Bertin stayed with Bishop during this period at NYU.

CELIA BERTIN— In September, before classes began, I went to visit Elizabeth and Alice [at New York University]. I was working on research, interviewing people in New York, for my book about Marie Bonaparte. I had learned long before I was thinking of writing this book that Elizabeth didn't believe in psychoanalysis. She hated, for instance, Helen Deutsch.

I stayed with Elizabeth for a few days. That's when Elizabeth had an accident during the night. There was crying. Elizabeth had fallen in the bathroom. Alice and I took her to the hospital, St. Vincent's, where Lota had died. That's when I heard about Lota's death.

✦   ✦   ✦

Bishop did not have to teach during the 1978–79 academic year. She intended to accept a position at Brandeis University, but she was awarded a Guggenheim Fellowship, to write a book of poems. During this academic year she served on the National Book Award Committee, awarding the prize for poetry to James Merrill for Mirabelle: Book of Numbers. Bishop was also busy with a number of other college and university engagements, including a reading at the University of Rochester in October 1978.[1] In April 1979 she visited Bryn Mawr College, to advise the college library on its Marianne Moore Poetry Collection.[2] In May 1979 Bishop traveled to Dalhousie University in Halifax, Nova Scotia, to accept an honorary degree. She visited with her friend Zilpha Linkletter and her cousin Phyllis Sutherland.

ZILPHA LINKLETTER— [When] Elizabeth was here for her honorary degree from Dalhousie, we had dinner at quite a nice restaurant overlooking the harbor. She was troubled by her asthma. She didn't talk about it ordinarily. I asked Elizabeth if her living in Boston on the waterfront was the best place for her with her asthma. Her comment was that her doctor thought she ought to go to Arizona, but she said, "Who wants to live in Arizona?"

I enjoyed Elizabeth. I found her quiet humor very compatible. We could relate to one another even though she was a literary, artistic type, and I'm not particularly artistic. I was in economics and public administration. Notwithstanding the considerable reputation she had at that time, she was so down-to-earth. You had no sense all the time that you were talking to somebody that [renowned]. I really didn't appreciate what an outstanding person Elizabeth was. She didn't act as if she were.

PHYLLIS BOWERS SUTHERLAND— The last time we saw Elizabeth was in May [1979], and she had been up the fall before. I was disappointed with the presentation of the honorary degree at Dalhousie. They didn't tell anything about her. She was just presented with her scroll, and there was a reception afterward. A professor who was supposed to be her right-hand man didn't introduce her around. When we left, we went down for a drink, and Elizabeth said, "I must go because Zilpha is waiting for me and we are going someplace tonight. I'm going back tomorrow." When we got up to the bedroom, she laid the citation out on the bed and said, "Now, where am I going to put that? I could paper two rooms now." She told me to keep all the letters she had written to my mother and me, especially the ones she had signed personally. She said that someday they would be worth a lot of money.

Elizabeth used to come in the spring and fall. She loved the fall, the colors. I remember taking her to Scrabble Hill, and we drove the old roads where she used to go. She used to be here to visit Mom when she had become old, and she would say, "I hope that never happens to me. I never want to go through what Aunt Grace is going through." I just took it for granted that she was frightened after what her mother had gone through that it could happen to her. She said to me, "I'd come home often, but it's so hard for me. I can't see Aunt Grace that way." [Grace died in 1977.]

One day, after Mom took sick and when Elizabeth had started at Harvard, she visited. I said, "Let's go for a drive, Elizabeth. Where would you like to go?" "Oh, someplace way back where it is quiet." There's an old cemetery way back up in the woods, so I said, "Let's get a six-pack, Elizabeth, and I'll show you where to go." I took her back to this old, old cemetery. It's just a well-kept and beautiful spot. We sat there and talked all afternoon. She said, "It's so quiet here. All I can hear is the river and the cars in the distance. This is where I'd like to be buried."

✦   ✦   ✦

Throughout 1979 Bishop worried about her illnesses. She feared that she was becoming a burden to Methfessel. Anne Hussey saw a vigorous, if frail, Bishop that spring. Others who saw Bishop that summer, whether at North Haven or while she and Methfessel were traveling in Europe, sensed Bishop's decline. Some acquaintances of Bishop also noted her developing a new reflective nature.[3]

ANNE HUSSEY— When our house was being built in Connecticut, Elizabeth had to see it. She and Alice visited in May of 1979, which was actually the last time I saw her. The house was barely framed. The stairs were pieces of left-over, uneven lumber tacked together. There was no railing. The stairwell was open all the way down to the basement, which was pretty far because the house is built on the side of a hill. We told Elizabeth not to go up it. It was too dangerous.

Before we knew it, she was halfway up, and you couldn't drag her back down. Elizabeth was rather frail, but determined. The problem was getting her back down, which we did by her sitting down step by step, with one of us in front and one behind her, step by step. This was accompanied by a certain amount of hilarity. She compared it to bobsledding. Elizabeth was driven by curiosity and determination. She didn't like people who complained about their health or complained about anything much. She didn't want to hear about illnesses; she wanted to overcome them.

ILSE BARKER— Elizabeth and Alice were in England in 1979 before and after a Swan Hellenic Tour. I felt that there was something wrong with Elizabeth's health, although it was Alice, of course, who had the attack of appendicitis while they were here in London. They were staying in a little pension, and Alice developed terrible pains. They got a local doctor who sent her to St. George's Hospital for observation, but they couldn't make up their minds what was the matter with her. Elizabeth spoke to me on the telephone for a long time, late that night, worried, upset, just talking. Then suddenly the pain went away, and they were told they could travel. They came to us as arranged for two days, and then I drove them to Gatwick to catch their plane to Venice.

At the end of their trip, I picked them up at Gatwick (at two in the morning). Alice seemed perfectly OK, but Elizabeth, I thought, was not well. She said she had enjoyed the trip very much, but she did complain about the heavy schedule and didn't go on all the excursions. She had trouble with her asthma when walking up steep hills and found herself sitting down halfway up a mountain.[4]

LLOYD SCHWARTZ— The last time Elizabeth went to Nova Scotia to see her Aunt Grace, she was very depressed because Grace didn't recognize her some of the time. Elizabeth was terrified of growing old, especially of losing her faculties and having to be put in a nursing home. I don't think she was a hypochondriac—she had good reason to worry, with so much evidence around her. Elizabeth was especially worried about her memory. She had lapses. When she had a few drinks, she would start to repeat things. That was the most noticeable symptom, the earliest symptom that she had been drinking. She would tell you exactly the same story she had told you ten minutes before. Elizabeth knew she had these lapses of memory and was scared.

I went to North Haven for a weekend in 1979, and Elizabeth was not in good spirits. Her back was bothering her. She had gotten a chill in her sacroiliac from picking lingonberries out on the front lawn. She was always doing that kind of domestic thing. She made wonderful marmalade and jam. Nettle baskets. Her back wasn't in great shape to begin with, and she probably shouldn't have been sitting out on the damp grass. Frank was there too. It had been much more festive a couple of years before.

PEGGY ELLSBERG— The last time I was in Elizabeth's apartment was in June 1979. She called me and asked if I could come over. I think I came that day. When I got there, she was somewhat agitated. She was reading *The City of God* by Saint Augustine, and she was near the end. She said, "I want to believe this. It's one of the most exciting things I've ever read. I called you because I know you are Catholic and I want to hear what you have to say." I can't remember what I said. I remember her taking one of my hands in both of her hands and saying, "If only I had a daughter, if only I'd had a child, I wouldn't feel so bad now." That was the last time I saw her. The subject that day was immortality and everlasting life and life after death. I remember saying to her, "I have no child, but I have no doubts about immortality." She said, "That's why I called you."[5]

JERRY REICH— When I was with Elizabeth in North Haven in 1979, we stumbled into talk of dying, and Elizabeth did say, "Well, when I go, I want to be cremated, and I want a big party." She wanted a big party, with all her friends, lots to drink, and balloons. She may have told this to Alice because this is what happened—except for the balloons.

I did have to go over to Elizabeth's one night in the last week or two. There was a late call, and she said, "I really want to see you." We had the most intense exchange that we'd ever had. That was the last time I saw her. She was not sober, lying in bed, talkative and upset. A lot was on her mind: her concern for Alice, her own inadequacy, how little she'd written, and back to Alice, and back to her meager work. The two themes of that night were how little she'd done compared with others and her worries for Alice.

✦　✦　✦

Bishop remained, throughout her life, an unbeliever, even an aggressive doubter, as Richard Wilbur remembers from one incident.

RICHARD WILBUR— The only time that I remember Elizabeth being undelectable, being cross with me, was on the day of a party at John Brinnin's house. When we had taken to the out-of-doors and were having drinks and would soon move on to croquet, Elizabeth took me up on it when I mentioned that we had just been to church. She said something like, "Oh, dear, you do go to church, don't you? Are you a Christian?" I said, "Well, yes, going to church, I am likely to be a Christian." Elizabeth said, "Do you believe all those things? You can't believe all those things." I said, "Like most people, I have my days of believing nothing, and I have my days of believing much of it, and some days I believe it all."

Then Elizabeth began mentioning points of Christian doctrine that she thought it intolerable to believe. She said, "No, no, no. You must be honest about this, Dick. You really don't believe all that stuff. You're just like me. Neither of us has any philosophy. It's all description, no philosophy." At that point Elizabeth shifted to talking about herself and lamenting the fact that she didn't have a philosophic adhesive to pull an individual poem and a group of poems together, but she was really quite aggressive at that point. It surprised me because of her bringing up, [from which she] had many Christian associations, cared about many Christian things, and had got [them] into her poems here and there. I think that's what she was left with, the questions, if not the answers, of a person with a religious temperament.

✦   ✦   ✦

On 6 October 1979, Bishop died in her apartment, from a cerebral aneurism, while she was dressing for dinner at Helen Vendler's. Methfessel found her on the floor in her bedroom when she came to Lewis Wharf to pick her up. Chester Page remembers a conversation he had with Bishop shortly before she died, and Helen Vendler recollects the night of her death.

CHESTER PAGE— The last time I called Elizabeth she said she was feeling depressed. Her speech was rather slurred, and she said she had not had a productive summer. I said, "So what? You have lots of time." Elizabeth said, "That's just it, I don't." I said, "Don't be silly." Elizabeth didn't say she was not feeling well. I thought, had she had a premonition or what? I know she called Margaret Miller the night before she died.

HELEN VENDLER— The night she died, Elizabeth was supposed to come to my house for dinner. Harry and Elena Levin, Frank Bidart, and some others had already arrived, and then the phone rang. It was Alice saying that she had gotten to Elizabeth's apartment to pick her up and that she had found her on the floor, half-dressed, dead. Frank said he would immediately join Alice there. We sat around eating dinner in a very uncomfortable way and then cut the evening short.

There were several phone calls in the course of the dinner. The police had come. There was something about their wanting to seal the apartment. The coroner had to certify an unattended death. Then Frank called to say that the police didn't want to let them stay. Alice and Frank had to say that they were her heir and literary executors. Frank called again, just after people had left, and said that he was bringing Alice to my house and they would have dinner. Elizabeth was supposed to give a reading the next day, and they started calling people to try to reschedule and rearrange that. They asked me if I would write the obituary and phone it in to the New York Times. The Times asked how they could know this wasn't a hoax. This struck me with such shock that I asked if they wanted to speak to either Alice or Frank. This reassured the obituary editor, and he said no. At about two in the morning Frank and Alice left. They were both so courageous about trying to get everything arranged and to do everything right.

✦　✦　✦

Bishop was to have read her poetry on 7 October at Harvard with Mary Lavin in a benefit for the Boston magazine *Ploughshares*. Lloyd Schwartz and Robert Pinsky were involved in rearranging this evening.

LLOYD SCHWARTZ— We decided on a reading of Elizabeth's poems rather than canceling the event, partly because Mary Lavin was also scheduled to read, and canceling wouldn't have been fair to her. Frank was too shaken to read. I was supposed to introduce Elizabeth, so I ended up being a kind of master of ceremonies for this part of the program. The readers were Robert Pinsky, Aileen Ward, Amram Schapiro, David Ferry, and myself. We each agreed to read two or three of our favorite poems. We met at Sanders Theatre just before to make sure we weren't going to overlap. No one had picked anyone else's poem! I think everyone read wonderfully—I remember it being a very positive experience. Cathartic. Many people didn't realize Elizabeth had died, so some sort of makeshift sign had been posted. When DeWitt Henry came out at the beginning of the reading and announced that Elizabeth had died the night before, there was an audible gasp of shock from a large part of the audience. I think a couple of people left. Introducing Mary Lavin, Rosellen Brown movingly addressed the issue of why the reading should proceed.

ROBERT PINSKY— There was a reading, a benefit for *Ploughshares*, that Elizabeth was supposed to give at Sanders Theatre the night after she had died. Somebody called me up and said they were thinking of doing a reading by Elizabeth's friends. My first response was we shouldn't do it. It seemed more appropriate to cancel and give people their money back. They decided to go ahead and have people read poems by Elizabeth. We each read a few poems, and I saw I had been wrong. The evening was quite moving because there was no memorial quality to it, no funerary atmosphere to the occasion. Nobody attempted a eulogy. People were quite minimal in alluding to what the occasion represented and just read these incredibly beautiful and amusing poems. People were quite upset still, but the event had no lugubrious quality. There was laughter. We were all moved by very wonderful poetry we heard from a variety of voices. I remember a quality of celebration.

You could almost date the phenomenon of Elizabeth's reputation surviving her death in a way that doesn't characterize most artists, from that occasion. Artists' reputations tend to dip or decline for a while after death. Bishop's has risen. One way I explain that to myself is that it wasn't buoyed up by personality. Elizabeth hadn't developed a kind of showmanship that American poets often are led to have. She didn't have a lot of pals all over. She seemed able to and eager to take in people of many kinds, rather than any clique or guild. She didn't live in the United States, and her reputation wasn't buoyed up by giving many poetry readings, by having any place where she taught, with a constituency of colleagues or students. Hers was a pure reputation based upon the quality of her work, and so when the personality is withdrawn, no artificial support is withdrawn.

✦   ✦   ✦

At her request, Bishop's body was cremated and the ashes were buried in Hope Cemetery in Worcester, with the remains of her mother and father. Methfessel inherited Bishop's estate and became the literary executor. Bidart was coexecutor, and he, Methfessel, and Anne Hussey met in Worcester one afternoon to inter the ashes. There was also a memorial reading in New York that fall, which David Kalstone remembers attending.

DAVID KALSTONE— The memorial reading at the YMHA was very interesting because there were perhaps eight poets, each of whom read two or three poems. Most of them read poems that one ordinarily hadn't heard Elizabeth read. One had that impression of wonderful ventriloquism, the qualities of her voice which each of them had managed to pick up not only in his reading of the poem but also in his [own] writing. I suppose the show was stolen by James Merrill, who got up and recited "The Shampoo" from memory. Mark Strand read "At the Fishhouses." Frank Bidart did "The Moose." One was aware suddenly of a range of voices that you weren't always aware of when you heard Elizabeth read her own poems. [This reading touched on] areas of her poetry either that she felt were too private to touch in public or that she just wasn't comfortable reading aloud.

On 21 October there was a service in memory of Elizabeth Bishop at Agassiz House in Cambridge. Methfessel spoke and Bidart read from Bishop's poems. The other participants ranged from friends she had made during her final years in Cambridge and Boston (including Anne Hussey, Helen Vendler, and Octavio Paz), to her close friend from Walnut Hill, Frani Blough Muser.

Louise Crane and Margaret Miller attended the service. All sang some of Bishop's favorite hymns—"We Gather Together," "Rock of Ages," "A Mighty Fortress is our God," and "Dear Lord and Father of Mankind." Lloyd Schwartz read the last poem Bishop had written, "Sonnet."[6] Elizabeth Bishop had become her poems.

Elizabeth Bishop's art, so modest in its surfaces, so magnetic in its depths, has compelled the attention of three generations of readers. Poems such as "At the Fishhouses" or "In the Waiting Room" now claim a place in the lyric tradition as certain as "Tintern Abbey" or "Ode on a Grecian Urn." Poets as diverse as John Ashbery and James Merrill, Mark Strand and Amy Clampitt, C. K. Williams and Jorie Graham name her as a major influence on their work, variously revering her perfection of tone, her social, moral, and psychological insight, her visual accuracy, her formal invention. What experiences inform this sensibility, so anguished, yet so resilient? We inquire of the life as of a source of light.

Yet Bishop was not self-revealing in an autobiographical sense. In her early poems she was almost impersonal, though, like the hidden but audible alligator in "Florida," she has many "distinct calls" that make the poems tremble with feeling. She shares the elusive intensity of the "man-moth":

> If you catch him,
> hold up a flashlight to his eye. It's all dark pupil,
> an entire night itself, whose haired horizon tightens
> as he stares back, and closes up the eye. Then from the lids
> one tear, his only possession, like the bee's sting, slips.

We know what it costs the bee to surrender his sting; the man-moth is a tortured figure in his Chaplinesque way. Yet, as his agonies are expressed, they have been distilled into a rejuvenating substance, "cool as from underground springs and pure enough to drink."

Geography III turned from what some saw as the evasions of abstraction and description to a poetry at once more intimate and more expansive, in which personal anxieties, sufferings, and joys are understood in their social and cultural setting. Bishop's private sense of homelessness spoke to a larger cultural displacement. It was this volume, with its unsentimental glimpse into the abyss of social definitions, the inadequate constructions of language and knowledge, the constricted transcendence of art, the incidental but profound solaces of nature, that hurled Bishop from poet's poet to voice-of-her-time. She seemed to have found a way out of both the straitjacket impersonality of modernism and the maniacal flailings of confessional poetry. In an era dominated by the etiolated "workshop poem," she gave vital direction.

But the genius that could imagine "In the Waiting Room" or "Crusoe in England" is already present, in a minor key, in such early poems as "The Weed" and "The Bight." Bishop's deep connection to the lyric tradition is part of what makes her modern revisions so compelling. How can we locate ourselves in a world bereft of its transcendental fictions? Here is a poet who has taken in Herbert, Hopkins, Wordsworth, Baudelaire like bread and wine, but who finds these nourishments are not enough to sustain a faith. She must, like her Crusoe, rely on what is "home-made."

No quality has drawn more praise for Bishop than her perfection of tone, for it is at once an aesthetic and a moral quality. Bishop had, through her experience, an imagination for disaster; she does not flinch from what troubles her sight, nor does she suppress apocalyptic feeling. Yet the sense of tragedy, her art suggests, is most felt where least dramatized. Tutored by Marianne Moore, she respects the virtue of restraint, but her own natural reticence has none of Moore's defensive armor. It involves, rather, a saving humility in the claims of the suffering self, a will to cast oneself into the larger pageantry of the mutable world and the surrealism of everyday life. Honest feeling is usually mixed; moments of sensuous delight offset a moral gloom; the weight of loss and change is counterbalanced in an occasional levity as life's iridescence flashes across a somber surface. "Awful but cheerful" is the delicate balance her poems often hold. Two powerful faculties maintain this balance against the dark vision at the core of Bishop's work: a sense of humor and a sense of beauty.

Bishop's social vision sometimes runs to black humor, as in the grotesque vision of "Pink Dog." Beneath the systematic gaiety and garish disguises of Carnival, the poem tells us, lies a naked world of human need that embarrasses society and provokes its violence. But more often Bishop's humor has a calming affect, checking apocalyptic feeling. As she peers into the "[c]old, dark, deep and absolutely clear" sea in "At the Fishhouses," her hypnosis is temporarily broken by a seal:

He stood up in the water and regarded me
steadily, moving his head a little.
Then he would disappear, then suddenly emerge
almost in the same spot, with a sort of shrug
as if it were against his better judgment.

In "Filling Station" the humor partakes of that affection we feel for the American primitive. This "oil-soaked, oil-permeated" and inflammatory life manages a "big dim doily / draping a taboret / (part of the set), beside / a big hirsute begonia." There is something pathetic, yet endearing and affirming, in our effort to establish beauty and order in the "over-all / black translucency" of our lives.

But Bishop's idea of beauty is not restricted to these grotesques. There is a more sublime beauty, not man-made but sometimes evoked in human orders, which rescues her from despair. Beauty in Bishop's world is not classical, not neat or symmetrical, and never predictable. It arises mysteriously, as the undecodable writing of fireflies at night, the dazzling dialectic of rivers, lost tributaries and distant smoke trails, birds disappearing into pinpoints of sky, whatever releases the eye into curve and variety. For all the psychological depth to Bishop's descriptions, one also feels that observation, like art, was a fundamental good in her experience, a triumph over personal suffering. Beauty in the outer world emerges as a sudden clarity out of mist, a shaft of sunshine breaking through clouds to illuminate stones on a beach. Bishop's idea of beauty (and her idea of danger) is associated with freedom, especially sudden release from a confining medium. Her own celebrated inventiveness with meter and stanza form partakes of this idea. No poem expresses this delight more compactly than "Sonnet" (Bishop's last poem to appear in The New Yorker), which seems, in its wavering dimeter and unruly rhymes, a pattern of her thought about life and art.

Caught—the bubble
in the spirit-level,
a creature divided;
and the compass needle
wobbling and wavering,
undecided.
Freed—the broken
thermometer's mercury
running away;
and the rainbow-bird

from the narrow bevel
of the empty mirror,
flying wherever
it feels like, gay!

All these ways of measuring suddenly yield to a measureless spirit, and the words themselves seem to spring free of the sonnet's hold. Yet the escape from measure has something eerie about it. The self released from its search for balance and direction finds indeterminate space, but loses all form. Encoded in this little poem are memories of many earlier poems (the divided heart in "The Weed"; the crazy-compass wanderings in Brazil and "Elsewhere" in Questions of Travel; the momentary loss of self-identity in "In the Waiting Room," among others). A life and life's work is summed up as the dialectic of captivity and freedom, of fixed form and poetic extravagance, of social norms and personal deviance. But the ultimate freedom, she knew, is beyond art and life. The mirror must be empty to release the rainbow-bird; the thermometer must be broken for the liquid to escape.

Bonnie Costello

1. CHILDHOOD, 1911–1927

1 John William Bishop was born in White Sands, Prince Edward Island. His father had been a ship's carpenter who emigrated from England in 1819 to work at the dockyards at St. John, New Brunswick, and to operate a small farm. When John William was eleven, his parents immigrated to Lonsdale, Rhode Island, where he took a job in a cotton mill. John W. Bishop himself had little formal schooling. Family legend has him running away from home at twelve with a box of carpentry tools. He learned the trade at the age of fourteen while working for a builder in Providence. From this point he was on the path to becoming a self-made man.

At twenty-one John W. Bishop traveled to Worcester, the second largest city in Massachusetts, where he went into business for himself in 1874. He built a large stable as his first contract. In 1880 he took George H. Cutting as a partner, and Cutting and Bishop became a leading construction firm in Massachusetts. This business was dissolved in 1895 when John W. Bishop formed the company bearing his own name, with capital of $200,000. He eventually established offices in Boston, New York, Providence, and New Bedford. Bishop was to oversee the construction of hundreds of buildings in the Northeast, among them office buildings in Boston and Montreal; academic buildings at Princeton, Harvard, Brown, and McGill; hospital buildings in Providence and Worcester; industrial buildings and mills in New York, Rhode Island, and Massachusetts; numerous public libraries and churches; and several palatial residences in Newport. He was known for his analytical powers of mind as well as his ceaseless energy. Men in the business world were impressed with his talent for organizing large projects into discrete departments and tasks, his industriousness, and his comprehensive understanding of the construction business. Bishop's grandfather was also respected as a fair, honest businessman.

In 1870 John W. Bishop married Sarah A. Foster from Holden, Massachusetts, even though their marriage initially had not been endorsed by her parents. The Fosters traced their lineage to the earliest settlers of New England, and Bishop the self-made immigrant was a less than socially suitable suitor. Elizabeth's Aunt Florence, an avid member of the DAR (Daughters of the American Revolution), kept alive the Foster's pride in their heritage, as well as their snobbishness.

2 William Bishop attended public schools and Classical High School in Worcester, leaving the latter to become a timekeeper in his father's business. He then became a brickmason, a journeyman, an estimator at the Providence office for several years, and finally a vice-president in the company and manager of the Worcester office.

3 Was Bright's disease used as a euphemism for liver problems stemming from drink? Elizabeth claimed later in her life that her own difficulties with alcohol came from the fact that a grandfather, her father, and three uncles were drinkers, although there is no information to bear out this statement. (See Elizabeth Bishop to Anny Baumann, 17 January 1951, Special Collections, Vassar College Libraries.) None of the Bishop relatives remember anything about alcoholism regarding Bishop's father or grandfather.

4 Layton interview.

5 Layton interview.

6 Chisholm interview.

7 Patriquin interview.

8 Nelson interview.

9 Bowers interview.

10 Chisholm interview.

11 Patriquin interview.

12 Bowers interview.

13 Bowers interview.

14 Bowers interview.

15 Bowers interview.

16 People in Great Village recollect Arthur.

DONALDA MACLACHLAN NELSON—Art would come to the store wanting to buy lemon essence, which had a bit of alcohol in it. My parents caught on after a while that he was drinking too much of it. One day my father had taken it off the shelves [and placed it] underneath someplace. Art asked Dad for some. Dad said he didn't have any. Art was about to leave, and he turned around, looked at Dad and said, "You say you have no lemon essence?" in a tone of voice [that implied Dad was] lying. My father was so amused that "you say you have no lemon essence?" came to be a term we used in the family if we didn't quite believe what you were saying.

17 Forbes interview.

18 NANCY ORR MORRILL—Grandpa was good to his entire family, but he was very domineering. We couldn't say much because he gave us things we wouldn't have had. He ran the house; it was his home. When I was in bed almost a year with rheumatic fever, there wasn't a week that Grandpa didn't drive [to Providence] to see me or send his chauffeur with a bag of gifts. He rented two houses for my family in South Chatham [Massachusetts], a house for my mother and myself, and one for my brother and sister and the maids, whom he also hired. He would drive from Worcester once a week.

Grandpa had worked in the mills in Whitinsville [Massachusetts]. When you went to Providence in those days [from Worcester], you had to go through Uxbridge and Whitinsville, and I can remember him pointing out to me and my brother a little old house where he had lived. When he got wealthy, he put bathrooms in every one of those houses. He never forgot that he had no education. That's why every one of his grandchildren was educated, [although] his own children weren't. I used to say that he liked his grandchildren better than his own children.

19 KAY ORR SARGENT—[Family was] a very [important part of my grandparents' life]. There was a big fuss one Christmas when my family couldn't go [to Worcester] because I had

come down with the mumps. I remember Mother calling Worcester and the twins on the top step howling that Santa wouldn't come because we couldn't go to Grandpa's. Santa came by limousine. Ronald [the chauffeur] drove to Providence with all the Christmas presents.

At the time of Uncle Jack and Aunt Ruby's wedding, [Grandpa had] a big picture of the whole family [taken]. Uncle John Coe was too far away to get there. Grandpa was so disappointed that Uncle John wasn't there that he had the photographer stick a head of John in the picture, which wrecked the photography.

20   Sargent interview.

21   Sutherland interview.

22   Sargent interview.

23   Ms., Special Collections, Vassar College Libraries.

24   Sutherland interview.

25   Elizabeth Bishop, "An Interview with Elizabeth Bishop," by Ashley Brown, *Elizabeth Bishop and Her Art*, Ed. Lloyd Schwartz and Sybil P. Estess (Ann Arbor: University of Michigan Press, 1983), 292.

26   PHYLLIS SUTHERLAND—Mom had a great sense of humor. Nothing escaped her. She was always writing little things to Elizabeth. [There was] one [poem] about a cow going through somebody's hedge and [someone] coming out after it:

> There was a cow in our town,
> And she was wondrous wise.
> She ran through Cassie's lilac bush
> And brushed off all the flies,
> And when she found all the flies were off
> With her mighty mane
> She legged it through the churchyard gate,
> And got them on again,
> And as she stopped and stuffed and stuffed, and fatter got,
> We licked our chops and said,
> "My, wait till she strikes the pot."
> At last the dreadful day arrived,
> The terrible deed was o'er,
> And Nellie, once our joy and pride,
> Lay on the old barn floor.
> "The angel's called our darling Nell,"
> Said Pa to Mr. Root.
> "I'm glad she died," said R. S. Root.
> "She's only good for soup."

I remember Mom telling about Elizabeth doing cartwheels out on the veranda [at the farm]. She was quick on her feet and seemed to enjoy the farm so much.

27   Sargent interview.

28   Sargent interview.

29   Sargent interview.

30   Muser interview.

31   Elizabeth Bishop, "An Interview with Elizabeth Bishop," by Ashley Brown, *Elizabeth Bishop and Her Art*, Ed. Lloyd Schwartz and Sybil P. Estess (Ann Arbor: University of Michigan Press, 1983), 292.

32   Muser interview.

2. WALNUT HILL, 1927–1930

1   Ruby Willis, Confidential information given by Elizabeth's guardian, John W. Bishop, 27 July 1926, Walnut Hill School.

2   Florence Bigelow to Mrs. John W. Bishop, 12 December 1927, Walnut Hill School.

3   Ruby D. Bishop to Miss Bigelow, 17 December 1927, Walnut Hill School.

4   Ruby D. Bishop to Miss Bigelow, 20 February 1928, Walnut Hill School.

5   John W. Bishop to Miss Helen Farwell, 2 April 1928, Walnut Hill School.

6   Disney interview.

7   Elizabeth Bishop, "An Interview with Elizabeth Bishop," by Ashley Brown, Elizabeth Bishop and Her Art, Ed. Lloyd Schwartz and Sybil P. Estess (Ann Arbor: University of Michigan Press, 1983), 292.

8   During her junior-year Christmas in Nova Scotia, Bishop received one of Miss Prentiss's sentimental notes: "Come up the path through the fir trees and white birches to my little cottage by the sea and by the fireside where nothing is 'developed' save friendliness and contentment. . . . Meanwhile Christmas Joys and the star-shine of a poem, and my love." Bishop passed this letter to Frani Blough, along with her Aunt Grace's observation penciled at the top that there was an "aching void" at the center of this woman's life (Eleanor Prentiss to Elizabeth Bishop, 31 December 1928, Special Collections, Vassar College Libraries).

9   Ruby D. Bishop to Miss Bigelow, 2 November 1927, Walnut Hill School.

10 Sheehan interview.

11 Helen M. Farwell to John W. Bishop, 27 May 1929, Walnut Hill School.

12 Ruby Willis, Confidential information given by Elizabeth's guardian, John W. Bishop, 27 July 1926, Walnut Hill School.

13 Elizabeth Bishop to Frani Muser, 5 September 1929, Special Collections, Vassar College Libraries.

14 Ruth Mulligan, copy of a letter to Miss Florence Bishop, 13 September 1929, Walnut Hill School.

15 Elizabeth Bishop to Frani Muser, January 1930, Special Collections, Vassar College Libraries.

16 Eleanor Prentiss to Frani Muser, 9 March 1930, Special Collections, Vassar College Libraries.

17 Later in her life, Bishop told the odd story that she had applied to Vassar a year earlier, but that her application had been rejected because of her poor grades on the entrance exam in mathematics. No evidence supports this recollection. See Elizabeth Bishop, "An Afternoon with Elizabeth Bishop," by Elizabeth Spires, Vassar Quarterly (Winter 1979): 8.

18 [College recommendation for Elizabeth Bishop sent to Wellesley and Vassar] Walnut Hill School.

19 The Lantern, 1930. Walnut Hill School, 18.

20 The Lantern, 1930. Walnut Hill School, 32.

3. VASSAR, 1930–1934

1   Elizabeth Bishop, "An Afternoon with Elizabeth Bishop," by Elizabeth Spires, Vassar Quarterly (Winter 1979): 8.

2   Muser interview.

3 Frani Blough Muser heard Bishop express some reservations about this escapade: "Elizabeth was dissatisfied with Eleanor for getting her into this mess. As far as Elizabeth thought of it, they took off rather in the spirit that we used to go up and look at the sunrise [at Walnut Hill]. Eleanor had other ideas, I guess, and got them in trouble with the police. So Elizabeth hated that whole thing."

4 Miriam Steeves to Miss Girard, 9 March 1932, Walnut Hill School.

5 As a result of curriculum reform in 1927, students at Vassar in the 1930s had much more freedom to arrange their own curricula than had students in the past. This change in curriculum was similar to, if less ambitious than, that taking place in other women's colleges such as Bennington and Sarah Lawrence. The new curriculum, which required a broad and general distribution of courses for freshmen, placed the onus upon students in their sophomore year to create their own program of concentration in a single discipline with complementary courses in related disciplines. There was also a curriculum review in the fall of 1933, with additional changes occurring in the spring of 1934.

Freshman were required to select four courses of three hours each, one from each of four groups: arts (including English), foreign languages and literatures, natural sciences (including mathematics), and social sciences. A freshman who wished to establish a special foundation in one area could petition to have one of these required courses postponed to her sophomore year. Bishop did so. She deferred her science course (zoology) to her sophomore year and elected arts courses—English 165 (Shakespeare), Music 230a (Analysis of Design), and a one-credit pianoforte lesson. The English course was in the standard freshman curriculum, but the music course demanded prerequisites that Bishop was allowed to bypass. During the second semester of her freshman year, she took Music 105, Introduction to Theoretical Music. This course was the prerequisite for Music 230a, which had given her trouble the previous semester. Sophomore year she took Music 210, Harmonic Writing. Junior year she took Music 140, Music as Literature, her final music course at Vassar.

Bishop's sophomore year curriculum in English consisted of English 120 (Old English, Beowulf), English 240 (English Literature in the Seventeenth and Eighteenth Centuries, open to sophomores by permission), and English 255 (English Drama, open to sophomores by permission); in junior year, English 243 (English Prose from 1800 to the Present Time), and English 350 (Contemporary Prose Fiction, with an added two hours for extra credit); and in senior year, English 480 (Studies in Critical Theory), English 500 (Independent Study), English 312 (The Contemporary Press), and English 335 (American Literature).

6 Barbara Swain to Anne Stevenson, 22 March 1964, Elizabeth Bishop Papers, Washington University Libraries.

7 Warren interview.

8 Warren interview.

9 Muser interview.

10 Muser interview.

11 Sheehan interview.

12 Smith interview.

13 Elizabeth Bishop to Frani Muser, 17 July 1933, Special Collections, Vassar College Libraries.

14 Gaines interview.

15 Gaines interview.

16 Gaines interview.

17 Smith interview.

18 In addition to writing for the *Vassar Miscellany News*, Bishop had roles in two plays on campus during her sophomore year. One was a small part in the spring production of *The Canterbury Tales*. Mary McCarthy played Arcite in "The Knight's Tale." Bishop received a good review in the *Vassar Miscellany News*, 16 November 1932, as a humorous henpecked husband in Karl Vollmoeller's expressionistic play *Uncle's Been Dreaming*: "Elizabeth Bishop gave [an] excellent comedy characterization. Using a soft, gentle voice, and unfinished gestures, Miss Bishop was splendid as the poor little man who was told to do nothing but smile and say 'Hm,' and at the wrong moment."

Bishop seems not to have been interested in the celebrated Vassar Experimental Theatre, under the direction of Hallie Flanagan. In part, their productions were too propagandistic for her. During her freshman year, Bishop must have attended a performance of the Experimental Theatre's *Can You Hear Their Voices?* written by Flanagan and a student. It was wildly successful. The play dramatized the effects of a recent Arkansas drought on the farmers and was based on a series of newspaper articles by Whitaker Chambers. The set was a number of screens covered with newspaper and magazine pages. As the *Vassar Miscellany News* reported on 6 May 1931, the audience was so moved by the human misery they saw on the stage, including a mother's strangling of her own baby to save it from the pain of starvation, that they paused after the performance to let their emotions settle before applauding.

19 The *Vassar Miscellany News*, 25 November 1933, Vassar College Libraries.

20 Elizabeth Bishop, "An Interview with Elizabeth Bishop," by Ashley Brown, *Elizabeth Bishop and Her Art*, Ed. Lloyd Schwartz and Sybil P. Estess (Ann Arbor: University of Michigan Press, 1983), 294.

21 Smith interview.

22 Elizabeth Bishop, "An Interview with Elizabeth Bishop," by Ashley Brown, *Elizabeth Bishop and Her Art*, Ed. Lloyd Schwartz and Sybil P. Estess (Ann Arbor: University of Michigan Press, 1983), 293-94.

23 Warren interview.

24 Eunice Clark, her sister Eleanor, and Muriel Rukeyser founded their own literary magazine, *The Housatonic*, the previous summer. On 25 May 1932, the *Vassar Miscellany News* announced that *The Housatonic* would "deal with the culture and traditions of New England in their changing social and economic backgrounds. . . . In general the editorial plan is to work, through a critical survey of New England economics, politics, social conditions and culture, past and present, to a positive view for the future." The magazine received notice in the *New York Herald Tribune*. See also Eunice Clark Jessup, "Memoirs of Literatae and Socialists 1929-33," *Vassar Quarterly* (Winter 1979): 17.

EUNICE CLARK JESSUP—Muriel came to live with us that summer when Eleanor and I got out a magazine, *The Housatonic*. We had a wonderful time. Denise Dryden, the business manager of the *Miscellany News*, came along to handle the business end of it. We only did it for a summer vacation. We never planned more than four issues. Eleanor and I both got jobs without any trouble on the basis of that. I immediately started writing for *Common Sense*.

25 *Vassar Miscellany News*, 11 March 1932.

26 *Vassar Miscellany News*, 13 December 1933.

27 *Vassar Miscellany News*, 10 January 1934.

28 Arthur Mizener to Elizabeth Bishop, 1946, Special Collections, Vassar College Libraries.

29 *Vassar Miscellany News*, 11 November 1933.

30 The issue of what is or is not propaganda was a hotly contested one at Vassar in the
    1930s. In May of Bishop's senior year, A. E. Austin, Director of the Hartford Atheneum,
    and two artists, the painter M. Jean Lurcat and the Swiss architect M. William Lescaze,
    were on campus discussing the relationship between art and propaganda. The *Vassar
    Miscellany News* of 12 May quotes Austin as saying, " 'When form is outdone by propa-
    ganda the result is poor art. . . . Rivera, for instance, does not produce great art since he
    over-emphasizes subject matter to the detriment of form.' " However, Lurcat felt that
    " 'what we call propaganda, in a derogatory sense, is the expression of ideas with which
    we disagree. Art is termed propaganda, in the derogatory sense, only when the art is
    poor, in which case the propaganda element is disagreeably obvious.' " Lescaze felt that
    " 'all art is propaganda. Whatever the artist creates must express his individual point of
    view.' "
31 Smith interview.
32 Elizabeth Bishop to Frani Muser, 22 October 1933, Special Collections, Vassar College
    Libraries.
33 Bishop's article on Hopkins's metrics ("Gerard Manley Hopkins: Notes on Timing in His
    Poetry," *Vassar Review*, February 1934) received the highest praise of any in the magazine
    from the *Vassar Miscellany News*, as did "The Last Animal" (*Vassar Review*, April 1934), a
    pathetically comic story of a zoology professor, his son, and the last animal on the earth.
        Elizabeth Bishop's notes on the timing in Gerard Manley Hopkins' poetry are the
    masterpiece of the issue. They are penetrating criticism of real originality and are
    brilliantly successful in defining some of the almost intangible qualities in Father
    Hopkins' poetry. Although dealing with a subject of much subtlety and complexity,
    Elizabeth Bishop through her vigorous and varied metaphor has succeeded in
    making her position perfectly realizable, and what is more, thoroughly alive. This
    essay contains the best sort of criticism, penetrating without dissecting, soundly
    based, without being pedantic. (*Vassar Miscellany News*, 17 February 1934)
        Without doubt, Elizabeth Bishop's "The Last Animal" is the most finished and
    most interesting piece of work, well placed in a position of prominence. It has been
    a long time since Vassar has had anything approximating a humorous story, and this
    one by the techniques of understatement and a kind of dry common sense succeeds
    in combining comedy and pathos to a degree worthy of *The New Yorker*. (*Vassar
    Miscellany News*, 2 May 1934)
34 Julia G. Bacon to Mrs. Anne Elvin, 21 January 1963, University of Washington Library.
35 In December 1933 Bishop hoped this translation would be produced as the final Hall
    Play of her senior year, although this production did not materialize. In the spring of her
    senior year, Bishop wanted to find a composer to write music to complement her
    translation. As late as 1950 Margaret Miller encouraged her to complete the translation.
        Bishop was also interested in writing plays or small operas of her own. She traveled to
    Hartford in March 1934 for the premiere of Gertrude Stein and Virgil Thomson's *Four
    Saints in Three Acts*; she was anxious to hear Virgil Thomson's music and had not heard
    anything by him before. Stein's work, and Bishop's interest in Eliot's *The Rock*, at least
    temporarily roused Bishop to write her own drama or masque that spring. Bishop had
    written about Stein in "Times' Andromedas" (*Vassar Journal of Undergraduate Studies*, 1933).
    Bishop must also have viewed the first major exhibition of Picasso's work in the United
    States on display at the Hartford Atheneum at that time.
        A. E. Austin, director of the Atheneum in Hartford, visited Vassar in May 1934 and
    spoke of the importance of the innovation of Gertrude Stein. According to the *Vassar*

Miscellany News of 12 May 1934, Austin believed that " 'Gertrude Stein represents the only possibility of opera in English which avoids the pitfall of the ridiculous. The opera, while amusing, witty and slight is yet more honest than the grand-opera 'shell of pomposity'.' "

One student recollects the general tone of creativity at Vassar during this period.

HARRIET TOMPKINS THOMAS—It seemed we were constantly discovering the work of new and very good writers during our years at Vassar. A professor named Alan Porter was a great favorite of mine. He'd already published several books of poetry, and he seemed to be connected with a New York group of literati. We all felt that that was very glamorous. Gertrude Stein came to Vassar, and Archibald MacLeish. I attended the premiere of *Four Saints in Three Acts* in New York. Agnes Rindge, an art instructor, also had connections with this avant-garde group of literary, musical, and artistic people in New York. This heady feeling of creative excitement penetrated down to us at Vassar. After all, we had only just become conversant with the work of the great innovators of the twenties and before—Gertrude Stein, Joyce, Picasso, Hemingway, Schoenberg, and so on. It was a stimulating time; one, almost, of cultural shock.

36 McCarthy interview.

37 Bishop wrote to Donald Stanford about allowing the meter of a poem to emerge as the poem was being written. She wanted to capture the mind itself in the act of thinking. She drew a distinction between her own poetry, a poetry of action, and Stanford's, a poetry she perceived as at rest. Bishop was interested in writing that captured objects and thoughts in as immediate a state of perception as possible.

In these comments Bishop is using the terms of "The Baroque Style in Prose" by Morris C. Croll (*Studies in English Philology, A Miscellany in Honor of Frederick Klaeber* [Minneapolis: University of Minnesota Press, 1929] 427−56). Two typed pages of notes from this article are among Bishop's papers in Special Collections, Vassar College Libraries, including the following about baroque stylists: "Their purpose was to express . . . not a thought, but a mind thinking, or, in Pascal's words, *la peinture de la pensee*. They knew that an idea separated from the act of experiencing it is not the idea that was experienced. The ardor of its conception in the mind is a necessary part of its truth; and unless it can be conveyed to another mind in something of the form of its occurrence, either it has changed into some other idea or it has ceased to be an idea, to have any existence whatever except a verbal one."

38 See also Donald E. Stanford, "From the Letters of Elizabeth Bishop, 1933−1934," *Verse*, 4, no. 3 (November 1987): 19−27.

39 Muser interview.

40 Smith interview.

41 "Foreword," *The Nineteen Thirty Four Vassarion*, published by the Senior Class, Vassar College, Poughkeepsie, New York. Special Collections, Vassar College Libraries.

42 Smith interview.

4. NEW YORK, EUROPE, AND KEY WEST, 1934−1940

1 See also Harriet Tompkins Thomas, "Travels with a Young Poet: Elizabeth Bishop," *Vassar Quarterly* (Winter 1985): 21−25.

2 In the fall of 1935 Bishop was thinking about writing a masque, a stylized dramatic entertainment, in the manner of Ben Jonson: she imagined a Henry James character

walking in a garden, talking about manners, attended by a retinue of angels. Frani Muser suggested to Bishop that they collaborate on such a work, with Muser writing the music.

Muser believed that she and Bishop could write a chamber opera free of Wagner's influence, an opera that would be "a new idea, had by a few select people sitting around after dinner, then polished up." Their collaboration was to be "something really funny and amusing not heavy" (to Elizabeth Bishop, 7 October 1935, Vassar College Library, Special Collections). Coincidentally, Margaret Miller, who was studying in New York, was considering writing a thesis on Italian baroque in the masque costumes of Inigo Jones, who had designed some scenery for Jonson (to Elizabeth Bishop, 16 November 1935, Vassar College Library, Special Collections). Miller encouraged Bishop to write a poem about Versailles that would be free from surrealism (to Elizabeth Bishop, 17 January 1936, Special Collections, Vassar College Libraries).

3   Wheeler interview.
4   Helfman interview.
5   Elizabeth Bishop to Frani Muser, 20 October 1938, Special Collections, Vassar College Libraries.
6   Elizabeth Bishop to Marianne Moore, 4 February 1936, Marianne Moore papers, Rosenbach Museum and Library.
7   By August 1936 Bishop had published eight poems in a range of good magazines since the spring of 1935. Although it is difficult to tell how much writing Bishop did in Europe, by the autumn of 1937 she would have five additional poems and two pieces of prose published, three of the poems based on experiences and observations in France.
8   Elizabeth Bishop to Frani Muser, 28 July 1937, Special Collections, Vassar College Libraries.
9   Elizabeth Bishop to Frani Muser, 9 August 1937, Special Collections, Vassar College Libraries.
10 Elizabeth Bishop to Marianne Moore, 24 November 1937, Marianne Moore papers, Rosenbach Museum and Library.
11 BETTY BRUCE—By 1930 everything had collapsed [in Key West]. The sponge industry had gone bad because of disease in the sponge beds. The cigar industry had stopped because by law you had to have hand-rolled cigars to make cigars in Key West. The industry had gone in for manufacturing them by machinery, and also Tampa had taken over. The sugar crop had fallen out of the market in Cuba, which was the big transportation between [Florida and Cuba], and Dole had started their pineapple operation. [There was] a tariff on the Cuban pineapples. There was just no work in this town. The city and the county both went bankrupt and the federal government had to come in 1932–33.

The WPA FERA came up with the promotional idea to revitalize the island by making it a center for writers and artists and to doctor up some of the houses for boarding houses. The WPA went in and renovated the officers' houses there and rented them to people like John Dewey and Ned Bruce. Of course, it was a very cheap place to come to. Key West had always been an artists' colony, but it had not been promoted; Winslow Homer and some of the other painters, for one reason or another, had just drifted in. Audubon had come because of the birds. There had been painters in and out. Remington and [others] came as newspaper illustrators. They didn't spend much time.

12 ROBERT FITZGERALD—Elizabeth told us one really astounding story. She said Pauline Hemingway had substantially written a Hemingway story about the fellow who goes out to salvage a wreck and sees the blond woman's floating hair through the porthole. Elizabeth said that this story had been told apparently by a charter man, one of the locals,

and that Pauline had remembered and taken it down mentally and had written the story. I've never been quite able to believe it, but it was like [Elizabeth's] blow against Hemingway, whom she disliked.

Elizabeth had an incident to illustrate her dislike. Some local goof had come up to Hemingway, who was drinking with some friends, and cracked him on the shoulder, and said, "How are you, Hem?" Hemingway, who didn't even know the oaf, rose to his feet and slugged him. Elizabeth felt this was very cruel, macho Hemingway at his worst. The fellow meant no harm, oafish as he was.

13 Elizabeth Bishop to Marianne Moore, 15 December 1939, Marianne Moore papers, Rosenbach Museum and Library.

14 Quoted in Elizabeth Bishop to Marianne Moore, 8 June 1940, Marianne Moore papers, Rosenbach Museum and Library.

15 Elizabeth Bishop to James Laughlin, 9 November 1940, Special Collections, Vassar College Libraries.

16 Charlotte Russell interview.

5. KEY WEST AND NEW YORK, 1941–1948

1 Sauer interview.

2 Boyden interview.

3 Marjorie Stevens to Elizabeth Bishop, 25 September 1944, Special Collections, Vassar College Libraries.

4 Gold interview.

5 Lovell Thompson to Elizabeth Bishop, 8 March 1946, Houghton Library.

6 Edward Weeks, "Prize Poet," *Atlantic Monthly* (August 1946): 148.

7 HOWARD MOSS—Elizabeth actually came to *The New Yorker* through Mrs. White. I think she needed the money and was sort of finished with *Partisan Review* in a way. I think she felt guilty [about leaving *Partisan Review*]. When I became poetry editor [in the late 1940s], there was a natural link because she knew that I adored her poems. There wasn't ever a poem I didn't take. The editing was meticulously done, which she liked, and *The New Yorker* would get back to Brazil, whereas very few [other] magazines would.

8 See Robert Lowell, "Elizabeth Bishop's *North & South*," *Collected Prose*, ed. Robert Giroux (New York: Farrar, Straus and Giroux, 1987), 76–80.

9 Elizabeth Bishop to Carley Dawson, 21 August 1948, University of Oregon Library.

6. WASHINGTON, D.C., AND YADDO, 1948–1951

1 Elizabeth Bishop to Robert Lowell, n.d., Houghton Library.

2 Hanson interview.

7. BRAZIL, 1951–1957

1 Rosalina Leão interview.

2 William Alfred also witnessed an incident of sparring between Bishop and Moore.
    WILLIAM ALFRED—Elizabeth didn't talk much about poetry. She told me that once

she'd sold three or four poems to *The New Yorker*, one right after another, and apparently Miss Moore hadn't had any luck that year. Elizabeth went over to Brooklyn to have dinner, and she said Miss Moore had a can opener in the kitchen. There was a kind of chill in the air, so in order to make conversation Elizabeth said, "Oh, what a charming can opener. It looks like a little Mexican." Marianne Moore said, "Save that for *The New Yorker*, Elizabeth."

3 Rosalina Leão interview.
4 Jackson interview.
5 Elizabeth Bishop to Ilse Barker, 27 October 1955, Princeton University Library.
6 Quoted in Elizabeth Bishop to Loren MacIver, 26 January 1952, Special Collections, Vassar College Libraries.
7 Elizabeth Bishop to Ilse Barker, 12 October 1952, Princeton University Library.
8 Elizabeth Bishop to U. T. and Joseph Summers, 21 April 1953, Special Collections, Vassar College Libraries.
9 U. T. Summers interview.
10 Sauer interview. Howard Moss also recollects Bishop at this time.

    HOWARD MOSS—I tried to find a place for Elizabeth [in 1957]. I went looking and scouting and asking people, and actually she and Lota found one for themselves eventually. We saw each other quite often. Once I met Elizabeth for lunch at the Algonquin. She had just gotten back from Brazil. She hadn't been drinking, and she looked marvelous. She had lost about twenty pounds. Lota and Elizabeth and I went to E. B. White and Mrs. White's for drinks once. We had an awfully nice time. I liked Lota. She was foreign and she was interesting—obviously extremely intelligent—and had a lot to say about Brazil.

11 Quoted in Robert Lowell to Elizabeth Bishop, 15 August 1957, Special Collections, Vassar College Libraries.
12 Robert Lowell to Elizabeth Bishop, 9 August 1957, Special Collections, Vassar College Libraries.
13 Elizabeth Bishop to Robert Lowell, 15 August 1957, Houghton Library.

8. BRAZIL, 1958–1965

1 Elizabeth Bishop to Ilse Barker, 24 March 1958, Princeton University Library.
2 Elizabeth Bishop to Joseph and U. T. Summers, 5 December 1958, Special Collections, Vassar College Libraries.
3 Magu Leão interview.
4 Brown interview.
5 Rosalina Leão interview.
6 Mark Strand interview.

9. SEATTLE, 1966

1 Bishop could find some level of comfort with certain academics. When the philosopher Susanne Langer visited Seattle and Bishop met her, Bishop was at first wary, according to Wesley Wehr: "Elizabeth was very, very jumpy, saying that she didn't know anything about philosophy and wouldn't know what to talk about. She and Susanne immediately found a common ground talking about the problems of teaching. It was a very nice visit."

2   Wehr interview. Later that semester Wesley Wehr and Gary Lundell traveled with Bishop
to visit the painter and sculptor Phil McCracken and the painter Guy Anderson.

WESLEY WEHR—[Elizabeth, Jean Russell, Gary Lundell, and I spent] a nice afternoon
going up to Loomis Island to see the McCrackens. We also took Elizabeth to meet Guy
Anderson, and, God knows why, Guy Anderson suggested that we go across the street to
the Lighthouse Restaurant Tavern. It was so loud in there that Guy and Elizabeth couldn't
have had an exchange if they had wanted to. They barely spoke. There we sat and suffered
through our drinks. Maybe because Guy is very shy, he arranged it that way. Elizabeth
said how much she enjoyed meeting him. He seemed like a very charming man. In the
car Elizabeth said, "Wes, did you notice that young fisherman, the boy that sat next to
me? God knows what kind of mother complex he's got. He spent the whole time sitting
with his hand on my knee. I just ignored him, of course."

Elizabeth pointed out that the so-called Northwest Mystics seemed actually to be
rather gregarious. She was very quick to pick up on the urban streak. They may profess to
live in wildernesses, but they know who has painted what on Ferry Street and what sold
at what price at Sidney Janis two days ago.

JEAN RUSSELL—One weekend I took Elizabeth to visit Ann and Phil McCracken. Phillip
is a sculptor and a painter. He and Elizabeth got along very well. Phil was telling about
having applied for a Guggenheim and not having won it. The piece that he had sent did
not arrive. I remember Elizabeth saying, "Well, Phil, if you ever win one, you're in," and
then she enumerated the ones that she had won. She said that it's that first one, whether
it's a Guggenheim, or a Ford, that is the magic word.

3   Brett Millier employs the pseudonym "Suzanne Bowen" in Elizabeth Bishop: Life and the
Memory of It (Berkeley: University of California Press, 1993). For consistency and conve-
nience, and with Professor Millier's permission, the authors are doing likewise.

4   Wehr interview.

5   Matchett interview.

6   Wehr interview.

10. BRAZIL, 1966–1967

1   It was at this time that Bishop wrote "Under the Window in Ouro Prêto," which she
dedicated to Lilli Araújo. Araújo remembers Bishop sitting in the window of her house
across the street from Casa Mariana, observing her own house, then going across the
street to observe Lilli's house, all the time taking in the flow of residents in the town.
Bishop had drinking spells of two to three weeks at this time. Once workmen came to
Araújo to tell her that Bishop needed to be collected at a workman's bar in town. Bishop
needed constant supervision. Her book on Brazil was still stalled.

2   Da Costa interview.

3   Mark Strand interview.

4   Elizabeth Bishop to Anny Baumann, 20 January 1967, Special Collections, Vassar College
Libraries.

5   Elizabeth Bishop to Dorothee Bowie, 18 January 1967, Special Collections, Vassar College Libraries.

6   Elizabeth Bishop to Anny Baumann, 3 July 1967, Special Collections, Vassar College
Libraries.

7   Da Costa interview.

8   Although Howard Moss did not see Bishop during this period, he recollects a later discussion with her.

HOWARD MOSS—Elizabeth did say that Lota had been building this park and that she had become obsessed by it. The political situation had become such that she had gotten into a kind of maze. Lota was a person who thought that by common sense she could solve everything. She was a rational person. She suddenly found herself in a paranoid mirror where she couldn't. Then she became obsessed with something that was unsolvable.

9   Elizabeth Bishop to Dorothee Bowie, 20 December 1967, Vassar College Libraries, Special Collections.

11. SAN FRANCISCO, 1967–1969

1   In the fall of 1968 Bishop also wrote a brief gallery note for Wesley Wehr, who remembers the details of her helping him.

WESLEY WEHR—[At one point during Elizabeth's time in San Francisco] Morris Graves was having a showing of his private collection at the Humboldt Gallery. It turned out that Morris owned a painting of mine that was in the show but marked not for sale. Suzanne and Elizabeth mentioned me to the gallery, so when I did contact the Humboldt Gallery, they said there had been a certain interest in me because I painted a picture that Morris would not sell. When I went down, I took some pictures and showed them to the dealer, and before I knew it interest in my work had already started.

I asked Elizabeth if she would write a blurb [for me to use with an exhibition]. The Humboldt Gallery wanted to use an abbreviated version, and Elizabeth was furious. It was reprinted in 1973, for the Shepherd Gallery in New York, and just a bit of it in the Victoria, British Columbia, Art Museum catalog a few years ago. It was something to have Elizabeth Bishop being that supportive, that encouraging.

2   Confusion on the part of some regarding the nature of the relationship between Bishop and Bowen could lead to misunderstanding, as one friend of Bishop's in San Francisco recollects.

MAJORIE BRUSH—Elizabeth called [me on Howard Moss's recommendation], and she and Suzanne came to see me. Elizabeth showed that charming gaiety of hers right away. We had no trouble with [becoming friends]. In fact, that made a little trouble about Suzanne, because I wasn't very astute, and I would get so excited about talking about books with Elizabeth or in my eagerness to hear Elizabeth's stories about her childhood and about her visiting [Ezra Pound in] St. Elizabeths, I would begin to ignore Suzanne.

I went to dinner one night, and Elizabeth was very excited about the fact that she had bought an old filing cabinet made of wood. They had prepared a charming dinner for me, and I was just having a great time, and suddenly Suzanne left the table. She was angry that Elizabeth and I were having such a good time. I misunderstood Suzanne. I thought because she had the little child perhaps she was like an au pair who also was helping Elizabeth. Elizabeth attended to the dinner, and I thought that was the end of it, that I was not going to be able to have my pleasure in knowing Elizabeth. But that did not turn out to be the case.

[When I wanted to give Elizabeth a tour] of the beach and Telegraph Hill, my goddaughter, who is just about Suzanne's age, [paid] attention [to her]. [Suzanne felt comfortable with me after that.] In fact, she came to see me from Brazil one time and brought me a present, little Brazilian cigars, and a message from Elizabeth.

3   Elizabeth Bishop to Dorothee Bowie, 8 September 1968, Special Collections, Vassar College Libraries.
4   Quoted in Louise Crane to Elizabeth Bishop, 28 January 1969, Special Collections, Vassar College Libraries.
5   Wehr interview.
6   Elizabeth Bishop to Frani Muser, 24 February 1969, Special Collections, Vassar College Libraries.

12. OURO PRÊTO, 1969–1970

1   Merrill interview.
2   Jose Nemer interview.
3   Bidart interview.
4   Elizabeth Bishop to Anny Baumann, 7 September 1969, Special Collections, Vassar College Libraries.
5   Elizabeth Bishop to Anny Baumann, 19 November 1969, Special Collections, Vassar College Libraries.
6   The Nemers were closest to Bishop at this time and recollect how she seemed to have developed a mistrust of all those around her in Ouro Prêto.

JOSE ALBERTO NEMER—Elizabeth was very fragile, very lonely. She was very vulnerable to feelings of guilt. She did not know how to handle them. Elizabeth mentioned she was very hurt that the common friends of Lota and her had blamed her for having contributed to Lota's death. It was a very formidable point for Elizabeth. She carried an enormous weight. Elizabeth was so fragile that many times she received mail from writers in the United States, very well-known writers. Some of them she abominated, and when they wrote her she wouldn't open the envelope and she would drink and drink. Only receiving a letter would do it. Elizabeth was terrified, I don't know what of.

LINDA NEMER—At points Elizabeth was quite ill here. [Once] she thought she was going to die. She asked me to handle the [arrangements] and to have her body sent to the United States. Elizabeth gave several names of people to call, and then she asked me to be very careful in breaking this news to a special aunt [Grace, in Nova Scotia].

JOSE—Elizabeth was over-sensitive. My girlfriend arrived at two in the afternoon one day when there was a festival going on and I wasn't at home. Elizabeth hadn't been drinking. When I came home, she was drunk. She told me, "[Your girlfriend] has been here looking for you." Then she called to me and said, "Who were the two young men who accompanied her?" I said I didn't know. She went on drinking during the night, and the next day she repeated to me, "Who were those young men? Who were they?" For two more days Elizabeth went on drinking, insisting, "Who were those young boys?" I didn't know.

Two days later I met my girlfriend. She was embarrassed because she had [just] met these boys who had given her a ride to Elizabeth's house and in order to call to Elizabeth, they [had used a slang term] that young boys used to call [a young woman]. It was something so simple [like this that could trigger Elizabeth's suspicion].

Whenever Elizabeth started to drink, she would go on for days. At night I would wake up because Elizabeth would drink and she would cry loudly, and then laugh loudly, too, laughing and crying. It was something that you couldn't help hearing. The situation would go on until I would convince Elizabeth that I would take her to the hospital, and she would agree. Sometimes Elizabeth herself asked me to take her to the hospital for detoxification. After that I would take her to my family's house for a few days. In the hospital Elizabeth would ask for watercolors and also for mystery books, which she devoured, and ice cream. I would take one book in the morning and then [go] back in the afternoon and change it for another one. [She would stay in the hospital] five days [to] one week each time.

In one of those drinking fits, there was a festival going on. My friends wanted to borrow a record of Renaissance music to tape record. Since I was living in her house and had access to everything, I thought that it would be okay if I lent it to them. I was sure they would return it. I didn't ask Elizabeth for it, because she was drinking. A few days later, when she was better, the four friends who had borrowed the record arrived for dinner and returned the record to Elizabeth. I wasn't home yet. [Ours] had always been a relationship of equal to equal. Elizabeth didn't say anything to me, but from this day on, I had the impression she became a little suspicious of me and lost that trust. If somebody came to Elizabeth and said something against somebody else, she was very easily influenced by that.

13. CAMBRIDGE, 1970–1973

1 One scene when Bishop "hit bottom" is recollected by two of her friends.

MARY MEIGS—When Elizabeth was first living in Cambridge, I brought her my blue-glass finger bowl with "Lizzie" etched on it—I thought it would please her. She unwrapped it very carefully. Almost immediately she saw a tiny crack and exclaimed, "But there is a crack in it!" "Crack" was the word she used, not "There's a flaw in it." It struck something so deep in her, the connection between Lizzie and being cracked. I thought later it might have recalled her mother's insanity.

Some time later there was a phone call, out of the blue, which was utterly mysterious to me. Elizabeth was quite incoherent and said, "You did a terrible thing." I said, "What? What Elizabeth? Tell me, what was it?" After more incoherence, she hung up. I thought that call harkened back to the blue "Lizzie" bowl. I couldn't think of any other terrible thing that I had done. It has haunted me ever since.

MARY-CLAIRE BLAIS—[I was not there, but it seems to me that] Elizabeth was just too sensitive. There's something that seems so ridiculous about this to normal people. But for someone like Elizabeth, this crack was unbearable. She was extremely sensitive to invisible things that really could kill her.

2 Elizabeth Bishop to Dorothee Bowie, 2 November 1970, Special Collections, Vassar College Libraries.

3 Elizabeth Bishop to Dorothee Bowie, 7 November 1970, Special Collections, Vassar College Libraries.

4 Elizabeth Bishop to Dorothee Bowie, 2 January 1971, Special Collections, Vassar College Libraries.

5 Vendler interview.

6 Pinsky interview.

7 Hussey interview.

8 Vendler interview.

9 Howard Moss recollects other aspects of Bishop's relationship with The New Yorker.

HOWARD MOSS—Elizabeth was absolutely wrong [when she claimed that The New Yorker would not publish translations]. I don't know why she said that. I would have published all the Andrade [translations] if I had seen them. There may have been some misunderstanding. The same thing happened with another [piece], and I don't know quite why. There's a story ["Memories of Uncle Neddy"] that I think we rejected. When it came out in *Southern Review* [Fall 1977], I saw it first; then the editor of fiction saw it. It killed us. He said, "Did we get it?" And it turned out we had. There were seven people reading prose at *The New Yorker* at that time. I still don't know what had happened.

What did come to me after Bishop's death was the Moore piece ["Efforts of Affection: A Memoir of Marianne Moore"]. I was disappointed in it. I thought it wasn't really Elizabeth's top prose. There was a struggle going on there. The struggle was still there after she was dead. It wasn't what I read Elizabeth for.

10 Engel interview.

11 During the fall of 1970 Lota's nephew and Bishop's close friend Flavio committed suicide. His wife recollects this event.

REGINA CÉLIA COLÔNIA—Flavio killed himself with a gun on the thirteenth of November 1970. I didn't know when I married Flavio that he had tried to kill himself twice before I met him. Flavio had to fight his way through difficult circumstances—the splitting up of his parents among other events. I believe it was also confusing for him to go to court against his mother in favor of another person who was not part of his family, as Flavio told me he did for Elizabeth over Lota's will.

At the end of 1970, however, everything was apparently coming together and working fine. We had just married. He had recently been promoted to Second Secretary. He had a promise to be sent to Washington, D.C., to work at our embassy, which is considered an important post. There was reason to believe that he was finally happy. At that moment he killed himself.

A few months before he died, Flavio prepared a book of his articles. He dedicated it to Elizabeth, but it was never published.

12 Merrill interview.

13 One student whom Bishop frequently mentioned in 1972 to her friends and colleagues was John Peech, a graduate student in physics who was also studying with her for a second year. Bishop admired his talent as well as a certain naïveté and freshness in his personality—once Peech read Herbert's "Love Unknown" in class, pronouncing all the "f's" as "f's," not "s's." (Elizabeth Bishop to Lloyd Frankenberg, 8 January 1972, Vassar College Library, Special Collections.) Anne Hussey, who was one of Bishop's closest friends and confidantes in Cambridge, was a good friend of Peech and often saw him and Bishop together.

ANNE HUSSEY—John Peech was my good friend. He was a young man who looked like an old Ben Franklin, though he was not fat. He was a physicist, and a musician, and a maverick. John had been in Elizabeth's class her first year. He was very uneven. John published only two poems in his lifetime. He either got hot and wrote a really great one, or he had a lot of fizzle. Of course, he was a very busy man. He managed to read enough to be well-read enough to be in the game, but very often it was last minute. There was a poem that he withdrew that had to do with the physics department and atomic power, a poem that had been accepted by *The New Yorker*. He withdrew it because he knew it was going to get him in trouble. John and I were not part of the Cambridge poetry groupies or what Elizabeth called the Cambridge Poetry Operators. I believe we were resented somewhat for our need to be separate. Elizabeth was very conscious of this younger group in Cambridge, and of feeling old, and of not wanting to alienate them. So she was very gracious to a number of people with whom she might not have had a great deal in common.

John was a dramatic person, very intense, but scattered. He was criticized for being a dilettante, for doing a little of this and a little of that, and not ever settling on one thing. He was really very accomplished on the piano, and had performed semiprofessionally here and there. He won the concerto contest at Harvard, playing Bartók. He couldn't be without crisis. He suffered magnificently. John gave one disastrous concert in the fall of 1975, at which there had been many mistakes, both musically and technically. Elizabeth, Alice, my husband, and I attended this concert together. Afterward, Cal, who was also there said, "John, I thought you were Christ on the cross. That's a compliment." I think the drama of being a genius was something John enjoyed. He was a wonderful ham, and I can say that because I was very fond of him. His very expansiveness became difficult for Elizabeth. She became tired. She simply could not talk on the phone for that long, often more than an hour. She could not get involved with all his problems and subsequently saw less of him. He was too full of his own problems, and she said she felt to some degree that he was emulating Cal, wanting to suffer in the same way he suffered. I think that may have hurt her feelings.

14   David Weimer recollects Bishop's visit to Rutgers.

DAVID WEIMER—Elizabeth was, I suspect, to the end of her life very unsure of what she had achieved. Whenever she got an honor, it sort of astonished her. I dimly remember that when she came to Rutgers to get an honorary degree, she said things to the effect that she didn't know why they were giving her [this honor].

I often felt sorry for Elizabeth, I confess. All this talent, intelligence, cultivation, and achievement, but she was so unsure of herself. At her age and with all that accomplishment behind her, Elizabeth still felt that she hadn't really accomplished anything much and her poems really weren't very good. Elizabeth said something about how people who introduce her always mention the Pulitzer Prize. The implication was very clear that nothing had really come her way in terms of a great award since then. Another part of herself knew she was very smart, very gifted. She was confident at least in the sense that she knew how smart she was.

My wife and I rode with her from one part of the campus to another, along with two other recipients of honorary degrees, Kurt Waldheim and Ralph Nader. I cannot imagine a more anomalous trio.

15   In a letter to Gary Fountain (27 July 1993), Lloyd Schwartz related an incident that illustrates Frank Bidart's understanding of Bishop's literary style:

A word about Frank Bidart, and why poets like Elizabeth and Robert Lowell trusted him so much. Practically the first thing I did when I got back from my first trip to Brazil, in the spring of 1990, was call Frank and read him my "discovery"— the love poem ("Dear, my compass / still points north") that Elizabeth had written to Lilli Correia de Araújo, the Danish innkeeper of the little 18th-century hotel in Ouro Prêto where Elizabeth used to stay. She even "illuminated" the poem with tiny water-color images in the margins. As far as I know, Elizabeth kept no copy of this poem when she returned to the U.S. It's the only poem in which she explicitly compares her life in Brazil with her childhood in Nova Scotia.

Frank was as excited as I was about this "find" and asked me to make a copy for him. When he read it on the page, he seemed somewhat less enthusiastic than he had seemed over the phone. When I asked him why, he said that he thought there was something a little blurry about the big transition to the last stanza—the transition that turns the fairy-tale imagery into a love poem. It would have been more characteristic of Elizabeth, Frank thought, to indicate this dramatic shift of tone with a dash at the beginning of the first line of the last stanza. But there was no dash in the version I copied.

Lilli had first shown me the poem in Elizabeth's handwriting, which I couldn't really decipher (her tiny chicken-scratching was notorious); Lilli then let me see a copy Elizabeth herself must have typed out so that Lilli could read it (this typed version had similar watercolors in the margins), and that's the page she allowed me to copy. I was extremely careful—I was sure that I transcribed the poem accurately, paying especial attention to punctuation (after all, I knew I'd show this to Frank).

When I returned to Brazil the following year, I asked Lilli if I could see the original handwritten version again. "Why do you want to look at that again?" she asked, typically blunt and suspicious. But she brought out the original version, which she kept framed in her private quarters behind the breakfast room of the inn. This time I already knew the poem by heart, so I could make out what was previously too hard to read. Imagine my astonishment to see in Elizabeth's own unmistakable hand the very dash at the beginning of the last stanza that Frank was so sure she needed there.

16 Angelo Osualdo, a friend of the Nemers who met Bishop at this time, recollects her illness.

ANGELO OSUALDO—I was a very good friend of Jose and Linda Nemer. I knew about Elizabeth as a great American poet who lived in Brazil. Before living in Ouro Prêto from 1977 to 1983 as Municipal Secretary of Culture and Tourism, I always went [there] for weekends, and I stayed at Elizabeth's house with Jose or Linda around 1971 or 1972. At this period she was in the United States, so I knew the house before I met Elizabeth.

One of these times, Elizabeth was there and Jose brought me to meet her. From then I went to her house many times, to have tea or a drink together and talk about Brazilian culture and literature. Elizabeth talked about many [Brazilian writers] with emotion. At this time I was the editor of the literary supplement of the Minas Gerais newspaper, *Supplemento Literario do Minas Gerais*. During this period this supplement was going through a period of great renewal in all the cultural circles of Brazil. Elizabeth was kind enough to give me a poem translated into Portuguese by Emanuel Brasil, which I published with an illustration.

Even though Ouro Prêto is the most important historical city in Brazil, there is very close by an aluminum factory, which contaminates the air. It made [Elizabeth's asthma] grow worse. Elizabeth smoked, drank, became very nervous, very tense, and she had to go to the hospital for treatment during the crisis period of those attacks. The last time I saw Elizabeth she had a horrible asthma crisis. She went to the hospital, and I paid her a visit together with Jose Alberto, who took her ice cream. It soothed her throat. We were both in the room when the nurse came in to give her an injection, and she was horrified of injections. She did not let us leave the room. We went to the window to look out, and we were looking at the hospital yard, at sunset—it was very sad—and at the same time as we were doing this, we could hear Elizabeth screaming as the injection was being [administered]. My last impression of Elizabeth is of her scream. [That memory] is stopped in time. It was the last time I saw her.

17 Hussey interview.
18 Engel interview.
19 Engel interview.

20 Another example of Bishop's uneasiness with academics was her relationship with Helen Muchnic's companion, Dorothy Walsh.

HELEN MUCHNIC—Elizabeth and I got on famously because our interests were more or less the same. It was of literature we talked for the most part. Elizabeth read whatever happened to catch her attention. She read for enjoyment, not for any set purpose, and her comments on books, like her remarks on everything else—people, objects, ideas—were positive, forceful, immediate. She had strong likes and dislikes, but her judgments were perfectly consistent, arising as they did from a firm, ingrained sense of values. Whatever the context, what she demanded was accuracy, precision, concreteness, and, above all, genuineness. She abhorred pretense, flimsy thinking, self-aggrandizement, affectation, sentimentality, and in a favorite term of disapproval, "How Chi-chi," would damn any manifestation of these. If a poet used a plant or flower in his verse, he had better know its botanical properties as well as the scansion and sound of its name, while economists, politicians, and philosophers had better shape their theories on concrete experience and specific cases, not cloudy ideologies. These, of course, are the qualities that distinguish her own work, the apparent simplicity of which is the ultimate simplicity of something deeply felt and completely understood.

Alice and Elizabeth would sometimes stay with Dorothy and me in Cummington, visits that we always enjoyed and looked forward to. But at first Elizabeth kept Dorothy at a distance, insisting on addressing her as Dr. Walsh, to which Dorothy, nonplused, puzzled, taken aback, retaliated by calling her Dr. Bishop (on the strength of her honorary doctorate). This estrangement, of course, did not last, and they became very good friends once Elizabeth realized that her initial distrust of Dorothy was based on a mistake. The mistake, it seems to me, was a characteristic misinterpretation. Dorothy was a philosopher. Her mind played naturally with the abstractions that to Elizabeth, until she discovered otherwise, seemed attempts at showing off. However, everything changed once she realized that Dorothy's bright generalizations were not meant to impress but to convey and share her genuine appreciation, knowledge, and delight in art. (After all, aesthetics was her chosen specialty.) Once this happened, everything changed and they talked a lot together, exchanging views on poetry, etc.

21 Penelope Laurans Fitzgerald recollects how her relationship with Bishop developed.

PENELOPE LAURANS FITZGERALD—The first time I saw Elizabeth for any length of time was in the fall of 1974, when she asked Robert to bring me for drinks at Lewis Wharf, soon after she moved in. I was teaching at Yale and commuting on weekends to Cambridge, so I was often there only between Thursday evening and Sunday. Elizabeth and Robert had been getting to be increasingly good friends, and I think Elizabeth was curious about what I was like. At the time Robert had not been long separated from Sally Fitzgerald, and there was gossip in Cambridge. I felt the invitation to drinks was an invitation to be looked over, more or less, not in any bad sense, but just in the sense that Elizabeth was curious about who it was Robert loved, and also curious about someone who might potentially be brought into the family.

I say family and I mean family because in a sense there was a circle of people around Harvard, principally writers, which formed a kind of family, a special little band at the time. Most of these people came and went frequently, some were never there more than a semester a year, some were junior people who left for jobs after a while, but nevertheless there was a loose family community from which people slipped in and out, a community always being augmented by visitors.

When I say I think Elizabeth was curious and wanted to look me over, I want to define more of that curiosity. Elizabeth had a natural human curiosity, of course, but she also had a kind of curiosity that was beyond that. She was also capable of being curious in an almost disinterested way. She was curious about me, but then she was curious about everything, and she was partly curious about me in the same way she was curious about everything. Her question was, Who is this person? and she really wanted to know in the same way she wanted to know what kinds of birds existed in a certain geography. This doesn't mean that she didn't like people or wasn't a quite social person when she was not depressed or ill, or that she couldn't be friendly or wonderful company or vulnerable or dependent. It's just that there seemed a certain emotional distance in Elizabeth's relationship to people, undoubtedly stemming from her early life, a kind of coldness perhaps, even when she was suffering and confiding in you.

During the first meeting with Elizabeth, I don't think I said very much at all, but my very innocuousness may have helped me pass the test because Robert and I together began to see more of Alice and Elizabeth. It helped that Robert and I both liked Alice very much, and grew to be very fond of her, and that we all seemed to be able to have pleasant times together. I really grew very fond of Elizabeth as a person—since I taught her poems I learned to separate the poems from the person (though they were clearly all of a piece). I'm sure Elizabeth never felt about me the way she felt about Robert, but I do think she changed over time from seeing me just as Robert's girl who was inoffensive, to seeing me as a real person she liked.

The turning point in our relationship, I think, was when I asked Elizabeth to come and do a reading at Yale. She did not really want to do the reading, since she hated to read, but the money was attractive, she was at least a little curious about Yale and flattered about being asked down, and, I think, she knew I would take care of her, protect her. Our agreement was that she would come down by train, give the reading at 8:00 p.m. and then, late as it was, I would immediately drive her back to Cambridge. I was very nervous, of course, because with Elizabeth not really wanting to come, not being in perfect health, and not really liking to give readings, anything could have gone wrong, but it didn't.

Harold Bloom introduced her to a packed house and he was at his very best. Elizabeth, of course, was a great favorite of Harold's, part of his canon from the very beginning, even before she was so famous—and, well, let us say that Harold helped to make Elizabeth famous by his impassioned teaching of her work to so many of his brilliant students who then became brilliant teachers of her work themselves. In any case, Harold gave a magnificent introduction. Elizabeth took the stage and began reading, and I at last felt I could take a big breath. She had read for no more than ten minutes (with me standing in the wings congratulating myself) when all of a sudden she stopped, turned toward me and said loudly enough for everyone to hear, "Is that enough now, Penny?" I very nearly fainted. Of course, when I said it wasn't enough, she dutifully went on and read more in that completely natural, direct, unaffected way that was her trademark. But Elizabeth must surely be one of the few poets in the whole history of poetry who gave such short readings that she would always leave an audience hungry for more—which was as it should be.

Anyway, going home that night, leaving about ten o'clock, the hour, the excitement, the trip, the dark of the car finally helped me cement my relationship with Elizabeth. We gossiped a lot, talking in shorthand about people and situations we knew very well— Elizabeth was at that time particularly distressed about Cal and his quoting of Elizabeth Hardwick's letters in his sonnets, and she chewed the situation over from a hundred angles, always coming back to the same point of view. She was disapproving of Cal—irritated at him and particularly irritated at him for requiring her disapproval. When I think about it now, our conversation that night was very much like the conversation the woman in "The Moose" drowsily overhears going on behind her. We were talking about family histories in a way made more intimate by the hour and the situation. When we were tired of talking, we sang hymns. There we were, barrelling down the Massachusetts Turnpike, singing "A Mighty Fortress is Our God" and "Abide with Me," remnants of both our boarding school youths. After that night, I never felt uneasy around Elizabeth again.

22 See also Dana Gioia, "Studying with Miss Bishop," The New Yorker, 15 September 1986, 90–101.

23 Bishop and Fitzgerald also talked about the nature of poetry.

ROBERT FITZGERALD—I like very much what happened with Elizabeth over a copy of my Illiad. She had it on her desk in her little office in Kirkland House and wanted me to inscribe it for her, which I did. She said, "My, what a lot of work." Elizabeth was very careful about praising the work of her friends and contemporaries and never went in for it in a big way, which was intensely honorable of her. I remember many lunches with her when the talk would sometimes circle around poetry. I remember her saying that one of her friends, a prose writer, had chided her for trying so hard to find some accuracy about the way in which a goat's eyes were formed, because she had to have it accurate for a poem ["Crusoe in England"]. And the prose writer said, "What does it matter whether they're perpendicular or horizontal?" And Elizabeth said, "I suppose that's the difference between prose and poetry. Poetry has got to be true."

At one of these lunches Elizabeth brought me a copy of "One Art" and said, "This is my first villanelle." She inscribed it "With love . . ." That's how she talked about poetry, by bringing me one. Elizabeth also would occasionally say she wanted to take my versification course because she didn't know anything about versification. I think she was perfectly sincere. She would have students join her course after having gone through mine who would talk about what they'd learned. Elizabeth was curious, I think. She would have liked to be there and listen to some of this.

Bishop's concern with the specific details of poems extended to the work of her fellow poets and the interpretation of her own work.

RICHARD WILBUR—Elizabeth had the greatest impatience of untruth in and out of poetry. I published a poem in The New Yorker called "Shad Time," which was about the time of the year when the shad run and the shad [bush] blooms on the bank. I put in all the other phenomena of the season, and Elizabeth liked the poem very well. But she said to me, very firmly, "In the center stanza of that poem your grammar is wrong. You've got an incomplete sentence, and you don't have an incomplete sentence anywhere else." Elizabeth said this to me not tutorially—she sounded more disappointed than anything else because she had come to expect perfect grammar of me, or complete grammar. Elizabeth said it about three times during one evening. I assure you, I went and fixed it.

DAVID KALSTONE—[In] a piece that later became a chapter in my book [Five Temperaments], I wrote about "In the Waiting Room." At one point I talk about the moment when Elizabeth hears her aunt's scream inside [the doctor's office] and then realizes it was "me: / my voice." I commented on the fact that I thought [the word] "inside" was wonderful because it allowed you to think of the aunt inside and something coming from inside Elizabeth herself. Elizabeth said, "Oh, dear, I hadn't really thought about that and maybe I ought to try and clarify that." In other words, she didn't want that double meaning. She wanted the sense that the child was astonished to discover and include the scream, but she didn't want any confusion about where the scream was actually taking place.

14. CAMBRIDGE AND BOSTON, 1973-1977

1   Lushington interview.

2   HELEN VENDLER—I asked Lowell once why he had published the sonnets using his wife's voice. (He had done the same thing with letters Elizabeth Bishop had sent from Brazil.) I said to him that I could understand his writing them, but why did he feel that he had to publish them? He could have let them be published after all concerned were dead.

Lowell said that he wouldn't have been able to write any new poems. He would have kept tinkering with those. As long as he had a poem that wasn't published, he kept working on it. In the case of *Notebook* he kept working on the poems even after they were published, and did another version of *Notebook*, and then did them over again for *History*. Lowell said it was very hard for him not to tinker with a poem as long as it was under his hand. He had to get it out in print.

I think he must have been very much surprised by the criticisms, because he damns himself more by letting us see Lizzie's view, naked with her grief and accusation, than if it had been filtered through his view of her. He doesn't enunciate any grievances against her. He just lets her enunciate grievances against him.

3   In 1973 Bishop also approved the production of a broadside of her poem "The Fish."

M. TAYLOR BOWIE—In 1973 I was working as a manager for a bookseller (and a great fisherman) David Ishii. He had become familiar with Elizabeth's poetry, particularly "The Fish," which I liked, too. David said, "I think it would be nice to print up some copies and have her sign some." He talked to John Sollid, a printer, gave him the text of the poem and [asked him to] do something simple but nice. So John produced thirteen copies of this, kept one and gave David the other twelve. Then David [asked] me [if I thought] Elizabeth would sign them. I wasn't sure. I hadn't thought through all the ramifications of contract and things like that. I spoke to mother about it, and she said she would ask Elizabeth.

DOROTHEE BOWIE—Elizabeth said it was absolutely against the contract.

TAYLOR—When I actually talked to Elizabeth [when she was in Seattle for the Roethke reading] and showed [her] the broadsides, she said [that signing would] be OK [but that I was not to] tell anyone about it. David said that these were not for sale anyway. He wanted to give a few to [his] friends, which he did. So she signed all twelve.

DOROTHEE—Elizabeth asked for two, one to go to me and one for Frank Bidart.

4   Merrill interview.

5   Leithauser interview.

6   During her trip to Florida that winter, Bishop met Carol Crotty, who talked with Bishop about her own experiences in Brazil.

CAROL CROTTY—Elizabeth and I were friends in the seventies in Florida, when Charlotte [Russell] introduced us. Elizabeth came to Fort Meyers Beach [in 1974] to stay several weeks. We discovered that we had Brazil in common. I had this great nostalgia for Brazil and loved to speak Portuguese. I had spent quite a bit of time in Ouro Prêto and knew it quite well. Elizabeth told me that Melo Franco de Andrade, Head of the National Patrimony, said, "We have the most beautiful house here in Ouro Prêto. It has the most beautiful roofline of all of them, and if somebody doesn't buy this house and preserve it and restore it, it's going to collapse." Elizabeth bought the house.

One thing I remember very well is that Elizabeth, the Russells, and I had a plan to all go early in the morning, around six or so, to Corkscrew Swamp. Elizabeth was an ardent birdwatcher. I had been in an awful auto accident and was shaky on my legs. Elizabeth leapt out of that car after we drove into Corkscrew, went up to the office, commandeered a wheelchair, and pushed me [along] a boardwalk that had been built by the Audubon Society. This was ⅝ of a mile out and back. With her own physical ailments, Elizabeth was so kind and so thoughtful of others. Elizabeth was so natural and so concerned about the ordinary people she invited into her life.

7 An incident relating to Bishop's sense of privacy and Methfessel developed in the summer of 1977 at North Haven.

MARY MCCARTHY—Elizabeth and I had a falling out that I was unaware of for years. I didn't find out about it until practically her death. [The incident occurred] when Elizabeth lived in the summer in North Haven. We had a date to go over there with Cal Lowell and spend the day. Cal was conducting the negotiations for that visit. And at the last minute—we'd already engaged the boat and everything—Elizabeth canceled it.

Cal [eventually] told me that he thought the real reason Elizabeth didn't want me to come over there was that I would observe her relationship with Alice, [because] she was convinced that I had put Lota in The Group. None of that was true. That all was rather crazy. I was very much upset to hear this, for I had seen Elizabeth in between at Vassar and had been very friendly and nothing had been said. Yes, [I did write her a letter about this misconception]. I know she couldn't have gotten the letter—it was mailed from Paris, perhaps the day before she died.

McCarthy's letter arrived after Bishop's death in October 1979. The letter is in the Vassar College Library. Frank Bidart recollects Bishop telling him this story, and two others of Bishop's friends recollect comments she made to them about Mary McCarthy.

FRANK BIDART—Elizabeth said that she never read The Group, but from what people said to her, she was convinced that she was the model for Lakey. She knew that Mary McCarthy insisted she wasn't, but she thought she was. She was bitter about this, very angry. The first time I met Elizabeth, in Kirkland House, she said that she had made a million dollars for Mary McCarthy in The Group. She had known McCarthy very well and had helped McCarthy through various crises. There's a chapter of the book which was originally a short story, about Dotty being fitted for a pessary; Elizabeth had indeed gone on a similar first trip to the doctor with McCarthy.

Because of the figure of the countess in The Group, she was very sorry that she had ever let McCarthy meet Lota. In the last summer of Lowell's life, when Elizabeth and Alice were staying at North Haven, the Lowells were at Castine, and McCarthy lived in Castine. McCarthy wanted to come over with the Lowells for a day trip, and Elizabeth wouldn't let her come. Elizabeth said that she didn't want Mary to meet Alice, because she felt it would end up as another episode in a novel. She certainly didn't forgive McCarthy.

DAVID JACKSON—Elizabeth told one of the funniest stories about Mary McCarthy's first marriage. Apparently you weren't even supposed to be engaged in those days—strictly against the rules at Vassar. All of Mary McCarthy's buddies were in on this plan, and they were setting up an apartment someplace in New York, and everybody went in to fix it up and do the work to get it going. Elizabeth ended the story by saying, "I have slept spoons with Mary in a day bed, and I wouldn't trust her to this day because she particularizes so.

She would take me into a gathering of new friends saying, 'I want you to meet Elizabeth Bishop, my lesbian friend.' "

GRETCHEN KEENE SMITH—In a conversation with Elizabeth about Mary, Elizabeth said, "Oh, yes, I understand that people say that Mary used me for one of the characters." She said it in a bemused fashion but made no further comment on it. But we went on to talk about Mary some more, and I wondered if this annoyed Elizabeth or if other things might annoy her that Mary had done or said about her or other people. Elizabeth said, "Well, yes, people feel that way about Mary, but you know Mary always gives you that feeling that she was the little girl who wasn't invited to the party." I think that weighed heavily with Elizabeth and her kindness toward, her tolerance of Mary.

8 Joseph Summers interview.
9 Frederick Morgan interview.
10 In February Bishop gave a reading at the Boston Public Library.

MONROE ENGEL—Elizabeth's readings were unlike any readings I ever went to, in part because of her reluctance to do the readings. There was a reading at the Boston Public Library one night, and it was advertised as an hour's reading. The person who introduced Elizabeth arrived late. Elizabeth was there punctually. Say the reading was to start at eight. By the time Elizabeth had been introduced and started reading, it was 8:30. At nine she looked at her watch and said that it was time to end the reading. Everybody groaned in protest, so she went on for another ten or fifteen minutes, reminding me of Marianne Moore, who was always prepared to walk off after twenty minutes.

JANE SHORE—At the Boston Public Library, Elizabeth gave a very short reading, perhaps twenty-five minutes or so. The audience wouldn't let her leave the stage. Elizabeth asked for requests, and people started shouting titles of poems they wanted her to read. Someone asked Elizabeth to read "Sestina," and I remember her looking up and saying, in that slightly quizzical and amused voice of hers, "You like that poem?" I couldn't tell if it was kind of a staged modesty that she had or if she really was surprised that someone would ask her to read that poem.

11 HAROLD LEEDS—Elizabeth and I shared Anny Baumann, and we also shared a specialist Anny used. We were each of us sent, Elizabeth first and me a year or two later, to a man whose specialty was stomach, the intestines, the colon, and all those. The examination is not a very agreeable one, and Elizabeth said that after he had performed this examination, the doctor said to her, "I must tell you, the only thing that has ever impressed my daughter is that you were coming to my office today." I don't think anyone is subjected to that kind of examination unless they are looking for something [very serious].

12 Vendler interview.
13 Vendler interview.

15. BOSTON, 1977–1979

1 U. T. SUMMERS—Elizabeth said, "If I come [to read at the University of Rochester], I want a lot of money because it takes so much out of me." Tony Hecht got the money for her to come, and we had a lovely time. Elizabeth said she didn't like to eat and talk much before the reading. We had dinner with Elizabeth and the Hechts the night before, and they didn't invite anybody else. I got the impression Elizabeth didn't want to see anybody else. There were a lot of people furious because they didn't see her. I think she finally got to

where she really did rather like to be celebrated. She didn't like being exploited just as a literary object.

JOSEPH SUMMERS—[The reading went] very well. Elizabeth was a much more confident reader than she [had been in the past]. She was embarrassed with the notion that anybody would try to make his or her poetry sound good or pretentious. She sort of underplayed it. Auden used to do that in his earlier things. He would flatten out every one of his jokes and read them so deadpan you wouldn't know it was a joke. That was sort of the way Elizabeth was. There was a good audience. Some people had trouble hearing. Everybody was impressed. I think Elizabeth was pleased. She was annoyed, though, when U.T. sent her a clipping and somebody had said she looked like a grandmother. She said they wouldn't do that kind of thing with Robert Frost.

U.T.—The ferocity of her comeback was wonderful.

2 BARBARA THACHER—When Marianne Moore died, Bryn Mawr College raised a fund in her name for the study of poetry. The endeavor was part of Bryn Mawr's Tenth Decade Campaign, of which I was chairman. Elizabeth Bishop was exceptionally nice about joining and helping work on the committee for the fund. She gave a talk at the Lincoln Center branch of the New York Public Library and another at the college. She included some delightful Moore reminiscences from an article she was writing at the time. She also served until her death as the Marianne Moore Consultant in Poetry to the Bryn Mawr Library.

I don't think this task was onerous. She came to the college once a year, looked over the poetry collection and made some notes on books of new poetry she thought we ought to have. She would spend a night or two at the President's House, which she liked doing because she liked sleeping in one of the brass beds M. Carey Thomas had brought back from India. It had all kinds of animals worked into the screen of the footboard.

Elizabeth liked Bryn Mawr and was grateful to the college for the Donnelley Award she had once received, which permitted her to take her important trip to Brazil. And Bryn Mawr was very pleased and proud to have her interest and attention. I remember asking Laurence Stapleton who she thought was the outstanding poet in the U.S. at that time, and she said Elizabeth Bishop, without a question.

3 HAROLD LEEDS—The last time we saw Elizabeth was in the summer of 1979.

WHEATON GALENTINE—We started out to take a one-week stay [in North Haven] and liked it so much. Elizabeth made us so welcome, we stayed two weeks.

LEEDS—Elizabeth felt very much at home in that house and loved the landscape. She was always up before anybody, six or before, and she liked to prepare breakfast for us. She liked that time alone.

GALENTINE—I was getting up rather early, and I would go downstairs and talk to Elizabeth. It's very interesting because she had a lot of scientific interests that one wouldn't exactly associate with a literary person. She was interested in astronomy and used to talk about space flight. Elizabeth knew a lot too. She knew facts. Elizabeth was also interested in the scientific side of plant growth, which is something that interests me, because I've done a lot of photography of plants. We would talk about how they grow and why.

LEEDS—Elizabeth complained a little bit about not getting enough work done that summer. We would go for walks. Wheaton and I went swimming briefly every day. It was too cold to swim. We got out quickly. We usually went out for an excursion in the afternoon.

GALENTINE—One day we went out through a forest and found chanterelle mushrooms.

LEEDS—Chanterelles that would be $35-a-pound in our local New York market.

4 In the fall of 1979 Bishop was involved in printing a broadside of "North Haven," illustrated by Kit Barker.

ILSE BARKER—In the autumn of 1979 Elizabeth wrote that someone in California, Herb Yellin, had been asking her for years to do a broadside. She now decided to agree to this if Kit would do a drawing for "North Haven." Kit loved the view of Mount Megunticook from the house on North Haven. He made many paintings and watercolors of it.

When it was printed, Kit liked the broadside, but he had meant the drawing to be in black ink. Elizabeth too was horrified when she saw the bright blue. She wrote that she had tried to match the blue of the drawing with a blue pen for her signature. She signed 156 copies fifteen days before she died.

5 Sally Fitzgerald talked with Bishop about Flannery O'Connor and retained some impressions of Bishop's attitude toward religion.

SALLY FITZGERALD—Elizabeth and I talked about Flannery O'Connor, and Elizabeth spoke highly of her, as a friend. *Mystery and Manners*, that little book of Flannery's essays and talks, had been published by 1970, when I first knew Elizabeth, but nothing had been done on the letters. These were not released [for editorial preparation] until 1974. I didn't even know that Elizabeth and Flannery had had this correspondence. When work on the letters was begun, Elizabeth very kindly gave me those she had. Later she wrote to me and said that she liked *The Habit of Being* very much.

I think Elizabeth understood that Flannery really believed. Elizabeth herself didn't know really very much about it [Catholicism]. She thought that a bottle she had sent Flannery [from Brazil], holding a wooden cross, a cock, a ladder, and a sign [INRI] was a crucifix. Flannery disabused her of this notion and told her that these were the instruments of the crucifixion but not a crucifix. Flannery was delighted with this gift. The objects inside—a bottle was evidently blown around these things—are very primitive. Elizabeth was fascinated by sacramentals, possibly because they were quaint. She didn't seem to have a strong interest in Christianity, or any particular religion, although in the last note she sent to me she said she was going out on the balcony to catch a glimpse of the Pope [who was visiting Boston]. She knew I was Catholic, and Robert [Fitzgerald] was Catholic, and Bill Alfred was Catholic, and she wondered about us all.

6 LLOYD SCHWARTZ—I was thrilled to be asked to read "Sonnet" at Elizabeth's memorial program. *The New Yorker* had kept the poem for over a year, and Elizabeth had been getting very impatient about its publication (she finished "Pink Dog" later, but it was published eight months before "Sonnet," apparently because it was ready just in time for Mardi Gras). In the flurry of preparation for the memorial, no one seemed to be able to locate a copy of "Sonnet." Alice asked me to call Howard Moss and have him dictate it to me. When the poem appeared posthumously a week later, one line was different. *The New Yorker* had "Caught—the bubble / in the spirit-level, / contrarily guided" instead of "a creature divided." The rest was exactly the same. It's not entirely clear where *The New Yorker* version came from, whether it represented an earlier or later version of the poem than the one Howard Moss read to me over the phone. Elizabeth doesn't seem to have shown the version *The New Yorker* printed to anyone beforehand, which was not her usual practice. When Alice, Frank, and I met with Robert Giroux to go over the contents of *The Complete Poems*, we all agreed that what Howard Moss had dictated to me was the superior version.

WILLIAM ALFRED, playwright, editor, and translator (of Old English and Middle English poetry), is a professor of English at Harvard University. His *Hogan's Ghost* was produced on Broadway in 1965, and its musical version, *Cry for Us All*, was produced in 1970. Interviewed on 8 December 1984 in Cambridge, Massachusetts.

LILLI CORREIA DE ARAÚJO lives in Ouro Prêto, Brazil, where she operates a hotel, Chico Rei. Interviewed May 1985 in Ouro Prêto.

JOHN ASHBERY is a translator and the author of poetry, plays, essays, and a novel. Among his many awards and honors are the Pulitzer Prize, the National Book Award, and the National Book Critics Circle Award, all in 1976 for his poetry collection *Self-Portrait in a Convex Mirror*. He received a MacArthur Fellowship in 1985 and is the Charles Stephenson Professor of Literature at Bard College. Interviewed on 25 April 1984 in New York City.

ILSE BARKER publishes her writing and translations under the pseudonym Kathrine Talbot. Among her translations are *When the Nightbird Cries* by Lilli Palmer (1989) and two books by Leonara Carrington (1988, 1989). *Return*, a novel, was published in 1959, and her poems and stories have been published in numerous magazines and anthologies. Interviewed on 9–11 June 1989 in Petworth, West Sussex, England.

MARGARET MANN BEMIS settled in New Hampshire with her husband to raise their two children after serving in the Women's Army Corps in World War II. Interviewed on 4 March 1989 in Marlborough, New Hampshire.

CELIA BERTIN has published books on a range of topics; her books include the biographies *Marie Bonaparte: A Life* (1982) and *Jean Renoir: A Life in Pictures* (1991). A study of women during the Nazi Occupation in World War II is forthcoming. She has recently been a visiting scholar at the Center for European Studies at Harvard University. Interviewed on 25 February 1989 in Epping, New Hampshire.

FRANK BIDART has published numerous articles and several books of poetry, among them *In the Western Night: Collected Poems, 1965–1990* (1990). He teaches at Wellesley College. Interviewed on 18 July 1985 in Cambridge, Massachusetts.

MARY-CLAIRE BLAIS was awarded the Prix France-Canada and the Prix Medicis of France for *Un*

Saison dans la Vie d'Emmanuel (*A Season in the Life of Emmanuel*), one of her novels. She has also published poetry, plays, and essays. She lives in Montreal. Interviewed on 1 July 1989 in Kingsbury, Quebec.

HAZEL BOWERS taught school in Nova Scotia for thirty-two years and was also school principal in Great Village and Londonderry. In the 1930s she and her husband bought the house owned by Elizabeth Bishop's grandparents in Great Village, Nova Scotia, where she still lives. Interviewed on 21 September 1985 in Great Village.

DOROTHEE BOWIE served for several years as assistant to the chairman of the English Department at the University of Washington, Seattle. Interviewed on 22 October 1985 in Seattle.

M. TAYLOR BOWIE, JR., a specialist in old and rare books, operates Bowie Company in Seattle. Interviewed on 22 October 1985 in Seattle.

STEVE BOYDEN was the director of the Audubon House in Key West, Florida. Interviewed on 17 March 1989 in Key West.

HILARY BRADT is a publisher (Bradt Publications) and travel writer. Interviewed on 6 June 1989 in Farnham Common, England.

ASHLEY BROWN, a professor of English at the University of South Carolina, has written and edited books on a number of modern poets, including Allen Tate, Wallace Stevens, and Elizabeth Bishop. *The Achievement of Wallace Stevens* was published in 1962 and *The Poetry Reviews of Allen Tate, 1924–1944* in 1983. Interviewed on 15 October 1988 in New York City.

BETTY BRUCE lives in Key West, where her family has lived for several generations; she was historian at the Key West Library for a number of years. Interviewed on 16 March 1989 in Key West.

MAJORIE EDWARDS BRUSH currently lives in San Francisco. Interviewed on 17 October 1985 in San Francisco.

HENRY CARLILE, who has won a number of awards for his writing, is a professor of English at Portland State University. His poems, stories, and reviews have been widely published; his latest collection of poems is *Rain* (1993). Interviewed on 27 January 1991 by telephone from Portland, Oregon.

REGINA CÉLIA COLÔNIA, a fiction writer who has received many literary prizes in Brazil, is also a journalist, a poet, and a photographer. She has published a book of poems *Sumaimana* (second ed., 1984) and three collections of stories: *Canção para o Totem* (1977), *Sob o Pé de Damasco, sob a Chuva* (1984) and *Os Leõs de Luziãna* (1985). Her works have been translated into a number of foreign languages. Regina Colônia has served as acting consul general and head of the Brazilian Trade Bureau of the Brazilian State Department in Atlanta, as well as serving on other missions to Europe and Africa. She received an M.S. from the Georgia Institute of Technology, where she is currently completing her Ph.D. in experimental psychology. She is also a vice-president for research and development at Modus OSI Technologies, in Boca Raton, Florida. Interviewed on 19 March 1989 in Smyrna, Georgia.

JOANNA DOS SANTOS DA COSTA worked for Lota de Macedo Soares and Elizabeth Bishop in Rio de Janeiro and Petrópolis. Interviewed in May 1985 in Rio de Janeiro.

CAROL CROTTY has lived and traveled extensively in Brazil. Interviewed on 30 August 1988 in Farmington, Connecticut.

CARLEY DAWSON spent her professional life starting and running stores for her mother's perfume business, Mary Chess, in London (where she lived for twenty years), New York, and Washington, D.C. She is currently writing in Santa Fe, New Mexico. Interviewed on 27 December 1990 in New Lebanon, New York.

PAULA DEITZ, coeditor of The Hudson Review, is a freelance writer and critic whose work has appeared in numerous publications. Interviewed on 16 February 1989 in New York City.

JOAN COLLINGWOOD DISNEY has pursued a lifelong love of literature through reading, teaching, and her own private writing. Interviewed on 8 October 1988 in Lynn, Massachusetts.

ROBERT DUNCAN, an editor and poet, was largely responsible for establishing San Francisco as a center for contemporary American poetry. Among his numerous books, poems, and plays are Fictive Certainties: Five Essays in Essential Autobiography (1979) and Ground Work: Before the War (1984). He was the first recipient of the National Poetry Award, in 1985, in recognition of his lifetime contribution to the art of poetry. Robert Duncan died in 1988. Interviewed on 15 October 1985 in San Francisco.

PEGGY ELLSBERG has a Ph.D. from Harvard in church history, has taught in the English departments at Harvard and Vassar, and currently teaches in the English department at Barnard. Her poems, articles, reviews, and essays have been widely published; she is the author of Created to Praise: The Language of Gerard Manley Hopkins (1988). Interviewed on 9 February 1991 in Farmington, Connecticut.

MONROE ENGEL has written fiction, including Fish (1985) and Statutes of Limitations (1988), nonfiction, including The Maturity of Dickens (1959), and numerous articles, reviews, and stories. He was director of the Writing Program at Harvard University. Interviewed on 19 January 1991 in Cambridge, Massachusetts.

PENELOPE LAURANS FITZGERALD is associate dean of Yale College and a lecturer in English. She has edited The Third Kind of Knowledge, Memoirs and Selected Writings (1993) by Robert Fitzgerald. Interviewed on 6 November 1984 in Hamden, Connecticut.

ROBERT FITZGERALD, Boylston Professor of Rhetoric and Oratory at Harvard University, wrote four volumes of poetry and translated The Odyssey (1961 Bollingen Award for the best translation of a poem into English), The Illiad (1974), The Aeneid (1984), and Greek drama (some with Dudley Fitts). Among his numerous other works are edited editions of the prose and poetry of James Agee and a posthumous collection of his own memoirs and essays. Robert Fitzgerald died in 1985. Interviewed on 6 November 1984 in Hamden, Connecticut.

SALLY FITZGERALD coedited Mystery and Manners, Occasional Prose by Flannery O'Connor (1969), edited The Habit of Being: Letters of Flannery O'Connor (1979), and is writing a biography of O'Connor. Interviewed on 19 January 1991 in Cambridge, Massachusetts.

ROBERT FIZDALE AND ARTHUR GOLD, duo pianists famous for their recordings and their concerts throughout the world, also wrote biographies of Misia Sert and Sarah Bernhardt, and The Gold and Fizdale Cookbook. Arthur Gold died in 1990. Interviewed on 6 July 1984 in Water Mill, New York.

CASSILDA CHISHOLM FORBES lives in Great Village, Nova Scotia, on a family farm formerly operated by her husband. She taught school for twenty years throughout Nova Scotia and has raised three daughters who are also teachers. Interviewed on 23 September 1985 in Great Village.

A. L. FRANCIS lives in Fort Myers Beach, Florida, where, at one time, he worked for Louise Crane. Interviewed on 4 April 1985 in Fort Myers Beach.

JOSEPH FRANK is Professor of Comparative Literature Emeritus at Princeton University and Professor Emeritus of Slavic Literature at Stanford University. His numerous publications include literary studies and a multivolume biography of Dostoevsky in progress, the most recent volume of which is Dostoevsky: The Stir of Liberation, 1860–1865 (1990). Interviewed on 21 December 1988 in Princeton, New Jersey.

JOAN B. GAINES, daughter of the artist Eulabee Dix, worked for public relations companies in New York City and Washington, D.C. Interviewed on 25 October 1985 in Seattle.

JONATHAN GALASSI, an executive editor at Farrar, Straus & Giroux, has published Morning Run (1988), a volume of his poetry, and two volumes of translations of the work of Eugenio Montale. He served as poetry editor of the Paris Review for ten years. Interviewed on 27 February 1985 in Brooklyn, New York.

WHEATON GALENTINE is a documentary filmmaker. Interviewed on 18 October 1984 in New York City.

DANA GIOIA is a poet, translator, and critic. His recent work includes a book of poems, The Gods of Winter (1991); a translation of Mottetti by Eugenio Montale; and Can Poetry Matter? Essays on Poetry and American Culture (1992). Interviewed on 15 July 1992 in Hastings-on-Hudson, New York.

ROBERT GIROUX, chairman of the editorial board at Farrar, Straus & Giroux, has edited Elizabeth Bishop, The Collected Prose (1984) and One Art: Selected Letters of Elizabeth Bishop (1994), in addition to other works. Interviewed on 11 November 1990 and 18 December 1990 in New York City.

CLEMENT GREENBERG, a major critic of art and American culture since the 1940s, was an editor for the Partisan Review, an art critic for The Nation, and a book reviewer for the New York Times. Among his many publications are books on Joan Miro (1948), Matisse (1993), and Hans Hoffman (1961), and Art and Culture: Critical Essays (1961). His numerous essays and reviews have been published in Clement Greenberg: The Collected Essays and Criticism (4 volumes, 1986, 1993). Interviewed on 15 April 1989 in New York City. He died in 1994.

THOM GUNN has published several books of poetry, including The Passages of Joy (1982) and The Man with Night Sweats (1992). The Occasions of Poetry: Essays in Criticism and Autobiography was published in 1982. Among his many awards is a MacArthur Fellowship (1993). Interviewed on 16 October 1985 in San Francisco.

PAULINE HANSON was resident secretary of Yaddo, the writer's colony in Saratoga Springs. The title poem from her first collection, The Forever Young, was set for orchestra and voice by Herbert Elwell and performed by the Cleveland Symphony Orchestra; The Forever Young and Other Poems (1957) and Across Countries of Anywhere (1971) are her two other volumes of poetry. Interviewed on 25 September 1990 in Brookline, Massachusetts.

ROBERT HEILMAN was chairman of the English Department at the University of Washington in Seattle for twenty-three years. He has written nine books; The Ways of the World (1978) was awarded the Christian Gauss Award in 1979. Interviewed on 24 October 1985 in Seattle.

ELIZABETH SEAVER HELFMAN has written numerous books for children and young adults, among them Blissymbolics: Speaking Without Speech, about symbolic language that allows the handicapped to communicate without speech or writing and for which she won in 1981 the Golden Kite nonfiction award from the Society of Children's Book Writers. Her most recent book is On Being Sarah (1992). Interviewed on 19 December 1984 in Southbury, Connecticut.

JOHN HOLLANDER has most recently published Tesserae and Other Poems (1993) and Selected Poetry (1993), a collection from fourteen earlier books. Among his four volumes of criticism is Rhyme's Reason: A Guide to English Verse (1981). He is A. Bartlett Giamatti Professor of English at Yale University. Interviewed on 17 September 1984 in New Haven, Connecticut.

RICHARD HOWARD, poet, critic, and translator, has published several volumes of poetry, most recently Like Most Revelations (1992). His Untitled Subjects (1969) was awarded the Pulitzer Prize for poetry in 1970; his translation of Baudelaire's Les Fleurs du Mal won an American Book Award in 1984. Interviewed on 14 April 1985 in New York City.

ANNE HUSSEY has published poems in a number of magazines, including The Atlantic and The New Yorker. Her "Baddeck" and other Poems (1978) was nominated for the Pulitzer Prize. Interviewed on 2 October 1988 and 5 January 1989, in Farmington, Connecticut.

DAVID JACKSON has written short stories and newspaper articles. One story, "Pigeon Vole," was made into a film in 1972, and a travel narrative, "Mexico," was published in England in 1982. He shares residences in Key West, Florida, and Stonington, Connecticut, with the poet James Merrill. Interviewed on 5 May 1984 in Stonington, Connecticut.

EUNICE CLARK JESSUP wrote for Common Sense and Fortune and published poetry in a number of magazines, including Poetry and The Nation. She wrote Handbook of the War, about U.S. defense policy in 1939–40, and a book on the financing of the Swedish welfare state. She translated the Fables of La Fontaine into English verse for an edition illustrated by Alexander Calder (1948). Mrs. Jessup died in 1987. Interviewed on 25 October 1984 in Wilton, Connecticut.

DAVID KALSTONE was a professor of English at Rutgers University. Among his published works are Five Temperaments: Elizabeth Bishop, Robert Lowell, James Merrill, Adrienne Rich, and John Ashbery (1977) and Becoming a Poet: Elizabeth Bishop with Marianne Moore and Robert Lowell (1989). David Kalstone died in 1986. Interviewed on 9 October 1984 in New York City.

BARBARA CHESNEY KENNEDY has exhibited her paintings in several galleries in Tucson, Arizona, and her work is in the permanent collections of the University of Arizona Museum and the Tucson Art Museum. Interviewed on 12 October 1985 in Tucson.

JAMES LAUGHLIN, editor, short story writer, essayist, and poet, founded New Directions in 1936, which has published many important modern writers including Ezra Pound, William Carlos Williams, H.D., Vladimir Nabokov, Octavio Paz, Tennessee Williams, Delmore Schwartz, Thomas Merton, Kenneth Rexroth, Denise Levertov, and Gary Snyder. He has been presented numerous awards and honorary degrees, and in 1977 he received the American Academy and Institute of Arts and Letters Award for Distinguished Service to the Arts. Among his many works are the poetry collection The Bird of Endless Time (1989), Random Essays: Recollections of a Publisher (1989), and Random Stories (1990). Interviewed on 2 October 1984 in Norfolk, Connecticut.

ELSEE F. LAYTON, after graduating from Acadia College, taught and worked as a director of religious education at a number of churches, among them one in Willington, Connecticut, before returning to Great Village, Nova Scotia, her original home. Her father founded and operated the general store next to the Boomer homestead, and this store is currently operated by her nephew. Interviewed on 25 September 1985 in Great Village.

ROSINHA AND MAGU LEÃO live in Rio de Janeiro where their professional lives have included landscape architecture. Interviewed on 20 May 1985 in Rio de Janeiro.

HAROLD ELIOT LEEDS is an architect and retired teacher of design. Interviewed on 18 October 1984 in New York City.

BRAD LEITHAUSER has published his third novel, Seaward (1993), and his third volume of poems, The Mail from Anywhere (1990). His articles have been widely published, and among his many awards is a MacArthur Fellowship. He currently teaches at Mount Holyoke College. Interviewed on 23 April 1986 in Middletown, Connecticut.

ZILPHA LINKLETTER is director of Economic Development for Nova Scotia at the Department of Trade and Industry in Halifax. Interviewed on 3 February 1989 in Halifax.

GARY A. LUNDELL is an archivist at the University of Washington Libraries. When he met Elizabeth Bishop in 1966, he was a graduate student in anthropology and linguistics at the University of Washington. Interviewed on 23 October 1985 in Seattle.

BEATRICE LUSHINGTON, the widow of Theodore Roethke, married another gifted English teacher in 1972 and is now herself a retired teacher in the Old Town of Hastings, England, where she is trying to find time to write about life with Roethke. She is an amateur cook, gardener, and painter. Interviewed on 18 June 1989 in London.

MARY MCCARTHY, novelist, literary critic, essayist, and autobiographer, was one of America's prominent modern intellectuals. She received numerous awards and honorary degrees. Her novel The Group (1963) chronicled the life of several Vassar College friends for seven years following their graduation. Among her collections of essays are Ideas and the Novel (1980) and Occasional Prose (1985); she also translated the works of Simone Weill. Mary McCarthy died in 1989. Interviewed on 23 July 1985 in Castine, Maine.

SANDRA MCPHERSON is a widely published poet. Her book The Year of Our Birth (1978) was nominated for a National Book Award; her most recent book of poems is The God of Indeterminacy (1993). She teaches at the University of California at Davis. Interviewed on 17 October 1985 in Davis, California.

ROBERTO BURLE MARX, Brazil's preeminent landscape artist, designed gardens throughout the world. He died in 1994. Interviewed on 27 May 1985 in Rio de Janeiro.

WILLIAM H. MATCHETT was a professor of English at the University of Washington in Seattle. He has published two books of poetry—Fireweed (1980) is the more recent—articles and several other books, among them Poetry: From Statement to Meaning (with Jerome Beaty, 1965) and the Signet edition of Shakespeare's King John. Interviewed on 24 October 1985 in Seattle.

MARY MEIGS is an artist and writer whose paintings have been shown in New York City, the Boston area, and Montreal. She has published in numerous periodicals, and her books include The Medusa Head (1983) and In "The Company of Strangers" (1991). Interviewed on 1 July 1989 in Kingsbury, Quebec.

JAMES MERRILL is a poet, novelist, playwright, and nonfiction writer who has received numerous awards and honors. His Selected Poems was published in 1992, and his prose collection Recitative, in 1986. He has twice been awarded the National Book Award for his poetry (in 1967 for *Night and Days* and in 1979 for *Mirabell: Books of Number*); his *Divine Comedies* (1976) was awarded the Pulitzer Prize; and *The Changing Light at Sandover* (1982) won the National Book Critics Circle Prize. Interviewed on 10 May 1984 in Stonington, Connecticut.

AGNES MONGAN was curator of drawings, and for two years director, at the Fogg Art Museum at Harvard. Among her published works are *Drawings in the Fogg Art Museum* (1946), *Ingres. In Pursuit of Perfection: The Art of Jean-Auguste-Dominique Ingres* (1993), and *David to Corot: French Drawings in the Fogg Art Museum* (1991). Interviewed on 13 January 1989 in Cambridge, Massachusetts.

FREDERICK MORGAN founded *The Hudson Review* in 1947, which he coedits with his wife, Paula Deitz. He has published seven books of poems (most recently, *Poems: New and Selected*, 1987), two volumes of translations, and two collections of prose parables. His book of poems *A Book of Change* was nominated for the National Book Award in 1972. Interviewed on 16 February 1989 in New York City.

NANCY ORR MORRILL is a cousin of Elizabeth Bishop. She was active in a range of volunteer organizations, including serving as president of the Worcester Girls Club, and president of the Memorial Hospital Aid Society in Worcester. Her husband managed Morrill Lumber Company. Interviewed on 4 March 1989 in Worcester, Massachusetts.

MARY STEARNS MORSE followed a dancing career with an active life rearing children in Brazil. Interviewed on 18 May 1985 in Rio de Janeiro.

HOWARD MOSS was the poetry editor of *The New Yorker* for nearly forty years. He published numerous books of poetry, and *Selected Poems* (1971) was awarded the National Book Award. His other writings include critical work on Proust, plays, and a collection of criticism entitled *Writing against Time* (1969). He taught at several universities. Howard Moss died in 1987. Interviewed on 24 January 1985 in New York City.

HELEN MUCHNIC was a member of the Smith College faculty from 1930 to 1969, first in the Department of English, then in the Russian Department. Her publications include *An Introduction to Russian Literature* (rev. ed., 1964), *From Gorky to Pasternak* (1961), and *Russian Writers: Notes and Essays* (1971). Interviewed on 15 August 1988 in Cummington, Massachusetts.

FRANI BLOUGH MUSER worked as a musicologist at the New York Public Library and on individual projects of music research. She also held an editorial position with the magazine *Modern Music*. Interviewed on 7 August 1984 in Cornwall-on-Hudson, New York.

JOHN BERNARD MYERS, an art dealer and writer, was involved in many projects in the New York City art world, including editing *View* and managing the Tibor de Nagy Gallery, of which he was a partner, from 1951 to 1970. He presented and published the work of many well-known New York artists and poets. His writing included essays and articles for a number of publications and his own memoir, *Tracking the Marvelous* (1983). John Myers died in 1987. Interviewed on 9 July 1985 in New York City.

DONALDA MACLACHLAN NELSON spent her childhood in Great Village, Nova Scotia, to which she and her husband retired in 1978. She was a teacher and raised two sons; her husband held various administrative positions in education in Nova Scotia. Interviewed on 21 September 1985 in Great Village.

JOSE ALBERTO NEMER is an artist and teacher of art who has lived in Belo Horizonte and Ouro Prêto, Brazil. Interviewed on 24 May 1985 in Belo Horizonte, Brazil.

LINDA NEMER currently owns and occupies Casa Mariana, the house Elizabeth Bishop owned in Ouro Prêto. Interviewed on 24 May 1985 in Belo Horizonte, Brazil.

ELODIE OSBORN was director of circulating exhibitions at the Museum of Modern Art in New York City. Interviewed on 31 January 1985 in Salisbury, Connecticut.

ANGELO OSUALDO has worked as the director of the Patrimonio in Ouro Prêto, Brazil. Interviewed on 26 May 1985 in Belo Horizonte, Brazil.

CHESTER PAGE came to know Marianne Moore, Bryher, Elizabeth Bishop, and Djuna Barnes (about whom he has written) when he was a young pianist. He is an assistant to Louise Crane. Interviewed on 5 February 1986 in Brooklyn, New York.

G. ARTHUR PATRIQUIN lived and worked in Great Village, Nova Scotia, where he and his wife, Elizabeth, raised their two children. Interviewed on 21 September 1985.

STELLA PEREIRA lives in Rio de Janeiro. Interviewed on 18 May 1985 in Rio de Janeiro.

ROBERT PINSKY, who has written four books of poetry and three of criticism, teaches at Boston University. His most recent works are the poetry collection The Want Bone (1990) and the essay collection Poetry and the World (1968). Interviewed on 16 October 1985 in Berkeley, California.

KATHA POLLITT received the National Book Critics Circle Award for her book of poems Antarctic Traveller (1983). Her poems, reviews, and essays have been widely published. Interviewed on 9 September 1988 in New York City.

JERRY REICH was for several years head of the design department in the chemical plastics division of General Tire and Rubber. Interviewed on 25 February 1989 in Epping, New Hampshire.

ALASTAIR REID, poet, translator, essayist, and author of books for children, has been a staff writer for The New Yorker since 1959. He has taught at a number of colleges and universities and has translated the works of Borges, Neruda, and Vargas Llosa. A collection of his work, Weathering: Poems and Translations, was published in 1988. Interviewed on 24 October 1990 in New York City.

MAIA WOJCIECHOWSKA RODMAN is a poet, novelist, translator, and author of children's fiction. Among her numerous works are the novel The People in His Life (1980) and Shadow of a Bull (1964), for which she won the Newbery Medal. Interviewed on 23 July 1990 in Mahwah, New Jersey.

NED ROREM, composer, diarist, and essayist, has had his symphonies, instrumental pieces, operas, and songs performed by the major artists and conductors of his time. Among his many published writings are Settling the Score: Essays on Music (1988) and the most recent volume of his famous series of diaries, The Nantucket Diary of Ned Rorem, 1973–1985 (1987). Interviewed on 9 October 1984 in New York City.

CHARLES AND CHARLOTTE RUSSELL have worked and lived throughout their adult lives in and around Fort Myers Beach, Florida. Interviewed on 18 April 1985 in Fort Myers Beach.

JEAN RUSSELL was secretary to the president of Burlington Northern Railroad for many years. She was one of the first collectors to encourage painters of the Pacific Northwest. Interviewed on 25 October 1985 in Seattle, Washington.

KAY BISHOP ORR SARGENT raised two daughters and volunteered for various community and church organizations in Salem, Massachusetts, where her husband, Oliver, worked as a banker-lawyer for State Street Bank and Trust Company. Interviewed on 11 January 1989 in Salem, Massachusetts.

MARTHA WATSON SAUER, a watercolor painter, lives in Key West, Florida, with her attorney husband, Robert Sauer. They spend a great deal of time traveling to foreign countries, where she fills sketchbooks with pen-and-ink drawings from which she composes award-winning watercolor landscapes. Her paintings have been exhibited in Miami Beach, Mexico City, Key West, and Savannah, Georgia, and are in numerous private collections. Interviewed on 16 March 1989 in Key West, Florida.

LLOYD SCHWARTZ has published two books of poetry, most recently *Goodnight, Gracie* (1992), written articles on Elizabeth Bishop, and coedited *Elizabeth Bishop and her Art* (1983). He is a professor of English and codirector of the Creative Writing Program at the University of Massachusetts, Boston. His comments on and reviews of classical music can be read in the *Boston Phoenix* and heard on National Public Radio's "Fresh Air." He received a Pulitzer Prize for criticism in 1994. Interviewed on 20 September 1984 in Somerville, Massachusetts.

ROBERT B. SHAW, a professor of English at Mount Holyoke College, has written a critical work on John Donne and George Herbert and three books of poems, including *The Wonder of Seeing Double* (1988) and *American Studies* (1994). His reviews and essays are widely published in journals. Interviewed on 20 December 1990 in South Hadley, Massachusetts.

RHODA WHEELER SHEEHAN lives an active life that includes community responsibilities in Adamsville, Rhode Island. She taught German, English-as-a-second-language, and American literature, among other subjects, for many years at Bristol Community College in Fall River, Massachusetts. Interviewed on 4 December 1985 in Adamsville, Rhode Island.

JANE SHORE has published her poetry widely, and her second book, *The Minute Hand* (1987), was the 1986 Lamont Poetry Selection of the Academy of American Poets. She teaches at George Washington University. Interviewed on 8 September 1988 in North Bergen, New Jersey.

GRETCHEN KEENE SMITH has lived in a number of cities in the United States, most recently Seattle, Washington, where she and her husband raised two children. Interviewed on 22 October 1985 in Seattle.

DONALD STANFORD is a poet, critic, editor, Alumni Professor Emeritus at Louisiana State University, and founder of the *Southern Review*, which he edited from 1963 to 1983. He has contributed to numerous periodicals and edited two volumes of the *Dictionary of Literary Biography*. *Cartesian Lawnmower & Other Poems* (1984), *Revolution and Convention in Modern Poetry* (1983), and his edition of *The Selected Letters of Robert Bridges* (1983) are among his numerous published works. Interviewed on 18 November 1984 by telephone from Baton Rouge, Louisiana.

ANNE STEVENSON is a poet and critic who has taught at a number of universities, most recently in England and Scotland. She has contributed to the *Times Literary Supplement* and other periodicals in Great Britain and the United States. Hers was the first published critical study of Elizabeth Bishop (1966). Among her numerous other publications are *Selected Poems, 1956–1986* (1987), *Bitter Fame: A Life of Sylvia Plath* (1989), and the poetry collection *The Other House* (1990). Interviewed on 17 June 1989 in Langley Park, Durham, England.

JULIA G. STRAND lives in Salt Lake City, Utah, with her family. Interviewed on 15 June 1985 in Salt Lake City.

MARK STRAND, poet, translator, and critic, has published several books of poems, including *Selected Poems* (1980); the 1992 combined reissue of his two early books of poems, *Reasons for Moving* (1968) and *Darker* (1970); and *Dark Harbor, A Poem* (1993). He has translated poems by Rafael Alberti and Carlos Drummond de Andrade, edited anthologies, and written books on art and photography (including *William Bailey* [1987]), children's books (including *Rembrandt Takes a Walk* [1986]), a collection of short stories, and numerous articles on painting and photography. He was awarded a MacArthur Fellowship in 1987 and was poet laureate of the United States in 1990. Interviewed on 15 June 1985 in Salt Lake City, Utah, and 14 February 1991 in New Haven, Connecticut.

JOSEPH SUMMERS is Roswell S. Burrows Professor Emeritus at the University of Rochester, where he has taught since 1969. Among his publications are *George Herbert—His Religion and Art* (1954), *The Muse's Method—An Introduction to "Paradise Lost"* (1962), and *Dreams of Love and Power: On Shakespeare's Plays* (1984). His most recent book is a collection of previously published and unpublished essays on Renaissance literature (1993). Interviewed on 23 February 1985 in Rochester, New York.

U. T. SUMMERS, a Vassar graduate, worked for Houghton Mifflin when Elizabeth Bishop's first book of poetry, *North & South*, was published. U. T. and Joseph Summers raised a family in various academic settings. She taught for sixteen years at the Rochester Institute of Technology and wrote more than fifty columns for a Rochester newspaper. Her name was her father's creation, prompted by her having been born at the University of Texas Hospital. Interviewed on 23 February 1985 in Rochester, New York.

PHYLLIS SUTHERLAND and her husband, Ernest, have been lifelong Nova Scotia residents. Ernest was the production manager of a woodworking plant, and Phyllis has raised their daughter, Miriam. Ernest Sutherland died in 1986. Interviewed on 23 September 1985 in Tatamagouche, Nova Scotia.

BARBARA THACHER is a trustee of Teachers College, Columbia University, and has served on a number of child welfare and education boards including New York's WNET (Channel 13), the New York City Board of Higher Education (CUNY), and as chairman of the Board of Bryn Mawr College, which awarded her its M. Carey Thomas Prize. She and her husband, Tom, have six children and seven grandchildren. Interviewed on 10 December 1988 in New Canaan, Connecticut.

THOMAS THACHER is a retired partner of a New York City law firm. He also served for five years as New York State Superintendent of Insurance. Interviewed on 10 December 1988 in New Canaan, Connecticut.

HARRIET TOMPKINS THOMAS has been a freelance writer and editor with Little, Brown in Boston and Fitzhenry and Whiteside in Canada. She has four children and eleven grandchildren. She lives in Toronto, where she writes occasional articles. Interviewed on 29 November 1984 in Toronto, Canada.

ROSALYN TURECK, noted concert artist, author, editor, and conductor, has lectured and taught at numerous educational institutions. She performs on various musical instruments, antique and modern, including the harpsichord, clavichord, fortepiano, contemporary piano, Moog Synthesizer, and pipe organ. She has won many honors and competitions, has made numerous recordings, and in the course of world tours has performed with the world's major orchestras. In 1958 she was the first woman invited to conduct the New York Philharmonic. Among her publications is *An Introduction to the Performance of Bach* (three volumes, 1960); she has also written books and articles, and edited musical texts. Interviewed on 13 April 1989 in New York City.

SHIRLEY CLARKE VAN CLEEF was in public relations at Children's Hospital Medical Center in Boston and raised a family of three children. She writes poetry. Interviewed on 12 October 1985 in Tucson, Arizona.

HELEN VENDLER is A. Kingsley Porter University Professor at Harvard University and the author of several books on poetry, including *On Extended Wings: Wallace Stevens' Longer Poems* (1969) and *The Odes of John Keats* (1983). Many of her essays have been published in collected editions, the most recent of which is *The Music of What Happens* (1988). She has been elected and appointed to prominent professional positions and awarded many honorary degrees and academic distinctions. She is poetry critic for *The New Yorker*. Interviewed on 26 September 1990 in Cambridge, Massachusetts.

MARY ST. JOHN VILLARD taught drama at independent schools and worked for the James Weldon Johnson Community Center and the Public Education Association. She also had a long association with Vassar College as alumnae director, alumnae president, alumnae trustee, and chairman of the board of trustees. She died in 1986. Interviewed on 6 November 1984 in New York City.

ELEANOR CLARK WARREN is the author of novels, nonfiction books, stories, essays, and reviews. *Camping Out*, a novel, was published in 1986, and the nonfiction work *Rome and a Villa*, first published in 1952, was expanded and reissued in 1971. She published *A Memoir* in 1977. Interviewed on 20 November 1984 in Fairfield, Connecticut.

WESLEY WEHR is an affiliate curator of paleobotany at the Thomas Burke Memorial State Museum in Seattle. His paintings have been exhibited in New York, San Francisco, Switzerland, and Germany. Although paleobotany is his major field of research and publication, Wehr has also published his own poetry and articles on Elizabeth Bishop. Interviewed on 22 October 1985 in Seattle.

DAVID WEIMER was a professor of English and American literature for forty years at Rutgers University and elsewhere. He is now enjoying retirement as a traveler, chess player, and author of a nearly completed novel entitled *The Sicilian Hoard*. Interviewed on 12 June 1989 in London, England.

MONROE WHEELER, who in his early professional life was a book designer and printer-publisher, was involved in a number of projects and held several positions at the Museum of Modern Art, including director of the membership department, director of publications, and director of exhibitions. Interviewed on 4 February 1986 in New York City.

CHARLOTTE WARD WILBUR divides her time between Key West, Florida, and Cummington, Massachusetts. Interviewed on 11 October 1984 in Cummington, Massachusetts.

RICHARD WILBUR has received many awards and honors for his poetry and translations, among them the 1957 Pulitzer Prize and National Book Award for his poetry collection *Things of This World*, the 1963 Bollingen Prize (corecipient) for his translation of *Tartuffe*, and the 1989 Pulitzer Prize for *New and Collected Poems*. His translations of Moliere and Racine have been widely produced in the English-speaking world. He has taught at several colleges and universities and was appointed second poet laureate of the United States from 1987 to 1988. Interviewed on 11 October 1984 in Cummington, Massachusetts.

Academy of American Poets, 190
Acadia University, Wolfville, Nova Scotia, 7
Adams, Leonie, 62, 114
Agee, James, 337
Alcoholism, EB's struggles with
  Bidart's comments on, 272–73
  Brazil and, 145–47, 180, 225, 227, 258,
    266–67, 370n6
  EB's father and, 358n3
  EB's Uncle Art and, 10
  Key West and, 111–13
  Lota's concern about EB and, 145–47,
    150–51, 192, 223
  Moore's concerns about EB and, 96
  New York and, 118–19
  San Francisco and, 247, 252
  Seattle and, 202–3, 220
  Washington, D.C., and, 109–10, 114,
    117
  Yaddo and, 121–24
Alfred, William, 239, 249, 286, 303
  recollections of, 269–70, 275, 285, 305,
    309, 366n2
Allen, Ross, 71–72
Almyda, Mrs. (Key West housekeeper), 73,
  77, 85, 92
Alves, Manuelzinho (Brazilian servant),
  140–41, 156, 184
Amazon River trip, 164–66
American Academy and Institute of Arts and
  Letters, 336

Ames, Elizabeth, 121–22, 124
Amy Lowell Travelling Fellowship, 149–50,
  285–86
Anderson, Guy, 368n2
Anemia, 340, 344
Araújo, Lilli, 197–98, 200, 235, 254–55,
  368n1, 373n15
Archera, Laura, 164
Arendt, Hannah, 152
Armstrong, Phyllis, 114
Ashbery, John, 155
  recollections of, 337–38
Asthma
  in Brazil, 142, 178, 225
  in Cambridge, 188–89, 281, 286, 292,
    345
  in EB's childhood, 15–17
  in Europe, 67, 69–70
  in Key West, 74
  in New York, 61–62, 99
  in Ouro Prêto, 292, 374n16
  in Seattle, 201, 215
  at Yaddo, 123
The Atlantic, 100
Auden, W. H., 109, 191, 381n1

Bacon, Julia G., 55
Bahia, Salvador, 197–99
Bandeira, Manuel, 142, 145, 147
Bard Poetry Conference (1948), 103–8

Barker, Ilse
  recollections of, 122–24, 186–87, 224,
    316, 341, 343–44, 347, 382n4
  Yaddo and, 119, 122
Barker, Kit, 186, 223–24, 343, 382n4
  Yaddo and, 119–20, 122–23, 139
Baumann, Anny, 129, 161, 167, 228, 335,
    340, 380n11
  EB's alcoholism and, 124–25
  EB's letters to, xi
  Lota's death and, 231, 234, 236
  qualities of, 96–97
Baumgarten, Bernice, 149, 153
Beach, Sylvia, 65
Bemis, Margaret Mann, recollections of, 20–
    21, 26, 30
Bernardes, Sergio, 131, 139, 196
Berryman, John, 244, 324
Bertin, Celia, recollections of, 319–20,
    343–44
Bidart, Frank, 3, 286, 316–19, 335, 373n15
  EB's death and, 349–51
  recollections of, 128, 140–41, 149, 270–
    73, 290–91, 379n7
    on EB's drinking, 272–73
    EB's feminism and, 327
    on EB's mother, 5
    on EB's output, 339–40
    on EB's relationship with Lowell, 271–
      72
    on EB's relationship with Methfessel,
      272–73, 332–33, 336
    on EB's relationship with Miller, 70
    on Lota, 128
    on meeting EB, 270–73
    on "One Art," 332–33
    on Robert Seaver's death, 68
Bishop, Elizabeth
  academic world and, 294–95
  art and, 7, 16, 118, 123
  childhood of, 1–19, 28
    birth of, 2–3
    death of playmate and, 11–12
    father's death, 3
    under guardianship of Uncle Jack, 18–
      19
    with maternal grandparents in Great
      Village, 5–12

  mother's mental illness, 3–5
  with paternal grandparents in Wor-
    chester, Mass., 12–16
  with Shepherdsons in Revere, Mass.,
    16–18
curiosity of, 346, 375n21
death of, 260, 349–52
depression and, 28, 85, 125–26, 145,
    330–36
education of, 8–9, 62
  Vassar College and, 36–59, 362n18
  Walnut Hill School and, 20–35
idea of beauty of, 355–56
interest in fishing, 9, 72
languages and, 179, 194–95
loneliness of, 96, 178–80, 308, 333
memorization and, 311
over-sensitivity of, 370n6, 371n1
personal style of, 136
posthumous reputation of, 351, 353
privacy of, xi, xiv, 74–75, 116, 189, 272,
    309, 316, 328–29, 333, 379n7
self-assurance of, 28, 179
self-doubt and, xii, 96, 201–2, 205–6
sense of her own difference, 28–29
sense of homelessness, 354
struggle between strength and weakness,
    xi–xii, 12, 342–43
suicidal tendencies of, 126, 252–53,
    333–34
taste of, 22–23, 92–94, 248, 321–24
uncompleted commissions and, 273–76
wit of, 28, 75, 116, 156–57, 178, 248,
    276–77, 342
Works
  "Americanism," 17
  An Anthology of Twentieth-Century Brazilian
    Poetry (translation), 240, 300
  Aristophanes' The Birds (translation),
    55, 57
  "The Armadillo," 108, 293
  "Arrival at Santos," 193
  article on Marianne Moore, 316
  "At the Fishhouses," 339–40, 353–55
  "The Ballad of the Burglar of Babylon,"
    194, 246
  "The Baptism," 11
  "The Bight," 354

"Brazil, January 1, 1502," 164
"Casabianca," 80, 159
"The Colder the Air," 80
The Complete Poems, 1927–1979, 56
The Complete Poems of Elizabeth Bishop (1969 edition), 242–43, 263–64
"Conversation," 159
"The Country Mouse," 12, 14–15
"Crusoe in England," 265, 333, 354, 377n23
"Dear, my compass / still points north," 373n15
The Diary of "Helena Morley" (translation), 147–48, 153–54, 184
"Dimensions for a Novel," 56
"Efforts of Affection: A Memoir of Marianne Moore," 372n9
"Elsewhere," 356
"The End of March," 290
"Faustina," 291
"Filling Station," 154, 160, 355
"The Fish," 248, 378n3
"Five Flights Up," 316
"The Flood," 51
"Florida," 71–72, 353
gallery note for Wesley Wehr, 369n1
"The Gentleman of Shalot," 80
Geography III, 245, 290, 339–40, 353–54
"Gerard Manley Hopkins: Notes on Timing in His Poetry," 363n33
"Gwendolyn," 11, 142
"House Guest," 179
"Hymn to the Virgin," 56
"In Prison," 72
"Insomnia," 159
"In the Village," 22, 142, 147, 242
"In the Waiting Room," 15, 35, 353–54, 356, 377n23
"Jerónimo's House," 72
"Large Bad Picture," 7
"Letter to New York," 159, 208
"The Man-Moth," 65, 353
"Manuelzinho," 134, 140–41, 208, 326
"Memories of Uncle Neddy," 9–10, 322, 372n9
"A Miracle for Breakfast," 121, 337

Modern Architecture in Brazil (translation), 148
"The Moose," 99, 245, 289–91, 377n21
"The Mountain," 159
"Mrs. Sullivan Downstairs" (unfinished story), 16
"North Haven," 344, 382n4
North & South, 81, 98–101, 149, 318–19, 337
"One Art," 332–33, 377n23
"Over 2,000 Illustrations and a Complete Concordance," 108, 337
"Paris, 7 A.M.," 64
parody of Yeats's "A Prayer for My Daughter" (uncompleted), 140
"Pink Dog," 141, 354, 382n6
"Poem," 7, 290, 322
poem about Vassar toilets, 43
Poems: North & South—A Cold Spring, 98, 149, 159, 193
printed in Walnut Hill yearbook, 19
"The Prodigal," 123–24, 344
Questions of Travel, 154, 160, 190, 192–93, 322, 339, 356
"The Riverman," 141, 164
"Roosters," 117
"The Sandpiper," 208
"Santarem," 290
"Sestina," 380n10
"The Shampoo," 141–42, 147, 193, 351
"Songs for a Colored Singer," 98, 158–59, 328
"Sonnet," 352, 355–56, 382n6
"Thank-You Note," 324
"Then Came the Poor," 50–51, 56
"Three Sonnets for Eyes," 52
Time-Life book on Brazil, 172–73
"Times' Andromedas," 363n35
"Trouvée," 227–28
"Under the Window in Ouro Prêto," 195, 368n1
"The USA School of Writing," 61
"Visits to St. Elizabeths," 115, 159–60, 263–64, 299
"The Weed," 354, 356
"While Someone Telephones," 120

Bishop, Florence (EB's aunt), 13–15, 23, 31–32, 161, 357n1
Bishop, Gertrude May Boomer (EB's mother), 2–5, 100
  death of, 58–59
  mental illness of, 3–5
Bishop, John Warren (EB's "Uncle Jack"), 13–14, 17–19
  EB's years at Walnut Hill School and, 20–21, 23, 29–30
Bishop, John William, Sr. (EB's grandfather), 2, 12–14
Bishop, Marion (EB's aunt), 13
Bishop, Ruby (EB's aunt), 18–19, 21, 23, 31
Bishop, Sarah A. Foster (EB's grandmother), 13–14, 357n1
Bishop, William Thomas (EB's father), 2–3
Blais, Barie-Claire, 86
  recollections of, 337, 371n1
Bloom, Harold, 376
Bloom, Hyman, 104
Bloomfield, Morton, 268
Blough, Frani. See Muser, Frani Blough
Blue Pencil (Walnut Hill School literary magazine), 33
Bly, Robert, 189, 208
Blythwood clinic, Greenwich, Conn., 113
Bogan, Louise, 100, 105, 161
Books Abroad / Neustadt International Prize for Literature, 335–38
Boomer, Arthur (EB's "Uncle Neddy"), 9–10
Boomer, Elizabeth Hutchinson (EB's grandmother), 3, 5–7, 10–11
Boomer, Grace (EB's aunt). See Bowers, Grace Boomer
Boomer, Mabel Pigott (EB's "Aunt Hat"), 10
Boomer, Mary (EB's aunt), 6–8, 17, 245
Boomer, Maud (EB's aunt). See Shepherdson, Maud Boomer
Boomer, William Brown (EB's grandfather), 5–6
Borden, Fannie, 57
Boston. See Cambridge, Mass.; Harvard University; Lewis Wharf, Boston
Boston Public Library, poetry reading at, 380n10

Botsford, Keith, 175
Bowen, Suzanne [pseud.]
  in Brazil with EB, 254–59, 263–65
  difficulties between EB and, 256–57, 263–66
  EB in Cambridge and, 273
  EB's Brazialian will and, 226
  EB's life with, in San Francisco, 238–41, 243–44, 246–53
  EB's Seattle relationship with, 205–6, 219–21, 369n2
  Lota's death and, 232, 237
  New York trip with EB, 245–46
Bowers, Grace Boomer (EB's aunt), 2, 4, 7, 99, 346–47
  EB's childhood and, 16–17
  poem by, 359n26
Bowie, Dorothee, 215, 221
  recollections of, 5, 202–3, 218, 378n3
Bowie, M. Taylor, recollections of, 218, 378n3
Bowles, Paul, 249
Bowplate (freighter), 126–27
Boyden, Steve, recollections of, 79, 99
Bradt, Hilary, recollections of, 233, 240–42, 250–53, 257, 264–65, 283–84
Branco, Castelo, 193
Brant, Mrs. ("Helena Morley"), 147–48
Brasil, Emanuel, 230, 242, 335
Brasilia, 163–64, 183
Brazeau, Peter, xi, xii–xiii
Brazil, 127–200, 222–37, 254–68. See also de Macedo Soares, Lota; Ouro Prêto, Brazil; Petrópolis
  EB's anecdotes about, 335
  EB's arrival in, 127–28
  EB's July 1966 return to, 222
  EB's literary output in, 142, 145, 147–50, 157, 163, 226
  EB's National Book Award and, 263–64
  Flamingo Park in, 168–69, 178, 190–92, 194–97
  life at Samambaia and, 138–41
  Lota's friends in, 142–45, 171–72, 194–95, 234–37, 255, 259
  Lota's sickness and, 222–26
  Lowell's visit to, 175–76
  military coup in, 184–86

music in, 191, 266
Order of Rio Branco award and, 282
politics in, 129, 167, 172, 183–86
renovation of Rio apartment and, 173–74
response to Lota's death in, 234–35, 253, 255
social class and, 179–80
Time-Life book on, 172–73
travel in, 164–66, 197–99
Breen, Miss (shipmate on *Bowplate*), 126
Brevard, N.C., 89–90
Bright's disease, and EB's father, 3, 358n3
Brinnin, John, 300, 309, 319, 348
Brodsky, Joseph, 331
Brooks, Cleanth, 189
Brooks, Gwendolyn, 315
Brown, Ashley, 229–30
    recollections of, 142, 190–93, 197–202, 257–58, 284–85
Brown, Rosellen, 350
Brown University, honorary degree from, 289
Bruce, Betty, recollections of, 75–78, 84, 88–89, 365n11
Brush, Majorie, recollections of, 115, 369n2
Bryn Mawr College, 345, 381n2
    Lucy Martin Connelly Fellowship, 125, 128–29

Cal. *See* Lowell, Robert
Calder, Alexander ("Sandy"), 135, 177
Cambridge, Mass., 269–321. *See also* Harvard University
    Brattle Street apartment in, 282, 285
    EB's first months in, 269–73
    friendships and, 282–84, 298–99
    illness with asthma in, 286, 289
    Kirkland House in, 269–71
    memorial service for EB in, 351–352
    professional obligations and, 273–77
    teaching at Harvard and, 277–82
Camp Chequesset, Wellfleet, Mass., 18
Cape Breton Island, Canada, 2
Cape Cod, 43–44
Carlile, Henry, recollections of, 207–9, 215–16, 220–21, 306–7
Carter, Elliot, *A Mirror on Which to Dwell*, 336
Casa de Reposuo, 225

Chapelbrook Foundation grant, 166, 186
Chesney, Barbara. *See* Kennedy, Barbara Chesney
Chestnut, Anny Laurie, 85
Chico Rei (hotel), 197–98
Children, EB's appreciation of, 152, 187–88, 253, 256, 306
Clark, Eleanor. *See* Warren, Eleanor Clark
Clark, Eunice. *See* Jessup, Eunice Clark
Clarke, Shirley. *See* Van Cleef, Shirley Clarke
Cleaver, Eldridge, 251
Cleaver, Kathleen, 251–52
Cocteau, Jean, 160
Coe, John (EB's uncle), 359n19
Coe, Priscilla (EB's cousin), 32
Colônia, Regina Célia, recollections of, 261–63, 372n11
Columbia University, 62
Con Spirito, 50–52
Cootchie (Key West character), 72–73
Copland, Aaron, 155–56
Cozzens, Mrs. James Gould. *See* Baumgarten, Bernice
Crane, Louise, 132, 135, 328, 330, 352
    with EB in 1930s, 64–87 *passim*
    EB's breakup with, 85–87
    EB's career and, 62
    Margaret Miller and, 68–70
    at Vassar, 41–43
Crane, Mrs. W. Murray, 42, 64, 86
Cromer, Robert, 264
Crotty, Carol, recollections of, 378n6
Cummings, E. E., 94, 153, 172
Cummings, Mrs. E. E., 161
Cutting, George H., 357n1
Cuttyhunk Island, 47, 60, 67

Dalousie University, Halifax, Nova Scotia, 345
Daniels, Miss (teacher at Walnut Hill School), 24
Dartmouth College, 316
Darwin, Charles, 190
Davis, Ellabelle, 83, 85–86
Davis, Phil, 55
Dawson, Carley, recollections of, 101–3, 109–10, 114
de Chambrun, Countess, 64–65

Deitz, Paula, 338
  recollections of, 322
Delaney, Beauford, 120, 122
de Moraes, Vinicius, 175, 237, 328
DesBrisay, Ella, 99–100
de Sousa, Decio, 225–27, 230, 233, 237
Dewey, Jane, 77–79, 117–18, 161, 229,
  282
Dewey, John, 77–79, 91, 98
Disney, Joan Collingwood, recollections of,
  27–28
Dos Passos, John, 163–64, 178
dos Santos da Costa, Joanna, recollections of,
  141, 169–71, 200, 222–24, 227,
  235
Douarnanez, France, 63–64
Duncan, Robert, 244, 250
  recollections of, 248–49

Eaton, Bertram Knight, 7
Eberhart, Richard, 101, 105
Eczema, 15, 18–19
Eliot, T. S., 51, 109, 172, 192, 325
Elitism, 179–80, 326
Ellsberg, Peggy, recollections of, 280–82,
  322–24, 347–48
Engel, Monroe, 303, 325
  recollections of, 292–93, 295, 329,
  380n10
England, 186–90, 223–24
Europe, trips to, 62–70, 186–90, 292
Evett, Bob, 122–23

Farrar, Straus, and Cudahy, 149, 153–54
Farwell, Harriet, 28–31
Feminism, EB's view of, 327, 329–30
Ferrin, John, 75
Ferry, David, 350
Fisher, Nate, 9
Fitts, Dudley, 56
Fitzgerald, Penelope Laurans, recollections
  of, 295, 301–3, 329–32, 375n21
Fitzgerald, Robert, 1, 279, 296, 299
  recollections of, 301–3, 331, 365n12,
  377n23
Fitzgerald, Sally, recollections of, 382n

Fizdale, Robert, 150, 158, 161
  recollections of
    on EB's prominence, 155–56
    on Kathleen Cleaver interview, 251–52
    on Lota, 135–36, 138, 233–34
    on Marianne Moore, 137
    on visit to Ouro Prêto, 255–56
Flamingo Park, 168–69, 178, 190–92,
  194–97, 229
Flanagan, Bill, 159
Flanagan, Hallie, 48, 54, 362n18
Flanner, Janet, 320
Florida, 1974 trip to, 330, 332–34, 378n6.
  See also Key West, Fla.
Forbes, Cassilda Chisholm, recollections of,
  8
Ford, Harry, 154
Foster, Dr. (EB's psychiatrist), 124
Foster, Sarah A. (EB's grandmother). See
  Bishop, Sarah A. Foster
Fowlie, Wallace, 121
Francis, A. L., recollections of, 334
Frank, Joseph, 129, 176
  recollections of, 115–17
Frankenberg, Lloyd, 77, 93–94, 100, 117,
  125, 161, 282
  Bard Poetry Conference and, 103, 105–6
Frankenbergs. See Frankenberg, Lloyd; Mac-
  Iver, Loren
Fraser, Kathleen, 287
Friendships
  aging of friends and, 282
  aid from friends and, 1–2, 62
  in Cambridge, 282–84, 298–99
  in EB's childhood, 14, 18–19
  EB's gifts and, 22–23, 28, 95, 109, 267,
    270, 306, 318–19
  EB's thoughtfulness and, 270, 379n6
  in San Francisco, 243–44, 247–50
  at Vassar, 36–38, 40–44
  at Walnut Hill School, 20–23
Frost, Robert, 114, 119, 291
Frye, Northrop, 299

Galapagos Islands, 284
Galassi, Jonathan, 282
  recollections of, 277–78, 342

Galentine, Wheaton, recollections of, 41, 96–97, 228, 231, 381n3
Gay rights movement, EB's view of, 327–29
Gide, André, 65
Gilkey, Richard, 205
Gioia, Dana, recollections of, 295–300
Giroux, Robert, 81, 149, 161, 172, 192, 263–64
  publishing relationship with EB, 153–55, 242–43, 339
  recollections of, 153–55, 242
Gold, Arthur, 150, 158, 161
  recollections of, 135–38, 155–57, 233–34
Goodman, Mitch, 250
Gotham Book Mart party, 109
Goulart, João, 172, 185
Goyen, William, 122
Graves, Morris, 205
Great Village, Nova Scotia, 99, 316
  EB's childhood in, 3, 5–12, 16
Greenberg, Clement, recollections of, 92–93
Greenslet, Ferris, 100
Greenwich Village, 227–28
Gregory, Horace, 62
Guggenheim Fellowship, 100, 345
Guggenheim Museum, 190, 253
Gunn, Thom, 247, 249
  recollections of, 243–45, 249–50

Haieff, Alexi, 119, 161
Haiti, travels in, 110–11
Hall, Donald, 187–89
Halpin, Evelyn Huntington, 43
Hanson, Pauline
  The Forever Young, 119, 121
  recollections of, 119–22, 150–51
Hardwick, Elizabeth, 175, 244, 309, 376
Harrison, Jim, xi
Harvard University
  EB's attitude toward, 301–3
  EB's first teaching position at, 1, 267–68, 277–82
  EB's permanent appointment at, 294–95, 302–5
  EB's retirement from, 340

  EB's teaching at, 277–83, 287–88, 292–94, 301, 311–13
  faculty skepticism about EB at, 295–96, 301
  Fogg Art Museum at, 143–44
  1968 poetry reading at, 249, 268
  Phi Beta Kappa poem at, 289–91
  treatment of writers at, 302–5
Hatfield, Ann, 174
Hecht, Tony, 380n1
Heilman, Robert, 199, 202, 216
  recollections of, 217–18
Heiss, Cordie, 89–90
Helfman, Elizabeth Seaver, recollections of, 45–47, 68
Hemingway, Ernest, 76–77, 104, 365n12
Hemingway, Pauline, 77–78, 89, 96, 104, 110, 113, 365n12
Henry, DeWitt, 350
Holiday, Billy, 43, 75, 84, 86, 104, 328
Hollander, John, recollections of, 305–6
Honorary degrees, 245–46, 289, 345, 373n14
Houghton Mifflin, 81, 97–100, 103, 108, 148–49, 153
  Poetry Prize Fellowship, 98, 103
Hound and Horn, 55–56
Howard, Richard, recollections of, 276–77, 330
Humboldt Gallery, 369n1
Humphries, Rolfe, 215, 217–18
Hunt, Barbara, 16
Huntington, Evelyn. See Halpin, Evelyn Huntington
Hussey, Anne, 351
  recollections of, 276, 293–94, 310–14, 346, 372n13
Hutchinson, Elizabeth (EB's grandmother). See Boomer, Elizabeth Hutchinson
Hutchinson, George (EB's uncle), 7
Hutchinson, John (EB's uncle), 7
Hutchinson, William (EB's uncle), 7
Huxley, Aldous, 139, 163–64, 178

Illness. See also Alcoholism, EB's struggles with; Asthma; Mental illness
  in EB's childhood, 15–19
  EB's concerns about, 342–43, 346–48

Inacio, Jair Afonso, 198
Ingram Merrill Foundation award, 253
Innes-Taylor, Lloyd, 89
Ishii, David, 378n3
Italy, 70, 186

Jackson, David, recollections of, 166, 379n7
Jarrell, Randall, 100, 181, 190–91, 298
Jazz, 75, 83–84
Jessup, Eunice Clark, 48–53
   recollections of, 49, 51, 362n24
Jones, Inigo, 365n2

Kalstone, David, 306, 318
   recollections of, 322, 351, 377n23
Kazin, Alfred, 119–20
Kazin, Pearl, 126, 153
Keene, Gretchen. See Smith, Gretchen Keene
Kennedy, Barbara Chesney, 16–17, 45–47,
   245
   recollections of, 21–23, 25–26, 34–35,
   43–45, 68
Kenney, Leo, 205
Kentfield, Calvin, 119, 122
Key West, Fla., 70–89, 110–13
   as artists' colony, 365n11
   first winter in, 70–72
   life in, 74–79, 82–83, 88–89
   second winter in, 70, 72–79
   624 White Street house in, 73–75, 87,
      99
   Square Roof brothel in, 82–83
   Ten Thousand Islands canoeing trip and,
      83–84
Kirkpatrick, Ralph, 104
Kirstein, Lincoln, 56
Kizer, Caroline, 205
Klein, Kenneth, 94
Kylso (adopted son of Lota), 131–32, 152

Lacerda, Carlos
   Flamingo Park project and, 167–69, 190,
      194–95
   Lota's friendship with, 163, 167–68,
      171, 177
   Lota's involvement in politics and, 175,
      193–94
   political turmoil around, 184–86, 190

Lage, Alfredo, 132
Langer, Suzanne, 367n1
Laughlin, James, 79–83
   recollections of, 80–83
Laurans, Penelope. See Fitzgerald, Penelope
   Laurans
Lavin, Mary, 350
Layton, Elsee, 17
   recollections of, 3, 5
Laytons (neighbors of Boomers), 6
Leão, Magu, 168, 236
Leão, Rosalina, 161
   recollections of, 132–33, 140, 145–46,
      148, 164–66, 168, 236–37
Leeds, Harold, recollections of, 41, 96–97,
      228, 231, 380n11, 381n3
Leithauser, Brad, recollections of, 280, 308,
      328–29
Lesbianism, EB's discretion about, 86, 249,
      327–30
Levertov, Denise, 250
Lewis, C. Day, 224
Lewis Wharf, Boston, 1–2, 307, 321–24,
      330
Library of Congress, poetry position at, 110,
      114–19, 253
Life and Letters Today, 62, 65
Life magazine picture, 109
Linkletter, Zilpha, recollections of, 99–100,
      345
Lispector, Clarice, 175
Literary criticism, EB's view of, 298
Literary output of EB
   EB's feelings about size of, 95, 316, 332,
      339, 348
   EB's feminism and, 327
   first year in Brazil and, 142, 145
   in San Francisco, 240, 242–43
Living Theater Company, 284–85
Lockwood, Helen, 37, 51, 53–55
Lowell, Harriet, 175
Lowell, Robert ("Cal"), 109, 115, 120,
      126, 166, 187–88, 191, 228, 246,
      337
   Bard Poetry Conference and, 103, 105,
      107–8
   competitiveness between EB and, 313–
      14, 339

death of, 341–42
EB's disagreements with, 271–72, 309, 341, 376, 378n2
EB's feelings about, 342
EB's National Book Award and, 263–64
EB's 1957 visits with, 160–61
EB's position at Harvard and, 1, 267–68, 271
EB's relationship with, 100–103, 106–8, 117, 244
Harvard and, 303–5
Lota's death and, 232
students' views of, 278, 280–81, 311–15
use of wife's voice by, 309, 376, 378n2
works
    The Dolphin, 309, 341
    "For the Union Dead," 193, 297
    Imitations, 341
    "Thanks Offering for Recovery," 322
Lulu (Brazilian cook), 139–40
Lundell, Gary, recollections of, 219

Ma, Yo-Yo, 326
McCarthy, Eugene, 263
McCarthy, Mary, 50, 60–62, 379n7
    recollections of, 43, 48, 152–53, 379n7
McCracken, Ann, 368n2
McCracken, Henry Noble (Vassar College president), 49
McCracken, Phillip, 368n2
McCurdy, Miss (teacher at Vassar), 55
MacDonald, Dwight, 161
MacIver, Loren, 94–95, 103, 105, 114, 117, 161, 172, 282
    art of, 77–78, 93, 98, 149, 322
    EB's use of New York apartment of, 227, 231, 246
MacLachlan, Muir, 316
MacLachlans (friends of EB's grandparents), 99
MacLeish, Archibald, 114
McPherson, Sandra, 208, 306
    recollections of, 209–12
    "To a Night Worker," 210–11
The Magazine, 56
Mandlebaum, Allen, 305–6
Marlowe, Sylvia, 335
Marshall, Margaret, 62

Marx, Roberto Burle, 168, 171
    recollections of, 196–97
Matchett, William, recollections of, 216–17
Matisse, Pierre, 94
Meigs, Mary, recollections of, 85–87, 94, 97, 371n1
Men, EB's interest in
    EB's sexuality and, 328
    facade of, 64–65
    Vassar years and, 44–47
Mental illness
    EB's fears of, 107–8, 241–42
    of EB's mother, 3–5, 28–29
    others' concerns about EB and, 28–29
Meredith, William, 263
Merrill, James, 253, 306, 345, 351
    recollections of, 108, 128, 266–67, 292
Metaphor, EB on, 208
Methfessel, Alice, 273, 319, 330–36, 344
    early kindnesses to EB and, 272, 282–83, 286, 292
    EB's death and, 349–51
    travels with EB and, 307, 316, 336, 347
Mexico, 91, 330–31
Midlin, Enrique, 171, 174
Miles, Josephine, 249–50
Miles, Marianne, 248
Millay, Edna St. Vincent, 121
Miller, Margaret, 117, 349, 352, 365n2
    accident involving, 68–70
    EB's Christmas with, 61–62
    EB's Vassar years and, 41, 43–44, 52
    relationship with EB, 61–62, 67, 70, 99
Mindlin, Henrique, 148
Mizener, Arthur, 52
Mongan, Agnes, 166, 336
    recollections of, 143–44, 336
Mony, Bob, 206
Moore, Marianne
    death of, 316
    EB's alcoholism and, 96
    EB's career and, 62, 67, 73, 80, 98, 100
    EB's friendship with, 109, 137, 228, 246, 335
    EB's meeting with, 57–58, 155
    etiquette of visiting with, 135
    "The Monkeys," 208
Morash, Georgie, 8

Morgan, Frederick, 326–27, 338
Morocco, 66
Morrill, Nancy Orr, recollections of, 32, 358n18
Morse, Mary Stearns, 126, 135, 259
    recollections of, 129–32, 141, 144–45, 147, 174, 184–85, 200, 225, 227, 230, 234–35
    on EB and Lota's friends, 145, 234
    on EB's drinking, 147
    on Lacerda, 184–85
    on Lota, 129–32, 144, 200, 225, 227, 230
    on Lota's death, 234–35
    on Manuelzinho, 141
    on Rio apartment, 174
Moss, Howard, 181, 194, 273, 382n6
    recollections of, 95–96, 275–77, 366n7, 367n10, 369n8, 371n9
Muchnic, Helen, recollections of, 53, 93–94, 246, 342–43, 375n20
Mulligan, Miss (teacher at Walnut Hill School), 32–33
Muser, Frani Blough, 282, 351, 365n2
    recollections of
        on EB's sense of poetry, 7
        Vassar and, 39, 42–43, 50, 55, 361n3
        Walnut Hill and, 24–27, 30–31
Museum of Modern Art (MOMA), 133, 143
Music
    in Brazil, 191, 266
    Dolmetsch clavicord and, 64, 95–96, 156
    EB's collaboration with Ned Rorem and, 158–60
    Louise Crane and, 75, 83–84, 328
    Vassar and, 38–40, 42–43
    at Walnut Hill School, 24, 26–27, 39
Myers, John Bernard, 253
    recollections of, 157–58

Nabokov, Nicolas, 175
Nantucket, 47
National Book Award, 263–64
National Book Award Committee, 345
National Book Award translation panel, 305
National Book Critics Award, 340
Nelson, Donalda Maclachlan, recollections of, 9, 99, 358n16

Nemer, Jose Alberto, 374n16
    recollections of, 259–61, 264, 370n6
Nemer, Linda, 374n16
    recollections of, 265, 370n6
Neruda, Pablo, 91
Neustadt Prize. See Books Abroad/Neustadt International Prize for Literature
Neway, Patricia, 159–60
New Democracy, 79–80
New Directions (publisher), 79
    "Five Young American Poets" series, 80–81
    "Poets of the Year" series, 81
New York City
    memorial reading in, 351
    in 1930s, 60–62, 67–68, 70
    in 1940s, 91–110
    in 1950s, 128–29, 150–62
    1960s trip to, 226–33
    1973 reading in, 306
The New Yorker, 142, 164, 193, 290, 371n9, 382n6
    first-reading contract with, 100, 226
    poetry reviews for, 273–76
The New York Times, 349
New York University, Berg Professorship at, 344
Nock, Albert, 63
North Haven Island, Maine, 319–21, 339, 343–44, 381n3
Nova Scotia, 2, 99–100, 189, 345–47. See also Great Village, Nova Scotia; Sable Island
Nova Scotia Hospital in Dartmouth, 4–5, 7, 9

O'Connor, Flannery, 162, 190–91, 382n5
O'Hara, Frank, 155–56, 158
One Art: Selected Letters of Elizabeth Bishop (Giroux, ed.), 242
Orr, Kay (EB's cousin). See Sargent, Kay Orr
Orr, Nancy (EB's cousin). See Morrill, Nancy Orr
Orr, Sarah (EB's aunt), 13
Osborn, Elodie, recollections of, 133–35, 151, 232–33
Osser, Maya, 245
Osualdo, Angelo, recollections of, 374n16

Ouro Prêto, Brazil
  EB's house in, 198–99, 223, 237, 254–
    55, 257–59, 378n6
  EB's 1969–1970 stay in, 254–68
  Living Theater Company incident in,
    284–85
  1960s vacations in, 197–99
  1970s trips to, 282, 291–92

Page, Chester, recollections of, 335–36, 349
Paris, E. Rosemary, 51
Paris, France. See Europe
Partisan Review, 72, 92–93
Partisan Review Fellowship, 149
Patriquin, G. Arthur, 8
  recollections of, 6, 11
Patriquin, Gwendolyn ("Gwendolyn Ap-
    pletree"), 11
Paulo (Brazilian gardener), 139–40
Paz, Marie Jo, 316, 331
Paz, Octavio, 316, 326, 331, 333, 351
Pedricki, Jean, 97–98
Peebles, Rose, 52–53
Peech, John, 372n13
Peele, George, 158
Pereira, Stella, 253
  recollections of, 144–45, 174, 176, 200,
    230, 234
Peru, 284
Petrópolis, Brazil
  EB's studio at, 138–39
  Lota's development of Samambaia at,
    130–31
  Lota's house at, 128, 131, 138–39, 150,
    156
  servants in, 139–40, 157, 179
Pfeiffer, Virginia, 110, 117
Pierpont Morgan Library, 330
Ping-Pong, 285, 319
Pinsky, Robert, recollections of, 350–51
Plath, Sylvia, Letters Home, 276
Ploughshares magazine, 350
Poetry, EB's sense of, 203–4, 211–13
  drafts and, 290–91
  EB's contrarian identity and, 299–300
  emergence of, 7
  meter and, 210–11, 364n37

precision and, 288, 297–98, 325
  truth and, 152–53, 278, 377n23
Poetry readings
  at Boston Public Library, 380n10
  EB's manner in, 280
  at the Guggenheim Museum, 253
  at Harvard University, 249, 268
  in late 1960s, 245–46
  in 1972, 289
  in 1974, 306
  for Poetry magazine in Chicago, 276–77
  at Rutgers University, 253
  at San Francisco State University, 250–51
  at University of Rochester, 380n1
  at Walnut Hill School, 253
  at Wesleyan University, 253
  at Yale, 376
Poetry Society of America, Shelley Memorial
    Award, 142
Politics
  art and, 93
  Cambridge and, 324, 326
  Lota and, 129, 167, 172, 183–86, 193–
    94
  San Francisco in the sixties and, 247,
    250–51
  Vassar and, 47–50
Pollitt, Katha, recollections of, 278–80,
    327–28
Porter, Alan, 364n35
Porter, Katherine Anne, 122–23, 161
Portinari, Candido, 129, 133, 142–43, 161
Portland State University, 306
Pound, Ezra, 80, 101, 114–15, 117, 120,
    248, 264
Prentiss, Eleanor, 23, 25, 360n8
Publishing world, EB's attitude toward, 80–
    83, 98–99
Pulitzer Prize, 149, 161, 187, 192

Racism, 292
Reed, Henry, 199, 202, 208, 210–11, 215–
    18, 224
Reich, Jerry, recollections of, 320, 348
Reid, Alastair, 180–81
  "Quarrels" (poem), 182
  recollections of, 181–84
Reitz, Robert, 77

Religion, 190–91, 382n5
in EB's childhood, 10–11, 104
EB's last days and, 347–49
Rexroth, Kenneth, 106, 247–48, 263–64
Rich, Adrienne, 329–30
Rockefeller Foundation grant, 219, 242
Rodman, Maia Wojciechowska, recollections of, 111–13, 118–19
Rodman, Selden, 110–11
Roethke, Beatrice, 205
Roethke, Theodore, 202, 207–10
Ronald (Bishop's chauffeur), 12, 16
Rorem, Ned, 299
recollections of, 158–60
Ruhle, Otto, 91
Rukeyser, Muriel, 114, 208
Russell, Charles ("Red"), 330
recollections of, 71–73, 83–85, 89–90
Russell, Charlotte ("Sha"), 5, 330, 334
recollections of, 71–73, 83, 90
Russell, Jean, recollections of, 368n2
Rutgers University
honorary degree from, 289, 373n14
poetry reading at, 253

Sable Island, 125–26
Sandburg, Carl, 119
San Francisco, Calif., 238–53
decision to live in, 237
life with Bowen in, 238–40, 246–53
political activity in, 247, 250–51
Saratoga Springs, N.Y. See Yaddo (artists colony)
Sargent, Kay Orr (EB's cousin), recollections of, 3, 13–14, 358n19
Sauer, Martha Watson, 282
recollections of, 74, 76–78, 84, 88–89, 150
Schapiro, Amram, 350
Schapiro, Meyer, 172
Schuyler, Jimmy, 155
Schwartz, Lloyd, 352
recollections of, 304, 316–19, 328, 330, 341–42, 347, 350, 373n15, 382n6
on dissertation about EB, 316–19
on EB's death, 350, 382n6
on EB's feminism, 330
on EB's health concerns, 347
on EB's sexuality, 328
on Frank Bidart, 373n15
on Harvard, 304
on Lowell's death, 341–42
Seattle, Wash., 201–21
EB's decision to go to, 199–200
EB's feelings about Brazil while in, 204, 219–21
EB's relationship with Bowen in, 205–6
first weeks in, 201–6
kindness of friends in, 206
visiting professorship in, 306
Seaver, Robert, 44–47, 64, 67–68
Sexton, Anne, 300, 310–11
Shaw, Robert B., recollections of, 305, 324–26
Sheehan, Rhoda Wheeler, 43–44
recollections of, 27, 334
Shepherdson, George (EB's uncle), 16–17
Shepherdson, Maud Boomer (EB's aunt)
EB's childhood and, 16–17
painting and, 7, 16
Shore, Jane, recollections of, 286–89, 304, 314–15, 380n10
Simile, EB on, 208
Smith, Gretchen Keene, 60–61
recollections of, 53, 61, 214–15, 380n7
Smith College, honorary degree from, 245–46
Soares, Flavio (Lota's nephew), 163, 176, 261–63, 286, 372n11
Soares, Lota de Macedo
adopted son of, 131–32, 152
artistic friends of, 142–45, 171–72, 194–95
background and personality of, 129–36, 177
death of, 231–37, 266–67
EB's decision to stay in Brazil and, 127–28, 266
EB's desire to write elegy for, 339
EB's difficulties with, 194, 197, 200, 218, 226–27, 232, 234
EB's relationship with, 128, 136–38, 141–42, 151, 157–58, 178, 182–84
EB's sense of guilt about, 70, 233–34, 257, 267

park job in Rio and, 167–69, 173–76, 178–80, 190–93
politics and, 129, 167, 172, 183–86, 193–94
provision of will of, 234–35
sickness of, 222–26, 229–30
work problems of, 235–36
Sollid, John, 378n3
Spain, 66–67
Spender, Stephen, 189
Spires, Elizabeth, 342
SS Königstein, 62–63
SS Mormacstar, 161–62
Stanford, Donald, 364
recollections of, 56–58
Stapleton, Laurence, 381n2
Steeves, Miriam, 39–40
Stevens, Marjorie, 99, 111–13, 161
EB's relationship with, 88–92, 113
Stevens, Wallace, 104
Stevenson, Anne, 318
recollections of, 187–89, 273–75
Strand, Julia, 335
recollections of, 283, 331
Strand, Mark, recollections of, 194–95, 223, 233
Sullivan, James ("Sully"), 76–77
Summers, Joseph, 230
Bard Poetry Conference and, 103–8
recollections of
on EB at Yaddo, 103–6
on EB's drinking, 125–26
on EB's relationship with Bowen, 246–47
on EB's relationship with Lota, 151–52, 224
on EB's retirement, 340
on Harvard, 304–5
on Lowell, 309–10
on reading at Rochester, 381n1
Summers, U. T.
Bard poetry conference and, 104–6, 108
recollections of
on EB at Yaddo, 103–6
on EB's relationship with Bowen, 247
on EB's relationship with Houghton Mifflin, 98

on EB's relationship with Lota, 151–52, 224
on Lowell, 309–10
on reading at Rochester, 380n1
Supplemento Literario do Minas Gerais, 374n16
Sutherland, Ernest, 16
Sutherland, Phyllis Bowers (EB's cousin), 16
recollections of, 345–46, 359n26
Swain, Barbara, 40
Swann, Emma, 337
Swenson, May, 119–21, 150, 232

Tate, Allen, 109, 115, 191
Tate, Carolyn, 109, 200
Taylor, Dr. (psychotherapist), 29–30
Teaching
EB's difficulties with, 206–7, 268, 283, 301–2, 316, 324–26
EB's style of, 206–14, 277–82, 287–88, 292–94, 311–13
Thatcher, Barbara, recollections of, 321, 381n2
Thatcher, Tom, recollections of, 320–21
Theater, 25–27
Thomas, Dylan, 114, 119–20
Thomas, Harriet Tompkins, recollections of, 47, 51, 62–66, 364n35
Thomas, John, 65–66
Thomas, Norman, 48–49
Thompson, Jan, 205
Thompson, Maureen, 89
Thomson, Virgil, 62, 159, 320
Time, Inc., 172–73
Time magazine, 190
Tompkins, Harriet. See Thomas, Harriet Tompkins
Trial Balances, 62
Tucson, Ariz., 245
Tureck, Rosalyn, recollections of, 94–95

University of California, Berkeley Campus, 245
University of Rochester, 306, 345, 380n1
University of Washington in Seattle, 306

Valdes, Gregorio, 74
Van Cleef, Shirley Clarke, recollections of, 36–37

Vargas, Getulio (president of Brazil), 167
Vassar College, 36–59
    cabaret event at, 49
    campus political activities at, 47–50
    Con Spirito and, 50–52
    death of EB's mother and, 58–59
    EB's application to, 33–34, 360n17
    EB's curriculum at, 38–40, 361n5
    EB's dating life at, 44–47
    EB's freshman year at, 36–41
    EB's literary focus at, 55–57
    EB's meeting with Marianne Moore and,
        57–58, 155
    EB's teachers at, 37, 39–40, 52–55
    escapades at, 37–38
    friendships at, 36–38, 40–44
    Miscellany News at, 47–49, 51–52, 54
    pot of Roquefort cheese and, 36
    summer vacations and, 43–44
    theater at, 362n18
    toilets at, 41, 43
    yearbook at, 58
Vassar Miscellany News, 47–49, 51–52, 54
Vassar Review, 50–52, 55
Vendler, Helen, 342, 351
    recollections of, 283, 300–301, 321–22,
        332–33, 349–50, 378n2
Villard, Mary St. John, recollections of, 47–
    48
Von Hagen, Victor Wolfgang, 119

Wagoner, David, 210
Walnut Hill School, 20–35
    academic life at, 23–25
    costume incident at, 28–29
    EB's admission to, 18–19
    EB's curriculum at, 24
    EB's friendships at, 20–24, 27
    EB's independence and, 22, 24, 30–33
    EB's teachers at, 24–25
    graduation from, 35
    poetry reading at, 253
    recommendation to Vassar from, 33–34
    summer vacations and, 30–32
Walsh, Dorothy, 246, 375n20
Wanning, Tom, 161
Ward, Aileen, 350

Warren, Eleanor Clark, 161
    recollections of, 37–38, 54, 124
Warren, Robert Penn, 161
Washington, D.C., 114–19
Weeks, Ted, 100
Wehr, Wesley, 307
    recollections of, 110, 203–6, 212–13,
        219, 367n1, 368n2, 369n1
Weimer, David, recollections of, 173, 176–
    80, 185–86, 239, 373n14
Weiss, Ted, 103–4, 107
Wellesley College, 306
Wescott, Glenway, 161
Wheeler, Monroe, 133, 161, 169
    recollections of, 42, 171–72
Wheeler, Rhoda. See Sheehan, Rhoda
    Wheeler
White, E. B., 367n10
White, Katherine, 100
Wilbur, Charlotte, 105
    recollections of, 106–7, 253, 308–9
Wilbur, Richard, 105, 181, 189
    recollections of, 106–8, 286, 308, 348–
        49, 377n23
    "Shad Time," 377n23
Williams, Tennessee, 79, 81–82, 113
Williams, William Carlos, 80, 105, 297
Willis, Ruby, 24–25, 29
Wilson, Edmund, 93, 98
Worchester, Mass., 2–3, 12–16
Wright, James, 208
Wright, Mrs. (Holly Inn landlord), 90
Writing. See also Literary output
    academia and, 299
    EB's approach to, 116–17, 260, 325–26,
        339–40
    EB's early interest in, 17
    letters and, 169–70
    somatic connection with, 300–301
    at Walnut Hill School, 25–27

Yaddo (artists colony), 113–15, 119–24
Yale University, 376
YMHA, New York City, 306, 351

Zabel, Morton Dauwen, 161